CROSSING the JORDAN

Israel's Hard Road to Peace

SAMUEL SEGEV

ST. MARTIN'S PRESS ☙ NEW YORK

Design by Bryanna Millis

Library of Congress Cataloging-in-Publication Data

Segev, Samuel
    Crossing the Jordan : Israel's hard road to peace / Samuel Segev.—1st ed.
        p.   cm.
    Includes bibliographical references.
    ISBN 0-312-15506-9
    1. Arab-Israel conflict—1967–1973. 2. Arab-Israeli conflict—1973–1993. 3. Arab-Israeli conflict—1993––Peace. 4. Israel—Foreign relations—United States. 5. United States—Foreign relations—Israel. 6. United States—Foreign relations—20th century. Segev, Samuel. I. Title.
DS119.7.S3818   1998
956.04—dc21   98-12227
                                                        CIP

First Edition: May 1998

10 9 8 7 6 5 4 3 2

CROSSING the
JORDAN

To Oudi and Arnon,
who were born between the wars,
who fought in the wars, and who now, finally,
taste the promising fruits of peace.

Contents

Preface

The declaration of principles and the letter of mutual recognition signed by Israel and the PLO on the White House South Lawn on September 13, 1993, were the direct result of a discreet cooperation between the dovish elements of the Israeli Labor Party, Egypt, Norway, a few Israeli Arab Knesset members, and a small group of PLO activists, both in Tunis and in the occupied territories. Without this cooperation, however, there would not have been an Israeli-Jordanian peace treaty and no modest beginning of economic normalization between Israel and some of the Persian Gulf countries.

The Oslo Accords closed an important chapter in the history of the Israeli-Palestinian conflict. It was, undoubtedly, the most important political event in 1993 and gave hope for a solution to one of the most complicated of the several dozen national, ethnic, and religious conflicts raging then and now all over the world. Historical and ethnic hatreds do not vanish instantly, as the tragic events in the former Yugoslavia have shown. The Arab-Israeli conflict is no exception. Yet, after eighty years of violent confrontations and bloodshed, the ground had been seeded with a few grains of realism, and a small seed of trust had begun to take root.

The declaration of principles reflected the limitations of each side's power. Israel, despite her proven military superiority, could not eliminate acts of terror and could not suppress the Palestinians' drive for self-determination and statehood. The Palestinians, the weakest part in the equation, were unable to throw Israel into the sea and eradicate the "Jewish cancer," as they called it, from the Arab body. The result was obvious: Israel recognized the PLO and the national aspirations that it represents; the PLO recognized Israel's right to exist within secure and demarcated borders in the Middle East. Although one cannot be sure of the ultimate harvest, one can confidently assert that the process thus begun is irreversible—and both Israel and the Palestinians have crossed the point of no return.

The agreement between Israel and the PLO was followed a year later—on October 26, 1994—by a formal peace treaty between Israel and Jordan, a country with which Israel had had covert relations for more than three decades. The ceremony, attended by President Clinton, was held in the Jordan Rift Valley, one of the deepest regions on earth. The site was a former minefield, cleared for the occasion, and since then has become one of two crossing points between Israel and Jordan. Morocco, one of the first Arab countries to have established covert relations with Israel, brought these contacts into the open and paved the way for formal diplomatic relations in the future. Tunisia, Qatar, Oman, and Bahrain hosted the multilateral negotiations, with Israeli participation. In preparation for future regional economic cooperation, Morocco hosted in early November 1994 the "Casablanca Conference," with the active participation of the United States and Israel. A second conference was held in Amman in October 1995, and the third conference in Cairo in the fall of 1996.

One cannot detach these historic events from the broader international spectrum. Toward the end of the twentieth century, the international scene dramatically changed. After close to fifty years of Cold War and ideological confrontations, the international community is consistently demonstrating its desire for generational change and political orientation. The Soviet Union is gone, and the Communist empire has disintegrated. The Berlin Wall has crumbled, reuniting the two Germanies. Despite the tragic events in Tiananmen Square, China is gradually moving toward democracy and a younger and more energetic generation of national leaders is emerging. President F. W. de Klerk ended the apartheid policy in South Africa and transferred, democratically, the reins of power to Nelson Mandela. Even Great Britain took an unprecedented step and opened a dialogue with the IRA.

Yet, the road to peace in the Middle East is mined by many obstacles. Syria, the most intransigent nation in the Arab world, is not fully engaged in the peace process. Repeatedly defeated on the battlefield, President Assad, whom Henry Kissinger once described as a modern Bismarck, is determined to be the victor at the negotiating table. Syrian intransigence has a direct effect on Lebanon. Egypt is facing a violent challenge from Islamic fundamentalists, and there is even doubt whether Saudi Arabia can contain the winds of "democratic evolution" that are sweeping the entire Persian Gulf region.

The Palestinians, of course, are not immune to these winds of change. However, like the French under the Bourbons, the Palestinians under Arafat learned nothing from their long and bitter history. Ever divided and hopelessly splintered into numerous feuding groups, they approach their way to statehood through a destructive effort to derail the process of reconciliation among themselves and between them and Israel. Opponents of the Oslo Accords have embarked on violent dissent, and by their terrorist actions they are likely to confirm what Abba Eban once said: "The Palestinians never miss an opportunity to miss an opportunity."

The most serious obstacle, however, remains Yasser Arafat, who proves to be unable to transform himself from a "revolutionary" to a "statesman." His ineffective and corrupt administration has eroded his credibility, and his leadership is being constantly challenged not only by his opponents but also by many of his closest companions. Arafat's refusal to reconstruct the PLO in a manner that would invest more power in a new generation of young and Western-educated Palestinians caused delays in the flow of funds pledged by donor countries through accountable and modern institutions. Private investors backed away from their initial interest and are afraid to take risks in this unstable situation.

The assassination of Yitzhak Rabin in November 1995 and the Likud's victory in the Israeli general elections in May 1996 have complicated further the already difficult situation. In the aftermath of his victory, the new Israeli prime minister, Benjamin (Bibi) Netanyahu, was judged according to his election slogans and not according to his deeds. Even before he formed his government, Netanyahu was labeled by the Arab countries as "the enemy of peace." Netanyahu's expansive settlement activity, the opening of an archaeological tunnel in Jerusalem, the beginning of construction at Har Homa, and the collective punitive actions against the Palestinians have deepened Arab mistrust of Israel.

The result is obvious. In both Israel and the occupied territories, there are growing calls for a reassessment of the Oslo Accords.

Caught between these conflicting trends, the United States continues to play the role of a "facilitator" and rightly refuses to impose its own blueprint for a solution. "We can assist the parties, but we cannot negotiate on their behalf," President Clinton has said on several occasions.

Despite all the obstacles, all parties remain committed to the peace process and none of them wants to be accused of derailing it. Both parties also want the U.S. to be more directly involved in the peace effort. This could eventually prove to be the best prescription for achieving peace in the Middle East.

In researching this book, and as an active journalist who covered the Middle East and the Arab-Israeli conflict for more than thirty years, I have talked to most of the Israeli participants in the peace process, including Moshe Dayan, Golda Meir, Yitzhak Rabin, Yitzhak Shamir, Shimon Peres, David Levy, Moshe Arens, Benjamin (Fuad) Ben-Eliezer, Shulamit Aloni, Yossi Sarid, and many Israeli Foreign Ministry and intelligence officials. I have also discussed the subject, on past occasions, with American, Egyptian, Jordanian, and Palestinian officials, including Abu Ala (the PLO executive who negotiated the Oslo Accords with the Israelis) and several commanders of the intifada, the Palestinian uprising in the West Bank and the Gaza Strip. In Israel, I had access to privileged information not available previously to the Western media. Other sources included leaders of the American Jewish community, who were briefed regularly by the Bush and Clinton administrations. Finally, during the writing, I went through a vast quantity of printed material in the United States, Israel, France, Egypt, Lebanon, and Jordan as well as various PLO publications.

Some of my Israeli sources prefer to remain anonymous. I respect their wish. They know who they are, and they all have my gratitude.

I wish to express special thanks to my beloved wife, Phyllis, who was deprived of so many hours of companionship throughout the many months when I sat behind closed doors.

My beloved sons, Oudi and Arnon, were a constant source of inspiration to me. They have shown great faith in me and encouraged me to write this book.

From the inception of this book to its completion, my dear friend George Dempster was always generous with his useful advice. Alexander Hoyt, my agent, who also became my friend, invested great effort in bringing this book to completion.

Jeremy Katz, my devoted editor at St. Martin's Press, and his successor, Tara Schimming, did a great editing job. Their talents are very much reflected in every chapter of this book.

TEL AVIV, ISRAEL
SEPTEMBER 1997

INTRODUCTION:
PERES'S DEFEAT

Six years after the Madrid Peace Conference, four years after the Oslo Ac-
cords between Israel and the PLO, two years after the assassination of Prime
Minister Yitzhak Rabin, and one year after Likud's Benjamin (Bibi) Netanyahu
became the youngest and the first directly elected prime minister of Israel, the
Arab-Israeli peace process is facing one of its more severe crises.

Israeli-Palestinian negotiations, which have been suspended several times
in the past three years, are being suspended again. Despite American and
Egyptian efforts to revive the stalled peace talks, relations between Israel and
the Palestine Authority remain tense and distrustful. Israeli relations with
Egypt remain frigid. Because of an unnecessary dispute on water transfer,
which was eventually resolved, and especially after a failed Israeli attempt to assassinate an Islamic Hamas leader in Amman, relations with Jordan grew more
tense. Morocco and Tunisia have frozen their normalization process with Israel,
and Morocco's King Hassan had turned down requests by Prime Minister Netanyahu, Foreign Minister David Levy, and the minister of the infrastructure,
Ariel Sharon, to visit Rabat. Qatar and Oman adhered to an Arab summit decision to freeze normalization with Israel. Oman closed its liaison office in Tel
Aviv. Qatar, however, acting under strong U.S. pressure, rejected Syria's pressure and decided to go ahead with its previous decision to host in Doha, in November 1997, the Fourth Middle East and North Africa Economic Summit,
with Israel's participation. The meeting was a total failure. Despite Secretary
Madeleine Albright's personal efforts, most Arab countries—including Saudi
Arabia, Egypt, Morocco, and Tunisia—boycotted the Doha conference. What
is more significant: No date was set for a fifth summit and no Arab country
agreed to host such a conference, before the stalled peace process is revived.

Yet, despite this latest crisis, what has been achieved shows a historic transformation. As a matter of fact, each stage in the Arab-Israeli peace process, in
the last twenty years, has been accompanied by a recurring cycle of hope and
despair. The experience accumulated since President Sadat's historic visit to
Jerusalem in November 1977 has shown that the euphoria generated by the
Egyptian president's visit was soon followed by a setback and the slightest

progress was accompanied by a sense of disappointment and frustration. Hence, if the same pattern continues, the chances for a future resolution of the Israeli-Palestinian conflict remain very real. Despite the reciprocal threats and the often inflammatory rhetoric, both Israel and the Palestinians know that their movement toward reconciliation and peace has crossed the point of no return. With Yasser Arafat controlling the lives of more than two million people in the West Bank and the Gaza Strip, no serious leader in Israel or in the Arab world really believes that this situation could be easily reversed. Therefore, while a new full-scale war between Israel and its Arab neighbors is not impossible, it is not very likely—at least not in the immediate future. In an interview with a French newsmagazine, Egypt's President Mubarak said: "Another war between Israel and the Arabs is simply out of the question. The only alternative to war is terrorism. A war, obviously, is planned and manageable; terrorism is not. . . ."[1] This has been Mubarak's position all along. Addressing an Arab summit in 1989, Mubarak said: "We fought for many years, what did we achieve? . . . Therefore, I am not prepared to take more risks. . . . Wars have generally not solved any problem."[2] Egyptian Foreign Minister Amr Mussa said the same thing. In an interview with an Israeli newspaper, Mussa said: "I am not talking about [military] confrontation or war. In my way of thinking, I believe that wars between Arabs and Israelis are over. We are engaged in a diplomatic struggle, but no wars. . . ."[3]

Mubarak's national security adviser, Dr. Ossama el-Baz, echoed the same opinion. In a long interview with a London-based, Saudi-owned daily newspaper, el-Baz said that a war option is "totally unimaginable." He said that a new war would be extremely costly and would change nothing on the ground. He also warned against exaggerated Arab expectations that the U.S. can "deliver" Israel. His conclusion was, therefore, that the Palestinians have no alternative but to continue negotiating with Israel.[4]

Israel and the Palestinians share the same view. Despite their present difficulties and their future crises, they both know that the war option is not practical at the present time. Arafat himself admitted it. In an interview with a London-based Arab weekly, Arafat said: "The international situation does not permit a new war. . . ."[5]

What makes the war option so unlikely is the unique nature of the Israeli-Palestinian conflict. Experience has shown that it is easier to solve a conflict between two neighboring countries separated by clearly demarcated and recognized borders than to solve a conflict between two neighbors sharing the same land. Hence, a solution of the Israeli-Palestinian conflict requires more patience, a lot of goodwill, creative thinking, and reciprocal concessions.

The latest crisis was caused by Israel's decision, on March 18, 1997, to start building a new neighborhood on mostly Jewish-owned land at Har Homa, a site on the southeastern edge of Jerusalem, which Arabs call Jabal Abu-Ghneim.

The United States had traditionally opposed the Israeli settlement activity in the West Bank and had opposed the building at Har Homa as well. The United States saw in the Israeli move an attempt to predetermine the final status of Jerusalem. Yet, the building at Har Homa placed the United States in a difficult situation. Contrary to Arafat's claim, the land at Har Homa was not taken from Arabs, but was legally bought and owned by Israel. The site is within the municipal boundaries of Jerusalem; U.S. Public Law 104-45 of November 8, 1995, recognized the undivided city of Jerusalem as the capital of Israel. The legislation fulfilled the clause in the American Democratic Party's platform calling for the transfer of the U.S. embassy in Israel from Tel Aviv to Jerusalem. To consolidate this position, the U.S. Senate passed on June 17, 1997, a major foreign relations bill that authorized $100 million for the construction of the new embassy in Jerusalem. The anticipated legislation would require the State Department to list "Jerusalem, Israel" as the birthplace of someone who was born in the city and who is entitled to an American passport. In addition, U.S. government documents must refer to Jerusalem as Israel's capital. However, since the Oslo Accords in September 1993, President Clinton has been trying to circumvent the issue of Jerusalem by refusing to take any step that could be interpreted as preempting negotiations between Israel and the Palestinians over the final status of the city. Clinton even threatened to veto the legislation, if passed.

As expected, Arafat reacted angrily to Israel's decision to start building at Har Homa. He suspended the negotiations with Israel and also suspended the cooperation between the security agencies of Israel and the Palestinians. Moreover, in an effort to prevent Palestinians from selling land to Israelis, the Palestine Authority ruled that any Palestinian who sold land to Jews would be executed. Indeed, within days, four Palestinian real estate dealers were knifed or shot to death. Finally, in a meeting with leaders of Hamas and Islamic Jihad, Arafat was understood to have given them the green light to resume their murderous attacks against Israel. Indeed, on March 21, 1997, a Hamas suicide bomber blew himself up in a café in Tel Aviv, killing three Israeli women and wounding many more. The suicide bomber belonged to a Hamas cell of six terrorists from a small village near Hebron; the cell has been responsible for the murder of twelve Israelis in three years. Following a tip-off by Israel, the PA arrested three members of the cell, while Israel arrested the remaining two.

Arafat took advantage of the universal condemnation of the Israeli building at Har Homa and, with the support of the Arab and Islamic world, called for an emergency meeting of the UN Security Council. Believing that the UN was not the proper forum to solve this problem, the United States twice vetoed a one-sided resolution sharply condemning Israel and calling for the cessation of the building at Har Homa. The Arab bloc called for two special meetings of the General Assembly. Despite strong U.S. opposition, the General Assembly passed two resolutions—with an overwhelming majority—condemning the Israeli action and calling upon the UN secretary general to report within sixty days whether Israel had complied with the UN decision. On July 15, 1997, for the third time in four months, the General Assembly adopted a resolution condemning Israel for continuing building in disputed territories. The action brought immediate criticism from the United States and Israel. They accused the General Assembly of reverting to the anti-Israeli crusades of the Cold War era. Ambassador Bill Richardson, the U.S. envoy to the UN, repeated Clinton administration criticisms of building at Har Homa, but added that hints of an economic boycott and threats to Israeli membership in the UN were "a throwback to the ugly credentials challenges of past decades." The newly appointed Israeli envoy, Dore Gold, accused the UN relief agencies in the region of gathering information for the secretary general, in contravention of their assigned tasks. Gold called the secretary general's report "hostile and one-sided."[6]

The three General Assembly resolutions were undoubtedly a moral victory for Yasser Arafat and a serious setback to Israel's claim to undivided sovereignty in Jerusalem. From an Israeli point of view, what was alarming in this new situation was the realization that the more "assets" Arafat had, the more intransigent and less flexible he became. In advance of the final status negotiations, Arafat became more aggressive in his demand for a sovereign Palestinian state, with East Jerusalem as its capital. In an interview for a London-based Arabic newsmagazine, Arafat said: "For me Jerusalem is the red light. If Netanyahu does not agree to a Palestinian state, with East Jerusalem its capital, then let him drink the salted water of the Dead Sea."[7] Thus, Palestinian violence and Israeli settlement-building activity had broken the "core bargain" struck in Oslo. In an effort to revive the stalled negotiations, President Clinton sent his special envoy, Ambassador Dennis Ross, to the Middle East to convey to the parties the U.S. concerns that Israel's activity in disputed areas and Palestinian attacks on Israelis were damaging the peace process. Officially and publicly, both sides agree that there is no alternative to an active American role in the peace process. Despite Palestinian efforts to involve Egypt, Russia, and Europe in this process, Yasser Arafat knows quite well that only the United States can influence Israel's position. At the same time, the U.S. role cannot be effective unless both sides accept the United States as their "honest broker." As one senior American official put it: "If we accept all Israeli positions, we risk losing the Arabs' trust; and if we respond positively to all Arab demands, we risk losing our capacity to influence Israel. . . ."

In a late-night meeting at the residence of U.S. Ambassador to Israel Martin Indyk, Ross told Israeli and Palestinian negotiators that he regarded himself as the "ladder" that could help them climb down the tree. Ross suggested the immediate resumption of the security cooperation between Israel and the Palestinians and three days of intense negotiations, to be followed by a summit meeting between Netanyahu and Arafat. As a confidence-building measure,

Ross also suggested a temporary suspension of settlement activity in the West Bank, the opening of the Gaza airport, and safe passage for the Palestinians between the Gaza Strip and the West Bank. The Palestinians rejected Ross's proposal. Feeling strengthened by the UN General Assembly's decisions, the Palestinians wanted a clear Israeli undertaking to freeze permanently—not just temporarily—all settlement activity, a demand that had been rejected by Israel both in Oslo and in Cairo. Palestinian negotiator Saeb Erikat said: "It's illogical to expect us to resume the negotiations while Israel continues to 'swallow' the land."

Israeli Defense Minister Yitzhak Mordechai, who participated in the negotiations at Indyk's residence, told Erikat that Israel was prepared to promise publicly that no privately owned Arab land would be confiscated. Such an undertaking, however, would not apply to state-owned land. The Palestinians rejected this offer as well.

Faced with this deadlock, Ross traveled to the Gaza Strip for an after-midnight meeting with Arafat. Ross reiterated his definition of his role as a "ladder" that could help the parties to climb down the tree. He suggested to Arafat not relying too much on the assumption that Netanyahu's downfall is "very close." On the contrary, Netanyahu might stay in power until the end of his term, in the year 2000. Therefore, Arafat should take note of this possibility and resume talks with the present Israeli government. Arafat rejected Ross's characterization of his role as a "ladder." He told Ross: "I can't climb down the tree by myself. Netanyahu has pushed me and the Arab and Muslim leaders up the tree. If I climb down alone, nobody in the Arab world will ever walk with me along the same path again. . . ."[8]

Realizing that a continued stalemate in the peace process is likely to affect the U.S. position in the Middle East and in the Persian Gulf region, Secretary Albright made her first trip to the region in the fall of 1997. Her immediate objective was to ensure a further redeployment of Israeli forces in the West Bank and to ensure a more effective security cooperation between Israel and the Palestinian Authority. She failed in her mission. Two separate meetings between Albright and Netanyahu (in Paris), and between Albright and Arafat (in London), did not produce any better results.

Determined to avoid a total collapse of the Israeli-Palestinian peace process, President Clinton invited Prime Minister Netanyahu and Chairman Arafat to meet with him in Washington, on January 20 and 22, 1998. The invitation signaled an important change in the U.S. role—from "facilitator" to an "active participant." Clinton submitted to Netanyahu and Arafat a U.S. proposal for a phased Israeli deployment—to be accompanied by a gradual Palestinian fulfillment of previous commitments. While the gap between Israel and the PLO remains wide, Clinton's initiative succeeded in keeping the process alive.

Before evaluating Netanyahu's performance during his first year in office, we have to dwell briefly on Shimon Peres's short tenure as prime minister and his defeat in the general elections on May 29, 1996. In the aftermath of Rabin's assassination, Peres inherited a rich bounty: world sympathy for the heavy price Israel had paid for the sake of peace with the Palestinians. It was obvious that despite their many weaknesses, the Oslo Accords paid Israel generous political and economic dividends. Peres inherited from Rabin a booming economy that was envied by many industrialized nations. In 1995 alone, the Israeli GNP was close to $90 billion—more than the combined GNP of Egypt, Syria, Lebanon, Jordan, and the Palestinians. Direct foreign investments in Israel increased dramatically, from $366 million in 1991 to more than $1 billion in 1995 and $2 billion in 1996.

No less impressive was the inheritance in the field of diplomacy. Although this trend began after the Madrid Peace Conference, in the aftermath of the Oslo Accords, Israel had achieved the widest breach ever in the wall of Arab and Muslim hostility. With normal relations with 168 countries, Israel became less isolated in the international scene. Because of strong U.S. pressure, Israel opened interest offices in Qatar and Oman and Saudi businessmen paid discreet visits to Israel. Two missions of American Jewish leaders visited Saudi Arabia and met with Saudi ministers and senior officials. Israeli tourism to Morocco and Tunisia grew steadily. Through third countries, Israel in 1995 exported to Algeria goods worth $600 million, and Algerian scholars attended, discreetly, Israeli academic seminars. Egypt's peace with Israel was always cool, but the peace with Jordan was warm and promising. Through Jordanian intermediaries, Israel exported even to Iraq—small quantities of food and medicine. As a result of Israel's reduced economic isolation, there has been an upsurge in trade with countries that refused to deal with Israel in the past. This was particularly true in Asia. Israel's exports to Asia rose from $2 billion in 1991 to more than $3 billion in 1994. Finally, Israel's economic growth has been assisted by a dramatic reduction of the defense budget. Because of Rabin's courageous decision to change the order of Israel's priorities, the defense budget was reduced from a peak of 35 percent of the national budget in 1975 to about 10 percent in 1995.

Because of this rich bounty, most Israelis took it for granted that Labor under the leadership of Shimon Peres would easily win in the general elections scheduled for November 1996. Some Labor leaders, including the party's secretary general, the Tunisian-born Nissim Zvilli, urged Peres to call for immediate elections. He refused. Peres didn't want to be carried to the premiership by the sympathy and grief generated by Rabin's assassination. He wanted his presumed victory to be based on his own personality and on his record in the peace process.

Since he assumed the premiership in November 1995, Peres was driven by a desire to prove to his critics that his vision of a "New Middle East" was not a fantasy. He sincerely believed that economic relations and open borders would eventually lead to a political solution. Addressing an international conference of Jewish journalists in Jerusalem, Peres predicted that the Middle East would become like the European Economic Community (EEC). He said that in a world run by the United States, the Arab countries would turn democratic, since despots would be overthrown by the Western-educated elites, who would want to live as comfortably as their colleagues in the West. "Borders will be insignificant," Peres said, "since the New Middle East will cooperate with Israel, especially in the fields of energy and communications. The Arab world will also become technologically proficient and computer-literate. By the year 2000, Israel will have diplomatic relations with twenty-one or twenty-two Arab countries. . . ."[9]

Peres's "vision," unfortunately, had no connection with the realities of the region. Despite the optimistic predictions, Islamic fundamentalism continued to spread in Egypt, Algeria, and Sudan, and a more dangerous, Iran-inspired Islamic terrorism began to take root in the Arabian Peninsula and the oil-rich Persian Gulf countries. Islamic opposition to the continued American military presence in the Persian Gulf became more vocal. Islamic extremism was rising in the West Bank and the Gaza Strip as well. After the evacuation of six cities and 450 villages, Israeli security agencies questioned Arafat's ability, or willingness, to honor his written commitments to curb terrorism and end violence.

Complicating Labor's situation at that time was the growing feeling in Israel that in the absence of Rabin's "brakes," Peres and his team would rush to conclude an agreement with Arafat "at any cost." This feeling was already apparent in the wake of the signing of the Oslo Accords. Yossi Beilin, who initiated the secret negotiations with the PLO in Oslo, and who became a minister in Rabin's and Peres's cabinets, was asked in Boston about the security importance of the Jordan Valley, which was defined by all Israeli governments as the "defensive border" of Israel. Beilin replied: "This whole subject is related more to symbols than to security realities. Since the 1967 Six-Day War, Israel considered the Suez Canal as its defense line against Egypt. This concept collapsed in the 1973 Yom Kippur War. The same could be said about the Jordan Valley. We have to change this concept. . . ."[10]

As expected, Beilin's statement in Boston caused an uproar in the Labor Party, and especially in the kibbutz movement, many who were encouraged to settle in the Jordan Valley by the various Labor governments. During a cabinet meeting on November 24, 1993, Shimon Shetreet, the hawkish minister of economic planning, urged Rabin to dismiss Beilin for undermining Israel's negotiating positions. Rabin ignored the suggestion, because he did not want a conflict with Peres—Beilin's patron—at that time.[11]

The reaction of the Jordan Valley's settlers was more blunt. In a meeting with their representatives in Tel Aviv, Yossi Beilin reiterated his belief that the security value of the Jordan Valley was "unimportant." He told the settlers that they had only one choice—to return to Israel proper or to stay in the Jordan Valley, under Palestinian rule. The settlers were shocked. One of them lost his cool and shouted: "For God's sake, Yossi, shut up!"[12]

Realizing that the Oslo process created many divisions within Israeli society, Peres sought to heal the wounds and to rebuild a bridge to the religious parties. Rabin's assassination showed him to what extent he needed a Jewish consensus in order to continue the peace process. He knew that he could not govern a Jewish state based on a Jewish minority supported by Israeli Arabs. Hence, he sought to turn a new page in Labor's relations with the religious parties, which Rabin alienated. As a clear signal to the religious parties, Peres appointed the moderate Rabbi Yehuda Amital as a minister without portfolio in his cabinet. After both the Likud and the National Religious Party accepted the Oslo Accords as a fait accompli, Peres wanted to secure the religious vote in the Knesset so that he would not be totally dependent on the Arab vote. The religious parties, however, refused to grant him this "security valve." Peres's efforts drew fire from the pro-Rabin ministers and from the left-wing coalition partner, Meretz. "Peres's rapprochement with the religious parties gave legitimacy to the same groups which produced Yigal Amir, Rabin's assassin," complained Shimon Shetreet, a respected professor of law at the Hebrew University and the only minister in Rabin's cabinet who abstained in the vote on the Oslo Accords.[13]

Regarding the peace process, Peres decided to concentrate on the Israeli-Syrian track. In this respect, he was assured of total U.S. support. Indeed, even before President Clinton's arrival in Jerusalem to attend Rabin's funeral, U.S. Ambassador Martin Indyk informed Peres that Clinton would like to meet with him before his return to Washington. "Itamar, is Peres familiar with all that was achieved in the Israeli-Syrian track?" Clinton asked Professor Itamar Rabinovich, the Israeli ambassador to Washington, at Mount Herzl Cemetery. "Please make sure that before we meet at the King David Hotel, Peres is fully briefed on the subject."[14]

Indeed, thirty minutes before his meeting with Clinton, Peres was briefed by Rabinovich on the latest developments in the Israeli-Syrian track. Peres was shocked. He suddenly realized how close Rabin was to achieving a breakthrough with Syria, without his knowledge. In a discussion with President Weizman, Peres complained: "I am amazed how much information Rabin concealed from me. . . ."

In his meeting at the King David Hotel, Peres assured Clinton that he would continue Rabin's policies, and he was even prepared to accelerate the pace of the peace negotiations with Damascus. Peres urged the U.S. president to try to persuade President Assad to agree to an Israeli-Syrian summit meeting, under U.S. auspices. Clinton promised to try.

In an effort to enhance the prestige of the new Israeli prime minister, Peres was invited in December 1995 to meet with President Clinton at the White House and address both houses of Congress. Peres returned to Israel equipped with Clinton's goodwill and American political and military support. On the regional level, Peres explored with Clinton the idea of a strategic alliance between Israel, Turkey, and Jordan, to be joined later by Iraq, after Saddam Hussein's downfall. This idea was also discussed with Defense Secretary William Perry during his visit to Israel in January 1996.[15] While Israeli relations with Turkey have always been warm and the military cooperation is expanding constantly, the idea of a formal tripartite alliance with Jordan has not materialized yet.

In advance of the resumption of talks between Israel and Syria, Secretary of State Warren Christopher came to the Middle East for another round of talks with Prime Minister Peres and President Assad. In a meeting in Jerusalem on January 11, 1996, Peres urged Christopher to persuade Assad to meet with him, in an effort to convince the Israeli public that Syria wants peace. Egypt added its voice in Damascus in support of the Peres request. Returning from Damascus on January 12, Christopher gave Peres a Syrian negative reply. Assad said that a meeting with Peres could not take place before tangible progress was made. As a condition for such a meeting with Peres, Assad wanted a prior Israeli commitment to withdraw to the lines of June 4, 1967, and not just to the recognized international border.

Despite the wide gap in their positions, Israel and Syria decided to resume their peace negotiations. Remembering the experience in Oslo, where the talks were conducted in utmost secrecy and with no press or TV coverage, the United States invited the Israeli and Syrian delegations to hold their meetings at Wye Plantation, a secluded estate in Maryland. As in Oslo, however, Peres again preferred loyalty over competence: He removed Ambassador Rabinovich—a respected scholar and an expert on Syrian affairs—from the chairmanship of the Israeli delegation and replaced him with his protégé Uri Savir, who continued to serve as the director general of the Israeli Foreign Ministry, under Ehud Barak. Savir, a former consul general in New York, is an able diplomat but has no intimate knowledge of Middle Eastern affairs. Unlike Rabinovich, Savir had no experience in dealing with Syrian evasiveness and double- talk.

For a while it looked as though a breakthrough between Israel and Syria was possible. Despite the Syrians' reserved tone, Savir continued to radiate optimism. The Clinton administration also hoped that an Israeli-Syrian breakthrough was possible. However, when Syrian President Assad continued to oppose adequate Israeli security arrangements on the Golan Heights as a condition for Israel's withdrawal and when he refused to set a date for a meeting between him and Shimon Peres, it became clear that the hoped-for breakthrough with Damascus was very unlikely. Facing such a reality, Peres decided in early February to advance the parliamentary elections from October 29 to May 29, 1996.

Yet, even before Peres decided to advance the general elections, a dramatic event in early January was to have a critical effect on his political future. Yahya Ayyash ("the Engineer"), the leading bomb-maker of the Islamic group Hamas, was killed at his hideout on January 5 when his booby-trapped cellular phone exploded in his hand. Although Israel never admitted responsibility for Ayyash's death, Hamas blamed the Israeli security services for this action and promised revenge. In anticipation of such a retaliation, Peres met on January 24 with Yasser Arafat at the Erez checkpoint and handed him a list of twenty-four Hamas and Islamic Jihad activists who had been involved in terrorist attacks against Israel. Peres asked Arafat to arrest them and to confiscate their arms arsenals. Arafat knew most of the twenty-four Islamic activists personally, but he ignored Peres's request.

Arafat liked Peres and respected him. He considered him to be the real architect of the Oslo process. He wondered, however, if Peres had Rabin's courage and determination. Arafat feared Rabin and admired him. The night Rabin was assassinated, Arafat was meeting in Gaza with Portuguese President Mario Soares. Suddenly, his phone rang. "They shot Rabin," his aide told him. "The assassin is a Jew." Arafat turned pale and became emotional. "They shot my partner," Arafat told the Portuguese president.

"Rabin was a tough negotiator," Arafat told a group of Israeli journalists, "but once he signed an agreement, he implemented it to the letter."

Now Arafat was dealing with Peres alone. Would he be able to deliver?

Arafat's meeting with Peres came only a few days after he was elected as chairman of the Palestine Authority and after the election of an eighty-eight-member Legislative Council. The elections, on January 20, were monitored by a group of international observers and were considered to be relatively free. A number of Hamas activists in the Gaza Strip disobeyed their leaders in Jordan and Syria and participated in the elections. Arafat saw in this participation a sign that a reconciliation with the Islamic groups was possible. Hence, when he received from Peres the list of the twenty-four Hamas and Islamic Jihad activists, he decided to ignore Israel's request to arrest them, out of fear that such an arrest would lead to civil war. The result was disastrous. In the space of little more than a week, beginning on February 25, four suicide bombings in Jerusalem, Tel Aviv, and Ashkelon killed fifty-nine Israelis and wounded more than two hundred. This was a real blow to the peace process and to the personal prestige of the prime minister. Peres placed a draconian closure on the West Bank and the Gaza Strip. He imposed a strict curfew on the territories. The redeployment in Hebron was delayed and peace negotiations with the Palestinians were suspended until Arafat should fulfill his commitment to curb terrorism.

The suicide bombing in Tel Aviv on March 4, 1996, was particularly alarming, since it involved cooperation with an Israeli Arab. Said bin Hussein Suleimani, forty-six, a Bedouin from a small tribe in Jezreel Valley, made a living from transporting scrap between Gaza and Israel. He had a permanent crossing pass from Israel to Gaza, and he was well known to Israeli and Palestinian security services. On March 4, Suleimani was approached by Ramzi bin Kader Mohammed Abed, a bearded young man who introduced himself as a "student" at Bir Zeit University, near Ramallah. He claimed that he was caught in Gaza because of the closure and was unable to resume his studies at Bir Zeit. The "student" offered Suleimani $1,100 if he would smuggle him out of the Gaza Strip and drive him to his college. Suleimani could not resist the temptation to earn such a big amount in one day, and he smuggled the "student" out of Gaza. The moment they were out of the Strip, Ramzi Abed told the truck driver that he had changed his mind and wanted to be driven to Tel Aviv. He was dropped off at Dizengoff shopping mall. A few minutes later, the Islamic Jihad terrorist blew himself up, killing thirteen and wounding more than a hundred. That same evening, Suleimani was arrested and confessed his crime. On July 9, 1997, he was convicted and sentenced to thirty years' imprisonment.[16]

The suicide bombings had a devastating effect on the Israeli public. The Persian Gulf War had already shown how vulnerable the Israeli public was to "blind" missile attacks. The launching of Iraqi Scud missiles into Tel Aviv and other cities had shaken Israeli morale. The suicide bombings had the same effect. All of a sudden the "heart" of Israel became a target and the personal security of the Israelis was threatened. Peres was accused by his political right-wing opponents of withdrawing from one city after the other, ignoring the fact that Arafat was not living up to his security commitments.

"I am being haunted by a curse," lamented Peres. Heartbroken and helpless, Peres accused Iran of masterminding the bombings. Angry Israelis demonstrated in front of the prime minister's office in Tel Aviv and Jerusalem. Peres was in total shock. The new acts of terror made him more vulnerable to accusations that he was a weak leader, unable to provide security to his people. When Peres formed his government, in the aftermath of Rabin's assassination, some of his closest aides had suggested to him that he appoint the charismatic former chief of staff General (Res.) Ehud Barak as defense minister. Such an appointment could have instilled a sense of confidence in the traumatized Israeli public. Peres refused. Like Rabin, he wanted to hold both the premiership and the Defense Ministry. Now, in the wake of the suicide bombings, Peres was again advised to appoint Barak as defense minister, and he again refused.

The change in the public's mood was reflected in the polls. Peres was losing ground and his popularity was waning. His threats to Hamas and Islamic Jihad were not taken seriously. It was obvious that Peres had become a prisoner of his own assurances that once the evacuation of the big cities in the West Bank was completed, Arafat would turn forcefully against the Islamic groups. Thus, Peres found himself in the unbearable situation of being unable even to criticize Arafat publicly, lest the criticism be perceived as an admission that the Oslo process had failed.

What Peres could not say was said by some of his associates. In a meeting with Israeli military correspondents, a high-ranking army officer said: "The problems with the Palestinians are still ahead of us. It was possible for us to make peace with Egypt and Jordan. In certain circumstances, it would be possible to make peace with Syria as well. With the Palestinians it's different. The maximum that we can expect is coexistence. Peace with the Palestinians requires a long period of cultural education. Both sides are not yet engaged in this education process."[17]

The new wave of murderous terrorism led several ministers and army officers to caution against relying on Arafat's security services. Addressing a Jewish gathering in London, the minister of health, General (Res.) Ephraim Sneh, said: "Israel without Rabin lacks the moral authority to make more concessions to the Palestinians. Israel must be now more cautious and make much smaller concessions than it made in the past."[18]

In an effort to demonstrate leadership and to calm public fear, Peres revived an old decision of Rabin's to establish a special antiterrorism command. It backfired. Commenting on his decision, General Uri Saguy, the former head of military intelligence, said: "After the signing of the Oslo Accords, we warned that Oslo was very problematic and that terrorism was likely to intensify. We cautioned that each vacated Palestinian city would become a training base, a logistical center, and an operational headquarters for planning and launching terrorist attacks against Israel. We were ignored at the time. Now it has happened. If the government understands only now the full implications of Oslo, then it is very irresponsible behavior. . . ."[19] Peres dismissed this criticism by saying: "This is a very pessimistic description of the situation. . . ."[20]

The sharpest criticism came from General Ilan Biran, the officer who commanded the Central Command and who is currently the director general of the Israeli Defense Ministry. A graduate in political science of Georgetown University, this tough warrior was a member of the Israeli negotiating team with the Palestinians and clashed with Peres on several occasions. In a memorandum to the chief of staff, in May 1994, Biran said that because of his weakness, Arafat would not be able to fight terrorism and would not disarm Hamas and Islamic Jihad. He recommended, therefore, a cautious approach in Israel's dealings with the Palestine Authority. He adopted the same cautious approach when, as a member of the negotiating team of the 1995 interim agreement, he insisted on maximum security for Israeli settlements and the roads leading to them. "Peres's boys" were very unhappy with General Biran and suggested that he resign from the negotiating team. He ignored the advice. In interviews with Israeli newspapers after the new wave of terrorism, Biran said: "Even before the Israeli withdrawal from Jericho, we warned that the city would become a shelter for terrorists. It happened. Then we warned that the evacuation of the big cities in the West Bank would affect our ability to penetrate Hamas and Islamic Jihad. The army's position was again ignored. Now it is proved that Arafat did not do what he promised to do. . . ."[21]

The United States was aware, of course, of Peres's delicate situation. In a telephone conversation with the Israeli prime minister, President Clinton asked: "What can I do for you, Shimon?" Peres answered: "I appreciate your interest. I know how busy you are, I really don't want to bother you. . . ." Clinton insisted: "Don't worry about me. I have all the time for you and for Israel. . . ."[22]

Indeed, in an effort to avoid the total collapse of the peace process, Clinton responded positively to Peres's idea and arranged a very impressive antiterrorist summit in Sharm el-Sheikh, an Egyptian resort city on the shores of the Red Sea. The summit was attended by thirty heads of state, including fifteen Arab kings, presidents, and foreign ministers. It recommended an international effort and regional cooperation in combating terrorism. In addition, Clinton promised Peres very advanced high-tech equipment that Israel had been denied in the past. It soon became clear, however, that for such a cooperation to succeed, it should not be formally institutionalized, and because of Arab sensitivities, it should be very discreet.

In the aftermath of the Sharm el-Sheikh summit, Israeli security agencies registered some success in breaking a number of Palestinian terrorist cells. The most impressive success was the tracking down of Hassan Salameh, the deputy commander of Iz el-din el-Qassam, the military wing of Hamas. Salameh, twenty-six, was arrested in a Hebron hospital after being shot and wounded by Israeli soldiers. In his interrogation, Salameh admitted that he was responsible for planning the three suicide bombings in Jerusalem and Ashkelon in February 1996 that killed forty-six Israelis. He revealed that he had been trained in Syria and Sudan and had infiltrated back into the Gaza Strip—via Egypt—in December 1994. In July 1997, he was sentenced by an Israeli military court to forty-six times life imprisonment.

The Israeli government increased its pressure on Yasser Arafat to honor his written commitments and to arrest the most wanted Hamas and Islamic Jihad terrorists. Acting under the dual pressure of the United States and Egypt, Arafat's security agencies rounded up many prominent Hamas activists, but none of them belonged to Iz el-din el-Qassam. Nevertheless, in an effort to assure the traumatized Israeli electorate that his antiterrorist policy was succeeding, Peres said that Arafat's actions "were moving up a rung."[23]

Because of Arafat's actions against Hamas and Islamic Jihad, Iran got directly involved in terrorist acts against Israel. On April 12, 1996, a "British tourist" carrying a forged British passport under the name of Andrew Jonathan

Neuman was blinded and lost both legs and his left arm in a powerful explosion at his Lawrence Hotel room in East Jerusalem. Police investigators said that a powerful explosive charge hidden in a transistor radio, which was intended to explode in a crowded site in Tel Aviv, went off prematurely. The police said that Neuman's real identity could not be established yet. The only hint about his identity came from General Moshe (Bougi) Yeelon, the head of Israel's military intelligence, who said that "Iran was trying to bring down the Labor's government, in the general elections of May 29, in an effort to destroy the peace process." The right-wing Likud opposition party, unaware of the intelligence in Yeelon's possession, accused the Israeli military of trying to help Labor's election campaign. Only months later, after being elected as prime minister, Netanyahu became aware of Neuman's identity. Indeed, on July 10, 1997, Israeli security services revealed that "Andrew Jonathan Neuman" was a Lebanese Shiite whose name was Hussein Miqdad and who had served as an accountant at the pro-Iranian Hezbollah's office in Beirut. Miqdad told his interrogators that he had been recruited by Iran and had been instructed to detonate a bomb in a crowded site in Tel Aviv. Without revealing their modus operandi, Israeli security agents hinted that "Neuman" had been under surveillance from the moment he received his visa at the Israeli consulate in London until his explosive charge went off prematurely at his hotel room in Jerusalem.[24]

While the various security measures helped prevent any further terrorist acts before election day in Israel, on May 29, the suffering resulting from the draconian closure of the West Bank and the Gaza Strip and the delay in the redeployment in Hebron were to have a devastating effect on the conduct of Israeli Arabs during the election campaign. The closure "strangled" the Palestinians. They lost their jobs in Israel. They were unable to get new food supplies or receive medical treatment in Israel. "The Palestinians felt as though Israel were trying to transform the Gaza Strip and the West Bank into a kind of Albania under the Communist regime," said General (Res.) Danny Rothschild, the former coordinator of Israeli policies in the territories.[25]

Israeli Arabs were appalled by the sudden transformation of Peres from a superdove to a superhawk. Both Israeli Jews and Arabs suspected his motives, and his credibility sank. Peres, however, did not take the Arab anger seriously. Since Labor returned to power in 1992, the Rabin government had allocated large amounts for building roads and improving health, education, and social services in Arab villages. Many Israeli Arabs were appointed to key government positions, and their political influence was growing constantly. Yet, Israeli policymakers underestimated the depth of their national feelings and their solidarity with the Palestinians. Peres and other Labor leaders were convinced that when it came to national elections, Israeli Arabs had no choice but to support Labor against Likud. They were wrong.

In April 1996, the crisis between Peres and Israeli Arabs grew even deeper.

Because of the stalemate in Israeli-Syrian negotiations, the pro-Syrian and Iran-inspired Lebanese Hezbollah intensified its attacks on Israeli soldiers in South Lebanon. Israeli casualties were mounting. Since Damascus gave Hezbollah its tacit approval to intensify its attacks in the self-declared Israeli security belt, seven Israeli soldiers had been killed and more than thirty wounded. Israeli intelligence reports indicated that Hezbollah was using villages as cover for its operations.

Peres was aware, of course, of the fact that he was perceived as a "weak leader." Despite his enormous contribution to Israel's security—through arms procurements, establishing the aircraft industry, and building the Dimona nuclear center—Peres suffered from the fact that he had never served in the army. Contrary to the directness of Rabin, he was always soft-spoken and elegantly dressed. Now, as defense minister, he wanted to be "more Rabin than Rabin." Wearing battle dress, he paid frequent visits to army bases and made a tremendous effort to win the trust of the army's high command. In face of the mounting escalation in South Lebanon, Peres decided on April 11 to launch Operation Grapes of Wrath against Hezbollah bases. In an effort to minimize the number of casualties, the army planned a "surgical operation" based on air and artillery power and high technology. For the first time since the war in Lebanon in June 1982, Israeli jets and helicopters attacked targets in the outskirts of Beirut.

Understanding Peres's electoral needs, President Clinton turned a blind eye on Operation Grapes of Wrath. In the days preceding the Israeli attack, American diplomats in Damascus made an intense effort to persuade President Assad to rein in the Islamic fundamentalists. To no avail. As far as Syria was concerned, Assad saw no difference between Labor and Likud.

In the first few days, Operation Grapes of Wrath went quite well. Lives were spared and villagers who sheltered Hezbollah terrorists were urged to move northward, in the direction of Beirut. The idea behind this action was to put pressure on Syria and Lebanon to rein in Hezbollah. It was argued that more than one million Syrians worked in Lebanon, and hence it was in Assad's interest to stabilize the situation in South Lebanon. Assad did not move. The sight of tens of thousands of Lebanese refugees, shown daily on TV evening broadcasts, shocked Israeli Arabs and alarmed Jordan's King Hussein. On April 16, the Jordanian monarch sent his prime minister to Jerusalem in an effort to persuade Peres to put an end to the military operation. The Israeli prime minister refused. An Arab diplomatic intervention in the United States and Europe also failed.

Then came the least expected tragedy. On April 18, a group of Hezbollah guerrillas found refuge at a UN camp in Qana, where thousands of Lebanese refugees were concentrated. Israeli artillery pounded the camp by mistake, killing more than a hundred Lebanese—many of them women and children—

and wounding many more. World public opinion was moved by this tragedy and turned immediately against Israel. Arab countries denounced Israel for its brutality, and anti-Peres sentiments deepened among Israeli Arabs. On April 22, Arab Knesset members spoke vehemently against Peres and called for his resignation. One, Abdul Wahab Darawsheh, was particularly harsh in his criticism. He said: "Peres is the biggest disappointment of the peace camp. He is a murderer of women and children. I want to make it clear. Israeli Arabs are going to punish Peres for his brutality and they are not going to vote for him on election day. If Peres loses the elections, let it be. Let Peres go to hell. . . ."[26]

The Qana tragedy limited Israel's ability to end the military operation on its own terms and brought an uninvited diplomatic intervention to end the crisis. On April 26, following an intense dual effort by Secretary of State Warren Christopher and French Foreign Minister Herve de Charette, a cease-fire was declared and a new monitoring group, consisting of Israel, Lebanon, Syria, France, and the United States, was established to monitor events along the Israeli-Lebanese border. From an Israeli point of view, Operation Grapes of Wrath was a total failure.

With his wings clipped, Peres left for Washington to meet with President Clinton and address the annual conference of the American-Israeli Public Affairs Committee, (AIPAC), the pro-Israel lobby in the United States. During his visit to Washington, Peres and Clinton signed a counterterrorism agreement and the United States also agreed to step up the joint Israeli-American effort to develop the Arrow tactical antiballistic missile. In a hardly disguised effort to signal his "endorsement" of Peres in the general elections, Clinton told AIPAC: "I pledge to you today that no one can break this strong relationship between our two nations. . . ."[27]

After addressing the Washington Institute for Near East Policy, Peres returned to Israel to concentrate on his election campaign, which still lacked a sense of direction. Peres's decision to advance the general elections from November to May 29 was probably the biggest gamble in his entire political career. Being more popular abroad than at home, Peres had led the Labor Party in the past into four defeats. He now entered his fifth race under a new electoral system by which—for the first time—Israelis cast two separate ballots, one for the candidate to the premiership and the other for the election of the Knesset members. At the time, the Likud Party opposed the new system—the only dissenting voice was that of Benjamin Netanyahu. Among the Labor leaders, Rabin supported the new legislation, while Peres opposed it. He feared that the new law would give the directly elected prime minister "dictatorial powers." However, in the aftermath of Rabin's assassination, Peres no longer opposed the new electoral system. He underestimated Netanyahu and he was certain that he would easily win election.

The election campaign was dull and highly personalized. In contrast to

Netanyahu's aggressive campaign, Peres projected civility and statesmanship. In his campaign, Peres did not use Rabin's assassination; he wanted to be elected because of his own record. In the wake of the suicide bombings, both Peres and Netanyahu moved to the center. In his effort to win the "floating vote," especially the votes of those who feared his peace policies, Peres introduced a "security valve": He promised the electorate that in case of an agreement with Syria or the Palestinians, he would put the agreement to the Israeli public, in a referendum. Peres revised Labor's platform by omitting the opposition to the establishment of a Palestinian state or to a territorial compromise on the Golan Heights. As for Jerusalem, Labor's platform emphasized that the city would remain Israel's undivided capital.

For a while it looked as though things were moving in Labor's direction. The peace process was on track. Suicide bombings had stopped. The eighty-eight-member Palestinian Legislative Council was elected and Arafat was improving his governing skills. In late April, Arafat convened the 450 members of the Palestine National Council (PNC), the Palestinian parliament-in-exile, for a special meeting in Gaza, for the purpose of amending the PLO Covenant and deleting all paragraphs calling for Israel's destruction. In order to assure the needed two-thirds majority, Israel allowed all PNC members, including the most wanted terrorists, to attend the Gaza session. Nevertheless, the leaders of the most radical Palestinian groups, whose main offices are in Damascus, did not come to Gaza. They were warned by Syria of an Israeli trap, and they feared they would be arrested and brought to trial for the many acts of terrorism they had conducted in the past thirty years.

Israel followed the deliberations in Gaza with great interest. The result, however, was very disappointing. Arafat published a short communiqué in English claiming that he had fulfilled his commitment to revise the PLO Covenant. Commenting on Arafat's statement, and without even reading the text of the relevant resolution, Peres said: "This is the most significant ideological development in more than one hundred years of conflict between Israel and the Palestinians." The United States followed Israel's lead. A State Department spokesman said that Arafat had "proved himself deserving of American assistance." Similar positive comments came from Europe and world capitals elsewhere. In only a few days it was apparent that Arafat's statement was misleading. While the exact text of the PNC resolutions was not immediately released, Bulletin No. 8 of El-Fatah—Arafat's group in the PLO—published the full Arabic text of the resolution, as follows:

- The PNC decides to amend the Palestinian Covenant by deleting those sections which are in contradiction to the Letters of Mutual Recognition which were exchanged between Israel and the PLO on September 9, 1993.

- The PNC authorizes the Legal Committee to redraft the Covenant and to submit the new language for approval by the PLO's Central Committee, at its first meeting.

The acting chairman of the PNC, Salim Zaanoun, explained that "there were no specific sections in the Covenant that were deleted." He said that the PNC legal committee would redraft the PLO Covenant within a period of six months. If approved by the PLO's Central Committee, the new text would then be submitted to another session of the PNC for final approval.[28]

Needless to say, the new text of the PLO Covenant was not drafted, and to this date there is still no word when, if at all, a new text will be submitted to the PNC.

The publication of the official Arabic text of the PNC resolution constituted a severe blow to Peres's prestige. His quick endorsement of the vague English text was perceived by his political opponents as an attempt to mislead the public in order to help him win the May 29 elections.

Commenting on this episode, A. M. Rosenthal wrote in his *New York Times* column: "It turned out to be part hype, part hoax and part Middle East comedy. The [PNC] resolution was passed in secret. So many versions in Arabic, Hebrew and English were whipped around the world, that it was like that hilarious contract scene in *A Night at the Opera* where Chico Marx keeps ripping off paragraph after paragraph. . . ."[29]

Then came the hardest blow of all. On May 3, the *Jerusalem Post* published what was described as a four-month investigation that detailed informal discussions between Israeli and Palestinian teams on the final status of the West Bank. The negotiations, which began in Stockholm in October 1993, lasted two years and produced an unsigned thirteen-page document, later known as the Beilin–Abu Mazen agreement. According to the "agreement," Israel would accept a demilitarized Palestinian state, whose capital would be Abu Dis—a small village that was part of Jerusalem during the Jordanian rule. Temple Mount would be under Muslim religious authority. Jerusalem, without the Old City, would remain undivided, under Israeli sovereignty. The status of the Old City would be subject to further negotiations. The Palestinian refugees would not return to Israel, but would be allowed to return to the Palestinian state. Finally, Israel would annex about 10 percent of the West Bank, in return for a stretch of land in the Israeli Negev, thus extending the size of the Gaza Strip. As for the settlements, part of them would be annexed to Israel and part would remain under Palestinian sovereignty.

Beilin presented the document to Peres on Saturday, November 11, just one week after Rabin's assassination. Peres was not enthusiastic about it. Foreign Minister Ehud Barak also had reservations. What was more important, both Abu Mazen and Yasser Abed Rabbo, a member of the Palestine Authority, disclaimed the document. They said publicly, on several occasions, that the ideas mentioned in the document were Beilin's, but Abu Mazen had never accepted them. Because of repeated assertions by Beilin that such an agreement was indeed reached, Abu Mazen published in May 1997 a very sharp denial and expressed the hope that this denial would put an end to Beilin's claim. In an interview with a London-based Arabic daily, Abu Mazen said: "There is no document called the Beilin–Abu Mazen agreement, nor was any formal or informal document approved by the PLO institutions. Honestly speaking, no Palestinian would ever dare to accept what was attributed to me in that so-called 'agreement.' No Palestinian would ever accept any alternative to Arab Jerusalem, East Jerusalem, sanctified Jerusalem that was occupied in the 1967 war. We will never trade East Jerusalem for Abu Dis. East Jerusalem is our future capital. . . ."[30]

Beilin claimed that Peres didn't know about his secret negotiations with Abu Mazen.[31] Other Labor leaders doubted it. They argued that secret talks lasting two years could not have been conducted, for the second time, behind Rabin's back, without Peres's knowledge. This was not the time, however, to deal with this subject. Facing a tough election campaign, Peres and other Labor leaders made an extreme effort to keep the issue of the Beilin–Abu Mazen "agreement" secret. It did not help. The contents of the document were leaked to Likud and caused tremendous damage to Labor. Within days, the country was flooded with Likud slogans such as "Peres will divide Jerusalem" and "Bibi is good for the Jews." The presumed agreement confirmed Israelis' fear that Peres was in a hurry to reach an agreement with Arafat at any cost, and that he was prepared to compromise even on Jerusalem. This was undoubtedly one of the reasons for Labor's defeat in the general elections of May 29, 1996.

Some Israeli commentators compared Peres's downfall to Winston Churchill's defeat in the aftermath of his glorious victory in World War II. While the comparison is valid, it would take several years to determine the real causes of Labor's defeat. According to data available so far, it is safe to conclude that Peres's defeat was owed to a combination of factors. Generally speaking, Peres had the support of the established Jewish Ashkenazi community, the leftist Meretz Party, and the majority of Israeli Arabs. Netanyahu had the support of his right-wing Likud Party, the religious parties, the Russian immigrants, and the underprivileged Sephardic Jews.

The religious support of Netanyahu was of particular interest. Netanyahu is a secular Jew. He does not observe the Sabbath, nor does he keep a kosher kitchen. Like President Clinton, Netanyahu was attacked for his extramarital experiences. "We supported Netanyahu not for his Jewish values, but because of his nationalistic positions," explained one of the religious leaders.

The official election results showed that Netanyahu won by a very slim majority: 50.49 percent to 49.51 percent. The difference between Netanyahu and

Peres was less than thirty thousand votes. This figure, however, is misleading. Not only did Jewish voters elect Netanyahu by a 55–45 majority, but there were also 150,000 voters (among them twenty thousand Arabs) who cast blank slips in the ballot boxes. One of the reasons for this protest vote was Arab and leftist Meretz disenchantment with Peres's "iron fist policy" in Lebanon and in the territories. Tanya Reinhart, a leftist activist who led the "White Slips Revolt," wrote: "Peres brought upon himself his defeat. He inherited [from Rabin] two peoples—the Israelis and the Palestinians—who were ripe for peace. Instead of leading them, Peres did everything in his capacity to show them that the Likud was justified in its opposition to peace. . . . He imposed a draconian closure on the territories, he delayed the redeployment in Hebron, he suspended the final status negotiations, and he demonstrated his iron fist in Lebanon. If this is the new Israeli policy, why vote Peres? Netanyahu knows better how to implement it."[32]

This was the interpretation of the left. A similar disenchantment was shown by the Sephardic Jews, who in 1992 had voted overwhelmingly for Rabin. Two of Labor's most prominent Sephardic leaders, former housing minister Benjamin (Fuad) Ben-Eliezer and former ambassador to Madrid and now Knesset member Professor Shlomo Ben-Ami, complained about their party's shortsightedness when it rejected General Yitzhak Mordechai's efforts to join Labor. Defense Minister Mordechai, a moderate and a supporter of the peace process, is now the most popular minister in Netanyahu's cabinet. Ben-Eliezer said: "Mordechai is a legend among Sephardic Israelis. The Iraqi-born general is a war hero. A paratrooper, he is the only army general who served in all three commands—Central, South, and Northern Command. He is known for his respect for family values and for Jewish tradition. When he retired from the army, he spoke with Peres about his political future. He wanted to become either a minister or the head of the General Security Service. Peres underestimated him and turned him down. Mordechai went to Netanyahu, who embraced him warmly. Mordechai, together with Moroccan-born David Levy, another moderate, won for Likud the majority of the Sephardic vote in the poor development towns."[33]

Finally, there was the personal aspect. Many of the 130,000 Jews who cast white slips in the ballot boxes did so because of personal distrust of Peres. Because of his poor credibility and his manipulative nature, Peres lost the trust of many of his supporters. One of them said: "Peres never kept a promise. On some occasions, he wanted to keep his word, but he was afraid of the precedent. . . ."[34] If we add the 130,000 Israelis who cast white slips in the ballot boxes to the number of those who voted against Peres, we must conclude that Peres lost by a much bigger margin.

Netanyahu's victory confounded the pollsters and caused some concern among the Palestinians, in the Arab world, and in the United States and Europe. One week after he formed his cabinet, on June 18, 1996, the new Israeli prime minister met with President Clinton at the White House and addressed both houses of Congress. In a joint press conference with Clinton, Netanyahu reiterated his commitment to continue the peace process, according to the Oslo Accords "and on the basis of reciprocity." Asked about his settlement policy, Netanyahu revealed that under the heading of "natural growth," Rabin expanded the settlements by fifty thousand additional settlers. "You surely don't expect me to do less than what Rabin did," he said.

Netanyahu's visit to Washington proved that it was hard to step into Rabin's shoes. Clinton's friendship with Rabin was unparalleled in American-Israeli history. Some of Clinton's aides confided to several Jewish leaders that "Bibi tried to be a little too casual" with the president. They revealed that on several occasions, Netanyahu called the U.S. chief executive "Bill" in front of his aides, while even Hillary Rodham Clinton called her husband "Mr. President" in public.[35]

The U.S. presidential election campaign gave the new Israeli prime minister the grace period that he so needed. Clinton's effort at that time was limited to keeping the peace process from going backward. The United States urged the Arab leaders to give Netanyahu a chance, and to work with him rather than against him. U.S. officials told their Arab counterparts that they should not misinterpret Netanyahu's sternness during his campaign as belligerence. As for the Palestinians, Clinton kept Arafat going by ensuring him a continued flow of financial assistance.

In early July, Netanyahu met with Egypt's President Mubarak and Jordan's King Hussein. Both gave him the grace period that he asked for and shielded him from early media attacks. Netanyahu also sent his political adviser, Dore Gold, to the Persian Gulf to appease the fears of Qatar and Oman and to assure them of the new government's intention to continue the peace process.

However, shortly afterward, the first signs of disappointment with Netanyahu's performance began to surface. The new Israeli prime minister came to power with no real experience in government. A former ambassador to the UN, Netanyahu served as deputy foreign minister under David Levy, and during the Madrid Peace Conference he excelled mostly in the field of information and public relations rather than in policy planning. Being the first-ever directly elected prime minister, Netanyahu had only a vague idea about the functioning of the new structure. In the United States, a new administration has a long period of transition between election day and the inauguration, but Netanyahu did not have this luxury. He came to the prime minister's office totally unprepared for the enormous task that he was facing. He did not have a blueprint for his first hundred days, and he had to learn from his mistakes while governing. Like President Clinton during his first two years in office, Netanyahu marched from one crisis to another, driven by events rather than directing them.

The new electoral system brought into the scene groups and parties with no political experience. As a result, twelve out of eighteen members of Netanyahu's cabinet were new and had no past experience in government. Contrary to his aggressive election campaign, in the aftermath of his victory Netanyahu projected an image of an indecisive leader who succumbed to pressure and had no sense of direction. His attempt to create a national security council and a council of economic advisers—similar to the institutions at the White House—was torpedoed by the ministers of defense, foreign affairs, and finance. Netanyahu did not understand that despite the new electoral system, Israel's political culture remained basically parliamentarian; it was not an American-style presidential system. Netanyahu did not want the charismatic Ariel Sharon in his government, but he was forced to yield to David Levy's pressure and created a special Ministry of the Infrastructure for the enigmatic war hero. Within a year, two of the Likud's pillars, Benny Begin and Dan Meridor, resigned their ministerial posts. They accused the prime minister of betraying the Likud's ideology and of running a government riddled with sleaze.

Netanyahu's peace team also lacked the necessary professional competence. He appointed David Levy and General Yitzhak Mordechai as his ministers for foreign affairs and defense. Both brought with them rich experience—Levy in government, Mordechai in the army. Both are also moderates and supporters of the peace process. Their appointment was a good signal to both the United States and the Arab world that the new Israeli government was committed to the continuation of the peace negotiations with both the Palestinians and the Syrians. However, instead of taking advantage of the vast experience accumulated at the Defense Ministry and Foreign Ministry, Netanyahu tried to run everything from the prime minister's office. This proved to be a miserable effort. The appointment of senior officials at the prime minister's office was made without thorough background checks, and as a result, within a very short period six officials resigned or were forced to quit.

If Peres's peace team was unfamiliar with Middle Eastern affairs and was not sufficiently qualified to negotiate with the Palestinians, Netanyahu's personal team was even less qualified for this complicated task. Except for his diplomatic adviser, the American-born Dore Gold, who earned his Ph.D. in Middle Eastern affairs at Columbia University and had spent several years at the prestigious Jaffe Center for Strategic Studies at Tel Aviv University, none of Netanyahu's team had the necessary experience to negotiate with the Palestinians. Rabin had several excellent private channels that he used occasionally, and successfully, for his dealings with Yasser Arafat. They were Yossi Genossar, the former deputy director of the General Security Service, and Ephraim Sneh and Benjamin Ben-Eliezer, both of whom had served in the West Bank and had excellent and trustful relations with the Palestinian leaders. Netanyahu had no such channel. The newly elected prime minister appointed the cabinet secretary, Danny Naveh, a young lawyer with no experience in Middle Eastern affairs, as his negotiator with the Palestine Authority. He also appointed his friend and confidant, the attorney Yitzhak Molcho as his "back channel" to Arafat and Abu Mazen. The Jerusalem-born Molcho was fluent in Arabic and was a good negotiator, but he needed time to study the thick files of the negotiations with the Palestinians and to win their trust and confidence.

Here again, it took almost a year and many crises before the new Israeli negotiating team was reorganized. Foreign Minister David Levy became responsible for the negotiations with the Palestinians, with Cabinet Secretary Danny Naveh a member of his team. Attorney Molcho would continue to serve as Netanyahu's back channel to Arafat, but would report to both the prime minister and the foreign minister. Dore Gold was appointed as ambassador to the UN and his place as political adviser was taken by Dr. Uzi Arad, a veteran of the Mossad who had studied and worked in prestigious think-tank organizations in the United States.

Netanyahu began his term as prime minister in an atmosphere of crisis. He hoped to continue the diplomatic and economic momentum with the Arab world while at the same time slowing down the implementation of the various agreements with the Palestinians. This did not happen. Despite U.S. advice to respect the democratic process in Israel and to give the newly elected prime minister a chance, the Arab world could not easily recover from the shock of Netanyahu's election. Arab leaders, especially Egypt's President Mubarak and Yasser Arafat, could not "forgive" Netanyahu for winning the election and defeating Shimon Peres. Egypt and Syria were determined to help topple the new democratically elected Israeli government.

Shortly after Netanyahu's election, an Arab summit was convened in Cairo to discuss the new situation in Israel. Such a summit had been considered several times in the past, but Arab leaders had been unable to overcome their divisions resulting from Iraq's invasion of Kuwait. This time, however, with the exclusion of Iraq, they managed to project a common anti-Netanyahu front. The Arab leaders rejected the Israeli idea that security takes preference over peace. They insisted that the new Israeli government fulfill all the agreements signed with the previous Labor government. Rejecting Netanyahu's statement in Washington that he was prepared to resume negotiations with Damascus "without preconditions," the Arab summit supported President Assad's position that the negotiations be based on the principle of "land for peace," and that they should be resumed from the point where they were suspended in March 1996.

The Arab summit's decisions were accompanied by various military and diplomatic actions. A Hamas terrorist cell killed five Israelis in two drive-by shootings near Beit Shemesh, southwest of Jerusalem, and revived fears of renewed terrorism. Then on August 12 there came a sudden redeployment of Syrian commando units from Beirut to the Golan Heights and intensified violence by Hezbollah in South Lebanon. Conflicting evaluations by various intelligence agencies aroused fears of a renewed war with Syria. It was obvious that the Arab leaders were testing Netanyahu, the way Nikita Khrushchev tested the newly elected John Kennedy in the Cuban missile crisis in 1961. Like Kennedy, Netanyahu was not deterred. On the contrary, the Israeli army countered by conducting "maneuvers" in the Golan Heights and by adding $300 million to the defense budget to replenish the stockpiles and supplies it had let run low in recent years. All Israeli military experts were unanimous in their evaluation that the Syrian army was no match for the Israeli army. Yet, some of them feared that President Assad would be tempted to use "shock therapy" by initiating a "limited war" and by launching Scud missiles into Israeli urban centers. The purpose of such an initiative, it was argued, would be to enable Assad to negotiate from a position of strength. A prompt U.S. diplomatic intervention in Syria defused the tension. The Clinton administration simply could not afford a new war in the Middle East while the president was busy in his own election campaign.

A more troublesome situation existed between Israel and the Palestinians. Shortly after Netanyahu assumed the premiership, President Ezer Weizman urged him to meet with Yasser Arafat to complete the redeployment in Hebron and to ease the closure of the West Bank and the Gaza Strip. Still a prisoner of his own election campaign, Netanyahu refused. Instead, he authorized lower-level discussions between his diplomatic adviser, Dore Gold, and Abu Mazen and between various Israeli and Palestinian teams. As a gesture of goodwill, the Palestine Authority agreed to close three of its offices that were operating illegally in East Jerusalem.

What was annoying in these low-level negotiations was the degree of unpreparedness of the Israeli teams. "The 'new' Israeli negotiators were totally unaware of the progress that had been made and the understandings reached between the Palestine Authority and the Labor government. They didn't even carefully read the Oslo Accords and the interim agreement. There were cases where the Israelis raised a certain problem. We referred them to the texts that have been already approved," Saeb Erikat, the chief Palestinian negotiator, told Israeli correspondents.

In August 1996, in a move aimed to please his nationalist and religious supporters, Netanyahu renewed the incentives to the settlers in the West Bank and the Gaza Strip that had been withdrawn by the Rabin government. In the face of mounting criticism in the Arab world, the United States, and Europe, the Israeli prime minister explained that such a move was necessary to meet the "natural growth" needs of the settlers.

Netanyahu's refusal to meet with Yasser Arafat remained the most irritating issue in Israeli-Palestinian relations. During his election campaign, Netanyahu denounced Arafat in very strong terms. Upon taking office, however, he knew that a meeting with the chairman of the Palestine Authority was inevitable. He began to prepare the ground for such a meeting by allowing Foreign Minister David Levy and Defense Minister Yitzhak Mordechai to meet with the Palestinian leader. He even eased the closure of the territories and considerably increased the number of Palestinian workers who were allowed to cross for work in Israel. As for his own meeting with Arafat, he still found it difficult to ignore his past promises, and he kept delaying it as much as he could.

Terje Larsen, the Norwegian scholar who had masterminded the secret negotiations in Oslo and who had been appointed by the UN to monitor the financing of the various projects in the Gaza Strip, flooded Netanyahu with cables urging him to meet with Arafat. The former Israeli prime minister, Shimon Peres, met with Arafat and found him frustrated and despairing. He also called for a meeting between Netanyahu and Arafat. Netanyahu, however, spoke with arrogance, even contempt, about the Peres-Arafat meeting. He said: "Arafat should realize that there is a new government in Israel. Peres has no importance anymore. It is as though [President] Bush should address a Republican Convention and declare his intention to raise taxes. . . ."

President Clinton was very unhappy with this situation, but his hands were tied by the presidential election campaign. Early in his administration, Clinton took a strategic decision to drop the confrontational approach of President Bush and to work with the government of Israel, not against it. With Rabin and Peres, it was easy. They were both committed to peace, and they both accepted the principle of land for peace. With Netanyahu, however, it was different. Nevertheless, Clinton did hope that after his reelection he would be able to work with Netanyahu. Until then, Clinton had to keep his cool. He could not afford any public criticism of Israel, especially when his Republican rival, Bob Dole, was sniping at him on every occasion.

Addressing the annual conference of B'nai B'rith in Washington, Dole accused Clinton of interfering in Israel's domestic affairs by supporting Labor's Peres against Likud's Netanyahu. In addition to his declared position on Jerusalem, Dole also told the Jewish gathering that if elected president he would not pressure Israel to withdraw from the Golan Heights.

Clinton's point man on the Jewish campaign trail was Vice President Al Gore. Addressing the four hundred Jewish delegates to the Democratic National Convention in Chicago, Gore said that the Democratic platform would clearly state that undivided Jerusalem was Israel's capital. He added that the platform would call for the continuation of the peace process in order to achieve "peace with security," a slogan used by Netanyahu. Gore assured the Jewish delegates that Clinton would work with Netanyahu to achieve this goal.[36]

Toward the end of August, Netanyahu knew that the time had come for a meeting with Arafat. Increasingly frustrated, Arafat appealed to President Ezer

Weizman. The president was prepared to invite Arafat to meet with him at his private residence in Caesarea, but he agreed to postpone the meeting until after a meeting between Netanyahu and Arafat. In early September, Netanyahu was due to visit the United States to address—together with Al Gore—a festive dinner in New York to celebrate the fortieth anniversary of the Conference of Presidents of Major Jewish Organizations. A meeting with President Clinton, at the White House, was scheduled for September 9. Netanyahu knew that he couldn't see Clinton without having met Arafat. Indeed, following an intensive and secret negotiation between Dore Gold, Abu Mazen, and the Norwegian intermediary, Terje Larsen, Netanyahu and Arafat finally met and shook hands, on September 4, at the Erez checkpoint on the border between Israel and the Gaza Strip.

This was a major political event, and it was welcomed in the United States and in the entire world. The meeting was seen as another proof that the new Israeli prime minister was indeed committed to the continuation of the peace process and to the implementation of the various accords with the Palestinians.

Netanyahu's meeting with Arafat generated a new wave of goodwill in the United States, which was reflected in Al Gore's speech at the Conference of Presidents. Gore said: "History will record that Israel has never had a better friend in the White House than President Bill Clinton. Just as we once walked side by side in partnership for peace with Yitzhak Rabin, we are proud to walk by your side, Mr. Prime Minister, in your search for peace with security. The United States recognizes that Israel's aspirations for peace must be balanced with demands for security, and it is the Israelis who must determine how to keep this balance. . . ."[37]

This positive atmosphere, however, was squandered by the sudden Israeli decision to open an archaeological tunnel exit in the Old City of Jerusalem. The opening was marked by too many blunders. Netanyahu and Jerusalem's mayor, Ehud Olmert, opened the Western Wall tunnel in the early-morning hours of September 24, with no press or TV coverage and with no proper explanation of the tunnel's importance as a tourist attraction that would benefit both Israel and the Palestinians. Ignoring the sensitive nature of the action, especially in an area so close to Temple Mount, Netanyahu left a few hours later for England and Germany. While in the air, he received the first reports about the riots in East Jerusalem and in other parts of the West Bank. Palestinian leaders accused Israel of digging a tunnel under Temple Mount, thus endangering the Muslim holy shrine. This was, of course, a false accusation, but nevertheless it was believed in the Arab and Muslim worlds.

The next day, for the first time since the Palestine Authority took charge of six cities and 450 villages in the West Bank, Palestinian policemen in Ramallah and Nablus opened fire on Israeli soldiers, causing a serious crisis of confidence from which Israel never recovered. In these clashes, seven Israelis and sixteen

Palestinians were killed and many more were wounded. Netanyahu cut short his visit to Europe and rushed back home. He finally understood that his action had pushed Israel to the wall and drawn sharp attacks from Arab and Western leaders. Jordan's King Hussein was enraged. Two days before the opening of the tunnel, Netanyahu had sent his diplomatic adviser, Dore Gold, to Amman to brief the Jordanian monarch on the results of his recent trip to the United States. He had not been given even a hint about the opening of the tunnel.

Egypt took a particularly maximalist position against Israel. The Egyptian media mocked Netanyahu as "rotten" and compared him to Adolf Hitler. President Mubarak warned of a new intifada and called for an immediate closure of the tunnel. Like Syria earlier, Egypt conducted large-scale military maneuvers along the Suez Canal. In an interview with an Israeli newspaper, Egypt's foreign minister, Amr Mussa, said: "In any final status agreement, Israel must withdraw completely to the 1967 cease-fire lines and abandon all claims to its settlements in the territories. Some of the settlements could remain under a Palestinian sovereignty, just as Arabs live within Israel. Under no circumstances would the settlements be incorporated into Israel." Mussa faulted Arafat for closing three Palestinian offices in East Jerusalem. He added: "We now advise the Palestinians not to make any more concessions. This is not a maximalist position. To establish a Palestinian state is not a maximalist demand. Without a full withdrawal and the establishment of a Palestinian state, I don't think there would be peace."[38]

Mubarak threatened to cancel the third regional economic summit, which was due to be held in Cairo in November, with Israeli participation. Normalization with other Arab countries was slowed down or suspended. The disruption in the peace process had adversely affected Israel's economy, and foreign investments were reduced, especially in the fields of construction, telecommunications, and tourism.

In an effort to avoid the total collapse of the peace process, Clinton on October 1 urgently called a summit meeting at the White House, with the participation of Mubarak, King Hussein, Netanyahu, and Arafat. The Jordanian monarch was most outspoken in that meeting. "You are no Yitzhak Rabin," Hussein told Netanyahu, and his remarks were immediately leaked to the American media. Both Mubarak and Hussein urged Netanyahu to close the tunnel. He refused. While admitting that the opening of the tunnel had been mishandled, Netanyahu was convinced that yielding to Arab pressure—especially after Palestinian policemen opened fire on Israeli soldiers—would destroy his image at home and undermine his authority among his coalition partners.

In order to avoid a stalemate, Clinton suggested concentrating on the future problems rather than on the mistakes of the immediate past. First priority was given to the redeployment in Hebron. The president assigned Ambassador

Dennis Ross to this task and instructed him to stay in the region as long as necessary.

Ross and his team made two trips to the Middle East, one before and one after the presidential election. In October, Ross worked with Netanyahu and Arafat for twenty-three days. Toward the end of December, he came for another twenty-two days, which ended on January 15, 1997, in an agreement for the redeployment in Hebron. This was a major victory for American diplomacy and a personal success for Ross. This victory was made possible through very positive and creative assistance from King Hussein. "One of the major obstacles to overcome was the low level of trust between Israel and the Palestinians," Ambassador Ross told a meeting of the Conference of Presidents of Major Jewish Organizations, in New York, on January 30, 1997.[39] Ross said that in the past there had been a low level of trust between Rabin and Arafat as well, until some time in 1995, when they started to trust each other. The mistrust between Arafat and Netanyahu ran much deeper. Therefore, the United States this time had to play a much more active role in order to bridge the gap between the two parties.

Ross dealt not only with the issue of redeployment in Hebron, but also with the remaining issues from the interim agreement of September 1995, which were not yet implemented. The issues included the release of prisoners, a safe passage between the West Bank and the Gaza Strip, the opening of the airport in Gaza, and various economic problems. Finally, on January 15, Netanyahu and Arafat convened in the presence of Ross, and at their mutual request, he prepared a note for the record, summarizing what they agreed upon in their meeting. The two leaders agreed that the Oslo peace process must move forward. The Israeli redeployment in Hebron must be completed within ten days. The first phase of the three further redeployments in the West Bank would be carried out during the first week of March 1997. In a side letter to Netanyahu, dated January 15, Secretary Christopher assured the Israeli prime minister that the United States had conveyed to Chairman Arafat its view that the process of redeploying the Israeli forces remained the exclusive responsibility of the Israeli government. Christopher's letter also made it clear that all three phases of the further redeployments must be completed not later than mid-1998. Thus, while Israel had gotten an extra year for the redeployments, as compared with the original agreement between Peres and Arafat, it was now reaffirmed that the redeployments must be completed before the end of the negotiations on the final status of Jerusalem and the West Bank.

The note for the record reaffirmed Arafat's commitment to complete the revision of the Palestinian Covenant, to fight terrorism and end violence, to strengthen the security cooperation with Israel, to combat terrorist organizations systematically and destroy their infrastructure and confiscate illegal arms, and finally to reduce the size of the Palestine police, pursuant to the interim agreement.[40]

Unlike the interim agreement (Oslo II), which was approved by the Knesset with a majority of one single vote (61–59), the protocol on the redeployment in Hebron was approved by a very impressive majority, 87–17, with only sixteen abstentions. The political implication of such an accord was obvious: The Likud and the religious parties associated with Netanyahu's coalition government were no longer opposed to the principle of land for peace. That was the most significant signal that the Netanyahu government had conveyed to the international community about its peace policies in future.

For a while it seemed as though the peace process was back on track. A few weeks later, however, came another cold shower. As had happened with the opening of the Old City tunnel in September 1996, two events in March 1997 squandered the goodwill generated by the Hebron agreement. On March 7, Israel had announced that as part of the three further redeployments, it would transfer to the Palestine Authority 9 percent of the West Bank territory. According to the interim agreement, the West Bank was divided into three parts: Zone A, which was under the total control of the Palestinians; Zone B, which was under the administrative responsibility of the Palestine Authority but under joint Israeli-Palestinian security responsibility; and Zone C, which was still under the exclusive control of Israel. Acting according to Secretary Christopher's letter of January 15, 1997, Netanyahu announced his intention to transfer 7 percent of land from Zone B to Zone A, and only 2 percent from Zone C to Zone A.

Arafat exploded in anger. He believed that Netanyahu was humiliating him deliberately by offering him land in Zone B, which was already under his administrative jurisdiction. He wanted each of the three phases to include 30 percent of the West Bank. Arafat informed Netanyahu and the United States that he refused to accept this meager Israeli redeployment. Unfortunately, Arafat again misunderstood the significance of the Israeli move. What was important in this first phase of the redeployment was not the size of the land to be transferred, but the principle: The Israeli prime minister had been elected on a platform maintaining that the entire territory that was under the British Mandate was "the Land of Israel." Now, however, Netanyahu emerged again as a leader who was ready for a territorial compromise. Once the principle of redeployment in Hebron was approved by the overwhelming majority of the Knesset, the size of the additional withdrawals, and not the principle, would be negotiable.

This new reality, however, was overtaken by another, more serious event. On March 18, with the approval of the full Israeli government but without prior consultation with the Palestine Authority, Israel sent its bulldozers to start building the infrastructure of a new Jewish neighborhood at Har Homa, a Jewish-owned site on the southeastern edge of Jerusalem, which Palestinians call Jabal Abu Ghneim. This was too much for Arafat to swallow. Taken against the background of the surprise opening of Jerusalem's Old City tunnel, Arafat saw in the construction at Har Homa a deliberate attempt by Israel to predetermine the final status of Jerusalem.

Arafat's response was instant. That same day, March 18, Arafat met in Gaza with leaders of Hamas and Islamic Jihad. According to Israeli intelligence reports, Arafat gave the Islamic fundamentalist leaders the green light to resume their suicide bombings in Israel. This was a flagrant violation of all Palestinian commitments to Israel. Arafat denied the accusation and claimed that it was an Israeli attempt to divert attention from the Har Homa crisis. The United States too expressed some doubts whether such a green light was given. Its credibility being questioned, Israel submitted immediately to the United States an "irrefutable proof" that such a green light had indeed been given. Three days later, there was no need for any further proof. On March 21, a suicide bomber blew himself up in the Apropo Café in Tel Aviv, killing three Israeli women and wounding forty-seven.

As expected, the Arab reaction to the construction at Har Homa was very negative. In addition to two anti-Israel votes in two emergency sessions of the UN General Assembly, Arab countries suspended all normalization activities with Israel. The United States, Europe, and the Arab world called on Netanyahu to suspend the building at Har Homa. He refused. To his many critics, Netanyahu said: "Finally, Arafat will now understand that there is a new government in Israel. . . ."[41]

Out of fear that both Israel and the Palestinians would lose control of events, King Hussein sent a very angry letter to Netanyahu criticizing the Israeli prime minister for his behavior. In a gesture of courtesy, Jordanian Prime Minister Abdul Karim Kabariti sent a copy of this letter to Yasser Arafat. One of Arafat's aides leaked the contents of the letter to the Israeli press. It caused a furor both in Amman and in Jerusalem. In a very unusual move, King Hussein accepted Kabariti's "resignation" and appointed former prime minister Abdul Salam Majali to succeed him.

The renewed crisis with the Palestinians led many Israeli officials and political observers to consider new approaches to the peace process. In a meeting of the Israeli Foreign Ministry's policy planning staff, David Afek, the director of the ministry's research center, warned that if Israel would not come out with a new initiative, "it will be increasingly isolated on the international scene and the peace process will die."[42] Indeed, it was in this context and at the height of this commotion that the Israeli prime minister launched a surprise initiative, proposing to plunge immediately into negotiations on the final status of the territories. Netanyahu pledged to end these negotiations in six to nine months' time. Both Egypt and Arafat rejected this proposal.

It is not difficult to explain the logic behind this initiative. While serving as interior minister in Yitzhak Rabin's cabinet, Ehud Barak—the former chief of staff who is now the chairman of the opposition Labor Party—expressed some reservations about the territorial aspects of the interim agreement with the Palestinians. He told Rabin that by agreeing to three phases of further redeployments in the West Bank, Israel ran the risk of being left with no bargaining cards for the final status negotiations. These negotiations were to determine the final status of Jerusalem, final borders, water resources, and the resettlement of the refugees. Rabin dismissed Barak's argument. He explained that since he alone would determine the extent of the redeployment in each phase, Israel would retain enough "territorial cards" for the final status negotiations.

Netanyahu acted according to Rabin's way of thinking when on March 7 he submitted to Arafat his proposed map of redeployment in the West Bank. Arafat's rejection of the Israeli proposal led Netanyahu to adopt Barak's ideas. Arafat's opposition to the new Israeli initiative was to be expected. Just as Netanyahu sought to keep as much territory as he could for the final status negotiations, Arafat sought to get as much territory as he could before the final status talks began.

Nevertheless, Netanyahu did not abandon his initiative. As a matter of fact, even before the redeployment in Hebron, Netanyahu began to think in terms of a final settlement of the Palestinian problem, rather than in terms of interim arrangements. In this respect, he was very much influenced by an article written by Henry Kissinger, who as secretary of state under presidents Nixon and Ford had formulated the U.S. position on the Palestinian problem. Writing on "the bottom line of the Middle East peace process," Kissinger said: "The time has come to address two of the great unmentionables of the peace process: Palestinian statehood . . . Israel's frontiers" and Jerusalem. According to Kissinger, the PLO could not hope to attain statehood for its people until it dropped from its covenant the mandate to eradicate Israel. Moreover, Palestinian statehood had to be made absolutely conditional on an agreement regarding its frontiers, which could not be those of 1967. Israel could not leave, as no country could, all of its major cities within mortar range of the enemy and connected by tenuous corridors, with the one between Haifa and Tel Aviv being only nine miles wide. Finally, in Kissinger's view, the issue of Jerusalem could not be discussed until legal status and borders were settled.[43]

Two days later, some of Netanyahu's aides launched a "trial balloon" regarding the final status of the West Bank. They said that the prime minister's idea was to create a Palestinian entity "which is similar to Puerto Rico or Andorra."[44] The example of Andorra is of particular interest. This tiny European entity is a sovereign member of the UN, with voting rights equal to those of any other member state. The Oslo Accords did not explicitly grant statehood to the Palestinians, but the present conditions appear to be riper for such a solution. According to John Whitbeck, a British attorney specializing in international law, the following conditions are necessary for the recognition of a sovereign state:

- The existence of a well-defined territory that no other entity claims sovereignty over.

- The presence of a permanent population within that territory.

- An effective control of the territory and its population.

- The will and capacity of the governing authority in that territory to carry out all its obligations toward the international community and to fulfill the clauses of a treaty.

- Finally, the ability of the governing authority to conduct foreign policy and to establish diplomatic relations with other countries.[45]

Part of these conditions already exist in the areas under Palestinian authority. The Palestinians already have their own flag, a national anthem, and a sizable police force. As an "observer" at the UN, the PLO has a vast net of diplomatic representation. The only thing that is not yet defined is the size of the territory that the Palestinian entity would control and its final borders.

As became manifest in all previous crises, both Israel and the Palestinians realized that the solution of their conflict was too heavy a load for them to lift. They both needed the American hand. This point was stressed by Yasser Arafat, President Mubarak, King Hussein, and Benjamin Netanyahu, who came to the United States in March and April 1997 to meet with the new Clinton administration. This was also the first time that the Middle Eastern leaders had met with the new secretary of state, Madeleine Albright.

In his meeting with President Clinton, Netanyahu reiterated the logic behind his proposal to move forward to the final status negotiations. Realizing that too much was at stake, Clinton again sent his tireless envoy, Ambassador Dennis Ross, to the region. Despite the Palestinian rejection of the Israeli proposal, the U.S. position was cautious, but not totally negative.

Ross did not achieve much on this trip. In an effort to revive the stalled negotiations between Israel and the Palestinians, Ross suggested a package: Israel should temporarily suspend the building at Har Homa and the Palestinians would resume their security cooperation with Israel. Both sides rejected the American's package. The Palestinians insisted on a total freeze of Israeli settlement activity, not only at Har Homa but throughout the West Bank. Israel insisted on the need to continue building in the existing settlements, in order to accommodate "natural growth." Loyal to his modus operandi, Ross did not publicly say anything that could compromise his efforts in future. However, in a secret cable to Jerusalem, Avi Primor, Israel's ambassador to Bonn, quoted officials at Chancellor Kohl's office as having told him: "Ross returned from the Middle East very disappointed. He blamed Israel for the present crisis."[46]

A few days later, an Israeli daily said that "American diplomats have concluded that about 25 percent of the houses in the Israeli settlements in the West Bank and the Gaza Strip are empty. Hence, there is no justification for Israel to continue enlarging the settlements for natural growth."[47] Netanyahu reacted immediately to this report. He said that the American figures "were false and groundless."[48]

In an effort to avoid a total deadlock, Prime Minister Netanyahu asked Egypt's President Mubarak to try to mediate between Israel and the Palestinians. Following a summit with Netanyahu at Sharm el-Sheikh, Mubarak sent his national security adviser, Ossama el-Baz, to Gaza and Jerusalem to try to work out a solution. El-Baz shuttled several times between Netanyahu and Arafat, but to no avail.

Almost two years after Netanyahu's installation as Israel's prime minister, the Palestinians and the Arab world are still depicting him as an "enemy of the Arab nation." Many Arab leaders believe that it is very difficult, if not impossible, to reach an agreement with Netanyahu. This is mostly due to the change in attitudes and negotiating tactics of the Likud-led government. Despite its initial opposition to the Oslo Accords, the Netanyahu government accepted what was done by Labor as done. It was determined, however, to put an end to Labor's bargaining approach, which Netanyahu characterized as give-and-give. The Israeli prime minister ruled out surrendering additional territory without a reciprocal concession by the Palestinians. "Labor's gifts," said Dore Gold, Netanyahu's former political adviser, who became the new Israeli ambassador to the UN, "filled Arafat with expectations that he would sweep the table. Palestinian leaders told us that they expected to receive from Peres and Beilin a return to the 1967 lines. Now they know that they will receive from Netanyahu much less than what they expected to receive from Peres."[49]

Yet, now that he has moved to the center, even Netanyahu understands that his acceptance of the agreements with the Palestinians means a "generous" territorial compromise and a tacit acceptance of a Palestinian state. It is in this context that on June 4, 1997, Netanyahu presented to the inner cabinet his concept of Israel's future borders. He called it the "Allon Plus Plan"—an enlarged version of the original formula presented in 1968 by then Israeli deputy prime minister Yigal Allon. According to Netanyahu's plan, Israel should retain the Greater Jerusalem area (comprising the municipal boundaries as enlarged after the Six-Day War), the Jordan Valley, a security belt east of the 1967 armistice lines, and a bloc of Israeli settlements in the Etzion region, near Hebron. According to Netanyahu's plan, about 40 percent of the West Bank would be transferred to the Palestine Authority.[50] In its broad lines, Netanyahu's concept very much resembles the ideas of the late Yitzhak Rabin and the incumbent Labor leader, Ehud Barak.

Yasser Arafat and other Palestinian leaders rejected the Israeli plan outright. "This is not a basis for negotiations on the final status of the West Bank," said Ahmed Qrei (Abu Ala), the speaker of the Palestinian Legislative Council, who conducted the secret Oslo negotiations. Qrei added that the Palestinians insist on the establishment of an independent Palestinian state with East Jerusalem as its capital, and also on the solution of the 1948 refugee problem.

The conflicting Israeli and Palestinian positions should not come as a surprise. These are only the opening bargaining positions. Once the Likud-led coalition government accepted the principle of a territorial compromise, the size and scope of such a compromise are to be determined by the outcome of the negotiations. Or, to paraphrase George Bernard Shaw, now that we know what Netanyahu professes, the only question is the price.

As happened so many times in the past, both Israel and the Palestinians painted themselves into a corner, which makes the American role even more difficult. After the failed mission of Ambassador Dennis Ross, the United States said it would wait to see whether Egyptian mediation efforts bore fruit. President Mubarak's prediction that "progress will be achieved in ten days" has not come true, but the United States remained reluctant to resume its efforts. Some American officials have privately said that they are allowing the parties to stew in their own juices. Convinced that neither side has a better alternative to no agreement, the United States preferred to wait until both sides were ready to pay the domestic price of their inevitable mutual concessions. The question is, of course, whether Israel and the Palestinians will reach this conclusion before or after the outbreak of a new wave of uncontrolled violence.

Finally, in a major foreign policy address on August 6, 1997, Secretary of State Madeleine Albright outlined an important shift in the U.S. role in the peace process; not a mere "facilitator" but an "active participant" in the efforts to achieve peace in the Middle East. Following Albright's trip to the region, it is now President Clinton himself who has become directly involved in the peace efforts. Such an active U.S. participation could prove to be the best way to prevent the outbreak of a new wave of uncontrolled violence in the entire region.

RABIN AND CLINTON

Of the nine prime ministers who have governed the State of Israel since its establishment in May 1948, Yitzhak Rabin was undoubtedly the most pro-American. While Israel has always enjoyed bipartisan support in the United States and all American presidents have proved their friendship to Israel and their commitment to its security and survival, President Bill Clinton is already being perceived by both Israel and large segments of American Jews as the most pro-Israel president since Harry Truman. In a rare and unique demonstration of friendship, but also as a clear message of continued support for the peace process, Clinton led a U.S. delegation that included three presidents, three secretaries of state, the entire bipartisan Congressional leadership, and the leaders of the American Jewish community to Rabin's funeral. Clinton's gesture prompted eighty-five other heads of state and prime ministers—including King Hussein of Jordan, President Mubarak of Egypt, the Prince of Wales, President Chirac of France, Chancellor Kohl of Germany, and the prime minister of Morocco—to come to Israel and pay their respects to their courageous fallen colleague who strove to change forever the political face of the Middle East.

Everything in Clinton's and Rabin's personalities would lead to the conclusion that a friendship between them would be illogical and practically impossible. Yet the personal friendship between Clinton and Rabin was genuine. Rabin was one of Israel's most revered war heroes and survived three wars with the neighboring Arab countries, and then late in life transformed himself into Israel's leading soldier of peace. In contrast, Clinton, even as a student, was a "peacenik," ideologically opposed to the war in Vietnam, and became the commander in chief of the U.S. armed forces without even serving a single day in the military. Rabin, the first Israeli-born prime minister, was a secular Jew and was by nature shy and introverted. Clinton, a young Baptist from Hope, Arkansas, is very sociable and a great communicator. Rabin, with no formal academic education, had his career shaped in the military and, like Dwight D. Eisenhower, moved to diplomacy and politics after glorious military victories. Clinton was a Rhodes scholar and a lawyer, and he came to the White House after having served as the governor of Arkansas.

There is also a difference in the characters and beliefs of the two leaders. Rabin rarely attended religious services in synagogues, but Clinton is a practicing Baptist and regularly attends services in church. In addition to his political and strategic considerations, Clinton's friendship with Israel also has a religious and spiritual dimension; together with his pastor, Clinton visited Israel in the seventies. On several occasions, and again in his speech to the Israeli Knesset in October 1994, Clinton told the story of his pastor's deathbed warning: "God will never forgive you if you ever betray Israel." In that speech Clinton pledged publicly, "I will never let Israel down. . . ." Rabin's fascination with America had no religious or spiritual dimension—it was purely pragmatic. He liked the executive power vested in the president and wanted to imitate him. He envied the simplicity of the two-party system. Although he was raised in a "socialist" family, he disliked the Histadrut—the powerful trade union federation—and preferred free enterprise and the market economy.

The Israeli prime minister was totally inept at small talk. His language was on occasion abrasive and even hurtful. He was impatient with those he considered fools and contemptuous of and rude to those who opposed his views. During his ambassadorship in Washington, I served as the Israeli daily *Maariv*'s bureau chief in the United States. For almost three years, I worked with Rabin on a daily basis. Members of his embassy used to complain that he never allowed a dissenting opinion. He used to open his morning staff meeting with a long monologue on the subjects to follow, and he would end the meeting with the remark, "And those who don't agree with this view are either fools or don't understand what is going on in America." Needless to say, none of the junior diplomats would agree to expose themselves as fools.

Like President Clinton, Rabin greatly respected American Jews, for their political and economical achievements and for their contributions to America in general. He had, however, a problematic and at times even acrimonious relationship with American Jews. Rabin was a secular Israeli who had studied in an agricultural school, and consequently his Jewish education was very limited. American Jews, on the other hand, do not have the ability to be secular Jews in a Jewish state. Perforce, the synagogue is the center of American Jewish life. On several occasions, I observed his pain when he had to attend a religious service. But Rabin's problems with American Jews did not stop there. The Israeli prime minister resented what he perceived as the repeated attempts by American Jewish leaders to encroach on his authority by approaching the U.S. administration on Israel's behalf. He insisted that official American–Israeli business be conducted only by the governments. He limited the lobbying effort by AIPAC, the official pro-Israel lobby in the United States, to Capitol Hill only. Rabin reiterated this position in a meeting with the Conference of Presidents of Jewish Organizations (an umbrella group) shortly after he returned to power in 1992.

Rabin was absorbed by one subject: the Arab-Israeli conflict. I remember one day, during the presidential campaign of 1972, I went to talk to him about the differences between the American and Israeli political parties. It did not take me long to realize that he was very uncomfortable with the subject. Indeed, after a few sentences he shifted the conversation and gave me a long exposition on President Nixon's Middle Eastern policy, with which he was pleased, and explained at length why it would be "disastrous for Israel" if Senator George McGovern were to win the election. He was delighted when this did not happen. Rabin's opinion on Nixon was not based on intimate knowledge of the person or on his domestic policy, but rather on his foreign policy goals. Rabin believed that the "Nixon Doctrine," if applied correctly in the Middle East, was a good policy for America in the post-Vietnam era.

Rabin sincerely believed that Nixon's reelection would serve Israel's national interest. It was in this context that he suggested that I get in touch with Pat Buchanan, one of Nixon's aides and one of the Republican presidential contenders, with the purpose of writing a "nice article" for *Maariv* on Nixon's pro-Israeli policies. Indeed, Buchanan liked the idea. He proposed an interview with the First Lady, and he strongly implied that during the interview, the president would pop in to say hello to his wife. I could take that opportunity to ask the president a few questions on his policy toward Israel. However, when I suggested the subject to my editors in Tel Aviv, I received an unbelievable answer: "Pat Nixon is not interesting for us. If Buchanan cannot arrange an exclusive interview with Nixon alone, then it's better to drop the subject altogether." Rabin was much disappointed, but he didn't give up. He gave a personal interview to Israeli radio, praising Nixon's policies. The interview provoked immediate angry protests from American Jewish leaders, most of them Democrats, who interpreted the interview as a statement of support for Nixon's reelection.

Rabin's opinion of Nixon's foreign policy was greatly influenced by Henry Kissinger, Nixon's national security adviser and later his secretary of state. Rabin admired Kissinger and had great respect for his intellect and his analytical abilities. For his part, Kissinger held Rabin in high esteem for his analytical abilities and his precise descriptions of given situations. From long personal friendship, Kissinger knew that Rabin was very cautious in his moves but determined and unshakable once he reached a conclusion. In his memorable interview on CNN after Rabin's assassination, Kissinger said that "Rabin had the ability to face reality and follow it wherever it might lead him, and however painful this might prove to his own instincts." Rabin had certainly proved it in his approach to the PLO and to Yasser Arafat. Kissinger also valued Rabin's views on Vietnam. On one occasion, Rabin was the only military man who predicted the exact location of the next Vietcong offensive. At the same time, Rabin trusted Kissinger, and whenever Rabin was in the United States, even when not in government, he never missed the opportunity to meet with the former secretary of state and to chat with him on a variety of subjects. The last time they met in New York was two weeks before Rabin was assassinated.

Rabin's victory in the June 1992 elections presented American Jews with a real dilemma. For the previous fifteen years of right-wing Likud governments, prime ministers Menachem Begin and Yitzhak Shamir had conveyed to Jews in the Diaspora a sense of Israeli isolation and insecurity. They stressed repeatedly the theme that the PLO was a terrorist organization bent on Israel's destruction "in stages," and that total Israeli control of the West Bank and the Gaza Strip was vital to Israel's security and survival. By rejecting the formula of "land for peace," the successive Likud governments embarked on a massive construction of Jewish settlements in densely populated Arab regions. When President Bush linked the grant of $10 billion in loan guarantees to Israel, for the absorption of Soviet Jewish immigrants, to a freeze of new settlements in the territories, an ugly confrontation developed between the Bush administration and American Jews. Despite his persistent denials, Secretary Baker was accused of having said that since American Jews voted traditionally for the Democratic party, "fuck the Jews." Baker's denials were simply disbelieved. The result was obvious. The overwhelming majority of American Jews voted for Clinton and helped defeat George Bush.

Rabin, however, painted for American Jews a totally different picture. As a Jerusalem-born Israeli whose family was not affected by the Holocaust and who successfully fought and defeated the various Arab armies, the new Israeli prime minister projected strength and self-confidence. He told his audiences that Israel was not isolated and that the world was "not against us." Having met with President Bush on several occasions in the past, he was confident that he would be able to forge with him a decent working relationship. After a short visit by Secretary Baker to Jerusalem, Bush invited Rabin to meet with him at his vacation home in Maine. As expected, Rabin accepted the formula of "land for peace" and was prepared to freeze the building of new settlements in the territories. In return, Bush granted Rabin the $10 billion in loan guarantees that had been denied to Shamir.

Rabin's close ties to Bush were not mirrored in his relationship with the American Jewish community. With no apparent reason, Rabin lashed out at AIPAC in brutal language. Addressing the Jewish leadership on August 13, 1992, Rabin said, "You have waged battles that were lost in advance. By generating unnecessary conflicts with Reagan, over the sale of AWACS reconnaissance planes to Saudi Arabia, and with Bush over the loan guarantees, you caused Israel considerable damage. You did not bring Israel even one single cent. . . ." This was, of course, an exaggeration, and Rabin's blunt language did not endear him to the American Jewish establishment.

Rabin's approach to peace sharpened even more the antagonism between him and the American Jewish leadership. Clinton was aware, of course, of this acrimonious relationship, and he was concerned that the dispute would undermine Rabin's authority and limit his ability to compromise in the peace process. Clinton was therefore determined to come to Rabin's help. Appearing together with Rabin at the annual meeting of AIPAC in Washington in May 1995, Clinton departed from his prepared text and told the national Jewish leadership: "In the Middle East, as nowhere else, two forces are locked in a deadly struggle. On the one side a strong Israel, backed by a strong America, building peace with its neighbors. But on the other side, these continuing desperate attempts of fanatics, eager to keep old and bloody conflicts alive. We can beat them. We must beat them. But we are going to have to work at it. We cannot grow weak, we cannot grow weary, and we cannot lose our self-confidence. If we give up on the peace, if we give up on our freedoms, if we walk away from what we are, and what we can become in the United States, but most of all in Israel and in the Middle East, then they—those dark forces—will have won. So, I ask you in closing, stand for the future. Stand with Yitzhak Rabin, this brave man, in his attempt to make peace and don't stop until the job is done."

During his diplomatic and political career, Rabin met or worked with seven U.S. presidents—Johnson, Nixon, Ford, Carter, Reagan, Bush, and Clinton. However, it was only with Clinton that he was able to forge a warm personal relationship. Clinton liked Rabin's directness and honesty and found him very credible. He knew that whatever Rabin promised, he delivered, despite Rabin's slim electoral majority. His political survival became dependent on the support of various small factions in the Knesset.

The close ties began to surface in March 1993, when the newly elected Rabin came to Washington to meet with the equally new president of the U.S. Rabin met with Clinton at a time when the strategic situation in the Middle East had completely changed. With the collapse of the Soviet empire and the end of the Cold War, the United States became the only superpower in the world. Consequently, Israel's Arab enemies were left without a super patron. Iraq's defeat in the Gulf War and the destruction of its military infrastructure had altered the military balance in the Middle East in Israel's favor, producing a unique opportunity for Israel to negotiate peace from a position of strength. Isolated in the Arab world and burdened with enormous debts, Saddam Hussein did not pose any imminent threat to Israel. Instead, he was desperately seeking contacts with Israel, as a venue to Washington. Rabin also knew that Boris Yeltsin was too preoccupied at home to try to play Moscow's past role as a "spoiler" in the Middle East. His dependence on American economic and financial assistance left Yeltsin with no choice but to follow the American lead in the Middle East.

Furthermore, the smooth absorption of 600,000 Soviet Jews, with the generous U.S. aid in the form of $10 billion in loan guarantees, frustrated the PLO dream of defeating Israel demographically. Arab diplomats in Moscow had made several appeals to the Soviet government to halt the exodus of Soviet Jews to Israel, but to no avail. As a result, Arab countries reached the inescapable conclusion that if they didn't compromise with Israel, they would probably lose their last chance to prevent Israel from settling the new immigrants in the West Bank. The PLO, so Rabin reasoned, could not afford to miss this opportunity. Discredited in the Arab world (except in Egypt) because of Yasser Arafat's support of Saddam Hussein, the PLO had lost the generous financial support of Saudi Arabia and the other oil-rich principalities. The PLO was broke. Salaries to rank and file were not paid for months, and PLO offices abroad were closing one after the other. Generally speaking, the PLO in 1993 was in the worst position since its defeat in the Lebanese war in June 1982. Therefore, Rabin reasoned, Arafat did not constitute a threat to Israel's security. As for Syria, being deprived of Soviet military and economic assistance, President Assad too had no alternative but to continue the process begun in Madrid in October 1991.

Convinced of Israel's geostrategic importance to the United States in the Middle East, Rabin constantly sought to commit the United States to maintaining Israel's qualitative (if not numerical) superiority over the various Arab armies. With the new realities of the post-Soviet world, he wanted to move forward and so sought a new strategic understanding with the United States for the pursuit of peace in the Middle East.

This was an appealing prospect to the new president, and it laid a good basis for the first Clinton-Rabin encounter at the White House in March 1993. During that meeting in the Oval Office, Rabin told Clinton, "I have been a warrior, a general, for too long. In forty-five years of warfare, I have seen too much bloodshed. It's enough. It's time now to try and make peace. The Israeli people gave me a mandate to take calculated risks for peace." Clinton responded: "If you are going to do that, my role, the U.S. role, is not to tell you how to do it, or when to do it. My role is to try to minimize those risks that you will be taking."

The effort to minimize those risks was indeed impressive. In the following months and years, Clinton and Rabin agreed on several projects that would enhance Israel's military capabilities and ensure its armed superiority. The United States promised to continue financing research and development of the Arrow antimissile missile; joint development of Nautilus, a laser-guided system that would intercept ground-to-ground missiles and rockets; joint development of Delilah, a remote-controlled plane capable of destroying radar systems even when not in operation; and joint development of a remotely controlled plane capable of detecting the launch of ground-to-ground missiles (like the Scud).

Rabin understood that in the wake of the Persian Gulf War, the United States had a national interest in improving the defensive capabilities of its allies in the Gulf area. Hence, he did not oppose the sale of additional quantities of arms to Saudi Arabia and the United Arab Emirates. He only asked that certain technologies be omitted from the proposed sale, so that Israel's technological superiority would be maintained.

For its fifty years of existence, Israel had been a staunch ally of the United States. Yet, this first encounter between Clinton and Rabin at the White House dramatically changed the nature of this alliance. From a U.S. commitment to Israel's security and survival and a partnership in preserving the territorial integrity of the pro-Western Arab countries, there emerged now an informal new alliance in pursuit of a comprehensive peace in the Middle East and regional stability.

One cannot explain this unique partnership without dwelling briefly on the nature of American-Israeli relations in the last five decades. Immediately after its establishment in May 1948, Israel declared its neutrality between the two superpowers. This decision was taken in appreciation of the Soviet support for the 1947 UN Partition Plan of Palestine and the establishment of the State of Israel. However, with the heating up of the Cold War, Israel's founding father and its prime minister, David Ben-Gurion, made the historic decision to abandon his neutrality and to join the American-led free world. Ben-Gurion reasoned that as a young democracy, Israel could not support the totalitarian regime of Joseph Stalin. Ben-Gurion also had a pragmatic reason for his decision: To fulfill its Zionist destiny and to ensure its security, Israel had to absorb more and more Jewish immigrants. In addition to the survivors of the Holocaust dispersed all over Europe and the Jews in the Arab lands, the two biggest Jewish communities in the world were in the Soviet Union and in the United States. Stalin, however, would not allow Soviet Jews to emigrate to Israel, going so far as to suppress their Jewish identity. As a result, the only remaining Jewish reservoir was in the free world, and the only country in the world capable of assisting Israel in its absorption was the United States.

Ben-Gurion's alliance with the United States was consistent and unshaken. Nevertheless, in the absence of a coherent American Middle Eastern policy and because of inconsistencies in the American attitude toward the pan-Arab, pro-Soviet Gamal Abdel Nasser, Israel was forced to seek additional alliances in Europe—first in France, and later also in West Germany. Israel's alliance with France began in the early 1950s and reached its peak in October 1956. In retaliation for Nasser's nationalization of the Suez Canal and in response to repeated terrorist attacks against Israeli settlements, Israel joined with France and Great Britain in an attack against Egypt. Known as the Suez Campaign, this tripartite attack was launched without the prior knowledge of the United States. An infuriated President Eisenhower forced the three countries to withdraw from Egyptian territories.

During that period, Israel's relations with France came close to a formal military alliance. France agreed to supply Israel with a nuclear reactor, located in Dimona, which remains to this date the single most effective deterrent against any surprise Arab attack. The champion of Israel's French and European outlook was Shimon Peres, and he remained so until after the Six-Day War, in June 1967.

Yet, despite this apparent tilt toward Europe, Ben-Gurion never lost sight of the fact that Israel's real interest lay only with the United States. Immediately after the Suez Campaign, after being reelected for a second term, President Eisenhower announced the Eisenhower Doctrine. It was, in effect, the first American peace plan for the Middle East, but failed in large part because the Arab world was not yet ready for a peaceful settlement of its conflict with Israel.

In an effort to contain the nationalist and subversive policies of Egypt's Nasser, the CIA sought to build an informal regional framework that included (in addition to Israel) Turkey, Iran, Ethiopia, Saudi Arabia, Jordan, and Lebanon. Although there were no direct links between Israeli intelligence agencies and the Arab countries, it was still possible to exchange information, either through Turkey and Iran or directly through the CIA. This network became particularly important in February 1958 when Egypt and Syria formed the United Arab Republic (UAR). In July 1958, a military coup overthrew the pro-Western monarchy in Iraq and established a pro-Nasserist and pro-Soviet republic in Baghdad.

Jordan and Lebanon felt immediately the effects of the combined subversion effort by Cairo and Damascus and requested American help. Eisenhower ordered the immediate landing of the Marines in Beirut. At the same time, British paratroopers were rushed from Cyprus and, with the permission of Israel, flew over Israeli territory to land in Amman. As the result of a combined effort by the United States, Turkey, Israel, Jordan, and Saudi Arabia, the UAR was dissolved in September 1961. This major setback to Nasser marked the beginning of the end of his sway in the Arab world.

It was during these turbulent years that Yitzhak Rabin was introduced to the American military. As head of the training branch in the general headquarters, General Rabin toured American military installations, met with senior American officers, and exchanged views about the explosive situation in the Arab world. He was tremendously impressed by the quality of the American armament, the aggressiveness of the officer corps, and the discipline of the troops. He was particularly impressed by the Green Berets and by the 82nd Division at Fort Bragg. Upon his return to Israel, he immediately introduced the practice that all infantry officers—not only those who were assigned to the special units—be trained as paratroopers. This decision bore fruit in the Six-Day War when the Israeli officers proved to be far superior to those of the various Arab armies.

The close American-Israeli cooperation on the regional level led the United States gradually to abandon its traditional policy of not supplying Israel with American arms. In a meeting in New York in 1961, Prime Minister Ben-Gurion presented the newly elected President Kennedy with a request to buy U.S. Hawk antiaircraft missiles to help defend Israel against the Soviet-equipped Egyptian, Syrian, and Iraqi air forces. While Kennedy recognized the need for such a supply, he nevertheless made it conditional on Israel's acceptance of U.S. inspection of its nuclear facilities in Dimona. Ben-Gurion rejected this condition outright. He told Kennedy that as prime minister of Israel, he had a responsibility for the Jewish people at large. After two thousand years of exile and persecutions, not to mention the Holocaust, Israel had to have a deterrent against its Arab enemies. "I can assure you, Mr. President," Ben-Gurion told Kennedy, "that Israel would not be the first to use nuclear weapons in the Middle East. We are allies, and allies must be trusted." After lengthy negotiations between the two governments, Ben-Gurion finally agreed to American inspection of the nuclear reactor only, not the entire Dimona complex. Eventually, even this limited inspection was canceled by President Nixon, at the urging of Rabin, who was then ambassador.

Kennedy's decision to supply Israel with Hawk missiles was a major policy change, and it was obvious that this token supply of defensive weapons would not remain an isolated case. No doubt the American arms market would be soon wide open to Israel. Kennedy's decision came at a time when an important change began to become evident in Franco-Israeli relations. With the end of the Algerian war in July 1962, President de Gaulle reoriented his Middle East policy toward the Arab world and the Persian Gulf. While not totally abandoning his informal alliance with Israel, and with no immediate suspension of contracted arms supplies, de Gaulle became more selective on future weapons sales. At the same time, French relations with the United States became more tense, in view of de Gaulle's decision to take a more independent line within NATO and toward the Soviet Union and Communist China. As far as Israel was concerned, the signs were obvious, but neither Ben-Gurion nor Foreign Minister Golda Meir was prepared to admit publicly that the "special relationship" with France was coming to an end. In particular, Shimon Peres, who in his capacity as deputy defense minister orchestrated this special relationship and became closely identified with it, continued to work tirelessly for keeping the Paris channel open. Not for long.

In June 1963, Ben-Gurion resigned as prime minister. He was succeeded by Finance Minister Levi Eshkol. Golda Meir retained her position as foreign minister and Shimon Peres retained his position as deputy defense minister. However, Abba Eban, the most brilliant ambassador to Washington and to the UN in Israel's history, became deputy prime minister. Whereas Peres symbolized a continued French connection, the appointment of Abba Eban signaled a reorientation of Israeli foreign policy toward the U.S.

With the inauguration of Lyndon Johnson, this change in direction became evident. More than any of his predecessors, Johnson was a staunch supporter of Israel, and he had no illusions about Nasser's ambitions in the Arab world. He saw in Israel a stabilizing factor in the Middle East and treated Israel as a trusted ally that deserved to be supplied with American arms and military equipment. In welcoming Eshkol to the White House in the early summer of 1964, LBJ pledged that never again would an Israeli prime minister enter the White House through the back door. This was an allusion to Kennedy's insistence that his meeting with Ben-Gurion in 1961 be held in New York and not in Washington.

Johnson translated his words into deeds: He authorized the sale of Skyhawk warplanes to Israel, thus abandoning Kennedy's policy to limit arms supplies to Israel to defensive weapons only.

Yitzhak Rabin was at the time the chief of staff of the Israeli army, and he welcomed Johnson's decision wholeheartedly. He saw the Skyhawk as the "next-generation" plane of the Israeli air force and hoped gradually to replace the French equipment with American arms. Rabin was also opposed to the Ben-Gurion–Peres policy of "self-reliance" and to their decision to research, develop, and manufacture Israeli warplanes and missiles. He believed that American arms were not only superior but also cheaper. At a time of economic recession and growing unemployment, and in the face of growing difficulties in absorbing the thousands of new immigrants who were pouring into the country each month, this was a very convincing argument. Over Peres's objection, Prime Minister Eshkol cut funds for research and development and for expanded military production. Rabin's victory brought an increased tension with Peres, who not only acquired the French arms and the nuclear reactor but also built a modern aircraft industry capable of producing planes, missiles, and sophisticated high-tech equipment. This tension, with varying degrees of intensity, continued until very recently and became part of Israeli political folklore.

Shortly after he led his army into Israel's greatest military victory in the Six-Day War, Rabin asked Prime Minister Eshkol to appoint him as the next Israeli ambassador to Washington. In one of her many interviews after her husband's assassination, Leah Rabin said that many of their friends scoffed at the time at the idea, saying, "What would you do standing around at cocktail parties with a tie on and a drink in your hand?" He replied, "Now that we won the war, it is time to make peace with our Arab neighbors, and Washington is the only key to making peace."

Rabin came to Washington in the summer of 1968, toward the end of Johnson's presidency. The presidential campaign was very tense and was dominated by the war in Vietnam and the Soviet support for North Vietnam's insurgencies against Laos and Cambodia.

When Nixon entered the White House, on January 20, 1969, neither he nor his national security adviser, Henry Kissinger, was unknown in Israel. Rabin had met both of them in Israel long before the election. As a future presidential candidate who was very interested in international affairs, Nixon had embarked in June 1967 on a Middle East tour. His first stop was in Morocco, where he met with King Hassan. On June 6, while on his way from Rabat to Cairo, Nixon heard that a new Arab-Israeli war had broken out. Nixon diverted his plane and landed in Tehran, where he met with the shah of Iran and discussed with him the security problems in the Persian Gulf area. As soon as the hostilities ended and a cease-fire went into effect, Nixon flew to Tel Aviv; he was the first dignitary to land in Israel after the Six-Day War. After meetings with Prime Minister Eshkol, Defense Minister Dayan, and Foreign Minister Abba Eban, Nixon met with David Ben-Gurion and had a long talk with Chief of Staff Rabin. The discussion was an eye-opener to the future ambassador to Washington. Rabin knew, of course, about Nixon's obsession with Communism and had a general idea about Nixon's "kitchen debate" with Nikita Khrushchev in Moscow. He was very impressed, however, with Nixon's understanding of the Middle East. Nixon fascinated Rabin with his description of his philosophical discussion with Ben-Gurion, whom he called an "Old Testament prophet." Ben-Gurion urged Nixon to reach out to Communist China, because without China there would be no world peace and no international military balance.

Years later, as ambassador to Washington, Rabin told me how Nixon perceived his Israel policy at the time. "The United States," Nixon told Rabin, "has two permanent interests in the Middle East—a strategic interest in the Persian Gulf and a moral commitment to Israel." Nixon did not think of Israel as a strategic asset to the United States. He valued the intelligence-sharing between the two countries but he thought that the United States had enough technology to gather the intelligence itself. However, like most of his predecessors, he was morally committed to the security and survival of Israel. He knew that America's allies in Europe and elsewhere would judge its credibility according to its attitude toward Israel. "If America abandons Israel, no other ally would ever trust the United States," Nixon told Rabin.

Rabin met Kissinger several years earlier. The brilliant professor from Harvard ran a three-month summer seminar for potential leaders in various countries. Yigal Allon, an Israeli general in the 1948 war, a strategic thinker, and a cabinet member under Ben-Gurion, attended the seminar in 1957. This was Kissinger's first meeting with an Israeli of that stature, and a real friendship developed between them. During a four-hour drive from Boston to New York, Allon expounded his views on the situation in the Middle East. Allon complained that on two occasions—in 1948 and again in 1956—the United States had forced Israel to withdraw from the Sinai, without assuring Israel peace in return. Kissinger observed that this should not happen again and that Israel should always insist on quid pro quo—an opinion he has continued to hold.

In early 1961 as a guest of Yigal Allon, Kissinger came for his first visit to Israel. Sitting on the porch facing Lake Kinneret at Allon's home, Kissinger was introduced to Allon's friend General Yitzhak Rabin. In 1966, Kissinger came again to Israel, this time as guest of Chief of Staff Yitzhak Rabin. He lectured at the National Security College and met with most of Israel's political leaders. At a luncheon hosted by Shimon Peres, to which I was invited, Kissinger asked all participants who would be the next prime minister, after Levi Eshkol. Each gave a different name, but none of us predicted that it would be Golda Meir. Kissinger was particularly impressed by Rabin's ability to discuss issues reaching far beyond the current situation. Allon recalled that Rabin was much concerned with the dilemma of security and democracy in a small Jewish state that had no natural resources, but was burdened with a large and growing Arab population, and was surrounded by a hostile Arab world.

At that time, Kissinger was not in government and therefore was not inhibited from talking about his Jewish background. He told Allon and Rabin that he would never forget that thirteen members of his family perished in the Holocaust, nor would he ever forget what it had been like to live as a Jew in Nazi Germany. He felt confident that the new breed of Israelis were capable of assuring Israel's security and survival.

Rabin's ambassadorship was characterized by many contradictions. On the one hand, he enjoyed the full support of Prime Minister Golda Meir. However, by reporting directly to her, he lost the trust and confidence of Foreign Minister Abba Eban. Although he lacked any diplomatic skill (he was called in Israel "the undiplomatic diplomat"), Rabin brought to Washington a welcome freshness in Israeli thinking and a sense of directness in his dealings with the administration. He did not have the oratorial skills of Abba Eban (no other Israeli leader or diplomat has), and his command of the English language during his first six months in Washington was limited. His deep voice, however, combined with the aura of victor in the Six-Day War, carried weight and authority. He was very proud of his achievements, and rightly so. In private conversations with Israeli journalists in Washington and with American Jewish leaders, Rabin often said that he gave Eshkol and Golda "better boundaries than those that existed under King David or King Solomon." Because of his early acquaintance with Nixon and Kissinger, he had good access to both the White House and the State Department. He had equally good access to Congress and to the Washington press corps.

Facing criticism in Jerusalem and among American Jews that his Republican bias could undermine the traditional bipartisan support for Israel in Congress, Rabin developed the theory that it was good for Israel to have one branch of the American government controlled by the Republicans and the other branch controlled by the Democrats. In this way, he reasoned, Israel would always enjoy bipartisan support and a pro-Israeli U.S. Middle East policy. He also said that except for Eisenhower, who had forced Israel to withdraw from the Sinai in 1957 with no Arab concession in return, Israel always favored the incumbent president. He could not understand why he was being criticized in Israel because of his close relationship with the president and his national security adviser. A few years later, when he returned to Washington as prime minister and faced the same criticism after his meeting with President Ford, he quoted Henry Kissinger as saying, "Israel is the only country in the world that would criticize its prime minister for having good relations with the president of the United States and his secretary of state."

Rabin's first months as ambassador were rather tense. He had to fight two particularly damaging initiatives by the State Department, the Rogers Plan and a policy statement concerning the future status of Jerusalem. The Rogers Plan, the first American attempt to impose a solution in the Middle East, was immediately derailed by Golda Meir. The tough-minded Israeli prime minister convinced Nixon that Israel would never accept such a solution. Instead, she urged the president to persuade the Arab leaders to negotiate directly with Israel. Indeed, this became the official U.S. policy and remains in effect to this date.

The policy statement on Jerusalem had a more lasting effect. On July 1, 1969, the U.S. ambassador to the UN, Charles Yost, told the UN Security Council that the United States considered East Jerusalem an "occupied territory" and, hence, subject to the provisions of the international law governing the rights and obligations of an occupying power. This was a major blow to Israeli diplomacy, especially in light of the fact that Resolution 242 does not explicitly mention Jerusalem and therefore, according to the Israeli interpretation, does not fall under the definition of "occupied territory." Rabin lobbied Congress and tried hard, and in vain, to change the Nixon administration's view. It took years of diplomacy before the United States agreed to the definition that the issue of Jerusalem should be left to the negotiations on the final status of the West Bank.

Through his friendship with Kissinger and with Assistant Secretary of State for Middle Eastern Affairs Joseph Sisco, Rabin built with the United States a unique relationship that proved itself on two very important occasions. First, in the spring of 1970, the Soviet Union escalated the war of attrition between Israel and Egypt along the Suez Canal by building an integrated air defense system manned by Soviet technicians. Moscow also sent Soviet pilots to fly MiG-21s in combat missions. By March 31, there were more than sixty Soviet pilots and four thousand missile personnel in Egypt. By June 30, the numbers had doubled. This was the first time that the Soviet Union had deployed combat forces outside of Europe. On April 18, 1970, Soviet pilots tried to intercept two Israeli Phantoms over Egyptian territory. Because of bad weather, the Soviets missed their targets. This was a new, dangerous situation in the Middle East. Acting on instructions from Jerusalem, Ambassador Rabin leaked the story of the encounter to the *New York Times* on April 18. The leak was not intended to prepare the ground for a request that the United States also deploy troops in Israel to balance the Soviet deployments in Egypt. Israel never asked for foreign troops to help in her defense. Instead, Israel wanted an immediate and positive reply to a request made by Golda Meir in September 1969 for the supply of an additional twenty-five Phantoms and one hundred Skyhawks. Kissinger was in favor, Secretary of State William P. Rogers was opposed, and Nixon decided to keep the Israeli request on hold. Everyone knew, however, that the situation was explosive and needed an immediate solution.

Early in June 1970, Secretary Rogers gave Soviet Ambassador Dobrynin a letter warning against the deployment of Soviet personnel in the Suez Canal area. Entry of Soviet personnel into the combat zone, the letter warned, "could lead to serious escalation with unpredictable consequences to which the United States could not remain indifferent." The Soviets ignored the warning. In the next few weeks, Soviet and Egyptian missile crews shot down five Israeli Phantoms. This new development caused great concern in Israel and in Washington.

Nixon and Kissinger decided, at Rabin's urging, to show Moscow and Cairo that the United States would not let the balance of power shift against Israel. Nixon ordered that electronic countermeasure equipment be dispatched to Israel immediately. Its installation on Israeli planes would protect them against the Soviet and Egyptian missiles. However, the equipment proved to be inadequate. After several more encounters in the Suez Canal area, Rabin informed Kissinger that the Israeli government intended to draw the line; it decided to challenge the Soviet pilots. On July 30, four Israeli Phantoms and four Israeli Mirages set up an air ambush in the Gulf of Suez. The Soviets fell into the trap and sent sixteen MiGs to intercept the Israelis. Within seconds, four Soviet MiGs were downed with no casualties to Israel.

The Soviets did not react publicly to this embarrassing incident, and papers in Moscow reported that the four pilots had been killed in a car accident. Analyzing this incident, Israeli and American officials reached the conclusion that Soviet restraint was not because of fear of Israel, but only because the Soviet leadership concluded that Israel would not have dared to challenge the Soviet Union if it had not received "strategic cover" from the United States.

The second occasion was even more dramatic. In September 1970, Palestinian terrorists hijacked five passenger planes and landed them in a deserted airport in East Jordan. After lengthy negotiations, the Palestinians freed the passengers but blew up the planes. Unable to ignore this challenge to his authority, King Hussein launched an all-out attack against PLO bases in Jordan. Syria rushed to the rescue of the Palestinians and sent an armored battalion across the border with Jordan. With the blessings of Golda Meir and Moshe Dayan, Rabin forged a strategic axis with the United States aimed at saving the Jordanian throne. Israel concentrated troops along the borders with Jordan and

Syria. Kissinger warned Dobrynin of the consequences of the Syrian intervention, and in order not to leave any doubt about its intentions, the United States sent the Sixth Fleet to the eastern Mediterranean. This combined American-Israeli effort was enough to deter Syria from further intervention, and the Jordanian army proved able to push the Syrian forces back to their bases. Even more important, King Hussein continued the drive against the PLO, expelling all Palestinian armed groups from his kingdom and restoring his authority.

Despite these unique diplomatic achievements, Rabin was criticized in Jerusalem as being "too subordinated" to Kissinger. The late Moshe Dayan observed, "Since the days of Ben-Gurion, all Israeli prime ministers sought to forge friendly and harmonious relations with the United States. There were occasions, however, when each of them had to say no to America. Ben-Gurion said no to Kennedy on the issue of American inspection of Israel's nuclear complex in Dimona; Golda Meir said no to Nixon on the issue of the Rogers Plan and again on various developments during the Yom Kippur War; Begin said no to Carter on the issue of the PLO and the Soviet involvement in the peace process. With Rabin, it never happened. He always followed the American line."

Indeed, except during the administration of Carter, whom he distrusted, Rabin coordinated all his moves with the United States and won the trust of the various administrations by never acting behind their backs. This was again demonstrated in the nature of the close relationship that Rabin had developed with President Clinton and his peace team, a relationship based on absolute trust and mutual respect.

Rabin ended his ambassadorship to Washington in March 1973. He was succeeded by Simcha Dinitz, the director general of the prime minister's office and Golda Meir's confidant. For the next nine months, Rabin was unemployed. For an unknown reason and despite Rabin's proven successes, the prime minister did not offer him any government or public position. It was a public snub that he definitely did not deserve.

The seed for this snub, however, could have been noticed several weeks earlier. In February 1973, Golda Meir paid her last visit to Washington during Rabin's ambassadorship. Rabin went out of his way to arrange a royal treatment for her. She was to stay at Blair House, across from the White House, and her shopping bag was to be filled with additional quantities of arms and military equipment. Even the joint communiqué was drafted in advance and included many friendly pronouncements. However, on February 21, in the midst of the preparations for Meir's visit, a civilian Libyan jetliner flying over the Mediterranean lost its way and flew over the Sinai Desert, toward the Israeli nuclear research center at Dimona. It ignored repeated calls for identification and, fearing that the plane was on a spying mission, the Israelis sent air force planes to intercept it. The Libyan pilot ignored signals to follow the Israeli planes for landing in Israel. Within seconds, the plane was shot down, and all of its 106 passengers—among them the Libyan minister of information—were killed. The only survivor, the navigator, was taken to an Israeli hospital and was returned to Libya after three years of intensive medical treatment. Washington was shocked by the incident, and Israel received sharp criticism for its action. In the face of growing condemnation, Rabin became panicky. He was concerned that Meir's visit would be clouded by the Libyan incident. His flood of cables to Jerusalem reflected that fear. Quite surprised by her ambassador's reaction, the Israeli prime minister wondered whether Rabin was ripe for national leadership.

As it happened, Meir's visit to Washington was very successful. President Nixon hosted a state dinner at the White House, attended by cabinet secretaries, Congressional leaders, and the leaders of the American Jewish community. When Nixon rose to offer a toast in honor of Prime Minister Meir, it became clear that the state dinner was also a farewell party for Ambassador Rabin. After paying tribute to Meir's courage and leadership and speaking warmly about Israeli-American relations, Nixon praised Rabin's talents and successes in Washington. Turning to Meir, Nixon said jokingly, "If you don't have a place for Rabin in your government, I will be more than happy to have him in my cabinet."

The Israeli prime minister took Nixon's "joke" very seriously. She saw it as an attempt to twist her arm and force her to appoint the pro-American Rabin in her cabinet. The next day, at a press briefing with Israeli correspondents at Blair House, she was asked what Rabin's next job would be. She replied dryly: "We shall see how he behaves in Israel. . . ." When told about Meir's remark, Leah Rabin said, "What chutzpa."

A few months later, in October 1973, Israel went through the very traumatic experience of the Yom Kippur War. Having no official position, Rabin spent hours at the operations center. But neither Golda Meir nor Moshe Dayan wanted him there; they preferred Haim Barlev, the cool-headed minister of commerce and industry who served as chief of staff during the war of attrition along the Suez Canal. Rabin was appointed to coordinate the fund-raising for the war effort.

Shortly after Henry Kissinger had arranged a cease-fire, new elections to the Knesset were held. Despite the traumatic experience of the war, the Labor Party won the elections, and Yitzhak Rabin for the first time became a Knesset member. It was months, however, before Golda Meir was able to form a new coalition government. Finally, on March 10, 1974, Meir presented her cabinet to the Knesset. Rabin became the new minister of labor.

Meir's cabinet, however, did not last long. On April 2, the Agranat Commission of Inquiry presented its preliminary report on the blunders that preceded the Yom Kippur War. The report blamed the chief of staff, General

David Elazar, for the army's poor preparedness. It exonerated both Golda Meir and Moshe Dayan, but nevertheless, public outcry forced the government to fall. Pending the election of a successor by the 611 members of the Labor Party's Central Committee, Meir continued to function as interim prime minister.

On April 22, in a tense and grim mood, the Central Committee met in Tel Aviv to choose between two candidates—Yitzhak Rabin and Shimon Peres. Rabin won by a slim majority. The seeds of bitter conflict and enmity between these two rising stars were sown then.

Rabin, fifty-two, was not only Israel's youngest but also its first Israeli-born prime minister. He was politically inexperienced, and was flanked by two very experienced and powerful rivals—Peres as defense minister and Yigal Allon as foreign minister. Rabin presented his government to the Knesset on June 3 and won its confidence, again with a slim majority.

Lacking a firm party base, Rabin was considered a weakling throughout his first premiership. His main concern was Shimon Peres, the most hawkish member of the cabinet, whom he accused of trying to undermine his authority and to limit his ability to strike compromise deals with the various Arab governments.

One of Rabin's first functions as prime minister was to welcome President Nixon to Jerusalem. After Kissinger succeeded in brokering a separation-of-forces agreement between Israel and Syria on May 31, 1974, Nixon had decided to detach himself from the agonies of the Watergate affair and traveled to Jerusalem, Cairo, and Damascus. He was enthusiastically received in all three capitals. Watergate, however, continued to haunt him even during the tour. Officials in his entourage revealed to their Israeli counterparts that the moment he was through with his official functions, Nixon locked himself in his Presidential Suite at the King David Hotel and listened obsessively to the famous Watergate tapes.

During two days of discussions with Rabin, Peres, and Allon, President Nixon stressed the need for Israel to sign a separation-of-forces agreement with Jordan. Jordan had not participated in the Yom Kippur War and therefore there was no need for separation of any forces. Nevertheless, Rabin was prepared to make a "goodwill gesture" and was ready to transfer the city of Jericho, in the West Bank, to King Hussein.

On August 29, 1974, long after sundown, a Jordanian army helicopter landed at Atarot Airport, north of Jerusalem. As though trained for such occasions, Israeli air force officers rushed to the helicopter, saluted King Hussein and his prime minister, Zeid Rifai, and transferred them to an Israeli helicopter standing nearby, its engines warming up. Within seven minutes, the helicopter landed at a government guest house north of Tel Aviv, where Rabin, Peres, and Allon were waiting. King Hussein was very familiar with this place—most of his previous meetings with Golda Meir and other Israeli leaders had been held there. Thus, long before President Sadat came to Israel, in November 1977, King Hussein had been a frequent guest. Of the three Israeli leaders, Hussein only knew Allon, but the "click" between the king and the Israeli prime minister was instant. As is customary in such meetings, both Hussein and Rabin had first a detailed summary of the situation in the Middle East. Turning to Israeli-Jordanian relations, King Hussein explained his need for a separation-of-forces agreement, similar to those signed between Israel and Egypt and Syria. He insisted that Israel withdraw not only from the city of Jericho, as Rabin had suggested to Nixon and Kissinger, but also from a whole strip of land ten to twelve kilometers wide along the Jordan River. Hussein's idea contradicted the Allon Plan, which regarded the Jordan as the security border of Israel. The three Israeli leaders were unanimous in rejecting the king's request. Very bitter, Hussein observed, "The irony of the situation is that had I joined Egypt and Syria in the Yom Kippur War, I would have been much better off." Prime Minister Rifai said, "If you don't accept our proposal, Jordan would be forced to withdraw from any involvement in the affairs of the West Bank."

Meanwhile the PLO pressures on Jordan grew steadily. In support of the PLO position, Egypt's President Sadat announced that King Hussein had no authority to negotiate the future of the West Bank with the Israelis. Morocco's King Hassan took a similar stance. During a weekend discussion with Allon at Camp David, Kissinger urged the Israeli foreign minister to accept King Hussein's proposal. Sitting at his Madison Hotel room in Washington, Allon told me at the time, strictly off the record, that Kissinger warned him that "if Israel would not settle with Jordan, it would be forced to negotiate with Arafat."

Facing growing American pressure, Rabin flew to Washington in September 1974 for discussions with President Ford and Secretary Kissinger. The White House rolled out the red carpet for the Israeli prime minister, but the political discussions were tough. Rabin was shocked to discover how vulnerable the United States had become to Arab pressures as a result of the Arab oil embargo during the 1973 war. "It would take the industrialized nations six to seven years to free themselves from the grip of the Arab oil-producing countries," Kissinger told Rabin. He added, "We hate to be in such a situation, but until then we have no choice but to move forward and find interim solutions."

Upon his return to Israel, it became clear that Rabin accepted Kissinger's approach of "step-by-step" diplomacy. Rabin even devised his own expression—"a piece of land for a piece of peace." He said that while the Arabs would have to take steps to convince the Israeli public of their readiness to make peace, he was now prepared to draft several specific plans and draw the necessary maps for each stage. His position departed from previous governments' policies that consistently refused to draw maps before direct peace negotiations started.

As he feared, Rabin encountered stiff opposition from Peres, but the relations between the hawkish defense minister and Secretary Kissinger were equally tense. In private discussions with friends and Israeli journalists, Peres described Kissinger as "the most devious man" he had ever met. Kissinger described Peres as "a phony hawk" and on one occasion he even told Ambassador Dinitz in Washington that he was going to Israel "to save Rabin from the conspiracies of Peres."

On October 19, 1974, Rabin made another effort to reach an interim agreement with King Hussein. In a secret meeting near Tel Aviv, Rabin again suggested an Israeli withdrawal from the city of Jericho, and the Jordanian monarch again rejected the proposal as inadequate. One week later an Arab summit meeting in Morocco recognized the PLO as the "sole representative" of the Palestinian people, thus denying King Hussein any further involvement in the affairs of the West Bank and the Gaza Strip. For now, at least, an interim agreement between Israel and Jordan was excluded. In an effort to maintain the momentum, Kissinger turned to Egypt.

The separation-of-forces agreement that was signed between Israel and Egypt in the aftermath of the Yom Kippur War was due to expire in early 1975. In an effort to avoid the resumption of hostilities, Kissinger proposed that in return for a three-year cease-fire, Israel would withdraw from the strategic Mitla and Gidi Passes in Sinai and would also surrender the Abu Rudeis oil fields, in southern Sinai, that Israel had developed and was now exploiting. Kissinger explored the idea with President Sadat and found him very responsive. Kissinger traveled to Jerusalem for the same purpose. Even before he landed in Israel, he knew that his problem was not with Rabin or Allon, but with Peres.

At the insistence of Peres, Rabin told Kissinger that there would be no further withdrawals in Sinai without Sadat's agreeing to end the state of belligerency with Israel. Sadat rejected this Israeli condition, and Kissinger's mission ended in failure. President Ford put the blame on Israel. During an emergency cabinet meeting in Jerusalem, an urgent letter from President Ford was handed to Rabin. The U.S. president told the Israeli prime minister that in view of the recent development, the United States would have to "reassess" its policies in the Middle East.

Being all too familiar with the modus operandi of the U.S. administration, Rabin understood exactly what this reassessment meant. He also knew that the author of that presidential letter was Kissinger himself. On several occasions in the past, various American administrators had imposed embargos on arms supplies to the Middle East. This unusual "reassessment," however, was far more serious. An aid package of $2.5 billion, which included sale of additional F-15 planes and Lance ground-to-ground missiles to Israel, was put on hold. Day-to-day relations between American officials and their Israeli counterparts became very cool. Even the small group of Israeli journalists in Washington were made to feel that the reassessment was for real. In a series of background briefings with key American Jewish leaders, U.S. officials claimed that the aim of the re-assessment was not to punish Israel, "but to convince Jerusalem to move."

Indeed, over Peres's objection, Rabin sought a face-saving formula that would enable him to resume the negotiations for a new interim agreement with Egypt. On May 21, 1975, at the initiative of AIPAC, seventy-six U.S. senators addressed an open letter to President Ford urging him to end the reassessment of his policy toward Israel. Although not binding, the letter gave both sides the moral basis for the resumption of American-Israeli negotiations. On June 5, the Suez Canal, blocked since 1967, was reopened for international navigation. As a gesture of goodwill, Rabin withdrew several military units from Sinai, signaling thereby to President Sadat his willingness to move toward a peaceful settle-ment in Egypt. In mid-June 1975, President Ford met with President Sadat in Salzburg, Austria, and later he met with Rabin in Washington. Both leaders agreed to resume their talks on a new interim agreement. On September 3, 1975, Egypt and Israel signed the interim agreement, according to the terms proposed by Kissinger in March. The "reassessment" came to an end.

As part of the agreement, Israel was promised an American aid package of $2.2 billion in military and economic assistance. To compensate for the oil that Israel was extracting from the Abu Rudeis oil fields, which constituted about 55 percent of its annual consumption, Kissinger had arranged with the shah of Iran to increase his oil sales to Israel. Rabin, however, wanted a more direct commitment from the shah. Rabin traveled secretly to Tehran and in a meeting with the shah was promised that Iran would cover all of Israel's oil needs. Fi-nally, and again as part of the agreement, President Sadat agreed that some two hundred American technicians would man the Israeli electronic surveillance station in Sinai, to warn against an Egyptian surprise attack.

The new Israeli-Egyptian agreement widened the gap between Rabin and Peres, and the wounds of this infighting would not heal. By now, however, Rabin was more experienced and self-confident. In social gatherings and in pri-vate discussions, Rabin showed contempt for Peres and dismissed his opposi-tion to various terms of the interim agreement with Egypt as "not relevant." He also said that Peres's behavior convinced him "not to fall under Peres's thumb, the way Golda Meir was under Moshe Dayan's thumb."

The interim agreement opened a new chapter in the U.S. relations with Is-rael and Egypt. In October 1975, President Sadat was the first leader in Egypt's history to pay an official visit to Washington. He was received with pomp. In ad-dition to the festive ceremony on the White House South Lawn and the state dinner, Sadat was invited to address both houses of Congress, and his speech was interrupted many times by applause and standing ovations. A similar treat-ment was accorded to Rabin when he came to Washington in January 1976.

However, two months before Rabin's visit, Israel's attention was drawn once again to the Palestinian problem. On November 12, 1975, Harold Saunders, the deputy assistant secretary of state for Middle Eastern affairs, told the House Foreign Affairs Committee that the United States considered the Palestinian problem to be "at the heart of the Arab-Israeli conflict" and stressed the need for its solution. Coming in the wake of the "reassessment," Saunders's statement was perceived as another change of direction in American Middle Eastern policy. To calm the storm in Israel and among prominent American Jewish leaders, Kissinger dismissed Saunders's statement as a "misunderstanding."

Nevertheless, the statement did achieve its goal. It deflected for a while Arab pressures, and, what was more important, it convinced Rabin that he could not remain indifferent to changes in the international scene. He realized he must come up with some fresh ideas on how to continue the peace process. It was in that spirit that Rabin suggested in 1976 that Ford and Kissinger help arrange direct Israeli-Arab negotiations on further partial Israeli withdrawals, and the end of the state of war between Israel and its Arab neighbors. 1976 was an election year in the United States, and in an effort to appease the concerns of American Jews, Ford and Kissinger adopted Rabin's idea and began to explore it with various Arab leaders.

In November, however, Ford lost, and Jimmy Carter became the new U.S. president, with Cyrus Vance as his secretary of state. In shaping his Middle Eastern policy, President Carter deviated from all of Kissinger's methods. Instead of the step-by-step approach, Carter wanted an overall settlement. Kissinger excluded the Soviet Union; Carter wanted Moscow back. Kissinger used to tell the Arab leaders that Moscow could supply them with arms and help launch a war against Israel, in which they would again be defeated, but only the United States could help make peace; Carter invited the Soviet Union to take part in a revived Geneva Peace Conference. Finally, Kissinger defined the conditions under which the United States would recognize the PLO; Carter wanted to circumvent these conditions and to involve the PLO in the peace process.

This basic change of direction was not yet known publicly when Rabin came in March 1977 to meet with Carter at the White House. It was a disaster. Rabin was under the illusion that Carter would pick up where Ford and Kissinger had left off, continuing the step-by-step withdrawal in return for the end of the state of belligerency. He discovered that Carter had in mind a totally different approach. More troubling, this major change in policy was made without any consultation with Israel. This too was a deviation from previous practices. As a matter of fact, since 1969, the United States had not tried to act behind Israel's back, and it was to the credit of Rabin that he too coordinated every move with the United States. Therefore, when Carter suggested to Rabin recognition of the PLO and the granting of a "homeland" to the Palestinians, Rabin flatly said no. The president, however, was not dissuaded. While Rabin was still in the United States, Carter made his plan public. In a speech at Clinton, Massachusetts, and in a press conference on March 9, 1977, Carter divulged the contents of his discussion with Rabin. Furthermore, in a report in the *New York Times* on March 10, White House officials were quoted as having said that Carter found Rabin "rigid and stiff-necked." Carter did not leave Rabin much room to maneuver, and the Israeli prime minister returned to Jerusalem bitter and empty-handed. Rabin's failed mission to Washington, besides being a personal blow, undoubtedly led to Rabin's downfall later that year.

Rabin's problems, however, did not end there. While still in Washington, Leah Rabin, the prime minister's wife, went to cash a check in a local bank. Dan Margalit, the Washington correspondent of the Israeli daily *Ha'Aretz,* uncovered the fact that contrary to Israeli law, Leah Rabin had kept her U.S. bank account from the days of their ambassadorship in Washington. The public storm in Israel forced Rabin to resign. On April 7, 1977, Shimon Peres became the interim prime minister.

Rabin's resignation did not help the Labor Party and contributed to Peres's 1977 loss to Menachem Begin. For the first time since the establishment of the State of Israel, Begin formed a Likud-led coalition government. He appointed Moshe Dayan as his foreign minister and General Ezer Weizman, the former commander of the Israeli air force, as defense minister. Needless to say, with this new government, Carter's plans for a Middle Eastern solution had to be shelved. Begin and Sadat forced Carter to exclude the Soviet Union from the peace process. Sadat's dramatic visit to Jerusalem in November 1977 signaled his intention to strike a separate deal with Israel. Indeed, when Carter assembled only Begin and Sadat and their teams at Camp David, it was obvious that he had abandoned his plan to include the PLO in the peace process.

For almost fifteen years, the Labor Party remained in the opposition or participated as a less-than-equal partner in two governments dominated by the Likud. It was not until 1992 that Rabin and Labor returned to power.

THE   CONSPIRACY
THAT   NEVER   WAS

The signs were all there, but as it happened on the eve of the Yom Kippur War, in October 1973, these signs were totally ignored.

Since the beginning of 1993, even before the historic handshake between Prime Minister Yitzhak Rabin and PLO Chairman Yasser Arafat, there were increasing intelligence reports about plans by Jewish extremists to assassinate the prime minister of Israel. Nevertheless, the Shin Bet and the Israeli General Security Service (GSS), which is responsible for the protection of VIPs, did not consider the threats real. The GSS head, Carmi Gillon, though a brilliant and well-educated security agent, did not conduct even one thorough and substantive review of its protection methods. The tragic outcome was in retrospect foreseeable.

Rabin's assassination came at one of the darkest periods in GSS history. The security agency, whose record in combating terrorism was the envy of many countries and whose methods guided many other security agencies in the world, was caught off-guard. At forty-five, Carmi Gillon had been GSS chief for hardly a year. He was appointed to this important position not because of his operational skills but rather because it was believed that he could lead the GSS into the twenty-first century.

Gillon came from a family of lawyers. His grandfather, Gad Frumkin, was, during the British Mandate, Israel's first Supreme Court justice. His father, Colin Gillon, served as attorney general during the early years of the State of Israel. His mother is also a lawyer, and his brother, Alon, is the current registrar of the Israeli Supreme Court. Carmi broke the family tradition by studying political science and international relations. He began his career in the GSS as a junior officer in the VIP protection unit and was later assigned as a security officer in one of the Israeli embassies in Europe. He then headed the "Jewish Branch," which monitored the activities of right-wing and extremist religious groups in the West Bank and the Gaza Strip. His last function before becoming GSS head was as director of administration and personnel of this important security agency.

Because of Gillon's background, Prime Minister Rabin was very reluctant to appoint him. He wanted an army general to head the GSS. He even spoke with three of them, but all declined. Having no choice, Rabin appointed Gillon as GSS head. Without a military background, Gillon lacked operational experience, and he was unable to win the respect and allegiance of more experienced subordinates. As a result, eight senior operatives—five of them experts in Arab affairs with records of success in combating terrorism—left the service. The vacuum thus created was not easily filled.

Unlike the army, which operates on the basis of forces and missions, the Shin Bet, like the FBI, operates on the basis of experienced individuals, good intelligence, and clearly defined duties. If one military unit is unable to carry out a certain mission, another unit will do the job. The army is well adapted for this. The GSS is totally different. If a senior and experienced agent quits the service, it takes time before his successor is fully qualified for the job.

Furthermore, developments since the Six-Day War in 1967 brought a basic change in the organization and duties of the GSS. Until then, the small GSS agency dealt mostly with counterespionage—both Arab and Eastern European—and with potential subversion by Israeli Arabs. The Six-Day War changed all that. More than one million Palestinians came under direct Israeli military control, and the GSS had to build an infrastructure to combat the PLO and other Palestinian terrorist groups. Its successes were phenomenal.

In recent years, however, the GSS had several setbacks that damaged its reputation and exposed its methods to stricter judicial and parliamentary scrutiny. Human rights groups, both in Israel and abroad, complained about its methods of interrogation, thus reducing its ability to extract vital information from terrorist prisoners. It was several years before the GSS struck a proper balance between the ends and means of interrogation.

Carmi Gillon assumed the directorate of the GSS at a particularly critical time. It was no secret that the Oslo Accords neglected security problems. The Israeli foreign ministry team that negotiated the declaration of principles with the PLO was not qualified for this complicated task. The members of the team lacked the experience in Middle Eastern security affairs, and their military and security background was close to nil. Deputy Foreign Minister Yossi Beilin, initiator of the opening to the PLO, was a junior reporter for the Israeli daily *Davar* before becoming Shimon Peres's spokesman and aide. When Labor joined the national unity government in 1984, he became the cabinet's secretary under Peres and then moved with him to the Foreign Ministry. His Ph.D. thesis at Tel Aviv University had been on domestic Israeli politics. His military experience was as a signal corps NCO. Uri Savir, the director general of the Foreign Ministry under Peres, had similarly light experience. Savir was a talented career diplomat who had served in the United States and Europe. Like Beilin, he had accompanied Peres once to Morocco and had had access to files detailing Peres's secret encounters with Jordan's King Hussein. However, he had no personal experience in negotiating complex Middle Eastern problems. His military and security experience was also negligible.

It was no wonder, then, that immediately after the signing of the Oslo Accords, both the chief of the general staff, General Ehud Barak (later the foreign minister), and the chief of military intelligence, General Uri Saguy, criticized the way the Oslo Accords had been negotiated and saw great difficulties in their implementation on the ground. They proved to be right, especially concerning the GSS.

According to the Oslo Accords, the PLO undertook to end violence and to cooperate with Israel in combating terrorism. However, immediately after Arafat took control of Jericho and the Gaza Strip, his security services began harassing Palestinian informers of the GSS. The GSS evacuated many of the informers and their families into Israel. The Shin Bet, however, could not afford to remain without adequate intelligence and was determined to recruit new informers. This proved to be much more difficult. In the absence of direct Israeli control of the Gaza Strip and parts of the West Bank, there were very few incentives that the GSS could offer to potential informers. This, combined with the lack of honest and sincere cooperation by the Palestinian security services, resulted in suicide car bombings inside Israel and a growing number of attacks against Israeli military and civilian targets.

Unable to stop the terrorist attacks, the Rabin government faced a growing opposition to its peace moves, and threats against the lives of Rabin and Peres multiplied. Nevertheless, just as on the eve of the Yom Kippur War the political and military leadership ignored the abundance of intelligence about Egyptian and Syrian troop movements, the Israeli leadership dismissed the possibility that a Jew would kill a Jew.

The ironic part of this tragedy is that the ultimate head of the GSS is the prime minister. Back in 1975, when Rabin was prime minister for the first time, the Israeli government adopted a set of guidelines for the protection of VIPs and for coordination between the GSS and the police. It was also decided that the prime minister would define GSS priorities and would allocate the necessary funds for its operation. After the signing of the Oslo Accords, Rabin directed the GSS to concentrate on the struggle against the Islamic terrorist groups Hamas and Islamic Jihad, and less on the protection of VIPs. Rabin's actions, in fact, frustrated the GSS protectors at every turn. When an armored Cadillac was bought in the United States for the personal use of the prime minister, Rabin balked. After some time, Gillon persuaded Rabin to use the Cadillac, but he was less successful in his efforts to get him to wear a bulletproof vest whenever he addressed large crowds. He insisted that he felt safe in the midst of his people and he did not need the bulletproof vest. When the Finance Ministry appropriated funds for the GSS to recruit thirty additional bodyguards to counter the increased threats against various Israeli leaders, Rabin complained, "Your emphasis should be on the fight against Hamas and Islamic Jihad and not against Israeli religious extremists." In a discussion with several of his cabinet ministers, Rabin was reported to have lamented, "I am unhappy with the GSS head. He is so panicky. Instead of fighting Hamas, he keeps insisting on the need to increase the number of my bodyguards."[1]

A few months later, Rabin changed his mind about the performance of the GSS head. At a private social event, the prime minister told a friend, "You know, Carmi is a pleasant surprise. He is really okay."

Indeed, Gillon grew into his new position. He met with Arafat and his security chiefs and exchanged information with them about Hamas and Islamic Jihad. He also met with his counterparts in Egypt and Jordan and discussed possible cooperation in combating Islamic terrorism.

Unfortunately, as Gillon knew, the "Jewish threat" was no less real than the Islamic terrorism. Lacking professional authority and operational skill, Gillon was unable to impose his will on the prime minister, nor was he able to convey the seriousness of the Jewish threat to his subordinates. Testifying before the government-appointed Commission of Inquiry, after the assassination (the Shamgar Commission), Rabin's bodyguards at the Tel Aviv peace rally said that they had understood the threat to be the throwing of stones or tomatoes at the prime minister.

Yet the Jewish threat was not new, nor was it only a result of the Oslo Accords. Since the summer of 1988, the GSS has explored possible Jewish resistance to a political settlement that would involve an Israeli withdrawal from the West Bank and the Gaza Strip. Prime Minister Yitzhak Shamir, with the full knowledge of Defense Minister Rabin, directed the GSS to penetrate the various Jewish extremist groups.

Shamir's directive was based on one past experience. Back in 1984, the Arab anti-Jewish terror escalated and tension grew between the Jewish settlers and the local Palestinian population of the West Bank. The increasingly brutal attacks raised one serious question among the Jewish settlers: What was the nature and the degree of protection that the Israeli army was providing to the settlers? Some of the settlers believed that the protection was inadequate. Therefore, they decided to take the law into their hands and to "remind" the Arabs that Jewish blood had a high price. In April 1984, the GSS head at the time, Abraham (Avrum) Shalom, informed Shamir that he had uncovered a plot to plant explosives in several Arab buses. The plot was averted and twenty-five settlers were arrested. Some of those arrested were members of Gush Emunim (Bloc of the Faithful), an extremist religious group that was founded after the Six-Day War and held that the West Bank was an integral part of the State of Israel and that Jews had a divine right to settle anywhere in the Land of Israel. Others were sympathizers with radical American-born Rabbi Meir Kahane, who advocated a violent campaign against the Arabs, calling for their expulsion from the Jewish state. To the horror of most Israelis, this "hate the Arabs" campaign won Kahane, in 1984, a seat in the Knesset. Even after Kahane's assassination in New York in the early nineties, his organization continued its illegal activities both in Israel and in the United States and was constantly watched by the GSS and the FBI.

Around that same period, there emerged two new Jewish religious groups: Zo Artzenu (This Is Our Land), headed by Moshe Feiglin and Rabbi Benny Allon, who was the son of a former Supreme Court justice and was recently elected to the 14th Knesset; and Eyal, a small group of activists, some of them students at Bar-Ilan University, near Tel Aviv. Eyal members organized weekend seminars to discuss the dangers of surrendering territories to the Palestinians and amassed weapons to use against the Palestinians if such a need arose. Yigal Amir, Prime Minister Rabin's assassin, was an Eyal member.

One Eyal leader was Avishai Raviv, a disabled Israeli soldier, who had grown up in a secular family in Holon, near Tel Aviv, but had in recent years become an observant Jew. Raviv behaved as a real extremist. Between the summer of 1988 and November 1995, he was arrested eleven times on charges of illegal military training, incitement to kill Arabs, obstructing police activities, and participating in illegal demonstrations. In all these cases, he was interrogated by the police, but the files were closed and no further action was taken against him.[2] In one case, he was suspended from classes at Bar-Ilan University. Shamir's office intervened and he was allowed to resume his studies. After Rabin's assassination, Raviv was arrested again, along with several other religious activists. He was brought to Amir's cell. "I salute you. You really did it. You will now enter the history books, and for that I envy you," Raviv told Amir. Rabin's assassin, however, kept his mouth shut.[3]

A few days later, Rabbi Benny Allon exposed Raviv as a GSS informer. An Israeli TV commentator, Amnon Abramovitz, who is known for his close contacts with the Israeli General Security Service, went one step further. He revealed that Raviv's code name in the GSS was "Champagne."[4]

There was nothing abnormal in Raviv's "extremism," nor was it unusual for a security agency to penetrate extremist groups. To succeed, an agent has to espouse the positions of the other members of the group, in order to win their trust. His handler, however, should be in full control of his activities. This, apparently, did not happen in Raviv's case. Religious activists told police interrogators that on several occasions, Raviv told Eyal members, "Rabin should go." Moreover, Raviv had been linked to the infamous posters showing Rabin in Nazi uniform or wearing an Arab headdress similar to the one worn by Yasser Arafat. Was it a provocation sanctioned by his handler in the GSS, or was it Raviv's private initiative, aimed at exposing potential conspirators? There is no official answer to this question. The fact remains, however, that despite his zealous activity, Raviv was unable—or unwilling—to unmask the assailant who eventually murdered the prime minister.

Raviv's testimony before the government-appointed Commission of Inquiry remains classified. In the public part of its findings, the commission referred to this matter in the following general terms: "The commission addressed itself to the running of agents, the need for close supervision of problematic agents, and the need to prevent them from violating the law or engaging in provocations."[5]

The first substantive tip about a planned assassination of the prime minister reached GSS headquarters on June 16, 1995. Shlomi Halevy, a student at Bar-Ilan University and a reserve soldier in the intelligence branch of the Central Command, told the police the following story: "In early June, while in the washroom of Tel Aviv bus terminal, I heard a conversation between two persons. Unaware that I was in one of the cabins, they spoke freely in Hebrew with no accent. One of them told the other: 'This short, slim Yemenite is a real bastard. He said that he intends to kill the prime minister.' When asked by his friend if the Yemenite was armed, he answered: 'Yes, he has a licensed pistol. He seems to be very determined. . . .' "

Shlomi Halevy told the police that at the beginning he did not attach much importance to this discussion in the washroom. His girlfriend, however, convinced him that he couldn't keep this information to himself. Nevertheless, when he reported the story to the police, Halevy withheld some crucial information that could have helped uncover the potential assailant. Asked by the Commission of Inquiry why he did not tell all he knew, he answered that had he been asked by his interrogator, he would have answered.

The police officer who took this testimony transmitted it immediately to the GSS with the following remark: "The source [Halevy] appears to me as very serious. He is a reservist in military intelligence and has brains in his head." The GSS instructed "Champagne" to inquire who the "Yemenite" was. Shin Bet officials testified that Raviv did identify the man as Yigal Amir, but he reported that Amir was talking only about killing Arabs and did not mention Rabin as a possible target. Hence, the GSS did not pursue the matter any further.

Amir, however, contradicted this version. The assassin told the Tel Aviv court that Raviv knew of his plans to "liquidate" Rabin but did not take him seriously. He said that he shared his secret also with Margalit Harshefi, also a member of Eyal. Margalit told Amir that she would report him to the police, if he really intended to kill Rabin. He told her he was just joking.[6]

Raviv was rated by his GSS handler as "good agent." It is clear, though, that Raviv failed miserably in his mission. Although he was a leading member of Eyal, which he had helped found, he was always suspected by the other group members and never won their trust. Hagai Amir, the assassin's brother, also in jail on charges of "conspiracy to kill Arabs," told police interrogators that on one occasion he asked his brother to involve Raviv in efforts to get arms and ammunition. Yigal Amir objected. "Leave him alone," Yigal told Hagai. "Avishai pretends to be friendly, but he is a GSS informer. Everything that I tell him, he reports immediately to his bosses."

Who, then, is Yigal Amir, the man who committed the first ever political assassination in Israel? Amir was born to an Orthodox family of Yemenite descent and modest means. His father, Shlomo, is a religious scribe and his mother, Geula, a kindergarten teacher. Although Orthodox, Geula always maintained close contacts with secular Israelis. She drove a car, participated in classes of folk dances, and even ran for office, as a candidate for the Herzliyah municipal council.

Geula Amir never hid her feeling that slim little Yigal was the most accomplished of her eight children. He was always "her" child. After completing his elementary education, and contrary to his father's advice, young Yigal enrolled in one of the sixteen religious boarding secondary schools, which combined education with military service. His teachers described him as a "very motivated" student, with a high IQ. They also said that he always subordinated his emotional and physical needs to his rational motivation.

After graduating from the religious high school Kerem de-Yavneh, Amir joined the army and served in the elite Golani infantry brigade. After his military service, his academic achievements and high intelligence admitted him to Bar-Ilan University's law school. During the university's summer recess, he was sent by the religious youth movement to Riga, to teach Hebrew to young Latvian Jews. In Riga, Amir was happy to find a classmate from high school, who was soon to become the head of the GSS "Jewish Division." It was this friend who recruited Avishai Raviv to penetrate the various Jewish extremist groups.

Relatives and neighbors in Herzliyah describe Amir as a charmer. His classmates at Bar-Ilan said that because of his charm, his sense of humor, and his omnipresent smile, many women were attracted to him. Amir, however, had only one serious girlfriend, the young and beautiful student Hava Holtzman. After five months, Hava left him in order to marry one of his best friends at the university. Yigal Amir was devastated. He lost weight and became depressed and withdrawn. "Yigal was never again the same person," said his mother, Geula. His brother, Hagai, told police interrogators that Yigal became so depressed that he started talking of "sacrificing" himself. It was during this period that he started talking more intensely about his plans to kill Rabin. His personal depression became a political desperation, and more than ever before, he was determined to prove to himself and to others that he was not just talking but also capable of doing something big.

Dr. Gabriel Weil, a government psychiatrist who examined Amir at the court's request, said that Amir had difficulties communicating his emotional feelings. He attributed his constant smiles at the court's sessions to "symptoms of narcissism." He added that Amir's emotional makeup "indicates a deep identification with his people and he regards himself as God's servant and God's messenger." Other psychologists who also examined the assassin during the trial said that "Amir projected an intense desire to be loved by everyone, to prove himself, to his family and friends that he was capable of achieving more than others."

This characteristic of Amir—the need to prove his capabilities—was clearly reflected in what he told his police interrogators. He said that he "targeted" Rabin shortly after the signing of the Oslo Accords. His "target," however, was not Rabin the man, but rather the symbol—the prime minister of Israel. He added: "I never believed that I would be able to kill Rabin. I used to tell my friends, 'I must kill him, I must kill him.' They laughed. None of them believed that this 'charming, humorous, and intelligent Yemenite' was capable of doing it. Even I myself did not believe that I could do it. . . .' "

The four weeks that preceded Rabin's assassination were full of conflicting messages as to the public mood concerning the peace process. Despite proven successes in combating terrorism and Israel's improved status in the international arena, opposition to government policies grew stronger and stronger. In early October 1995, Likud-organized demonstrations became more violent. On October 5, the Knesset approved by one vote the Oslo II agreement, extending Palestinian self-rule in the West Bank and setting the timetable for the evacuation of six out of seven Palestinian cities in that region. Within hours, protesters demonstrated in Jerusalem with effigies of Rabin in a Nazi SS uniform. On Tuesday, October 10, Rabin attended a gathering of close to fifteen hundred English-speaking Israelis, most of them from the United States, Great Britain, and South Africa. The gathering was held at the Wingate Physical Training Institute, south of the coastal city of Netanya. Rabin expected a civilized encounter. Instead, he was greeted with boos and jeers, and he was hardly able to speak. "Rabin, resign!" they shouted repeatedly. Among the hecklers was an American-born rabbi from the Hebrew University in Jerusalem. Angry, red-faced, and frustrated, Rabin shouted back, "Shame on you, shame on you," and then left.[7]

The next few days were more rewarding for the Israeli prime minister. On the occasion of the UN fiftieth anniversary, Rabin traveled to New York, where he met with President Clinton and many other world leaders. At Rabin's urging, a small group of American Jewish leaders met with Yasser Arafat and assured him of their support of the peace process. As was his custom for many years, Rabin had a long lunch meeting with Henry Kissinger. Neither of them was, of course, aware of the fact that this was going to be their last meeting.

Back home, Rabin read with grave concern intelligence reports announcing Syria's resumption of financing of ten Palestinian groups in Damascus. According to one report, President Assad gave these groups $18 million to finance their terrorist activities against Israel and Yasser Arafat. The report said that Hamas leader Imad el-Alami was now operating from Damascus and instructing members of Iz el-Din el-Qassam—the military wing of Hamas—on their future targets in Israel.

On October 26, there came good news from Malta. Fathi Shqaqi, the leader and founder of Islamic Jihad, had been gunned down in Valletta, Malta's capital, on his way back from Libya to Damascus. Contrary to Syrian advice, Shqaqi—who was on Israel's most wanted list—had traveled in disguise and with faked passport to Tripoli, to meet with Kadhafi and his senior intelligence officials. Wearing a wig and thick sunglasses, Shqaqi sailed from Tripoli to Valletta and registered under an assumed name in a small hotel. Awaiting his flight to Damascus, he walked in the direction of the commercial area, to buy a few small gifts for his wife and children. Two young men with Middle Eastern features were waiting on a motorcycle not far from the hotel. One of them approached Shqaqi from the rear and shot him in the head, then fled with his friend on the motorcycle. According to the Maltese police, the whole operation took no more than twenty-two seconds. Arab press reports accused the Israeli Mossad of being behind this operation. Israel didn't even bother to deny it.

On October 29, Rabin and Peres headed a large delegation of cabinet ministers, senior officials, and businessmen to the second International Economic Conference in Amman. The conference, which was opened by King Hussein, was attended by Secretary of State Warren M. Christopher and ministers from most of the Arab countries. Syria and Lebanon did not attend, and Libya, Iraq, and Iran were not invited. The first International Economic Conference, in Casablanca, Morocco, in November 1994, was more ceremonial than substantive, but the Amman conference was more business-oriented and hence more successful. Rabin witnessed the signing of a "letter of intent" by the ministers of energy of Israel and Qatar, according to which Qatar would supply Israel with natural gas to meet Israel's energy needs. This was Israel's first public entry into the Persian Gulf market, and the agreement practically nullified the effects of the Arab economic boycott against Israel.

Upon his return to Israel, Rabin was very upbeat. In an Israeli TV interview—the last in his life—on November 1, 1995, Rabin spoke about the success of the Amman conference and the role that Israel had played there. A large part of the interview, however, was devoted to a sharp attack on the Likud party for failing to stand up against the extremist elements who were demonstrating daily in front of his home in Tel Aviv. He called the Likud leader, Benjamin Netanyahu, a "hypocrite" for suggesting meeting with him and discussing ways to reduce the verbal violence.

The next day, November 2, Rabin received a sober reminder that the two-month lull in terrorist attacks inside Israel was misleading. Two Palestinian suicide bombers were killed in the Gaza Strip while trying to blow up two school buses near an army checkpost. Miraculously, no Israeli casualties were reported. Rabin was angry. Yasser Arafat was either unable or unwilling to prevent such terrorist actions, nor was he willing to disarm Hamas and Islamic Jihad.

This was, then, the background to the peace rally that Rabin was to address Saturday night, November 4, at Kings of Israel Square in Tel Aviv. Well known to every Israeli, the square had become the preferred rallying place for all political parties and action groups. It was in this square that close to 400,000 Israelis gathered in June 1982 to protest the war in Lebanon. In face of growing public opposition to the Oslo Accords and the continued violent demonstrations against Rabin and Peres, two of their prominent supporters decided to organize this rally in Tel Aviv, in order to show the world that the majority of the Israelis did support the peace process.

Saturday was a relaxing day for the Rabins. After their routine Saturday-morning tennis game at their neighborhood country club, they lunched with friends in the coastal city of Herzliyah and then had a short rest before driving to the Kings of Israel Square. They were overwhelmed by the large crowds that spilled to the adjacent streets. According to police estimates, more than 150,000 people were gathered in the square that evening. They shouted again and again—"Rabin, Rabin"—and repeated the slogan of the evening—"Yes to peace, no to violence." Rabin was delighted. Never before had he addressed such a large crowd. The friendly welcome was such a contrast to the daily demonstrations in front of his residence, where he was called a traitor and was urged to resign.

Shortly before he arrived at the square, Rabin was alerted by the GSS to the possibility that an unknown assailant might commit an act of terror, in retaliation for the killing of Fathi Shqaqi in Malta. No specific warning, however, was given to the effect that the "unknown assailant" could be an extremist Jew. Rabin was confident that the GSS had taken all the necessary precautions to protect him, and he again refrained from wearing the bulletproof vest.

Unfortunately for Rabin, the GSS did not take all the necessary precautions to protect him. Carmi Gillon, the GSS head, was abroad. Despite repeated warnings about a possible retaliation by pro-Iranian terrorist groups and the sharpened debate with Jewish extremists, Gillon did not think to postpone his trip and take personal charge of the security measures for the protection of his prime minister and the large crowds that filled the square. In his testimony before the government-appointed Commission of Inquiry, Gillon presented an organizational thesis, whereby it was enough for him to define goals and their order of priority and to delegate authority to his subordinates. From that moment on, so Gillon testified, the responsibility was with his subordinates. The commission rejected this argument. It wrote: "The commission determined that the organization, alertness, and readiness of a GSS unit dealing with the sensitive matter of protecting the prime minister is a matter in which the GSS head cannot divest himself of responsibility for active supervision and monitoring."[8]

An equal blame was addressed to the head of the VIP protection unit, an experienced agent who had accompanied Rabin in October 1993 on his trip to China and Indonesia. The commission found that although this senior security official was at the square, Rabin's bodyguards were not alerted to the possibility that a Jewish assassin could target the prime minister, nor was Rabin's driver instructed on the shortest way to the nearest hospital, and the hospital was not put on alert. Worse, the large parking lot and the stairs leading to the balcony from where Rabin, Peres, and the other VIPs were to address the crowds were not "sterile," as they should have been. Hence, uninvited people were allowed to hang around. Yigal Amir, the assassin, was one of them.

On Saturday morning while Leah and Yitzhak Rabin were playing tennis, Yigal Amir, his father, Shlomo, and his brother, Hagai, were attending the morning service at their neighborhood's synagogue, Tif'eret Tze'irim in Herzliyah. Just before sunset, Yigal was back in the synagogue, attending the evening service and praying piously to God for success in his mission. Then he returned home, took a shower, shaved, and dressed in T-shirt and jeans. He loaded his 9mm double-action Beretta pistol with ten bullets, including the hollow-point type that expand on impact and can penetrate a bulletproof vest. He cocked his pistol and tucked it into his pants.

Amir boarded bus 274 to Tel Aviv. He got off the bus at the corner of Arlozorov and King Solomon Streets and walked two blocks southward to Kings of Israel Square. In order not to be identified with the religious and "to look like a leftist and a peacenik"—as he later told his police interrogators—he removed his black yarmulke and, with unexplained ease, entered the dimly lit parking lot and sat on a concrete planter, just across from Rabin's armored Cadillac.

Benjamin Avrushmi, a young man from Beit Shean and a personal friend of a policeman on duty, testified before the Commission of Inquiry that when he saw Amir leaning on a gray pickup truck near the stairs leading to the balcony where Rabin was addressing the crowds, he asked a GSS officer, "Who is this man?" The officer sent a policeman to inquire. "I am the driver of Aviv Gefen," said Amir nonchalantly, and he was allowed to stay.[9] Aviv Gefen is Israel's top pop star, who dodged military service by vowing to commit suicide if drafted. Gefen was among the stars performing that evening. Although supposedly he was Gefen's employee, Amir joked with the policeman about Gefen's looks. He said, "Just look at him, look how he wears lipstick and mascara. It's disgusting."

Rabin was addressing the crowds passionately. "I was a soldier for twenty-seven years," Rabin said. "I fought as long as there was no prospect for peace. But I believe that there is now a chance for peace. . . . I believe that the majority of the nation wants peace and is prepared to take the risks of peace. . . . You are here the proof that the nation wants peace and rejects violence. Violence is undermining the foundations of our society. It must be rejected. Violence is not the way of the State of Israel, democracy is our way. . . ."[10]

Rabin was very upbeat. He told Peres, his lifelong rival and now his partner in the peace process, that this was one of the happiest days in his life. He was moved by the warm atmosphere, by the outpouring of camaraderie and affection. Unprecedentedly, he joined a song in public, struggling courageously with the words of the "Song of Peace," which became a hymn of the peace movement in Israel.

While Rabin was singing the "Song of Peace," Amir was waiting, emotionless, in the dimly lit parking lot. He later told his police interrogators: "During the forty minutes that I was there, I hoped to be asked to leave. Had I been asked to go, I would have obeyed. I would have regarded the order as a message from God that it was not yet time to take Rabin's life. . . ."

The killing proved to be very easy. An amateur videotape of the assassination, shot from a nearby balcony by Roni Kempler, a thirty-seven-year-old accountant, showed, with chilling detail, Amir lounging about or sitting on the cement planter. The dark, fuzzy tape then showed Shimon Peres coming down the stairs, walking near Amir and greeting supporters. Then came Rabin. Amir was seen reaching for his gun, circling behind the prime minister, and extending his arm, followed immediately by a flash and three gunshots. The last image from the tape, screened on Israeli television, was of Rabin disappearing under a pile of security men, to screams of horrified onlookers who hit the ground.

Interviewed by Israeli TV, Kempler said that he had focused on Amir because from the moment he observed him he had a "gut feeling that something bad would happen." Kempler added that because there was so much talk about political assassinations, terror attacks, Amir looked to him like a potential assassin.[11]

Amir shot Rabin at point-blank range. It was so close that one of the bodyguards testified that "Rabin felt the gun at his back even before he felt the bullet." The second bullet hit the arm of bodyguard Yoram Rubin, and the third was fired at the prime minister from a distance of only twenty-five centimeters. Amir told the police: "I aimed for the center of his back. I saw Rabin fly forward. I saw a flash from the gun and boom as if he was getting hit. At such range, you don't have to be a great firing genius. . . ."

Rabin was rushed to the nearby Ichilov hospital, where Leah Rabin, President Weizman, Peres, and other dignitaries and close friends started to gather. At 11:14 P.M., Eytan Haber, Rabin's faithful and closest aide, announced the painful truth: "With horror, grave sorrow, and deep grief, the government of Israel announces the death of Prime Minister and Defense Minister Yitzhak Rabin, murdered by an assassin."

At Kings of Israel Square, which Tel Aviv Mayor Roni Milo quickly renamed Yitzhak Rabin Square, police had jumped Amir and thrown him to the ground. That is exactly what he had hoped would happen. After confessing his crime, he told police interrogators that during the evening service at the synagogue, he had prayed to God to enable him to kill Rabin without himself being hurt. "I did not want to be a dead hero," he said.

Police officer Mordechai Naftali, who interrogated Amir immediately after his arrest, was shocked by his calm. "He was cool as a fish. He asked me if Rabin was dead. When I said that he was, Amir smiled and said this is a cause for celebration. 'Let's drink *l'chayim,* let's toast the event.'" When he was asked what he had felt when he shot the prime minister, Amir answered that he had felt as though he had shot "an Arab terrorist."

Appearing before the Tel Aviv District Court, on November 6, 1995, Amir explained his motives as follows: "People were apathetic to the dangers of handing over the territories to the PLO, with its army of terrorists. What do you think, I killed Rabin because I am a murderer? I did it because this is the first time that an Israeli leader gave away the Land of Israel, an act that brought on deadly attacks against innocent Israelis. Therefore I wanted to alert the public to the dangers of the Oslo Accords." Amir concluded his statement to the court: "My only concern that night was that I would fail in my mission. No, I do not regret my action. On the contrary, now that God has made my mission successful, I feel it's good to go to jail for the sake of our country."

Shortly after Amir was arraigned, Jonathan Ray Goldberg, an American-born attorney who had immigrated to Israel from Houston and settled in the religious community Emmanuel, in the West Bank, told the court that he had been hired by "someone close to the family" to defend Yigal Amir. The announcement led to an immediate speculation that a Jewish dentist from Toronto, whose son, Dani, had studied with Amir and served with him in the army, was helping to pay the attorney's fees. In August 1995, Dani had been married in Israel and Amir had been among his guests. The right-wing Orthodox doctor owned a small hotel in Jerusalem. Immediately after he saw Amir's picture on TV, he flew to Israel and offered the family financial support. In Toronto, the dentist was considered to be well off, and he contributed generously to various Jewish causes.

Shortly after the opening of Amir's trial, attorney Goldberg withdrew from the defense team, and eventually the Israeli court appointed two lawyers to defend the murderer. In the following weeks, and during the court's sessions, the confessed assassin projected the image of a proud and self-confident defendant. His father, Shlomo, a religious scribe with a patriarchal beard, told reporters that he had pleaded with his son many times to repent, but in vain. Wearing a black yarmulke and a blue sweater over a clean white shirt, all the while chewing gum, Amir listened impassively to the various witnesses. Asked by the prosecutor if he hastened to kill the prime minister out of fear that someone else would kill Rabin before him and thus "steal" from him the "bravery," Amir replied: "I wanted an intelligent man to do it. I was afraid that an Arab would kill him. I wanted God to see that one of us did it. . . ."

On the eve of the verdict, Amir read a short statement in court. He said: "What I did was not for my sake. On the contrary. I brought hardship and damage to myself and to my family. I did it not out of hatred or jealousy, nor out of anger or a desire for vengeance. I did it only out of concern for the fate of the Israeli people who are being misled by their leaders. I killed Rabin for the sake of God, the Torah, the people of Israel, and the Land of Israel. I was obliged to kill Rabin, although it is contrary to my nature and my upbringing." That was the only "political" statement that Amir was allowed to make in public. Despite his repeated attempts to use the court as a platform for his ideology, Judge Edmond Levy steered the deliberations strictly to the evidence. In reading his verdict, Judge Levy said that his abominable crime of assassinating Prime Minister Rabin would forever remain "the Mark of Cain" on Amir's forehead.

Amir is serving his term in solitary confinement, in a high-security prison in Beersheba, the capital city of the Negev. He is not allowed to mingle with other prisoners, lest one of them assassinate him. He has a Bible and is allowed television, a computer, and one newspaper. He is also allowed to continue his law studies, to marry if he wants to, and to have conjugal visits. There has been no indication that he has such intentions. Nevertheless, these rights prompted Moshe Gross of New York, a religious activist, to inaugurate an "open line" that called for "candidates" to marry Amir. In a recorded message, the candidates were told that they should be eighteen to twenty-three years old, mentally and physically healthy and with "suitable ideological background." A group of rabbis would choose the prospective bride. . . . [12]

Rabin's assassination evoked memories of that of President Kennedy. Government agencies in Israel were flooded with letters and phone calls suggesting that Amir was not a lone assassin but part of a wider conspiracy. Right-wing and religious activists argued that the GSS had actually "plotted a faked assassination attempt" in an effort to discredit the opponents of the Oslo Accords. Rabbi Benny Allon, one of the leaders of Zo Artzenu, who was the first to blow the cover of Avishai Raviv as a GSS informer, claimed that "Raviv was part of a GSS conspiracy and he purposely incited anti-Rabin fanaticism." Left-wing activists, on the other hand, argued that "right-wing sympathizers inside the GSS" were actually behind Raviv's incitements and actions. They claimed that in recent years, the GSS recruited many agents who were not ideologically far from Amir's views. Hence, the argument went on, Rabin's protection was deliberately neglected.

Court-appointed attorney Gabi Shahar, a former police officer, raised the conspiracy theory in court. He argued that "Amir was a small fish in a vast conspiracy." He said that near the place where Rabin was shot, police had found a watch and eyeglasses that no one claimed to have lost. "It could well be," Shahar argued, "that the watch and the glasses belong to a second assassin, unknown even to Amir." He claimed that gaps and inconsistencies in the evidence raised doubts whether Amir was the real killer. "There are several missing links, there are stones that were left unturned. Together, they raise a reasonable doubt that the bullets that killed Rabin were not those fired by the defendant," he said.[13]

The court, however, was not convinced. Not only had Amir confessed his crime, but also the amateur videotape clearly and convincingly showed Amir as the sole assassin. The conspiracy theory was thoroughly investigated by the government-appointed Commission of Inquiry, and it was dismissed as baseless. The commission was headed by former chief justice Meir Shamgar, and its two other members were the former director of the Mossad, General Zvi Zamir, and the dean of Tel Aviv University law school, Professor Ariel Rosen-Zvi. After holding sixty-one meetings, during which it heard seventy-two witnesses whose testimony was documented in 6,385 pages of protocol, and after studying thousands of exhibits, the commission reached the conclusion that Rabin's assassination was a result of the GSS blunders and the collapse of the GSS protection system.

Rabin's assassination had proved the strength and vitality of Israeli democracy. Despite the shock and anguish, government power moved immediately and swiftly into the hands of Shimon Peres. Even the opposition cooperated in this swift transfer of authority. The head of the opposition, Likud leader Benjamin Netanyahu, stated publicly that the opposition would not take advantage of the tragedy, since in Israel "ballots and not bullets" would determine who would govern the country.

Taking advantage of the shock, Peres moved quickly to implement the Oslo II agreement. With opponents momentarily mute, Peres advanced the Israeli army withdrawal from six of the seven Palestinian cities and turned over the administration of hundreds of villages in the West Bank to Yasser Arafat. In normal circumstances, such a withdrawal would have sparked mass demonstrations. Now, it met no opposition. Painting himself as Rabin's political heir and calling the slain prime minister "my elder brother," Peres forced the Likud to accept the realities on the ground, making it practically impossible for the wheel to turn back.

Peres had also to deal immediately with an urgent problem—he had to restore public trust in the GSS and instill a sense of pride and self-confidence in its agents. As expected, immediately after Rabin's assassination, Carmi Gillon, the GSS head, tendered his resignation. Peres, however, asked Gillon to continue in his duties until the Commission of Inquiry ended its work and submitted its conclusions. As the Shamgar Commission drew closer to its goal, it became clear that in view of the serious security lapses, Gillon's departure was only a matter of time. Indeed, on Sunday, January 7, 1996, Gillon again tendered his resignation and Peres accepted it "with regret."

Gillon's resignation was linked to an extraordinary event—the killing of Yahya Ayyash, "the Engineer," the Hamas suicide-car maker who was on Israel's most-wanted list. Ayyash was behind several car bombings that killed dozens of innocent Israelis in Tel Aviv, Ramat Gan, Hadera, Netanya, and Afula. The operation was reminiscent of the sophistication and professionalism of the GSS that the Israelis had known and admired for so many years.

Ayyash had been hiding for months at Beit Lahiya, a small village in the Gaza Strip, at the house of Ossama Hamad, his roommate at Bir Zeit University. The telephone in Ayyash's hideout was out of order. Ossama's uncle, a builder with close ties to both Israeli and Palestinian authorities, gave him a cellular phone for temporary use. The cell phone also malfunctioned. The uncle took it for "repair." A few days later, it was returned, packed with explosives. On Friday, January 5, Ayyash's father called to say hello. When the Engineer picked up the phone, it was instantly detonated from a circling plane above the hideout, blowing off Ayyash's head.

The liquidation of Ayyash enabled Gillon to leave the GSS on a high note. Peres appointed Admiral Ami Ayalon, the former commander of the Israeli navy and a veteran of clandestine naval operations, as the new GSS head. Peres hoped that the appointment of a relative outsider would help polish the image of the disgraced secret service and rehabilitate its wounded reputation.

Rabin's assassination raised numerous questions to which no answers were forthcoming. People of all classes and political affiliations wondered how Israel had gotten to the point where a prime minister could be murdered by a Jewish radical assailant and violence became a tool for resolving political disputes.

As expected, under the impact of the shocking assassination, all fingers were directed to the right-wing and religious circles to which the assassin, Yigal Amir, belonged. Leah Rabin, the feisty widow of the slain prime minister, refused to even shake hands with Netanyahu, who came to console her after her husband's funeral. She accused him and his supporters of creating the atmosphere that led to the tragic assassination.

However, in Israel of November 1995, it was difficult, if not impossible, to define the social and political culture that led to this first-ever political assassination of an Israeli prime minister. Beyond the personal and national grief, the assassination raised an important question: In a democratic society, what is the line between legitimate opposition and an open incitement to political violence? Relevant to this basic question, there was another important issue: What is the limit of free speech and an honest interpretation of religion? Several prominent rabbis, for example, ruled that if ordered to evacuate settlers and settlements in the West Bank, soldiers were permitted by the Torah to disobey orders from their commanders. Amir identified with this ruling, but the overwhelming majority of religious officers and soldiers disregarded it.

Unlike the United States, where the freedom of speech is protected by the First Amendment, Israel still does not have a constitution, and freedom of the press and freedom of political opinion are protected by a set of ad hoc rulings by the Supreme Court. In the wake of Rabin's assassination, Labor leaders and left-wing parties accused Likud and nationalist rabbis of interpreting Jewish law in a manner that encouraged violence. They also accused right-wing thinkers of raising memories of the Holocaust to justify their opposition to the Oslo Accords. They brought as an example a comment by a respected author and winner of the Israel Prize for Literature, Moshe Shamir. Commenting on the ceremony in Oslo, in November 1994, during which Rabin and Peres were the recipients, together with Yasser Arafat, of the Nobel Peace Prize, Shamir said that the ceremony reminded him of cases in history "when prisoners of war were forced to dance in front of their captors." Shamir, who moved politically from the extreme left to the extreme right, likened the satisfaction in Israel for this Nobel honor to "a nation celebrating its own destruction."[14]

Moshe Shamir was not alone. Since the signing of the Oslo Accords, there had been many extremists in Israel who portrayed Yasser Arafat as "Hitler" and his PLO movement as a modern-day Nazi Party. Hence, if Arafat was Hitler and members of the PLO were Nazis, then anyone cooperating with them was a "collaborator" who deserved execution. Rabin himself was labeled a "traitor" and was described as head of the "Judenrat"—the much-hated Jewish councils that were established by the Nazis in ghettos and concentration camps. The religious and right-wing parties countered by accusing Labor and the left-wing parties of trying to delegitimize religion and of "terrorizing" the opposition into political impotence. They argued that Rabin's assassin had not grown up in a political vacuum. He was born into a culture that began to develop after the Six-Day War in 1967, when the West Bank and the Gaza Strip came under Israeli military control. While stating publicly that the newly occupied territories would serve as bargaining cards around the negotiating table, all Israeli governments—from Levi Eshkol and Golda Meir to Menachem Begin and Yitzkak Shamir—encouraged the building of new Jewish settlements in areas that were to be incorporated within the final borders of the Jewish state. They recalled that when the ultra-Orthodox nationalist movement Gush Emunim began in 1968 to settle in the city of Hebron, it was a Labor minister, Yigal Allon, who personally handed the group's leader, Rabbi Moshe Levinger, the first three Uzi submachine guns, for their self-defense.[15]

In May 1973, a few months before the Yom Kippur War, Defense Minister Moshe Dayan told an interviewer: "Israel should remain in the West Bank forever. . . . If you think that to feel at home in all of the West Bank is 'expansionism,' then yes, I am an expansionist. . . ."[16]

Labor's positions concerning the settlement movement began to change, however, in June 1981, after Shimon Peres was defeated, for the second time, by Menachem Begin in the general parliamentary elections. In an effort to sharpen the political difference between Labor and Likud, Peres expressed growing opposition to Jewish settlements in densely populated Arab areas in the West Bank and the Gaza Strip. In June 1992, Yitzhak Rabin gave his settlement policy a clearer definition. Rabin made a distinction between "security settlements," which he supported, and "political settlements" in densely populated Arab areas, which he opposed. Thus, the political debate in Israel about a future settlement of the conflict with the Palestinians became very acrimonious. It only intensified after Rabin and Peres recognized the PLO and signed with Arafat the Oslo Accords.

The government-appointed Commission of Inquiry, headed by former chief justice Meir Shamgar, was not asked to examine this loaded situation and the political and social culture that led to Rabin's assassination. The Shamgar Commission mentioned the subject in its report, but left it to the education system and to other political and social frameworks to debate it in depth.

THE SWEDISH CONNECTION

When George Bush was inaugurated as the forty-first president of the United States, on January 20, 1989, he inherited from the Reagan administration a failed Shultz peace initiative, a beginning of a dialogue between the United States and the PLO, a still-vibrant intifada, and a new version of an Israeli national unity government, headed by right-wing Likud leader Yitzhak Shamir.

Unlike Bush's landslide victory over Democratic candidate Michael Dukakis, the Israeli elections on November 1, 1988, gave the Likud a very small edge over Labor—forty Likud Knesset members versus thirty-nine Labor. Despite this minimal edge, however, Shamir was capable of forming a new government with the comfortable support of the religious and extreme right parties. Such a government was not to Shamir's liking. His relationship with the United States was already tense, and his policies were criticized by the Palestinians and neighboring Arab countries. In anticipation of a renewed peace effort by President Bush and his new secretary of state, James Baker, Shamir wanted some flexibility and did not want to become a prisoner of his extremist coalition partners. Despite his tense personal relationship with Shimon Peres, he still preferred a revived coalition with Labor. Shamir, however, made it absolutely clear that he would not accept a rotating premiership, as had been the case in the outgoing government, nor would he like to see Shimon Peres as his foreign minister again. In order to face the challenges of the new Bush administration, he wanted full control of Israel's foreign policy.

Shamir had a natural ally in Labor—Yitzhak Rabin. Pleased to see Peres defeated in the general elections, Rabin was absolutely delighted not to have his archrival as prime minister. He was quick to declare publicly that Shamir was right in refusing a rotating premiership, "because Shamir does not need us to form a new government." "Who authorized him to rush and give up the rotation?" an enraged Peres told his close associates. "I am still the chairman of Labor, and there is no party decision yet on the conditions of our joining a new national unity government with Likud."

Peres knew, however, that he had lost the game. Pressure was building up with Labor to join Shamir's government and for Peres to move to the Finance Ministry. The kibbutzim—those unique agricultural settlements that were the pearl in the crown of the socialist pioneers in Israel—were in deep financial trouble. With Israel becoming more and more industrialized, the kibbutzim's share of the national economy was shrinking constantly and their debts were accumulating by the day. Kupat Holim, the Histadrut's health fund, found itself unable to cover the rising costs of health care. With Peres at the Finance Ministry, it would be easier to secure the desperately needed financial help.

On the American scene, the opening of the official dialogue between the United States and the PLO was undoubtedly the most dramatic achievement of Reagan's second term. It was also the least expected publicly. Prime Minister Shamir was confident that such a step—if it would be made at all—would be undertaken by the Bush administration and not in the very last days of George Shultz as secretary of state.

The moves that led to the U.S. recognition of the PLO and to the opening of a dialogue with Yasser Arafat in Tunis were the result of a long-range Swedish diplomatic initiative, pursued with vigor and consistency, with the full knowledge of the United States and with the active support of Egypt and the Soviet Union. Augmenting these efforts, William B. Quandt, one of the most respected American specialists on the Middle East, and Mohamed Rabi'e, a Palestinian-American who headed the nonprofit Center for Educational Development, undertook some private diplomacy. Israeli sources qualified the center as an organization financed by Arab money, with the aim of promoting PLO causes in the United States. Quandt, who was on President Carter's team that negotiated the Egyptian-Israeli Camp David Accords, and Mohamed Rabi'e wrote in some detail about their roles in this private diplomacy.[1] The "Swedish connection" helped open the U.S.–PLO dialogue and eventually led to the Madrid Peace Conference and to the Oslo Accords, a fact that has never been fully revealed.

Despite the public appearance of "friendship and cooperation," the last year of Reagan's presidency was marked by increasing tension between the United States and Yitzhak Shamir's government. The cumulative effect of the war in Lebanon, the Israeli role in the Iran-Contra affair, the arrest of Jonathan Pollard on charges of spying for Israel, and the lack of progress in the Arab-Israeli peace process began to erode the traditionally friendly relationship between the two countries. The Palestinian uprising in December 1987 demonstrated to what extent Israel and the United States were divided. The Israeli government tried at first to minimize the intifada's importance; the United States concluded that there was a need for a new peace initiative, in which the Palestinians would be fully incorporated.

The intifada caught both Israel and the PLO by surprise. Defense Minister Yitzhak Rabin was in the United States, and he decided to continue his visit, as scheduled. "In a few days it will be over," Rabin told administration officials and American Jewish leaders. Prime Minister Shamir also dismissed the Intifada as a "passing phenomenon."

American officials, however, thought otherwise. For quite some time, Ambassador to Israel Thomas Pickering, a very talented career diplomat who had served earlier as ambassador to Jordan and who is now deputy secretary of state under Madeleine Albright, was whispering at the ears of Israeli officials that the situation in the Gaza Strip and the West Bank was "boiling." Other embassy officials were concerned when they learned that Israel did not have the necessary equipment to deal with mass demonstrations. Indeed, when the Intifada broke out, Israel did not have even clubs and had to use live ammunition against stone-throwing children.

Those of us who were born in Israel and had gone through previous Palestinian uprisings sensed immediately that the intifada was different, both in its scope and in its discipline. Although it was not initiated by the PLO and was totally spontaneous, Yasser Arafat saw the opportunity and took charge of it. He was successful in recruiting the diplomatic support and the necessary funds for its continuation. Arafat appointed Khalil el-Wazir (Abu Jihad), one of his closest lieutenants, as the intifada coordinator. Within days, Abu Jihad was able to subordinate the intifada commanders to his authority and to direct their actions. Pamphlets calling for strikes or demonstrations and signed by the "Unified Command of the Intifada" were promptly obeyed. Fully aware of their inferiority in firepower, the intifada commanders used the stone as their major weapon, thus evoking the biblical image of David and Goliath. Only this time, Israel was the Goliath, and the "children of the intifada" were the Davids.

Upon his return from the United States, Rabin vowed to suppress the uprising by force. After receiving an urgent shipment of clubs from the United States, Rabin instructed the army to minimize the use of live ammunition and to use rubber bullets and clubs. In an effort to enforce law and order, Rabin said, "You can break bones, if necessary." It soon became clear, however, that cameras became the most effective propaganda tool for the Palestinians. The daily images of Israeli soldiers chasing and beating stone-throwing children caused irreparable damage. Israel's repressive measures were criticized even by Israel's closest friends and allies.

Liberal American Jews were shocked by the way the intifada was being repressed. They phoned Shamir and Rabin, they sent letters of protest, but to no avail. "Israel is losing whatever goodwill remains in America. You must do something to restore peace and order. The TV pictures are killing you," said Jack Stein, past chairman of the Conference of Presidents of Major Jewish Organizations and one of the few Jewish leaders active in the Republican Party.

Other Jewish leaders went one step further. They urged Secretary Shultz to pressure Israel into accepting an international peace conference, as an umbrella for Israeli negotiations with a joint Jordanian-Palestinian delegation. Rabbi Arthur Hertzberg, one of the past vice presidents of the World Jewish Congress and a highly respected Jewish intellectual, and Michael Lerner, the editor of *Tikun,* a liberal Jewish newsmagazine published in California, lobbied separately for a Congressional statement that would support Shultz's peace initiative that was launched in March 1988.

During a visit to the United States in late March, Prime Minister Shamir lashed out against those American Jews who were pressuring the Reagan administration to "force" Israel into accepting an international peace conference. Addressing a particularly crowded meeting of the Conference of Presidents of Major Jewish Organizations, Shamir accused those liberal Jews of disloyalty to the State of Israel. Albert Vorspan, senior vice president of the Union of American Hebrew Congregations, an organization of more than eight hundred Reform synagogues in the United States and Canada, would not tolerate this language. He told Shamir that Israel should not always expect a "reflexive" support of American Jews. He also said that it was "dangerous" for Israeli leaders to imply that honest disagreements with Israeli policies represented disloyalty. "Israelis themselves are divided on this issue," he stated.[2]

It was at this moment that the "Swedish connection" was born. Its author was Sten Andersson, the dynamic Swedish foreign minister. His logic was very simple: If American Jews dared to express publicly their disagreements with Israel, and if they also lobbied Congress and the State Department to take action not acceptable to the government of Israel, then it would also be possible to "mobilize" liberal American Jews in support of a dialogue between Israel and the PLO and between the United States and the PLO.

There was nothing unusual in Sweden's decision to get more actively involved in the Arab-Israeli peace process. Until the Six-Day War in June 1967, Sweden was among the European countries friendliest to Israel. Despite the assassination in 1948 of Count Folke Bernadotte—the first UN mediator in the Arab-Israeli conflict—by members of Yitzhak Shamir's Lehi (the Stern Gang), relations between Israel and Sweden remained friendly and cordial. Count Bernadotte had been personally involved in rescuing Jews from Nazi-occupied Europe, and Sweden had provided refuge for Holocaust survivors. Bernadotte's assassination was perceived as directed not against Sweden, but against his "internationalization" plan for Jerusalem. The fact that Israel was governed for many years by a succession of socialist governments also helped to forge this friendly relationship. Olof Palme, the Swedish socialist prime minister, met regularly in the Socialist International with Israeli Labor leaders, including Golda Meir, Yigal Allon, and Shimon Peres, and strong bonds existed also between the trade unions of both countries. Swedes were particularly impressed by the kibbutz movement and by the highly developed social services in Israel. Over the years, thousands of young Swedes came to spend their summer vacations in Israel and to experience life in a kibbutz. Swedish Foreign Minister Sten Andersson even sent his thirteen-year-old son to an Israeli kibbutz in 1964.

The Six-Day War brought the first changes in Sweden's friendly relations with Israel. Sweden was moved by the plight of more than one million Palestinians who came suddenly under Israeli occupation. Palme and Andersson were both active in the Socialist International, and they both supported Austrian chancellor Bruno Kreisky's efforts to promote a dialogue between Israelis and Palestinians. During visits to Israel, Andersson had many angry exchanges with Golda Meir and other cabinet ministers over their refusal to recognize the Palestinians' right to self-determination. In the fall of 1974, an Arab summit meeting in Rabat recognized the PLO as the "sole representative" of the Palestinian people. As such, the PLO was granted observer status at the UN, and Yasser Arafat was invited to address the UN General Assembly. At the suggestion of Bruno Kreisky, who was the secretary-general of the Socialist International, and with the full support of Chancellor Willy Brandt of West Germany and Olof Palme of Sweden, Dr. Issam Sartawi, a Palestinian intellectual, was appointed as the first PLO observer in this international Socialist body. Shortly afterward, Olof Palme was among the first European leaders who met with Arafat in Algiers. In 1983, Sweden allowed the opening of a permanent PLO office in Stockholm, thus becoming a useful source of information on Palestinian developments and a site for secret meetings between the PLO and liberal Israelis.

In the spring of 1989, I was among a group of five Israeli correspondents who were invited by the Swedish Foreign Ministry for a week of briefings on how Sweden had succeeded in helping the United States to begin its dialogue with the PLO. Sitting in his spacious and elegantly decorated office in Stockholm, Foreign Minister Andersson told us that the Swedish connection was born in the aftermath of a visit that he made to Israel in March 1988. "I was profoundly shaken by the intifada and by the developments that followed," he said. "I sensed that attitudes had hardened on both sides. I had a very angry exchange with Shimon Peres, who was then the foreign minister. I urged him to talk to the PLO. He refused. So I decided to act on my own."

Andersson's visit to Israel and the West Bank came after two trips that Secretary Shultz had made to the Middle East, in late February and in early March. They produced very little. The first trip was particularly humiliating. In advance of Shultz's arrival in Israel, the American consul general in Jerusalem explored the possibility that a small group of local Palestinians would meet with the secretary in East Jerusalem. This was to be the first ever visit by an American secretary of state to Israeli-governed East Jerusalem. Moderate Palestinians, like Elias Freij, the mayor of Bethlehem—the only elected mayor in the West Bank at that time—accepted the invitation to meet with Shultz. "I told my friends that we must go and hear what Shultz has got to say," said Freij.[3] The position of Faisal Husseini and other local leaders was unclear.

Shultz came to Jerusalem via Moscow on February 25. The snow and the cold weather reflected exactly the political mood in the Israeli capital. Shultz was told that the "Unified Command of the Intifada" had circulated a pamphlet warning against any contact with him. Undeterred, Shultz went to the American Colony Hotel, in East Jerusalem, where his encounter with the Palestinians was to take place and which became the meeting place of the intifada activists with the foreign press. Shultz read his prepared statement to the empty hall, urging local Palestinians to negotiate with Israel.

This humiliating experience proved that the local Palestinian leadership was totally subordinated to Yasser Arafat. Even moderate leaders would never dare to ignore Tunis's instructions.

On March 4, 1988, Shultz returned to the Middle East, to submit his peace initiative in writing. It called for a ceremonial international peace conference, with the participation of the five permanent members of the Security Council. The conference would not be substantive, but would begin negotiations between Israel and a joint Jordanian-Palestinian delegation. Shamir responded that he needed time to think, but nobody doubted that he was opposed to the new American peace plan.

The Palestinians had no problem with an international conference. On the contrary, they supported it. It was Shultz who ruled out the participation of the PLO. Since no Palestinian would participate in peace negotiations with Israel without the PLO, King Hussein too would not participate in a peace conference without a Palestinian representation. It was this obstacle that the Swedes wanted to overcome, and so Andersson met with Shultz at the end of March 1988.

The Swedish foreign minister broached with Shultz the idea of recruiting the support of American Jews in an effort to influence the Israeli government position on the PLO. He told Shultz, "Just as you are influenced by the positions of American Jews, so is Israel influenced by them. The Israeli government is paralyzed. Shamir is stubborn and inflexible and Peres has no power to act on his own. If we can bring a group of American Jews to meet with the PLO in Stockholm, this might help to convince Shamir to meet with the PLO and the door could then be open for a dialogue between the United States and the PLO."

Shultz did not dispute the logic behind Andersson's idea. However, realizing the impact of such a move on domestic American politics, especially in an election year, he did not want to commit himself. He did not say no, nor did he say yes; he only wanted to remain in the picture.

Following the Swedish tradition of "active neutrality" in foreign affairs, Andersson put together a team of able diplomats to carry his initiative forward.

The team included Deputy Foreign Minister Pierre Schori; the head of the ministry's Middle East department, Mattias Mossberg, reputed to have close contacts with the PLO; and Andersson's principal secretary, Anders Bjurner. Andersson told his aides that the initiative should be secret and no one at the ministry should be privy to it. In order to avoid leaks or electronic interception, the foreign minister instructed his aides that sensitive communications with the State Department should be in person and not by diplomatic cables. The addressee in Washington for these communications should be Shultz's aide Charlie Hill, and it was up to him to decide whom to invite to participate in the meetings with the Swedish diplomats.

April, however, was not a good time for launching the Swedish effort. On April 7, Yasser Arafat traveled to Moscow, at the invitation of Gorbachev. It was his first visit to the Soviet capital since 1983. The timing of the visit was carefully chosen. It was in advance of Shultz's visit to Moscow, to prepare for the Reagan-Gorbachev May summit. The Middle East was included in the summit's agenda. Gorbachev and Arafat shared the view that Shultz's initiative did not meet the Palestinians' aspirations. It did not recognize the PLO, nor did it acknowledge the right of the Palestinians to self-determination. The PLO had nothing to gain from it.[4]

Toward the end of April, a commando unit stormed the villa of intifada co-ordinator Abu Jihad in the Tunisian resort city of Hammam el-Shatt and killed him in front of his wife. The PLO accused Mossad of organizing this daring raid. Israel never confirmed its involvement.

In an effort to avoid a new cycle of revenge and retaliation, on May 6 Andersson sent Anders Bjurner to Tunis with a letter of condolences for Yasser Arafat. While expressing sympathy with Arafat, the Swedish foreign minister urged restraint. At the same time, Andersson sent Pierre Schori to launch his initiative with American Jews. Schori's first contact was with an old friend from the anti–Vietnam War movement, Stanley Sheinbaum, a wealthy Los Angeles economist and publisher. Sheinbaum, a liberal Jew and a philanthropist, was also active in the American branch of the Israeli Peace Now movement. He was also a member of the board of the Tel Aviv–based International Center for Peace in the Middle East, which was founded in 1982 by Dr. Nahum Goldman and whose international chairman remains Abba Eban. At Sheinbaum's suggestion, he and Schori met in New York with the chairman of the International Center's American branch, Rita Hauser, a prominent lawyer, a former U.S. representative to the UN Human Rights Commission, and a Republican with close contacts to George Bush. Hauser was a Peace Now activist as well.

Hauser, Sheinbaum, and Drora Kass, the center's New York director, found the Swedish connection appealing, and they promised to try to form a delegation of representative American Jews to meet with the PLO in Stockholm. They wanted, however, a clearer sign from Arafat to justify such a meeting. Schori was very encouraged by this meeting, and he swore his Jewish interlocutors to secrecy. They were not even to tell Abba Eban. Needless to say, Schori briefed the State Department about his conversations.

In the meantime, events were heating up inside the PLO. After his return from Tunis, Andres Bjurner reported to Andersson that he sensed that the PLO's mainstream, El-Fatah, was turning more moderate. Mattias Mossberg was conveying the same message. He reported that Faruq Kaddumi, the head of the PLO political department, was very hostile to any departure from the PLO militant approach. On the other hand, Mahmoud Abbas (Abu Mazen), who was responsible for the contacts with liberal Israelis, was very supportive of a political settlement.

Developments in June confirmed Swedish reports that a moderating trend was indeed emerging in Tunis. In advance of an Arab summit meeting in Algiers, Secretary Shultz returned to the Middle East in a fruitless effort to keep his initiative alive. Unlike previous occasions when he had stayed at the King David Hotel in Jerusalem, this time the secretary established his headquarters at Cairo's Sheraton-Heliopolis Hotel. It was a gesture of goodwill, in appreciation of President Mubarak's consistent support of the American peace initiatives and the moderating role that he played in the Arab world.

"Shultz is waging a war of attrition against Shamir. He is trying to wear him down," Avi Pazner, the prime minister's aide, told me after attending the meeting in Jerusalem between the U.S. secretary of state and the Israeli prime minister. "Shultz knows that Shamir is unlikely to change his position on the international peace conference and he also knows that no development is expected before the November elections in both Israel and the United States. Why can't he just stay in Washington until then?"

American officials who accompanied Shultz on this tour were also more outspoken. Sitting at the bar of the Sheraton-Heliopolis, one senior American official told me, "not for attribution," that the secretary had grown impatient with Shamir and had become tougher in his criticism of the Israeli prime minister's attitude. He said that in May, both President Reagan and Shultz had met with Shimon Peres at the White House and had been very impressed with him. Asked to characterize the secretary's meeting with Shamir in Jerusalem, the official said, "Shultz was talking to the wall."

Shultz's main purpose on his June trip to the Middle East was to try to moderate the Arab positions in the Algiers summit meeting. This was achieved. Indeed, both President Mubarak and King Hussein urged the other Arab leaders "not to close doors" and to keep the lines of communication with Washington open. In his memoirs, Shultz said that after the summit, Palestinian moderates were leaking to the press that the PLO was now ready to play a role in the peace process and that it might also accept a "two-state" solution, thus recognizing Israel's right to exist.[5]

Shortly afterward, Arafat's spokesman Bassam Abu Sharif released a document suggesting direct negotiations with Israel. Abu Sharif called for peaceful coexistence with Israel and for an independent Palestinian state. He claimed that the document was "official PLO policy." A shortened version of the document appeared in the *New York Times* and other Western publications around the world.[6] While Arafat remained silent, another senior PLO official, Salah Khalaf (Abu Iyad), the man who masterminded the assassination of the eleven Israeli athletes in Munich in 1972, criticized the article and said that it did not represent the PLO's official policy. Therefore, Hauser and Sheinbaum called Pierre Schori in Stockholm and asked him to try to get Arafat's official endorsement of Abu Sharif's article.

Acting on Hauser's request, the Swedish foreign minister wrote on July 6, 1988, to Arafat suggesting a formal endorsement of his spokesman's article. Andersson said that he had received many calls from "prominent Jews in Europe and in the United States" and therefore a formal endorsement of Abu Sharif's article "would significantly improve the climate of the political debate, not only in Israel but also in the United States."[7]

Andersson also felt that it was now time to transform the impact of the intifada into concrete political gains. He sent Mattias Mossberg to Tunis, in an effort to advance the idea of a meeting in Stockholm between the PLO and a group of "distinguished American Jewish personalities." He found Arafat amenable to the idea, but the PLO chairman wanted more time to decide. Mossberg then went to Washington, to brief Charlie Hill, Shultz's aide, on his talks in Tunis.

During the next three months, the PLO intensified its "peace offensive" in an effort to seek for itself a role in the Middle East peace process. At the request of Pierre Schori, Hauser and Sheinbaum started to think about who among the prominent American Jews could be induced to travel to Stockholm to meet with PLO representatives. They had in mind Rabbi Alexander Schindler, the president of the Reform movement in the United States; Rabbi Arthur Hertzberg, a prominent Jewish intellectual and a supporter of Peace Now; and Philip Klutznick, a Chicago entrepreneur, an honorary president of B'nai B'rith, and a former housing secretary in President Johnson's cabinet.

In the meantime, independently of the Swedish effort, the PLO sought a direct channel to Washington. Mohamed Rabi'e, a Palestinian-American with close ties to Arafat, contacted William B. Quandt of the Brookings Institution and raised with him "hypothetical questions" whether the United States would respond positively to the PLO's acceptance of the U.S. conditions and would open a dialogue with the Palestinian body. According to Israeli sources, Rabi'e did not act on his own but was Arafat's messenger. On September 3, Quandt presented Richard Murphy, assistant secretary of state for Middle Eastern affairs and a former ambassador to Damascus, with a PLO document implying acceptance of U.S. conditions, but also demanding American acceptance of Palestinians' right to self-determination. Israeli sources revealed that a similar document was circulated earlier in Moscow and Cairo and that it was at a Soviet suggestion that Arafat accepted the U.S. conditions. After being shown the PLO document, Shultz told Murphy, on September 12, that if the PLO would meet the American conditions—namely, acceptance of UN Resolutions 242 and 338: recognition of Israel's right to exist, and renunciation of terrorism—the United States would immediately start a dialogue with the PLO. Shultz made it clear, however, that the United States would not grant the Palestinians a right to self-determination.

In the meantime, Prime Minister Shamir got wind of the PLO efforts to open an indirect channel to the United States. Much agitated, Shamir wrote on September 12 to Shultz, warning him that flirtation with the PLO, even if indirect, would weaken the local Palestinian leadership in the West Bank and in the Gaza Strip and would close the door for their future integration in the peace process—a thinly veiled expression of Israel's dissatisfaction.

Realizing that the exchanges between Murphy and Quandt were, in fact, a back channel to the PLO, Shultz decided to put an end to this private diplomacy. In his book, Shultz revealed that in October the PLO sent a query via a CIA channel whether it was true that Shultz would not negotiate via Quandt.[8]

What was left, then, was the Swedish connection. This was a convenient, discreet channel that gave the U.S. government deniability. Andersson visited the UN with Mattias Mossberg, who met with Rita Hauser, Stanley Sheinbaum, and Drora Kass again. They discussed the possibility that at the end of their meeting with the PLO in Stockholm, the two delegations would issue a joint statement calling for peace and mutual recognition of Israel and the PLO. As in the past, Mossberg reported to Charlie Hill and Dan Kurzer about his meeting with the three American Jews. In early October, Sweden conveyed to Arafat the substance of Mossberg's discussions and asked him to fix a date for the proposed meeting in Stockholm.

PLO officials told Mossberg that the Palestine National Council (PNC) was due to meet in Algiers in mid-November and to expect a very important statement. They thought that the meeting with the Jews should be held after the PNC meeting. The officials also hinted that because of the importance of the PNC statement, Arafat might wish to go to New York in order to participate personally in the annual UN debate on Palestine.

In late October, Arafat gave his final consent to the proposed meeting between the PLO and the group of American Jews in Stockholm. He confirmed that the meeting would take place only after the PNC meeting in Algiers. He designated Khaled el-Hassan, one of the founding fathers of the PLO and the head of the PNC's political committee, to head the PLO delegation. The choice of Khaled el-Hassan was very symbolic: He was the first senior PLO official who had met officially, in 1974, with then deputy director of the CIA Vernon Walters, under the auspices of King Hassan of Morocco. When told about the meeting, Secretary Kissinger was very upset, because it contradicted U.S. policies at the time. He forbade any future meetings. By assigning el-Hassan to the Stockholm meeting, Arafat sent a message to Washington that he expected the road to be open for official U.S. dialogue with the PLO.

Encouraged by this development, the Swedish foreign minister sent invitations for the Stockholm meeting, scheduled for November 21–22. On November 15, the PNC met in Algiers and published the long-awaited statement, proclaiming an independent state of Palestine, "on our territory with Holy Jerusalem as its capital." The lengthy declaration was written by the exiled Arab-Israeli poet Mahmoud Darwish. At the end of the declaration, a reference was made to the effect that "Independent Palestine would enter into confederation with Jordan."[9]

As expected, Israel dismissed the Algiers Declaration as containing nothing new. There was still no recognition of Israel, there was no renunciation of terrorism against Israel, and there was a reference to the right of 1948 Palestinian refugees to return to their homes, which were now in Israel. The United States, on the other hand, while recognizing that the Algiers Declaration did imply a two-state solution, did not find the declaration sufficient for recognition.

The scene now moved to Stockholm. On November 20, Rita Hauser, Stanley Sheinbaum, and Drora Kass flew to the Swedish capital for two days of secret meetings with the PLO. Before leaving for Stockholm, Hauser met in Washington with Richard Murphy, assistant secretary of state for Middle Eastern affairs, while Sheinbaum met at the White House with General Colin Powell, Reagan's national security adviser. Both Powell and Murphy welcomed the Stockholm meeting and defined to their interlocutors the exact American position on a dialogue with the PLO.

The gathering in Stockholm was opened by Sten Andersson. He called for an international peace conference and for Israeli-Palestinian negotiations on the basis of UN Resolutions 242 and 338 and for recognition of the Palestinians' right to self-determination. Andersson then left the room, leaving behind Pierre Schori and Mattias Mossberg to help the two delegations establish a dialogue and draft a joint statement.

From the outset, Rita Hauser made it clear that she and her colleagues had come to Stockholm as private American citizens only. They did not represent any American Jewish organization. She further declared that they did not come to negotiate, "because only Israel can negotiate," but rather to clarify some of the inconsistencies in the Algiers Declaration. In response to this gentle prodding, Khaled el-Hassan assured the delegation that the PNC "had accepted Israel as a state in the region." The PNC also accepted Resolutions 242 and 338 as a basis for negotiations on peace and self-determination for the Palestinians and "rejected terrorism in all its forms." The PLO team wanted to include a reference to the 1948 Palestinian refugees in the joint statement. In the face of strong opposition from the Jewish team, the subject was dropped.

The PLO team flew to Tunis, where the PLO Executive Committee approved the text of the joint statement. At the suggestion of Khaled el-Hassan, the Swedish foreign minister sent Pierre Schori to Washington to brief Secretary Shultz on the Stockholm discussions and to hand him a copy of the joint statement. "I told the Swedes," wrote Shultz in his memoirs, "that I regarded the statement as an improvement on what had come out of the PNC conference, but it was not yet even close to meeting the U.S. conditions for a dialogue with the PLO."[10] According to Rita Hauser, Shultz rejected the text of the joint statement because unless it was made public, it had no value.[11] Arafat agreed to come to Stockholm the first week of December, but he insisted on making the document public only in the presence of the American Jews who had participated in drafting it. He also wanted to know if the publication of the joint statement would be enough for the United States to open a dialogue with him. Andersson informed Shultz of the new development and asked him to spell out exactly what were the U.S. conditions for opening the dialogue with the PLO. Shultz sent his conditions via the Swedish embassy in Washington. Shultz told the Swedish ambassador that the American position was nonnegotiable. The PLO would have to do the changing.[12]

Andersson invited Rita Hauser and her colleagues to return to Stockholm, but he wanted to upgrade the delegation by including representatives of the various Jewish organizations. Here, however, Hauser faced a problem. None of the leaders of the American Jewish establishment would agree to meet with Arafat. The three prominent leaders whom she had in mind—Rabbi Alexander Schindler, Rabbi Arthur Hertzberg, and Philip Klutznick—were active supporters of Peace Now, but all three declined the invitation. Only few days earlier, Shultz had created a furor in Washington by denying Arafat a visa to come to the United States to address the UN General Assembly on the grounds that the PLO was a terrorist organization. Despite pressure from Presidents Ford and Carter and from Egypt and Saudi Arabia, the secretary stood firm. In view of this uproar, how could respected American Jewish leaders go to Stockholm and meet with Arafat, thus exposing Shultz to criticism that he was "more Jewish than the Jews"!

Hauser and Drora Kass persuaded Professor Abraham Udovitch, the chairman of the Middle East department at Princeton University, and New York attorney Menachem Rosensaft to attend. Rosensaft had one advantage that the other members of the delegation lacked. He was the president of the Labor Zionist Alliance, an eight-thousand-member-strong American organization affiliated with the Israeli Labor Party. In his capacity as president of LZA, Rosensaft was also a member of the Conference of Presidents of Major Jewish

Organizations. In addition, like the other members, Rosensaft was a supporter of Peace Now and favored a dialogue with the PLO.

The talks in Stockholm convened on December 6, at the heavily guarded Haga Palace, with five American Jews, eight members of the PLO Executive Committee with Yasser Arafat, and a team of four Swedes, led by Andersson. Arafat was given an official welcome in Stockholm, and Swedish Prime Minister Ingvar Carlsson cut short a visit to Paris in order to welcome the chairman of the PLO.

However, even before the discussions began, Rosensaft faced a serious personal problem. The night before, the Swedish Foreign Ministry had announced the forthcoming gathering between an American Jewish delegation and the PLO and had released the names of the participants. The news created a storm in Israel and in the American Jewish establishment. Even the Labor Party, with which the LZA was affiliated, was caught by surprise. Sworn to secrecy, Rosensaft did not consult with Labor leaders, nor did he inform the LZA board members of his intention to meet with Arafat. When he arrived at the Haga Palace, Rosensaft was handed an urgent cable from Jerusalem. Simcha Dinitz, the president of the World Zionist Organization and the chairman of the Jewish Agency, urged Rosensaft not to participate in the meeting with Arafat. Dinitz, a former Israeli ambassador to Washington and former director general of Golda Meir's office, warned Rosensaft that if he were to participate in the meeting, "Mr. Leket [the international chairman of the Labor Zionist Movement] will demand that you resign from all official Jewish positions." Both Dinitz and Leket were members of the Israeli Labor Party, and both belonged to Labor's hawkish wing. Rosensaft decided to ignore the warning. Years later, Rosensaft told me: "All these past years, I supported a dialogue between Israel and the PLO. How could I avoid such a dialogue, when it involved me personally?"[13]

Rosensaft introduced himself to Arafat as "a son of two Holocaust survivors from Auschwitz and Bergen-Belsen, as a Jew, and as an American who is totally and completely committed to the State of Israel, to the people of Israel, and to the future of Israel." Arafat interrupted him, saying: "This makes the two of us committed to the future of the Israeli people. Are the two of us also committed to the future of the Palestinian people?"[14]

The meeting between Arafat and the five American Jews, on December 6, lasted six hours. The PLO representatives made their acceptance of a public joint statement conditional on Israel's acceptance of a Palestinian state. Hauser and her colleagues rejected this condition. They told the PLO members: "We are not Israelis—only Israel can negotiate. We are here to dialogue, to clarify PLO's intentions." She pressed Arafat on the 1968 Palestinian Covenant that called for Israel's destruction. Arafat replied that the recent Algiers Declaration "nullified and abrogated" those sections of the covenant.

During a coffee break, Arafat told the American Jews that he had once saved Henry Kissinger's life. He claimed that radical Palestinians in Beirut wanted to shoot down Kissinger's plane during one of his Middle East shuttles. Arafat communicated the information to the CIA station chief in Beirut, and Kissinger's plane was redirected to another flying corridor. "Nobody even said thank you," he complained.

While the PLO and Hauser's team were debating the text of the proposed joint statement, with the active assistance of Pierre Schori, Andersson was on the phone with Shultz in Washington, with Arafat beside him, trying to clarify if the wording of the joint statement conformed to the U.S. conditions for a dialogue with the PLO.[15] The main point of disagreement was Arafat's insistence on the Palestinians' right to self-determination, which Shultz categorically rejected. At Andersson's insistence, Arafat finally agreed to accept Shultz's conditions. The Swedish ambassador to Washington informed the secretary that Arafat would announce his acceptance of the U.S. conditions at the joint press conference with the American Jews the next day.

When the two delegations gathered for the press conference, Arafat got cold feet and did not utter publicly his acceptance of the U.S. conditions. He did, however, submit a "qualified acceptance," in the form of a letter to Sten Andersson, in which he reiterated his reference to a Palestinian state.[16]

The Stockholm Statement was immediately denounced by Israel and by mainstream American Jewish organizations. It brought the five American Jews hatred, vilification, and contempt. In a written statement, Morris B. Abram, the chairman of the Conference of Presidents of Major Jewish Organizations, said that "these American Jews naively permitted themselves to be used by Arafat, as willing dupes, prepared to broadcast his latest deceptions."[17] Of the five Jewish participants, Rosensaft faced the most severe consequences. His colleagues on the board of the Labor Zionist Alliance wanted him to resign. There was even a doubt whether he would be allowed to participate in future meetings of the Conference of Presidents. The Labor Party doves in Israel, however, came to his assistance. Abba Eban even threatened to cut all his connections with the international Labor Zionist movement if Rosensaft was removed from the presidency of the American branch. The storm soon passed.

The drama, however, was not over; it only moved from Stockholm to Geneva, where Arafat was to address the UN General Assembly on December 13, 1988. In advance of his speech in Geneva, Arafat sent emissaries to Moscow, Cairo, and Rabat to brief the leaders of the three countries on the Stockholm discussions and to seek their support for his position. The Swedish foreign minister was again most active. He spent hours with Arafat in Geneva, trying to persuade him to meet the U.S. conditions for a dialogue with the PLO. He succeeded. Andersson immediately informed Shultz, on December 12, that Arafat would announce his acceptance of the U.S. conditions in his UN speech.

Despite previous disappointments, Shultz felt confident enough this time to call the Israeli ambassador to Washington, Moshe Arad, to inform him about the new developments. Arad was taken aback. He certainly had not expected this to happen in the last days of the Reagan administration. It did not take long before Prime Minister Shamir cabled Shultz: "Please do not react to Arafat's statement until you have heard from Israel." Shamir warned: "There will be great difficulty in our relationship if the United States moves to open a dialogue with the PLO." Shultz was undeterred. He told the Israeli prime minister that if the PLO met the U.S. conditions, the United States would move promptly. Shultz explained to Shamir that that was a long-standing American position and the United States had every intention of honoring it.[18]

Arafat, however, again proved to be Arafat. In his UN speech, he stated his acceptance of the U.S. conditions in a conflicting way. Shultz was outraged. Despite the fact that President-elect Bush and his future secretary of state, James Baker, thought that Arafat had met the American conditions, Shultz was not satisfied. He wanted a clearer PLO commitment. Andersson was again at work. "You have gone that far, you cannot allow yourself to miss this opportunity for a dialogue with the United States," the Swedish foreign minister told Arafat. Finally it was agreed that Arafat would hold a press conference to "interpret" his UN speech. On December 14, Arafat announced his acceptance of the U.S. conditions. He read, almost word by word, the text dictated by Shultz.

A few hours later, Shultz went to the State Department's press room, where he announced the opening of the dialogue between the United States and the PLO. He designated Robert Pelletreau, the U.S. ambassador to Tunis and an experienced diplomat in Middle Eastern affairs, as the sole channel of communication with Arafat's organization. Aware of the anxiety and anger in Israel, and the disappointment of American Jews, Shultz concluded his short statement by saying: "Nothing here may be taken to imply an acceptance or recognition by the United States of an independent Palestinian state. The position of the United States is that the status of the West Bank and the Gaza Strip cannot be determined by unilateral acts of either side, but only through a process of negotiations. The United States does not recognize the declaration of an independent Palestinian state. The U.S. commitment to the security of Israel remains unflinching."

Two days later, Ambassador Pelletreau had his first meeting with Salah Khalaf (Abu Iyad), a senior PLO official in Tunis. A new chapter was opened in the history of the Middle East. Despite Israeli objections and temporary suspension, this U.S.–PLO dialogue was never totally interrupted and it would eventually lead the Bush administration to the Madrid Peace Conference.

THE MADRID
PEACE CONFERENCE

The Madrid Peace Conference, which opened on October 30, 1991, was one of the major foreign policy successes of the Bush administration. Nevertheless, and despite the tremendous excitement of Israelis and Arabs sitting together at the beautiful Hall of Columns in Madrid's eighteenth-century royal palace, Israel and the Arab delegations knew quite well that the conference in itself was not a definitive act. It was only a framework for negotiating a settlement of one of the most intractable conflicts of this century.

There is a basic difference between the impressive signing ceremony of the Israeli-Egyptian peace treaty on March 26, 1979, and the equally impressive Madrid Peace Conference. When Egypt's President Anwar Sadat and Prime Minister Menachem Begin put their seal on the treaty that ended the conflict between the most populous Arab country and the only Jewish state in the world, they knew that the treaty was a definitive act. Negotiated tirelessly by President Jimmy Carter, the treaty's terms were clear and not in dispute. President Sadat gave Israel total peace, in return for Israel's total withdrawal from Sinai, including the dismantling of all the Israeli settlements in this desert separating Israel from Egypt.

This was not the case in Madrid. President Bush and Secretary Baker were aware that the gap between the parties was still very wide. Hence, from the very beginning, they expected many tactical shifts, angry exchanges, and frequent suspensions of the negotiations. They were not deterred by this prospect, however. It was a part of the "game of nations."

The political ambiance in 1979 was also different from that of 1991. When the Israeli-Egyptian peace treaty was signed, the two superpowers were still engaged in their bitter Cold War. The collapse of the pro-Western regime in Iran and the Soviet invasion of Afghanistan demonstrated how vulnerable was the American national interest in the Persian Gulf. Thus, the peace treaty was generally perceived as contributing to the security and stability of the entire region. The Madrid Peace Conference was opened in a totally different international atmosphere. The end of the Cold War had left the United States as the only superpower. Iraq's defeat in the Persian Gulf War had dramatically altered the regional balance of power in Israel's favor and had reduced the threat to the oil-rich Persian Gulf countries. The war had shown that the United States was very much aware of its national interest and did not hesitate to use force to defend it.

The end of the Cold War and the defeat of Iraq had theoretically relieved the United States of any immediate pressure to embark on a new peace initiative. Nevertheless, the United States and its Western allies were committed to an Arab-Israeli peace process. While rejecting Saddam Hussein's repeated attempts to link his invasion of Kuwait to the continued Israeli occupation of Arab lands, Bush had promised his Arab coalition partners that once Kuwait was liberated, he would turn aggressively to the solution of the Arab-Israeli conflict. Bush even made this promise public. In a speech to the UN General Assembly on October 1, 1990, Bush said that in the aftermath of Iraq's unconditional withdrawal from Kuwait, "new arrangements will be built to . . . settle the conflicts that divide the Arabs from Israel."[1]

In the aftermath of the war, the United States perceived a new sense of realism in the various moderate Arab countries. Israeli restraint in the war had altered perceptions and raised the possibility of a settlement with the Jewish state. The moderate Arab countries, foremost among them Egypt, Saudi Arabia, and Kuwait, believed that PLO support of Saddam Hussein had isolated Yasser Arafat and that his coffers were empty. Hence, they argued, it was possible that he would accept anything that he could extract from Israel.

Indeed, among the various Arab parties, the Palestinians were the most eager to settle with Israel. In the years since the Camp David Accords, the increased number of Israeli settlements in the West Bank and the Gaza Strip had made the situation intolerable. In 1978, settlers numbered 10,000. By 1991, they had increased to 130,000. The massive Jewish immigration from the Soviet Union made the problem even more pressing. Between the years 1987 and 1991, more than 400,000 Soviet Jews arrived in Israel. "Our immediate goal is to stop and freeze the Jewish settlements in the West Bank," said Elias Freij, the respected and moderate Christian Arab mayor of Bethlehem. He added, "If we can't stop the settlement activity and avoid its expansion, then the negotiations will be pointless. What land would we talk about, if Israel takes it all?"[2]

This Arab fear is not new. Since its inception at the beginning of the twentieth century, the Palestinian national movement consistently opposed the issues of Jewish immigration and settlement. In the aftermath of the Second World War, the Palestinians even opposed the immigration of 100,000 Holocaust survivors. After the establishment of the State of Israel, the Arab opposition to this twin problem remained unchanged. Before the gates of the Soviet Union were open, Palestinian leaders hoped that because of higher Arab birth rates, demography would eventually tip the balance in their favor. Now they saw this hope again shattered.

When President Bush and Secretary Baker embarked on their new initiative, in March 1991, they came to the conclusion that Syria must be included in the U.S. peace efforts. As a participant in the U.S.–led coalition against Iraq, Syrian President Assad won a certain degree of acceptance and respectability in Washington.

Exclusion was no longer an option. Already in September 1990—after the Iraqi invasion of Kuwait but before the Persian Gulf War—Syria indicated its readiness to negotiate peace with Israel. In a letter to the UN secretary general, the Syrian foreign minister wrote that an international peace conference could be sponsored by the two superpowers alone.[3] In appreciation of this new, moderate position, and especially because of Syria's joining the anti-Saddam coalition, President Bush met with President Assad in Geneva in late November 1990. Bush promised Assad what he was saying in public: After the liberation of Kuwait, the United States would turn to the Arab-Israeli conflict and would try to solve the problem of the Golan Heights as well. Realizing that the moderate Arab states would not agree to exclude Syria from any future peace effort, Secretary Baker spent many hours with Assad to extract from him agreement to attend the Madrid Peace Conference. Israeli diplomatic reports quoted European leaders as having said that "Assad was very keen to make the point that without him, there would be no Madrid."

Like most Israelis, however, Prime Minister Shamir was very suspicious of Assad's intentions. Israeli intelligence sources revealed that despite Syria's poor economy, Assad spent the $2 billion he received as aid from Saudi Arabia on T-72 tanks and Scud missiles. The intelligence estimate said that while Assad definitely wanted to regain the Golan Heights, its continued occupation by Israel did not cause him an intolerable headache. Assad's agreement to participate in a peace conference with Israel therefore did not mean that Syria was desperate to regain the Golan. Assad could wait until his conditions were met.

Israeli evaluations of the situation in the aftermath of the Gulf crisis were of a different nature. The destruction of the Iraqi war machine had definitely reduced the threat to Israel. It had also eliminated—temporarily, at least—the danger that Saddam Hussein would join Syria or Jordan in a new military adventure against the Jewish state. Israeli military and political analysts observed that while Israel should continue to be able to defeat any combination of Arab armies, the lessons of the Persian Gulf War could not be ignored. Israeli policymakers admitted, in private background discussions, that they were aware of the new realities in the region. They trusted the U.S. commitment to Israel's security and survival. Without spelling it out publicly, they knew that should Israel face an "existential threat," the United States and other Western countries would rush to its rescue, as they did with Kuwait. Israel, however, was not Kuwait, and Israelis were too proud to depend on outside assistance for their defense. Israeli military doctrine had always been one of "self-reliance." The conclusion was that Israel should definitely move toward peace with its Arab neighbors, but slowly and with caution.

This suited the character of the Israeli prime minister just fine. Yitzhak

Shamir was a tough bargainer. Less sentimental than Menachem Begin and certainly no visionary or dreamer like Shimon Peres, Shamir most resembled the ever-cautious Yitzhak Rabin. Shamir did not trust the Arabs, and he was very suspicious of President Bush and Secretary Baker. He knew, however, that the mood in Israel, after the traumatic experience with the Iraqi Scud missiles, was for peace. He also knew that the Israeli people would not let him miss any opportunity for peace.

There was a lot of symbolism in the choice of Madrid as the site for this historic gathering. After the early eighth century, when Muslim conquerors invaded Europe and were stopped at the gates of Poitiers (A.D. 732), Spain became an example of Arab-Jewish coexistence. When King Ferdinand and Queen Isabella expelled the Jews from their kingdom, on March 30, 1492, many of those who did not convert to Christianity fled to Morocco. They lived there side by side with their Arab neighbors and enjoyed the protection of the Moroccan kings and sultans. Hence, despite the offers of several European capitals to host the conference, Secretary Baker persuaded his Soviet counterpart and cosponsor, Boris Pankin, to convene it in Madrid.

Backed by the tremendous logistical and security capabilities of the United States, the Spanish government did a remarkable job in organizing this conference. In less than ten days, the Spanish press office accredited more than five thousand journalists, installed 3,500 telephone and fax lines, and supplied more than a thousand desks and typewriters in different scripts for the use of the thousands of correspondents who flocked to Madrid. Security at Efema, the press center, also known as the Crystal Pavilion, was very tight. Every piece of equipment was X-rayed, and the fenced compound was guarded by hundreds of security agents and armed civil guards. Security was equally tight at the Hotel Victoria, reserved for the Palestinians, and the Princessa Husa Hotel, which accommodated the Israelis.

Security was indeed the toughest problem that faced the organizers. Immediately after Baker sent the invitations to the Madrid Conference, the participants sent their security officials to work out the necessary arrangements for their respective delegations. Although theoretically the PLO was "not present" in Madrid, in practice all the security arrangements for the Palestinian delegation were made by the PLO. Arafat sent one of his security chiefs, Atef Bsiso, to Madrid to coordinate security arrangements with the FBI and the Spanish authorities.[4] Bsiso was the former aide of Abu Iyad, and was also personally involved in several terrorist attacks against Israel.

The conference was held in the magnificent Hall of Columns in the royal palace, where the Spanish kings normally hold their state banquets. Busts of Spanish kings and nobles lined the immense tapestry-hung walls, and glittering chandeliers of crystal and bronze swung from the ceiling, further ornamented by a large Renaissance fresco framed by carved cherubs.

Shortly before he left for Madrid, Shamir had created a storm within his own Likud Party. The peace conference was convened at the level of foreign ministers. Shamir, however, decided to take charge of the Israeli delegation, and he appointed his aides to the key posts in the Israeli team. Terribly offended, the Israeli foreign minister, David Levy, decided not to attend the Madrid Conference.

The rift between Shamir and Levy had to do not only with their personal qualifications, but also with intra-Likud rivalries. When he formed the Likud-led government in June 1990, Shamir wanted his ally Moshe Arens, the American-educated former ambassador to Washington, to remain as foreign minister. Levy, however, commanded substantial influence within the Israeli-Moroccan community, the lynchpin of Likud's victory. Shamir was forced to appoint Levy to this important position. Levy was politically moderate and a pragmatist. Shamir feared that Levy would be blinded by the glamour of Madrid and would offer concessions contradicting the Likud platform. The brutal way in which he pushed Levy aside and the public insult to his "Moroccan" foreign minister were among the reasons that eventually led to Shamir's downfall in June 1992.

As soon as he arrived in Madrid, on Tuesday, October 29, Shamir met with President Bush and Secretary Baker. He was shocked to learn that he had been misled about the composition of the joint Jordanian-Palestinian delegation. After months of tough negotiations, it was agreed that the Palestinian team would not include official PLO members, or Palestinians who carried Jerusalem residence cards, or Palestinians from the Diaspora, or deportees who had been expelled from the West Bank and the Gaza Strip because of their terrorist or subversive activities. It was also agreed that the joint Palestinian-Jordanian delegation would be headed by the Jordanian foreign minister. In Madrid, however, Shamir was told that the joint Jordanian-Palestinian delegation would remain unified, but would have two chairmen. Each of them had been allotted equal time to address the conference. The meaning of this decision was obvious—the joint delegation was a farce and the Palestinians had won their right to be considered as a separate entity.

Another source of irritation was the "entrance" of the PLO to Madrid, through the back door. Dr. Haidar Abdul Shafi, a respected seventy-two-year-old physician from the Gaza Strip, who was among the founders of the PLO and chaired the first Palestinian legislature in Gaza in the early 1950s, was the head of the Palestinian delegation to Madrid. However, Faisal Husseini, a resident of East Jerusalem and the most prominent unofficial PLO activist in the West Bank, came to Madrid as a member of a "steering committee" composed of three Palestinians from the territories and three from Tunis. The head of this steering committee was the PLO executive Dr. Nabil Shaath. Thus, everything that had been rejected by Shamir—Jerusalem residents, deportees, and PLO officials—was present in Madrid.

Having been manipulated—or so he thought—Shamir consulted with his aides. He clearly understood what it meant for him to walk out of the Madrid Conference and return to Israel. He would be blamed for the collapse of the conference and would expose Israel to harsh criticism and possible sanctions. His aides suggested that in light of his tense relationship with Bush, he had better swallow this bitter pill. There were other pills for Shamir to swallow in the next two days.

In order to drag Shamir to Madrid, the United States acceded to his condition that the peace conference would be one single ceremonial opening, to be followed by separate face-to-face negotiations between Israel and the various Arab delegations. Shamir agreed that the first round of the face-to-face negotiations would be held in Madrid, but would be considered as part of the ceremonial session. The Israeli prime minister did not want American participation in the face-to-face talks. He argued that once Israel and Egypt had signed a peace agreement between them, there was no need for outsiders to broker similar accords between Israel and other Arab parties. This argument was hardly convincing. Since the establishment of the State of Israel not one single accord with any Arab government had been achieved without outside intervention, American or international. The Arab-Israeli armistice agreements, in 1949–50, were negotiated with the assistance of the UN. In the aftermath of the Yom Kippur War, it was Henry Kissinger who arranged for the separation-of-forces agreements. Finally, had it not been for the stubbornness and patience of President Carter, there would have been no Israeli-Egyptian peace agreement. Instead, Begin and Sadat would have been at each other's throats.

Shamir's real reason for refusing American participation in the face-to-face talks was his knowledge that the United States's long-held opinions concerning Israel's final borders were closer to the Arab position than to Israel's. Every American president from Johnson to Bush envisaged an Israeli withdrawal to the 1967 lines, "with minor modifications." The U.S. interpretation of UN Resolution 242 was "land for peace." In the face of strong Israeli resistance, Baker agreed not to publicize this.

The U.S. promise proved to be meaningless. While the invitations to Madrid did not mention the principle of land for peace and merely stated that the negotiations would be based on Resolutions 242 and 338, the private letters of assurances that Baker addressed to the various Arab parties clearly mentioned this principle. In his letter of assurances to the Palestinians, dated October 18, 1991, Baker quoted President Bush's speech of March 6, 1991, in which he said that the negotiations would be based on Resolutions 242 and 338 and on the principle of land for peace. As to East Jerusalem, Baker's letter to the Palestinians reads: "Nothing Palestinians do in choosing their delegation members in this phase of the process, will affect their claim to East Jerusalem, or be prejudicial or precedential to the outcome of the negotiations." While stating that Jerusalem must never again be divided, the United States assured the Palestinians that it did not recognize Israel's annexation of East Jerusalem or the extension of its boundaries.[5]

Baker handed the first draft of his letter to Hanan Ashrawi, the spokesperson of the Palestinian negotiating team, in Amman, on September 20, 1991. Ashrawi told Baker that she was going to show the letter to Arafat. Although according to an Israeli law that was still in effect it was illegal for Ashrawi to meet with PLO officials, Baker did not object. He only asked her not to circulate the letter, lest it be leaked, "and then it would create problems with Israel."[6]

The Madrid Peace Conference opened on Wednesday, October 30, with remarks by King Juan Carlos, who welcomed the participants and shook hands with the head of each delegation. In addition to Presidents Bush and Gorbachev, there were Shamir, the foreign ministers of Egypt, Syria, Lebanon, and Jordan, and the Palestinians. Prince Bandar bin Sultan, the Saudi ambassador to Washington, an observer from the UN, and a representative of the European Community were also present.

Although the conference was cosponsored by the United States and the Soviet Union, it was obvious that America was running the show. Gorbachev's presence in Madrid attracted little attention, his speech even less. Most of Gorbachev's speech was devoted to Soviet problems, and he said very little about peace in the Middle East and Moscow's role in the process.

President Bush's speech was balanced and well articulated. He said: "Peace will only come as a result of direct negotiations, compromises, give and take. Peace cannot be imposed from outside, not by the U.S. or anyone else. . . . We come here to Madrid as realists. We don't expect peace to be negotiated in a day, or a week, or a month, or even a year. It will take time. Indeed, it should take time—time for parties so long at war, to learn to talk to one other, to listen to one another. . . . What we envision is a process of direct negotiations proceeding along two tracks. One track is between Israel and the Arab states, the other between Israel and the Palestinians. Negotiations are to be conducted on the basis of Resolutions 242 and 338. Soon after the bilateral talks commence, the parties will convene to organize multilateral negotiations as well. . . . Peace cannot depend upon promises alone. Real peace must be based upon security for all states and peoples, including Israel. For too long, the Israeli people have lived in fear, surrounded by an unaccepting Arab world. Now is the ideal moment for the Arab world to demonstrate that attitudes have changed, that the Arab world is willing to live in peace with Israel and make allowances for Israel's reasonable security needs. . . . Peace must be also based on fairness. . . . This applies above all to the Palestinians. Israel has now an opportunity to demon-

strate that it is willing to enter into a new relationship with its Palestinian neighbors. . . . Throughout the Middle East we seek a stable and enduring settlement. We have not defined what this means. Indeed, I have no maps showing
where the final borders are to be drawn. Nevertheless, we believe that territorial compromise is essential to peace. . . ."[7]

At the end of the conference's first day, it was obvious that Israel was on the
defensive in Madrid. Among the Arab delegations, the Palestinians were the
most forceful, and their sentiment was that of ecstasy and triumph. "Today, sitting together, at the same room with Bush, Gorbachev, and Shamir, we feel as
though we have placed the foundation stone for the Palestinian state," Saeb
Erikat, a professor of political science at El-Najah University in Nablus and a
member of the Palestinian negotiating team, told a group of Israeli journalists
in Madrid. For him, it was not only a question of pride, but rather a feeling that
the United States had finally recognized the Palestinians' right to have their
own national entity. Erikat, spectacled and with a bushy beard, provoked Shamir
that morning by entering the Hall of Columns wearing a headdress similar to
that of Arafat. Shamir complained to Baker about this "provocation," but certainly he would not walk out from a peace conference because of a headdress.

That evening, however, came a much more serious provocation. In his constant effort to prove his "presence" in Madrid, Arafat summoned the entire Palestinian delegation—more than a hundred people, including negotiators, advisers,
security personnel, and administrators—to come and meet with him in Algiers.
There was nothing urgent in this unusual summons. Arafat had given the delegation all the necessary instructions and had approved the text of the Palestinian
speech that was to be delivered the next day. Arafat's only reason for this move
was to demonstrate who was the Palestinian boss. He correctly reasoned that the
disappearance of an entire delegation could not remain unnoticed, especially in
a city flooded with security agents from so many countries. Indeed, shortly after
the delegation took off for Algiers, Israeli security officers told Shamir about
the Palestinian surprise. He said nothing, but shrugged his shoulders.[8]

The Israeli mood on Thursday, October 31, was somber and businesslike.
Shamir was the first of five speakers that day. If he had any misgivings about the
U.S. attitude—and he had many—they were certainly not reflected in his
speech. In his forty-five-minute address, Shamir dealt with the historic past, the
situation at the present time, and his vision for the future. There was nothing
unusual in the speech. He did not repeat his not-one-inch approach, nor did he
call for territorial compromise, nor did he give any hint of possible compromise
concerning Jerusalem or the Israeli settlements in the territories. Nevertheless,
while he made no rhetorical gestures, the tone of Shamir's speech was realistically consistent with a desire to negotiate. He suggested publicly what had
already been secretly rejected by the United States. He invited the Arab
countries to face-to-face negotiations in the Middle East, with a first round in
Israel. The Arabs rejected this invitation. They wanted to remain in Madrid, al-

though eventually they settled for Washington. However, Shamir's message was clear: Israel had come to Madrid to negotiate. Despite the continuing provocations by the Palestinians, he did not seize several opportunities to walk out.[9]

After the remarks by the Jordanian foreign minister, it was the Palestinians' turn to deliver their message. The appearance of Dr. Haidar Abdul Shafi, the most prominent PLO supporter in the Gaza Strip, was the high drama of the day. The Palestinians had finally found their place among the nations, at a major Middle East peace conference, and they made no effort to conceal their pride. Abdul Shafi expressed this sentiment, clearly and loudly. His speech had been written by Hanan Ashrawi, with inputs by him and others, and had been faxed to Tunis for Arafat's approval. Arafat wanted an explicit reference to the PLO and an allusion to him personally. Baker, however, had promised Shamir that there would be no mention of the PLO in the Palestinian opening statement. If there was, Israel would walk out. After several angry telephone calls between Baker and Ashrawi and between her and Arafat, the reference to the PLO was replaced by the general term "our acknowledged leadership."

Abdul Shafi opened his speech by saying: "We come to you from a tortured land and a proud, though captive people, having been asked to negotiate with our occupiers, but leaving behind the children of the intifada and a people under occupation and under curfew, who enjoined us not to surrender or forget." As Abdul Shafi continued to hammer in his message, Shamir sat with a poker face, drumming his fingers, writing notes furiously, and passing them to aides sitting behind him.

Like Shamir's, the Palestinian political message carried no surprises. Repeating all the known claims for self-determination, suspension of Jewish settlement activity, East Jerusalem, etc., Abdul Shafi accepted publicly the two-stage approach for a solution—an interim period of five years and final status negotiations. Before the Persian Gulf War, Arafat had rejected this approach.

Abdul Shafi dared Shamir twice to walk out—first, when he mentioned "our acknowledged leadership clearly and unequivocally recognized by the community of nations, with only few exceptions," and then with a selective quote from Yasser Arafat's speech to the UN General Assembly in 1974. On that occasion, Arafat—pistol on hip—ended his speech with the following sentence: "I have come to you bearing an olive branch and a freedom fighter's gun. Don't let the olive branch fall from my hand." In Madrid, Abdul Shafi deleted the reference to the "freedom fighter's gun" and left only the "olive branch." It was obvious that the quote itself was not important—what was important was the allusion to Arafat.[10]

In a remarkable manifestation of self-restraint, the Israeli prime minister did not fall into the PLO's trap. He knew quite well that whatever the provocation, Israel could not afford to walk out. He would have ample time to pay back the Palestinians for their Madrid manipulations.

The Syrian foreign minister's speech was certainly the most aggressive and most abusive of the day. Syria had suppressed Islamic insurgency in the city of Hama by slaughtering more than twenty thousand people, and it was indeed bizarre to hear its foreign minister accusing Israel of inhuman treatment of the Palestinians in its efforts to suppress the intifada. While ignoring the fact that President Assad was denying the small Syrian Jewish community the right to leave the country and reunite with their families, Foreign Minister Faruq el-Shara'a devoted a large passage of his speech to the "humane treatment" of the Jews living among the Arabs "in grace, dignity, and tolerance." The Syrian minister argued that he was mentioning these "historical facts" only because, according to him, the "Jews being in control of the world media have distorted the picture and the world does not know the truth about the Arab-Israeli conflict." As expected, the Syrian minister called for total Israeli withdrawal not only from the Golan Heights and South Lebanon, but also from the West Bank, the Gaza Strip, and Jerusalem.

The next day, Friday, November 1, was devoted to rebuttals and to closing remarks by Secretary Baker. In that session, el-Shara'a staged a small "media sensation." He held up an old British police poster from the 1940s, showing Shamir as a wanted man for acts of terrorism against the British mandatory government in Palestine. When the Syrian foreign minister staged that show, the Israeli prime minister was already on his way back home, trying to reach Israel before the Sabbath.

In his closing remarks, Baker described the role Washington would play in the next phase of the negotiations. He said: "We have our own positions and views on the peace process, and we will not forgo our right to state them. But as an honest broker in Middle East negotiations, we also know that our critical contribution will often be to exert quiet, behind-the-scene influence and persuation. . . . We will do our part, but we cannot do your part as well. The U.S. and the Soviet Union will provide encouragement, advice, proposals, and views to help the peace process. None of this, however, will relieve you, the parties, of the obligation of making peace. If you won't do it, we certainly can't. We cannot want peace more than you do. . . ."[11]

With the end of the ceremonial part of the Madrid Peace Conference, the formal role of the United States and the Soviet Union came to an end. As Baker had said in his closing remarks, the United States had some ideas how to bridge the gap between the parties, but Baker could not advance them unless both sides wanted him to do so. Israel, however, opposed any direct American involvement in the face-to-face negotiations and feared an imposed solution. The Arabs, on the other hand, wanted the United States to continue playing an active role in the peace talks. They believed that without such a U.S. presence, there would be no progress in the peace talks.

What made the situation even more complicated was that both Shamir and Arafat were suspicious of American intentions. The PLO chairman feared that the United States and Israel were trying to build an "alternative leadership" in the West Bank and the Gaza Strip. With the PLO excluded from the negotiations, the PLO role would be eliminated, and the negotiating team in Madrid could become the "alternative Palestinian leadership." This fear was clearly expressed on October 20, 1991, during a sharp exchange between Arafat and Mahmoud Abbas (Abu Mazen), the PLO official responsible for coordinating the talks with the Israelis and liberal American Jews. After lengthy deliberations, the PLO executive finally approved the composition of the Palestinian negotiating team. Abu Mazen picked up the phone and called the PLO representative in Amman and asked him to transmit the names of the Palestinian negotiators to King Hussein and to the prime minister of Jordan. Arafat burst into the discussion and told his representative in Amman that the list was not yet final and that there could be some more changes. Abu Mazen was shocked. Arafat's intervention meant that the names of the Palestinians could not be communicated to the various parties involved in the preparations for Madrid. He had this angry exchange with Arafat:

Abu Mazen: "What a shame. For the last forty-eight hours, King Hussein and his prime minister have been asking for the names. Baker, the Soviet Union, and the Spanish government were all anxious to get the names. . . ."

Arafat: "We are the wild card in the Middle East equation. They can wait. . . ."

Abu Mazen: "This was true long ago, not anymore. You forget that until a few weeks ago, you were 'wanted'—alive or dead—because of your support of the Iraqi invasion of Kuwait. Your picture was displayed everywhere, side by side with Saddam Hussein. . . ."

Arafat: "That's true. I am still 'wanted.' The United States wants to eliminate me and create an alternative leadership to the PLO, in the West Bank and the Gaza Strip. The United States wants to steer the developments in the direction of Jordan. The Americans prefer a dead Arafat, or at least impotent. . . ."[12]

One could hardly expect a breakthrough in Madrid. Indeed, despite its success in its very convening, the Madrid Conference was more a big TV show than a peace conference. Sitting face to face with the Israelis for the first time since Camp David, the Arab delegations could not resist the temptation to grandstand. It was obvious that no Arab delegation could afford to be perceived as moderate or soft, lest it be accused of treason. The Israelis, the Syrians, and the Palestinians came to Madrid reluctantly, not because they were convinced that the time was ripe for reconciliation, but because the United States wanted them to come. Hence, facing the TV screens, they continued in Madrid their rhetorical confrontations, exactly as they were doing back home. President Carter faced such a possibility when he got himself involved in the Israeli-Egyptian peace negotiations. His success at Camp David was owed mainly to the fact that he got Begin and Sadat outside of Washington, with no TV cameras or press leaks.

Nevertheless, President Bush and Secretary Baker did not despair. They considered the public maximalist views to be bargaining positions. They believed that once the parties moved to the face-to-face negotiations, they would try to reach a fair settlement. Before coming to Madrid, Baker urged Israel and the Palestinians to exchange some "confidence-building measures" (CBM). He urged the Palestinians, for example, to announce the end of the intifada, in return for Israel's announcing the suspension of the settlement activity in the West Bank. This did not happen in Madrid and was not likely to happen in the separate, bilateral face-to-face meetings that Secretary Baker had scheduled for Sunday, November 3, in three different locations in Madrid. The meetings were scheduled between Israel and Syria, Israel and Lebanon, and Israel and a joint Jordanian-Palestinian delegation. Syria, however, rejected this plan. Syrian Foreign Minister Faruq el-Shara'a told Baker that such an arrangement would further divide the Arab delegations. He suggested, instead, three separate meetings but at one single site, either simultaneously or successively. When Baker insisted on the original schedule, el-Shara'a said that in such a case Syria would not participate in the scheduled meetings and he would fly back to Damascus.

An angry Baker spent most of Saturday on the phone, trying to recruit the support of Egypt and Saudi Arabia, in a desperate effort to convince the Syrians to change their mind. Indeed, Saudi King Fahd, President Mubarak, King Hussein, and even Yasser Arafat called President Assad and urged him not to wreck the conference. They knew that should the Syrians boycott the bilateral discussions with the Israelis on Sunday, the entire world would forget the ceremonies and would only remember that the Arabs didn't want peace. Assad was still noncommittal. The only encouraging and positive development on that Saturday in Madrid was that both the Jordanians and Palestinians informed Baker that they would come Sunday to the scheduled meeting with the Israelis regardless of the Syrian decision. As for the Lebanese, nobody really expected them to raise an independent voice.

On Sunday morning, at the scheduled hour, the Israelis and the members of the joint Jordanian-Palestinian delegation met for three hours at the Palacio de Parcent, a three-story baroque-style annex of the Spanish Ministry of Justice building. The meeting dealt with procedures and explored the venues for further meetings, and it went quite well. The Syrians and the Lebanese, who were to meet with the Israelis at the Palacio de Viana, two miles away, didn't show up. It was an Israeli PR coup that Deputy Foreign Minister Netanyahu, who was in charge of the Israeli information team in Madrid, did not fail to exploit.

The drama, however, was not over yet. Realizing that they were unable to impose their will on the Jordanians and the Palestinians, the Syrians finally succumbed to Arab, American, and European pressure and decided to meet face to face with the Israelis. At 10:00 P.M., Sunday, November 3, 1991, the Syrians and the Lebanese rolled up to the gates of the Palacio de Parcent for their separate but simultaneous meeting with the Israeli delegation. The meeting lasted five hours and was inconclusive. Emerging from the meeting, an exhausted Yossi Ben-Aharon, the director general of the prime minister's office and the head of the Israeli negotiating team with Syria, told reporters that the meeting had been a disaster. Even the coffee breaks had been unpleasant. The Syrians would not shake hands and would not discuss anything, merely repeating their question "When will Israel withdraw from the Golan?" They even refused to discuss the venue of the next round of the direct negotiations. When Ben-Aharon suggested moving the talks to the region and expressed readiness to hold them even in Damascus, the Syrians replied: "Why? What's wrong with Madrid?" The Syrians refused any comment to the waiting reporters.

No discussion of the events in Madrid is complete without an explanation of the complex, mutually suspicious relationship between President Bush and Prime Minister Shamir.

Nothing in Bush's career, whether as vice president, or director of central intelligence, or as ambassador to the UN, indicated any public anti-Israeli bias. On the contrary, both the Israeli political body and American Jewish leadership praised the outstanding humanitarian job that Vice President Bush had done in the discreet effort to rescue Ethiopian Jews and airlift them to Israel. Uri Lubrani, the former Israeli ambassador to Ethiopia and Iran and the coordinator of both Operations Moses and Solomon, told a gathering of the Conference of Presidents in New York that were it not for Bush's efforts with Sudanese President Jaafar Nimeiry, Ethiopian Jews would not be in Israel today.

Nevertheless, American Jewish leaders, most of them Democrats, described Bush, in private discussions, as a "cold fish" with no emotional attachment to Israel. "Bush is no Reagan," they said. Jack Stein, the former chairman of the Conference of Presidents of Major Jewish Organizations and one of the very few Republican Jewish leaders, disagreed. Stein, whom Bush appointed as an ambassador and a member of the U.S. mission to the UN under Ambassador Thomas Pickering, agreed that "Bush is not emotional," but he insisted that the president's commitment to Israel was unshaken.

American Jewish leaders were uneasy about James A. Baker as well. Baker, the friend and ally whom Bush appointed as his secretary of state, was described as a fair and no-nonsense lawyer who in the determined pursuit of a deal could become blunt and brutal. American Jewish leaders were disturbed by a *Time* magazine profile of the new secretary of state, in which Baker told his interviewer: "Shooting turkeys consists of getting them where you want them, on your terms. Then you control the situation, not them. You have the options—pull the trigger, or don't. It doesn't matter, once you have gotten them where you want them. The important thing is knowing that it is in your hands, that you can do whatever you determine is in your interest to do. . . ."[13] American Jewish leaders and Israeli officials feared that Baker would apply his turkey-hunting theory to his Middle East policy and to his dealings with Israel as well.

The Israeli Foreign Ministry's evaluation of the new administration's Middle East policy was based on Bush's record as Reagan's two-term vice president. Despite his reluctance to publicly oppose Reagan's pro-Israeli policies, the Likud component of Shamir's national unity government regarded Bush as "pro-Arab." Because of Bush's personal friendship with the Saudi ambassador to Washington, Prince Bandar bin Sultan, one leading Likud minister said: "Bush sees the Middle East through the eyes of an oil baron from Texas and a Saudi prince eager to play a discreet role in the politics of the Middle East."[14]

The Israeli profile of Bush included the following instances in which the vice president held positions considered to be anti-Israel:

- In June 1981, after Operation Opera—the destruction of the Iraqi nuclear facility near Baghdad—Bush called for punitive actions against Israel.

- Also in 1981, in meetings at the White House, Bush sharply criticized Israel and AIPAC for their effort to block the sale of AWACS planes to Saudi Arabia.

- In 1982, during the war in Lebanon, Bush supported Defense Secretary Caspar Weinberger in his efforts to impose sanctions on Israel.

- In 1984, at the urging of Egypt and Saudi Arabia, Bush tilted toward Iraq and supported the decision to allow Egypt to sell Iraq arms and other military equipment.

- In 1985–86, Bush was very critical of the pro-Iranian role that Israel had played in the Iran-Contra affair.

- Finally, Bush and Baker disliked AIPAC and shared the view that Israel had too much influence in Washington.

While Likud treated Bush as pro-Arab, the Labor component of the national unity government, and especially Rabin and Peres, did not find Bush's and Baker's positions on the Arab-Israeli conflict or on arms sales to the Arab countries different from those of their predecessors.

The interesting thing was that some of the Arab countries, and especially the Palestinians, felt the same uneasiness about the new Republican administration. Like Israel, the Palestinians did not know much about the president's future approach to the Arab-Israeli conflict. They knew, of course, that both Bush and Baker supported Secretary Shultz's decision to open the dialogue with the PLO in December 1988, and they were assured that this dialogue would continue. They were suspicious, however, of the new Middle East team that the president and the secretary had assembled. Baker inherited from Shultz Dan Kurzer, the Jewish head of the State Department's Israeli desk and a consistent supporter of opening a dialogue with the PLO. Baker kept him in the same position. The secretary added two additional Jews who were not exactly "in tune" with Kurzer to his Middle East team. They were Dennis Ross and Aaron Miller. At the same time, General Brent Scowcroft, the national security adviser, appointed Richard Haas (another Jew) as director of Near East and South Asian affairs at the White House, a position that Ross had occupied during the Reagan administration.

The most senior official in Baker's Middle East team undoubtedly was Dennis Ross, a brilliant researcher who had worked at the State Department and in the Pentagon and who had expertise in Soviet affairs and Soviet policies in the Middle East. Baker had met him during the Bush presidential campaign when Ross served as foreign policy adviser. Baker was very much impressed by Ross's analytical capabilities and his ability to define goals and means in a clear and logical way. He put him in charge of the policy planning staff at the State Department. Ross brought with him Aaron Miller, who wrote extensively on Palestinian affairs.

Dennis Ross was born in 1948 to a Jewish family of Russian extraction. In 1970, as a student, this baby boomer from San Francisco visited Israel for the first time. Although Ross was always aware of his "Jewishness," his Jewish identity grew even stronger after he met his wife of twenty-five years. Ross was a freshman in college when the Six-Day War broke out. Already he had come to the conclusion that the United States was preoccupied with Vietnam and paid too little attention to the Arab-Israeli conflict. When he became the senior member in Baker's Middle East team, Ross tried to rectify what he considered a blunder of the Johnson administration and devoted much of his time to the Arab-Israeli conflict. His approach was clear and sound. In order for the United States to safeguard its national interests, there was an urgent need to initiate a Middle East peace process, especially now that both Israel and the Arabs trusted America. However, there was an equal need for direct negotiations. The United States could play the role of "facilitator" and help shape goals and priorities, but it could not substitute for one of the parties. Ross knew, of course, that the Arab-Israeli conflict could not disappear overnight. However, being patient and persistent and possessed of a sense of humor, he was prepared for many ups and downs. He was not deterred by the prospect of frequent crises and last-minute maneuvers by the parties concerned.

Before joining the Bush administration, both Dennis Ross and Richard Haas took part in a bipartisan study group that toured the Middle East in the summer of 1988. The study group was organized by Martin Indyk, the director of the Washington Institute for Near East Policy, a pro-Israeli research center that within a relatively short period had earned a reputation as one of the most influential think-tank groups in Washington. Indyk, who President Clinton appointed as the first Jewish-American ambassador to Israel, is now assistant secretary of state for Middle Eastern affairs under Secretary Albright.

While opposing the Likud doctrine of "not one inch," both Ross and Haas were known to prefer a low-key, step-by-step approach to the Arab-Israeli conflict, based on the principle of land for peace and a reasonable territorial compromise. They were reported to be leaning toward Rabin's tendency to try to build an alternative Palestinian leadership in the territories, rather than recognizing the PLO. However, once Schultz had opened the dialogue with the PLO, no one on Baker's team challenged this new reality and none recommended the suspension of the U.S. dialogue with Yasser Arafat in Tunis.

This was not, however, the view of Prime Minister Shamir. With Moshe Arens as foreign minister in his new national unity government, Shamir was in full control of Israel's foreign policy. Or so he thought. Shamir embarked immediately on a campaign aimed to suspend the U.S. dialogue with the PLO. During a three-day annual leadership trip to Israel, in early February 1989, hundreds of members of the forty-seven organizations within the Conference of Presidents of Major Jewish Organizations were exposed to a concerted effort aimed at urging them to pressure the Bush administration to reverse Shultz's decision. Government spokesmen used a clash between the Israeli army and a PLO-affiliated group in South Lebanon as proof that Arafat's commitment to renounce terrorism was "worthless." The effort failed, however. The consensus in the Jerusalem meeting was that upon their return to New York, American Jewish leaders would meet with Baker and ask for "reassessment" (not suspension) of the dialogue with the PLO. That was the first indication that as in Israel, the American Jewish leadership was divided on its approach to peace. This division would weigh heavily on future peace moves by Bush and parts of the Israeli political body.

Indeed, in its meeting with Baker, the Conference of Presidents realized that it had a weak case. The Palestinian group that was involved in the clash with the Israeli army in South Lebanon belonged to the Popular Front for the Liberation of Palestine (PFLP), based in Damascus. In a meeting in Cairo, on February 20, 1989, President Mubarak told Arens: "Be realistic. No matter what promises Arafat had made to the United States, he is unable to control all factions of the PLO. . . . Hence, regardless of what Arafat said, terrorism, unfortunately, will continue."[15]

Meanwhile, pressure was building up on the new Shamir government to agree to an international peace conference with PLO participation. French President François Mitterrand, President Mubarak, British Prime Minister Margaret Thatcher, and Soviet General Secretary Mikhail Gorbachev all conveyed to Israel the same message. Soviet Foreign Minister Eduard Shevard-nadze even suggested that Moscow host a PLO-Israeli dialogue under the auspices of the superpowers. In return Moscow would reestablish diplomatic relations with Israel.

Shamir rejected all these pleas. He was more interested in the American position. In advance of Shamir's visit to Washington in April 1989, Arens came to Washington for a meeting with Bush and Baker. In what became a pattern in the U.S. relationship with the Likud component of the Israeli government, Arens was welcomed by a front-page story in the New York Times, quoting a "senior administration official" that the United States expected both Israel and the PLO to take steps to ease tensions in the West Bank and the Gaza Strip in preparation for future negotiations on the final status of the territories. The report, by diplomatic correspondent Thomas Friedman, whom the Israeli embassy in Washington described as close to Baker, added that the administration had some ideas about the final status and it wanted Arens to convey these views to Shamir.[16]

In their meeting with Arens, Bush and Baker did not explore any new ideas. Instead, they wanted to see what was in Arens's bag. The Israeli foreign minister said that the new Israeli government was in the process of formulating a peace initiative based on the assumption that Israel's negotiating partners would be Palestinians from the West Bank and the Gaza Strip, and not members of the PLO. Bush raised with Arens the issue of the settlements in the West Bank. He left no doubt that the United States was opposed to their expansion.

The next day, the New York Times reported that the administration had told Arens that the way to break the deadlock was through a two-tier peace process: Israelis and Palestinians would take specific and immediate steps to reduce tensions between them; shortly thereafter, they would begin discussions on a final settlement for resolving Israel's security concerns and the Palestinians' quest for self-determination.[17] Bush was to articulate this same position eighteen months later at the Madrid Peace Conference.

Upon his return to Israel, Arens reported his discussions in Washington to the cabinet, and he told his colleagues that he was not exposed to any American pressure, nor had he heard from Bush or Baker any new ideas. When asked about the contradictions between his report and the Times reports, David Levy, the housing minister, volunteered an answer. He said: "It's very simple. Arens speaks English, but doesn't understand English." Levy's quote was immediately leaked to the Israeli press and became a part of Israeli political lingo for many months.

On April 6 in Washington, Shamir presented an outline of a peace initiative consisting of four elements: a call on all Arab states to negotiate peace with Israel; a call on the three signatories of the Camp David accords (Israel, Egypt, and the United States) to convene at the foreign-minister level to review their status; free elections in the West Bank and Gaza in advance of the final status negotiations between Israel and the democratically elected Palestinian representatives; and an international effort to help alleviate the sufferings of the Palestinian refugees.[18]

According to Shamir, the outline was well received in Washington, and he promised Bush that he'd submit a detailed plan in the near future. On Sunday, May 14, the Israeli government approved the peace plan, consisting of a preamble and twenty paragraphs. The plan was prepared in collaboration with Defense Minister Yitzhak Rabin, and it was based on the Camp David Accords and UN Resolutions 242 and 338. It called for an interim period of five years of Palestinian autonomy to be followed by negotiations on the final status of the West Bank and the Gaza Strip. The plan rejected the idea of a Palestinian state and ruled out PLO participation in the peace negotiations. Instead, the plan suggested free elections in the territories to elect representatives who would negotiate with Israel on the details of the autonomy.[19]

For the time being, at least, the Bush administration appeared to be satisfied that it had gotten something to work with. The PLO and Egypt, however, rejected Israel's peace plan immediately. Arafat shunned it because he was excluded from the process and because he feared the creation of an alternative leadership under Israel's control in the territories. Arafat believed that he had regained the international support that he had lost after his expulsion from Beirut in 1982. A few days before Israel published its plan, Arafat was officially received in Paris by President Mitterrand. On the first day of his visit, an estimated twenty thousand French Jews marched in the direction of the Arc de Triomphe in a noisy and emotional protest against Arafat's red-carpet reception. In the heavily Jewish Pletzel district in Paris, shopkeepers rang their burglar alarms for five minutes to express their anger. The PLO Charter, which calls for the destruction of Israel, was the main concern of the French Jews. The French Jewish community is the fourth-largest in the world (after the United States, Israel, and the Soviet Union) and the largest in Western Europe. Interviewed on French TV on May 2, 1989, Arafat borrowed from French Foreign Minister Roland Dumas the expression *caduque* to describe his view that the charter was null and void.

Israeli officials were quick to dismiss Arafat's interpretation. Yossi Ahimeir, Shamir's aide, told Israeli Radio that Arafat's statement was not believable "because we all know that Arafat is a chronic liar."[20]

In Washington, however, a State Department spokesman welcomed Arafat's comment. He only wondered whether it represented the official view of the entire PLO. He said that the most convincing way to dispel any doubt about the Palestinian Charter would be for the PNC (Palestine National Council) to confirm Arafat's remark. "This is a stronger wording than he has used in the past, when Arafat said that the PNC resolutions of last winter [November 15, 1988] superseded the Charter. It is positive to see him say this. We would like to see more of this approach," the State Department spokesman said.[21]

Encouraged by the friendly welcome in Paris and the continued dialogue with the United States in Tunis, Arafat felt secure enough to reject the Israeli peace initiative. Egypt too was critical of the Israeli plan. Like Arafat, Mubarak was opposed to the exclusion of the PLO from the negotiating process. His public opposition was intended to deter local Palestinians from engaging in any binding dialogue with Israel.

Faced with the reality that Israel's peace initiative was practically deadlocked, Baker decided on shock therapy. Addressing the May 22 annual meeting of AIPAC in Washington, Baker dropped a bomb. He opened his remarks by praising Israel's peace initiative and describing the strength of the strategic partnership between Israel and the United States. Then, totally unexpectedly and certainly unnecessarily at this early stage and at this forum, Baker told the crowd that the U.S. interpretation of UN Resolution 242 was "land for peace" and hence any negotiation would end in some kind of territorial withdrawal. Then came his message to Shamir: "For Israel, now is the time to lay aside once and for all the unrealistic vision of Greater Israel. Israeli interests in the West Bank and Gaza—security and otherwise—can be accommodated in a settlement based on Resolution 242. Forswear annexation. Stop settlement activity. Allow schools to reopen. Reach out to the Palestinians as neighbors, who deserve political rights."

Baker had a similar message for the Arabs and the Palestinians: "Speak with one voice for peace. Practice constructive diplomacy. Recognize Israel as a partner in trade and human contact. Understand that violence will not work and that no one will 'deliver' Israel to you."[22]

Baker's remarks were received in silence and total shock. Jewish activists from across the country had come to Washington to rub shoulders with government officials and congressmen and show appreciation of their devoted activity on behalf of Israel. They had not come to be lectured on how the United States wanted Israel to behave. Since its founding by Sy Kenan in the early 1950s, AIPAC had hosted many U.S. national leaders. No one had ever thought to drop such a bomb on such a devoted pro-Israel crowd. "This was the night of the long knives," said one of AIPAC's top executives. Others said, "Baker decided to take off his diplomatic gloves." It was clear that Baker's speech had backfired.

However, whenever American Jewish leaders complained to Baker about what they believed to be his anti-Israeli policy, Baker would answer, "But my Middle East team is entirely Jewish. They all love Israel, they all visited Israel and worked there, and some are even fluent in Hebrew. You really could not believe that all of them are anti-Israel."

The response to Baker's shock therapy was instant. In a letter addressed to Baker and drafted that same night, ninety-four senators and hundreds of representatives urged the administration to endorse "strongly and publicly" the Israeli peace initiative. Although not binding, the letter was a major victory for AIPAC. It signaled to Bush and Baker that this organization would not be intimidated into supporting U.S. policies that would not meet Israel's basic security needs.

In the weeks that followed, Israel's security situation worsened considerably. In addition to the intensified terrorist activity inside the territories and along the Israeli-Lebanese border, a growing number of Palestinians were murdered by radical Palestinian groups on charges of collaboration with Israel. Accordingly, on July 18, 1989, the Israeli Foreign Ministry circulated among its embassies abroad a report compiled by Israeli intelligence indicating that the PLO, contrary to its assurances to the United States, had not, in fact, abandoned terrorism. The report detailed seventy acts of terror—ten of them inside pre-1967 Israel—carried out by Arafat's faction in the PLO. More dramatic was the arrest of a young Danish woman who was involved in a plot to assassinate Danish Chief Rabbi Malkior, who was visiting Israel at that time. The woman, who was not named, had fallen in love with a PLO agent in Copenhagen and become pregnant. She was accused of trying to smuggle into Israel $70,000 to finance the plot. Arafat would not comment on the report, nor would the United States show any inclination to suspend its dialogue with the PLO.[23]

In the second half of 1989, all U.S. and Arab efforts were directed at persuading the PLO to allow Palestinians from the West Bank and the Gaza Strip to enter into negotiations with Israel on the basis of an improved version of Shamir's plan. As the gap between Labor and Likud widened within the national unity government, the Israeli domestic scene witnessed a unique and unprecedented diplomatic experience. Both Egypt and the United States began to treat the Israeli government as though it were two governments. Every piece of information that was communicated to Shamir and Arens was automatically communicated to Yitzhak Rabin and Shimon Peres as well. At the same time, Labor dovish elements, headed by Deputy Finance Minister Yossi Beilin (whom Rabin nicknamed "Peres's poodle"), began to meet in Jerusalem with local Palestinians who were identified with the PLO. Peres and Rabin were maintaining a regular and intensive contact with Egypt. One cabinet minister, Ezer Weizman, was reported by the Israeli Security Service to have met in Geneva with Nabil Ramlawi, a PLO executive, and to have had occasional telephone conversations with Arafat himself. Shamir wanted to dismiss Weizman from his cabinet. However, in the face of a Labor threat to dissolve the national unity government, Shamir agreed to keep him in the government but excluded him from the ministerial committee on security and foreign affairs. Thus, in mid-1989, Shamir knew quite well that the Labor component of his national unity government was negotiating with the PLO, directly or indirectly.

In early September 1989, Rabin left for Washington for a meeting with Defense Secretary Dick Cheney. A few days earlier, Egyptian Foreign Minister Ismat Abdul Maguid met with Baker and presented him with general ideas about a ten-point peace plan that President Mubarak was drafting. Without informing Shamir in advance, Rabin also met with Baker and offered some comments about Mubarak's plan, even exploring a list of Palestinians who could be acceptable to both Israel and Egypt as possible interlocutors in a peace process. Rabin's meeting with Baker had a deeper meaning. It really meant that Rabin, who was associated with the preparation of the rejected Israeli peace plan, was now ready to shift his support to the Egyptian plan. Rabin qualified Mubarak's ten-point proposal as "a big and important step forward." Seven of Mubarak's points dealt with the procedures for the elections in the territories; one called on Israel to accept the principle of land for peace; another demanded that all settlement activity be halted. The last point called on Israel to agree to the participation of East Jerusalem Palestinians in the proposed elections. All three last points had been rejected in the past by Shamir, and there was no indication that he was likely to change his position in the near future.[24]

Upon his return to Israel, Rabin reported to the inner cabinet about his discussions in Washington. At that stage, Mubarak's plan had not yet been officially presented to Israel. Therefore, there was no need for the government to take an immediate decision. Arens was due to leave for New York on September 19 to attend the UN General Assembly. He was expected to meet there with both President Mubarak and Secretary Baker. They would certainly discuss the Egyptian proposal in detail. A decision would be taken, then, upon Arens's return.

The UN General Assembly of September 1989 will be remembered as the most bizarre in Israel's diplomatic history. Israeli politics, which are notorious for intensity, sank in those days to a record low. Just before Arens's arrival in New York, Peres, already there, was meeting with the same people that the foreign minister was expected to meet and conveying opposite views to them. As a personal snub to Arens, and as a clear signal to the Israeli public that the United States favored Labor over Likud, President Bush met with Peres in the Oval Office. As a compensation, Bush met also with Arens for a photo op, in a New York hotel, just minutes before the president hosted a dinner for the heads of delegations attending the General Assembly. The difference in decorum was yawning.

The Israeli public found itself confused by the conflicting messages that Arens and Peres were conveying in the United States. Arens told the United States that "Shamir wants peace," but he ruled out talking to the PLO, or to any Palestinian who had been deported from the West Bank and Gaza because of terrorist or subversive activity, any Palestinian who was not a permanent resident of the territories, any Palestinians who were associated with the leadership of the intifada, and any Palestinians from East Jerusalem. Who was left, then, for negotiations with Israel? A cartoon in the *Jerusalem Post* portrayed the "acceptable Palestinian" as a pro-Israeli Palestinian informer of the GSS, armed with a pistol and asking for permission to emigrate.

Peres, on the other hand, said at a press briefing in Washington that he supported Mubarak's ten-point plan because it had a better chance of implementation than the original Israeli peace initiative. Peres found Mubarak's document "fascinating" for what it left out. In Mubarak's plan, there was no reference to the PLO, there was no mention of self-determination and a Palestinian state, and there was no requirement that Israel withdraw to the 1967 lines. He concluded his press briefing by saying: "The Palestinian partner for negotiations that exists would not be acceptable to Shamir; the one acceptable did not exist."[25]

Despite this conflicting approach to negotiations, the Israeli inner cabinet met to discuss Mubarak's ten-point guideline. By then, the Egyptian proposal had been officially submitted to Israel. In a last-minute effort to have his plan approved, Mubarak appealed on Israeli TV to the Israeli people to exert pressure on Shamir to approve the Egyptian proposal. Such blunt Egyptian interference in Israeli domestic politics was unprecedented. Egypt also invited a group of Israeli journalists to meet in Cairo with Arafat. Since it was illegal for Israelis to meet with PLO officials unless the meeting was in the context of a press conference, the Egyptian Ministry of Information had arranged one. Arafat assured the Israeli people of his desire for peace and called on the Israeli government to recognize the PLO and negotiate with him directly.

Despite this psychological pressure, the Israeli inner cabinet was evenly divided and Mubarak's guideline was rejected. Shamir argued that accepting Egypt's plan was tantamount to signing a letter of capitulation.[26]

The public debate about the Egyptian plan was accompanied by a sharp, discreet exchange between Egypt and Likud. Arens summoned Egyptian Ambassador Mohamed Bassiouni—a former general in the Egyptian intelligence and a former military attaché in Damascus and Tehran—and accused him of interfering in Israel's domestic affairs. "Ask President Mubarak," Arens said angrily, "if he would now reciprocate by allowing Shamir to appear on Egyptian TV, and if he would grant the Israeli ambassador in Cairo the same freedom of diplomatic activity that you are enjoying here."

A Likud minister told Israeli journalists off the record that Shamir and Arens had toyed for a while with the idea of declaring Bassiouni persona non grata. They abandoned the idea because of intraparty considerations. The minister explained that since the Israeli-Egyptian peace treaty had been signed by Menachem Begin, it was politically considered a Likud achievement. Shamir feared that expelling the Egyptian ambassador would generate a similar move by Mubarak. People would then say that Begin had built the peace with Egypt and Shamir had destroyed it.

The diplomatic vacuum created by the rejection of the Egyptian plan was filled instantly by the United States. On October 6, Baker interjected himself into the process. He phoned Arens and suggested what was to become known as Baker's five-point plan. Its purpose was to make Shamir's own initiative more acceptable to the Palestinians but less generous than Mubarak's ten-point guideline. Peres and Rabin supported Baker's proposal immediately. Shamir and Arens asked for clarifications. In order to avoid any future misunderstandings, on October 23, Arens put the requested clarifications in writing. They were all aimed at excluding the PLO from the process and denying Palestinians from East Jerusalem the right to participate in the elections to the autonomous authority in the West Bank and the Gaza Strip. Baker forwarded the requested Israeli clarifications to Egypt for comment.

In the meantime, Shamir was scheduled to leave for New York on November 15 to address the annual meeting of the Council of Jewish Federations in the United States and Canada. More than three thousand people were expected to attend. For many years, it had been the practice that once notified about the forthcoming visit, the State Department would schedule a meeting between the president and the prime minister of Israel. This year, however, there was a total silence. When various Jewish leaders contacted the State Department, Baker or his aides would simply say that the White House had not scheduled a date yet. It was obvious that the administration was trying to use the anticipated meeting with the president as a stick to force Shamir to accept Baker's five points, without all or part of the requested clarifications. In defiance of this personal snub, Shamir announced that he would address the Jewish gathering whether he was invited to the White House or not. On November 10, just five days before Shamir's departure, Baker informed Arens that the president was looking forward to his meeting with the prime minister.

By early December, there was still no answer from Cairo about the requested Israeli clarifications of Baker's plan. Israeli intelligence sources reported that after a stormy debate, the PLO Executive Committee in Tunis had rejected Baker's plan. Arafat informed Mubarak that as the sole representative of the Palestinian people, the PLO insisted on being included in any negotiations under the umbrella of an international peace conference.

Baker's efforts were, then, completely deadlocked.

Developments in early 1990 changed the international climate dramatically. The brutal Communist regime in Romania collapsed and President Nicolae Ceausescu was executed by a firing squad. In the wake of perestroika and glasnost, the Eastern European nations were moving away from the Soviet Union toward political freedom and democracy. Then came the least expected development of all—the gates of the Soviet Union swung open and thousands of Jews were allowed to emigrate to Israel. In the early 1970s, during the short period of détente, Soviet President Brezhnev had allowed a sizable number of

Jews to emigrate to Israel. Shortly after the Yom Kippur War in 1973, the immigration gates were again closed. In 1987, for example, only two thousand Soviet Jews emigrated to Israel. In 1988, thanks to the efforts of Reagan, Mitterrand, and Thatcher, Gorbachev allowed some thirteen thousand Soviet Jews to emigrate. In early 1990, it became a flood, and by the end of the year, a total of 185,000 Soviet Jews had arrived in Israel.[27] It was a blessing to Israel and to the Jewish people. Unlike the previous waves of immigrants, the Soviet immigrants were rich in talents and skills—they were scientists, engineers, physicians, and musicians in the thousands. A popular joke among Israelis in those exciting days was that if a Russian came off the plane without a violin, it meant he was a pianist.

The mass immigration of Soviet Jews revived the old dispute between Israel and the United States about settlement activity in the West Bank and the Gaza Strip. In an effort to absorb the increasing number of immigrants, Israel embarked on a worldwide fund-raising campaign called Operation Exodus. Israel had also asked the United States for $400 million in loan guarantees for the same purpose. In a meeting with Arens in Washington on February 23, 1990, Baker said that the U.S. administration could not agree to settling the Soviet immigrants in the territories. He wanted a public Israeli commitment to prohibit Soviet Jews from settling there. This was the first time that an American government had linked a humanitarian issue to a political decision. Arens explained to Baker that no Israeli prime minister, not just Shamir, would agree to such a linkage.[28] Finally, after a strong lobbying effort by the American Jewish community, a compromise formula was found, according to which Israel would not "encourage" Soviet Jews to settle in the West Bank and the Gaza Strip. Shamir, however, was soon to realize that there was a big difference between approval of a loan guarantee and the actual release of the money.

The new developments in the Eastern bloc had brought two new political realities to the Middle East. The formerly Communist countries were rushing to reestablish diplomatic relations with Israel, thus ending thirty-five years of Israeli political isolation in Eastern Europe; and radical Arab countries, foremost among them Iraq, Syria, Libya, and the PLO, had suddenly lost their automatic Communist support and had now to readjust to the new international realities.

The entity most immediately affected by the new situation was the PLO. At the insistence of Egypt, Arafat dropped his condition for a personal involvement in the peace process, and he was now prepared to reengage in negotiations—via Egypt—about the implementation of Baker's plan. Arafat was still insisting, however, that the Palestinian negotiating team should include two deportees and at least one Palestinian from East Jerusalem who had another residence in the West Bank. Faisal Husseini, for example, was a resident of East Jerusalem but also had residence in Jericho. The Palestinian list would be presented to Israel and the United States by Egypt, after consultation with the PLO.

This moderated PLO position was worked out in Washington in late January 1990, in two secret, separate meetings between Baker and Rabin and the Egyptian foreign minister. The precise makeup of the list was not totally resolved. Rabin agreed, however, that Egypt and the United States would provide a list of Palestinians acceptable to Israel, and Israel would not ask too many questions about the origin of the list. This was a semi-acceptance of the possibility that the PLO would be the discreet "kingmaker." This was the same formula that Moshe Dayan and Menachem Begin had accepted in 1979, during discussions with Egypt about the autonomy to the Palestinians. Rabin, however, was not authorized by Shamir to negotiate on behalf of the Israeli government, nor was his compromise acceptable to Shamir and Arens. Both of them, as is known, voted at the time against the Camp David Accords.

Nevertheless, the bargaining over the Baker-Rabin compromise continued. In a meeting with Baker in Washington on February 23, 1990, Arens presented an Israeli counterproposal, aimed at eliminating the role of the PLO in future negotiations. He insisted that the Palestinian list that would be presented by Egypt should also be approved by Israel. Without defining it as such, Arens practically wanted a veto power over the composition of the Palestinian representation. Arens ruled out the possibility that Shamir would agree to include in the list any Palestinian from East Jerusalem.

On March 7, Shamir convened the inner cabinet to decide on a moderated Palestinian position as presented to Baker by Egypt. Labor ministers supported the compromise worked out in Washington between Rabin and Baker. Likud ministers approved Shamir's position as presented to Baker by Arens. Rabin burst out in anger. His compromise was accepted by Egypt and had a good chance of being implemented. Shamir's position was not acceptable to Egypt and the Palestinians would certainly reject it.

That same evening, Rabin was interviewed by Israeli TV on the two conflicting approaches to Baker's five-point plan. Rabin was angry, especially when he was asked about East Jerusalem. "I fought in Jerusalem in 1948," he said. "Motta [former chief of staff Motta Gur] liberated East Jerusalem in 1967. Who are these Likudniks who are now lecturing us on how to protect Jerusalem? Arens? Nissim? They did not even serve in the army and they have contributed nothing to Israel's security."[29]

If this outburst proved anything, it proved that the fate of the national unity government was sealed. Indeed, on March 13, at the opening of a special cabinet meeting, Shamir read a short letter addressed to Shimon Peres advising him that he was fired from the government. Shamir explained that the reason for such a dramatic and unprecedented move was Peres's subversion and his constant effort to topple the government. Visibly shaken, his face pale and his voice trembling, Peres hit back. "I don't recognize you as my prime minister," Peres said. Immediately afterward, all Labor ministers, including Rabin, submitted their resignations and left the room.

For a while it looked as though Peres would be able to form a new narrow-based government, without Likud. At the end, however, it was Shamir who formed the new government without Labor. On June 11, 1990, the new Shamir government was sworn in by the Knesset. The Moroccan-born David Levy became the new foreign minister, and Arens moved to succeed Rabin as defense minister. A new chapter opened in Israel's stormy politics.

The immediate victim of the new developments in Israel was the conditionally approved $400 million in loan guarantees to help absorb Soviet immigrants. When Shamir publicly undertook "not to encourage" Soviet Jews to settle in the territories, he had not mentioned East Jerusalem. For him, united Jerusalem was the capital of Israel. That was not the view of the Bush administration. When told that thousands of Soviet Jews were settling in the neighborhoods surrounding Jerusalem, Bush was enraged. He was convinced that Shamir had lied to him. He sharply attacked Shamir's settlement policy in the West Bank and in East Jerusalem.[30]

That was a dangerous escalation in the Bush-Shamir dispute. The very fact that the president mentioned East Jerusalem as an "occupied territory" gave Shamir the final excuse to say no to Baker's five-point plan. Shamir argued that the president's remarks about East Jerusalem proved that he was not an "honest broker" and was not "objective." Tensions between Israel and the United States had never been so high.

In the spring of 1990, regional developments were affecting the Palestinians as well. The Persian Gulf crisis was already in the air, and arguments between Saddam Hussein and Kuwait over oil prices and production intensified. Having lost the support of the Communist bloc and facing Egypt's inability to affect Israeli positions, Arafat was inclined to embrace Saddam Hussein. The PLO chairman pinned his hopes on Saddam's April 1 speech, in which he announced that Iraq possessed binary chemical weapons, which, he threatened, he would use against Israel. "By God, we will make the fire burn half of Israel, if Israel tries to do anything against Iraq," he boasted.[31]

This, however, was not mere boasting. Israeli intelligence officials reported to Shamir's government on April 4 that Iraq had indeed become the largest producer of chemical agents in the world. Mustard gas and nerve agents were produced in three facilities in Sammara, Falluja and Salman Pak, built with German and European technology.[32]

This belligerent Iraqi posture appealed to Arafat, and he thought it could become a viable alternative to the ineffective Saudi influence on the United States and the determination of the oil-rich Persian Gulf principalities to win American support for their own survival by ignoring the Arab-Israeli conflict.

The first sign of this Palestinian tilt toward Iraq came on May 30, 1990, on the Jewish holiday of Shavuot. Jews around the world celebrate on Shavuot the "birth" of the Ten Commandments, which Moses received from God on Mount Sinai. Secular Israelis, however, celebrate Shavuot also as the "Harvest Holiday," packing the beaches and the public parks and attending joyful folk-dance festivals. In two assaults, three hours apart, a pro-Iraqi faction of the PLO, the Palestine Liberation Front (PLF), mounted a seaborne guerrilla raid and tried to land sixteen heavily armed terrorists on one of the popular beaches south of Tel Aviv. The terrorists, in two dinghies, were intercepted by the Israeli navy. With the assistance of the border police, the Israeli sailors killed four terrorists and captured the remaining twelve on their vessels. It was just a miracle that none of the sunbathing Israelis were hurt.

In their interrogation, the terrorists admitted that they had been commissioned by their leader, Abul Abbas, "to kill as many Jews as possible." Abul Abbas had been responsible for the 1985 hijacking of the cruise ship *Achille Lauro* and the murder of the American passenger Leon Klinghoffer. In 1987, he was elected by the Palestine National Council (PNC) to represent his faction in the eighteen-member PLO Executive Committee. Abul Abbas's main base was Baghdad, and he received generous financial assistance from both Libya and Iraq. His relationship with Arafat was known to be very close. Abul Abbas carried out his raid while Arafat was in Baghdad attending an Arab summit meeting that pledged millions of dollars to the PLO.

Israel submitted all the information relevant to the raid to the United States and asked for an immediate suspension of the American dialogue with the PLO. American Jewish leaders added their voice to this request, and congressmen from both parties urged the White House to halt the dialogue. At a senior White House staff meeting on May 31, Bush decided to sharply condemn "the cowardly raid to target innocent people" and asked Arafat to expel Abul Abbas from the PLO Executive Committee. As to the suspension of the dialogue with the PLO, Bush and Baker were hesitant. Bush wanted to keep open his line of communication with Arafat. He believed that this dialogue was the only realistic hope for future progress in the Middle East peace process. Britain and France stood behind Bush. The U.S. president therefore decided to buy time, hoping that the public storm would calm down. It didn't. Unwilling to antagonize his new Iraqi patrons, Arafat refused to condemn the raid or to expel Abul Abbas from the PLO Executive Committee. He claimed that only the PNC was authorized to take such a punitive action.[33]

On June 8, in a desperate effort to save the dialogue with the PLO, Bush spoke by phone for fifteen minutes with President Mubarak, stressing the seriousness of the situation. Sweden, which had been instrumental in opening the U.S.-PLO dialogue in 1988, on June 9 sent a special envoy to Baghdad to persuade Arafat to take action against Abul Abbas. In vain.[34]

By mid-June it had become obvious that the White House delaying tactic was not working. On June 11, Vice President Dan Quayle and Defense Secretary Dick Cheney addressed an AIPAC conference in Washington and added their voices to those calling for the suspension of the dialogue with the PLO. That same day, Seymour Reich, the chairman of the Conference of Presidents of Major Jewish Organizations, met in Washington with General Brent Scowcroft, the national security adviser, and emphasized to him the need to take action against Arafat. America's credibility was at stake, Reich told Scowcroft. "I think that what they are trying to do is coax words out of Arafat. That serves no purpose, because if this does not come from the heart, it's false. It's theatrics," Reich told Israeli correspondents in Washington. What was more effective, however, was the Congressional pressure. Seven senators and thirty-six representatives introduced resolutions calling on Bush to suspend the dialogue with the PLO. On June 20, 1990, realizing that Congress would pass the resolutions by an overwhelming majority, Bush finally suspended the dialogue with the PLO.

The suspension of the eighteen-month dialogue with the United States was a major setback for Arafat. His relationship with President Mubarak deteriorated after Egypt decided to abandon its efforts to mediate between the United States and the PLO. "We tell them [the PLO] you have to solve by yourself your problem with the United States," Mubarak told the Egyptian press.[35]

In his effort to resume the dialogue with the United States, Arafat made an unusual move. He addressed a letter to Menachem Rosensaft, the president of the Labor Zionist Alliance in the United States and one of the five prominent American Jews with whom he had met in Stockholm on December 6, 1988. The letter was written in Arabic on June 21, the day after Bush suspended the dialogue with the PLO, with an English translation dated June 25, and was postmarked from Tunis on July 4. Arafat's letterhead contained a map of the "State of Palestine," stretching from the Mediterranean to the Jordan River and including the area that is Israel. The letter was notable for its silence about the aborted Abul Abbas raid, but its message was clear: Arafat wanted to negotiate peace. He blamed Israel for rejecting Baker's plan and pledged to end the "chain of violence." Arafat apparently naively believed that the five American Jews whom he had met in Stockholm would now join in counterpressure on the Bush administration to resume the dialogue with the PLO. His letter to Rosensaft was brought to the attention of the State Department but had no effect on the administration's position.

Iraq's invasion of Kuwait, on August 2, 1990, drew the world's attention from the Arab-Israeli conflict to the Persian Gulf crisis. After the suspension of the U.S. dialogue with the PLO, and in solidarity with Arafat, the Palestinian leadership in the territories suspended all its contacts with the American consulate in East Jerusalem. Arafat's notorious embrace of Saddam Hussein, however, had shown some conflict in perception between the PLO leadership in Tunis and the Palestinians in the territories. Realizing that the occupation of Kuwait undermined the moral basis of the intifada, Hanan Ashrawi, while in Geneva, tried to reach Arafat in order to persuade him not to support Saddam's move.[36] It was too late; Arafat was already on his way to Baghdad. Indeed, the Persian Gulf crisis caused the intifada to fade gradually away. TV coverage of Palestinian demonstrations in the territories dropped to zero, and foreign correspondents were reassigned to Saudi Arabia and Kuwait. With the lack of world interest, demonstrations in the territories stopped.

This new development affected Israeli-Palestinian relations as well. Liberal Israelis, like Knesset member Yossi Sarid, who for years had supported a dialogue with the PLO and endorsed Palestinians' right to self-determination, expressed doubts whether the dialogue was needed at all. "He stabbed the peace process in the back," Sarid said of Arafat's support of Saddam.

Throughout the Persian Gulf crisis, and in the many months of tough negotiations that led to the Madrid Peace Conference, there was no subject more irritating in American-Israeli relations than the issue of the settlements. President Carter considered the settlements to be illegal. President Reagan did not believe they were illegal, but he considered them an "obstacle to peace." President Bush sharpened the debate by the inclusion of East Jerusalem into the equation.

In September 1990, David Levy, Shamir's new foreign minister, came to New York to attend the UN General Assembly. Known as a moderate and a pragmatist, Levy was well received in Washington. He met with President Bush at the White House and had a very fruitful discussion with Secretary Baker. With the assistance of the very able and experienced deputy director general of his ministry, Eitan Bentzur, a former political counselor at the Israeli embassy in Washington, Levy reached an agreement with Baker for unfreezing the $400 million in loan guarantees. Realizing that the controversy between Israel and the United States over the settlements in the West Bank and the Gaza Strip was unlikely to be solved soon, Levy separated the loan guarantee from the settlements. As a former housing minister, he knew quite well that money was fungible and could be moved from one part of the budget to another. Hence, Levy agreed to a language that would require Israel to report to the United States on how the money was spent. He did not consider the language of the agreement restrictive to a degree that it could affect Israel's ability to continue its settlements policy.

Bush and Baker were impressed by the manner in which Levy handled this sensitive subject. After their tense relationship with both Shamir and Arens, they found Levy very easy to communicate with. Bush, in particular, wanted steady communication with Israel and considered Levy to be a "channel of reason." Bush, as is well known, is not a great orator, but he is very good in one-on-one conversation. He would often pick up the phone and talk to world leaders on the burning issues of the moment. He could not do that with Shamir. The Israeli prime minister was very discreet and introverted and could not engage easily in relaxed discussions. "Shamir is still in the underground—he is afraid to talk even to himself," his aides used to joke. Now Bush thought that he had found in Levy a "telephone pal" in Israel.

It was in this context that I received one day an urgent telephone call from my friend Jack Stein, a close friend of Bush's and a respected American Jewish Republican leader. Stein said that he wanted to talk to me confidentially. He had a message to convey to Levy from the White House. In order to avoid leakages, he did not want to use the official diplomatic channel of the Israeli consulate in New York but preferred to pass the message to Levy through me. He said that before leaving the United States, Levy should call the White House to thank the president for receiving him at the Oval Office. The White House switchboard was already alerted to this eventuality, and should Levy call, the operator would put him through to the president immediately.

I met with Levy at the Plaza Hotel in New York. When I gave him Stein's message, he was very flattered but also very hesitant. "I am a new foreign minister," he said. "How could I do such a thing to Shamir? He will be very offended that Bush is talking to me and not to him. No, I won't do it."

After Levy's return to Israel, he came under sharp attack for his agreement with Baker. Cabinet ministers, especially Defense Minister Arens, expressed concern that the language on East Jerusalem would restrict Israel's ability to continue building there. Within a few days it became clear that the Shamir government would not approve the Baker-Levy agreement. The loan guarantee was again frozen.[37]

In December 1990, a few weeks before the start of Desert Storm, Shamir came again to Washington and met with Bush at the White House. It was a pleasant meeting, attended on the American side by Secretary Baker and General Brent Scowcroft. Shamir had on his side the newly appointed Israeli ambassador to Washington, Zalman Shoval. Without Bush's spelling it out, it was clear that the war in the Persian Gulf was inevitable. Bush was anxious to get from Shamir a clear commitment not to attack Iraq preemptively, and if retaliating for Iraqi Scud missile attacks not to act without prior consultation with the United States. Bush assured Shamir that there would be no trade-off with Iraq against any aspect of U.S. commitments to Israel. He made it clear, however, that he did not want Israel to join the anti-Saddam coalition that he had built. Arab governments had warned that if Israel joined, they would leave. They explained that they could not be perceived in the Arab world as joining hands with Israel in a war against another Arab country.

Shamir promised Bush full cooperation in his effort to defeat Saddam Hussein. Bush and Shamir established two new secure channels of communications, one between the Pentagon and the Israeli Ministry of Defense and the other between the White House and the prime minister's office in Jerusalem. This second channel was handled exclusively by General Scowcroft and Ambassador Shoval.

Despite the relaxed mood, Bush was somewhat surprised when Shamir raised the issue of Jordan. The Israeli prime minister said that he could understand the president's anger at King Hussein's support of Saddam Hussein. Nevertheless, the administration should see the wider spectrum of the region. The king had his own domestic problems. It was not in the interest of the United States, Israel, and the pro-Western Arab countries to push Jordan further into Iraq's arms.

Finally, Shamir raised with Bush—for the first time—Israel's need for $10 billion in loan guarantees to help in the absorption of the massive Jewish immigration. Shamir said that Israel's economic and social infrastructure was not prepared for such an enormous task. The worldwide Jewish generosity was heartening, but the amounts raised were not adequate. Bush was sympathetic, but he promised to deal with this subject only after the Persian Gulf crisis.[38]

Bush had also shown great interest in the way the Ethiopian Jews, whom he had helped to rescue, were being absorbed in Israel, and he promised to unfreeze the $400 million loan guarantee that had been approved long before. He reminded Shamir, however, of his position on the settlements issue.[39]

Shamir's attitude during the Persian Gulf War was, indeed, exemplary. Despite constant pressures from Arens and other ministers, he rejected any retaliation against Saddam Hussein for launching thirty-nine Scud missiles into Israel. Not only did he promise Bush to show restraint, but he made a similar promise to King Hussein, whom he met secretly in London on January 5, 1991, just few days before the war started. Shamir's position could be summed up this way: The United States was a very important political, military, and economic ally of Israel. It was equally important to make sure that the United States helped Israel and didn't hurt Israel. Therefore, any action that Israel might consider should take into account Washington's positions and interests in the region.

However, as the Persian Gulf War came close to its end, it became clear that the tensions between Israel and the United States concerning the peace process in general and the settlements in particular had not disappeared but only been temporarily shelved. This came to a public expression on February 11, 1991, following a meeting between Arens and Bush, Cheney, and Baker in Washington. Accompanied by Ambassador Shoval, Arens raised in the meeting the problem of the damages suffered by Israel because of the war. Arens surprised the president and Defense Secretary Cheney when he told them that the effectiveness of the Patriot missiles that the U.S. had rushed to Israel to defend against the Scuds was 20 percent "at best." Cheney was stunned. He had been certain that the Patriots would be much more effective.

In a separate meeting with Baker at the State Department, the issue of the

$400 million in loan guarantees was also raised. Despite the fact that the guarantees had been approved a year before, the money was not yet released. Asked by Reuters News Agency about this problem, Ambassador Shoval—an educated and articulate diplomat who had given up his seat in the Knesset for this ambassadorship—replied: "We sometimes feel that we are being given the runaround, although to the best of our knowledge, Israel has fully complied with the requests that were raised in this connection."[40]

The White House reacted angrily to this innocent remark. In an unprecedented act in modern diplomatic history, President Bush issued a statement in which he said: "Shoval's Reuters interview was outrageous and outside the boundaries of acceptable behavior by the ambassador of a friendly country. . . . The secretary of state made this clear to the ambassador yesterday, and the president protested to Prime Minister Shamir by cable this morning. . . . We deserve better from Israel's ambassador."

There was no explanation for such presidential behavior. There had never been a precedent—never had an ambassador of a friendly country been castigated publicly and in such an angry manner by the president of the United States. Secretary Baker wrote in his memoirs that he even asked the State Department's legal advisers if it was possible to declare Shoval persona non grata. This overreaction, however, boomeranged. The director general of the prime minister's office, Yossi Ben-Aharon, summoned U.S. Ambassador Bill Brown and protested sharply against this brutal treatment of Shoval. American Jewish leaders bombarded the White House with phone calls, and various congressmen expressed their disapproval and regret. In a discussion in Tel Aviv, Shoval said that both General Scowcroft and Richard Haas had advised the president not to issue his statement. Baker, however, "overpowered" Bush and insisted on castigating Shoval.

No matter what the real motive behind Bush's and Baker's overreaction was, Israeli officials and many political observers were convinced that the president and the secretary of state were setting the stage for the numerous confrontations that Israel and the United States were to have on the long way to Madrid.

STALEMATE IN WASHINGTON

Despite its undeniable success, the Madrid Peace Conference did not ease the tensions between Israel and the United States. On the contrary, it intensified them. Despite the four rounds of bilateral face-to-face negotiations in Washington between Israel and three Arab countries and the Palestinians, and despite one round of multilateral negotiations on regional economic development, President Bush was unable to go beyond his initial success. By June 1992, the peace process, in which Secretary Baker and Ambassador Dennis Ross had invested so much patience and energy, appeared to be going nowhere.

The lack of progress that characterized most of 1992 was not owed only to the fact that it was an election year in both Israel and the United States. It was due mostly to an American error in judgment as to how much pressure the Bush administration could apply to force the Shamir government to accept the new regional balance of power that emerged in the aftermath of the Persian Gulf War. During his election campaign, Bush referred to Israel as a "strategic ally" whose Western values "buttressed the alliance in its vulnerable area." However, when this "vulnerable area" faced its greatest challenge from within—the Iraqi invasion of Kuwait—Bush had frozen his "strategic ally" and excluded it from the impressive coalition that he had successfully built to defeat Saddam Hussein. In an effort to maintain his "Arab coalition" intact, Bush had moved away from President Reagan's approach of building Israel's trust in U.S. mediation. Instead, he adopted a style of strong public discord with Israel, designed to modify its policies and to force Israel into accepting an almost total withdrawal to the pre-1967 cease-fire lines. Prime Minister Shamir's intransigence, his lack of flexibility, and above all his poor communication abilities further complicated the U.S.-Israeli dialogue, but they were not the only causes for its deterioration.

Domestic political instability in Israel and the disarray in the PLO's leadership were additional elements that brought the peace process to a stalemate. In addition to the widening gap in Israel between Labor and Likud over the road to peace, Shamir faced a serious and genuine crisis within his own right-wing coalition parties. In January 1992, three small extreme right-wing parties left

Shamir's coalition, giving him no alternative but to reach an agreement with Labor on dissolving the Knesset and advancing the parliamentary elections to June 23, 1992.

These sharp divisions within the Israeli political body enabled both the United States and Egypt to interfere actively in Israel's domestic affairs, trying to isolate Shamir and eventually helping in his downfall. The tool that the United States had used in implementing this strategy was Israel's request for $10 billion in loan guarantees to help absorb the massive Soviet Jewish immigration. The policy target, however, was the freezing of all Israeli settlement activities in the West Bank and the Gaza Strip, including East Jerusalem. Thus, the intensity of the Bush-Shamir discord, the president's determination to achieve his policy goals even at the price of alienating the overwhelming majority of American Jews, and his perceived pro-Arab bias—real or imagined— were among the main reasons that brought the bilateral negotiations in Washington to a standstill.

Secretary Baker himself, in a revealing private discussion with Hanan Ashrawi, the Palestinian spokesperson in Madrid and Washington and currently a "minister" in the Palestine Authority, seemed to partly confirm this conclusion. Baker's meeting with Ashrawi took place shortly after President Clinton's victory, and its details were reported by Mahmoud Nofal, a former commander of the military wing of the PDFLP (Popular Democratic Front for the Liberation of Palestine, based in Damascus) and for some time Yasser Arafat's national security adviser. Nofal was part of the team that monitored from Tunis the secret negotiations in Oslo and had access to all documents relating to the Palestinian-Israeli negotiations. In a recent series of articles, published in a London-based Arabic daily, Nofal wrote: ". . . Arafat believed that Baker was fair with the Palestinians. Therefore he wanted Ashrawi to hear Baker's assessment of the situation, before he and Bush left the White House. . . . Ashrawi quoted Baker as having told her that had Bush been reelected, he would have pushed the peace process even more aggressively, especially after Rabin's victory over Shamir. . . . He added that 'we [Bush and Baker] have paid the price for our confrontation with Shamir, and for our position on the loan guarantees. . . .' As to the future, Baker is reported to have told Ashrawi: '. . . Don't expect any serious pressures on Israel from the new administration. President Clinton owes it to his Jewish constituency. So, my advice to you—don't delay the peace process. Try to get now from Israel whatever you can get. . . .'"[1]

The Israeli request for $10 billion in loan guarantees was the single most serious issue during Shamir's tenure as prime minister that doomed the peace process to a stalemate. Indeed, shortly after the end of the Persian Gulf War, Israel renewed its request for the loan guarantees. In a meeting with Secretary Baker, Deputy Secretary Larry Eagleburger, and Ambassador Dennis Ross, Ambassador Shoval said that Israel had two requests: one for $1 billion as a compensation for war damages caused by Desert Storm, and the other for $10 billion in loan guarantees, for the absorption of Soviet Jewish immigrants, as Prime Minister Shamir had mentioned in his December 1990 meeting with President Bush.

The administration's evaluation of the damages caused to Israel was $200 million only. After further clarifications, Baker concluded that Israel would receive as compensation $700 million and an additional battery of Patriot ground-to-air missiles. As to the $10 billion in loan guarantees, Baker asked Shoval to delay the formal request until after Labor Day. Shoval spoke to Shamir by phone, and the prime minister agreed to the delay.[2]

In May 1991, Israel began to explore informally the Congressional position on the Israeli request for loan guarantees. Because of its restraint during the Gulf crisis, Israel enjoyed at that time a short period of grace in the United States. The Congressional response was very encouraging. Accordingly, on September 6, a few weeks before the opening of the Madrid Peace Conference, Israeli Finance Minister Yitzhak Modai and Ambassador Shoval submitted the formal request to Deputy Secretary of State Eagleburger. President Bush's reaction was instant. In a press conference that same day, Bush announced that he would ask Congress to defer "just for 120 days" the consideration of the Israeli request. He said that this deferral was important for the peace process. Bush said that it was "very, very important" to do everything possible to give peace a chance.[3]

Shamir was in total shock. Years later, he explained: "This was the first time in the history of American-Israeli relations that there was political and economic blackmail. Even President Carter, whose relations with Rabin and Begin were not always smooth, never used the U.S. economic assistance to Israel as a political stick. What President Bush was practically telling us was very simple: If you won't behave yourselves and if you won't accept the principle of land-for-peace, you won't receive the loan guarantees."[4]

Congressional reaction to the president's request was ambivalent, and, interestingly enough, American Jewish leaders were also divided on this issue. Not only Republican Jewish leaders like Max Fisher and Jack Stein but also liberal Jewish Democrats like Rabbi Alexander Schindler and others did not want a confrontation with President Bush on the eve of the Madrid Peace Conference. They did not consider the deferral for 120 days a disaster. The Israeli opposition parties also shared this view.

Nevertheless, on September 12, AIPAC mounted a major lobbying effort on Capitol Hill in support of the Israeli request. More than a thousand Jewish activists from across the United States met with their senators and congressmen and asked for their support. When told about it, Bush overreacted. After all, even if the Congress would be responsive to Israel's humanitarian needs, no decision was expected before the Madrid Peace Conference.

Nevertheless, in a televised news conference, Bush made an emotional appeal to the American people: ". . . A debate now on this issue could well destroy our ability to bring one or more of the parties to the peace table. . . . If necessary, I will use my veto power to keep that from happening. . . ." Bush then moved to a frontal attack on AIPAC. He said: ". . . We are up against some very powerful political forces, very strong and effective groups that go up to the Hill. . . . We have got one lonely little guy down here, doing it. . . . But I am going to fight for what I believe. It may be politically popular, but probably not. . . . The question for me is not whether it is good 1992 politics, what is important here is that we give the [peace] process a chance, and I don't care if I get [in the elections] only one single vote. . . ." That, however, was not all. In a clear distortion of history, Bush went on to say: ". . . Just months ago, American men and women in uniform risked their lives to defend Israelis in the face of Iraqi Scud missiles, and indeed Desert Storm, while winning a war against aggression, also achieved the defeat of Israel's most dangerous adversary. . . ."[5]

Bush's statement shocked Israel and the entire American Jewish community. Israelis were particularly upset by the president's saying that American men and women had risked their lives in their defense. Not only had Israel been excluded from the coalition against Saddam Hussein, but Bush had practically twisted Shamir's arm to prevent Israel from retaliating for the Iraqi Scud attacks, and had sent to Israel what proved to be totally ineffective Patriot missiles. Now Bush was telling the American people that American soldiers had risked their lives in Israel's defense. The angry Israeli reaction was reflected by the entire Israeli press. Editorial writers and political analysts "reminded" President Bush that it was Israel that had suffered human losses and material damage, and that by not responding to the Iraqi Scud attacks, Israel had served the American national interest.

No less sharp was the American Jewish reaction. Thomas Dine, the extremely effective executive director of AIPAC and a former aide of Democratic Senator Frank Church of Idaho, who was the main target of the president's attack, called Bush's televised press conference "a day of shame." In an interview with Israeli radio and TV, Dine said that "Bush's remarks were an affront to the entire Jewish community, since he put a question mark on their right to lobby on behalf of subjects close to their hearts."[6]

A few days later, on September 16, Secretary Baker tried to reassure Israel that there would be no further delay in approving the loan guarantees beyond January. In a joint meeting in Jerusalem with Shamir, David Levy, and Arens, Baker said: "My advice to you is to call off the dogs and strike the loan guarantees off your agenda, for the next 120 days." When Shamir told Baker that as a matter of principle he could not accept the linkage between a humanitarian problem and the peace process, the secretary interrupted him and said: "You have no choice. If you want the loan guarantees, you will have to accept our position on the settlements. . . . You have to stop settling in the territories; we are not going to fund settlement activity. . . ."[7]

There is no credible explanation of why Bush and Baker were so eager for a confrontation with Shamir, on such a sensitive issue, on the eve of the Madrid Peace Conference. Some Israeli politicians believed that Bush acted apparently on the assumption that when the dust settled down, the divided Israeli people and the equally divided American Jewish community would accept the new reality. Developments in the next few weeks would prove that the president was wrong. In the short range, however, Bush won his battle. Neither Congress nor the American Jewish community was prepared for a confrontation. They agreed to defer the consideration of the Israeli request for another 120 days.

In an effort to meet Israel's immediate needs, Jewish communities all over the world were called to the flag. They embarked on an emergency campaign, and their contributions to Operation Exodus and their purchase of Israel bonds almost doubled. Some communities even borrowed money from commercial banks and mortgaged their community centers as collateral against future pledges by wealthy individuals. The fund-raising effort was so successful that Meir Rosenne, the international president of Israel Bonds and a former ambassador to Paris and Washington, suggested to Shamir that he withdraw the request for the loan guarantees and to continue to rely on the Jewish people. Shamir rejected the idea. He thought that withdrawing the Israeli request, in these circumstances, would be a betrayal of those in the Congress and in the Jewish community who were prepared to confront the Bush administration on the issue.[8]

The confrontation between Bush and Shamir was resumed immediately after the Madrid Peace Conference. It was not limited to the issue of the loan guarantees but also included subjects related to the peace process. Invited again to address the annual meeting of the General Assembly of the Council of Jewish Federations, in Baltimore, Shamir left for the United States in mid-November 1991. His meeting with Bush and Baker at the White House was on November 22. The meeting was devoted mostly to the next phase of the bilateral negotiations between Israel and its Arab neighbors. Shamir reiterated his position that the face-to-face negotiations should be held in the region, alternating between Israel and the three Arab countries—Jordan, Syria, and Lebanon. Since the Arabs had already rejected this idea, Baker said that he would explore the possibility of holding the talks in Rome or in Nicosia (Cyprus). Pending an agreement on the venue between all parties concerned, Baker suggested holding the first two rounds in Washington. Shamir refused.

"Why are you so opposed to Washington?" Bush asked. "You have here so much influence in Congress and in the media."

The Israeli prime minister explained that his opposition to Washington was not aimed at the United States. He simply feared that the Arab delegations, in-

stead of negotiating seriously with Israel, would prefer to talk to the U.S. officials, hoping that Bush would "deliver" Israel to them.[9] The subject remained
open for further consultations.

The next day, however, while still in New York, Shamir was surprised to
learn that Hanan Ashrawi, the Palestinian spokesperson, had told ABC in
Jerusalem that the Palestinians had agreed to hold the first round of the bilateral negotiations in Washington, on December 4. The Israeli prime minister
was furious. In his meeting with the president and the secretary the previous
day, he had not been told that the parties had already been invited to Washington. Asked to comment on the ABC report, the State Department confirmed it
and added that the U.S. diplomats had been instructed "not to haggle" over any
condition. All they had to do was convey a short message to the parties involved:
That was the proposal—Washington, D.C., on December 4.

Angered and frustrated, Shamir decided to put an end to this confrontational American modus operandi. His position was that the United States was
not running the peace process, it was only facilitating it and helping the parties
to meet. It was up to the parties to decide what kind of help they needed.

However, knowing that Shamir was opposed to the Washington venue, the
Arab delegations rushed to confirm their acceptance of Baker's proposal. Realizing that he had no choice anymore about the venue, the Israeli prime minister
decided to challenge the secretary on the date. He informed Baker that Israel
would not attend the meeting in Washington on the fourth "because of
Hanukkah." He proposed December 9 instead. Everybody knew, of course,
that Hanukkah is not a religious holiday and that even observant Jews work during it. So the administration ignored Shamir's objection and went ahead with
the proposed date of December 4, as planned. Baker had informed the parties
that the State Department had prepared three separate rooms where the meetings would be held: one for Israel and the joint Jordanian-Palestinian delegation, another for Israel and Syria, and yet another for Israel and Lebanon.

I covered that first round of the bilaterals in Washington, for the Israeli
daily *Davar* and for the French newsmagazine *L'Express*. Indeed, it was quite a
power play to watch. The Israeli delegation, as Shamir had instructed, did not
show up on the fourth. The Palestinians, although they were advised that the Israelis would not come, and over the objection of Baker, decided to score points
with the press. They sent Hanan Ashrawi to the State Department's diplomatic
entrance, on C Street, to talk to the media. She was really harsh. When told that
the Israeli spokesman, Benjamin (Bibi) Netanyahu, had scheduled a press conference for later in the day to explain Israel's absence, she said: "Instead of
holding a press conference, the Israelis should have come to negotiate. All the
Arab delegations are here, only the Israelis did not show up. They don't want
peace. It's time for the United States to stop allowing the tail to wag the
dog. . . ."

On December 9, the day proposed by the Israelis, it was the Arabs' turn to play their game. They informed the State Department that the ninth was the anniversary of the intifada, the Palestinian uprising, and that all the Arab delegations would be attending two "memorial services" at the Washington Cathedral and at the mosque. Eventually, the bilateral negotiations began the next morning, on December 10, and they lasted until the nineteenth.

Some correspondents who did not know the background to this "haggling" thought the whole episode was "childish." For the Israeli delegations, however, it was a message well conveyed. In his invitations to the parties, Secretary Baker proposed an agenda of his own, to facilitate their dialogue and to build mutual trust. To Israel and Lebanon, for example, he suggested that as a confidence-building measure (CBM) the Israeli-trained and -financed "South Lebanese army" withdraw from the city of Jezin, on the crossroad from southern Lebanon to Beirut. To Syria and Israel he suggested a preliminary "what if" discussion: If Israel withdrew from the Golan Heights, what would the Syrians be prepared to give in return, and if Syria would give Israel full peace, what would Israel be prepared to give in return, etc. Israel rejected this "proposed agenda." It wanted to make sure that the Arab delegations understood that these were direct, face-to-face negotiations, with no intermediaries, no mediators, and even no cosponsors. It was up to the parties to negotiate their own agenda. Israel wanted to convey to the Arab delegations the clear message that the United States could not "deliver" Israel to them.

Indeed, in the next few days and weeks, U.S. officials limited their role to administrative problems only. Despite persistent Arab requests that the United States offer proposals of its own, to bridge the gaps between the two parties, Ambassador Dennis Ross sent the delegates back to the negotiating table.

The Palestinian negotiators raised in Washington a principle issue about their own status. Encouraged by their success in Madrid, they wanted to repeat it in Washington. Without prior coordination with the head of the Jordanian delegation, the Palestinians insisted on being recognized as a separate delegation and had asked the State Department for a room of their own for negotiating with the Israelis. Both the United States and Israel rejected that demand. The Palestinians decided to boycott the talks. In a telephone conversation with Eli Rubenstein, the cabinet secretary who headed the Israeli delegation to the talks with the Jordanians and the Palestinians, Prime Minister Shamir insisted on keeping the "Madrid Framework" intact. He said that recognizing the Palestinians as a separate delegation would mean recognizing the Palestinians as a separate entity. He was not prepared to give the Palestinians such a prize even before the start of the negotiations. In an effort to avoid the collapse of the process at this early stage, the three senior negotiators—Israel's Rubenstein, Jordan's Abdul Salam Majali, and the Palestinian Dr. Haidar Abdul Shafi—sat for days on a couch in one of the State Department corridors trying to find a solution. They wasted the whole first round on this "corridor diplomacy." Only at the beginning of the second round, in mid-January, was a face-saving formula reached: The Palestinians would have a separate room, but at least one Jordanian would join their delegation, while one Palestinian would join the Jordanian delegation. Both Israelis and Palestinians claimed victory.

This behind-the-scene minicrisis received little attention in the American media. The front pages of the American press in those days were filled with stories about John Sununu's resignation as White House chief of staff, and the William Kennedy Smith rape trial in Florida.

While the Palestinians continued to draw the media's attention, inside the negotiating rooms the picture was totally different. Both the Israelis and the Jordanians were stunned to realize how inexperienced and how unprepared their Palestinian counterparts were. Most of the Palestinian negotiators were from academia. Their past "negotiating experience" was random meetings with liberal Israelis, in encounters organized and funded by well-meaning American and European organizations. In Madrid, they had Dr. Nabil Shaath as their "invisible mentor," while Abu Mazen coordinated the whole effort from Tunis. Nabil Shaath did not come to Washington this time. Shaath was a prominent PLO executive, and the United States did not want to antagonize the Israelis, so it did not grant Shaath an entry visa, although he had visited the United States many times in the past. The result was constant rifts and tensions between the Palestinian negotiators.

Arafat had been aware of such a possibility even before Madrid. In a meeting in Tunis, on October 20, 1991, the PLO Executive Committee was supposed to approve the list of the Palestinian delegation to Madrid. Faisal Husseini faxed to Arafat, from Jerusalem, a list of twenty-five candidates—all of them from academia. In his note to Arafat, Husseini said that he had preferred "talent" over "reputation." When he saw the list, Arafat rejected it outright. He said: "The academicians have my full respect. But what is their popular support? What is their experience? Are they known in Hebron, or in the refugee camps? Of course not. I don't see the name of Elias Freij—the respected Christian mayor of Bethlehem. Freij is the only elected mayor in the West Bank. He has good standing in the Catholic Church. The pope likes him. He is a man of dignity and experience. We are going to Madrid in the worst possible conditions. The opposition to our move is very substantial. Therefore we need every bit of experience and popular support."[10]

Over the strong objection of Husseini, Arafat deleted a few names from his list and added the names of Elias Freij and Nabil Ja'abari from Hebron as negotiators. Arafat also turned to President Mubarak for assistance. While the majority of the Palestinians were closer geographically and demographically to Jordan, Arafat felt closer to Egypt. He studied engineering in Cairo, he adored Gamal Abdel Nasser, and after the expulsion of the PLO from Beirut in 1982,

Mubarak was the first to offer him a comforting hand. Arafat needed the Egyptians' long experience in negotiations with the Israelis. He knew that his delegation was inexperienced and had no negotiating skills. Therefore, Arafat accepted Mubarak's offer and attached two former Egyptian ambassadors to the Palestinian Washington delegation as legal advisers. The two Egyptian diplomats—Taher Shash and Hassan Abdul Latif—were very experienced and they participated in most of the peace negotiations between Egypt and Israel. In a meeting with Ambassador Shash at the Grand Hotel (now the Westin) in Washington, the Egyptian diplomat said: "They [the Palestinians] are still young and unskilled. They still don't know the difference between an academic paper and a diplomatic document. But they are very motivated; they will learn. I suggested to Cairo to persuade Arafat to send Nabil Shaath to Washington as soon as possible. I discussed this problem with the State Department as well."[11]

Indeed, at Arafat's request, Egypt persuaded the United States to grant Shaath the necessary entry visa so that he could come to Washington for the second round of the bilateral negotiations. Baker agreed, on condition that Shaath would be "anonymous" in the United States and would not grant any press interviews. What was even more interesting, Israel agreed to turn a blind eye to Shaath's presence in Washington. Thus, from early 1992, Shamir knew that he was now negotiating indirectly with the PLO.

As a matter of fact, Shamir knew this reality even before Madrid. He also knew that although the United States had suspended its official dialogue with the PLO on June 20, 1990, the Bush administration continued its indirect contacts with the PLO, through Egypt, Morocco, and the local Palestinians in the territories. On March 12, 1991, during Baker's first trip to the Middle East, after the Persian Gulf War, the secretary met with a group of twenty Palestinians at the American consulate in East Jerusalem. The matter of the discussion was immediately leaked, and Shamir got a full report. In order to avoid future leaks, the number of Palestinians who later met with Baker was reduced to three only—Faisal Husseini, Hanan Ashrawi, and Zakariya Agha (from the Gaza Strip).

Baker's discussion with the Palestinians on March 12 was indeed very alarming. Baker told the group that he wanted them to hear it from him personally: In dealing with the peace process, the White House would not yield to any "domestic pressure." The implication was obvious: Bush would not be deterred by AIPAC and by its influence on Capitol Hill. So when Bush said it publicly, six months later, Israel was not surprised.

In a recent meeting in Tel Aviv, I asked Shamir if he had known of the PLO presence in Madrid and Washington, and if so why he had continued to oppose recognition of the PLO and to pretend that Arafat did not exist. Shamir answered: "Of course I knew. I had full knowledge about the regular contacts between the local Palestinians and Arafat and his associates. I knew also about their trips to Tunis and Algiers. For me, Arafat represents a Palestinian state, which I strongly oppose. If it was up to me, I would continue to ignore Arafat, even today."[12]

The second round of the bilateral negotiations, which opened in Washington on January 13, 1992, was accompanied by a particularly intense wave of violence in the territories. In the face of the inability of the army to suppress the intifada, Israeli settlers—especially from Kiryat Arba, in Hebron—took the law into their own hands and embarked on a rampage of Arab villages. They smashed cars, threw stones, and fired in the air in the deserted streets. Facing growing criticism from his own cabinet colleagues, Defense Minister Moshe Arens declared his intention to deport twelve suspected leaders of the Intifada. Pending a verdict by the Israeli Supreme Court, the PLO and the Arab countries asked for an emergency meeting of the UN Security Council. At U.S. initiative, the Security Council met on January 6 and voted Resolution 726, which sharply condemned the Israeli policy of deportations and called on Israel to desist from such actions. Thus, Israel suffered a double defeat—it did not deport the intifada leaders and it was sharply condemned for its intentions.

At the opening of the second round of the bilateral negotiations, the head of the Palestinian team, Dr. Abdul Shafi, read a long memorandum outlining the Palestinian demands. At the suggestion of Eli Rubenstein, it was agreed to keep the deliberations secret. While Israel maintained secrecy, the details of these discussions were later leaked by a Palestinian source. In his memorandum, Abdul Shafi repeated in essence the same demands that he had already raised in Madrid: acceptance of the principle of land for peace, Israeli recognition that Resolution 242 applied to the West Bank and the Gaza Strip and hence Israel should withdraw from them, an end to the settlement activity, a Palestinian state with East Jerusalem as its capital, the right of 1948 refugees to return to their homes, etc. At the end of the session, Abdul Shafi left the memorandum with the Israeli delegation.[13]

The next day, January 14, it was Rubenstein's turn to reply. He told Abdul Shafi that when he studied the Palestinian memorandum, he was "very upset" and he even thought to return it, because the memorandum was submitted on behalf of the "Palestinian delegation." He wanted to emphasize, "for the record," that as far as Israel was concerned, there was no Palestinian delegation but a Jordanian-Palestinian delegation. As to the contents of the memorandum, Rubenstein said that from a historical perspective, it was unclear if there ever was a Palestinian people. Ethnic features did not necessarily mean political identity. The Iraqi Kurds were only one example. Rubenstein rejected the claim that Resolution 242 applied to the West Bank and the Gaza Strip as well. Rubenstein, a lawyer and a scholar in Middle East studies, argued that when Israel took control over these areas in 1967, there had been no Palestinian sovereignty. Those areas were controlled by Jordan, but except for Great Britain and

Pakistan, no other country in the world—not even the Arab countries—recognized the annexation of these territories to Jordan. Hence, the terms of the Geneva Convention regarding "occupied territories" did not apply in this case. Finally, Rubenstein said, it had been agreed with the cosponsors that the issues of East Jerusalem, settlements, and Israeli withdrawals would be discussed in the second phase of the negotiations and not as part of the interim agreements. Therefore, there was no need to raise these issues at the present stage.

The head of the Israeli delegation then submitted a proposed agenda to discuss the modalities and the jurisdictions of PISGA—the Palestine Interim Self-Governing Authority. He explained that according to the Israeli interpretation, there would be no border between Israel and the autonomous region and freedom of movement would be guaranteed. Foreign affairs and security would be in Israeli hands throughout the entire interim period of five years.[14]

On the third and last day of the second round, Abdul Shafi handed Rubenstein three documents. One of them dealt with the Palestinian interpretation of PISGA. It included all the attributes of an independent state, without calling it so. Then he told the Israeli delegation that henceforth the Palestinians would refuse to discuss any subject other than the cessation of Israeli settlement activity. As to the proposed Israeli agenda, Abdul Shafi returned it to Rubenstein, claiming that it was addressed to the joint Jordanian-Palestinian delegation and not to the Palestinian delegation.[15]

The deliberations in the two other groups did not produce any progress either. The heads of the Israeli negotiating team with Lebanon, Ambassadors Yossi Hadass and Uri Lubrani, told the Lebanese delegation that Israel had no territorial or water claims in Lebanon. Israel was ready to withdraw from South Lebanon, provided its security needs were met and the future of the Israeli-financed "South Lebanese Army" was assured. Hadass suggested accepting as a basis for negotiations the Israeli-Lebanese agreement of May 17, 1983, which had been brokered by Secretary Shultz and U.S. Ambassador Philip Habib, and which was unilaterally abrogated by President Amin Gemayel, under heavy Syrian pressure. Finally, Lubrani suggested forming a joint Lebanese-Israeli military team to discuss the security problems in South Lebanon.

As expected, Lebanon demanded Israeli commitment to total and unconditional withdrawal from South Lebanon, according to UN Resolution 425, prior to further discussions on any other subject. The Madrid Framework, however, was based on Resolutions 242 and 338, not on 425. The Lebanese would not move from their intransigent position, and the negotiations reached a dead end.

As in Madrid, the least pleasant meeting was between the Israeli and the Syrian teams. The head of the Israeli delegation, Yossi Ben-Aharon, said that his counterpart, Ambassador Muwaffaq Allaf, concentrated on one subject only: Israeli withdrawal from the Golan Heights. Allaf said that there was no need to discuss any agenda, because the only subject that mattered was the Israeli withdrawal. Yossi Ben Aharon said that Israel wanted to know what were the Syrian definitions for peace, and how "normal" Israeli-Syrian relations would be. Since both sides dug in their heels, the result was obvious—a deadlock.

With minor variations, these same arguments were repeated in the future rounds of negotiations, and no progress was in sight.

Before the end of the second round, Secretary Baker met separately with the various delegations. The head of the Israeli teams, Yossi Ben-Aharon, suggested that the next round be held in the Middle East or in Europe, between February 10 and 23. Baker said that he would consult with the Arab delegations on the time and place of the next round before any invitations were issued.

Of Baker's three meetings with the Arab delegations, the most revealing discussion was undoubtedly that with the Palestinians. After congratulating Abdul Shafi on the way he handled himself in the negotiations, Baker gave him one piece of advice: "Don't give the Israelis any excuse to walk out." When Abdul Shafi raised the issue of the settlements, Baker suggested not focusing on this issue, because the United States was already taking care of it. He said that the issue of the loan guarantees was in the hands of Congress. He did not want to be quoted, he said, but he hinted that it was the administration's intention to seek a further delay in the consideration of the Israeli request for loan guarantees.

Indeed, if Baker's remarks to the Palestinians proved anything, it was that Shamir's suspicions about the administration's attitudes toward him were vindicated. Bush had no intention of giving him the loan guarantees. By the time the second round of negotiations in Washington ended, Israel and Congressional leaders were exploring various forms of compromise on the loan guarantees. It was suggested, for example, that Israel would receive $2 billion in loan guarantees for the first year, and the remaining amount would be negotiated at a later date. It was also suggested that in accordance with the Baker-Levy agreement of October 1990, any funds spent on settlement activity would be deducted from future amounts. Bush refused all compromises. He wanted a clear Israeli commitment to stop all settlement activity as a condition for the loan guarantees. The president knew, of course, that Shamir would never make such a commitment, but he believed that Labor and other left-wing Israeli parties would.[16] Bush adopted this position at a time of serious political instability in Israel. Loyal to their party's platform to push for electoral reform, two Tsomet Knesset members left Shamir's coalition, and on January 5, they voted with the opposition on new legislation according to which the future prime minister would be elected directly by the people and not only by his party. The law was to go into effect in 1996. Of all Likud Knesset members, only Benjamin Netanyahu voted with the opposition. It proved to be the decisive vote. The new electoral reform was approved by one vote only, 57–56.

Ten days later, on January 15, Shamir lost his parliamentary majority. The three Tehiya Knesset members and the two Moledet Knesset members also left the coalition. Instead of being toppled by a no-confidence vote, Shamir reached an agreement with Labor, on February 4, to dissolve the Knesset and to advance the parliamentary elections from October to June 23, 1992. Until then, Shamir would remain at the head of a minority government, with no risk of being toppled. The dissolution of the Knesset generated an earthquake in the Labor Party. Sensing that for the first time in fifteen years they had a real chance to regain power, many Labor activists deserted the party chairman, Shimon Peres, and pledged allegiance to Yitzhak Rabin. The most prominent among those who defected were Gad Yaacoby, a former minister of economic planning, and two "stars" of Labor's young leadership—Knesset member Haim Ramon and General (Res.) Ephraim Sneh, the former head of Israel's civil administration in the West Bank and a liberal with a good reputation among the Palestinians.

That was a moment that Rabin had been waiting for since 1977, when he resigned the premiership over the issue of an illegal bank account that he and his wife, Leah, kept in Washington. The Israeli people had forgiven him long ago, and it was now time for a comeback. In an atmosphere loaded with tension and emotions, Labor's Central Committee, on February 19, deposed Peres and elected Rabin as the party's new chairman and its candidate for prime minister.

Rabin's candidacy did not generate a similar change in Likud's leadership. Terribly splintered, Likud again rallied behind Yitzhak Shamir. As in a Greek tragedy, Likud walked with open eyes into its defeat. Shamir was seventy-seven years old. Although older than Rabin by only seven years, Shamir was considered by the majority of the Israeli people to be a man of the past, a leader who symbolized immobility. His horizons were closed and he was incapable of offering his peace-hungry people any hope, or any new creative solution to the fifty-year-old Arab-Israeli conflict.

The Bush administration welcomed the new developments in Israel. This was an election year in the United States as well. Therefore, while determined to continue denying Shamir the $10 billion in loan guarantees, Bush took some steps to pacify the agitated American Jewish community: He moved actively to repeal the infamous 1975 UN resolution that equated Zionism with racism. This was a single-handed victory of U.S. Ambassador to the UN Thomas Pickering. This talented and very experienced diplomat, who successfully led the anti–Saddam Hussein effort at the UN during the Persian Gulf crisis, had served earlier as the U.S. ambassador in Jordan and Israel. He had excellent relationships with King Hussein and with Shimon Peres, and he had also good working relationships with Shamir and Rabin. His friendship with both Israel and Jordan was never in doubt. Capitalizing on the goodwill generated by Israel's restraint during the Persian Gulf War, and on the new world order that resulted from the collapse of the Soviet empire, Pickering succeeded—with great patience and skill—in mastering the necessary majority to repeal the anti-Zionist resolution. It was a great moral victory, not only for Israel and the United States but also for all those nations that resented the resolution's unjust and immoral attitude toward the liberation movement of the Jewish people.

The developments in Israel had a direct effect on the U.S.-Palestinian dialogue as well, and on attitudes within the PLO leadership. In discussions with the Palestinians, the U.S. peace team, headed by Ambassador Dennis Ross, tried to direct the Palestinian negotiating team away from the media and more toward serious negotiations with Israel. In reply to repeated Palestinian requests that the United States put its own ideas on the table, Ross encouraged them to invest more time in the negotiations. Israeli intelligence reports suggested that the Palestinians' inability to concentrate on the negotiations was a result of the confusion in Tunis and also of a power struggle at the top of the PLO leadership.

Ever suspicious of U.S. intentions toward him, and permanently obsessed by the fear of the emergence of an "alternative leadership," Arafat established a modus operandi that was impossible to cope with. On October 20, 1991, on the eve of the Madrid Peace Conference, the PLO Executive Committee decided that Arafat would be the top policymaker, but the day-to-day coordination between Tunis and the negotiating teams would be handled by Abu Mazen. In this role, Abu Mazen sent Dr. Nabil Shaath first to Madrid and then to Washington to guide the Palestinian delegation. Arafat, however, also sent "his" man to Washington. He was Akram Haniyeh, a talented journalist who had been expelled from the West Bank by the Israeli authorities because of his subversive activities. In Tunis, he became the liaison between Arafat and the Palestinian leadership in the territories. Cool-headed, intelligent, and discreet, Haniyeh was among the very few who pleaded with Arafat not to support the Iraqi invasion of Kuwait. Using different code names, he would phone or fax Arafat's instructions to the local leadership in the territories. Haniyeh also organized the secret trips of Faisal Husseini and Hanan Ashrawi from Israel to Tunis and Algiers, with the full cooperation of the French and British secret services in Paris and London. In Washington, however, Haniyeh's job was to report directly to Arafat, while Shaath reported to Abu Mazen. Furthermore, of all the Palestinian delegation members, Arafat trusted the bushy-bearded Saeb Erikat the most. Thus, in addition to getting Haniyeh's reports, Arafat would phone Erikat, hear his views, and give additional instructions. On several occasions, the Palestinian negotiating team received conflicting instructions, not to mention the suspicions that this situation had aroused among the various negotiators.

At the end of the second round in Washington, Abu Mazen decided to put an end to this messy situation. After a sharp exchange with Arafat, Abu Mazen packed his papers and left for Rabat, where he had a home and where he maintained a good relationship with King Hassan and several of his ministers. The Arafat–Abu Mazen rift came at a time when the PLO had to decide on its participation in the Moscow Multilateral Conference, which was due to open on January 28. Forty countries were to participate in this meeting, including Israel and six Arab countries. Abu Mazen approved a Palestinian participation at the Moscow Conference as part of the Jordanian delegation, based on the Madrid Framework. Arafat disapproved. He wanted a separate Palestinian delegation. Abu Mazen argued in vain that the PLO's credibility was at stake and that such a move was not coordinated with the cosponsors or with the various Arab countries. In the face of Arafat's insistence, Abu Mazen left Tunis in anger and stayed in Morocco for over a month.

The Palestinian appearance in Moscow was a disaster. On January 27, just before dawn, Hanan Ashrawi and three members of the Palestinian negotiating team were instructed by Tunis to leave that same morning for Amman, where a small chartered plane would fly them to Moscow. In the Russian capital, they would be joined by four PLO officials, and together they would form the Palestinian delegation to the Moscow Conference. Ashrawi and her friends did not prepare position papers and did not know the agenda or the subjects that were to be discussed.

Shortly after their arrival in Moscow, the Palestinians were informed that their list of participants was unacceptable. Secretary Baker and Russian Foreign Minister Boris Pankin, the cochairmen of the conference, told the delegation that of the eight Palestinians, they could approve only the three who had participated in the Madrid Peace Conference and in the Washington negotiations. The Palestinians replied that either all eight or none must be accepted. "So, it's none," replied Baker and Pankin. The next morning the Palestinians flew back to Tunis and Amman, their wings clipped.

The Israeli delegation, headed by Foreign Minister David Levy, followed with great interest, but no surprise, the debate between the sponsors and the Palestinians. "What was amazing to us," said one participant to the group of Israeli journalists in Moscow, "was the fact that none of the six Arab foreign ministers came to the rescue of the Palestinians. They didn't lift even one finger to extricate the Palestinians from the messy situation that they themselves created. They were even angry at Arafat's modus operandi and of his attempts to unilaterally change the rules of the game."

The Moscow Conference established five committees to study regional cooperation, in the fields of economic development, water resources, environment, arms control, and refugees. The committee on the refugees, headed by Canada, was suggested by Egypt and was approved over the objection of Israel. During Shamir's tenure as prime minister, the five committees met only once, in May 1992. The multilateral committee on the environment met in Tokyo, arms control in Washington, economic cooperation in Brussels, water resources in Vienna, and refugees in Ottawa. None of the committees produced any tangible results, nor were they expected to.

On January 29, and in the absence of Abu Mazen, Yasser Arafat convened the steering committee in Tunis to discuss the recent developments in Israel. Arafat said that the Israeli crisis was serious and genuine, but he was concerned that Rabin and not Peres was elected chairman of the Labor Party. All PLO contacts in Israel were "Peres's boys" and Arafat was not familiar with them. It was Abu Mazen who handled these contacts. Arafat did not suggest any plan for action. He only said: "If Rabin is the future prime minister of Israel, we definitely have a problem."[17] The developments in Israel created a situation that left Arafat with no choice. He had to yield to Arab and PLO pressure and ask Abu Mazen to return to Tunis. Arafat traveled in person to Rabat to plead with Abu Mazen and to promise him not to interfere anymore in his decisions.

By March 1992, the United States, Israel, and the Arab countries seemed resigned to the idea that no progress was to be expected in the Arab-Israeli peace process before the next Israeli elections. On March 7, the senior members of the Palestinian negotiating team came to Tunis on their way back from the third round of negotiations in Washington. The third round opened on February 24 and ended on March 5. In meetings with Abu Mazen and other members of the steering committee, Dr. Haidar Abdul Shafi, the head of the negotiating team, was the most outspoken. He argued that the enthusiasm for the peace process was gone. The face-to-face negotiations in Washington had produced nothing. Eli Rubenstein, the head of the Israeli team, was a "nice man," but he was trying to wear down the Palestinians by legalistic arguments and endless Talmudic jokes. He, Abdul Shafi, and several commanders of the intifada in the Gaza Strip were of the opinion that the Washington talks ought to be suspended.

Faisal Husseini reported on his discussion with Baker. He said that when he raised with the secretary the issue of the continued Israeli settlement activity, Baker told him to put this issue aside. Baker was reported to have said: "Your role on the subject of the settlements and the loan guarantees is negligible in comparison to what the United States is doing. Don't forget that this is the first American administration that is taking such a tough position on the Israeli settlement activity. Israel won't get the loan guarantees unless it declares publicly that it will halt all settlement activity. Israel is on the eve of new elections, so we don't expect Shamir to make such a commitment."[18] Abu Mazen ended the meeting by saying that despite the lack of progress, there was no choice but to continue the negotiations. The United States wanted the talks to continue and had already issued the invitations for the fourth round in Washington, on April 27. The Israelis suggested moving to Rome, but all the Arab delegations preferred to continue the talks in Washington.

On March 12, 1992, Abu Mazen convened the steering committee in

Tunis, with the participation of Arafat, to discuss the future elections in Israel. The committee first dealt with the multilateral negotiations. At the suggestion of Abu Mazen, the Palestinians agreed to participate in the five committees for regional cooperation, according to the Madrid Framework, that is, as part of the Jordanian delegation. Arafat appointed Ahmed Qrei (Abu Ala) as the co-ordinator for the Multilateral Track. Abu Ala, a former banker, was a few months later to become the negotiator of the Oslo Accords.

The discussions then focused on the Israeli elections. Both Arafat and Abu Mazen reported on their discussions with Egypt and Morocco and with the Palestinians in the territories. Abu Mazen stressed the absolute necessity of keeping the details of this discussion secret, so as not to adversely affect Labor's chances of winning the elections. He said that he would meet shortly with the Israeli Arab Knesset members—Abdul Wahab Darawsheh, Hashem Mahamid, and Muhamad Miari—and with the head of the Islamic movement in Israel, Ibrahim Nimer Hussein. He would impress on them the necessity that the Israeli Arabs cast their votes for the Labor Party and for Meretz, so as to ensure Shamir's defeat.[19]

After the signing of the Oslo Accords, there were rumors in Israel that the PLO had encouraged Israeli Arabs to vote for the Labor Party. This is, however, the first time that a senior PLO participant in a policy-planning meeting confirmed that the PLO had indeed interfered in the Israeli elections. Abu Mazen's meetings in Cairo were confirmed also by other sources. According to these sources, Egypt coordinated the entire effort. The chief coordinator was Dr. Ossama el-Baz, President Mubarak's national security adviser, who had been involved in the Arab-Israeli conflict since President Sadat's visit to Jerusalem in November 1977. Short and aggressive, Ossama el-Baz had earned his Ph.D. from Harvard University. In Egypt he was known as advocating a tough line vis-à-vis Israel. His brother, Dr. Faruq el-Baz, was a naturalized American and a senior researcher at the Kennedy Space Center.

El-Baz's pointman in Israel was Mohamed Bassiouni, the Egyptian ambassador. A former general in the military intelligence and a former military attaché in Damascus and Tehran, Bassiouni had come to Israel in 1981, first as deputy chief of mission (DCM); a few years later he was promoted to the rank of ambassador. During his service in Tehran, Bassiouni became familiar with Israel's activity in pre-Khomeini Iran and had also a good knowledge of the PLO's role in the Islamic Revolution. Bassiouni occupied a unique place in Israeli diplomatic history as the longest-serving ambassador in Tel Aviv.

During his sixteen years in Israel, Bassiouni had built a vast network of contacts, ranging from President Weizman to the mayor of the smallest Arab village in Israel. His Syrian-born wife, Nagwa, was fluent in Hebrew and was welcome in every Israeli home and at every social function. It was Bassiouni's idea to use the political power of Israeli Arabs in the service of the PLO.

There was nothing unusual in the constant effort by various political groups to court the Israeli Arab voter. Since the first Knesset elections in 1949, there had always been an Arab representation in the Israeli parliament. As their number grew constantly, because of a high birthrate and family reunifications, Israeli Arab voters were courted by all Israeli parties, with no exception. Traditionally, however, they voted for Labor or Labor-affiliated Arab parties. In recent years, however, and in an effort to get a slice of the Arab pie, Likud and Meretz included an Arab in their national lists for the Knesset elections. The Arab vote, then, had always been and would continue to be an integral part of Israeli politics. What was new in the 1992 elections was the joint effort by Egypt and the PLO to channel the Israeli Arab vote to parties that were closer to their ideologies and to their national goals and aspirations. The Likud candidate, Benjamin Netanyahu, made good use of this point in his bid for the premiership, on May 29, 1996. In the very last days of his campaign, he flooded the country with bumper stickers reading: "Netanyahu—good for the Jews," implying that his Labor rival, Shimon Peres, was good for the Arabs.

In the United States, meanwhile, President Bush's efforts to mend his fences with the American Jewish community were facing growing difficulties. An increasing number of American Jews came to see Bush and Baker as hostile to Israel. The president's continued denial of the loan guarantees was interpreted as intended to prove to his new "Arab allies" that he was a man true to his word. Just as Bush had gone to war against Saddam Hussein, he would now demonstrate his iron fist to Shamir. Bush's offensive remarks about AIPAC were perceived as a real challenge to the right of American Jews to lobby on behalf of Israel. Even those who opposed Shamir's policies and in different circumstances would have supported the administration's Middle East policies turned their backs on Bush.

In March 1992 came the hardest blow of all. In his weekly column in the *New York Post,* Mayor Ed Koch wrote about a Republican campaign strategy meeting at the White House at which the issue of the loan guarantees to Israel had been mentioned. Koch wrote that one of the participants remarked that because of the administration's position on this issue, Bush might lose the Jewish vote, and Baker interrupted him by saying: "Fuck the Jews—they don't vote for us anyway. . . ."

It was a shocking story. Baker issued an immediate denial. He also told Jack Stein and other Republican Jewish leaders that he had never made such a remark. Many American Jews—not just Republicans—believed him, but the damage was done, and it was enormous. The overwhelming majority of American Jews, including those who voted for President Reagan, decided to vote for Bill Clinton.

The Jewish anti-Bush sentiment in the United States was not reflected in Israel. On the contrary, the president's constant clashes with Shamir convinced many Israelis that as long as Likud was in power, relations with the United

States would not improve. The United States was Israel's only ally and its main source of military, economic, and political support. Thus, the "change of guards" in Labor and the replacement of Peres by Rabin gave the Israelis the preferred alternative to Shamir. Unlike Peres, whom Israelis considered distrustful and manipulative, Rabin was trusted. His past record as chief of staff and as ambassador to Washington assured Israelis of his ability to give them peace with security and to mend fences with the United States.

On June 23, 1992, Yitzhak Rabin won the election and had reduced considerably Likud's power in the Knesset. The prospects for a renewed momentum in the peace process had never looked more promising.

LABOR BACK IN POWER

The celebrations in Tel Aviv on that election night of Tuesday, June 23, 1992, resembled a mini-carnival in Rio. Moments after the TV anchorman announced that the exit polls showed that Labor's Yitzhak Rabin had defeated Likud's Shamir, the crowds poured into the streets and the public squares, kissed and hugged, sang and danced enthusiastically. Overfilled cars moved slowly among the crowds, honking loudly as they drove past Labor's headquarters on 110 Hayarkon Street. Across from Labor's building, at the grand ballroom of the Dan Hotel, which was Labor's election headquarters for that night, the same ecstatic atmosphere prevailed. Colorful balloons were in the air, champagne bottles passed from hand to hand, and Labor activists, kissing and crying, congratulated each other for an undeniable victory. When Yitzhak Rabin, the big winner, came to the ballroom to declare victory and to thank his supporters for their hard work, he looked like a Caesar addressing his cheerful battalions waiting for their share in the spoils of war. Indeed, after fifteen years of uninterrupted Likud rule, Rabin had brought Labor back to power, giving a new sense of security and hope to a peace-hungry people.

It was a new Rabin who was born that victory night. He was not the shy, inexperienced politician who had inherited the premiership from Golda Meir in 1974, constantly subverted by Shimon Peres and upstaged by the late Yigal Allon. It was a very experienced Rabin, confident of himself and with the right mixture of toughness and moderation. He was not as stubborn as Shamir, nor was he as dovish as Peres. He was a centrist, as Labor had always been before it drifted to the left under Peres's fifteen-year chairmanship.

Rabin's mandate was clear: to lead Israel into peace with security, through negotiations from a position of strength. Unlike Shamir's Likud, Rabin was ready for a territorial compromise, and he accepted the principle of land for peace. Looking at Peres, surrounded by his many supporters, Rabin said in his deep, loud voice: "I alone will form the cabinet, I will lead the coalition negotiations, and I will let nobody, nobody, interfere in my decisions. The days of political maneuvers and blackmail are gone. . . ." Rabin's remarks reflected the sentiment of the moment. The next few months, however, would prove that the prime minister–elect had overstated his power and his ability to lead a party still controlled by Peres.

Rabin's victory was welcomed all over the world, but reactions were mixed in the Arab world and among the Palestinians. While pleased at Shamir's downfall, the Palestinians were less than happy that it was Rabin and not Peres who had assumed the premiership. Faisal Husseini, the most prominent PLO representative in Jerusalem, who met regularly with Israelis and who understood Israeli politics, said: ". . . I can't say that I am happy that Rabin came to power. Nevertheless, with Rabin, at least, we can do business. We have great expectations that the Washington negotiations will resume very soon."[1] Husseini expressed the hope that Rabin would become the Israeli version of France's General de Gaulle: Just as the late French president, who was elected in 1958 by the nationalists and the right parties, then ignored his voters and granted the Algerians their independence, so would the hawkish Rabin grant the Palestinians their political rights.

Yasser Arafat rushed to Cairo to consult with President Mubarak on the next move in the peace process. His office in Tunis issued a strongly worded statement calling for total Israeli withdrawal from the territories, including East Jerusalem; for the suspension of all settlement activity; and for holding elections at the earliest. "The intifada will continue and intensify until the Palestinian flag flies over the walls of Jerusalem and over the State of Palestine," the statement said.[2]

Arafat's greatest fear was that Rabin, despite Labor's dovish face, would continue the policies of his predecessor and drag the Washington talks on endlessly. The Palestinians were outraged by a comment Shamir made about the negotiations. Without conceding Likud's worst defeat in twenty-three years, and without even congratulating Rabin for his victory, Shamir said that it was his intention to continue the Washington talks for at least ten years. The defeated prime minister said: "It is very painful to me to accept the reality that in the next four years [of Labor's rule] we will not be able to increase the number of settlers in the territories. Had I been reelected, it was my hope to increase the number of settlers to half a million. Without this demographic revolution in the territories, there will always be a danger of establishing a Palestinian state."[3]

Despite the Palestinians' fears, the reaction in the Arab world to Rabin's victory was more balanced. Egypt, in particular, whose active interference in the Israeli elections had brought about Shamir's defeat, was pleased with its own success. "The fall of the abominable Shamir," headlined the mass-circulation Cairo paper *Al-Akhbar*, and a leading columnist in that paper called Shamir "Frankenstein."

The election results had left Rabin with few choices as to the composition of his cabinet. Having won forty-four seats in the Knesset and having reduced Likud's power to thirty-two seats, his immediate and most natural partner was the left-wing Meretz Party, which won twelve seats. Adding to these five seats won by two small Arab parties, Rabin was able to block any attempt by Shamir to form a new government with the religious and the extreme right parties. Rabin, however, was reluctant to rely on the Arab vote. Just one week before the elections, in the only TV debate with Shamir, Rabin had pledged not to bring the Arab parties into his coalition. This was the consistent policy of all Israeli governments, whether led by Labor or Likud. It was Israel's founding father, David Ben-Gurion, who had ruled that as long as there was no peace with the Arab countries, Israeli governments could not rely on the Arab vote in matters related to national security or to war and peace. Moreover, Rabin disliked Meretz, and especially its two most prominent leaders, Shulamit Aloni and Yossi Sarid, who made no effort to conceal their secret contacts with the PLO and their support of a Palestinian state.

Determined not to be a "prisoner" of Meretz, Rabin turned first to the moderate religious Sephardic party Shas (six Knesset seats) and to the center-right Tsomet Party (eight seats). However, after meeting with Tsomet's leader, Raphael (Rafful) Eitan, who had been chief of staff during the war in Lebanon, Rabin had to drop Tsomet from his list; Eitan insisted on the continuation of the settlement activity in the West Bank, and he rejected Rabin's distinction between "political" and "security" settlements.

On July 13, Rabin presented to the Knesset his sixteen-member cabinet, supported by sixty-two Knesset members: Labor, forty-four; Meretz, twelve; and Shas, six. Together with the passive support of the five Arab Knesset members, he had a comfortable majority to lead the country in the next four years. In addition to the premiership, Rabin retained the defense portfolio, and he appointed Shimon Peres as deputy prime minister and minister for foreign affairs. Loyal to his pledge on election night that he would select his own ministers, Rabin did not consult with Peres about the composition of the new government. He even kept him guessing what portfolio he would get, if any. Peres supporters, however, let it be known that if Peres did not get either defense or foreign affairs, Peres would prefer not to join the government. Rabin remained silent.

Eventually, after ten days of waiting, Peres took the initiative and called Rabin. They met on Friday afternoon, July 3, at Rabin's Tel Aviv residence. "Yitzhak, you won and I accept the result," Peres told the prime minister–elect. "The question now is whether we can push the cart together, to achieve the peace that we both want." I knew Rabin very well and I had known Peres for more than three decades. I knew that as far as Peres was concerned, Rabin was governed by his emotions, not by his brain. He could never get over what he wrote in his memoir, that Peres was a "tireless schemer" and that he had used "bolshevik" tactics to subvert him. For Rabin, Peres always remained the Israeli version of "tricky Dick" and, like Nixon, was not to be trusted. Therefore, before appointing him as his foreign minister, Rabin wanted to make sure that the distribution of responsibilities between them was clearly defined. Uneasy with the dovish face of his potential coalition partners, Rabin wanted full control of the bilateral negotiations with the Arabs and the Palestinians in Washington and total responsibility for the relationship with the United States. Peres would be responsible for the multilateral negotiations on future regional cooperation. Peres knew, of course, that without meaningful progress in the bilateral negotiations, the multilateral track was meaningless. Peres had no choice. The division of responsibilities proposed by Rabin was similar to the arrangement between Shamir and his foreign minister, David Levy. Peres accepted this reduced role in the peace process.

Rabin did not want Yossi Beilin, the super-dove and "Peres's poodle," as he called him, as deputy foreign minister. In addition to disagreeing with Beilin's political positions and his support for a Palestinian state, Rabin had a personal grudge against Beilin: At the peak of the tension between Peres and Rabin, Beilin, as a former journalist in *Davar,* had written a letter to the editor, under an assumed name, in which he criticized Rabin's qualifications as a national leader. But Peres insisted on Beilin as his deputy, and he eventually got his way. Beilin became the coordinator of the five multilateral committees that were supposed to study regional development projects. It did not take long before the multilateral track became Peres's connection to the back channel in Oslo.

In presenting his government to the Knesset, on July 13, 1992, Rabin invited the Jordanian-Palestinian delegation to meet with him in Jerusalem for informal talks on how to revive the stalled self-rule talks in Washington. He also said that he was prepared to travel to the various Arab countries to negotiate peace. "I am prepared to travel to Amman, to Damascus, and to Beirut, today, tomorrow. For there is no greater victory than the victory of peace," Rabin said. The prime minister's speech contained two important messages—one to the Israelis and the other to the Palestinians. Rabin told the Israelis: ". . . In the last decade of the twentieth century, the atlases and history and geography books no longer present an up-to-date picture of the world. Walls of enmity have fallen, borders have disappeared. Powers have crumbled and ideologies collapsed. States have been born and states have died and gates of emigration have been flung open. . . . It is our duty . . . to see the new world as it is now. . . . No longer are we necessarily 'a nation that dwells alone.' No longer is it true that 'the whole world is against us.' We must overcome this sense of isolation that has held us in its thrall for almost half a century. We must join the international movement toward peace, reconciliation, and cooperation that is spreading over the entire globe, lest we be the last to remain, all alone, in the station." This passage was a sharp departure from the ghetto mentality of both Begin and Shamir, who invoked the Holocaust on every occasion.

Rabin's message to the Palestinians was an impassioned plea. He told

them: "To you, the Palestinians in the territories, our foes today and our partners to a peaceful coexistence tomorrow, I wish to say: We have been fated to
live together on the same patch of land. . . . We lead our lives with you, beside
you, and against you. You have failed in the war against us. One hundred years
of bloodshed and terror against us have brought you only suffering, humiliation,
bereavement, and pain. You have lost thousands of your sons and daughters,
and you are losing ground all the time. For forty-four years now, you have been
living under a delusion. Your leaders have led you through lies and deceit. They
have missed every opportunity, rejected all our proposals for a settlement, and
taken you from one tragedy to another. . . . You who have never known a single
day of freedom and joy in your lives, listen to us, if only this once. We offer you
the fairest and most viable proposal . . . an autonomy, with all its advantages and
limitations. You will not get everything you want. Neither will we. So once and
for all, take your destiny in your hands. Don't lose this opportunity that may
never return. Take our proposal seriously—to avoid further suffering, humiliation, and grief; to end the shedding of tears and blood. . . ."[4]

Rabin's message was clear: He was addressing the Palestinians in the territories, not the PLO in Tunis. It was not surprising. As defense minister in
Shamir's government, Rabin used to say that "the Palestinians who carry on
their shoulders the burden of the intifada deserve our attention. They are our
interlocutors, not those living in luxurious villas in Tunis." Yet, he knew quite
well that the Palestinians in the territories reported to Tunis and received their
instructions from Arafat. How would he bridge this gap between the desirable
and the realizable? Only time could tell.

The Arab reaction to Rabin's speech was very restrained. He was not the
first Israeli prime minister who had invited them to negotiate peace. Even
Shamir, whom President Bush practically dragged to Madrid, made the same
call to the Arab leaders. Hence, the Arab leaders were not yet prepared to roll
out the red carpet for Rabin. They preferred to judge him according to his
deeds, not his words. They read very carefully Henry Kissinger's description of
Rabin. The former secretary of state, who was considered Rabin's mentor in
balance-of-power diplomacy, said: "If any of his interlocutors are counting on
influencing him by charm or legalistic skill, they are heading for disillusion-
ment. Small talk is not his forte; personal charm not his specialty. Redundancy
taxes his patience; the commonplace does not capture his attention. He is as
tenacious as he is intelligent. . . . American and Arab leaders are not likely to
find Mr. Rabin a jolly companion on their journey through the thickets of Middle East diplomacy. But he is relentless in separating the chaff from what is essential. These qualities will now stand him in good stead, for the protagonists
need to disenthrall themselves from the attitudes that have produced the impasse. . . ."[5]

Immediately after Rabin won the Knesset's vote of confidence, he got a congratulatory phone call from Bush. The president told the newly sworn-in prime minister that he was looking forward to working with him "to deepen U.S.-Israeli partnership and to promote the peace with security that the Israelis have rightly yearned for so long." Bush also informed Rabin that he was sending Secretary Baker to the Middle East, "next week," to get the ball rolling again on peace talks. Finally, Bush invited Rabin for further talks at his summer house in Kennebunkport, Maine, in early August.[6]

Bush welcomed Rabin's victory with great relief. After his tense relationship with Shamir, here was an Israeli leader with whom he could work easily. Bush was pleased that his strategy to help defeat Shamir, by denying him the $10 billion in loan guarantees and by publicly denouncing his settlement activity in the territories, had succeeded. And, what was more important, working closely with Rabin could help convince American Jewish voters that Bush was not anti-Israel, merely anti-Shamir.

Rabin knew Bush quite well, from the days when the president was the U.S. ambassador to the UN and the Israeli prime minister was the ambassador to Washington. Since then, they had met on several occasions, including once in Jerusalem, in July 1987, during the then vice president's Middle East tour. Rabin had always attached great importance to his relations with the United States and to the American role in the peace process. He was eager, therefore, to restore as soon as possible the good and trustful relationship that Israel had always had with all U.S. administrations. He said: "The more the U.S. can say it is bringing peace to the area—assisted by Israel acting in its own interest—the more Israel will serve the mutual interest, in creating stability and leaving less room for the extremists."[7]

Since Rabin's Knesset speech did not contain any specifics on Palestinian self-rule or on the Golan Heights, Arab leaders were now waiting to hear from Secretary Baker what direction Israel's peace policy would take. They especially feared that Rabin would strike a separate deal with the Palestinians, leaving behind Syria, Lebanon, and Jordan. King Hussein was so alarmed about such a possibility that on July 16, just three days before Baker's arrival, he flew to Latakia to meet with President Assad and to coordinate their positions. Watching this development, Rabin was not particularly alarmed. He was even encouraged by an intelligence report according to which both Assad and King Hussein were still opposed to an independent Palestinian state and also had reservations about an enhanced Egyptian role in the Arab-Israeli peace process.

Arab leaders did not have to wait for Baker's arrival in order to learn about Rabin's future policies. Among Israeli politicians, Rabin was unique in that what he said publicly during the election campaign was to become his official policy as prime minister. In his TV debate with Shamir, on June 16, 1992, Rabin stressed the following three points:

- No Palestinian state.

- No return to pre-1967 borders.

- A united Jerusalem, "Israel's eternal capital," under Israeli sovereignty.

In his address to Labor's Central Committee, on March 26, 1992, Rabin outlined his political platform as follows:

- A pledge to conclude an autonomy agreement with the Palestinians within a period of six to nine months. This period was later extended to nine to twelve months. As part of the autonomy agreement, there would be a complete demilitarization of the West Bank, so that between the Mediterranean and the Jordan River, no army other than the Israeli army would be deployed. Rabin explained that unlike Shamir, he would not object to a total separation between the Jordanian and the Palestinian delegations, instead of the faked "joint Jordanian-Palestinian delegation." He went on to say that after the agreement with the Palestinians, he would move quickly to negotiations with Jordan and then with Syria and Lebanon.

- A total freeze of all "political settlements" in densely populated Arab areas, but continuation of "security settlements" in Greater Jerusalem, the Jordan Valley, and the Golan Heights. Rabin assured the settlers that he would not uproot one single settlement. He said: "Settlers need not fear—I would not dry out their settlements. They will continue to be provided with security and municipal services. But I would not spend millions on expanding political settlements."

- A change in the order of national priorities. Money that was allocated to "political settlements" would now be directed to modernizing the infrastructure, mostly roads and communication systems; housing projects for new immigrants, young couples, and the underprivileged; expansion of schools and hospitals; and research and development in various high-tech fields.

A day earlier, on March 25, Rabin explained his settlement philosophy vis-à-vis the United States. Addressing a Labor rally in Jerusalem, he said: "I will not accept a U.S. linkage between the peace process and the $10 billion in loan guarantees. I cannot accept the condition that we cannot build Jewish neighborhoods in Jerusalem, or that we cannot expand existing settlements in the Jordan Valley, or on the Golan Heights. Based on my past experiences, I am confident that if the Americans are convinced that we are focusing only on Jerusalem and on our borders, it will be possible to reach an agreement with them."

Rabin was very explicit in his interpretation of Palestinian self-rule. In an interview with *Newsweek* on March 30, 1992, he said: ". . . They would run all their internal affairs. They would not have a foreign policy, or control of security and defense. . . ." Finally, on June 1, 1992, Rabin wrote in the *Jerusalem Post:* ". . . I am unwilling to give up one single inch of Israel's security. For the sake of peace, however, I am willing to give up many inches of sentiments and territory, as well as 1.7 million Palestinians. That's the whole doctrine in a nutshell. We seek a territorial compromise, which will bring peace with security, a lot of security. . . ."

In his determination to negotiate peace from a position of strength and regional superiority, Rabin had very good cards in his hand. These were:

- The impressive military might of Israel.

- The common Arab perception that Israel was a nuclear power.

- The unique Israeli relationship with the United States.

- A robust economy. The 5.5 million Israelis (of whom 800,000 are Israeli Arabs) produce $85 billion a year, more than the GNP of 75 million Egyptians, Syrians, Lebanese, Jordanians, and Palestinians combined.

- The absorption of more than 700,000 Soviet Jews, many of them scientists, doctors, engineers, and musicians. This outstanding elite of the collapsing Communist empire was absorbed in only seven years. With the anticipated $10 billion in loan guarantees, they were expected to be fully integrated into the Israeli society and economy before the end of the century.

- Finally, in the aftermath of the Cold War and the Madrid Peace Conference, the end of Israel's isolation in the international arena. Thirty-five countries—including Russia, China, and India—had resumed or established diplomatic relations with the Jewish state, and others were to follow very soon.

Rabin, however, was realist enough to understand that the dreams and aspirations of many in the Arab world had not changed. He also knew that to abandon the drums of war and pursue the promise of peace, he had to take risks and make considerable territorial concessions. Because of the good cards in his possession, he was prepared to take these risks. He was prepared to follow President Kennedy's maxim in his inaugural address: "Let us never negotiate out of fear, but let us never fear to negotiate."[8]

Unlike Shamir and Likud, Rabin and Peres shared the view that UN Resolution 242 meant territorial compromise, i.e., land for peace. They also shared
the view that the Madrid framework, according to which Israel was negotiating
simultaneously with all the Arab parties, was unlikely to succeed, because no
Arab negotiator would dare to express a moderate position in the presence of
the others, lest he be accused of "treason." Rabin was determined, therefore, to
try to separate the Arab delegations. He reasoned that each Arab party had its
own problems and might be encouraged to strike a separate deal. Rabin was
convinced that it was easier to solve the Jordanian and the Lebanese problems,
but King Hussein would not dare to move before the Palestinians, while
Lebanon was under total Syrian control. He therefore followed Ben-Gurion's
and Moshe Dayan's approach: dealing first with Egypt and leaving Syria to the
end. Having already concluded peace with Egypt, Israel should now concentrate on the Palestinian, then on the Jordanian problems and only at the end
deal with Syria and Lebanon. Events in the coming weeks, however, would
show that this negotiating strategy was not fully accepted by the United States,
and Rabin was ready to modify his position so as to strike a harmony with the
U.S. approach.

While Rabin and Peres agreed on the broad lines of the desired settlement
with the Palestinians, they differed in their tactical approach to this important
issue. Both Rabin and Peres knew, of course, that Shamir was negotiating indirectly with the PLO. If there was any doubt about it, this doubt was dispelled
five days before the Israeli elections. On Thursday, June 18, the Palestinian negotiating team, including Dr. Haidar Abdul Shafi, Hanan Ashrawi, and Faisal
Husseini, crossed into Jordan for a public meeting with Yasser Arafat in
Amman. The reason given for this unusual step was that the Palestinian negotiators wanted to congratulate Arafat on his recovery from surgery to remove a
cerebral blood clot. The meeting, in the presence of all members of the PLO
Executive Committee, was shown on Israeli TV. The meeting posed an embarrassing dilemma for the Likud. To arrest the Palestinians would risk unraveling
the entire process. To do nothing would mean recognizing the PLO role in the
Washington negotiations. "It's a provocation," commented Shamir. "A proper
response will be given in due course."[9] Shamir's aides said that if he had been
reelected, he would have thrown the entire negotiating team into prison. Concerned about such an outcome, American officials met with the Palestinians in
Amman and suggested they not return to Jerusalem before the Israeli elections.
Indeed, the Palestinians returned to the territories on June 29. They were arrested at the Allenby Bridge, but after a short interrogation they were all released.[10]

Based on this reality, Peres was ready to accept Arafat as a negotiating partner and to incorporate the PLO in the Washington negotiating team. Rabin was
opposed to this approach. He preferred to maintain the status quo, especially

since the 1986 Israeli law banning all contacts with the PLO was still in force. Rabin did not know at the time that while in the opposition, Yossi Beilin had already met twice with a Norwegian intermediary—in May and June 1992—and that a third meeting was due to take place in the near future, to prepare for the opening of a secret back channel to the Palestinians, in Oslo.

Secretary Baker arrived in Jerusalem on Sunday, July 19, the first stop in a tour that took him also to Jordan, Syria, Egypt, and Saudi Arabia. In advance of Baker's arrival, Benjamin (Fuad) Ben-Eliezer, the new Israeli housing minister and one of Rabin's most trusted allies in the Labor Party, announced a total freeze of all settlement activity in the territories. In his meeting with Baker, Rabin said that he was committed to stopping the building of new settlements, but because of natural growth and family reunifications, he would still need limited expansion of the existing settlements. Based on information supplied by Ben-Eliezer, Rabin gave Baker the following figures: sixty-five hundred new housing units that had been approved by the Shamir government but whose construction had not started would be canceled. On the other hand, about ten thousand units that were in various stages of completion would have to be completed. Baker agreed. It was a significant American gesture and it showed to what extent Bush was eager to strike a good working relationship with the new Rabin government. This was in sharp contrast to the president's tense relationship with Shamir. Eventually, and as a result of this Baker-Rabin understanding, the number of Israeli settlers in the West Bank and the Gaza Strip increased from 110,000 in 1992 to 145,000 in 1996.[11] Prime Minister Benjamin Netanyahu was to make good use of these figures when he met with President Clinton at the White House, in July 1996. In an answer to a question during a joint press conference with Clinton, Netanyahu said that he had shown these figures to the U.S. president and observed: "You certainly don't expect us [Likud] to do less than what Labor did. . . ."[12]

Rabin told Secretary Baker that unlike Shamir, who wanted to move the negotiations to Rome, he was prepared to keep Washington as the venue for the next round of the bilateral negotiations. He described his concept of Palestinian self-rule as including a "territorial element," and he defined the future agreement with the Palestinians as "more than an autonomy, but less than a sovereign state." Here again, Rabin's readiness to surrender territory in the West Bank and in the Gaza Strip was a clear departure from previous Likud policies.

Speaking about the Golan Heights, Rabin raised the idea that Israel would recognize Syrian sovereignty over this strategic plateau, but that in return Syria would lease it to Israel for an extended period. Rabin asked Baker to try to explore this idea in Damascus. As expected, President Assad rejected the Israeli proposal as a "nonstarter." Commenting on Rabin's idea, Issa Darwish, the Syrian ambassador to Cairo, said: "Is there really a sane leader who would lease his homeland to Israel?"[13] Syria's rejection of the "lease" idea was to be expected. In July 1978, during a meeting with President Sadat in Vienna, Shimon Peres, as head of the opposition, asked the Egyptian president if he would agree to lease the two newly built Israeli air bases in Sinai. Sadat said no. Peres asked the question at the request of Moshe Dayan, who was at the time Menachem Begin's foreign minister. Peres also asked Sadat if he would agree to leave the Israeli settlements in Sinai until the year 2010. Sadat replied angrily: "Never. I want you to know that I am a farmer, and to a farmer the land is sacred. I am ready to sell Israel water from the Nile, but not land. . . ."

In his analysis of the situation in the Middle East, Rabin told Baker that he was now prepared to take the risks of peace, because the regional balance of power was in Israel's favor. He feared, however, that within a decade, a Syria equipped with long-range Chinese-made ground-to-ground missiles, a rehabilitated Iraqi army, a nuclear Iran, and a region influenced by Islamic fundamentalism would pose new dangers to Israel. Hence, in negotiating peace, he had to take these dangerous possibilities into consideration. Baker did not challenge this analysis.[14]

The next day, July 20, Baker met in East Jerusalem with the group of Palestinian negotiators, including Faisal Husseini and Dr. Hanan Ashrawi. Baker was upbeat. He told the Palestinians that he had found Rabin very forthcoming and that it was now the Palestinians' turn to show flexibility. The Palestinians, however, came with a totally new set of demands. They said that it was now time for the United States to resume the dialogue with the PLO and to urge Israel to negotiate directly with Yasser Arafat. They expressed concern that before the U.S. presidential elections, President Bush would grant Israel the $10 billion in loan guarantees. They wanted the release of all Palestinian prisoners from Israeli detention camps, a total freeze on any settlement activity whether "political" or "security," and the lifting of all "economic restrictions," which the Palestinians called "collective punishment."

Baker was aware of this hardened Palestinian position even before he came to the region. He also knew that there were Palestinians, like Haidar Abdul Shafi, the head of the negotiating team in Washington, who favored suspension of the talks with the Israelis in the event Bush granted the loan guarantees to Rabin. Baker did not appear to be much concerned with this Palestinian extremism. The Palestinians were "too weak" to impose their position on the other Arab parties. Through normal Arab diplomatic channels, especially Egyptian, the United States conveyed to the Palestinians the message that it was time for them to back off from their maximalist positions. Bush wanted them to come forward with reasonable proposals to match Rabin's flexibility. Or, as one senior administration official put it: "The Arabs did their share to get the peace process started [in Madrid]. The fact is, however, that for the last eighteen months, they have been sitting on the fence, watching Bush fighting with

Shamir. It was a great show, but it's over and now the Arabs' moment of truth is coming. . . ."[15]

Indeed, at the end of his meeting with the Palestinians, Baker got what he wanted. The Palestinians would resume the negotiations in Washington. Baker had received similar promises from Jordan's King Hussein and Syria's President Assad. At the end of the trip, Baker was able to announce the resumption of the Washington talks on August 10. The date was later changed to August 24.

On July 21, while Baker was still in the area, talking to King Hussein and to President Assad, Rabin flew to Cairo for a meeting with President Mubarak. This was his first visit to Cairo as prime minister. The last meeting between Rabin and Mubarak had been in the summer of 1989, when as defense minister in Shamir's government, Rabin went to Cairo to work out a formula on the Palestinian representation in the peace process. The very fact that the Israeli prime minister went to Cairo even before he traveled to the United States was much appreciated by Mubarak. It showed that Rabin recognized Egypt's leading role in the Arab world and was aware of its contribution to the peace process. Here too, there was a clear departure from the policies of Shamir, who opposed an active Egyptian role in the peace process. Rabin knew that since the expulsion of the PLO from Beirut in 1982, Yasser Arafat had been totally dependent on Egypt. Hence, if Mubarak was able to moderate Arafat's positions, such a role would certainly help to advance the peace process.

Indeed, Mubarak was pleased with Rabin's visit. It enhanced Egypt's position in Washington and it signaled to the various Arab countries that Egypt's leading role could not be ignored. Rabin's visit was more than timely. Since Shamir's downfall, Mubarak had been trying to convene an Arab summit meeting to discuss future developments in the region. Saudi Arabia and Kuwait had rejected this Egyptian initiative. They had still not forgiven King Hussein and Yasser Arafat for their support of Saddam Hussein's invasion of Kuwait. Furthermore, President Assad and King Hussein were not very enthusiastic about an enhanced Egyptian role in the peace process. They suspected that Mubarak wanted to use them as a card in his negotiations with the United States for additional economic assistance. In appreciation of Rabin's gesture, Mubarak "reciprocated" by shielding his Israeli guest from the Egyptian media's harassment. Hence, when Rabin was asked by Egyptian correspondents about his past and present attitudes toward the Palestinians, Mubarak intervened by saying: "The man [Rabin] is only one week in office. Give him a chance. . . ."[16]

A few days after his return from Cairo, on August 9, Prime Minister Rabin left Israel for his meeting with President Bush at Kennebunkport. He was accompanied by his wife, Leah, and by a small group of aides. Shortly before he left for the United States, Rabin was faced with the dilemmas of domestic American politics. Israeli Ambassador to Washington Zalman Shoval sent him a "top secret" cable recommending that during his short visit to the United

States, he should also meet with the Democratic candidate, Bill Clinton.[17] Prominent American Jewish leaders who were active in the Democratic Party knew quite well—and so did Rabin—that in his efforts to win at least a portion of the American Jewish vote, Bush would now grant Rabin the $10 billion in loan guarantees that had been denied to Shamir. They were concerned that in return for such a "gift," Rabin would reciprocate by publicly praising Bush's positions on Israel, as Rabin had with President Nixon in 1972. Despite his impressive victory in the Persian Gulf War, Bush was facing serious economic problems and unemployment was on the rise. Many public opinion polls had shown that the president was trailing Clinton. Hence, many Jewish Democrats believed that there was now more than a fair chance that Clinton would become the next president of the United States, and they did not want Rabin to compromise that chance. One of those Jewish activists, attorney Stuart Eisenstadt, traveled several times to Jerusalem, met with Israeli officials and journalists, and tried to convince them that Clinton's pro-Israeli views were sincere, not just election rhetoric. Eisenstadt, who was later appointed by Clinton as the U.S. ambassador to Brussels and later became the deputy secretary of commerce, had several convincing cards at his hand: Just before the New York Democratic primary, Clinton addressed the Conference of Presidents of Major Jewish Organizations and committed himself for the first time to "a united Jerusalem under Israeli sovereignty." The Democratic platform on the Middle East, and especially the section on Jerusalem, was far more positive to Israel than the Republican platform. The Democrats recognized undivided Jerusalem as Israel's capital, and recommended moving the American embassy from Tel Aviv to Jerusalem. After he won the Democratic nomination, Clinton was scheduled to appear again before the Conference of Presidents in October, and was expected to pledge his total support of Israel and its security. "Many of the participants were very impressed by what Clinton had to say. He appeared to us very sincere," said Malcolm Hoenlein, the energetic executive vice chairman of the Conference of Presidents.[18]

Rabin was not totally convinced by these arguments, but he saw no reason not to meet with Governor Bill Clinton. However, as a confidence-building measure, Rabin informed Bush of his intended meeting with Clinton. "It's fine with me," Bush said.

As expected, Rabin's meeting with Bush was very successful and his welcome by American Jews was very warm. Under Shamir, American Jews were in constant conflict with the Bush administration. Now they felt great relief. They were not forced anymore to choose between their president and Israel. On August 11, at the conclusion of his two-day talks with the Israeli prime minister, Bush announced an agreement on the "principles" for granting Israel $10 billion in loan guarantees. "I am committed to assist Israel with the task of absorbing immigrants. I am delighted that we have agreed on an approach that would assist these new Israelis, without frustrating the search for peace. . . . The prime minister has persuaded me that Israel is sincere about peacemaking," Bush said. Asked to comment on Rabin's new policy, which made a distinction between "political" and "security" settlements, Bush said: "We see a very different approach to settlements. We salute the prime minister for his courage. I know it wasn't easy."

Briefing Israeli correspondents in Washington, Rabin said that the first installment of the loan guarantees would go into effect on October 1. In case of an "abuse," the president would suspend further installments, at his exclusive discretion. Any amount that was spent in the territories would be deducted from future installments. Without being specific, Rabin implied that money spent within the "municipal boundaries" of Jerusalem would not be deducted. This was a real victory for the new Israeli prime minister. In the past, in dealings with Shamir, Bush and Baker had insisted that the new Jewish neighborhoods surrounding Jerusalem were "occupied territory." That was the essence of the Baker-Levy agreement in the fall of 1990 on the grant of $400 million in loan guarantees.[19]

"I wasn't surprised that Bush granted Rabin the $10 billion in loan guarantees," said former prime minister Yitzhak Shamir. "The moment Rabin accepted the principle of land for peace, there was no problem anymore. That's what Bush wanted all along."[20]

Returning to Israel on August 14, Rabin set the peace wheels in motion. Despite his earlier reservations about negotiating simultaneously with all the Arab delegations in Washington, he was convinced by Secretary Baker and his peace team, headed by Dennis Ross, to keep the Madrid framework intact. They argued that it had taken many hours and much patience to put the Madrid procedures together. Should Rabin insist on changing the procedures, the Arab countries—and certainly Syria—would do the same, and the whole peace process would unravel. Baker did not say it explicitly, but Rabin understood that President Bush was desperate to resume the peace talks before the presidential elections, so that he could show a major foreign policy success. Rabin agreed, therefore, not only to resume the talks with all the parties, but also to accelerate the pace by holding two successive rounds of negotiations, until the second half of September—the eve of Rosh Hashanah, the Jewish New Year.

Rabin returned from Washington fully convinced that it would be tactically wrong to leave Syria outside the negotiations room. Even before he left for Washington, he had hinted at such an eventuality. In an Israeli TV interview on July 15, just two days after he became prime minister, Rabin revealed the contents of a discussion he had had during the elections campaign with settlers on the Golan Heights. He told them that he did not rule out a partial withdrawal from the strategic plateau. He explained to the settlers that in 1974, when Henry Kissinger negotiated the separation-of-forces agreement between Israel and Syria, he had agreed to return to Syria the city of Kuneitra. "For the return of Kuneitra, a stretch of land of two kilometers only, we had seventeen years of calm. Would I miss a similar opportunity in future? Of course not," Rabin said.[21] He made it clear, however, that even if there was a chance for a peace agreement with Syria, Israel would not come down from the Golan Heights.

Appearing before the Knesset's Foreign Affairs and Security Committee after his return from Washington, Rabin spoke about the resumption of the bilateral talks in the U.S. capital. He repeated his commitment not to withdraw totally from the Golan Heights, but added: "This does not mean that we have to cling to every centimeter of land there."[22]

Rabin wanted to meet with President Assad, publicly or in secret. He asked the United States, Egypt, and Morocco to propose such a meeting to the Syrian president. Morocco's King Hassan wanted Assad to meet with Rabin under his auspices in Rabat, just as he had arranged in 1977 the secret meeting of Moshe Dayan and an Egyptian envoy, prior to Sadat's historic visit to Jerusalem.[23] Assad rejected all these proposals. "It's too early now, maybe later . . ." Assad said.

Rabin spoke about his desire to advance the negotiations with Syria with former French prime minister Pierre Maurois, who had become the new chairman of the Socialist International. Rabin said: "At the beginning, I wanted to concentrate on the Palestinian track. After I detected some signs of moderation in Damascus, I changed my mind. Assad, especially, began to prepare his people for peace with Israel."[24] One of these signs of Syrian moderation was observed publicly in the United States. Addressing the annual meeting of the UN General Assembly in New York, Syrian Foreign Minister Faruq el-Shara'a proposed "total Israeli withdrawal, in return for full peace." El-Shara'a, however, did not explain what he meant by full peace, and he repeated the old Syrian position that Israel had to commit itself to total withdrawal before negotiating the nature of peace.

This being the case, Rabin made a very significant change in the composition of his negotiating teams. He appointed Professor Itamar Rabinovich, the rector of Tel Aviv University and a respected expert on Syria, as the head of the "Syrian team," succeeding Yossi Ben-Aharon, the director general of Shamir's prime minister's office. Rabinovich, who was also to succeed Ambassador Shoval as the Israeli ambassador to Washington, earned his Ph.D. from UCLA under the supervision of the late Professor Malcolm Kerr, the well-known American scholar in Middle Eastern studies who, as president of the American University in Beirut, was murdered a few years later by Hezbollah terrorists in Lebanon. Rabinovich wrote extensively on Syria, and his last book, *The Road Not Taken,* on missed opportunities with Syria, had been published in 1991. The very appointment of Rabinovich was a clear signal by Rabin to President Assad that Israel was sincere in its intentions to negotiate peace with him.

Rabin reappointed the cabinet secretary Elyakim (Eli) Rubenstein as the head of the Israeli team negotiating with Jordan and the Palestinians. Ambassador Uri Lubrani was reappointed as head of the team negotiating with Beirut. In reappointing Rubenstein and Lubrani, Rabin demonstrated how skillful he was in choosing his closest associates. Although he had "inherited" both Lubrani and Rubenstein from Shamir, Rabin did not consider them to be rightwing Likudniks. They were civil servants who rose to prominence under Labor governments—Lubrani since the days of Ben-Gurion and Rubenstein as a very close aide of Moshe Dayan. Lubrani, a former ambassador to Ethiopia, Uganda, and Iran, had been the coordinator of Israeli policy in Lebanon since the end of the war in that ravaged country in 1982. Rubenstein had participated in Dayan's secret meetings with Morocco's King Hassan and King Hussein, and, like Lubrani, he had skill and experience in negotiating sensitive issues. Like Rabinovitch, they were both experts in Middle Eastern affairs, and they understood the nuances and the double-talk that are so common in the Arab world. Nevertheless, Rubenstein's reappointment drew fire from both the Palestinians and Labor's doves. The Palestinians, in particular, had hoped that Rabin would choose one of "Peres's dovish boys" who were supportive of a dialogue with the PLO and of the establishment of a Palestinian state. When this did not happen, they accused Rabin of being no different from Shamir. The effort to circumvent the Washington talks, in the direction of Oslo, was now accelerated.

As a goodwill gesture toward the Palestinians, Rabin released eight hundred Palestinian prisoners who had been involved in various activities of the intifada. He also canceled the deportation of eleven Hamas activists, which had been ordered by his predecessor, Moshe Arens, but been suspended following the sharp condemnation of Israel by the UN Security Council. Rabin set target dates for agreements with the Palestinians: December 1, 1992—an agreement on the elections procedures; February 1, 1993—an agreement on the jurisdiction of PISGA (Palestine Interim Self-Governing Authority); May 1993—elections to PISGA.

Rabin now had one serious problem to overcome—himself. Rabin had spent most of his career in the army, fighting successfully against the Arabs. He disliked the Palestinians and he hated Yasser Arafat. In recent years, especially since the intifada, he had gradually changed his positions, but his basic attitude remained resentment and contempt. As a matter of fact, until the intifada in December 1987, he had not meet with the Palestinians even once, although he had been a defense minister who controlled their lives for so many years. The Palestinians felt Rabin's resentment, and they hated him too. For them, he was the "bone breaker," the defense minister they loved to hate.

Having known both Moshe Dayan and Yitzhak Rabin, I can't resist the temptation of comparing their attitudes toward the Palestinians. Like Rabin,

Dayan fought the Arabs most of his life. Unlike Rabin, however, Dayan spoke Arabic, showed respect for the Arab culture, and did not treat the Palestinians with contempt. He spent days with the various Palestinian leaders in the West Bank and the Gaza Strip, trying to understand their problems and overcome obstacles. I remember one day, in the fall of 1968, when Nablus was under curfew because of a mini-uprising in the city. Dayan spent hours with the nationalist poet Fadwa Tukan, trying to understand the source of her hatred of Israel and the Jews. He was also eager to explain to her how wrong she was about Israel and the Zionist movement. Although a hawk, Dayan sided with the liberals, before the Six-Day War, who opposed Ben-Gurion's policies of restricting the movements of Israeli Arabs and controlling their lives through military government. Dayan went even further. Contrary to the advice of the security services, he invited Israeli Arabs and Palestinian leaders from the West Bank and the Gaza Strip to the marriage of his daughter, Yael. Except for Dayan and Yigal Allon, no other Israeli leader opened his house for Arab guests, whether socially or in family events. The Palestinians responded in kind: They feared Dayan, but respected him very much.

Rabin was totally different. He was not creative and original as Dayan was. He had trouble getting close to the Palestinians. Not only did he not speak their language, he had difficulty understanding their mentality and adjusting to their customs. He didn't understand their nuances and their double-talk. After the intifada broke out in December 1987, it took him six months to understand that it was not a passing phenomenon, but a general uprising of a people that had nothing to lose. He then came to the conclusion that there was no military solution to the intifada, and that Israel wouldn't be able to continue to rule 1.5 million Palestinians while denying them political rights. He then started talking about a two-stage solution: first an end to violence, and then negotiations with the local Palestinian leadership.

Two people are to be credited with the gradual change in Rabin's positions—Shmulik Goren, a veteran of the intelligence community who later became the coordinator of Israeli policies in the territories; and especially General (Res.) Ephraim Sneh, the head of the civil administration in the West Bank. Sneh was the son of the late Moshe Sneh, the former chief of staff of the Haganah, the Israeli underground during the British Mandate, who, after the establishment of the State of Israel, moved from the center right to the extreme left, then to the Communist Party. Like his father, Ephraim had studied medicine. He had participated in the daring Israeli commando raid on Entebbe and fought in Lebanon. Short and heavily built, Sneh was fluent in Arabic and had a good reputation among the Palestinians. He had left the army because of policy differences with Likud's defense minister, Moshe Arens. He joined the Labor Party and became the minister of health in Rabin's government. It was in his capacity as administrator of the West Bank that he had persuaded Defense Minister Rabin to start meeting with the local Palestinian leadership if he did not want to negotiate with the PLO.

The first meetings were a disaster. According to both Goren and Sneh, Rabin was not "Mr. Nice Guy"—he was cool, he hardly smiled at the Palestinians—but he understood their plight and he was genuinely looking for a solution. Gradually, Rabin's attitude toward the PLO began to change. The pragmatist Rabin understood that once the United States opened its dialogue with the PLO, in December 1988, Israel too would have to accept this new reality. He knew that even after the suspension of the official dialogue with the PLO, in June 1990, the United States had continued its contacts with Arafat, not only through the CIA, but also through Egypt, Morocco, and Tunisia and through the Palestinians in the West Bank. Rabin was therefore prepared to accept this American formula of indirect contact with Arafat, and to withhold the formal recognition of the PLO as a bargaining card in future negotiations. This cautious approach was in sharp contrast to Peres's position. The Israeli foreign minister, who was influenced by Egypt and by the Europeans, was ready to recognize the PLO and to negotiate directly with Yasser Arafat. He was to translate this position into a political deed, through his secret channel to Oslo.

Shortly after Baker's visit to the Middle East and Rabin's return from his successful trip to the United States, Russian President Boris Yeltsin sent his deputy foreign minister for Middle Eastern affairs, Victor Posavaliuk, to the region. Despite his pressing domestic problems, Yeltsin responded favorably to President Bush's request and sent Posavaliuk in an effort to moderate the positions of the Syrians and the Palestinians. Posavaliuk, fifty-five, was a graduate of the prestigious Moscow Center for Middle East Studies, which had formerly trained Soviet spies for duties in the Arab world. The incumbent Russian foreign minister, Yevgeny Primakov, was also a graduate of that school. Posavaliuk was fluent in Arabic and had served as ambassador to Jordan and Iraq. One of his classmates at Moscow's Middle East Center was the Russian opposition leader Vladimir Zhirinovsky, who had studied Turkish language and history. In discussions with senior officials in Jerusalem, Damascus, and Tunis, Posavaliuk explained that in the aftermath of the Cold War, Russian Middle Eastern policy was based on cooperation and not on confrontation. He did not think that improving relations with Israel should adversely affect Russian relations with the Arab world, and vice versa. He invited Israeli Foreign Minister Shimon Peres, Syrian Foreign Minister Faruq el-Shara'a, and PLO executive Abu Mazen to discussions in Moscow in the second half of August. In an interview with a Lebanese paper published in London, Posavaliuk said that the purpose of the discussions between Russian Foreign Minister Andrei Kozyrev and Peres, el-Shara'a, and Abu Mazen was to encourage them to show more flexibility in the bilateral negotiations in Washington.[25] Peres, however, used this occasion to urge Kozyrev to use Russia's influence in

Damascus to persuade President Assad to end his boycott of the multilateral negotiations and to participate in the five committees that were discussing regional cooperation in various fields. Syria refused. Israeli diplomatic reports from Moscow attributed Kozyrev's failure to some contradictions in the Russian policy toward Syria. While Yeltsin and Kozyrev were more pro-American and wanted Syria to participate in the multilateral committees, Yeltsin's rival at the time, Vice President Aleksandr Rutskoy, supported Syria's hard line toward Israel.

Shortly afterward, the old strains between Peres and Rabin had begun to surface again. Despite their effort to work in harmony, their old rivalry was revived. It was not public, nor acrimonious as in the past. Yet, it was evident to everyone who knew both of them. Peres, in particular, was bitter and depressed. He felt that he had been unjustly removed from the chairmanship of the party and as a result had lost his chance to be the prime minister again. He was sure that after the historic changes in the international scene, he was better qualified than Rabin to meet the challenges of the new world order.

In the past, at the peak of their rivalry, Rabin and Peres had not spoken to each other for four years, from 1977 to 1981. Even now, in 1992, they were constantly on each other's mind. Peres, however, much more restrained and more composed, would tell his supporters: "It's true we don't like each other, but we both abide by party discipline. After all, we are not serving an ego, we are serving a country." Peres was experienced enough to understand that reviving the old public rivalry with Rabin would destroy both of them. Therefore, Peres instructed his staff: "I want full cooperation with the prime minister's office. Everything should be coordinated. We don't need public confrontations anymore." That instruction proved to be very difficult to follow. Being excluded from the bilateral peace negotiations, Peres felt he was "exiled" from his own government. In an effort to console himself, he told friends and close associates that the bilateral negotiations were meant to solve problems of the past, while the multilateral negotiations, which were now his responsibility, would create the future.

One must admit that in addition to the differences in their personalities, Rabin and Peres differed in their political philosophies. Peres belonged to the group of politicians and scholars who believed that after the Cold War, military power was no longer the dominant key to peace and stability among nations. Economic power was the key. Owing to modern technologies, the "costs of wars"—not only in terms of human losses but also in economic expenditures—had become so costly that small nations could not afford wars anymore. Hence, the whole concept of balance of power had to be revised, giving preference to geo-economics over geo-strategy. Peres thought that in an era of peace, nations should beat their swords into microchips and . . . tourism. Peres gave expression to this belief in his recently published book *Battling for Peace*. He wrote:

"Today more than ever, the measure of a country's strength is not just how many troops it has, but how many tourists. . . ."[26]

Indeed, the moment he assumed the responsibility for the five multilateral committees (arms control, economic cooperation, water resources, environment, and refugees), Peres started traveling all over the world, promoting ideas about joint Israeli-Arab development projects to be financed by the big industrialized nations. Within a relatively short period, Peres traveled to Russia, France, Great Britain, the United States, Egypt, and Canada. In discussions with skeptical world leaders, he tried to sell his ideas about a "New Middle East." His "vision" was that regional development projects would eventually break the deadlock in the bilateral negotiations as well.

In his book *The New Middle East*[27] and in public speeches, Peres explained that he was trying to recruit the financial support of the European Community, Japan, and the oil-rich Persian Gulf countries for projects ranging from a Middle East development bank to a water desalination plant in the Gaza Strip that would be powered by a nuclear reactor. He wanted to computerize the public schools in the Arab world and to construct a net of regional superhighways that would link all countries of the region. In an effort to solve the shortage of water resources, Peres suggested that Turkey sell water to countries like Israel and Jordan and that desalination plants be built. Peres believed that creating a new economic dynamism would allow the opening of the borders to free trade and tourism; the standard of living in the region would constantly improve and would permit headway in the territorial dispute as well.[28]

The trouble with this vision was that Syria and Lebanon—the two most important links in this chain—were not participating in the multilateral track. President Assad had already made this very clear in Madrid. Assad had told Secretary Baker that he would not discuss regional cooperation unless Israel committed itself to a total withdrawal from the Golan Heights. Neither Shamir nor Rabin was willing to give Assad such a commitment before he defined the nature of peace that he would give in return. Undeterred by the "stubbornness" of both Assad and Rabin, Peres continued to travel, marketing his ideas to any world leader who would listen. Peres asked French President Mitterrand to urge Assad to join the multilaterals. He also suggested raising the level of the steering committee of the multilateral negotiations to that of foreign ministers, instead of senior officials, so that he personally could participate. Assad refused. "We were looking all the time for countries to invite Peres and to listen to his ideas," senior foreign ministry officials told me at the time. "Abroad, he felt terrific. Here at the office, he was eating his heart out because he was not involved in the Washington negotiations. We simply could not watch him suffering. Such a creative man, and yet in such a political desert. . . ."

The problem, however, with Peres's ideas was that he ignored two basic facts:

- The oil-rich Persian Gulf countries were not prepared to share their wealth with the poorer and more populous Arab countries. Since Egypt's President Gamal Abdel Nasser raised, in the mid-fifties, his slogan "Arab wealth—to all Arab nations," Persian Gulf countries had preferred to be protected by their Western customers rather than by their Arab brothers. Over the past thirty years, those countries had contributed large amounts of money to the Palestinian terrorist groups and to both Egypt and Syria. These amounts, however, were more "protection money" than genuine investment in the development of those countries.

- All Arab countries—including Egypt, with which Israel had signed a peace treaty in March 1979—were still suspicious of Israel and of its ambitions in the area. Therefore it would be a mistake for Israel to lead such an effort of change and modernization in the Arab world. Israel would be regarded as a "tool of imperialism" and would become the scapegoat for corrupt Arab rulers who were incapable of improving the standard of living of their own peoples.

In contrast to Peres, the "dreamer and visionary," Rabin, the pragmatist and military strategist, remained also the political realist. Despite the end of the Cold War, Rabin still considered geo-strategy and not geo-economics the key to regional balance of power and political stability in the area. He did not ignore, of course, the fact that in the aftermath of the demise of the Soviet empire, military threats on a global scale had diminished. However, the dangers of local and ethnic wars had increased. Bosnia, Somalia, and the Iraqi invasion of Kuwait were only the most recent examples. Therefore, matters related to national security were still Rabin's highest priority in absolute terms.

This conflicting perception of geo-strategy versus geo-economics resulted in two different approaches to the peace process. Peres accepted the Egyptian and the European view that the Palestinian problem was the key to the Arab-Israeli conflict. In a private discussion with Rabin, in August 1992, Peres suggested reconsidering the Israeli position on the PLO and negotiating directly with Arafat. Rabin refused. After his return from Washington, Rabin aligned himself with the American view that there could be no comprehensive peace in the region without Syria. While both Rabin and Peres shared the view that Syria should be left to the end, they differed sharply on tactics. After his lengthy discussions with Secretary Baker's peace team, Rabin became convinced that Syria should not be left out and that President Assad should get the feeling that the bilateral negotiations in the United States were sincere. Peres, on the contrary, believed that peace in the region could be achieved even without Syria. Challenging a statement by Henry Kissinger that there could be no war without

Egypt and no peace without Syria, Peres wrote in his 1995 memoir that he was not certain if this axiom was ever true. He said: ". . . there can be peace, or beginning of peace, without Syria . . . and there can be a war without Egypt. Today, the Syrian threat to Israel is greatly reduced. The Syrians have suffered a string of setbacks. Their army is dug into line after line of fortifications, stretching back more than thirty-five miles from the Golan Heights to Damascus. . . ."[29]

Rabin's attempt to move cautiously in the direction of Syria made Arafat nervous and Mubarak uneasy. Both feared that Rabin would strike a separate deal with Assad, leaving the Palestinians behind. Both wished Peres were the prime minister of Israel. A senior Egyptian diplomat in Tel Aviv put it to me very bluntly: "Rabin's efforts in the direction of Syria are unlikely to succeed. The emphasis should remain on the Palestinians. We [Egypt] must find a way to bring Peres into the bilateral track. If Rabin alone would continue to handle the bilateral negotiations, there would be no movement in the peace process. Rabin would become another Shamir. That's not good."[30] The Egyptian diplomat's view was shared by West Bank Palestinians and by the PLO leadership in Tunis. Thus, Peres's "Palestinian preference" and Egypt's and the PLO's determination to discredit Rabin's understanding with President Bush regarding Syria had set the stage for the secret Oslo channel.

Contrary to all published reports suggesting that the preparations for the Oslo channel began in September 1992, it is now confirmed that the idea was first suggested to Knesset member Yossi Beilin in May 1992. Terje Rod Larsen, the director of FAFO, a Norwegian research organization, conducted in 1991 a field research in the refugee camps of the Gaza Strip. Professor Yair Hirschfeld, a dovish Labor activist and a member of Mashov, the elitist, left-wing, and pro-Palestinian group created by Beilin within the Labor Party, was partly involved in Larsen's research. In a meeting in Tel Aviv with both Beilin and Hirschfeld, Larsen suggested that should Labor win the June general elections, he could help open a secret channel of communication with the PLO in Tunis.[31] Since that meeting, Larsen had become a key player in the secret Oslo channel. Larsen, forty-eight, had been born in Bergen to a family of fishermen. In 1982, while teaching at the University of Oslo, the tall, blond, handsome lecturer met Mona Juul, his student, eleven years younger. They fell in love. He divorced his wife to start a new life with Mona Juul. After graduating, she joined the Norwegian foreign service, and in 1990 she was assigned to Cairo. Larsen joined his wife, and it was during that period that he started conducting his research, on behalf of FAFO, on the living conditions of the Palestinian refugees in the Gaza Strip. The work earned him the praise of the UN and also the trust and confidence of the Palestinians.

In mid-June 1992, just a few days before the general elections, Larsen returned to Israel. The chances for a Labor victory were quite promising. In a meeting at the American Colony Hotel in East Jerusalem with Beilin, Hirschfeld, and Palestinian activist Faisal Husseini, Larsen again suggested opening a back channel in Oslo for negotiations with the PLO. Larsen's idea was that the Oslo channel would not replace the public bilateral negotiations in Washington but would complement them. Whatever was concluded in Oslo would be submitted to the Washington teams for formal approval. Beilin and Husseini endorsed this idea. In that meeting in East Jerusalem it was also agreed that should Beilin be appointed by Rabin and Peres to a position that would enable him to be involved in the peace process, both he and Faisal Husseini would handle the Oslo back channel.

It was not the first time that Beilin and Faisal Husseini had met. Professor Hirschfeld, whose specialty was the Middle East, maintained close contacts with the local Palestinian leadership in the territories. In August 1990, while Labor was still in the opposition, Hirschfeld had arranged for Beilin to meet at the Hotel Notre Dame in Jerusalem with Faisal Husseini, Hanan Ashrawi, and Dr. Sari Nusseibeh, a moderate Palestinian intellectual and a professor at Bir Zeit University, near Ramallah, whose Jerusalem family held important positions under the British mandate and the Jordanian rule. Since that meeting, Beilin and Husseini had met several times, once at Husseini's home in East Jerusalem.

Shortly after the elections, when Beilin became deputy foreign minister under Peres, the efforts to open the secret channel to the PLO in Oslo resumed. In a meeting in Jerusalem in August 1992, Sari Nusseibeh told Yair Hirschfeld that the bilateral negotiations with the Palestinians in Washington would lead nowhere. If the new Labor government was sincere in its desire to reach an agreement with the Palestinians, it had to do three things: talk to Arafat, as an expression of recognition of the PLO; talk to Abu Mazen, as the coordinator of the negotiations with Israel; and talk officially to Faisal Husseini, as the uncontested Palestinian leader in the West Bank and as the possible back-channel negotiator.[32]

Beilin brought the Hirschfeld-Nusseibeh discussion to Peres's attention. In his meeting with Rabin, Peres suggested that he would meet with Faisal Husseini. Rabin refused. Had Rabin agreed to a Peres-Husseini meeting, it could have legitimized future meetings between Beilin and Husseini, and possibly other PLO representatives, in Oslo. As a matter of fact, and while the Israeli and Palestinian teams were negotiating in Washington, Jan Egland, the Norwegian deputy foreign minister, came to Israel to discuss the back channel in Oslo. He was accompanied by Larsen and his wife, Mona Juul, who was also Egland's secretary. After being hosted at an "official" dinner by his Israeli counterpart, Yossi Beilin, Egland, Larsen, Mona Juul, Beilin, and Hirschfeld moved to a second hotel, where they had a "business meeting" on Palestinian matters. It was at that meeting that the opening of the back channel in Oslo was decided.

Egland informed the gathering that the Norwegian government would cover all the expenses related to the Oslo initiative.

Rabin's refusal to allow a meeting between Peres and Husseini forced Beilin to look for an alternative PLO representative. In a meeting with Hirschfeld, Hanan Ashrawi suggested a little-known PLO banker, Ahmed Qrei, better known by his nom de guerre, Abu Ala. It was an excellent suggestion. Ahmed Qrei was appointed by Arafat as the coordinator of the five Palestinian teams in the Multilateral Track. As such he became Beilin's counterpart in that track. Meetings between them, in the context of the Multilateral Track steering committee, would look "natural" and would not arouse suspicions. Qrei, who is currently the chairman of the newly elected Palestinian legislature in the territories, had never been personally involved in terrorist activity. Born in 1938 in the small village of Abu Dis, near Jerusalem, he had been in Saudi Arabia when the Six-Day War of 1967 broke out. He joined the PLO and a few years later became Arafat's financial adviser, and as such he also headed the PLO investment corporation. Bald, witty, and gifted with a sense of humor, he was among those who supported a political solution with Israel, and he was known to have the full confidence of Abu Mazen. Thus he was fully qualified for the discreet behind-the-scenes negotiations with Israel. However, since the next meeting of the steering committee was to be held in London in early December, the first contact with Abu Ala would be made only then. Beilin claims that this behind-the-scenes effort with the Norwegians and the Palestinians was made without Peres's knowledge. Others, who are familiar with the intimate and trustful relationship between Peres and Beilin, doubt that very much. They believe that Beilin was only shielding Peres from the accusation that he was "again subverting" Rabin and working behind his back.

The secret agreement between Beilin and the Norwegians on a back channel in Oslo had an immediate effect on the sixth round of the bilateral negotiations, which opened in Washington on August 24, 1992. It was the first round held under the new Labor government in Israel, and it lasted one month, with a short recess for the Jewish High Holidays, in September. The talks opened in a hopeful and positive tone. Realizing that there would shortly be secret negotiations between Israel and the PLO in Oslo, Arafat and Abu Mazen instructed their team in Washington to be forthcoming and cooperative. During the first phase of this round, which lasted until September 4, both Israel and the Palestinians submitted their own proposals for an agenda. In an interview with a Lebanese daily printed in London, Abu Mazen said that the gaps between the two proposals were not "unbridgeable" and expressed the hope that the two parties would soon agree on a joint agenda and on the sequence of the subjects to be discussed.[33] Abu Mazen stressed, however, that the PLO rejected Rabin's repeated emphasis on Jerusalem as the "eternal capital" of Israel and also rejected Rabin's distinction between "political" and "security" settlements. He said that during his recent visit to Moscow, he had given Russian Foreign Minister Andrei Kozyrev a copy of the proposed Palestinian agenda.

This relaxed atmosphere found its expression also on the ground. There were no more massive anti-Israeli demonstrations, fewer Israeli cars were stoned in the territories, the stores were opened, and the prices of land and houses in the West Bank and the Gaza Strip were soaring. Newly confident Palestinians were spending more money, buying new cars and home appliances. The hope for an early political settlement led Faisal Husseini and Dr. Sari Nusseibeh to assemble a group of three hundred scholars and technocrats to prepare a blueprint for the future self-governing authority. The group, which was backed up by legal advisers, was divided into thirty-nine teams, all working on a voluntary basis, at the Orient House.

A senior member in the Israeli negotiating team cautioned, however, that despite the relaxed atmosphere in Washington, the differences in the basic positions of the parties remained unchanged. Israelis and Palestinians differed, for example, on the issue of the elections to the legislative body and on jurisdiction over land and water resources. The Palestinians wanted the legislative body to have a broad power that would enable it to become a constituent assembly of an independent Palestinian state. The same applied to the jurisdiction over land and water resources. Israel opposed both demands. The Palestinians also wanted the Palestinian police to be recruited not only from among the local residents of the territories but also from the already trained members of the Palestinian forces scattered among several Arab countries. Eventually, and in a mutual effort to end this phase of the negotiations in a "positive" tone, both sides agreed to concentrate at this stage on the proposed agenda and to leave the tough issues of Jerusalem, settlements, and the final boundaries to the "final status" negotiations.

The United States was much pleased with the slow progress made in Washington and was "cautiously optimistic" that such progress would continue. Addressing the annual convention of the Arab lobby in Washington, Assistant Secretary of State for Middle Eastern Affairs Eduard Djeredjian said that despite the existing gap in the positions of both Israel and the Palestinians, "the prospect for the Palestinians to attain self-rule became a real possibility."[34]

In advance of the resumption of the Washington talks, after the Jewish High Holidays in September and at the request of Secretary Baker, Russian Foreign Minister Kozyrev sent Arafat a personal letter urging him to accept Israel's proposal for an agenda and also the broad lines of the self-governing authority. Kozyrev implied that should Arafat reject the Israeli proposal, Moscow might not grant the PLO representative in Moscow diplomatic recognition as ambassador.[35]

Before they returned to Washington, members of the Israeli team were briefed by Rabin. The Israeli prime minister told Eli Rubenstein and his deputy, Eitan Bentsur, the deputy director general of the foreign ministry: "I want you to keep the ball rolling all the time. I guess this round would be the last before the U.S. presidential elections. Even so, don't act in a manner that would halt the negotiations. You have to be extremely patient. Try to avoid bogging down on principle issues. On the contrary, try to seek formulae that would be fair to both sides. Just keep up the momentum. . . ."[36]

As a gesture of goodwill and as a sign of moderation, Israel allowed Faisal Husseini to participate in the ninety-eighth session of the Arab League Foreign Ministers Council, held in Cairo on September 14. That was the first time that a Palestinian from the territories, especially from East Jerusalem, had been permitted to attend an Arab League meeting. Husseini urged the Arab foreign ministers to support the Palestinian claim to East Jerusalem. He said that the Washington negotiations were aimed to take "full control" of the West Bank and the Gaza Strip and not just limited administrative powers.[37]

Despite this Israeli gesture, however, the Palestinians returned to Washington with a hardened negotiating position. Contrary to Rabin's instructions to his team to "keep the ball rolling," Arafat's instructions ensured that no progress would be possible. Aware, of course, of Rabin's veto on meetings with Husseini, Arafat feared that the Norwegian effort for a back channel in Oslo would be put off indefinitely and there would be no recognition of the PLO in the near future.

On September 18, 1992, the Israeli negotiating team in Washington made public its ten-page proposal for a Palestinian Interim Self-Governing Authority (PISGA). It said that the purpose of the negotiations was to establish PISGA for an interim period of five years. The interim arrangements would create a new climate for future negotiations on the final status, without prejudging the outcome of these negotiations. Members of PISGA would be elected by the Palestinians in the territories. PISGA would consist of fifteen members whose jurisdictions would be in the fields of justice, agriculture, environment, finance (taxation and budget), health, industry, commerce, labor, police, transportation, communications, municipal affairs, religious affairs, social affairs, and tourism. Security, foreign affairs, Israeli settlements, and "interests vital to Israel" would remain in Israel's hands during the interim period. Israel suggested that the negotiations on the election procedures would be concluded in December 1992, negotiations on PISGA's jurisdiction would begin in February 1993, and the elections to PISGA would be held in April or May 1993.[38]

By the terms of this document, the PLO was excluded from participation in PISGA, "security settlements" were not precluded, PISGA would have no authority in Jerusalem, and the elected body would have administrative powers and no legislative jurisdiction. The Palestinians countered immediately with a proposal of their own for PISGA. They wanted an elected body with broad powers, close to a sovereign state, and a legislative body of 180 members. They insisted also on jurisdiction over land and water resources. Finally, they asked for the dissolution of two elite Israeli army units—Shimshon and Duvdevan—whose sole duty was to track down the intifada activists. The soldiers and officers in these two units spoke Arabic and, disguised as Arabs, arrested and sometimes killed intifada leaders. Both Dennis Ross and Eli Rubenstein told the Palestinians that those subjects were not relevant to the interim negotiations.[39]

In an effort to avoid a total collapse of the negotiations, American officials warned the Palestinians that nobody could predict what would happen after the presidential elections. If the Arabs continued to waste time and would not get down to substance, they were likely to lose the only honest broker they had—Jim Baker.[40]

But Arafat was in no mood to compromise. He worried that Israel and Syria were about to strike a separate deal, leaving the Palestinians behind. Once the head of the Israeli negotiating team with Syria, Professor Itamar Rabinovich, told his Syrian counterpart, Ambassador Muwaffaq Allaf, that Israel recognized that there was a "territorial aspect" to a possible settlement with Damascus, the Palestinians were certain that there was more than met the eye. The Palestinians' suspicions increased amid reports that the United States, Morocco, and Saudi Arabia were trying to arrange a summit meeting between Rabin and President Assad in Washington. The rumors were so persistent that on September 21 the Syrian embassy in Washington published a formal denial, stating that "there are no plans for President Assad to meet with Prime Minister Rabin, in Washington, at the present time."[41]

On September 21, 1992, the Palestinians submitted to the Israelis a new memorandum, suggesting dealing with the issues of Jerusalem, Jewish settlements, and boundaries.[42] These issues had been raised by the Palestinians in the past and been rejected by both Israel and the United States as being irrelevant to the interim negotiations. The very fact that the Palestinians raised them again proved that the PLO had reached the conclusion that the sixth round of negotiations between Israel and the Palestinians in Washington was about to fail. Acting upon instructions from Jerusalem, the head of the Israeli team, Eli Rubenstein, initiated a private, informal meeting with his Palestinian counterpart, Dr. Haidar Abdul Shafi. They both agreed that once the principle of formal negotiations was established and the psychological barrier was broken, it would be better to move to secret talks, away from the TV cameras and the daily press briefings. Secret talks would enable the parties to speak freely, off-the-record, and to exchange views, explore ideas, and identify areas of difficulties. Rubenstein and Abdul Shafi met privately three times, but they could not break the deadlock. Abdul Shafi wanted a formal Israeli recognition of the PLO. This Rubenstein could not promise.

The sixth round of the Washington negotiations ended with no breakthrough on any front. On September 23, Rabin asked Justice Minister David

Libai to delay his proposed legislation abrogating the 1986 law that banned all contacts with the PLO. "The time is not yet ripe for such a legislation," Rabin told Libai. That same day, Arafat accused Rabin of being "the other face of Shamir's coin."[43] The discrediting of Rabin had begun. In a meeting with the Chinese foreign minister in Jerusalem, Faisal Husseini said: "Contrary to his public statements, Rabin's policies are not different from those of Shamir." Dr. Nabil Shaath, the PLO coordinator of the Palestinian negotiating team in Washington, told a group of Arab correspondents: "Rabin got everything from President Bush—a meeting at Kennebunkport, the $10 billion in loan guarantees, a commitment to maintain Israel's qualitative superiority, and a public recognition that Rabin is 'a man of peace.' There is nothing more that Bush can offer to Israel. Since Rabin has nothing to gain anymore, he has no reason to become less intransigent."[44]

The discrediting of Rabin was part of a vast Egyptian-Palestinian campaign—indirectly supported by Israeli doves—to force Peres's involvement in the bilateral negotiations. In an interview with MENA, the Egyptian-owned Middle East News Agency, Munzir Dajani (Abu el-Izz), the PLO "ambassador" in Algiers, said: "Shamir's proposals for self-rule were more generous than those proposed by Rabin. If Israel will not moderate its positions, it would be fair to say that contrary to its pretense, Rabin's government is a 'cabinet of war' and not a 'government of peace.' "[45]

This hardened Palestinian position led to an impassioned plea from Eli Rubenstein to Abdul Shafi and his team: "Don't miss this historic occasion that Israelis and Palestinians are sitting around the same table. We have no hidden agenda. We came to negotiate with you seriously and in good faith. You can only gain from this process." The same message was conveyed to the Palestinians by U.S. Assistant Secretary of State Ed Djeredjian. He said: "You are hurting only yourselves. You are wasting your time on issues that are irrelevant to this phase of the negotiations."[46]

The Madrid Peace Conference in October 1991 had been one of the major foreign affairs achievements of the Bush administration, but after six rounds of talks in Washington, the peace process did not seem to be going anywhere. Both Bush and Secretary Baker were determined to crown their effort with some kind of breakthrough. As head of the U.S. delegation to the UN General Assembly, Secretary Baker met in New York with Foreign Minister Peres and with the foreign ministers of Egypt, Syria, and Lebanon. He urged them to make a last effort to achieve progress in the bilateral negotiations in Washington, before the U.S. presidential elections in November. Peres suggested another round of negotiations in Washington, on October 21. The Arab foreign ministers, however, were not very enthusiastic about this idea, though they did not reject it. Reporting to the cabinet on the Washington negotiations, Rabin said that because of the presidential elections in the United States, the peace process would now be put on hold until after the inauguration of the new administration, in January 1993. Reporting to Labor's Knesset faction, Rabin expressed some frustration with the negligible results of the Washington talks. He said: "We have given the Palestinians plenty of hints that we're serious. The trouble is that the Palestinians have no clear address and no coherent leadership. . . ."[47]

Despite the fact that the seventh round of bilateral negotiations was scheduled to reconvene in Washington on October 21, world public opinion had turned to the presidential campaign in the United States. What was becoming clearer every day was that many U.S. allies, mostly European countries and Japan, had set aside their traditional preference for Republican realism in foreign affairs. Like many world leaders, Rabin too was beginning to lose faith in President Bush's ability to win a second term. Rabin was intrigued by a report from one of the Israeli ambassadors in Europe indicating that the world's major industrial powers were not making any effort to help Bush's reelection. The confidential report said that while in 1988 both Germany and Japan helped strengthen the dollar, the Bundesbank in Germany had now rejected a Bush request to lower interest rates, while Japan refused to take action to reduce its huge trade surplus with the United States.

The Arab countries were the exception. In appreciation of President Bush's role in the Persian Gulf War, Kuwait had reversed an earlier decision to buy British tanks and decided to buy American tanks instead. Saudi Arabia, although short of cash, decided to buy seventy-two F-15 fighter-bombers. Syria's President Assad showed his goodwill by accepting to reconvene for a new round of negotiations in Washington, while President Mubarak undertook to persuade Arafat to do the same.

In a last effort to win a share of the American Jewish vote, President Bush promised Prime Minister Rabin to sell Israel top-of-line Apache attack helicopters and Black Hawk transport helicopters, and to preposition a larger quantity of U.S. military equipment in Israel. In a telephone conversation with Peres, Secretary Baker—who had moved to the White House to manage the troubled Bush campaign—said that the United States was determined to maintain Israel's qualitative edge over its numerically superior Arab neighbors. Baker added that Bush was trying to put America's "special relationship" with Israel back on track.[48] Bush and Baker also urged the Arab countries, including Syria and Lebanon, that had not participated in the multilateral negotiations to end the economic boycott of Israel. The Arab foreign ministers who had met with Secretary Baker at the UN General Assembly in New York refused.[49]

The last weeks of the Bush administration were characterized by a concerted effort to draft a declaration of principles between Israel and Syria. Baker's peace team believed that Assad might be tempted to agree to such a move, in return for the removal of Syria from the State Department's list of countries supporting international terrorism. Both Israel and Syria thought that the U.S. initiative was inadequate. Rabin, while cooperating with the administration's effort, believed that without a summit between him and Assad, nothing would move. Assad, on the other hand, was unwilling to attend such a meeting with Rabin without a prior Israeli commitment to total withdrawal from the Golan Heights.

Thus, when the Arab and Israeli delegations met for the seventh round of negotiations in Washington, on October 21, it was obvious that the peace process had reached a dead end. The delegates were more interested in the outcome of the coming presidential election than in fruitless arguments about a breakthrough that all of them knew was unattainable at that stage. Any anticipated progress would have to wait for the next U.S. administration.

RABIN'S BUMPY ROAD TO OSLO

*In the fall of 1992, all the elements needed for a new, secret channel of nego-*tiations between Israel and the PLO were in place.

The political paralysis resulting from a long American presidential campaign opened the door for other parties to try to fill the vacuum. Among the Europeans, France in particular tried to inject itself into the Israeli-Syrian track, without much success. In early October 1992, while in Bonn, Prime Minister Yitzhak Rabin read Israeli press reports according to which Foreign Minister Shimon Peres had urged President François Mitterrand to play a more active role in the Israeli-Syrian peace process. Rabin was furious. For weeks, the United States had been making a serious effort to arrange a summit meeting between him and President Assad, under President Bush's auspices. Assad refused. President Mubarak also tried to arrange a similar summit, under his auspices, in Cairo. Assad again refused. The Syrian president even rejected a proposal by NBC to interview him and Rabin separately but to air the interviews consecutively. Finally, the head of the Israeli negotiating team with Syria, Itamar Rabinovich, suggested to his Syrian counterpart, Muaffaq Allaf, that a secret back channel be opened between the two countries, but Syria refused. So why would Peres invite France to take part in such an effort? Besides, according to a written agreement between them, drafted by attorney and Labor activist Giora Eini, Peres was not to be involved in the bilateral negotiations between Israel and its Arab neighbors. Hence, immediately after his return from his visit to Germany, Rabin told Israeli correspondents: "There is only one channel of negotiations with Syria, and this channel is Washington."[1] Nevertheless, in late October, French Foreign Minister Roland Dumas came to the Middle East, but after meeting with Rabin and Assad, he understood that his mission had failed.

In the Middle East, both President Mubarak and Chairman Arafat were upset by Rabin's decision to follow the American lead and to give preference to the Israeli-Syrian track. Taking into account the long interregnum between election day in the United States and the inauguration of the new administration, on January 20, 1993, Mubarak and Arafat were determined to use this window of opportunity to refocus Israel's attention on the Palestinian track. They knew that they could get more from Israel while President Bush was still in power than under President Clinton.

Mubarak did not have to wait until after inauguration day to figure out how pro-Israel the new Clinton administration would be. In early October 1992, Clinton met for the second time in New York with the Conference of Presidents of Major Jewish Organizations and pledged to continue the peace process, to maintain Israel's military superiority, and to consider undivided, united Jerusalem to be Israel's capital. The Democratic presidential candidate described Israel as "our strongest democratic ally in the Middle East." While praising President Bush and Secretary Baker for their success in convening the Madrid Peace Conference, Clinton attacked the Republican administration for abandoning the Christians in Lebanon, and he criticized Bush for applying "one-sided pressure on Israel" by denying Prime Minister Shamir the $10 billion in loan guarantees to help absorb the massive Jewish immigration from the Soviet Union. "Many of the Jewish leaders were impressed by Clinton's commitment and they trusted him," Malcolm Hoenlein, the energetic executive vice chairman of the Conference of Presidents, told me.[2]

Later in October, Egyptian Foreign Minister Amr Mussa met with Governor Clinton in Washington. The Democratic candidate repeated to Mussa what he had earlier told the Jewish leaders in New York.[3]

Hence, playing their usual game between Rabin and Peres, Egypt and the PLO found in the Israeli foreign minister more than a silent partner in their effort to give the Palestinian track preference over the Syrian track. The basis for this effort had been laid down on October 8, 1992, during a visit of several hours that the Egyptian foreign minister had paid to Israel. It was the second visit to Israel by an Egyptian foreign minister in a decade. Mussa delivered a personal letter from Mubarak to Rabin, in which the Egyptian president urged Israel to define the parameters for a final settlement with the Palestinians. Rabin refused. In his reply to Mubarak, Rabin stressed the need to continue the bilateral negotiations in Washington for an interim agreement between Israel and the Palestinians. The negotiations on the final status of the West Bank and the Gaza Strip could begin in the third year of Palestinian self-rule. The Syrian subject was hardly mentioned in that discussion.[4]

Mussa's discussion with Peres was more meaningful. It dealt with two subjects. The first was Palestinian participation in the multilateral working group on regional economic cooperation, which was due to meet in Paris on October 29, and the working group on refugees, which was scheduled to meet in Ottawa on November 11. Israel had boycotted the previous meeting of the two committees because Arafat named two members of the Palestine National Council (PNC)—the PLO's "parliament-in-exile"—to head the Palestinian teams. Amr Mussa told Peres that Arafat had now agreed to replace the two PNC members that Israel had opposed. He expressed the hope, however, that once the Israeli law banning all contacts with the PLO was abrogated by the Knesset, there would not be a need to oppose other PNC members.

The second issue was far more important—the possible Israeli withdrawal from the Gaza Strip. This was not a new idea. Morocco's King Hassan had suggested it to Moshe Dayan in the summer of 1977. At the request of Dayan, Peres, in his capacity as the head of the opposition Labor Party, had suggested to President Sadat in their meeting in Vienna in June 1978 that Egypt retake control of the Gaza Strip. Sadat refused. In the fall of 1982, Morocco's King Hassan had suggested to President Reagan that after an Israeli withdrawal, the Gaza Strip should be placed under a UN or multinational trusteeship, or even an Egyptian trusteeship, until its final status was resolved. In the more recent past, Moshe Arens, the Israeli defense minister in Shamir's cabinet, had suggested a unilateral Israeli withdrawal from the Gaza Strip. Finally, under the pressure of mounting violence, Rabin had made the shocking remark that he wished the Gaza Strip were "drowned" in the sea. Peres, more restrained than Rabin and certainly more manipulative, had decided to revive the old Dayan idea and had suggested an Israeli withdrawal from Gaza. He found Amr Mussa more receptive to the idea than Egypt had been in the past. Peres wanted Egypt, and not Israel, to propose the idea to Arafat. Peres explained that if Israel were to propose "Gaza first," Arafat would reject it automatically. But if Egypt persuaded Arafat to suggest the "Gaza first" idea, Israel would immediately accept it.

Indeed, Mubarak conveyed the idea to Arafat and recommended that the PLO accept it. On October 18, 1992, the PLO's Central Committee met in Tunis to discuss the "Gaza first" proposal. There was something very new in that meeting. Despite the Israeli law banning all contacts with the PLO, two Israeli Arab Knesset members—Abdul Wahab Darawsheh and Taleb el-Sane'h—took part in the PLO's meeting. Upon their return, they met with Rabin and gave him a detailed report about their discussions with Arafat and other PLO executives. They told Rabin that both Mahmoud Abbas (Abu Mazen), the head of the steering committee monitoring the peace talks with Israel, and Nabil Shaath supported the "Gaza first" idea. Arafat, however, wanted a "symbolic" Israeli withdrawal in the West Bank, as an indication that "Gaza first" would not become "Gaza only."[5] The two Arab Knesset members also told Rabin that Tunisia was prepared to host a summit meeting between him and Arafat.[6]

Morocco and Tunisia gave their discreet support to the Egyptian-PLO initiative to refocus attention on the Palestinian track. Fully briefed by Arafat about the Norwegian initiative to open a secret negotiating channel between Israel and the Palestinians in Oslo, Tunisian foreign minister Habib Ben-Yahya went there in October 1992 for a meeting with his Norwegian counterpart. Ben-Yahya met there also with Terje Rod Larsen and his wife, Mona Juul, who had been involved in the early encounters in Israel between Deputy Israeli Foreign Minister Yossi Beilin and the Palestinian leader Faisal Husseini. Now, in Oslo, they all agreed to intensify their efforts in that direction.

Meanwhile, in Israel, a major shift in the political balance of power had occurred within the ruling Israeli Labor Party. Despite Rabin's victory in the general elections, Peres managed to retain his control of the party's institutions. Since Labor's secretary general, Micha Harish, had been appointed a cabinet minister, both Rabin and Peres had presented their own candidates to succeed him. Peres won: Nissim Zvili, a Tunisian-born dovish Labor activist, was elected as Labor's new secretary general. Peres was able to demonstrate his regained partisan power again when despite Rabin's reservations he orchestrated the election of Ezer Weizman—one of Israel's most colorful and popular leaders—as the new president of the Jewish state.

Peres's enhanced prestige had limited Rabin's ability to take any action against his problematic foreign minister. This was clearly manifested in late October 1992. At the end of the one hundred days of grace of his government, Rabin faced a well-orchestrated press campaign by the dovish elements of the Labor Party. Peres was not personally involved in this anti-Rabin campaign, but "Peres's boys" were. Through selected leaks to Israeli correspondents and commentators, Rabin was repeatedly asked why there had been no progress in the peace process; why Rabin kept his cabinet secretary Elyakim (Eli) Rubenstein at the head of the Israeli team negotiating with the Palestinians in Washington; and why there was no apparent improvement in Israel's economy. What was more serious, despite Rabin's request to delay legislation on the abrogation of the 1986 law banning all contacts with the PLO, Labor doves identified with Deputy Foreign Minister Yossi Beilin resumed their contacts with local Palestinians identified with the PLO.

In an effort to appease his dovish critics, Rabin considered the appointment of Knesset member Ephraim Sneh as the chief negotiator with the Palestinians in Washington. Sneh, a retired army general, a dove, and a former administrator of the West Bank, had in the past been a Peres supporter. On the eve of the 1992 elections, he had switched his allegiance to Rabin. Peres had never forgiven Sneh for his "betrayal," and he opposed Rabin's intention to appoint him as the negotiator with the Palestinians. Eli Rubenstein continued to hold this function.

This intense anti-Rabin activity within the ruling Labor Party was accompanied by a new wave of violence in the territories and in South Lebanon. Following a general strike of Palestinian prisoners in eight Israeli prisons, there were mass demonstrations in the territories. Israel imposed a curfew, and in several clashes more than two hundred Palestinians were injured. On October 25, 1992, five Israeli soldiers were killed by a massive roadside bomb in South Lebanon. That same day, an Israeli soldier was killed by Islamic Hamas terrorists near Hebron. On October 27, the pro-Iranian Hezbollah in Lebanon fired Katyusha rockets into the Israeli town of Kiryat Shmona. A fourteen-year-old boy, a new immigrant from Russia, was killed. Indeed, since the Madrid Peace Conference, there had been almost daily acts of violence—shootings in the West Bank, knifings in Jerusalem, assaults in the Gaza Strip, and ambushes in South Lebanon. In October alone, ten Israelis, twenty Palestinians, and twelve Lebanese were killed. Since the beginning of the intifada in December 1987, 100 Israelis and 950 Palestinians had been killed and an additional 500 Palestinians had been murdered by fellow Palestinians on suspicion of collaboration with the Israeli security services.

Obviously frustrated by this turn of events, Rabin told the Knesset on October 25 that "the Palestinians are again deluding themselves in believing that their approach of 'all or nothing' will lead them somewhere. They will end up with nothing. . . ." Rabin added that it was obvious that Arafat was instructing his negotiating team in Washington to harden its positions and to reject all Israeli proposals for self-rule.[7]

What made the situation more complicated was the renewed tension between Rabin and Peres. "There were times when it was very unpleasant to attend a cabinet meeting because of the high tension between Peres and Rabin," said Shulamit Aloni, the former minister of culture and communication and former chairman of the left-wing Meretz Party. "They looked to me like a couple married for thirty-five years, with no love but with mutual dependence. They lived together, apart."[8]

The election of Governor Bill Clinton as the new U.S. president came as no surprise to Israel and the Arab world. Despite Bush's genuine efforts to mend fences with Israel, American Jewish leaders had not forgotten his ugly confrontations with Prime Minister Shamir and his effort to link the grant of $10 billion in loan guarantees to a total freeze on new Jewish settlements in the occupied territories, which—according to Bush—included East Jerusalem. This was one of the reasons why Bush's share of the Jewish vote fell to less than half of the estimated 37 percent he had received in the 1988 elections.[9]

Until inauguration day, in January 1993, the Bush administration acted in the Middle East more as a fire extinguisher than as a power broker.

Clinton's election was accompanied by an intensified wave of violence in South Lebanon. In a meeting with Rabin, on November 12, Chief of Staff General Ehud Barak, Chief of Military Intelligence General Uri Saguy, and the officer commanding the Northern Front, General Yitzhak Mordechai (now defense minister in Netanyahu's cabinet), recommended a "limited" military operation against the pro-Iranian Hezbollah. This would be his first test as defense minister since Rabin formed his cabinet in July. Although it was his prerogative to sanction such an operation, Rabin preferred a cabinet authorization. To his shocked surprise, Rabin found himself in the minority. Peres and most of the ministers spoke against any military operation at this time. Rabin asked for a formal vote. Trying to avoid a situation where a prime minister was defeated by his own government, Peres changed his mind and supported a military action. So did the other ministers. Rabin's prestige was saved, but the vote had shown once again who held the real power.

This regained political power was demonstrated by Peres in the manner he handled the issue of Palestinian representation in the multilateral working group on refugees, which was held in Ottawa on November 11. Despite the understanding he had reached with the Egyptian foreign minister that the PLO would replace Dr. Elias Sanbar as head of the Palestinian delegation for being a member of the PNC, his successor, Dr. Muhamad Khallaj, was also a member of the PNC. Khallaj, a former professor of political science at Bir Zeit University, near Jerusalem, was married to an American and lived in Washington. He was known as an expert on the issue of Palestinian refugees and considered himself one of them.

I covered the Ottawa meeting for the Israeli daily *Davar,* and I had alerted my editors ten days in advance that Khallaj was also a member of the PNC. The Israeli ambassador to Canada, Yitzhak Shelef, did the same. The Israeli Foreign Ministry, however, did not react. Having received no objection, the Canadian government, which served as host and the gavel of the working group on refugees, issued accreditation to Khallaj and his team. In addition, just as the United States allowed PLO Executive Nabil Shaath to monitor the working of the Palestinian team in Washington, the Canadian government allowed Ahmed Qrei (Abu Ala) to come to Ottawa and monitor the work of the Palestinian team on refugees.

A few hours before the opening of the conference, the head of the Israeli team, former ambassador to Spain Professor Shlomo Ben-Ami, informed the Canadians that unless the PLO replaced Dr. Khallaj for being a member of the PNC, Israel would be forced to boycott the meeting. Marc Peron, the deputy director general of the Canadian Ministry for External Affairs, was shocked. He told Ben-Ami that Israel had known well in advance the composition of the Palestinian team and had not objected to Dr. Khallaj's presence. Should Canada withdraw Khallaj's accreditation at this late hour, all fourteen Arab delegations participating in the working group would walk out of the conference. Canada was not prepared to take that risk. Addressing a crowded press conference, Ben-Ami announced Israel's boycott of the working group because of the PLO's abuse of trust, and added that the Israeli delegation was "packing and returning home." He did not. Peres instructed Ben-Ami to remain in Ottawa. Peres immediately called Amr Mussa in Cairo. Yasser Arafat happened also to be in Cairo, for a meeting with Mubarak. Canadian Minister for External Affairs Barbara MacDougal and Dennis Ross, the U.S. coordinator of the peace process, called Peres and urged him not to withdraw. Eventually, and contrary to Ben-

Ami's advice, Peres instructed the team to reverse its previous decision and to participate in the working group on Palestinian refugees.

A new political fact was thus established. Without a formal cabinet decision and without admitting it publicly, Israel began negotiating officially with the PLO. Formal legislation abrogating the 1986 law that banned all contacts with the PLO would soon follow.

Through Dr. Elia Zureik, a Palestinian political scientist at Queen's College in Kingston, Ontario, who served as a spokesman for the Palestinian team, I asked to meet with Abu Ala. I was surprised to receive a prompt positive answer. "We have no problem meeting with Israelis," Abu Ala told me smilingly. "The problem was always with the Israelis. Until now, we have played Shamir's and Rabin's games and pretended that we were absent from the official dialogue, whether in Madrid or in Washington. No more. We are present and we want the Israeli people to know it. . . ." Ahmed Qrei had been working as a banker in Saudi Arabia when the Six-Day War broke out in June 1967. Unable to return to Jerusalem, in 1968 he had joined Yasser Arafat's El-Fatah group and assumed the name Abu Ala. Abu Ala said that he had never engaged in terrorist acts, and he had always handled the PLO's financial and economic portfolio. Before returning to his home village after he had negotiated the Oslo Accords, he lived in Tunis with his wife and five children.

Abu Ala told me that since the war of Lebanon in 1982, Israel had misread the PLO. He explained that after President Reagan announced his plan for a solution of the Arab-Israeli conflict, the PLO supported Saudi King Fahd's counterplan, which was approved by an Arab summit meeting in Fez, Morocco, in the fall of 1982. "The importance of that plan," Abu Ala explained, "was that for the first time the entire Arab world—including Syria's President Assad and Iraq's President Saddam Hussein—called for a political solution of the conflict with Israel. Unfortunately, Israel misread the message. . . ."

Before leaving his hotel room in Ottawa, Abu Ala told me with a smile: "I want you to know that you are the first Israeli I have met in my capacity as a PLO executive." Less than three weeks later, on December 4, 1992, he was conferring in London with Dr. Yair Hirschfeld, one of the two Israeli academics who opened the secret Israel-PLO channel in Oslo.

Obviously frustrated by the increased Palestinian violence and the constant undermining of his authority from within his own cabinet, Rabin wanted to free himself from the "bear hug" of the Labor doves and of his left-wing coalition partner, Meretz. He wanted to lure Tsomet—the center-right party headed by former chief of staff Raphael (Raful) Eytan—into his government. With the full knowledge of Peres, Rabin asked the discreet Labor activist Giora Eini to approach Tsomet and see if there was a genuine basis for this nationalist party to join a Labor-led coalition. After several exploratory meetings, Eini brought Eytan to Rabin's residence to draft an accord for Tsomet's joining the coalition.

Prematurely leaked to the press, Rabin's initiative was derailed by Labor doves and Meretz. "Had Rabin succeeded in his endeavor, the whole course of events would have looked different. Who knows? Maybe even Rabin's assassination could have been averted," Eini told me.[10]

While Rabin was exploring the possibility of enlarging his coalition, Peres was pushing harder his plan for "Gaza first" with the PLO. During a visit to Cairo, on November 16, Peres suggested to Dr. Ossama el-Baz, President Mubarak's political adviser, and to Egyptian Foreign Minister Amr Mussa that Israel could cede to the Palestinians the city of Jericho, as a proof that Israel would eventually withdraw from areas in the West Bank. It was a gesture full of symbolism. In January 1950, after the Arab defeat in the 1948 war, the Palestinian leaders of the West Bank met in Jericho and voted unanimously for the annexation of the West Bank to the Hashemite Kingdom of Jordan. After the Yom Kippur War of 1973, King Hussein asked Secretary Henry Kissinger to arrange an Israeli withdrawal from Jericho and a stretch of land along the Jordan River as part of a separation-of-forces agreement between Israel and Jordan, similar to the agreements that Kissinger had arranged with Egypt and Syria. Israel refused. Now, Peres, without a formal approval by the Israeli government and without even the knowledge of Rabin, suggested in Cairo an Israeli withdrawal from Jericho. That was a real incentive for the opening of the secret channel in Oslo.

Indeed, on December 4, Beilin attended a scheduled meeting in London of the steering committee of the five multilateral working groups created by the Madrid Peace Conference. The PLO was not a member of the steering committee. Nevertheless, and according to a prior arrangement with the Norwegian intermediary, Terje Rod Larsen, Abu Ala, the PLO coordinator of the Palestinian teams in the multilateral track, came also to London to meet with Dr. Hirschfeld. The travel expenses of Abu Ala and Hirschfeld were covered by the Norwegian government, so there was no need for Beilin to ask permission for Hirschfeld's scheduled meeting with Abu Ala.

After being introduced by Larsen, at the Forte Crest St. James Hotel, Abu Ala and Hirschfeld agreed to meet again on January 20, 1993, for a three-day "seminar," during which Israel and the PLO would explore various approaches to the solution of the Israeli-Palestinian conflict.

All these political moves were accompanied by a continued wave of violence in the territories. On December 7, three Israeli soldiers were killed in the Gaza Strip. Two days later, another soldier was killed in Hebron. Then came a most serious incident: A border policeman, Nissim Toledano, was kidnapped and knifed to death inside Israel, not far from Ben-Gurion Airport. His body was discovered two days later, on the road to Jericho. Rabin faced a real dilemma. He had promised the electorate peace with security. The peace process, however, was going nowhere, and even inside Israel, security was nonexistent. Facing mounting public pressure, Rabin knew that tough language was not enough anymore. He had to take bold action. At the recommendation of the army and security services, some fifteen hundred Hamas and Islamic Jihad activists were arrested. On December 16, Rabin won the unanimous approval of his government to expel the most militant 415 activists to Lebanon. In the five years since the beginning of the intifada, in December 1987, Israel deported a total of sixty-five Palestinians from the territories. Now, in one bold action, Rabin ordered the deportation of 415. Shimon Peres was not in the country at that time—he was visiting Tokyo. In his absence, not even one minister dared to oppose the move. It was a disastrous decision. When the twenty-two buses carrying the deportees crossed the Lebanese border, Israel was surprised to discover that the Lebanese army was already deployed just outside the self-proclaimed Israeli security zone. In coordination with Syria, Lebanon prevented the 415 deportees from crossing into Lebanon. The deportees were dropped in the no-man's-land between the security zone and the Lebanese army, exposed to the cold and rainy winter. None of the deportees belonged to Iz el-Din el-Qassam—the military wing of Hamas—and all were part of the civilian infrastructure of this militant Islamic movement. Many of them were academics, and their daily descriptions of their hardship and sufferings became the focus of world media for weeks.

The deportations were met with worldwide criticism, which eroded support for Israel abroad and weakened the prestige of the Rabin government at home. On December 18, the UN Security Council unanimously condemned Israel for its action and demanded the return of the deportees to their homes. What was even more embarrassing was that Hamas's infrastructure was too solid to be shaken by the deportations, and its message became even stronger than before. This was marked by a surge of terrorist attacks, mass demonstrations, and daily clashes with the Israeli security forces.

In a desperate effort to remedy the situation, Rabin announced his intention to shorten the period of deportation. He also called on the Arab countries to provide shelter and comfort to the deportees. Needless to say, none of them responded to Rabin's plea. On the contrary, fully determined to exact a maximum political price from this uncalculated Israeli action, the Arab governments increased their public pressure on Israel. Meeting in Damascus, on December 24, Arab foreign ministers decided to suspend the bilateral peace talks with Israel, which were scheduled to resume in Washington in February.

The outgoing Bush administration was very much annoyed by this situation. Both the president and the secretary of state, Larry Eagleburger, urged Rabin to find a quick solution to the deportees problem. UN Secretary General Boutros Boutros-Ghali was pushing for sanctions against Israel. Never before had the UN taken such drastic action against Israel. During the Cold War, Israel had always been shielded by the U.S. veto power. Now, with the disintegration of the Soviet Union, the situation had changed. It took a tremendous effort by the United States to persuade the Security Council to delay any action until after the inauguration of the new Clinton administration.

Despite his pledge during his presidential campaign to change his administration's priorities from foreign affairs to pressing domestic issues, Clinton's first crisis related to the Israeli-Palestinian conflict. He knew that if the Security Council tried to impose sanctions against Israel, he would have no choice but to veto the decision. This would undermine his administration's credibility among already suspicious Arab countries. On January 23, 1993, Clinton spoke by phone with Rabin. The president told the Israeli prime minister that the United States had succeeded in persuading the UN Security Council to delay any action until the expected ruling of the Israeli Supreme Court on the issue. Clinton made it clear, however, that should the Supreme Court declare the deportation illegal, Israel would have to return the deportees to their homes immediately. Rabin promised to abide by the rule of law.

On January 28, the Israeli Supreme Court upheld Rabin's decision and declared the deportations legal. On January 29, Secretary Christopher called Rabin and urged him to find a solution that would not force the United States to use its veto power. "In the long run it would be also in Israel's best interest," Christopher said. Working hand in hand with the United States, the Israeli government approved on February 1 a proposal according to which one hundred deportees would return home immediately and the rest would be released gradually, so that by the end of 1994 all the deportees would have returned home. "It's a step in the right direction," Christopher said.

While world public opinion was focused on Clinton's new administration, a new and dramatic chapter in the Israeli-Palestinian conflict opened in Oslo. Again without Rabin's knowledge and authorization, two Israeli academics, Dr. Yair Hirschfeld and Dr. Ron Pundak, met on January 20 in a secluded villa at Sarpsborg, near Oslo, with three official PLO representatives: Ahmed Qrei (Abu Ala), who managed the PLO's financial and investment portfolios; Maher el-Kurd, an economist who was fluent in English; and Hassan Asfour, Abu Mazen's assistant. It was rather a bizarre situation: The PLO team was official and authoritative, whereas the Israeli team had no official standing. However, because of the close relationship between Hirschfeld and Yossi Beilin, the PLO officials were right to conclude that the Sarpsborg meeting had at least the blessing of the Israeli Foreign Ministry. The meeting in Norway took place one day only after the Israeli Knesset abrogated, with a majority of one single vote, the 1986 law that banned any contacts with the PLO. The "Sarpsborg Seminar," which lasted three days, was one of nine other unofficial dialogues between Israelis and Palestinians that were being conducted at the time in various capitals, mostly Cairo and in Europe. From the Israel doves' point of view, the Sarpsborg Seminar had two advantages: Since no Israeli officials were involved, the talks were deniable; and unlike the Washington bilateral negotiations, which were held at the State Department, the Oslo "seminar" was held in secrecy, with no public pressure and with no rigid agenda.

Indeed, the Norwegians did their utmost to keep the discussions secret. Upon their arrival in Oslo, the teams did not go through the normal immigration and custom control. Terje Larsen drove the Israeli team to Sarpsborg, while Mona Juul, drove the Palestinians. The Norwegian intermediaries proved to be excellent hosts. They created a relaxed ambiance—informal dress, candlelight dinners, and many opportunities for informal and free dialogues. It was Larsen who, after a short introduction, raised the issue of "Gaza first" as a possible subject of discussion. Both teams were familiar with the idea, which had been raised by Foreign Minister Peres in Cairo. Abu Ala told the Israelis: "If the Gaza Strip is causing you so much headache, why don't you withdraw unilaterally?" Abu Ala said that he was ready to explore a possibility for an Israeli withdrawal, within a period of two or three years, after which the Gaza Strip would be placed under a UN trusteeship until its final status was agreed upon. Hirschfeld negated the idea of a unilateral withdrawal and hinted that Israel would be willing to hand over the Gaza Strip directly to the Palestinians rather than to a UN body. Such a move, however, was subject to an agreement between Israel and the Palestinians on a two-stage solution: first a withdrawal from Gaza and an interim period of five years of Palestinian self-rule; then final status negotiations. The teams spent much time discussing a subject that was dear to Peres—a mini–Marshall Plan for the development and the reconstruction of the Gaza Strip.

Encouraged by this development, Peres met with Rabin alone on February 9, 1993, and gave him—for the first time—a full report on the Oslo channel. Peres did not know it at the time, but Rabin was not surprised. The Israeli intelligence community had already reported to him about the Norwegian initiative.

The Israeli intelligence community never admitted that it had penetrated the PLO headquarters in Tunis. In the last three years, however, PLO officials and Arab news media had revealed that the PLO security services had exposed two Mossad agents in Tunis. The most discussed among the two was fifty-four-year-old Adnan Yassin, who was an aide to Hakam Bil'awi, the head of one of the Palestinian security services and also the PLO "ambassador" to Tunis. Yassin had come to Tunis from Jordan after the bloody clash between the PLO and the Jordanian army in September 1970. After the expulsion of PLO forces from Beirut in 1982, Yassim had handled in Tunis all the travel arrangements of PLO executives and kept an open eye on the Israelis and Palestinians who came to meet with Arafat and his associates in Tunis. According to his own admission, Yassin was recruited by the Mossad in Paris, where his wife was undergoing cancer treatment. Yassin was exposed by the Tunisian intelligence on October

25, 1993, shortly after his son imported from France a small Renault car and a lamp in which was concealed a mini-transmitter. The lamp was placed in Abu Mazen's office. Yassin is still being held at a PLO jail, in Hammam el-Shatt, near Tunis.

The second Mossad "mole" was identified by the PLO as "A.A. Ein," a Palestinian from the Gaza Strip who was arrested in Tunis on January 10, 1994. According to a Palestinian security source, A.A. Ein was recruited by the Israeli General Security Service (the Shin Bet) and was instrumental in exposing many intifada commanders and other Palestinian activists. Because of his success, he was transferred from the Shin Bet to the Mossad. After a short stay in England, where he built his new identity and cover, he moved to Tunis, where he was to penetrate the PLO headquarters. He was eventually exposed and arrested.[11]

Israeli intelligence sources would not, of course, confirm that Adnan Yassin and A.A. Ein were Mossad agents. Nor would they confirm that one of them, or both, reported to Mossad headquarters about the Oslo channel. The fact remains, however, that when Peres reported to Rabin about the Norwegian initiative, the prime minister was already aware of it. Rabin asked Peres to suspend the Oslo talks until after Secretary of State Warren Christopher's first visit to the Middle East, later in February, and until after his return from his own official visit to Washington, in mid-March.

Peres ignored Rabin's request. By his own admission, Peres wrote: "I sent word to our two unofficial emissaries that they might carry on their discussions along the general lines that I had approved, explaining that we would review the situation after Secretary Christopher's trip."[12]

While the Washington negotiations were officially suspended until the full resolution of the issue of the Hamas deportees, the two Israeli and Palestinian teams met again in Sarpsborg on February 11–12, 1993. The meeting did not produce any immediate tangible results. Abu Ala told Hirschfeld and Pundak that while the PLO was ready to discuss an Israeli withdrawal from the Gaza Strip, the Palestinians insisted that the withdrawal include the evacuation of the Israeli settlements. "The settlements," Abu Ala said, "could become a joint Israeli-Palestinian project." Needless to say, the Israeli team was not in a position to discuss such an issue. Hirschfeld brought from Jerusalem a proposal for a declaration of principles that would specify an Israeli withdrawal from the Gaza Strip and the gradual empowerment of an elected Palestine Authority of several civilian functions. The Palestinians rejected the Israeli draft as presented. The two teams agreed, however, that should an agreement eventually be reached, its details would be passed to the official negotiating teams in Washington for endorsement.

In fairness to Peres, one must add here that his working behind Rabin's back was not unique. Arafat did the same. In a letter to President Assad in January 1993, Arafat expressed concern that Syria would strike a separate deal with

Israel, leaving the PLO behind. The letter was carried to Damascus by Nassri Youssef, a member of El-Fatah's Central Committee, and was handed to Syrian Foreign Minister Faruq el-Shara'a. In his letter, Arafat warned that a separate Israeli-Syrian deal would constitute "a betrayal of the Palestinian intifada and would deal a severe blow to the common Arab effort to coordinate positions, in the face of a constant Israeli effort to split the Arab front." Arafat concluded his letter by renewing his commitment to Assad "to stand fast" in the face of the Israeli maneuvers, and he strongly denied the "baseless rumors" about secret Israeli-Palestinian negotiations.[13]

Assad was to make use of this letter in his refusal to deal with Arafat after the signing of the Oslo Accords in Washington.

When Secretary Christopher came in late February 1993 for his first swing through the Middle East, he confronted an Arab world that was uncertain how much attention the domestically oriented Clinton administration would pay to the Arab-Israeli conflict. Given the very nature of the presidential election campaign and Clinton's own career, spent exclusively in domestic politics, it was only natural that the Arab leaders suspected that Clinton would treat foreign affairs as a "stepchild." The Arabs knew that the new U.S. president would not repeat President Bush's mistake of focusing too much attention on the outside world. Clinton's inclination was reflected in his choice of his foreign policy team. Both Secretary Christopher and National Security Adviser Anthony (Tony) Lake kept a low profile and allowed foreign policy to remain on the back burner.

But the Arab-Israeli peace process was the exception. In line with Clinton's public promises, during his campaign, Christopher announced that the United States would become a "full partner" in the Arab-Israeli peace talks. As a clear sign of continuity in U.S. Middle Eastern policy, Christopher kept Secretary Baker's entire peace team, headed by Ambassador Dennis Ross. Gradually, Christopher even expanded Ross's power and authority. It was a very sound decision. A graduate of the University of California in Los Angeles, where he had written his doctoral dissertation on Soviet decision making, Ross, forty-eight, was by now the most experienced and knowledgeable American official in the field of the Arab-Israeli peace process. Although Ross had been a very close adviser of Secretary Baker, both Clinton and Christopher considered him so valuable that they had asked him to continue with the new administration.

The only significant change in the U.S. peace team was made at the White House. Martin Indyk, the director of the prestigious Washington Institute for Near East Policy, had replaced the very knowledgeable Richard Haas as Near East and South Asia director at the National Security Council. Like Ross, Indyk was an admirer of Prime Minister Yitzhak Rabin, and he too regarded an Israeli-Syrian settlement as a key to an overall settlement of the Arab-Israeli conflict.

Indyk, who later became the first Jew to be appointed as the U.S. ambassador to Israel, was born in London in 1951, where his father, a renowned Australian surgeon of Polish origin, was studying. He spent a year at Hebrew University, and several years later he returned to Israel and carried out doctoral research at Tel Aviv University's Dayan Center, where he met Professor Itamar Rabinovich, one of Israel's most respected experts on Syria. This was to become a lasting friendship between Rabinovich and Indyk, first as scholars and later as ambassadors of Israel and the United States in Washington and Tel Aviv. Imitating the experience of the Dayan Center, Indyk helped found the Washington Institute for Near East Policy in 1985. The institute quite soon became one of the most influential think-tank organizations, attracting senior administration officials and high-profile Israeli and Arab speakers. Indyk's institute drew national attention when, on the eve of the 1988 presidential elections, he brought to the Middle East a high-profile bipartisan team to recommend polity options for the next U.S. president. Cochaired by former vice president Walter Mondale and future deputy secretary of state Larry Eagleburger, the Presidential Study Group, as it was known, produced a very impressive paper, titled "Building for Peace." It recommended that the next president "nurture" peace rather than impose it.

Four years later, in the 1992 presidential campaign, Indyk again organized a bipartisan study group, which included foreign policy advisers from Bush's and Clinton's campaigns. After the election, the head of Clinton's transition team, Samuel (Sandy) Berger, asked Indyk to prepare for the president-elect the Middle East section in the transition paper. Indyk's road to the White House was wide open.

In his first visit to the Middle East, Christopher was accompanied by, among others, both Ross and Indyk. The visit was not intended to achieve an imminent breakthrough but to set the stage for the resumption of the bilateral peace talks in Washington. In his meetings with Israeli and Arab leaders, Christopher reaffirmed U.S. opposition to the deportation of the Hamas activists to South Lebanon as a violation of the Fourth Geneva Convention. He proposed to Rabin the inclusion of Faisal Husseini, the most prominent PLO activist in East Jerusalem, in the Palestinian negotiating team, in an effort to enhance the team's prestige in the territories. Rabin promised to give the idea a "positive thinking." This was a clear departure from past practice, which was accepted at the time by both Bush and Baker, prior to the convening of the Madrid Peace Conference. According to that practice, no Palestinian from East Jerusalem was allowed to participate in the peace negotiations. At the end of Christopher's trip, it was agreed by all parties that the ninth round of the bilateral negotiations would be resumed in Washington on April 27, 1993.

In mid-March 1993, Prime Minister Rabin became the first Middle Eastern leader to meet with President Clinton at the White House. It was more than a "courtesy visit" to a new administration. It was a visit intended to forge a new strategic understanding between Israel and the United States. Rabin, the strategic thinker, understood quite well that with the collapse of the Soviet empire, the strategic environment had changed dramatically. Now that the Cold War had ended and the United States was the only superpower, Israel's Arab enemies no longer had a superpower patron. This could open the road to peace, but it also provided Israel with a unique opportunity to play a more active role in the broader U.S. Middle Eastern strategy.

The Madrid Peace Conference was undoubtedly one of the major foreign policy achievements of the Bush administration. Bush, however, left to President Clinton many unresolved problems. Despite his defeat in Desert Storm, Saddam Hussein was still in power in Baghdad and was regarded by his people as the "guarantor" of their territorial integrity. Iran had embarked on a dangerous arms race, aimed at procuring from Russia, China, and North Korea modern technologies and nuclear capability. The Iranian Islamic revolution had inspired terrorist activity in Saudi Arabia and Bahrain. Financial and material Iranian assistance to Hezbollah in Lebanon and to Hamas and Islamic Jihad in the Israeli occupied territories was never interrupted. Conflicts over water resources between Turkey, Syria, and Iraq risked endangerment of regional stability. There were still many border disputes between Iran and its Persian Gulf neighbors. The rise of Iranian-inspired Islam in Sudan gave a new dimension to the eternal conflict between Cairo and Khartoum.

This double Iranian-Iraqi threat necessitated a more active American security role in the Persian Gulf and a permanent military presence in the region. This was important not only for the protection of American and Western oil interests but also for the protection of pro-Western moderate Arab regimes. Rabin wanted to discuss all these issues with the new Clinton administration and to see what role Israel could play in the region. Despite the lack of meaningful progress in the Arab-Israeli peace process, Israel remained the strongest and most trusted U.S. ally in this turbulent region. Rabin therefore wanted to add Israel's input before the new Clinton policy was formulated and approved.

Rabin's success was beyond expectations. Not only did he lay the foundations for a new strategic alliance between the two countries, but he also witnessed an intimacy in his personal relationship with Clinton that no other Israeli prime minister, before or after him, ever developed with a U.S. president. Despite the crisis with the Hamas deportees, the ambiance surrounding Rabin in Washington was warm and friendly. Unlike Bush, Clinton saw any direct pressure on Israel as counterproductive. Rabin was familiar enough with American politics to know that no U.S. president would want to suffer what Bush had gone through with Prime Minister Shamir. Besides, since Rabin's Labor-led government had embraced the land-for-peace formula, there was no need to prod Israel to move the peace process forward. Hence, the whole notion of U.S. pressure on Israel disappeared from Clinton's Middle Eastern view.

Before leaving for the United States, Rabin reviewed several files that dealt with Israel's alliance with Washington in the struggle against the Soviet Union and its Arab clients. Rabin wanted the Israeli defense planners to search for a new strategic rationale for the U.S.-Israeli relationship in the post–Cold War era. The ideas that were proposed ranged from prepositioning in Israel billions of dollars' worth of U.S. military equipment to employing Israel as a "strategic platform" to cope with potential conflicts with Iran or Iraq. They also recommended formulating a joint strategy against international terrorism and differentiating between Islam as a religion and terrorism waged under the banner of Islamic fundamentalism.

Concerning the peace process, Rabin committed himself again to the U.S. approach that preferred the Syrian track over the Palestinian. As defense minister in Shamir's national unity government, Rabin had helped put together the formula that enabled Palestinians from the territories to participate in the Madrid Peace Conference. Now, however, he became disillusioned with them. During a breakfast with the U.S. peace team at the Grand Hotel in Washington, Rabin expressed his frustration at the lack of progress on the Palestinian track. His analysis was quite pessimistic. Rabin said that he had watched how Arafat had gained total control over the Palestinian delegation to the bilateral peace talks in Washington. He no longer believed in the capacity of the Palestinians from the territories to make peace with Israel. Sam Lewis, the popular former U.S. ambassador to Israel who, under Christopher, headed the policy planning at the State Department, asked Rabin: "Well, if this is the case, why don't you deal directly with Arafat?" Rabin was quick to answer: "Because I can't accept his requirements. Arafat wants an independent Palestinian state, with East Jerusalem as its capital. No Israeli prime minister could accept such a condition."[14]

Rabin did accept Christopher's idea of bringing Faisal Husseini to head the Palestinian delegation to the bilateral negotiations in Washington. It wasn't long before both Rabin and Christopher reached the conclusion that the effort to bring Faisal Husseini to Washington changed nothing. On the contrary, it only strengthened the conviction that Arafat was the real boss and no one dared to challenge his authority.

Summing up Rabin's successful visit in Washington, President Clinton stated in a joint press conference at the White House on March 15, 1993: "Prime Minister Rabin told me that he is prepared to take the necessary risks for peace. He has told his own people the same thing. I have told him that our role is to help minimize those risks. We will do that by further reinforcing our commitment to maintain Israel's military edge."[15]

In a private briefing with Israeli correspondents, Rabin revealed that he had asked for access to the software of American fire-control radar and electronic warfare systems. This was indeed a very sensitive issue. In the past, the United States had not allowed American companies to make this technology available to Israel. The United States feared that Israel would copy U.S. ideas and inventions and eventually sell them to other countries. Thus, while Clinton supported Rabin's request, it was a few more months before the Pentagon agreed to make the technology available to Israel.

A few days after Rabin's return from Washington, the two Israeli and PLO teams met for the third time in Oslo. Rabin did not forbid the meeting, because he did not believe it would achieve anything. Rabin, however, made three conditions: The Washington channel would continue to be the official venue for negotiations; the Oslo channel should remain unofficial and secret; and the United States should be made aware of the unofficial dialogue between the two Israeli academics and the PLO.

By the end of March, Beilin had sent Hirschfeld to Washington to meet with Dan Kurtzer, the most pro-Palestinian in the American peace team. Hirschfeld showed Kurtzer the skeleton of a declaration of principles (DOP) that was being discussed in Oslo and told him that Abu Ala had agreed to the idea that any agreement reached in Oslo would be sent to the Washington teams for formal approval. Hirschfeld reported to Beilin that Kurtzer was "impressed" and encouraged Hirschfeld to continue the negotiations in Oslo. After Rabin's return from Washington and at the end of the third round of the secret talks in Oslo, it became clear that the Israeli government was pulling in two conflicting directions: Prime Minister Rabin and the United States were focusing on the Israeli-Syrian track, while Foreign Minister Peres and Egypt were focusing on the Palestinian track. The question could then be asked why Rabin did not exercise his authority and shut down the Oslo channel. Yossi Sarid, the former minister of the environment and the leader of the left-wing Meretz Party, gave me the following explanation: "In addition to the fact that Rabin did not believe in Oslo, Rabin was obsessed by his traumatic experience in 1976. Searching for peace with Egypt, Rabin went to Morocco and asked King Hassan to help arrange a meeting between him and President Sadat. When Labor lost the elections in May 1977, it was Moshe Dayan who reaped the fruits of Rabin's initiative. After a meeting in Rabat between Dayan and an Egyptian envoy, Sadat came to Jerusalem and a year later, under the auspices of President Carter, contracted peace with Menachem Begin. Rabin didn't want this to happen again. If there was the slightest chance for a breakthrough with the PLO, he did not want to miss it."[16]

Another former minister, Benjamin (Fuad) Ben-Eliezer, who was very close to Rabin, had another interpretation of the prime minister's tolerance of Peres's actions. He said: "Rabin never trusted Peres and was very suspicious of him. At a certain point, however, he reached the conclusion that a recognition of the PLO was probably unavoidable. Hence, when Peres started to push in the direction of Oslo, Rabin started to test the question in his mind whether Arafat would be able to meet Israel's basic requirements. Rabin defined these requirements very clearly: Security would remain Israel's exclusive responsibility; no Israeli settlements would be removed; Jerusalem would be an issue left for the final status negotiations. Rabin was prepared to deliver control to the Palestinians over the occupied territories in stages. Such a practice would enable him to stop forward movement at any stage if the Palestinians proved to be unable or unwilling to control the terrorist groups and should Israel's security be threatened. Once these requirements were clearly defined, Rabin saw in Peres a mere tool, and he was able, in most cases, to control this tool. . . ."[17]

Tool or not, in mid-April, a major "confidence crisis" had erupted between Rabin and Peres, and it threatened an end to the Oslo channel. In an effort to soften the Palestinian position in the ninth round of the bilateral negotiations, which were due to resume in Washington on April 27, Rabin scheduled a meeting with President Mubarak in Ismailiya on April 14. Peres informed Rabin that he had explored "in general terms" with Egyptian Ambassador Bassiouni the idea of an Israeli withdrawal from Jericho in addition to the withdrawal from the Gaza Strip. "So don't be surprised if Mubarak explores this subject with you," Peres said. In his meeting with Mubarak on April 14, Rabin was totally shocked. The Egyptian president and his national security adviser, Dr. Ossama el-Baz, presented him with a map showing PLO control not only of the city of Jericho but of the entire "district of Jericho," including the Allenby Bridge linking the West Bank to Jordan. The map also showed an "extraterritorial" corridor, across Israel's Negev Desert, linking the Gaza Strip to the city of Hebron.

Rabin rejected the map outright. He told Mubarak that the whole idea of Jericho was "symbolic"—to show the Palestinians that after the Israeli withdrawal from the Gaza Strip there would be withdrawals from the West Bank as well. Palestinian control of the crossing points between the West Bank and Jordan would constitute a security risk for Israel and was totally unacceptable. Rabin explained that Palestinian control of the bridges would prevent Israel from monitoring the flow of personnel and military equipment into the territories.

Rabin returned to Israel furious, and his distrust of Peres grew even deeper. In an angry exchange with Peres, Rabin threatened to shut down the Oslo channel. Peres claimed that in his discussions with the Egyptians, the issue of the crossing points was never mentioned. He expressed the hope that it would be possible to exclude the Allenby Bridge and the Rafah crossing point from the "Gaza-Jericho first" plan. In the absence of an agreement between Israel and Egypt, the idea of a withdrawal from Jericho was temporarily shelved.

In his instructions to Eli Rubenstein, the head of the Israeli negotiating team in Washington, Rabin said that in the course of the ninth round of the bilateral negotiations Rubenstein could raise the issue of a possible withdrawal from the Gaza Strip, but should not mention Jericho at all. Rabin also instructed the Israeli military governor of the Gaza Strip to explore the idea with one of Arafat's loyalists.

This turn of events had an immediate effect on Arafat's behavior and attitudes. In advance of the ninth round in Washington, Secretary Christopher invited Faisal Husseini to meet with him at the State Department. Husseini was very excited and suggested to Arafat that he (Husseini) should accept the invitation. Arafat said no, and he summoned Husseini to Tunis.[18]

It is very easy to explain Arafat's behavior. After being informed by Mubarak that Rabin had rejected the "Jericho map," Arafat lost interest in the Washington talks, which were controlled in Israel by Yitzhak Rabin. He wanted to concentrate on the Oslo channel, which was controlled by Peres and brought him closer to his goal of being recognized by Israel as its "valuable interlocutor." He wanted the United States to follow the same path. So why would he agree to let Faisal Husseini be perceived in Washington as the "alternative leader" of the Palestinians?

All these political maneuvers were accompanied by repeated waves of violence, some of them even coordinated between the PLO and Hamas. In late February 1993, following a lethal attack by a Palestinian suicide-car bomber on crowded Dizengoff Street in Tel Aviv, Rabin had imposed a temporary closure of the Gaza Strip, where the assailant had come from. In late March, two Israeli policemen were killed in their car near Hadera, inside the green line. Consequently, on March 28, Rabin imposed an unlimited closure on the territories, except East Jerusalem. Rabin's decision was explained by a totally new definition—separation. On April 4, Rabin told his cabinet that in the absence of a political solution, the closure was meant "to create a separation between Israel and the territories."

Despite the closure, however, the violence continued. According to the figures released by the Israeli army, 291 incidents targeting Israeli objectives were recorded in March 1993 and 235 incidents were recorded in April.

The ninth round of the bilateral negotiations opened in Washington on April 27 and lasted until May 13. This was the first round of peace talks sponsored by the Clinton administration, and there was obvious interest in how it would be handled. Secretary Christopher's opening remarks did not contain any surprises. He clearly implied a continuation of Bush's and Baker's peace policy. The Palestinian delegation wanted to boycott the talks because of the unresolved issue of the deportees. Arafat, however, could allow himself to be "generous." Since he was negotiating directly with Israel in Oslo, he instructed the "official" Palestinian team to attend the ninth round in Washington, but he made sure that his guidelines would avoid any progress. As far as Arafat was concerned, the bilateral Washington talks were only a "decoration" to the more substantive talks in Oslo.

In an effort to avoid a deadlock, the United States departed from its traditional role of "facilitator" and submitted to the parties, on May 12, a short document summarizing the points of agreement and disagreement between them.

The Palestinians rejected the American paper outright, claiming that before its submission, the United States had consulted with Israel. In order to refute this allegation, Israel too rejected the American paper. Thus, the ninth round of the Washington talks proved to be another futile attempt to bridge the gap between uncooperative parties.

This was not the case in Oslo. Abu Ala and his Palestinian team came in late April for their fourth round of secret negotiations with the two Israeli academics. The Norwegian hosts informed the parties that Secretary Christopher had invited the new Norwegian foreign minister, Johan Jorgen Holst, to Washington to discuss the Oslo channel. Both the Israelis and the Palestinians regarded the invitation as a clear proof that the United States was fully aware of the Norwegian initiative.

Abu Ala intensified his pressure on the two Israeli academics, to convince them that it was now time for Israel to have formal talks with the PLO. He specifically asked for Beilin's participation. "We are having here good and pleasant discussions," said Abu Ala, "but we cannot go on and have 'academic seminars.' We must have an Israeli counterpart." Indeed, the PLO pressure to formalize the negotiations in Oslo was the subject of another private discussion between Peres and Rabin, on May 14, 1993. Peres believed that the PLO negotiator, Abu Ala, was very credible and that it was possible to strike a deal with him. In his book, *Battling for Peace,* Peres revealed that he wanted to travel himself to Oslo, in order to negotiate with Abu Ala. Rabin rejected the idea, because he did not want to commit himself to such a tricky undertaking before the cabinet had even a chance to discuss it.[19]

Rabin was facing a real dilemma. When Rabin presented his cabinet to the Knesset, in July 1992, he promised to reach an agreement with the Palestinians within a period of nine to twelve months. The deadlock in the ninth round of bilateral negotiations in Washington convinced him that there was no longer a possibility of negotiating with the Palestinians of the "interior" without the PLO's consent. Yasser Arafat was the real power broker, not Faisal Husseini. All the intifada commanders were subordinated to Arafat, and they, not the Palestinian academics negotiating with Israel in Washington, controlled the masses in the West Bank and the Gaza Strip. The Oslo channel was then the only alternative venue for negotiations. What was equally painful to Rabin was Syrian intransigence. Despite several Israeli goodwill gestures and hints that a settlement with Assad would entail a "territorial dimension" on the Golan Heights, President Assad did not reciprocate. He was still insisting on total Israeli withdrawal from the Golan Heights, without clarifying what he was prepared to give in return. "My way or the highway"—that was Assad's attitude.

On the other hand, in order for Rabin to cross the Rubicon and start negotiating with the PLO, he had to overcome personal and ideological barriers. On the personal level, Rabin had to ignore an order he had given to the Mossad in

1974 to liquidate Arafat and his top aides who had been involved in the massacre of the eleven Israeli athletes in Munich in 1972. Golda Meir was the first to give such an order. When Rabin succeeded her as prime minister, in June 1974, he renewed the order. Arafat topped the Israeli hit list. Menachem Begin and Yitzhak Shamir followed the same policy. By the time Rabin returned to power, in July 1992, only Arafat and a very few of his associates who were involved in the Munich massacre were still alive. Rabin did not renew the order to the Mossad, but he still had a strong personal aversion to Arafat.

Rabin's ideological dilemma was even more serious. During his election campaign, he had told the electorate that he opposed the establishment of an independent state and that he would not negotiate with Arafat. How could he now explain his change of mind?

Finally, besides the ideological problem, there were many practical questions that were to be answered. Could Arafat be trusted, and could he deliver? Throughout his long military, diplomatic, and political career, Rabin had noticed that there was not one single Arab leader that Arafat did not lie to. Rabin was reading intelligence reports indicating that the PLO was on the verge of financial collapse. Except for the strong support of his Egyptian patrons, most of the Arab leaders kept their distance from Arafat and distrusted him. Because of Arafat's support of Saddam Hussein during the Persian Gulf War, all the Persian Gulf countries had suspended their financial contributions to the PLO. As a result, salaries to thousands of PLO officials were not paid for months. PLO offices in various capitals were closing. Subsidies to widows and orphans were not distributed. Arafat's personal prestige with the PLO was shrinking. In the territories, pro-Iranian fundamentalist groups like Hamas and Islamic Jihad were expanding their popular support at the expense of the PLO. Not to mention the ten Palestinian rejectionist groups that were based in Damascus and that with President Assad's encouragement were opposing Arafat's policies and undermining his authority in the territories. Rabin, then, had to make a decision: What was better for Israel—to take advantage of Arafat's weakness and to try and extract from him maximum concessions, as Shimon Peres and Egypt were recommending, or to wait for Arafat's downfall and then negotiate with the new Palestinian leadership?

Because of the secret nature of the problem, Rabin did not consult with his ministers, or with the army and the intelligence community. He made the decision by himself: He would negotiate with the PLO in Oslo. However, since he was still uncertain about Arafat's ability to deliver, Rabin insisted that the Oslo channel remain secret, and that the official venue for the negotiations with the Palestinians continue to be Washington.

In accepting the idea of negotiating with Arafat in Oslo, Rabin made the most important Israeli decision since Ben-Gurion declared the establishment of the State of Israel in May 1948. By formally negotiating with the PLO, Israel

practically recognized the existence of a Palestinian national liberation movement and accepted Yasser Arafat as the only representative of the Palestinian
people. Furthermore, the recognition of the PLO meant an Israeli admission
that there was one Palestinian nation, combining those who lived in the territories under Israeli occupation and those scattered in the Arab world, Europe,
North America, and Australia. While Rabin continued to insist publicly that he
was still opposed to an independent Palestinian state, Egypt and the PLO were
stressing the opposite—that the Palestinian road to self-determination and
statehood had just begun.

Rabin's decision to negotiate with the PLO had introduced a major change
in the division of responsibilities between him and Peres. According to a written agreement drafted by attorney Giora Eini, Peres was to be involved in the
multilateral negotiations for regional cooperation, but not in the bilateral negotiations between Israel and each of the Arab parties. By opening the Oslo channel, Peres made himself part of the bilateral effort between Israel and the
Palestinians. Having rejected the idea that Peres himself should travel to Oslo
to negotiate with Abu Ala, Rabin consented to Peres's decision to appoint Uri
Savir, the director general of the Foreign Ministry, as the Israeli negotiator with
the PLO. Savir, a second-generation diplomat, was an able and talented person,
but had no intimate knowledge of Middle Eastern affairs and no negotiating experience with the Arab countries. Like Deputy Foreign Minister Yossi Beilin,
Savir too had a very limited military background and no professional understanding of Israel's unique security problems. Savir's career had been shaped in
Europe, and before becoming director general of the Foreign Ministry he
served very successfully as Israel's consul general in New York.

What was even more problematic was Peres's decision to exclude the army
and the intelligence community from the Oslo negotiations. The net result was
obvious: Israel's security problems were not adequately addressed in Oslo. Had
the intelligence community been involved in the secret negotiations, it could
have given Savir and his team the professional expertise that they lacked. When
asked about the wisdom of excluding the army and the intelligence experts,
Peres answered angrily: "All these wise guys who criticize the modus operandi
and the negotiations with Arafat, and who pretend to know everything even before it happened, what is their criteria for expertise? What have they predicted?
Did they predict the Yom Kippur War? Did they anticipate the peace with
Egypt? Had our intelligence community detected the secret negotiations in
Oslo, we would probably have not had an agreement with the PLO. . . ."[20]

Peres attacked the intelligence community on other occasions. Former defense secretary Les Aspin, who chaired Clinton's Foreign Intelligence Advisory
Board, told a dinner forum in Washington that Peres told him during a visit to
Israel in April 1995: "There isn't one thing that has happened on this peace
process that those guys of the intelligence predicted, not one. You know, they

were telling us that Yasser Arafat will never agree to anything. They were telling us that King Hussein will never get ahead of Syrian President Assad. They were telling us this, they were telling us that—all of which has turned out to be wrong."[21]

Rabin's agreement to send Savir to Oslo was immediately communicated to the Norwegian intermediary, Terje Rod Larsen, who in turn informed the PLO in Tunis. This had created a mini-crisis there. Realizing that Israel was sending a senior official to Oslo, Arafat and Abu Mazen decided to elevate the level of their team as well. Abu Ala was a member of the El-Fatah Central Committee, but he was not a member of the PLO Executive Committee. Therefore they decided to send to Oslo Yasser Abed Rabbo, a member of the Executive Committee and also a member of the steering committee monitoring the negotiations both in Washington and in Oslo. Abu Ala was greatly offended. The appointment of Abed Rabbo meant that Arafat and Abu Mazen did not consider him senior enough to negotiate with Savir. He threatened to resign and not to go to Oslo. Meanwhile, Arafat faced another problem with Hakam Bil'awi, the head of the Palestinian external intelligence service and also a member of the steering committee. When he learned about the designation of Abed Rabbo as the negotiator in Oslo, he burst out in anger: "This is not a game—it's the fate of a land and of a people. I too can open a channel of my own to the Israelis. . . ."[22]

Faced with this double opposition from Abu Ala and Bil'awi, Arafat retracted the offer to Abed Rabbo and kept Abu Ala as the negotiator with Uri Savir in Oslo.

"I would like to introduce to you Abu Ala, your enemy number one," Terje Larsen said laughingly to Uri Savir when the Israeli and the Palestinian teams met on May 20 for the fifth round of their secret talks in Sarpsborg, near Oslo. Contrary to some concerns, the encounter was relaxed. In addition to the effort made by the Norwegian hosts, the personalities of Abu Ala and Savir contributed to the relaxed mood. Both were witty and had a sense of humor, although it soon became clear that Abu Ala was much more manipulative. Savir and Abu Ala decided not to concentrate on the historical past but to deal with the present and the future. Savir said that the failure of the ninth round of the bilateral negotiations in Washington had persuaded Rabin to move to Oslo. He added that both Rabin and Peres were now directing the Oslo channel, and that Peres was determined to reach an agreement as soon as possible.

In the absence of an agreement between Rabin and Peres and between them and Egypt on the issue of Jericho, Savir was instructed to limit his discussion in Oslo to "Gaza first" only. Replying to Abu Ala's proposal that after Israel's withdrawal, within a period of two to three years, the Gaza Strip should be placed under a UN trusteeship, Savir repeated what Hirschfeld and Pundak had told Abu Ala earlier, namely that Israel was prepared to withdraw within three or four months of the signing of the declaration of principles. Israel would be prepared to evacuate the Gaza Strip even before a detailed agreement on self-rule was concluded. This suggestion only confirmed the Egyptians' and the PLO's evaluation that Israel was anxious to leave the Gaza Strip as soon as possible and hence, Israel would be prepared to pay an additional price in order to achieve that goal. As for the UN trusteeship, Savir said, this could be formed jointly by the Palestinians and the Egyptians. When a similar agreement was reached concerning parts of the West Bank, the Jordanians could join the trusteeship with the Palestinians. Abu Ala was not convinced.

Despite Savir's restraint in not raising the issue of Jericho, Abu Ala raised it. It was obvious that he was fully briefed about Rabin's and Mubarak's summit meeting in Ismailiya on April 14. He was also familiar with Rabin's concerns about the crossing points between the West Bank and Jordan and between the Gaza Strip and Egypt. In an effort to quiet Israel's fears, Abu Ala suggested joint Israeli-Palestinian control of the Allenby Bridge linking Jericho to Jordan. Abu Ala presented this idea in a manner that would convince Israel that for the Palestinians it was a matter of "symbol," while the "real" security powers would remain at the hands of Israel. Abu Ala insisted that there should be a symbolic Israeli withdrawal from Jericho, otherwise Arafat would not be able to sell the agreement to his colleagues and to the Palestinian people. He added that Arafat was already facing growing opposition to his leadership. Without Jericho, "Gaza first" would be perceived by Arafat's opponents as "Gaza only."

Savir and Abu Ala spent some time redrafting the declaration of principles that had been drafted earlier by Abu Ala and Hirschfeld.

On May 28, responding to an earlier U.S. invitation, Norwegian Foreign Minister Johan Jorgen Holst traveled to Washington to brief Secretary Christopher and Ambassador Dennis Ross on the Oslo channel. Holst told Christopher that with Uri Savir leading the Israeli team, it was no longer an "academic seminar" but an official negotiation between Israel and the PLO. Holst stressed the point that the idea behind the Oslo channel was that whatever was agreed upon in Oslo would be eventually passed to the negotiating teams in Washington for formal approval. In a report to Peres, Holst said that Christopher was "enthusiastic" about the Oslo channel and encouraged him to pursue it.

A few days later, the Norwegian intermediary, Terje Rod Larsen, informed Abu Ala that Israel had added a legal adviser, Yoel Singer, to its team and suggested that the Palestinians do the same. Colonel (Res.) Singer, a veteran of the Israeli army legal system, was an expert in international law. After eighteen years of military service, he had moved to Washington, where he was employed by the respected law firm of Sidley & Austin, which represented, among other clients, the Israeli Ministry of Defense and the Israeli military industries. Singer was chosen by Rabin, who knew of his past involvement in drafting the Camp David Accords and the peace treaty between Israel and Egypt. Working

with Chief Justice Aharon Barak, who had been attorney general at the time of
Camp David, and with Dr. Meir Rosenne, the former legal adviser of the Israeli
Foreign Ministry and a former ambassador to Paris and Washington, Singer
had acquired vast experience in drafting treaties with Egypt. Rabin wanted him
to apply this experience to the Palestinian problem. Studying the protocols of
the Oslo and Washington negotiations, Singer prepared a list of more than fifty
questions that were to be presented to Abu Ala at the next Oslo meeting.

Ignoring Larsen's request to add a legal adviser to his team, Abu Ala, in
Tunis, was waging his own war against Arafat's modus operandi, forcing some
changes in the composition of his team. Ever suspicious, and constantly afraid
of plots and conspiracies against him, Arafat was uncertain whether Abu Ala
was reporting to him the full contents of the Oslo deliberations. Arafat persuaded Maher el-Kurd, a senior member of the Palestinian team, to send him
"personal reports" about the discussions with the Israelis. When Abu Ala discovered this practice, he threatened to resign. "Either you trust me or you
don't," Abu Ala told Arafat during an angry discussion between them. "If you
do, then you must accept el-Kurd's removal from my team." Arafat had no
choice but to agree. Abu Ala appointed his assistant in the PLO's economic department, Mohamed Abu Khosh, an economist who had studied in the United
States, to succeed el-Kurd.

By the time the Israelis and the Palestinians met again in Oslo, on June 14,
Rabin and Peres had agreed on a withdrawal from Jericho, but without Palestinian control of the bridges linking the West Bank to Jordan. Meeting with
Singer on June 10, in the presence of Peres and Yossi Beilin, Rabin made it absolutely clear that the Israeli army's redeployment—first in the Gaza Strip and
later in parts of the West Bank—was a matter of Israel's exclusive discretion. "I
want you to clearly define this subject in the declaration of principles," Rabin
told Singer. Rabin was prepared to accept a language that would require "consultation" with the Palestinians on the Israeli redeployment, but not their consent. Rabin accepted Singer's opposition to the idea of a trusteeship, as
suggested by Abu Ala. In a well-documented paper, Singer argued, based on international precedents, that all trusteeships in recent history were considered a
temporary arrangement leading to full independence. Since Rabin was still opposed to an independent Palestinian state, and he certainly would not commit
himself to such a course at the beginning of the negotiations, the whole idea of
UN trusteeship should be dropped. Rabin stressed the point that no Israeli settlement would be evacuated during the five-year interim period and that both
the settlements and the settlers would be protected by the Israeli army. As for
Jerusalem, the whole issue should be deferred to the final status negotiations.
Finally, the issue of Jericho. Although he and Peres had agreed on "Gaza-
Jericho first," Rabin instructed Singer that as a tactical move, he should con-
centrate on "Gaza first" and only if the Palestinians raised the issue of Jericho

enter into negotiation on this issue, stressing Israel's refusal to relinquish control of the crossing points.

Before the Israelis and the Palestinians began their new round of negotiations in Oslo, Abu Ala met privately with Hirschfeld and Pundak. He wanted to know more about Singer and his political views. They could not tell him much. Throughout his long military career, Singer had worked under both Likud and Labor governments, but he kept his political views to himself. In his report to Arafat, Abu Ala quoted Hirschfeld as having told him that Rabin had sent Singer to Oslo "because he did not want to rely solely on Uri Savir's reports." Abu Ala added that Hirschfeld and Pundak had suggested to him to be "patient and calm" even if he found Singer to be "aggressive and arrogant."[23]

Unlike the previous meetings in Oslo, which were friendly and relaxed, the meeting with Singer in June was more businesslike and was dominated by the numerous questions that Singer had raised. Abu Ala brought from Tunis a Palestinian proposal for a declaration of principles that made a reference to the status of Jerusalem and raised a question of principle: The PLO wanted the interim self-government to be composed of two bodies, executive and legislative. Singer rejected it outright. The PLO's draft for a declaration did not mention that the Israeli army would be responsible for the "external security" or for the defense of the Israeli settlements and settlers, but Abu Ala did say that his instructions were to be flexible on matters related to Israel's security. On the issue of the Gaza Strip, Uri Savir laid to rest the idea of a UN trusteeship, since, he said, Israel was prepared to withdraw within three or four months of the signing of the DOP and hand over the area to the Palestinians. As expected, Abu Ala again raised the issue of Jericho and made it clear that there would be no agreement unless there was a simultaneous withdrawal from the Gaza Strip and Jericho. Singer replied that he would discuss this subject with Rabin and Peres.

Meanwhile, and independently of the Oslo channel, the two "official" Israeli and Palestinian teams began on June 15 the tenth round of the bilateral negotiations in Washington. Now that Israel and the PLO were negotiating directly in Oslo, Arafat no longer saw a challenge to his authority and was not concerned that Israel and the United States would try to build an "alternative leadership" in the territories. Consequently, Arafat did not oppose a meeting between Faisal Husseini and Secretary Christopher and Ambassador Dennis Ross in Washington. The meeting did not produce much. Husseini continued to urge the United States to resume its suspended dialogue with the PLO. Relying on the assurances given by the Norwegian foreign minister that whatever was agreed upon in Oslo would be brought for formal discussion in Washington, Ross asked the Palestinian spokesperson, Hanan Ashrawi, if they brought anything from the secret channel. Ashrawi was taken aback. Although it was she who had proposed that Beilin and Hirschfeld meet with Abu Ala, she didn't know that there was a secret channel. Neither the Palestinians nor the Israelis had told her about it. However, pretending that she knew what Dennis Ross referred to, she replied diplomatically: "Nothing is final yet." Immediately after the meeting, Ashrawi called Arafat in Tunis. "Ross is no different from Rabin," Arafat told her. "They are both trying to destroy the little progress that was achieved through the good offices of Egypt." Arafat did not tell Ashrawi anything about Oslo.[24] Nabil Shaath, who was also in Washington, was kept in the dark too. Both Arafat and Abu Mazen called him "a mobile radio transmitter" and didn't share the secrets of Oslo with him.

When the tenth round of the bilateral negotiations opened in Washington, on June 15, both Israelis and Palestinians were of the opinion that there was no sense in continuing these discussions. Like his Palestinian counterparts, the head of the Israeli "official" team, Eli Rubenstein, knew nothing about Oslo. He sensed, however, that the Palestinians were constantly hardening their positions, making an agreement in Washington impossible. Rubenstein suggested to his Palestinian counterpart, Dr. Haidar Abdul Shafi, holding "private" discussions instead of the plenary sessions. Rubenstein and Abdul Shafi had met several times in private in the previous rounds, but this time the Palestinian refused.

In a desperate effort to avoid a deadlock, the United States began to play a more active role in the process. On June 30, Ross presented an informal document of "written ideas" relating to the issue of Jerusalem and to the extent of Palestinian self-governing powers. In a telephone conversation with Rabin, Rubenstein said that the U.S. paper was submitted in advance of a new visit by the U.S. secretary of state to the region. Secretary Christopher spoke by phone with President Mubarak and urged him to persuade Arafat to accept the U.S. paper.[25]

The U.S. paper supported Israel in several key areas. For example, the United States did not expect Israel to grant the Palestinians jurisdiction over all the territories during the five-year interim period. The paper stated: "The inclusion or exclusion of specific spheres of authority, geographic areas or categories of persons within the jurisdiction of the interim self-government, will not prejudice the positions or claims of either party." The American paper also recognized Israel's responsibility for "overall security" in the territories, rather than just "external security" as the Palestinians preferred. Both Israel and the Palestinians rejected the American paper. Nevertheless, both agreed to hold an eleventh round of talks in Washington, on August 31. Developments in the following weeks would render this date irrelevant.

Back in Tunis, Arafat convened the steering committee to hear a detailed report about the last round of secret negotiations in Oslo. Arafat was upset that Singer and Uri Savir again refrained from discussing the withdrawal from Jericho. "I know that Rabin and the Israeli army want to get rid of the Gaza Strip," Arafat told his colleagues. "I am ready to take Gaza, but only with Jericho. The road to Jerusalem goes through Jericho. We should tell the Israelis that without Jericho, there would be no deal. Otherwise, everyone would accuse us of giving away Jerusalem and the entire West Bank." Before answering Singer's numerous questions, Arafat and Abu Mazen went to Cairo to consult with Mubarak and his aides. Arafat was very pessimistic. At the previous rounds in Oslo, the negotiations had been handled exclusively by Shimon Peres, but Arafat now saw Rabin's fingerprints in every Singer question. Arafat feared that Rabin's effort to reassert himself as the chief negotiator with the Palestinians would complicate matters. Mubarak, however, and his political adviser, Dr. Ossama el-Baz, appeased Arafat's fears. They told him that they knew for sure that Rabin and Peres were serious in their intent to withdraw from the Gaza Strip. They expressed the hope that the issue of Jericho would also be resolved. "Just be patient," Mubarak told Arafat and Abu Mazen.[26]

The month of July was full of activity, with many mixed and sometimes conflicting messages from both sides. The Norwegian intermediary, Terje Rod Larsen, had scheduled another meeting in Sarpsborg on July 3, 1993. During that meeting, Singer presented Abu Ala with a new text of a declaration of principles, in proper legal form. As expected, the Israeli draft differed from the Palestinian draft in many key areas. Abu Ala rejected it outright. The discussions were tense and loaded and were accompanied by mutual threats to withdraw from the Oslo channel. In general terms it could be said that the differences in the two versions of the declaration reflected the contradicting objectives of the parties. Rabin wanted to give the PLO "more than an autonomy, but less than a sovereign state." In contrast, Arafat wanted all the attributes of an independent state.

After lengthy deliberations, one key issue was resolved: Both sides agreed on a language in the DOP that clearly defined the linkage between the interim and final solution. But the issues of Jerusalem, Jericho, and the Palestinian refugees were not solved. It was obvious by now that the same tough issues that prevented an agreement in Washington had resurfaced with the same intensity in Oslo. Having won de facto recognition by the Israelis' very willingness to negotiate with the PLO, Arafat saw no reason to moderate his positions on the principal issues.

With no apparent progress made, the Israeli and Palestinian teams returned for further consultations with their superiors. They returned to Oslo for a new round on July 12. The meeting opened on a positive note. Responding to an earlier suggestion by Hirschfeld, Abu Ala handed to the Israelis a letter by Arafat addressed "to the meeting." It was carefully composed but unsigned. Arafat assured the Israelis that "we deal with this channel in full seriousness." However, when it came to substance, Arafat was uncompromising. Abu Ala presented an amended DOP draft according to which the crossing points between the Gaza Strip and Egypt and between Jericho and Jordan would be under Palestinian responsibility, but "with international supervision and in co-operation with Israel."[27] Peres saw in the altered version a "softening" in the Palestinian position. Rabin disagreed. In addition to Israeli security concerns, Rabin took into consideration King Hussein's interests as well. Over the last thirty years, Israeli-Jordanian security cooperation and joint control of the bridges had prevented many actions that could have undermined the stability of both countries. Rabin was not prepared to compromise this cooperation with Jordan by handing over control of the bridges to the PLO.

Another alarming issue that Abu Ala had raised was a Palestinian demand for an "extraterritorial corridor" between the Gaza Strip and Hebron and a safe "air corridor" between the Gaza Strip and the West Bank. This issue had been raised by President Mubarak during his meeting with Rabin in Ismailiya on April 14, and it had been rejected. Now the Palestinians had raised it again. Singer again said no. Singer told Abu Ala that the request for a "corridor" was a provocation and suggested that he "forget it."

Finally, on the issue of Jerusalem, the modified Palestinian version of the DOP still insisted on the right of the Palestinians in East Jerusalem not only to vote, but also to stand as candidates for election. Singer and Uri Savir were greatly upset by this Palestinian attitude. They told Abu Ala that his proposal for a DOP had pratically "blown up" the Oslo channel. They accused the Palestinians of deviating from previous commitments and raising again problems that had already been rejected. With the encouragement of the Norwegian intermediaries, both sides tried to put on paper points of agreement and disagreement. Eventually, they managed to reduce the number of points of disagreement from twenty-nine to eight. The remaining points of disagreement related to the issues of Jerusalem, Jericho, the settlements, the refugees, and matters of jurisdiction.

At the end of this round of secret talks, it became evident that the Oslo channel had reached a dead end. In an effort to avoid a total collapse, Peres traveled to Cairo for an urgent meeting with President Mubarak. Peres told the Egyptian president that the talks in Oslo had exhausted themselves and that it was now time for decisions. Mubarak told Peres that Arafat wanted to meet with him in Cairo. It was clear that Mubarak wanted to take credit for breaking the deadlock. Peres refused. He did not have permission from Rabin for such a meeting, nor had Arafat shown the kind of moderation that would warrant such a meeting. Peres told Mubarak that Israel and the Palestinians must first reach an agreement; the time for meetings would come later. Peres used the Egyptian channel to transmit an urgent message to Abu Mazen in Tunis. The contents of the message were revealed by Mahmoud Nofal, a former member of Arafat's national security team. In his book *The Israeli-Palestinian Peace*, written in Arabic and published in Beirut in early 1995, Nofal wrote: "Peres informed Abu Mazen that Rabin and Secretary Christopher wanted to close the Oslo channel and bring the parties back to Washington."[28] A few months later, Abu Mazen himself confirmed the story. He said: "In mid-July, Peres sent me an urgent message saying that if we didn't reach an agreement within two weeks, everything would be lost. The Oslo channel would be exposed, Rabin would retract from further contacts with the PLO, and he himself [Peres] would fly. . . ."[29]

Indeed, during that period and through selective leaks, the Israeli and Arab press began publishing reports about secret Israeli-PLO negotiations aimed at reaching an agreement on a possible Israeli withdrawal from the Gaza Strip. In early July 1993, the usually reliable Saudi-owned paper *El-Hayat* reported from Washington that Israel and the PLO were holding secret talks in Oslo. The correspondent attributed his story to "sources close to the U.S. peace team." *El-Hayat's* news editor called Tunis for comment. He received an angry denial. "The only channel other than the one in Washington is the Egyptian channel. Ossama el-Baz's recent trip to Israel was in connection with this Egyptian effort," an aide to Arafat said. Arafat accused Dennis Ross and Martin Indyk of making this leak. He told his aides: "The Americans oppose any negotiation, if they are not part of it. They would not support any agreement with Israel, if they did not help achieve it. . . ."[30]

On July 15, Naomi Levitzki, a credible Israeli journalist with good access to the intelligence community, also reported that Israel and the PLO were holding secret negotiations "in Europe."[31]

Asked to comment on these reports, Rabin told the *Jerusalem Post* on July 15 that "bringing the PLO into the negotiations would not be helpful."

Facing the possibility that their initiative was about to collapse, Norwegian Foreign Minister Johan Jorgen Holst and his two aides, Terje Larsen and his wife, Mona Juul, flew to Tunis for an urgent meeting with Arafat. In a handwritten letter transmitted to Peres by Larsen, Holst said that he had been "very tough" with Arafat and accused the PLO of "deviating" from the substance of realistic proposals. He had told Arafat that there had already been five drafts of a DOP and none had been accepted. Time was running out. The PLO would never get a better deal than the one proposed by Israel.

Arafat, however, told Holst that he had a problem of "selling" the "Gaza first" package. He explained that unlike the West Bank, the Gaza Strip had no religious significance to Israel. Therefore it was easy for Rabin to offer a withdrawal from that region. However, if an agreement with Israel was to be reached, it would have to signal in a very tangible way that there would be Israeli withdrawals from the West Bank as well. Arafat added that without the "symbolic" Israeli withdrawal from Jericho, there would be no accord. Arafat agreed, however, to resume the Oslo talks on July 27, 1993.

In his discussion with Larsen and Mona Juul in Jerusalem, Peres asked them to make sure that Arafat understood that the seat of the Palestine Authority could not be East Jerusalem and that he could not return to the territories with the title of president, as he had been calling himself since November 1988. Larsen said that Arafat understood this. Peres added that if Arafat continued to insist on including the issue of Jerusalem in the DOP, then the whole process would collapse. Peres concluded his discussion by telling Larsen and Mona Juul: "We have to move fast. Don't let the Oslo channel become like the Washington channel, like chewing gum. . . ." Larsen said that that was Arafat's position as well.[32]

While Holst and Larsen were making a genuine effort to salvage the Oslo channel, several "private" initiatives were undertaken by various members of Rabin's cabinet. Shulamit Aloni, the head of the left-wing Meretz Party and the minister of communications, asked to meet with Abu Mazen in Tunis. Rabin approved her request, but Peres opposed it. Back in March, Carl Kahana, an Austrian-Jewish businessman and a close friend of Chancellor Bruno Kreisky, had tried to arrange a meeting between Aloni and Arafat. Peres vetoed that effort. In July 1993, however, Aloni, as a senior member of the coalition, insisted on her right to meet with Abu Mazen. Rabin overruled Peres and told Aloni that she could meet with the PLO executive, but he wanted a full report after the meeting.[33]

Hanan Ashrawi contacted Abu Mazen and conveyed Aloni's request to him. Abu Mazen asked Abu Ala to verify the purpose of the meeting. Abu Ala asked Hirschfeld and Pundak, who were subordinated to Peres and Beilin. The two academics were reported to have told Abu Ala: "Don't pay any attention to her. For your information, Rabin can't stand Aloni. He hates having been forced to include her in his cabinet."[34]

I asked Aloni about this exchange. She said that she was not aware of it, but knowing Peres's tactics, she would not be surprised if it was true. Abu Mazen did not meet with Aloni. Realizing, however, that she was a senior coalition partner and taking into account her many contacts with the Palestinians in the past, Abu Mazen arranged for the poet Mahmoud Darwish to meet with her in Paris. Darwish, the most prominent Palestinian poet, had written the Palestinian Declaration of Independence in Algiers in November 1988. He was also a member of the PLO Executive Committee. Unlike Aloni, who knew nothing about the Oslo channel, Darwish was familiar with the details of the secret negotiations, and he was being briefed by Arafat on a regular basis.

"Darwish was very inquisitive about Rabin's policies and intentions," Aloni told me. The PLO knew that Peres wanted peace with the Palestinians, but there was some uncertainty about Rabin. Darwish wondered why, if Rabin indeed wanted peace, he kept Eli Rubenstein as the head of the Israeli negotiating team in Washington. Rubenstein had been appointed by Shamir. Wasn't Rabin's failure to replace him proof that Rabin was continuing Shamir's policies? Darwish asked. Aloni explained that unlike Shamir, Rabin was sincere in his quest for peace. He was by nature more cautious and very slow in decision making. As for Rubenstein, Aloni explained, he was a good and trusted civil servant. "In any event," Aloni told Darwish, "the decision-maker is Rabin, not Rubenstein."

Immediately after this meeting in Paris, Darwish went to Tunis to report to Abu Mazen about his discussion with Aloni. Abu Mazen was reassured by Aloni's input. His conclusion was that Rabin was trying to feel the Palestinian pulse and to see to what extent Arafat was committed to the peace talks.

The Aloni-Darwish meeting was not the only feeler at that time. Much more serious was the one undertaken by Dr. Ahmed Tibi, a thirty-nine-year-old Israeli Arab gynecologist who had become an Arafat confidant. Born to a wealthy landowning family in Taibeh, an Israeli Arab town northeast of Tel Aviv, Tibi had studied medicine at Hebrew University and done his residency at the Hadassah Hospital in Jerusalem. He was married to Mayeh, an attractive dentist from Tul-Karm, in the West Bank. Tibi was fluent in Hebrew, and through his close contacts with the Israeli Labor Party's doves—especially with Health Minister Haim Ramon—he arranged for his bride a permanent residence in Jerusalem, as part of the Israeli plan for family reunifications.

Dr. Tibi had drawn national attention in Israel in January 1990 when he arranged for Ezer Weizman to meet secretly in Geneva with Nabil Ramlawi in an effort to convince the PLO to accept Secretary Baker's five-point plan for Palestinian representation in the peace process. Weizman's meeting with the PLO had not been approved by Shamir. When informed about it by the Israeli security services, Shamir had wanted to fire Weizman from his cabinet. Fearing, however, a crisis with the Labor Party, Shamir eventually had settled for the exclusion of Weizman from the ministerial foreign affairs and security committee.

Dr. Tibi had been introduced to Arafat in 1984 by Raymonda Tawil, a Palestinian journalist who ran a pro-PLO news service in Jerusalem. Tawil is the mother of Suha, Yasser Arafat's wife, and she took Tibi with her secretly to Tunis. Since that meeting with Arafat and Abu Mazen, Tibi had become the liaison between the PLO and the Labor doves. He became so identified with the PLO that in the 1996 elections, Likud distributed a bumper sticker that read: "The choice is between Bibi [Netanyahu] and Tibi." In a meeting with Ramon in Tel Aviv in July 1993, Tibi said that from messages that he was receiving from Tunis, he gathered that Arafat and Abu Mazen were uncertain to what extent Rabin was indeed committed to direct negotiations with the PLO. A few days later, Ramon submitted to Tibi four questions that were drafted by Rabin himself. The questions were.

- Is the PLO ready for a two-stage settlement—an interim period of five years, and then final status negotiations?

- Does the PLO agree that during the five-year interim period, not one single Israeli settlement would be evacuated, and that the whole issue of settlements would be deferred to the final status negotiations?

- Does the PLO agree that during the interim period, the overall security would remain Israel's responsibility? Moreover, does the PLO understand that once an agreement is reached, it would have to desist from any act of terror and violence?

- Finally, does the PLO agree that the final status of Jerusalem would be deferred to final status negotiations?

Tibi took the questions to Tunis, and Arafat told him that Abu Mazen would draft the answers. Indeed, a few days later, at a meeting at his home in Ramat Hasharon, near Tel Aviv, Ramon informed Tibi that "Rabin was very pleased with Abu Mazen's answers" and that the prime minister saw no problem in negotiating directly with the PLO.[35]

Finally, there was another feeler transmitted via Faisal Husseini. The Palestinian leader in East Jerusalem reported to Arafat that he had been approached by Knesset member Ephraim Sneh, one of Rabin's loyalists, who asked if Arafat would be prepared to negotiate secretly with Israel, outside the Washington venue. Arafat, however, misread Rabin. He interpreted the prime minister's feelers as maneuvers aimed at circumventing the Oslo channel. Arafat instructed Husseini to stop all contacts with Israelis—officials or non-officials—and to come immediately to Tunis. Some of Arafat's aides, who clearly disliked Husseini, sharply criticized him and accused him of becoming a "tool" in the hands of both Israel and the United States.

Arafat convened the steering committee to discuss Faisal Husseini's message. Arafat and Abu Mazen agreed that Rabin was "unhappy" with the Oslo channel and was trying to reassert himself as the prime Israeli negotiator by opening an alternative channel of negotiations with the Palestinians. Arafat told Abu Ala to inform Larsen about "Rabin's maneuvers." Abu Ala himself attacked Husseini and accused him of opposing any channel that he was not part of.[36]

This was, then, the general mood when the Israelis and the Palestinians met on July 27 for another round of secret negotiations in Oslo. It was obvious that having gone that far, Rabin and Arafat had no choice but to continue the Oslo channel until an agreement was reached. Unknown to Arafat at the time, Rabin told Singer that he could now discuss an Israeli withdrawal from the city of Jericho. After Holst's visit to Tunis, and his letter to Peres saying that Arafat could not sell the package of "Gaza first" without a withdrawal from Jericho, Rabin appeared resigned to the idea that this was a price that he had to pay. Indeed, in his instructions to Abu Ala, Arafat said that the Palestinians should

stress the issue of Jericho, "even at the risk of withdrawing from the secret negotiations in Oslo." Not all members of the steering committee shared Arafat's
view. When Arafat left the room, Abu Mazen and Yasser Abed Rabbo told Abu
Ala: "You should, of course, raise the issue of Jericho, as a bargaining card.
Rabin would never agree to withdraw from Jericho. So it's better to try to get
the best possible deal in the Gaza Strip. Arafat is so keen on having a strip of
land, where he could build a 'ceremonial state,' that he would settle for an Israeli withdrawal from the Gaza Strip only."[37]

Abu Mazen was wrong. At the opening of the July 27 meeting in Oslo,
Singer surprised his Palestinian counterparts by letting them know that Israel
was now prepared to withdraw from Jericho as well. He made it clear, however,
that the withdrawal was limited to the city's boundaries only and that the exact
details would have to be discussed at a later stage. In return, Abu Ala said that
the PLO now agreed that no Israeli settlements would be evacuated during the
interim period, and that the security of the settlers would remain in the hands
of the Israeli security forces.

Abu Ala phoned Arafat and Abu Mazen immediately and told them about
the new development. They were obviously thrilled and could not believe their
ears. Arafat's intransigence had paid off. "Try now to push harder and try to get
more concessions from the Israelis," they both told Abu Ala.

The Palestinians' appetite proved to be very big. At the end of this round of
the Oslo talks, the problems that were still to be resolved were the following:

- The issue of Jericho. Israel proposed to withdraw from the city of
  Jericho. Abu Ala presented the Israelis with a map from the time
  of the British Mandate, showing the "District of Jericho" stretching from the Jordan River up to Jerusalem's city limits.

- The issue of Jerusalem. Both Israel and the Palestinians agreed
  that the final status of the city would be determined in the final
  status negotiations. As a gesture of goodwill, Israel agreed that
  East Jerusalem Palestinians who did not hold Israeli identity
  cards would be allowed to vote for the Palestine Authority, in
  polls outside of Jerusalem—in Ramallah or Bethlehem. In contrast, the Palestinians insisted on the right of East Jerusalem
  Palestinians not only to vote but also to stand for election. Abu
  Ala suggested that East Jerusalem Palestinians would vote in
  their holy places—the Muslims in El-Aqsa Mosque, the Christians in the Church of the Holy Sepulcher.

- The size of the Palestinian police force. In the July 3 meeting in
  Oslo, Abu Ala asked for an Israeli "professional assessment" of
  the number of policemen required to enforce law and order in

the Gaza Strip once the Israeli withdrawal was completed. Abu Ala said that according to Palestinian estimates, the PLO would need "at least" sixteen thousand policemen in the Gaza Strip alone. Israel thought that the number was excessive, and it exceeded the total number of Israeli soldiers in the Gaza Strip.

Thus, while Rabin made the important concession of surrendering Jericho to Palestinian rule, the problems to be resolved were still enormous. Obviously frustrated, Peres wrote to Norwegian Foreign Minister Johan Jorgen Holst: "I must share with you my honest concern, that they [the Palestinians] may opt to aspire for a too perfect solution. . . . The vacuum may be filled by opposing forces, or with other initiatives, including the possibility of desired progress between Israel and Syria. Secretary Christopher is at this very moment visiting our region. . . ."[38]

Rabin, on his part, took a very unusual step: He sent Yossi Sarid, the minister of environment, to meet secretly with Nabil Shaath in Cairo. Sarid, a leading member of Meretz, the left-wing coalition partner, was the only cabinet minister at that stage to know of the Oslo channel. Both Rabin and Peres associated him with this secret. Rabin sent Sarid without Peres's knowledge, and he was booked on the El-Al flight to Cairo as "Yossi S." The Israeli security services had unveiled his identity, and despite his protests, they had assigned two bodyguards to accompany him.

At a meeting with Sarid at his Meretz Party headquarters, the spectacled, balding former minister told me: "Rabin was very distressed. He certainly didn't like the Oslo channel. He was all the time concerned that Peres was not telling him everything about Oslo and about his discussions with the Egyptians. He was particularly concerned about Jerusalem and the Israeli settlements during the interim period. Rabin was afraid that Peres would drag him to destinations that he clearly did not want to reach." Rabin had told Sarid that he was not sure that Nabil Shaath was aware of the Oslo channel. "Therefore, in your discussions in Cairo, make sure that you don't become his source of information. If he knows nothing—don't tell him anything." Indeed, Shaath knew nothing about Oslo, and his meeting with Sarid did not clarify the issues that Rabin wanted clarified.[39]

In view of the apparent deadlock, Singer suggested a deal to Peres: formal recognition of the PLO in return for meaningful Palestinian concessions. Singer said that the whole idea of negotiating secretly with the PLO and submitting the results to the Washington teams for formal approval was "impractical." The true story would leak to the press and Israel would gain nothing. "On the other hand, if we grant the PLO recognition, Arafat would have to reciprocate by a counter-recognition of Israel, and a commitment to end terrorism," Singer said. "Forget it," Peres replied. Singer asked Peres for permission to try to convince Rabin. The prime minister told Singer that he was afraid that a Palestinian autonomy, combined with a recognition of the PLO, would be too hard for the Israeli public to stomach. Nevertheless, Rabin allowed Singer to raise this issue with Abu Ala, as a purely "private" initiative.[40]

In early August, Abu Ala returned from Oslo very pessimistic. He told Arafat and Abu Mazen that when he suggested to Singer replacing the word "Palestinians" with the word "PLO" in the declaration of principles, Singer replied that he would accept this change only in return for a PLO commitment to have the Palestine National Council (PNC)—the Palestinian parliament-in-exile—abrogate the relevant clauses in the Palestinian Covenant that called for the destruction of Israel. Arafat commented: "I don't understand. Back in November 1988, I declared in Paris that the Covenant was *caduque*. Why would Israel insist now on formal abrogation?"[41]

In Israel, Rabin was now facing conflicting pressures. The chief of military intelligence, General Uri Saguy, submitted to Rabin a report according to which the PLO was on the verge of financial collapse. "The PLO is splintered and bankrupt. Arafat did not recover from his blunder during the Persian Gulf War, when he openly supported Saddam Hussein. The possibility that Arafat will disappear soon is very real," Saguy wrote.[42] On the other hand, Rabin was under growing pressure by Peres and Egypt to conclude the Oslo talks. Egyptian Foreign Minister Amr Mussa visited Israel and urged Rabin to strike the deal with Arafat. After his return to Cairo, Mussa reported to Mubarak that he wasn't sure Rabin wanted the Oslo channel. Mussa quoted Rabin as having told him: "Let Peres and Abu Mazen play and explore their ideas. They both know that nothing would come out of it. . . ."[43]

Rabin himself gave public expression to his doubts. Asked by Israeli TV on August 12, 1993, if he was considering a meeting with Yasser Arafat, Rabin replied: "Forget it. Certainly not in the near future." The interviewer pressed harder: Could such a meeting take place before the end of Rabin's term as prime minister? "I hope not," Rabin answered. "The negotiations should be conducted in Washington, with the Palestinian residents of the territories. . . ."

That was just one week before the DOP was finally initialed in Oslo. Was it a smoke screen? Not entirely. Rabin knew that the intelligence report about the possible financial collapse of the PLO was accurate. The telephone bills of Abu Mazen's office in Tunis had not been paid for months. Salaries were frozen and PLO offices abroad were closing because of lack of funds. There were rumors about widespread corruption, which caused tensions among the rank and file everywhere. In Jordan and Lebanon, widows and orphans were demonstrating because they were not receiving their pensions. In Libya, there was an armed clash between PLO members and the guards of the Palestinian "embassy" in Tripoli. In Algiers, PLO rebels took charge of the PLO office. Since Arafat was not accountable, nobody really knew if the financial crisis was genuine or a mere "exercise" aimed at persuading the United States to rush to the PLO's rescue.

During these past weeks, the United States had had a general idea about the Oslo channel, but was not familiar with the details. During his trip to the Middle East in early August, Secretary Christopher raised the Oslo issue very briefly with Rabin. He was told that the major issues had not been solved and that the gap between the parties was still wide. Christopher did not discuss the subject with Peres. He underestimated Peres's manipulative abilities and he simply could not believe that Peres, Egypt, and Norway could achieve in Oslo what the United States had failed to achieve in Washington.

In his meeting with Christopher, on August 3, 1993, Rabin asked the secretary to verify with President Assad whether Syria would be prepared to sign with Israel a contractual peace, independently of the other tracks and whether this peace would include normalization and formal diplomatic relations with Israel. Rabin proposed that the anticipated Israeli withdrawal from the Golan Heights would be gradual and would last five years. Each phase would be accompanied by Syrian confidence-building measures in the field of normalization. That was Rabin's preferred approach. However, anticipating a Syrian insistence on progress in the other tracks as well, Rabin told Christopher that he would be prepared to reach an interim agreement with the Palestinians as well. The American secretary of state asked whether such an interim agreement would include a withdrawal from Jericho. Rabin answered: If Assad accepts my "package," the agreement with the Palestinians would be limited to the Gaza Strip only. However, if Assad adopts a delaying tactic—the agreement with the Palestinians would include Jericho as well.

In a meeting in Damascus, on August 4, Christopher conveyed to Assad Rabin's "hypothetical package." Assad's reply was very disappointing. While welcoming Israel's readiness to withdraw from the Golan Heights, Assad countered by so many conditions that Rabin interpreted them as a rejection. Syria rejected, for example, that the phased Israeli withdrawal be extended over a period of five years and suggested instead a period of six months. Assad was ready for formal diplomatic relations, but argued that economic normalization is a subject of mutual agreement between the businessmen of both countries and cannot be imposed by the governments. Finally, Assad rejected Rabin's proposal to open a secret channel of communications with Israel and insisted that all contacts be held in Washington.

Not expecting any breakthrough with Syria, Rabin gave Peres, on August 5, the "green light" to pursue the talks with the Palestinians in Oslo. Meanwhile, Rabin faced a major crisis at home. Shas, the Sephardic fundamentalist party, which had six Knesset members, left the coalition government over matters unrelated to the peace process. Thus, Rabin was left with a minority government, supported by fifty-six Knesset members only. In order to survive, Rabin had to rely on the support of five Arab Knesset members, who were not part of his coalition. With his sharp political instincts, Peres immediately understood that this was the last chance to achieve a breakthrough with the Palestinians in Oslo. "It's now or never," Peres told Norwegian Foreign Minister Johan Jorgen Holst. Peres used a scheduled visit to Stockholm, on August 17, and invited Holst to the Swedish capital. Holst was visiting Iceland at that time. When reached by phone by Yossi Beilin, Holst said: "I am at your disposal any time, anywhere."

Holst came to Stockholm with Larsen and Mona Juul. The explanation given to the Swedes for this unusual visit was that Holst had come to solve with Peres an old dispute about a Norwegian consignment of heavy water that had reached the Dimona nuclear research center. The Swedes knew, of course, that Peres was scheduled to visit Oslo in two days, so that the "dispute" could be solved in Norway. However, always discreet, the Swedes pretended to have accepted the explanation. Their intelligence services, however, which monitored all foreign communications, had undoubtedly intercepted the seven-hour telephone conversations between Stockholm and Tunis and were able to provide the Swedish government with a full report on the historic development that occurred that night on their soil.

Holst's effort to establish contact with Tunis began immediately after the official dinner offered by the Swedish foreign minister in honor of Peres ended. Terje Larsen tried in vain to reach Abu Ala. He phoned Arafat directly. He told the PLO chairman that his "fathers" (Holst and Peres) were sitting beside him in Stockholm and they both wanted to try to solve the remaining three issues that were delaying an accord between Israel and the PLO.

Arafat drove to Abu Mazen's and Abed Rabbo's homes and told them about his conversation with Larsen. They all agreed to meet at Arafat's office at 1:00 A.M. Arafat then drove to Abu Ala's home and gave him the same message. Finally, two other members of the steering committee, Mohsen Ibrahim and Hassan Asfour, also went to Arafat's office. Abu Ala called Larsen in Stockholm and informed him that the PLO leadership needed another ninety minutes for consultations.

Arafat and the other members of the steering committee agreed that this was indeed a matter of now or never. The domestic crisis in Israel was genuine. After the departure of the Shas Party from the coalition, there could be a very undesirable result: In order not to rely on the vote of the five Arab Knesset members, Rabin might be tempted to resign and form a new coalition government, with the center-right Tsomet Party and the religious parties, but without the left-wing Meretz Party. In such a case, everything that had been discussed in Oslo would become irrelevant.

Abu Mazen called President Mubarak's adviser Dr. Ossama el-Baz and Egyptian Foreign Minister Amr Mussa. They both shared the sense of urgency that Peres and Arafat had. They were also aware of the fact that both Rabin and Secretary Christopher were unhappy with Oslo and preferred to return the negotiating process to Washington. Furthermore, during his recent trip to the Middle East in early August, Secretary Christopher had made no secret of preferring the Syrian track over the Palestinian track. Therefore, the Egyptian advice to the PLO was: "Don't miss this opportunity. Try to get the maximum now and you will bargain on the rest at a later date. What is crucial, however, is not to close any future options. Any language in the DOP should not preclude future bargaining on the interpretation of the various clauses."

In line with this Egyptian advice, the PLO steering committee instructed Abu Ala to try to shorten the five-year interim period and to advance the date of the final status negotiations. Peres rejected this demand outright. He argued that the time frame for the interim and the final status negotiations was based on the letter of invitation to the Madrid Peace Conference, and hence could not be changed.

When the formal "telephone negotiations" between Tunis and Stockholm were resumed, at 2:15 A.M., August 18, Norwegian Foreign Minister Holst opened the discussion by stating that there was an agreement between the parties that the issues of Jerusalem, the Israeli settlements, the refugees, and the future relations between the Palestine Authority and other parties would be deferred to the final status negotiations. He also said that the third version of the DOP, the one that was drafted by Singer, would serve as the basis for the negotiation. Holst started reading the DOP line by line. Every clause that was agreed upon became the final text. Other issues, like jurisdiction and the status of Jerusalem during the interim period, took a longer time to resolve and necessitated further consultations between Peres and Singer and between Arafat and Abu Ala.

On the issue of jurisdiction, it was finally agreed that after the election of the Palestine Authority, Israel would transfer six functions to the new governing body: education, health, social affairs, taxation, tourism, and internal security. The size of the police force and the types of its equipment were left for further negotiations, after the signing of the DOP. A request by Abu Ala that the economic functions be transferred to the Palestinians even before the elections was rejected.

As expected, the issue of Jerusalem took a very long time to solve. Having agreed that the final political status of East Jerusalem be discussed at the final status negotiations, the PLO also agreed that the seat of the Palestine Authority would be outside Jerusalem. Nevertheless, there were two Jerusalem-related subjects that had to be resolved: the right of East Jerusalem Palestinians to participate in the election process and the status of the existing Palestinian institutions in East Jerusalem. On the issue of the elections, it was agreed to disagree. Like the issue of the size of the police force, the nature of Palestinian participation in the election process was left for further negotiations, after the signing of the DOP.

More complicated was the problem of the existing Palestinian institutions in East Jerusalem. During the past years, and under the supervision of Faisal Husseini, the Palestinians had established in East Jerusalem an impressive set of institutions that were active in various fields. The most important of these institutions was the Orient House, which had become the unofficial headquarters of the PLO in Jerusalem and was frequented by foreign dignitaries and members of the diplomatic corps. According to the DOP, the Palestinians had no jurisdiction in foreign affairs during the interim period. Having accepted that the final status of East Jerusalem be deferred to the second stage, neither Abu Ala nor Yasser Arafat agreed to suppress the existing activities of the Orient House and the other Palestinian institutions in the city. After lengthy deliberations, Peres agreed that the existing Palestinian institutions would not be affected during the interim period. Abu Ala wanted this commitment to be included in the DOP. Peres refused. Instead, he agreed to write a letter to the Norwegian foreign minister confirming this commitment. His only condition was that the letter remain secret. It wasn't long before the text of Peres's letter to Holst was leaked to Likud Knesset member Benny Begin, who in turn leaked it to the press. Finally, there was the issue of Jericho. Since both sides could not agree on the extent of the Israeli withdrawal from Jericho—whether it would be limited to the city itself or cover the District of Jericho—Peres and Abu Ala agreed to defer this problem too until after the signing of the DOP.

Before Arafat and Abu Ala gave their final approval to the DOP text, there developed a short debate in Tunis between the members of the steering committee. Mohsen Ibrahim, one of Arafat's most loyal companions since the war in Lebanon in 1982, suggested delaying the formal initialing of the DOP until after a proper consultation between the PLO and Syria, Lebanon, and Jordan. Arafat and Abu Mazen disagreed. They argued that because of the nature of the government crisis in Israel, the PLO could find itself with a DOP but with no Israeli government to sign it. Any further delay, they argued, could be detrimental to the PLO's interests. That was also the view of the Egyptian foreign minister.

Finally, at 5:00 A.M., August 18, Abu Ala informed Holst that all problems were resolved and that the PLO was prepared to initial the DOP in Oslo the next day. The Israelis and the Norwegians in Stockholm could hear, through the telephone, the members of the Palestinian steering committee cheering and weeping with joy. Arafat asked one of his aides to bring a camcorder and a still camera to commemorate that historic event. Indeed, they all stood at Arafat's office for this photo of Arafat himself, Abu Mazen, Abu Ala, Yasser Abed Rabbo, Mohsen Ibrahim, and Hassan Asfour.[44]

Holst asked Abu Ala to return to Oslo that same day, together with his team, for the initialing of the DOP. He informed Abu Ala that Peres wanted Uri Savir and Yoel Singer to initial the DOP on behalf of Israel, with Dr. Yair Hirschfeld and Dr. Ron Pundak standing behind them. Abu Ala told Holst that he and Hassan Asfour would initial the DOP on behalf of the Palestinians.

What was left unresolved was the drafting of the letter of mutual recognition between Israel and the PLO. Holst informed Abu Ala that he had agreed with Peres that after initialing the DOP, the Israeli team would remain in Oslo to conclude the mutual recognition paper. He suggested that the Palestinians do the same. Holst clarified, however, that Israel's condition for mutual recognition was that the PLO renounce terrorism and agree to abrogate the relevant clauses in the Palestinian Covenant which were in contradiction to the DOP.

Peres phoned Rabin and informed him that the negotiations with the PLO were concluded and that the DOP would be initialed the next day in Oslo. The prime minister had no comment. His thoughts were somewhere else. That same morning, seven Israeli soldiers had been killed by a powerful roadside bomb that Hezbollah had planted in South Lebanon. It was President Assad's way of "reminding" Israel that it was Syria that was holding the key to a comprehensive peace between Israel and its Arab neighbors. The tragedy in South Lebanon only strengthened Rabin's belief that preference should have been given to the Israeli-Syrian track, not to the Palestinian track. Now, however, it was too late. In cooperation with Egypt, Peres had reached an agreement with the PLO, and it was impossible for Rabin to retract. The only problem that continued to bother him was whether the agreement with the PLO would indeed end fifty years of bloodshed and destruction, or would be only a long cease-fire that would come to an end once the PLO felt rehabilitated and strengthened. Rabin did not have a clear answer to that.

As part of the effort to "sell" the agreement to the Israeli public and to world Jewry, Rabin needed the active support of the American Jewish establishment. At his request, Uri Savir phoned Lester Pollack, the chairman of the Presidents Conference in New York, and invited him and Malcolm Hoenlein, the executive vice chairman of this prestigious organization, for an urgent meeting with Peres and Rabin in Jerusalem. Pollack and Hoenlein tried in vain to get a hint about the reason for this surprising initiative. "I can't discuss it over the phone," Savir said, "but believe me it's urgent and very important."[45]

While Peres and his team were making their way from Stockholm to Oslo, Abu Mazen had arranged with Egyptian Foreign Minister Amr Mussa to send Ambassador Taher Shash immediately to Oslo to review the final text of the DOP. Ambassador Shash, like Singer, was an expert in international law, and he was also involved in the drafting of the Camp David Accords and the Israeli-Egyptian peace treaty. After the Madrid Peace Conference, President Mubarak had put Shash at the disposal of the Palestinian delegation to the bilateral negotiations in Washington, and he advised the inexperienced Palestinian delegates on Israeli negotiating tactics. Shash was welcomed at the Oslo airport by Larsen, who handed him a copy of the DOP. A few hours later, Shash informed both Abu Ala and Larsen that the DOP text was fine and he had no comments on its legal language.

Peres's visit to Norway was public and official. He and his team were accommodated at the official government guest house, a three-floor building in the suburbs of Oslo. On the top floor there were an elegant reception hall and several meeting rooms. The Norwegians had allocated one room to each delegation. According to the arrangements made by Larsen, the official dinner in honor of Peres would end around 10:30 P.M. After all the guests were gone and Peres and his team "went to bed," the Norwegian secret service took charge of the guest house. They had set up several video cameras, and one secret service agent served as a photographer. Recognizing the historic significance of the event, the Norwegians brought to the reception hall the same table on which the agreement for Norway's secession from Sweden had been signed in 1905.[46]

Around 1:00 A.M., August 20, the guest house came to life again. Before proceeding to the initialing ceremony, the three delegations met in the Norwegian room. That was the first time that Peres and Abu Ala met face to face. Abu Ala was very emotional and excited, and he told Peres that he would like to have a "little chat" with him. Holst suggested that they meet in the Norwegian room after the ceremony. The ceremony itself was short. Holst expressed pride that his country had been able to achieve what the big powers had failed to achieve. He thanked Israel and the PLO for their cooperation with Norway and expressed the hope that this agreement would lead to a permanent peace between Israel and the Palestinians and between Israel and its other Arab neighbors.

Abu Ala could hardly control his emotions. Reading in perfect English the translation of his original speech in Arabic, Abu Ala stressed the historic significance of the moment. He thanked both Israel and Norway for making the Palestinian dream come true. After Uri Savir made his own remarks, the two teams initialed the DOP, and Holst affixed his signature as a witness.

Immediately after the ceremony, Abu Ala called Tunis and informed Arafat that the DOP was officially initialed. Arafat asked about the letter of mutual recognition. Abu Ala told him that the two teams would now proceed to draft the letter. He told Arafat again that Israel, in return for recognizing the PLO, was insisting that the PLO renounce terrorism and that the Palestine Covenant be amended so that all clauses calling for Israel's destruction were abrogated by the Palestine National Council. Abu Ala added that the letter would be completed before the formal signing of the DOP in Washington.

Sitting in the Norwegian room, Abu Ala thanked Peres warmly for the personal role he had played in this dramatic chapter in Israeli-Palestinian history. Peres asked Abu Ala about Faruq Kaddoumi, the PLO's "foreign minister." Abu

Ala said that Kaddoumi had been opposed to the Madrid Peace Conference and was opposed to Oslo as well. Peres asked Abu Ala to keep the agreement secret until after he and Holst returned from the United States, where they were expected to brief Secretary Christopher on the DOP. Peres was confident that the United States would support the move, since all U.S. governments had always said that it was for the parties to reach agreements between themselves. Peres had no doubt that the Israeli government would endorse the DOP and, despite the expected strong Likud opposition, Rabin would be able to surmount the obstacles facing him. Finally, Peres stressed the importance of the PLO's taking a firm position against terrorism. If Arafat did not discipline the various terrorist groups, the Israeli people would be disenchanted with Oslo. Peres was reported to have spoken with contempt about Faisal Husseini and Dr. Haidar Abdul Shafi, the head of the Palestinian team to the bilateral negotiations in Washington. "Had we relied on them, there would have never been an agreement between us," he said.[47]

After his return from Oslo, Peres met with Pollack and Hoenlein on August 25 and briefed them on the secret negotiations with the PLO. Immediately afterwards, the two American Jewish leaders went to meet with the prime minister.

"Rabin told us that we were the first to hear about the Oslo Accords. Neither the Israeli government nor the U.S. administration knew the details. Therefore, Rabin stressed, it was imperative to keep the subject secret until it was officially announced," Malcolm Hoenlein recalled. He said that Rabin asked Jacques Neriyah, his diplomatic adviser, to join the meeting as a note taker.

"Peres was euphoric and very upbeat, while Rabin was more low-key," Hoenlein said. He recalled that after Peres's report, he and Pollack asked Rabin many tough questions. They questioned the wisdom of rehabilitating Arafat at a time when he was so weak and faced financial collapse; they asked if Arafat could be trusted, after he had lied to so many people, Arabs and non-Arabs. Could Arafat "deliver," especially when the ten radical Palestinian groups in Damascus were not subordinated to him, while Hamas and Islamic Jihad were openly challenging his authority? What about Jerusalem? Finally, what would the United States say and what impact would Oslo have on the Syrian and Jordanian tracks?

Rabin replied: "All your questions are legitimate and I share some of your concerns." He explained that despite Oslo, the dangers to Israel had not disappeared. Oslo, however, was likely to split the Arab world, and this, in turn, could weaken the Arab front against Israel. He added that at a certain point he had to make a decision. He had reached the conclusion that the recognition of the PLO was inevitable. So it was better for Israel to strike such a deal with Arafat while he was weak. "The Palestinians do not constitute an existential threat to

Israel. The real threat comes from Iran and Iraq, which are striving to acquire nuclear capability and are arming themselves with long-range ballistic missiles," Rabin said. He said that he was still opposed to an independent, sovereign Palestinian state and that the issues of Jerusalem and the settlements were deferred to the final status negotiations. Rabin did not tell them, of course, about Peres's secret letter to Holst permitting the continuous functioning of the existing Palestinian institutions in East Jerusalem. Finally, Rabin said that he insisted on the gradual implementation of the Oslo Accords. "If the PLO proves to be unable or unwilling to combat terrorism, then the whole Oslo process would come to a halt," the prime minister concluded.

"This is the first time that I have heard about the Oslo Accords," admitted Jacques Neriyah to Pollack and Hoenlein. "No one in the prime minister's office, not even General Danny Yatom, the military secretary [now the director of the Mossad], knows about it. I doubt even if the chief of staff, General Ehud Barak, was informed about the secret negotiations in Oslo."[48]

Neriyah was right. Rabin did not tell any member of his staff about the secret talks with the PLO. He did not believe in the process and he was skeptical of its success. On the other hand, in case the Oslo channel did succeed—as eventually happened—he did not want to be counterpressured by the army or by his own staff.

Indeed, the counterpressures started to build immediately after Peres's return from Oslo. The first to express his reservations was the chief of staff. While supporting the principle of negotiating with the Palestinians, General Ehud Barak thought the Oslo process was flawed and did not take into consideration the complexity of Israel's security needs. Rabin showed Barak the Oslo Accords before they were submitted for government approval. In public comments, in press interviews, and in closed briefings, Barak explained his position in the following terms: "I fully support the strategic significance of the Oslo Accords, which would bring an end to the Israeli rule over another people and which would lead to a separation between the Israeli and Palestinian communities. If we don't want Israel to become another version of Beirut or Bosnia, there is no alternative but to separate the 5.5 million Israelis and the 2.5 million Palestinians. Hence, my opposition to Oslo was not based on the strategic level, but on the tactical level. In my view, Oslo gave the Palestinians too many cards, which would render our ability to preserve our security needs and to negotiate a good deal in the final status negotiations much more difficult. . . ."

Like Rabin, Barak was opposed to an independent, sovereign Palestinian state. In his view, an independent state could make life for Israel much more complicated. If such a sovereign Palestinian state was not totally demilitarized, it would be able to deploy ground-to-air missiles in the vicinity of Ramallah and Jenin, and would be able to hit any Israeli plane taking off from Ben-Gurion Airport or other military airfields in the central part of Israel.

Rabin also discussed the DOP with Ariel Sharon. Despite his reputation as a hawk, and one of the right-wing Likud hard-liners, Sharon was also a pragmatist. Rabin and Sharon had a solid history of personal relationship that was forged during their long military service and went beyond their political rivalry. Sharon was one of the victorious generals who fought under Rabin during the Six-Day War. When Rabin became prime minister for the first time, in June 1974, he appointed Sharon as his military adviser. When Sharon became defense minister under Menachem Begin, Rabin supported his strategy during the war in Lebanon in June 1982. Despite their political rivalry, Rabin and Sharon trusted and respected each other. Hence it was no wonder that Rabin discussed the Oslo Accords with Sharon before they were formally approved by the cabinet.

"Rabin told me that he knew that a withdrawal from Jericho is a mistake," Sharon said. Rabin explained that the PLO, with the support of Egypt, wanted a symbolic withdrawal in the West Bank as a proof that "Gaza first" would not become "Gaza only." "So give them Nablus, or Jenin, but not Jericho," Sharon urged. Rabin knew that that was impossible. He told Sharon: "We are in a stage of take it or leave it. I can't change anything now."[49]

Finally, Rabin consulted with General Benjamin (Fuad) Ben-Eliezer, his minister of housing. He was one of Rabin's trusted allies in the Labor Party, and Rabin valued his opinion as a former commander of the IDF forces in the West Bank. Ben-Eliezer spoke fluent Arabic, had carried out several secret missions in Lebanon, and had a good reputation among the Palestinians. Ben-Eliezer supported the peace process and had no problem with the recognition of the PLO. He was, therefore, surprised when Rabin told him: "Thank you for your support, but this is the last declaration of principles that I accepted. It's a minefield and is full of holes. . . ."[50]

While Rabin was quietly recruiting support for his decision, Peres and Holst were aboard a Norwegian executive jet plane heading for California for a meeting with Secretary Christopher and Ambassador Dennis Ross. Christopher was vacationing on the West Coast, but he had arranged to meet with Peres and Holst on August 27 at a small naval air force base near Santa Barbara. Peres took with him Yoel Singer and Avi Gil, the two aides who had put the last touches on the Israeli-Palestinian DOP. Rabin asked Ambassador Rabinovich to fly from Washington and participate in Peres's meeting with Christopher and Ross.

Contrary to previous assumptions, the United States was not totally surprised by what was achieved in Oslo. Not only did Norwegian Foreign Minister Holst and Israeli officials report to Washington about Oslo, but the CIA had a considerable amount of information about this secret channel of negotiations between Israel and the Palestinians. Contrary to what Abu Ala had told Peres, that there were "only six people in Tunis who knew about Oslo," there were many many more who were briefed about it, but they kept the secret. Arafat was fully coordinated with Egypt, while Abu Mazen regularly briefed King Hassan of Morocco and the Tunisian president. So it was not difficult for the CIA to obtain from those three countries the necessary information about the Palestinian-Israeli accord. Thus, when Peres told Christopher that the Palestinians had made "considerable concessions" in Oslo, the American secretary of state knew better: None of the tough issues had been resolved, only deferred.

Peres's and Holst's idea was to sell the Oslo Accords to Christopher so that he could present them to the negotiating teams in Washington as though they were an American initiative. The secretary and Ross wanted to be left alone for private consultations. When the meeting resumed, they told Peres that the United States could not accept his proposal. The American media would dig into the story and would uncover the truth. This would seriously damage American credibility and prestige. The United States would definitely support the Oslo Accords, and would encourage others to support them, but only as a Norwegian initiative. Christopher also said that now that the DOP was initialed and once the letter of mutual recognition of Israel and the PLO was drafted, the United States would allow a PLO representative to come to Washington for the signing ceremony at the White House.[51]

Ross asked Peres if King Hussein was in the picture. Peres said no. It later transpired, however, that like the United States, King Hussein was not totally surprised by the Oslo Accords. Was he briefed by the CIA or by a friendly neighbor? This is still not known. Ross also suggested that in drafting the letter of mutual recognition, Israel should insist on the PLO's not only renouncing terrorism, but also undertaking to discipline PLO member groups that would continue to engage in terrorism. This important point was eventually incorporated into the Israeli-Palestinian accord.[52] While Christopher acted as the perfect gentleman, other senior American officials did not hide their anger at the way the Oslo channel had been manipulated. "How could you do such a thing, working with Egypt behind our back?" Martin Indyk, the senior White House expert on the Middle East, asked Eitan Haber, the director of Rabin's office and his speechwriter. "This is not the way to deal with your best ally." Haber, however, was not the right address. Like all the other officials at the prime minister's office, Haber knew nothing about the secret channel in Oslo.

Other U.S. officials criticized the "serious mistake" of pushing the tough problems under the carpet. One official who had been involved in the Arab-Israeli peace process since the Madrid Peace Conference and who insisted on anonymity said: "Israel decided in Oslo to keep the chestnuts in the fire. Instead of trying to solve the problems Israel decided to defer the solution and to pretend that the problems were already solved. Israel would pay dearly for the nonprofessional way it negotiated in Oslo. Israel appointed the least-experienced team to negotiate the most complicated conflict. . . ."[53]

Later in December, at the end of a Middle East tour, Christopher's en-

tourage leaked to the *New York Times* the secretary's frustration with the
Israeli-Palestinian DOP. The secretary was quoted as having said that the DOP
"was long on flourish and short on precision."[54]

While Peres and Holst were in the United States, Abu Mazen went to
Moscow to brief Russian Foreign Minister Andrei Kozyrev on the Oslo Ac-
cords. Kozyrev congratulated the PLO for its achievement and promised Abu
Mazen that he would attend the White House ceremony.

After Peres's return from the United States, Rabin submitted the DOP to
the Israeli cabinet for approval. As expected, it was approved almost unanimously, with only one abstention. Rabin and Peres agreed that the DOP would
be signed at the White House by Peres and Abu Mazen on September 13.
Rabin did not want to attend the ceremony—it was not "his" DOP. Although he
approved it, he still had many doubts about it. However, Arafat decided to go to
Washington. He needed the limelight at the White House. Egypt and Morocco
intervened on his behalf and urged the Clinton administration to allow Arafat
to participate in the signing ceremony. Interviewed by Israeli TV on Friday
night, September 10, Rabin said that despite Arafat's intention, he would not
travel to the United States. A few hours later, however, Rabin was forced to
change his mind. On Saturday morning, September 11, at 5:00 A.M., Ambassador Rabinovich called from Washington. He told the prime minister that because of Arab pressure, both President Clinton and Secretary Christopher had
agreed to Arafat's participation at the White House ceremony. They wanted
very much for Rabin to participate in the ceremony as well. Then Haim Ramon,
the health minister, was on the line. He told Rabin that Dr. Ahmed Tibi had
called him from Tunis and said that Arafat was definitely going to Washington.
Tibi expressed the PLO's hope that Rabin too would go. Finally, Christopher
called. He told Rabin that Clinton would very much like him to participate in
the ceremony. Rabin yielded. The prime minister's aide, Eitan Haber, called
Kol Israel and announced Rabin's decision. Then he called Avi Gil, Peres's aide,
and told him about the change in the prime minister's plans. When Gil reached
the foreign minister at his official residence in Jerusalem, Peres had already
heard the news over Kol Israel.

Peres was enraged. He watched Rabin's TV interview the night before, and
he went to bed assured that the White House ceremony was "his show." Peres
got up early Saturday morning to review the speech that he was going to deliver
in Washington. He even had a list of guests he intended to take with him—a
widow whose husband had been killed in a terrorist act, an author, a scholar,
and several army officers. Everything had to be changed now.

"Why is he [Rabin] doing this to me all the time?" roared an angry Peres in
a telephone conversation with Giora Eini, the Labor Party activist who was always called to extinguish the fire between Peres and Rabin. "This schmuck
[Rabin] has caused me enough damage. Why does he continue to walk on me?
I brought the Oslo Accords. He never believed in them. Now he wants to go to

Washington? Fine. Let him go. Tell him that I am staying at home and I am re-signing my position as foreign minister."[55]

Eini calmed Peres down. Then he shuttled between Peres and Rabin ten times, and arranged for both of them to meet in his presence, that same evening, at Rabin's Tel Aviv residence. As always, the tireless and discreet Eini found the face-saving formula. They would both speak at the Washington cere-mony, but Peres would sign the DOP. When I asked Eini to confirm this episode, he refused to reveal the substance of his telephone conversations with Rabin and Peres. "All I can tell you is that it was tough and it wasn't easy this time to reconcile them," he said.[56]

The Oslo Accords were signed with pomp at the White House. The historic handshake between Rabin and Arafat electrified Israel and the Arab countries and thrilled millions of people around the world. Despite its many shortcom-ings, the DOP clearly enhanced the willingness of Israel to actively support the peace process. The first reactions of the American Jewish community were also very favorable.

Arafat left Washington totally rehabilitated. For him, it was a clear eleva-tion from superterrorist to recognized statesman. His past forgotten and his state-to-be assured, he was now hoping for huge amounts of money to pour into his empty coffers from all over the world.

The reactions in the Arab world were mixed and sharply divided. Egypt and the North African and Persian Gulf countries stood firmly behind the Oslo Accords, although not all of them supported Arafat. King Hussein was angry at Yasser Arafat for not sharing with him the secrets of the long negotiations in Oslo. However, once the DOP was signed, Jordan supported it. On September 14, only a day after the White House ceremony, the chief Israeli and Jordanian negotiators in Washington, Eli Rubenstein and Ambassador Fayez Taraouneh, concluded at the State Department the agenda for their future discussions. On November 1, Jordan's Crown Prince Hassan and Israeli Foreign Minister Peres met with President Clinton at the White House and established a permanent forum to study joint Israeli-Jordanian economic projects.

Syria's attitude was clearly hostile. Nevertheless, following a telephone conversation between Clinton and Assad, the Syrian president permitted his ambassador to Washington to attend the White House ceremony. Assad also promised not to actively oppose the Israeli-Palestinian accord. Yet, no one in the Arab world had any illusions that the PLO-Syrian crisis had been averted. On the contrary, it had deepened. In the past, Arafat's disputes with Assad cen-tered around three points:

- After the war in Lebanon in June 1982, the PLO was prepared to engage in a political dialogue with Israel; Assad wanted to control the Palestinian decision.

- After the expulsion of the PLO forces from Beirut, Arafat intended to establish an alternative PLO headquarters in Tripoli, in northern Lebanon. Assad expelled the remaining PLO forces from Tripoli and formed the block of ten rejectionist Palestinian groups in Damascus that openly challenged Arafat's leadership.

- Finally, Arafat sought an alliance with Saddam Hussein. Assad considered this move aimed against Syria's dominance in Lebanon.

After the Madrid Peace Conference, Arafat tirelessly warned against a "separate peace" between Israel and Syria. Arafat even sent Assad a personal letter pledging not to strike a separate deal between the PLO and Israel. Now, in collusion with Egypt, Arafat had again betrayed Assad's trust and concluded the Oslo Accords with Israel. The Oslo Accords were a recognition by both Israel and the Palestinians that time was not working in their favor. Consequently, neither Israel nor the PLO wanted to wait until they reached national consensus within their own camps. Nevertheless, and as events were to prove in the following months, the Oslo Accords became victims of their own signatories. In their effort to sell the DOP to the Israeli people, both Peres and Rabin called the DOP a peace agreement. By so calling the DOP, they raised expectations in Israel about the "peace fruits," translated by Peres into a "New Middle East." It wasn't long before this effort boomeranged. The road to peace was still bumpy.

GEFILTE FISH AND COUSCOUS: MOROCCO'S ROLE IN THE MIDDLE EAST PEACE PROCESS

The special Israeli air force plane landed smoothly at the heavily guarded Rabat-Sale airport. In the past, visits by Israeli dignitaries to Morocco have been shrouded in utmost secrecy. This time, however, there was no effort to conceal the event. The twelve-hour layover on Prime Minister Yitzhak Rabin's and Foreign Minister Shimon Peres's return from Washington to Jerusalem on September 14, 1993, was in full public view. In the absence of formal diplomatic relations between Israel and Morocco, there were no Israeli flags at Rabat airport, nor were bands mustered to play the national anthems of both countries. However, in what amounted to a public de facto recognition of the State of Israel, the top Moroccan leadership rolled out the red carpet for the two Israeli leaders. It was the second time in more than thirty years of secret diplomacy that an Israeli prime minister had been publicly welcomed in Morocco. The previous time, on July 22, 1986, Shimon Peres met with King Hassan at his beautiful winter palace at Ifrane, in the Atlas Mountains. To protest that break with Arab solidarity, an angry Syrian President Hafez Assad broke diplomatic relations with Morocco. The enigmatic Libyan leader Muammar Qadhaffi suspended the treaty of federation with Morocco that he had signed two years earlier. For this event, however, there were no Arab protests, only a sharp criticism by Iran, a fundamentalist country that was desperately seeking to end its international isolation and was trying to court even the pro-Western Morocco. Thus, acting as an icebreaker, a confident King Hassan was able to demonstrate the extent of the dramatic change that had suddenly come over Middle Eastern politics.

Yitzhak Rabin, the former chief of staff who led his army to victory in the Six-Day War of June 1967, was by nature shy and introverted. He was obviously moved when he landed at Rabat, for he knew he was closing a seventeen-year circle. In October 1976, during his first term as prime minister, he had traveled to Morocco disguised in a shaggy wig and dark glasses. An Israeli who accompanied him on that trip said that "Rabin looked more like a beatnik than a prime minister." During his two-day visit to Rabat and Fez, he had been escorted by a junior minister, Mohamed Karim Lamrani, who, a few years later, paid a secret visit to Israel. Now Prime Minister Lamrani, Foreign Minister Filali (King Hassan's in-law), the chief of Moroccan intelligence, General Abdul Haq Qadiri, and the leaders of the small Moroccan Jewish community were at the airport to welcome the Israeli prime minister.

After a strictly kosher meal at the official government guest house in Souissi, an elegant Rabat suburb, Rabin spoke by phone with President Mubarak and King Hussein and met briefly with the PLO representative in Rabat, who came to pay his respects to the leader who had granted recognition to his organization. Then he and Peres drove to King Hassan's summer palace at Skhirat, off the Rabat-Casablanca highway, where Rabin was received with pomp. A platoon of Moroccan paratroopers presented their arms in honor of the Israeli leader, who was also defense minister. Rabin shook hands with the commanding officer and said, "I hope that the day will soon come when we all serve as soldiers of peace."

King Hassan met with Rabin and Peres in the same room where, sixteen years earlier and under his auspices, the late Israeli foreign minister Moshe Dayan had met with an Egyptian envoy to pave the way for President Sadat's historic visit to Jerusalem. The king and his Israeli guests even sat around the same coffee table.

During the two-hour discussion, Rabin thanked the Moroccan monarch for his assistance in the negotiations with the PLO. Since March 1993, the king and his immediate associates had been fully aware of the secret Oslo channel. Abu Mazen, the PLO executive who together with Peres had signed in Washington the declaration of principles between Israel and the PLO, had regularly come to Rabat to brief the king on the progress made in Oslo or on the obstacles that were yet to be removed. Despite the absence of direct phone links between Israel and Morocco, King Hassan maintained regular phone contacts with both Rabin and Peres.[1]

In his discussion with the king, Rabin focused mainly on the means to reinforce the accord with the PLO. He explained the difficulties ahead and expressed concern about the divisions among the various Palestinian groups, even among Arafat's immediate aides. Rabin dwelt largely on the security problems in the West Bank and in the Gaza Strip and warned that without security for the Israelis, the accord with the PLO would collapse. The Israeli prime minister portrayed the dangerous situation in the Gaza Strip. He said that the 750,000 Palestinians there needed immediate financial assistance to rebuild their infrastructure and to provide jobs, housing, education, and medical services for their poor. He wanted King Hassan to try to convince the oil-rich Persian Gulf countries to open their hearts and purses to the Palestinians. Rabin said, "Why can't the oil-rich Arab countries contribute generously? What is an amount of two or three hundred million dollars to them?"

Hassan saw "God's will" in the fact that the agreement between Israel and the PLO had been signed in Washington two days before Rosh Hashanah, the Jewish New Year. He was also encouraged by polls in Israel that showed strong support for the accord with the PLO. "This is a very positive development," the king observed. Hassan agreed with Rabin's assessment that the Palestinians needed urgent economic and financial support and promised to use his influence with the oil-rich countries to provide the necessary amounts. As to bilateral relations with Israel, Hassan called for "economic peace" between the two countries. He said that he would expand tourism between Israel and Morocco, send a high-level economic delegation to explore possibilities for joint ventures in the fields of modern technology, and begin a modest cooperation in banking. The king also promised to continue to urge Saudi King Fahd to ease the Arab economic boycott, although, he added, such a move necessitated a unanimous decision by the Arab League and would undoubtedly depend on the progress in the peace negotiations with the other Arab countries.

As chairman of the Jerusalem Committee of the Organization of the Islamic Conference—a group of forty-five Arab and Muslim countries—Hassan could be expected to raise the issue of Jerusalem. He stressed a point that he always raised with foreign dignitaries—the need to show the world that the Mediterranean could become a sort of Lake of Tiberias around which the three religions, all descendants of Abraham, could build a solid springboard for their next generations. "You should remember," Hassan told Rabin, "that not only Jews, but also Christians and Muslims have religious interests in El-Quds El-Sharif"—the sanctified eastern part of the city within the Jerusalem walls. "Hence, there must be a solution acceptable to all three religions."

King Hassan's remarks on Jerusalem were similar to the position he had taken when he met with Pope John Paul II in the Vatican, a few years previously. Hassan and the pope agreed that Jerusalem should never again be divided, but they also agreed that the present status, whereby Israel claimed exclusive sovereignty over the entire city, should be modified. Hassan told the pope that he was speaking not only on his own behalf but also on behalf of all Muslim countries.[2] He stressed this point to Rabin as well.

Even before Rabin and Peres landed in Rabat, there were reports in the Israeli and world media that Morocco and Tunisia were about to establish full diplomatic relations with Israel. Such a diplomatic achievement would bolster support in Israel for the accord with the PLO. It was argued that Hassan, a ruler with flair who enjoyed dramatic gestures, would probably be pleased to gain the prestige of being the first Arab head of state, after Egypt's President Sadat, to establish full diplomatic relations with Israel. The United States was known to have encouraged Hassan to move in that direction, as did France.

King Hassan, however, felt that he had to be more cautious. Through his extraordinary gesture and thirty years of secret diplomacy with Israel, Hassan had proved his ability to play a special role in building bridges between Israel and its Arab neighbors. He had proved that he was prepared, on occasion, to go out on a limb, provoking the pique of and even outright denunciation by other Arab leaders. Despite his secure hold on power, the king was acutely sensitive to the strong Islamic winds sweeping across neighboring Algeria and the more distant Egypt. Hence he did not want to fuel the small fundamentalist flame in his own country. Accordingly, even before Rabin's arrival in Rabat, a senior Moroccan official told an Israeli newspaper that "the problem is not recognition, but the successful completion of the peace process."[3] Morocco gave expression to this position immediately after the Hassan-Rabin meeting in Rabat. In a brief statement, Hassan said that "the agreement between Israel and the PLO was a step toward a better future." Rabin's reaction was also guarded. He said, "I have heard warm and promising things about the future. . . . Today we made one more step toward diplomatic relations."[4]

The king suggested to his Israeli guests a visit to the magnificent newly built mosque in Casablanca and also the old and impressive Jewish synagogue Beth El. The suggestion had its own symbolism. It signaled the centuries-old coexistence of Jews and Arabs in Morocco. It was also a reminder to Rabin that Hassan, as a religious leader, could not be indifferent to the fate of the "other mosque," the El-Aqsa Mosque in East Jerusalem.

During the visit to the mosque in Casablanca, Rabin, barefoot and holding his shoes in his hands, was very composed. Peres, in contrast, was obviously excited. Rabin wrote in the Golden Book, in Hebrew, "To His Majesty King Hassan II, the builder of the most magnificent mosque in the world. Very impressive and very beautiful—all in the grace of God." Peres wrote, "King Hassan II is a great builder and a great believer. This Home of Faith is the most magnificent in Islamic history. Peace and faith walk here hand in hand."

The Israeli delegation drove on to the synagogue Beth El. Facing the arc, white yarmulkes on their heads, Rabin and Peres offered a silent prayer that their decision to negotiate with the PLO was correct. On their visit they were accompanied by the three most prominent and influential Jews in Morocco: André Azoulay, King Hassan's economic adviser and the highest-ranking Jew ever in the Moroccan royal court; Serge Berdugo, a former minister of tourism and the president of the small Jewish community; and Robert Assaraf, the former director general of ONA, the biggest economic corporation in Morocco, whose shares are partly owned by the royal family.

For Azoulay to accompany the prime minister of Israel during his short visit to Morocco was not only a great honor but also personally satisfying. Here was the height of his nineteen years of active militancy for an Israeli-Palestinian settlement. Azoulay, married to Katya—a beautiful intellectual and author—and father of three daughters, remembered very well how it had begun. Born in 1941 into the family of a mid-level government official, the young André left his beautiful hometown, Mogador, to study journalism and economics in Paris.

After graduation, he tried in vain to revive a failing political and economic newspaper. In 1968, he joined the research department of Paribas, a prestigious French bank, specializing in investments in Third World countries, mostly African. His sound analysis and in-depth understanding of the needs of developing nations won him the support of the bank's top executives. After several promotions, he became Paribas's vice president for public affairs. Recognizing his economic ability and his consistent effort to promote understanding between Jews and Arabs, King Hassan appointed Azoulay, in 1991, as his economic adviser.

Azoulay's heart, however, was in Israel. Captured by the euphoria that swept the Jewish world following the Israeli military victory in 1967, he decided to visit his relatives in the Jewish state. He was appalled by what he discovered. After his immediate excitement, he found deep frustration among the thousands of Moroccan Jews, even alienation, from the mainstream Ashkenazi establishment. He knew, of course, that in their values, culture, music, and cuisine, Moroccan Jews were closer to the populations of the Middle East than to the Eastern European Jews, who dominated the political, economic, and cultural life in Israel. He never expected, however, to find political discrimination—real or imagined. His conclusion was, therefore, that only a durable peace between Israel and its Arab neighbors would put an end to this situation.

After a visit to Israel in 1974, Azoulay and his friend Robert Assaraf established the organization Identity and Dialogue in Paris, whose aim was to promote understanding between Ashkenazi and Sephardic Jews and between Jews and Arabs. The organization won the immediate support of King Hassan. Azoulay and Assaraf raised funds, organized seminars, and gradually accumulated political influence and personal prestige. Within a very short time, the organization increased its membership from a dozen to more than a thousand members. In the following years, Azoulay established many contacts in Israel, mostly among liberal and left-wing activists who supported a peaceful settlement with the Palestinians. In early 1975, the PLO was granted the status of "observer" in the Socialist International. Azoulay, himself a member of the French Socialist Party, established immediate contact with the PLO observer, Issam Sartawi, who lived in Paris. A warm personal friendship soon developed between these two intellectuals. Azoulay and Sartawi had many things in common. They were both honest and socially motivated; they believed in peaceful coexistence between Jews and Arabs; and they both supported the formula of land for peace, according to Security Council Resolution 242. This friendship came to a tragic end in 1983, when Sartawi was gunned down in Portugal by a radical Palestinian who was opposed to his contacts with the Israeli liberals and with Jewish intellectuals in the Western world.

Azoulay's activity drew immediate fire from right-wing French Jews, who accused him of being an "Arab supporter. "Nevertheless, Azoulay's contacts with the PLO never stopped. Among others, he met with Yasser Arafat, Abu Mazen, and other prominent Palestinian leaders.

Rabin's visit to Morocco on September 14, 1993, was prepared for in the utmost secrecy. It was arranged by Rafi Edri, a former cabinet minister and deputy speaker of the Knesset, who himself was of Moroccan origin. After the initialing of the Israeli-PLO accord in Oslo, on August 20, 1993, it was agreed that the document be signed in Washington by Foreign Minister Shimon Peres and PLO executive Abu Mazen. At the suggestion of Edri, Rabin agreed to pay a visit to Rabat in order to thank the king for his ongoing efforts to broker peace between Israel and the Palestinians. In a secret meeting between King Hassan and Edri, on August 31, 1993, it was agreed that Rabin would visit Rabat in early October. In early September, however, Arafat made it known that he would attend the signing ceremony in Washington. Rabin, who had never had much esteem for Arafat, was not enthusiastic. On September 7, Edri met in Paris with Serge Berdugo and Robert Assaraf. They suggested that Rabin attend the Washington ceremony, so that like the late President Sadat, who had visited Rabat after signing the Camp David Accords in Washington, Rabin too would stop over in Morocco on his way back to Israel. "I have already spoken to Foreign Minister Filali," Assaraf told Edri, "and I found him very supportive. Should Rabin agree to advance his scheduled October visit to Rabat, Filali is convinced that King Hassan would be very pleased."

Edri returned to Israel Thursday night, September 9, and met with Rabin at his home the next day. The prime minister was still hesitant. Meanwhile, pressure began to build from Washington. Both President Clinton and Secretary Christopher spoke with Rabin by phone and urged him to attend the White House ceremony. On Saturday morning, September 11, Rabin finally agreed. Hence, advancing the Rabat visit on the way back from Washington became an utmost necessity. Instead of returning to Israel just after shaking hands with Yasser Arafat, it was better to return home after a public meeting with King Hassan.

Edri phoned General Qadiri, the director of Moroccan intelligence, and Robert Assaraf and told them about Rabin's decision. One hour later, Assaraf told Edri that Foreign Minister Filali had spoken to the king and that Hassan would be delighted to welcome Rabin in Rabat on his way back from Washington. His only request was to keep the visit secret until after Rabin's departure from Washington. King Hassan did not want an early leak to the press, lest there be Arab counterpressure to cancel the visit.

Rabin's stopover in Rabat necessitated some rescheduling in Washington as well. President Clinton had planned a state dinner at the White House in honor of Rabin and Arafat. After learning the reason for the change, the dinner was canceled. Arafat was not offended—the Moroccans had already told him about Rabin's impending visit but asked him to keep it secret. Shortly after the BBC

announced that Rabin was on his way to Rabat, President Clinton said, in a
brief communiqué, that he saluted King Hassan for his courage and had expressed the hope that other Arab countries would follow his lead.[5]

The secrecy enveloping the Moroccan trip had one amusing note. Rabin
was accompanied to Washington not only by Peres, but also by his senior coalition partner, Communications Minister Shulamit Aloni. Shortly after takeoff
from Washington, Rabin asked Aloni: "Have you ever been to Morocco?" The
flamboyant and often outspoken minister replied, "No, I have never been. I
have always dreamed that one day I would go." Rabin replied smilingly, "Well,
your dream has come true. We are on our way to Rabat."

It is impossible to understand King Hassan's liberal attitude toward Israel
and his regular meetings with Israeli leaders without awareness of the traditional moderate attitude of Morocco toward its Jewish minority. Throughout its
history, Morocco had always been the best example of Arab-Jewish coexistence
in an Arab country. Jews had always prospered in Morocco, and their rabbinical
centers in Fez and Meknés had left a lasting impact on the cultural life in Morocco and on Jewish culture and theology all over the world. There had been
close to half a million Jews in Morocco when the country won its independence
in March 1956. Most of them had since left for Israel, others for France, the
United States, Canada, and Latin America. Most of them felt gratitude for the
Alawite dynasty that had protected them from persecution, especially during
the Nazi occupation of North Africa in the Second World War. An estimated
ten thousand Jews remain in this warm and hospitable country, mostly in
Casablanca. Generally, they have been treated with tolerance, and some of
them occupy important positions in public life. Despite the small size of the
community, there still existed in Morocco a vibrant Jewish culture that had
never been extinguished.

In a private and unpublicized meeting with American Jewish leaders in
New York on October 2, 1991, King Hassan had said that throughout history,
Jews and Arabs had not always been enemies and they should not remain "enemies forever." In the aftermath of the Persian Gulf War, it was imperative for
Israelis and Palestinians to live in peace and prosper together. Israel, he said,
would always remain a "Jewish enclave" in a predominantly Arab area. Therefore, Hassan concluded, it was now time to give Israeli youth a chance to integrate into a region where their ancestors had left such a rich heritage.

Equally interesting was King Hassan's philosophy on war and peace and
the tools he used to achieve his foreign policy goals. In discussions with French
journalist Eric Laurent, Hassan said, "You wage a war only if you are sure of
your victory and if such a victory would guarantee peace for at least one generation. If you cannot guarantee such a result, don't provoke a war."[6] Hassan applied this rule to the Arab-Israeli conflict. Even before he became king, in
March 1961, Hassan had reached the conclusion that the Western world would

never let Israel disappear. In a secret meeting with Rabin in October 1976, Hassan had revealed that during an Arab summit meeting in Lebanon in 1958, he had suggested Arab recognition of Israel and the admission of the Jewish state to the Arab League. "The Arab leaders almost fell off their chairs," Hassan said.[7]

Shortly afterward, Hassan—who was at the time the crown prince—gave his patronage to a Mediterranean conference in Florence, organized jointly by the mayor of Florence, Giorgio Lapira, and by Joe Golan, the political secretary of Dr. Nahum Goldman, the president of the World Jewish Congress. Goldman was known then for his liberal approach to the Arab-Israeli conflict and for his support of Algerian independence. The conference was attended, for the first time, by politicians and scholars from Israel and Egypt. I attended that conference in my capacity as the Paris bureau chief of the Israeli daily *Maariv*. The conference did not achieve any meaningful results, the gap between Israelis and Arabs being still very wide. The only positive result was an invitation by Hassan to all participants to attend a follow-up conference in Casablanca. When I asked the crown prince if Israelis would also be able to attend, Hassan answered, "Absolutely. It never occurred to me to refuse a dialogue with a person only because he is an Israeli or Jewish. Throughout its history, Morocco has proved that it can serve as a model for Arab-Jewish coexistence." The follow-up conference never took place; tensions within the Arab world prevented it from being convened.

After he became king in 1961, Hassan put his philosophy into practice. He changed Morocco's foreign policy from nonaligned to pro-Western and gradually moved away from Egypt's pro-Soviet and pan-Arab policies. As a liberal who had graduated from a French law school in Bordeaux, he was very much at ease with Western culture and civilization, and he consistently sought the friendship and cooperation of the United States and France. Hassan admired the newly elected President Kennedy and had much respect for General de Gaulle's "parallel diplomacy," namely that routine matters should be handled by the Foreign Ministry, while more sensitive issues should be handled through the back channels of the intelligence community and by "special emissaries."

This back-channel diplomacy was practiced from the very beginning of King Hassan's reign. As a liberal monarch who believed in the freedom of movement of his citizens, he introduced a dramatic change in his country's immigration policies. He abolished all restrictions on Jews who wished to travel abroad. This move was welcomed in Israel and won the applause of the American Jewish community. It was a dramatic departure from past policies. After it won its independence in March 1956, Morocco joined the Arab League and espoused all its anti-Israeli resolutions. Morocco restricted the movement of Moroccan Jews, cut all communication links with Israel, and imposed an economic boycott of the Jewish state. Zionist activity was banned, Jewish institutions were closed, and contacts with American Jewish organizations were restricted. Interventions by Eleanor Roosevelt and by the United States and France were ignored. In the face of such a hostile anti-Israeli and anti-Jewish policy, Prime Minister David Ben-Gurion instructed the Mossad to mount a vast covert operation in Morocco, aimed at smuggling Moroccan Jews out of the country. In Casablanca, Tangier, Fez, Meknes, Marrakesh, and distant villages of the Atlas Mountains, Jews were assembled at night and transported in secret to Al-Huceima, a small fishing port on the African shore of the Mediterranean. Protected by armed Israelis and local Jewish volunteers, the clandestine immigrants then boarded small fishing boats and at great personal risk sailed to Gibraltar or to the Spanish port of Algeciras. The Moroccan secret services were unable to put an end to this Israeli covert operation, which was carried out with the discreet cooperation of France, Great Britain, and Spain.

When Prince Hassan was crowned king, in March 1961, the Mossad station chief in Casablanca was Alexander Gatmon. A survivor of the Holocaust and a former colonel in the Israeli air force, he had come to Morocco as a "British businessman, representing a German industrial corporation." His beautiful blond Belgian-born wife, Carmit, was introduced as his "mistress." The French-educated Moroccan elite were fascinated with this "beautiful couple," and it wasn't long before Carmit and Alex were "in" in all social circles in Casablanca. They were soon associating also with people close to the royal court. It was during one of these social events that Alex was introduced to a Moroccan cabinet minister. The Israeli Mossad agent decided to take a dangerous gamble. At the home of a mutual friend, he revealed to the minister that his name was Colonel Gat and that he was the Mossad station chief in Casablanca. "Israel and Morocco are not enemies," Alex told the Moroccan minister. "I am here only because of our concern for Moroccan Jews and for their well-being. If you will grant the Jews their freedom of movement and allow them to leave the country, we will be very grateful to His Majesty and we might even be helpful to your country."

The Moroccan minister was stunned. He was aware, of course, of the clandestine Jewish emigration, but he had never expected to be face to face with the man who had organized it. The minister immediately informed the king about his meeting with the Mossad agent. To his even greater surprise, the king instructed him to continue the dialogue with the Israeli. After lengthy and secret discussions in Paris and Geneva, an agreement was reached according to which Moroccan Jews would be free to emigrate to "Europe and Canada," but "not to Israel." The same formula was adopted in the early fifties by Yemen, Iraq, Syria, and Egypt. Therefore, King Hassan saw no reason not to apply the same arrangement to Morocco. One other condition was that the whole operation be conducted by an American Jewish organization and not by Israel. Indeed, as part of what was to become known as Operation Yakhin, more than

76,000 Jews were flown and shipped from Morocco to Marseilles, under the supervision of the American Jewish organization HIAS, and from there they continued their journey to their new homeland in Israel.

This liberal policy toward the Jews soon led to a more meaningful cooperation in the field of intelligence, dictated by strategic and regional considerations. After the dissolution of the United Arab Republic, the unnatural union between Egypt and Syria, on September 28, 1961, Egypt's President Nasser launched a brutal subversion campaign against the moderate, pro-Western regimes in the Arab world. The kings of Saudi Arabia, Jordan, and Morocco felt threatened by this Egyptian hate campaign and were determined to meet Nasser's challenge. In cooperation with the shah of Iran, they formed what could be called "the four kings alliance," whose sole purpose was to contain Nasser's subversion.

With the full encouragement of the CIA, Israel already had a close cooperation with Iran. In May 1963, King Hussein inaugurated what became an uninterrupted policy of occasional secret meetings with various Israeli leaders. Around that period, King Hassan also inaugurated his back-channel diplomacy with Israel. According to a recently published French book by Moroccan opposition activist Mou'men Diori, the Mossad helped in the reorganization and training of the Moroccan secret services and supplied the king with intelligence on the activities of Moroccan opposition leaders in Egypt and in other Arab countries. Diori said that Morocco had bought arms from Israel and several Moroccan fishing boats were equipped with Israeli-made electronic devices that helped monitor subversive activities along Moroccan shores.[8] According to the usually reliable and well informed French newsmagazine *Jeune Afrique* (September 29, 1993), General Ahmed Dlimi, the former director of Moroccan intelligence, visited Israel several times during the seventies. In addition, three Egyptian newspapers reported in January 1987 that Israeli army officers participated as "observers" in the joint American-Moroccan military maneuvers known as "the African Eagle," held in the Sahara in November 1986.[9] Finally, Ali Baiba, the "foreign minister" of the Polisario, claimed that during the period June 1986–June 1987, Israeli army officers visited the battle zones in the western Sahara three times and suggested building a security fence that would prevent the infiltration of Polisario guerrillas into Moroccan territory.[10]

Indeed, the secret security cooperation between Israel and Morocco was a direct result of the unprovoked tensions with Algeria and the war in the western Sahara. Ever grateful for King Hassan's liberal approach toward "his" Jews, Israel sought to reciprocate. A modest program to train Moroccan security guards was initiated by Isser Harel, Israel's first director of the Mossad. His successor, General (Res.) Meir Amit, gave this cooperation the dynamism and the diversity that led gradually to the current situation.

In the fall of 1963, Amit secretly visited Morocco, for the first time, in his capacity as Mossad director. It was a period of heightened tension between Algeria and Morocco, and the king was in the field, directing his army's operations against his aggressive Algerian neighbors. Escorted by his Moroccan counterpart, General Mohamed Oufkir, Amit came late at night to Hassan's headquarters. "We want to help you and can help you," Amit told the young monarch. Amit's military credentials were impeccable. He had been a very successful brigade commander and later, as chief of operations in the general staff, had planned the successful Israeli part of the Suez Campaign in 1956. Dayan saw in him a serious candidate for the post of chief of staff. However, during training in a paratrooper course, Amit broke his legs. After a long and painful recovery, he was appointed as chief of military intelligence, and in the summer of 1963 he became the second director of the legendary Mossad.

After Amit's meeting with King Hassan, reciprocal secret visits by Israeli and Moroccan officials became routine. Those visits were limited at the beginning to military and intelligence officials, but in recent years they had also included politicians, diplomats, and businessmen. Both the CIA and the French secret service were fully aware of this Israeli-Moroccan cooperation and at times encouraged it.

From the very beginning, however, it was clear that King Hassan was also looking for Israeli assistance in attracting Jewish, mostly American, investments in his country. Indeed, because of Israeli efforts, Baron Edmond de Rothschild visited Morocco and discussed various investment possibilities with Hassan; the British retail department store Marks and Spencer sent a delegation to Casablanca for the same purpose; former Israeli deputy minister of defense Zevi Dinstein, an economist, discussed with the king ways to enhance the export of Moroccan citrus produce; and former Israeli chief of staff the late General Mordechai Makleff went to Morocco in his capacity as chairman of Israeli Chemical Industries to discuss problems related to the export of Moroccan phosphates. Based on the Israeli experience in Iran, Israel also sent an expert in psychological warfare to assist in combating anti-Moroccan propaganda in the Arab world. Finally, Aryeh (Lova) Eliav, a former Knesset member and an expert in regional agricultural planning, who was responsible for the reconstruction of the Iranian region of Qazvin, also went to Morocco and discussed with King Hassan the possibility of developing the Ourzazat region, near Marrakesh. Upon Eliav's return, Moshe Dayan, who was then minister of agriculture in Levi Eshkol's cabinet, sent two additional experts to Morocco to examine the availability of water resources in the region and the financial costs of such a big project. After a one-month study of the region, the two Israeli experts, Gabi Tibor and Ephraim Shilo, presented their findings to the king. The development of the Ourzazat area was possible, but it was beyond Israel's financial capability.

King Hassan's involvement in the Arab-Israeli conflict brought a voice of moderation to the otherwise inflammatory rhetoric in the Middle East. He abhorred the cries to destroy Israel, throw the Jews into the sea, rape their women, etc., and considered them to be a kind of political aphrodisiac for the radical Arab regimes. Like Tunisia, Morocco also supported a political solution based on two states—Israel and Palestine. Hence, when Tunisian President Habib Bourguiba toured the Middle East in March 1965 and urged the Arab leaders to recognize Israel, King Hassan was the first to applaud him. In a summit meeting in Casablanca in September 1965, Hassan told the Arab leaders, "Let's face it. There are no two solutions to the Arab-Israeli conflict. Either we negotiate a political settlement, which is my preference, or we attack. If we reject negotiations, let us not lose time. Let's attack even if our armies are ill prepared and even if they are equipped with clubs and not with rifles. . . ." Evoking this episode years later, King Hassan recalled, "The Arab leaders did not take me seriously. I was only four years on my throne and they thought that I was miserably inexperienced. So they listened attentively to my speech but they did not hear it."[11]

Nevertheless, when the Six-Day War broke out in June 1967, Hassan sent some of his army units to help in the fighting against Israel. But by the time those units reached the Libyan-Egyptian border, the war was over. Hassan was shocked. He thought that the Arabs had suffered the most humiliating defeat in their history. In a radio-television interview, Hassan blamed President Nasser for the defeat. He said, "For weeks, Nasser was threatening Israel instead of attacking her. What would we, Moroccans, have done in the face of such threats? Instead of waiting for our destruction, we would have preempted. That is exactly what the Israelis did."[12]

The Arab defeat in 1967 only strengthened King Hassan in his belief that there was no military solution to the Arab-Israeli conflict. He was critical of some Arab leaders who used the "Palestinian problem" for their own purposes, and he was angry with the Palestinians who allowed themselves to be exploited by those leaders. In his first meeting with Yasser Arafat in 1968, Hassan was very blunt. He said, "I am ready to cooperate with you, provided you face the realities. You will never be able to defeat Israel. Terrorist acts directed from outside the occupied territories would never lead to the 'liberation' of Palestine. Instead of having more illusions and wasting the time of the Arab leaders, you had better negotiate with Israel."[13]

Arafat, however, was in no mood for compromise at that time. He had won Egypt's support and he had just returned with Nasser from a secret visit to Moscow, where he had been promised Soviet "humanitarian" assistance. Arafat did not understand at that time that by tilting toward the Soviet Union, he became part of the Cold War and that no matter how justified his cause, he was unlikely to win the support of the United States. It was years before the PLO understood that the Soviet Union would never risk a conflict with the United States for the sake of the Palestinians.

In 1969, King Hassan widened his involvement in Middle Eastern politics by opening a new channel to American Jews. Despite Arab protests and angry Israeli reaction, Hassan met in Rabat with Dr. Nahum Goldman, the president of the World Jewish Congress, who was known to be at odds with Israel's policy toward the PLO. Since the mid-fifties, both Golda Meir and the former director of the Mossad, Isser Harel, had been opposed to Goldman's "independent diplomacy" in North Africa. Anxious to maintain the close relationship with France, Meir objected to Goldman's contacts with the Algerian rebels, the FLN, and did not approve of his intervention on behalf of Moroccan Jews. Shortly after Hassan was crowned king, the issue of Jewish immigration was solved satisfactorily. However, because of Hassan's involvement in the Israeli-Palestinian conflict, Goldman sought to add his voice in support of the PLO. Golda Meir, then prime minister, was furious. "I don't need another foreign minister," she said. "Goldman's policies are not mine." Goldman, however, ignored Meir's request to cancel his trip to Rabat. "I am accountable to the Jewish people and not to Golda Meir," he said.

Hassan was much impressed by Goldman's liberal attitude and his creative thinking. He knew, of course, that Goldman's position was unlikely to influence Israeli policies, but he thought the encounter was a "good investment" for the future. Hassan also hoped that his meeting with Goldman would help him establish a more solid contact with the American Jewish community, which, in turn, would help him win the support of the U.S. administration and Congress for more generous American economic aid and military assistance.

The civil war in Jordan in 1970, the expulsion of the PLO from Jordan to Lebanon, the sudden death of Gamal Abdel Nasser, and the emergence of Anwar Sadat as the new president of Egypt had dramatically changed the situation in the Middle East. Back in 1955, while still crown prince, Hassan had paid a visit to Cairo and had met, among others, Anwar Sadat. Hassan found Sadat a devout Muslim and a firm anti-Communist. Hence, when Sadat was sworn in as the new Egyptian president, the question for Hassan was not if but when Sadat would make his first move toward the United States. Accordingly, when Sadat expelled the Soviet military advisers in 1972, Hassan was not surprised. He even saw in the Yom Kippur War in October 1973 a part of Sadat's "grand design" to negotiate a peaceful solution with Israel from a "position of strength." Although he had no illusions about the outcome of that war, he showed solidarity with both presidents Sadat and Assad by committing troops to their assistance. A Moroccan battalion was already in position on the Golan Heights, while six thousand soldiers were prepared to be airlifted to Egypt. Having no transportation means of his own, Hassan asked for Algeria's assistance. President Houari Boumedienne instructed his national airline, Air Algérie, to airlift the Moroccan soldiers to Cairo. Air Algérie's French pilots refused to take off, invoking international regulations that prohibited a civilian airline from transporting military personnel to a war zone. A few days later, King Hassan knew that the war was over. The Israeli air force had destroyed Syria's infrastructure, while Israeli ground forces had crossed the Suez Canal into Egyptian territory and advanced toward Cairo in the west and the port of Suez in the south. Sadat had no choice but to accept an immediate cease-fire that was arranged in Moscow by Secretary Kissinger and his Soviet counterpart, Andrei Gromyko. Hassan was among the first to applaud Sadat's decision. In recognition of Hassan's moderating role in the Arab-Israeli conflict and considering him to be among the best analysts of Middle Eastern politics, Henry Kissinger made Rabat his first stop in what was to become his "shuttle diplomacy."

On October 29, 1974, an Arab summit meeting in Rabat recognized the PLO as the "sole representative" of the Palestinian people. Following this decision, the UN General Assembly accorded the PLO a status of "observer" in the international organization and invited Yasser Arafat to address the assembly. King Hussein felt betrayed by the Moroccan king. Hussein thought that by endorsing the PLO as the sole representative of the Palestinian people, Hassan took away from him something "that belonged to Jordan." In the course of a frank discussion, Hassan told Hussein that he was wrong. Jordan, he said, could not deprive the Palestinians of their right to determine their own future. He argued that the PLO presented its case in a very militant way, so why would Jordan insist on paying a bill that was not hers? If in the future the PLO decided to go back to Jordan, fine. If not, it was better for Jordan to distance itself.[14] It took Hussein fourteen years to follow Hassan's advice.

King Hassan went one step further. Using his back-channel diplomacy, he arranged for the first ever contact between the CIA and the PLO. General Vernon Walters, the deputy director of the CIA, came to Rabat in the fall of 1974, and in the king's presence, he met with Khaled el-Hassan, one of the founding fathers of the PLO and an ally of both Saudi Arabia and Morocco. Walters was to meet again with Khaled el-Hassan in early 1975, but this didn't happen. When told about it, Henry Kissinger was furious. He was concerned that such high-level contacts between the United States and the PLO would interfere with his shuttle diplomacy. With President Ford's approval, Kissinger put an end to these encounters. However, low-level meetings between the CIA and the PLO continued without interruption.

In early 1975, two developments changed the nature of Morocco's involvement in Middle Eastern politics—the active use of Moroccan Jews, both in Israel and abroad, as a channel for influencing Israeli politics, and, following the Jordanian example, the inauguration of high-level secret meetings with Israeli political leaders.

After years of persistent complaints about alleged discrimination—real or imagined—against Israelis of Moroccan descent, a new ethnic group called the Black Panthers was formed in Israel. The very idea that Israelis of Middle Eastern background could be treated in Israel in a discriminatory way sent shock waves across the Jewish communities all over the world. Obviously moved, King Hassan invited Jews of Moroccan descent to return to Morocco. The invitation was totally ignored. Except for a very limited number, the overwhelming majority of Moroccan Jews preferred to remain in their new homeland, in Israel. This, however, did not discourage the Moroccan monarch, and he was determined to treat the Israelis of Moroccan descent as though they were still "his" citizens. Accordingly, Hassan revived an old Jewish tradition in Morocco, the pilgrimage to the gravesites of venerable rabbis, and he invited "his" Israelis to visit. The invitation was an instant success, and the number of Israeli pilgrims to Morocco grew constantly.

King Hassan's initiative, however, was more far-reaching. With an eye to the United States and to the American Jewish community, Hassan decided to expand his covert contacts with Israel to include meetings with its top political leadership. In the summer of 1975, shortly after he left his position as defense minister in Golda Meir's cabinet, Moshe Dayan was the first Israeli politician to visit Rabat and meet with King Hassan. The visit was arranged through the Mossad channel, and Dayan traveled in disguise. Although Dayan was now a private citizen, his views carried much weight, and hence the record of that meeting remains classified. An Israeli who was familiar with the discussion said that there was a mutual fascination between Hassan and Dayan. The Moroccan monarch was charmed by the man whom he regarded as a "hero and a legend." Dayan was fascinated with Morocco and was very much impressed by King Hassan, whom he described as a "liberal autocrat."

In October 1976, Yitzhak Rabin became the first Israeli prime minister to visit Rabat and to hold secret discussions with King Hassan. Accompanied by the director of the Mossad, General (Res.) Yitzhak Hofi, by the Mossad station chief in Paris, and by his military secretary, General (Res.) Ephraim Poran, Rabin flew aboard an Israeli air force plane to Paris. At Orly Airport, he was welcomed by General Ahmed Dlimi, the director of the Moroccan intelligence community, and aboard a Moroccan Mystere 20 executive plane they flew to Rabat. In the course of their long discussion, King Hassan and Rabin made a thorough review of the situation in the Middle East. Hassan was very concerned about the growing trend of radicalization in the Arab world. He was fearful of Islamic fundamentalism in Egypt and warned that if no progress was made toward a peaceful settlement with Egypt, President Sadat might be forced to return to Moscow's arms. King Hassan had already conveyed the same warning to Secretary Kissinger, and he wanted Rabin to be aware of it. Hassan stressed that it was in Israel's interest to cultivate the friendship of pro-Western, moderate regimes in the Arab world. He offered to arrange a secret meeting between Rabin and Saudi Crown Prince (later King) Fahd, whom he described as "very intelligent and very supportive of a peaceful settlement of the Arab-Israeli conflict." Hassan said that Prince Fahd was "the real power broker" in

Saudi Arabia. Fahd owned a summer palace in Marbella, a Spanish resort city on the Moroccan shores of the Mediterranean, and hence the secrecy of the meeting could be assured.

Rabin thanked King Hassan for his offer and showed great interest in meeting Prince Fahd. Rabin accused the Soviet Union of encouraging Syrian President Assad's intransigence and explained why Israel could not negotiate with the PLO. "Arafat and his associates have blood on their hands and no Israeli leader can negotiate with them," Rabin told King Hassan. As for Egypt, Rabin agreed with Hassan's analysis but said that the only way for Sadat to contain Islamic fundamentalism was to negotiate peace with Israel. Rabin asked King Hassan to help arrange a meeting between him and the Egyptian president and left with him two written questions for Sadat: What would Sadat ask in return for full peace? And in the event Sadat was still unprepared for full peace, what would he ask in return for the end of a state of belligerency?[15]

Much encouraged by his discussions with both Dayan and Rabin, King Hassan shared with President Sadat, King Hussein, and Crown Prince Fahd his discussions with the two Israeli leaders. Some intelligence reports suggested that Hassan shared this report with the shah of Iran as well. Needless to say, the United States was fully aware of this secret channel between Israel and Morocco and encouraged it. Rabin, however, never got Sadat's answers to his two questions. Shortly after his return to Israel, Rabin became embroiled in the financial scandal that forced him out of office. In the general parliamentary elections that followed in May 1977, the Labor Party was defeated and the right-wing Likud leader Menachem Begin formed the new Israeli government. Likud's victory sent shock waves all around the world. In Washington and Paris, in Tehran, Rabat, and Riyadh, presidents and monarchs wondered what effect Likud's victory would have on the peace prospects in the Middle East. They were relieved when Begin appointed General Ezer Weizman, the former commander of the Israeli air force, as his minister of defense and invited Moshe Dayan to become his foreign minister. Dayan had already met both King Hassan and the shah of Iran, and it was hoped that he would now try to reap the fruits of Rabin's secret visit to Morocco in October 1976.

Indeed, shortly after he assumed his new position, Dayan traveled secretly to Rabat to seek King Hassan's assistance in arranging a meeting between Begin and President Sadat. Dayan traveled to Morocco via Paris, disguised with a wig and a thick mustache and with no eye patch. His meeting with Hassan took place in Ifrane, in the Atlas Mountains, in a small chalet that the king had used for short "disappearances" during his bachelor days.

According to King Hassan's account, the moment Dayan sat down, Hassan asked him, "What do you think of the Golan Heights?" Although surprised by this unexpected question, Dayan answered with no hesitation: "The Golan is Syrian. However, this territory is vital to our security. If we are to make peace with Syria, we would need some time and both sides would have to take some confidence-building measures. We would need UN troops or multinational forces to separate us from the Syrians. The Israeli settlements on the Golan should stay, either under Syrian sovereignty or under special security arrangements that would be incorporated in the peace treaty. Only then would we be able to withdraw to the original Syrian-Israeli border."

Years later, King Hassan admitted that the issue of the Golan Heights was for him a kind of test case. Had Dayan answered in an unbending way, he would not have "wasted" his time and would not have undertaken his initiative with Egypt.[16] Dayan told the king that he was born in Kibbutz Degania, near Tiberias, but grew up in Nahalal, near Haifa. "In such a case," the king said, "you must speak Arabic." For the next few minutes, they chatted in Arabic before resuming their discussion in English. For King Hassan, the discussion in Arabic was a clear indication that the Arabs now had an Israeli interlocutor who spoke their language, understood their mentality, and respected their culture. Hassan's Israeli "raw model" was Abba Eban, who spoke fluent Arabic and some Persian. He had no respect for Golda Meir, who not only did not speak one word of Arabic but also showed contempt for the Moroccan-born Israeli Black Panthers.

Hassan told Dayan that he was ready to try to open a dialogue between Israel and Egypt, but he wanted Dayan to realize that there could be no peace in the Middle East without a solution of the Palestinian problem. He even encouraged Dayan to talk to the PLO. Dayan replied that for Begin and for himself, a dialogue with the PLO was taboo and that he would never talk to Yasser Arafat. Hassan, however, persisted and gave Dayan three examples:

First, when his father, King Mohammed V, was exiled by the French to Madagascar, everyone in France had been certain that he would never return to Rabat and that the issue of Morocco's independence was shelved. Yet, it was with him that the French negotiated Morocco's independence.

Second, when the Algerians rebelled in 1954, the French had refused to negotiate with the FLN. Yet after eight years of bloody armed struggle, France had accepted reality and granted the Algerians their independence.

Finally, for years the United States had been embroiled in the war in Vietnam. Eventually, Nixon and Kissinger faced reality and negotiated with the Vietcong.[17]

"These are very good examples," Dayan answered, "but the PLO is different and I will not talk to Arafat."

President Sadat was much encouraged by the report of the Hassan-Dayan discussion. He asked the Moroccan king if Dayan himself would come to the next meeting. When Hassan replied in the affirmative, Sadat said, "Very good. In that case, I shall send a special envoy to meet with him."

Sadat chose his old friend and close confidant Mohamed Hassan el-

Tuhamy for this sensitive mission. It was an excellent choice. A former intelligence officer who was among the first Egyptian officers to join Nasser's coup, on July 23, 1952, Tuhamy, like Sadat, was very conservative and very close to the Muslim Brotherhood Organization. As a religious man, he was an ardent anti-Communist, and he was very much opposed to Nasser's alliance with the Soviet Union as well as to the gradual "socialization" of the Egyptian economy. Because he was a man of principles, Tuhamy soon found himself isolated from all the power centers in Cairo. However, because of his relationship with Sadat, Tuhamy made a comeback. He was appointed as the Egyptian ambassador to the International Agency for Atomic Energy in Vienna. Austrian Chancellor Bruno Kreisky introduced him to one of his Jewish friends, Carl Cahana, a wealthy businessman with close ties to the Israeli Labor Party. Tuhamy also met with some Israelis in Vienna, thus becoming the first "official" contact between Sadat and Golda Meir's government. Partly because of Kreisky's persuasion, but mostly because of his own conviction, he became more and more convinced that peace with Israel was not only necessary but also possible. "We thought at the time that Tuhamy had gone out of his mind," General Kamal Hassan Ali—a former prime minister, foreign minister, and military intelligence chief—confided to one of his Israeli friends years later. Sadat shared Tuhamy's view, but when he became president, in September 1970, he preferred to keep him out of any official function. However, when King Hassan told him about Dayan's visit to Rabat, Sadat immediately sent Tuhamy to meet with the Israeli foreign minister, under Moroccan auspices.

Dayan returned to Morocco on September 17, 1977, for his first meeting with the Egyptian envoy. Accompanied by General Ahmed Dlimi, the director of Moroccan intelligence, and by a Mossad operative and a bodyguard, Dayan was first given a short rest at the official guest house in Souissi. They then drove him to the royal palace in Skhirat, off the Casablanca-Rabat highway. They entered through the back gate, normally reserved for discreet visitors. After removing his wig and putting his eye patch on, Dayan entered a large hall where he was met by the king, the Moroccan prime minister, and Tuhamy. There was a certain tension and hesitation in the air, but once Dayan and the Egyptian envoy had shaken hands, the atmosphere became more relaxed. The meeting lasted four hours and notes were taken by the Mossad operative, who later summarized the discussion into an eight-page report, which is still officially classified. The following excerpts from that report are being published here for the first time.

Hassan opened the meeting by saying that the encounter could open a new chapter in the history of the Middle East. He introduced Tuhamy as an envoy who enjoyed the full confidence of President Sadat. In Cairo, only Sadat and Vice President Mubarak knew of this meeting. Hassan said that the return of the occupied territory to its "legitimate proprietors" was most important. In his opinion, the territories occupied by Israel were being held as a "trust" and as a bargaining chip to assure Israel's security. Therefore, with mutual consent, other solutions for Israel's security had to be found. The Palestinian problem was very complicated. Morocco accepted Dayan's contention that the Palestinians endangered the security of both Israel and Jordan. Hence, the Palestinians should be a subject of collective Arab responsibility. The Arab nations should supervise the Palestinians and provide Israel with adequate guarantees to meet Israel's security needs. Hassan suggested that once Israel and Egypt found a solution to these two problems—withdrawal from Sinai and a solution to the Palestinian problem—they should immediately inform President Carter, so that the United States did not find itself ignored and left out of the process. Hassan expressed the hope that once Israel and Egypt reached an accord, Syria would immediately join the process.

Now it was Tuhamy's turn to speak. He addressed Dayan directly and said, "To meet you, Dayan, under His Majesty's roof, is a source of great satisfaction and pride to me. For many years I believed that we should meet one day on the battlefield. Now, because of King Hassan's efforts and because of the trust that President Sadat has in Begin and in you, we are meeting here in Morocco in an effort to find a lasting peace between our two nations. You and Begin are strong leaders. We are confident that you are capable of making tough decisions. President Sadat did not have much confidence in your previous government, but he has full confidence in you."

Tuhamy added: "I want to assure you that President Sadat is very sincere in his efforts to reach an agreement with you. The key to peace, however, is the return of the territories. It is a question of sovereignty, of national pride, and, I might add, a question of Sadat's own survival. If Begin will accept the principle of total withdrawal, then it would be possible to solve all the other issues. We understand your concern about the Palestinians. However, if we don't find a solution to their plight and to their national aspirations, they will become a powerful element that will endanger the stability of the entire region. We therefore think that it would be possible to establish a Palestinian enclave that would eventually be linked to Jordan, Egypt, and Saudi Arabia. Such a solution would also guarantee King Hussein's survival.

"We urge you to accept Sadat's word that he will honor his commitments. Sadat is a noble man. He is a man of principles and honor. If we find a common ground, I can assure you that Sadat will go with you to the end of the world, because Israel and Egypt have common, vital interests."

Tuhamy then raised a very sensitive issue—the problem of Jerusalem. He said: "'Sanctified Jerusalem' is a very important subject to us. We know your position. But we believe that you should come with a constructive plan that would meet the religious sensitivities of all concerned. An accepted formula would defuse Arab resistance. Sadat says that he is a soldier whose land was captured.

He wants peace but not surrender. Sadat can bargain about any subject, except for territories and sovereignty. We are certain that if you reach an agreement with Egypt, Syria and Jordan would immediately follow. I suggest that after we report to our leaders and discuss each other's positions, we meet here again, say within two weeks."

Dayan told Tuhamy that he had come to Morocco as the emissary of Prime Minister Begin. Hence he could not express any opinion about the subjects raised. He wanted to consult with Begin before making any commitments. However, it was important to clarify one subject: whether the Egyptian demand for total Israeli withdrawal from Sinai was a precondition to Begin's meeting with Sadat. He added, "We believe that Begin and Sadat should meet, even if they disagree on total withdrawal. Egypt should also understand that no matter what Begin's position would be, any agreement would have to be approved by the full cabinet and later by the Knesset. Right now, I am not in a position to say what Begin's position will be. He might agree to your demand for total Israeli withdrawal but he might also disagree. Nevertheless, Begin would like very much to meet with your president. In my opinion, your proposal for a solution is not so simple. For more than nineteen years, our settlements in the Jordan Valley were shelled by the Syrians, dug in in the Golan Heights. Who would guarantee that such Syrian attacks would not recur? How could we secure the free navigation of our ships in the Red Sea? We have legitimate rights in the West Bank, the Wailing Wall, the Jewish Quarter in the Old City of Jerusalem, the Mount of Olives, the Hebrew University on Mount Scopus, the new neighborhoods south of Jerusalem. What will happen to the Jewish settlements in the Golan Heights and in the West Bank?

"As for the Palestinians, there is no historical precedent of an agreement with an organization that is committed to the destruction of a sovereign state, a member of the United Nations. We have fought against each Arab country. Resolution 242 speaks about countries; it does not mention the Palestinians or the PLO. President Assad said that all Palestinians should go back to their homes. What would happen if they do? They will not go to the small 'enclave' that you are suggesting. They would pour into Israel. It would be a demographic disaster. We believe that they should be resettled elsewhere. I know the problems are tough and complicated, but we should definitely discuss them. The problem of cities with different religious interests could be solved. The same could be said about the Straits of Tiran and free navigation in the Red Sea. We trust President Sadat that we could find a solution to our problems with Egypt. We don't trust President Assad and we are not sure of his intentions. We can find a solution to all our problems with Jordan. But there can be no independent Palestinian state. Nonetheless, we should start discussing all these problems soon."

Dayan and Tuhamy agreed to meet again in Morocco after consulting with

Begin and Sadat. Dayan also agreed with King Hassan on a date for Begin's visit to Rabat—November 20—on his way back from an official visit to Great Britain. Hassan had only one request: Begin should come in disguise and the visit should be kept secret. The visit, however, did not materialize, because in the meantime Sadat captivated the world's imagination by announcing his intention to go to Jerusalem.

King Hassan was in Marrakesh when Sadat announced his trip to Jerusalem. He thought that whether Sadat succeeded in his gamble or not, he was already a winner. Hassan gave Sadat his full support for his courageous initiative. In a personal message to Begin, Hassan urged the Israeli prime minister not to miss this opportunity and not to dash Sadat's hopes.

Sadat's visit to Jerusalem was followed on December 25, 1977, by Begin's visit to Ismailiya. A few days later, Dayan flew to Rabat to brief King Hassan on the Ismailiya summit. Hassan said that he was so thrilled with the new developments that he was now prepared to invite Begin and his wife, Aliza, to make a public visit to Rabat. He had, however, two conditions: that Begin agree to a joint communiqué stressing Israel's readiness to solve the Palestinian problem, and that he be prepared to discuss the future status of Jerusalem. Begin rejected King Hassan's conditions, and his trip to Rabat was put off "indefinitely."

The political disagreement between Begin and King Hassan was sharpened by another development. In March 1978, Palestinian terrorists hijacked a bus near Haifa, and by the time it was stopped, just north of Tel Aviv, twenty-six of its passengers were already murdered. In retaliation, the Israeli army launched Operation Litani—a deep incursion into Lebanese territory with the aim of destroying the Palestinian infrastructure in South Lebanon. King Hassan sent Begin a personal message expressing regret at the Israeli military action and urging an "immediate" withdrawal from Lebanese territory. Begin rejected Hassan's request. Nevertheless, while the personal relationship between Begin and Hassan suffered irreparable damage, the overall relationship between Israel and Morocco, through the Mossad channel, was not affected.

Meanwhile, the peace negotiations between Israel and Egypt were bogged down and there was a growing fear that both nations would lose the momentum created by Sadat's historic visit to Jerusalem. At the invitation of the Socialist International, Sadat and the head of the Israeli opposition, Shimon Peres, agreed to meet in Vienna, under the auspices of Willy Brandt and Chancellor Bruno Kreisky. Peres sought and obtained Begin's and Dayan's approval for this meeting with President Sadat. Sadat and Peres met for five hours at the Hofburg Palace, the site of the Austrian chancellor's office and where, in 1815, Metternich chaired the Congress of Vienna that set a new balance of power in Europe, following the Napoleonic Wars. Later in the day, in his hotel room, Peres told me that at Dayan's request, he had asked Sadat if he would be willing to lease the Israeli airfields in Sinai for a period of fifty years and if he would agree to leave the Jewish settlements in northern Sinai until the year 2010. Sadat categorically refused. "We are a nation of farmers, and for us land is sacred. Israel would have to withdraw from Sinai to the last grain of sand," Sadat said.

From Vienna, Peres flew to Paris, where he boarded a special Moroccan executive plane that took him to Rabat for a secret meeting with King Hassan. This was Peres's first visit to an Arab country, and he was very much impressed by its warm hospitality and discreet approach to sensitive issues. The Moroccan monarch urged the Israeli leader to do his utmost to soften Begin's position. "Sadat took a very courageous step, at great personal risk, and it would be a real tragedy if such an opportunity was allowed to be missed," the king said. Peres told Hassan that the Jewish people never ruled over other nations and hence the Labor Party was committed to peace, based on a territorial compromise. "However, we are not the government, we are the opposition. Should Begin move toward peace with Sadat, we would support him with no reservations," Peres said. Hassan used this occasion to ask for an Israeli lobbying effort on Capitol Hill to support Morocco's position concerning the armed conflict in western Sahara.

Peres reported his discussion with King Hassan to Begin. The Israeli prime minister did indeed urge Israel's friends on Capitol Hill to support Morocco's position in this matter.

In early September 1978, just a few days before President Carter brought Sadat and Begin together at Camp David, King Hassan paid an official visit to Washington. After the state dinner at the White House, Carter and Hassan had a private discussion in the president's study. Hassan urged Carter to include the Palestinians in the talks at Camp David. Carter replied, "If you would convince the PLO to accept Resolutions 242 and 338, I promise you to receive the Palestinian leaders here, at the White House."[18] Arafat rejected the Camp David Accords and did not join the peace process. He joined, instead, the "Rejectionist Front," together with Syria, Iraq, Libya, and South Yemen. Several years later, Arafat realized that he had committed a grave mistake in joining the Rejectionist Front, thereby missing an earlier opportunity to settle with Israel.[19]

In March 1981, shortly after President Reagan's inauguration, King Hassan invited Peres, who was still in the opposition, to pay another visit to Rabat. Israel was embroiled at the time in a fierce election campaign, and Peres had great hopes of returning to power. Based on the results of 1977, when Israelis of Moroccan descent voted against the Labor Party and helped elect Begin as the new prime minister, King Hassan hoped that an invitation to Peres would be a signal to "his Jews" in Israel to vote this time for Labor. However, shortly after Peres notified Begin that he was invited for political discussions with King Hassan, the story was leaked to the Israeli press. Labor and Likud blamed each other for the leak. As a result, any political gain that Peres might have had was drowned in the acrimonious debate between the two rival leaders.[20]

As events were to prove in the coming weeks, Peres's "secret" trip to Morocco did not play any role in the Israeli elections, and Begin was reelected for a second term as prime minister. Peres did not understand at the time that Israelis of Moroccan descent voted against Labor in 1977 not because of its foreign policy but because of the way they were treated in Israel. In an interview with the Egyptian newsmagazine *El-Mussawar*, Hassan said that in meetings with Likud Knesset members, he had asked them why they joined Begin's party. They replied that in the past, Labor had discriminated against them and did not give them equal opportunities. Begin, in contrast, revived their pride in their heritage, appointed them to key positions in the cabinet and in the army, and treated them equally.[21]

The war in Lebanon in June 1982 had dramatically changed the PLO's fortunes, and Yasser Arafat had become more amenable to a political solution with Israel. Seriously beaten on the ground, his infrastructure destroyed, and his forces evacuated from Beirut and dispersed among seven Arab countries, Arafat realized that he was not in a position of strength and he was incapable of dictating any conditions. Hence, a few days after President Reagan announced on September 1, 1982, his plan for a settlement in the Middle East, Arafat accepted King Hassan's invitation to attend an Arab summit meeting in Fez, on September 6, to discuss a Saudi counterinitiative. The tone and substance of the speeches by Moroccan King Hassan and Saudi King Fahd reflected the general mood of the summit. According to some intelligence reports, Hassan and Fahd argued that President Sadat had proved that it was possible for him to regain Sinai without a war. So why should oil-rich Arab countries continue to finance a Palestinian military effort if a diplomatic process could achieve better results? To the surprise of all participants, Iraqi President Saddam Hussein supported this political approach. Embroiled in a bloody and costly war with Iran, Saddam needed the financial support of the oil-rich pro-Western Persian Gulf countries. He therefore urged Arafat to accept King Fahd's plan.

Although more reluctant, President Assad too joined the "peace chorus." Assad said, "Although I am, by nature, more cautious and more hesitant, I do not want to be the 'spoiler' and I do support King Fahd's peace plan."

The Arab summit in Fez was a turning point in the long history of the Arab-Israeli conflict. It was the first time since the establishment of the State of Israel, in May 1948, that an Arab gathering unanimously endorsed a political solution to the conflict with Israel. Nevertheless, the Fahd Plan was rejected by Israel, because it only implicitly recognized its right to exist within secure and recognized borders, and it also recognized the Palestinians' right to a state of their own. The Fez summit formed a committee of seven heads of state, chaired by King Hassan, that was to travel to various capitals in an effort to persuade the international community to support the Arab plan. For that purpose, King Hassan went to Washington for talks with President Reagan, while King Hussein went to Moscow.

In a meeting with Secretary of State George Shultz, King Hassan submitted a four-page memorandum expressing Arafat's readiness to negotiate a tripartite confederation between Israel, Jordan, and "Palestine." King Hassan was convinced that Arafat's proposal would have the effect of a "bomb." He was disappointed. Shultz told him that the United States would stick to the Reagan Plan and would not endorse any other plan. "A tripartite confederation means an independent Palestinian state. The United States does not support such a solution," Shultz told the Moroccan king.

Shultz's position was reaffirmed by President Reagan. During a one-hour meeting at the White House, in the presence of Vice President Bush and Secretary Shultz, Reagan told Hassan that the United States appreciated his efforts but Arafat's proposal for a confederation and the Fahd Plan "were not practical at this time."

Rebuffed by Reagan, King Hassan tried to influence the Israeli political body, through "his Jews" in Israel. That was not easy. Shortly after he succeeded Begin, Prime Minister Yitzhak Shamir asked the Mossad, which is subordinated to the prime minister's office, to arrange for him a meeting with King Hassan. He was rebuffed. Hassan said, "Shamir wants only to reap political fruits and to win the votes of the Moroccan Jews in Israel. Should Shamir come with a serious idea how to solve the Palestinian problem, then of course I shall meet with him. Otherwise, it is a waste of time. Neither of us has time for tourism."[22]

On another occasion, Hassan said, "Shamir belongs to another generation. I don't believe that at his age, Shamir is capable of changing. He is unable to make the necessary decisions towards peace."[23]

Hassan's observations about Shamir reflected a deep conviction that as long as the Likud Party remained in power in Israel, there was no chance for a peaceful solution of the Arab-Israeli conflict. Accordingly, King Hassan was determined to try to reverse the course by creating a situation that would enable the Labor Party to return to power in Israel.

In 1979, Rafi Edri, a Labor Knesset member of Moroccan descent, came to Morocco and established contacts with the leaders of the small Jewish community in Casablanca. Through André Azoulay, the vice president of Bank Paribas in Paris and the cofounder of the intellectual group Identity and Dialogue, Edri met in Casablanca with David Ammar, the president of the Moroccan Jewish community and the chairman of the board of ONA, the biggest economic corporation in Morocco, in which the royal family has a sizable share. In future visits to Rabat, Ammar had arranged for Edri to meet with the two most trusted advisers of the king—Minister of the Court Reda Guedira and Ahmed Alawi. He also introduced him to General Abdul Haq Qadiri, the director of the Moroccan intelligence service, who was also the liaison with the Mossad.

In early 1983, Guedira introduced Edri to King Hassan. That same year, the king had given his approval to a joint initiative of David Ammar and Robert Assaraf, another prominent Jewish leader and also the CEO of ONA, to hold in Rabat a large Jewish congress, with the participation of Israeli, American, French, and Canadian Jewish leaders. Edri became the point man for the congress in Israel. The Labor Knesset member told Prime Minister Shamir about the initiative. The choice of the Israeli participants, however, remained exclusively in Edri's hands. In May 1984, the congress opened in Rabat, with the participation of some forty Israeli Knesset members, scholars, and journalists, not all of them of Moroccan descent. That was the first time that Israeli politicians and journalists had entered Morocco publicly. The congress debates were widely covered by the Moroccan media, which sensed that this was a government-inspired initiative. Furthermore, the closing session of the congress was attended by all twenty-eight Moroccan ministers, thus giving public legitimacy to Morocco's contacts with Israel. To his many critics in the Arab world, King Hassan replied, "My conscience is clear. I do not accept any interference in my decision on whom to invite to my country. We are free to organize any congress that we want. It is our right and obligation to invite Jews of Moroccan origin to take part in such a congress."[24]

Back in Israel, if there were any hidden hopes behind this Congress, they were again dashed. In the Israeli parliamentary elections held in June 1984, neither Labor nor Likud won a clear majority. As a result, a national unity government was formed in Israel, with a rotating prime minister. Shimon Peres was sworn in as the prime minister, while Yitzhak Shamir was his foreign minister. Two years later, they were to switch positions. Hence, if any change was to occur in Israel's peace policy, it was to be achieved during Peres's tenure as prime minister.

Indeed, Peres immediately embarked upon an ambitious and intensive effort to achieve a breakthrough in the peace process. His efforts were directed at Jordan's King Hussein, in hopes of including Palestinian representatives to a joint Jordanian-Palestinian delegation to negotiate peace with Israel. The first indications appeared to be promising. With the encouragement of Egypt, Morocco, and Saudi Arabia, King Hussein and Yasser Arafat signed an agreement in February 1985 according to which both sides undertook to join efforts to solve the Palestinian problem. King Hassan, in particular, urged Arafat to be more flexible in his approach toward a negotiated solution. Hassan believed that with Peres as prime minister, the Palestinians were given two years of grace and therefore they should not again miss this opportunity. He was confident that should Arafat be more flexible and agree to a solution that could be accepted by the majority of the Israelis, Peres would call for new parliamentary elections. Should Peres win, Shamir would not return to the prime minister's office.

Following the Jewish congress in Morocco in May 1984, Rafi Edri established himself as Labor's "Mr. Morocco." With Peres as prime minister, Edri also became a new channel of communication between Rabat and Jerusalem. It was a convenient channel for both sides. Being constantly attacked by radical Arabs for his cooperation with Israel in the field of intelligence and military affairs, Hassan was able now to use a bona fide "Moroccan-Jewish" channel for his public contacts with the Jewish state. Peres, by using this unofficial "Edri channel," was now able to circumvent the Mossad, thus avoiding the need to report to Shamir or to the Knesset Foreign Affairs Committee on the various initiatives that he was undertaking. Accordingly, on August 9, 1985, Peres sent Edri to Rabat with a personal letter to Hassan suggesting a meeting. In September 1985, the UN was to celebrate its fortieth anniversary. Reagan, Gorbachev, Peres, and King Hussein were among the many heads of state who were to address the General Assembly in New York. Peres suggested that King Hassan too attend the special UN session. In such a case, President Reagan might be willing to have a Hassan-Peres meeting under his auspices at the White House.

Hassan welcomed the idea. At the time that this exchange between Hassan and Peres was taking place, Moroccan Jewish leaders were preparing to form a "World Assembly of Moroccan Jews." At the initiative of David Ammar, the president of the Moroccan Jewish community, and of Rafi Edri, the assembly was to convene in Montreal, in October 1985, with the participation of delegates from Morocco, Israel, the United States, Canada, and Latin America. Ammar was to be elected the assembly's first president and Rafi Edri the vice president.

When Edri handed King Hassan Peres's letter, the monarch thought that he would combine the two subjects—address "his" Jews in Montreal and attend the special UN session before moving to Washington for the proposed meeting with Peres at the White House.

Peres sent Nimrod Novik, his political adviser, to Washington to explore the idea with the White House. The United States, however, was not very enthusiastic. In August 1984, King Hassan had signed a surprising "federation agreement" with Libya's Muammar Qadhaffi. The United States was stunned. Although the United States understood that the purpose of the agreement was to end Libya's assistance to the Polisario rebels in the western Sahara, it still could not understand how a liberal monarch could sign such an agreement with a country that harbored international terrorists. As a sign of displeasure, Reagan delayed his answer about the proposed joint meeting at the White House. Obviously offended, Hassan told Peres that he had decided not to attend the special UN session in New York. Instead, he said, he was considering a public meeting with Peres in Morocco. During a press conference in November 1985, Hassan replied to a question by stating that he was prepared to invite Peres to Rabat, "if he would bring with him interesting and serious ideas about how to solve the Palestinian problem." Hassan used the same language that he had used in the past in reply to Shamir's initiative, and he did not expect any immediate Israeli reaction. He only wanted to lay the groundwork for the meeting. Peres, however, misread Hassan's intentions. Assuming that this was the beginning of a new round of "microphone diplomacy," similar to the TV exchange between Begin and Sadat prior to Sadat's historic visit to Jerusalem in 1977, Peres reacted immediately. In reply to a question, Peres said that he was pleased "to accept King Hassan's invitation." Hassan was furious. Peres had accepted an invitation even before it was officially extended. As a result, the idea for a Peres public visit to Rabat was shelved for the time being.[25]

The contacts between the two leaders, however, continued. As a result of intense "private diplomacy," through the "Edri channel," Hassan and Peres agreed to meet in Paris on or around December 10, 1985. For that to happen, they needed French President Mitterrand's agreement. On December 4, 1985, Reda Guedira, the Moroccan minister of the court, called Jacques Attali, Mitterrand's national security adviser, and told him that the king would like to meet with Peres under the French president's auspices. Shortly afterward, a similar call came from Jerusalem. Uri Savir, Peres's press counselor, conveyed the same message to Attali. Mitterrand refused. Although he feared a strong Arab reaction, he was even more concerned that the joint Moroccan-Israeli initiative would exclude the PLO from any future peace negotiations.

After further consultations, Guedira informed Attali that Hassan and Peres would be pleased if Mitterrand only greeted them at the Elysée Palace and then left them alone for private discussions. The French president again refused. Now it was Peres's turn to call. He suggested to Attali that the meeting with King Hassan take place in a Parisian hotel and not at the Elysée. Mitterrand again refused.

On December 18, while in Geneva, Peres phoned Mitterrand. King Hassan was to meet with Mitterrand in Paris the next day, and Peres wanted to join the discussion. He told Mitterrand that a public meeting with King Hassan, in the presence of the French president, would break additional psychological barriers and would have a tremendous impact in the Middle East. As to Mitterrand's fears that such a meeting would exclude the Palestinians, Peres explained that the proposed meeting with Hassan would deal only with the modalities of the negotiations and not with their substance. Mitterrand, however, was still adamant in his refusal, and he told Peres that he would explain his position to King Hassan in detail.

Peres did not give up. On December 20, he called Hassan in Paris. He suggested proposing to Mitterrand that he and the king meet first in a Parisian hotel and then Mitterrand would receive each of them separately at the Elysée. Hassan was reluctant. He told Peres that if he insisted on such a procedure, he himself should propose it to Mitterrand. When Attali broached the subject again with Mitterrand, the French president was angry. He told Attali to inform Peres to get in touch with Foreign Minister Roland Dumas. That was an elegant way of refusing again. Dumas, an attorney, had a considerable reputation for the defense of PLO terrorists in French courts. Among others, he had defended Abu Daud, the notorious mastermind of the massacre of eleven Israeli athletes at the Munich Olympic Games in 1972. As foreign minister, Dumas was very critical of Israel and very supportive of the PLO. On December 20, in the late-afternoon hours, Peres called Attali again. He told him that he was unable to reach Dumas. The French foreign minister had not returned his calls. Therefore he insisted on talking to Mitterrand again. The president told Attali that as far as he was concerned, the subject was closed and he did not want to hear about it anymore.[26]

In early 1986, inter-Arab relations were again in limbo. In February 1986, after a year of inconclusive discussions with Yasser Arafat, King Hussein announced that he revoked the agreement he had signed with the PLO a year before. Tension between Syria and Iraq, resulting from President Assad's support of Khomeini against Saddam Hussein, reached a dangerous point. There was also the Iraqi-Libyan split and a slight tension between Syria and Jordan. The Arab leaders, instead of focusing on the Palestinian problem, were devoting their energies to inter-Arab disputes. Morocco was the only Arab country that showed signs of political stability and enjoyed international respect. Indeed, in the spring of 1986, relations between Morocco and the United States improved considerably. On the occasion of the twenty-fifth anniversary of King Hassan's rule, President Reagan sent an official delegation, headed by William Casey, the director of the CIA, to convey to King Hassan his personal greetings. Reagan was even considering inviting Hassan to make an official visit to Washington in July.[27]

Peres seized on this opportunity to revive his old idea of a joint meeting with Hassan, under Reagan's auspices. Peres sent Knesset member Rafi Edri to Rabat to explore such a possibility. In June 1986, Reda Guedira informed Edri that King Hassan agreed to meet with Peres in Washington. President Reagan immediately issued the invitation to hold the meeting at the White House. In preparation for the White House summit, Peres sent Edri again to Rabat. In a meeting with the king, the Israeli envoy sensed that Hassan was having second thoughts. Reda Guedira was also hesitating. He told Edri that the king was concerned that the Arabs would attack Morocco for such a high-profile meeting. They would claim that the king was meeting with Peres in Washington not for the sake of the Palestinians but because he had "sold out" to the Americans. After a long day of consultations, Edri was called again to the king. Hassan informed the Israeli envoy that he wouldn't attend the White House meeting with Peres. He added that such a public meeting should have a "Moroccan flavor" and not be subordinated to a foreign patron.[28]

Indeed, on July 11, 1986, Hassan formally invited Peres to a public meeting with him in Ifrane on July 21. Peres was elated. In a few months he was due to transfer the premiership to Shamir, according to the rotation agreement between Labor and Likud. He wanted to finish his premiership with a bang. The public meeting with King Hassan in Ifrane could be the bang he hoped for. During the next five days, Edri and Guedira spent many hours in Rabat, passing back and forth drafts for a joint communiqué that was to be published at the end of the Ifrane summit. The final draft was worked out at the Hotel Crillon, in Paris, in a meeting between Reda Guedira and Edri, with the assistance of Uri Savir, Peres's press counselor. It was full of ambiguities, and Guedira did not like it. He told Edri that he hoped that Peres would bring with him a clearer text.

The logistical and security arrangements were made in Jerusalem by General Abdul Haq Qadiri, the director of Moroccan intelligence, and by his Israeli counterpart, Nahum Admoni. Hassan's only condition was that the invitation to Peres be made public only after the Israeli prime minister had landed in Morocco.

If this intense activity proved anything, it was that the United States, Israel, and Morocco shared the same sense of urgency concerning the peace process. President Reagan and King Hassan were aware, of course, of the fact that according to the rotation agreement, Peres was to shift duties with Yitzhak Shamir in November. Peres as foreign minister, under Shamir, would not be able to further the peace process against Shamir's will. And Shamir was unwilling to move. Hence, in the few months that remained until the rotation, all three leaders were concerned that the chance for a breakthrough was rapidly slipping away. It was this sense of urgency that prompted King Hassan to invite Peres to meet with him in Ifrane. The king had other ideas in mind. If the meeting with Peres went well, he intended to invite King Hussein and Peres for another meeting in Rabat, just before the rotation between Peres and Shamir. At a later stage, it was possible to organize a similar summit between Peres and the leaders of the Persian Gulf countries.

Before Peres's arrival, King Hassan contacted President Mubarak and invited him to Ifrane. Mubarak, however, made two conditions: that Peres agree, in no uncertain language, to an international peace conference; and that Peres declare support for the "national rights" of the Palestinian people. Peres refused.

Accompanied by Edri, by his immediate aides Nimrod Novik and Uri Savir, and by Mossad operative Ephraim Halevy, Peres flew to Meknes on July 21, aboard a special Israeli air force plane that was painted white and carried no Israeli signs. Welcomed at the airport by Minister of the Interior Driss Bassri and by General Qadiri, Peres and his party were driven to Ifrane for a late-night informal discussion with King Hassan. The official discussion was held the next day, on July 22. It was a disaster. Peres knew, of course, in advance of Hassan's intention to present him with Fahd's peace plan, which the Israeli government had already rejected. He was surprised, however, by the intensity of its presentation. Hassan explained that the Fahd Plan had the double merit of being approved by all Arab countries and it also implied an Arab recognition of the State of Israel. Further, it also reaffirmed the recognition of the PLO as "the sole representative" of the Palestinian people and its right to an independent state. Hassan feared that in the absence of peace, the danger of another war would rear its head. This would be a tragedy and a disaster greater than those Israel and the Arab countries had experienced in the past. He was particularly concerned about the possible use of arms of mass destruction, which could inflict an enormous number of casualties.

Hassan devoted most of his discussion to the Palestinian problem. "Look," he told Peres, "there are now in the occupied territories hundreds of thousands of young Palestinians who were born after 1967. They have no memories of their past, they have no flag, no identity, and no state. But they do have national feelings. They speak both Arabic and Hebrew. They live in your midst. Their frustration could lead them to rebellion and violence. Because of the Cold War, the Soviet Union is likely to exploit them by intensifying their feelings of frustration.

"I know you," the king added. "You are a democratic country, a country of values. You would not want to deprive the Palestinians of their basic rights, including the right to vote. Their birth rate is higher than yours. Since you won't be able to use force, you will be obliged to find a solution compatible with your security needs and their national aspirations."

Peres's reply was marked by an angry and impatient interruption by King Hassan. An Israeli participant recalled that Peres opened with a long review of the situation in the Middle East. After twenty minutes, Hassan lost his patience. Very uncharacteristically, for the king was known for his good manners, Hassan interrupted Peres and said angrily in French: *"C'est dommage pour le long trajet que vous avez fait"*—It's a pity for the long journey that you have made.

Peres was stunned but kept his cool. He agreed with Hassan's analysis, but not with his conclusions. Peres rejected Hassan's suggestion of opening a dialogue with the PLO and argued that Yasser Arafat was not a partner for peace. He used as an example King Hussein's tireless efforts to reach an agreement with Arafat, but to no avail. Peres added, "Arafat is so preoccupied with his own survival that he has forgotten the reasons for his struggle. The PLO has wasted everyone's time and continues to be an obstacle to peace." Peres told Hassan that Israel was prepared to negotiate with "authentic representatives" of the Palestinians in the territories, Palestinians who were in search of peace and were not engaged in terrorist activity. Israel was also ready to negotiate with Jordan.

After this long exchange, both Hassan and Peres were disappointed. The king was aware, of course, that in the past Israel had rejected Fahd's plan, and he was not so naive as to believe that Peres had changed his mind totally. He hoped, however, that in return for his public gesture, Peres would come to Ifrane with some fresh ideas for a solution. That had not happened. In an expression of deep frustration, Hassan told Peres, "If you refuse to negotiate with the PLO, you refuse to withdraw from the territories, and you oppose the establishment of an independent Palestinian state, we have nothing more to say to each other. Good-bye."

In an effort to save the meeting from total collapse, Edri suggested forming two working groups to draft proposals for a solution of the Palestinian problem. It was a formula accepted by both King Hassan and Peres. After all, it was not in Hassan's interest to send Peres back home frustrated and humiliated.

While his aides were meeting with their Moroccan counterparts, Peres sat alone in his room thinking about the political implications of his failed mission. His sense of frustration grew deeper when the working groups failed to reach an acceptable formula. Peres became even more pessimistic when on Wednesday, July 23, at 3:00 A.M., General Qadiri came to see Rafi Edri. The director of Moroccan intelligence told Edri that "the king is very disappointed." Qadiri added that the king was convinced that Peres had "exploited" him and had no serious intention of discussing a solution of the Palestinian problem. Qadiri asked what Peres's plans were. If the prime minister were to leave right away, then there would be a need to alert the airport and make the necessary arrangements. The message, then, was very clear. The king wanted Peres out of Morocco—right away.

Facing the prospect of a political disaster, Edri wanted to gain time. The visit was originally planned for forty-eight hours. If Peres returned to Israel right away, it would be obvious that his mission to Morocco had failed. Edri suggested, therefore, that the working groups reconvene, later that morning, for another round of discussions. The working groups met for another five hours. In an effort to translate the goodwill that emerged from the very public visit to Ifrane into the language of political deed, Peres guided his aides in assembling quotations from the Camp David Accords and from previous Israeli government resolutions. These were incorporated into a ten-point proposal that could please the Moroccans. They were indeed elated. In his "new" proposal, Peres suggested an "immediate" meeting with "authentic Palestinian representatives," seekers of peace and rejectors of violence, in an effort to find a solution that would take into consideration the Palestinian aspirations and Israel's security needs. Peres also agreed to an "international accompaniment" to a peace conference, the nature of which was to be agreed by the parties. Finally, Peres agreed that for the duration of the negotiations, Israel would not extend its sovereignty in the West Bank and the Gaza Strip.[29]

This document was presented to King Hassan and won his immediate approval. Peres was relieved. The first public visit of an Israeli prime minister to Morocco had not failed after all. After a twenty-minute private discussion with King Hassan, Peres flew back to Israel, determined to make the most of his perceived success.

Indeed, Peres's visit to Ifrane fired the imagination of the world and drew enthusiastic reactions from the United States and various European capitals. Even the pope gave his blessing and support. The Arab reaction was not uniform. As expected, President Assad attacked the Ifrane summit in crude language and broke diplomatic relations with Morocco. In a subsequent Arab summit meeting in Algiers, Libya's Qadhaffi came wearing gloves because, he explained, he did not want to shake hands with the man who had shaken Peres's hand. Egypt welcomed Peres's visit to Ifrane in unambiguous language. Jordan, Saudi Arabia, and the other Persian Gulf states denied the rumor that they had advance knowledge of the meeting and made do with that denial. All told, the Arab reactions were surprisingly mild and moderate and very different from what was expected.

Nevertheless, King Hassan felt a need to explain his invitation to Peres publicly. In a radio and TV interview and in personal messages to Arab heads of state, Hassan said that the Fahd Plan was "the only basis" for his discussions with the Israeli prime minister and that he had not deviated from the Arab consensus on the Palestinian problem.[30]

On July 29, 1987, Vice President Bush arrived in Israel as part of a Middle Eastern tour that took him also to Jordan, Egypt, and Morocco. In a meeting in Jerusalem, Peres urged Bush to encourage King Hussein to follow Hassan's path and to agree to a public meeting with Israeli leaders. The Jordanian monarch, however, did not feel strong enough to accept this proposal.[31]

The Hassan-Peres summit in Ifrane did not generate the hoped-for momentum in the peace process. It did, however, establish the path to follow. Peres's formula for an "international accompaniment" to the peace process was the basis for the joint sponsorship of the United States and the Soviet Union of the Madrid Peace Conference in October 1991. In the years to come, King Hassan was "present" at all the stages that eventually led to the historic handshake between Prime Minister Yitzhak Rabin and Chairman Yasser Arafat on the White House South Lawn on September 13, 1993.

Needless to say, King Hassan was fully aware of the secret Israeli-Palestinian negotiations in Oslo. During a joint press conference with President Clinton at the White House on March 15, 1995, King Hassan said: "I was not surprised when the declaration of principles between Israel and the PLO was signed in Washington. Both Israel and the PLO kept informing me about the progress they have made and the obstacles yet to overcome."[32]

Rabin also kept Hassan informed about his secret negotiations with Jordan. Shortly after he signed the "Washington Declaration" with King Hussein, on

July 25, 1994, Rabin sent Knesset member Rafi Edri to Rabat with a warm personal letter to King Hassan. In his letter, Rabin drew Hassan's attention to King Hussein's special role in the Muslim holy shrines in East Jerusalem.

Loyal to his promise to have "economic peace" with Israel, King Hassan hosted in October 1994 the Casablanca Conference for Regional Economic Cooperation, which was attended by a large Israeli delegation headed by Rabin and Peres. That same month, Israel opened in Rabat an "interest office"—one step short of full diplomatic relations. Shortly afterward, several Moroccan economic delegations came to Israel and signed contracts with Israeli high-tech and pharmaceutical corporations and encouraged tourism between the two countries. Finally, in early March 1995, Morocco opened its own "interest office" in Tel Aviv and urged other Arab countries to follow the same path and to end their economic boycott of Israel.

The timing of this last move was not accidental—it was in advance of King Hassan's official visit to the United States. Hassan came to Washington on March 15, as head of a large delegation of cabinet ministers, senior officials, and businessmen who were seeking American investments in Morocco. As a trusted ally of the United States, Hassan had met with all U.S. presidents since FDR. In the "arrow of crisis" stretching from Morocco to Pakistan, Rabat was always perceived as a rock of stability and King Hassan was considered a "pillar of peace" in the Middle East.

In his ninety-minute discussion with President Clinton—the first between the two leaders—Hassan said that he had come to Washington not only as the king of Morocco, but also on behalf of the Arab and Islamic worlds. Speaking about the Arab-Israeli conflict, the king said that as soon as the air cleared between Israel and the Palestinians, there was a sense of relief in the Arab world. While he thought that the peace process was irreversible, he was nevertheless concerned that the newborn peace was threatened by dangers, because it was not a full-fledged, comprehensive peace. Hassan urged Clinton to invest more energy in advancing the negotiations between Israel and Syria. He also acknowledged that the Palestine Authority was weak, and if it would not assert itself "very soon," it would grow even weaker.

As head of the Islamic Conference Jerusalem Committee, Hassan warned against the transfer of the American embassy from Tel Aviv to Jerusalem. He was also opposed to what he called the "constant Judaization" of East Jerusalem. While he acknowledged that Jerusalem could not be divided again, he stressed that any solution in Jerusalem should be acceptable to the three monotheist religions.[33]

Shortly after Hassan's return from Washington, Israeli-Moroccan relations faced their most serious crisis in many years. Prime Minister Rabin authorized the confiscation of land in East Jerusalem for the purpose of building a new Jewish housing project. Following an outcry in the West Bank and in the Arab world, the Arab League called for an Arab summit in Rabat on May 27, 1995. Rabin and Hassan understood quite well what could be the consequences of such a gathering. It could derail the entire peace process. Rabin sent Knesset member Edri immediately to Rabat with a personal letter to the king. In his letter, Rabin explained his domestic pressures and expressed concern that should his government fall and a Likud-led government be formed, the situation would become even more serious. In his reply, King Hassan wrote: "No matter how serious are your election concerns, they cannot justify your action. Confiscation of Arab land is a serious matter and is totally unacceptable."[34] Acting under discreet American pressure, Rabin suspended the land confiscation. King Hassan was relieved. He also suspended the Arab summit. Instead, and through Edri, he invited Peres and Arafat to meet with him in Rabat on May 27.

After meeting separately with Peres and Arafat, Hassan hosted a working dinner with the two delegations, which lasted four hours. According to one Israeli participant, the discussion was very frank and each side put its grievances on the table. Peres complained about the inefficiency of the Palestine Authority. He blamed the delays in implementing the Oslo Accords on the inexperience of Arafat's team. Peres explained that the delays in the redeployment in the West Bank were due to the lack of agreement on Israel's security needs. Arafat replied that not only Israel had security needs, the Palestinians too were concerned about their security. One of Arafat's aides said: "Israel should stop describing itself as a small country surrounded by Arab enemies. You are a regional power, you are a leading force in the Middle East." After intense deliberations, Peres gave July 1 as a target date for Israeli deployment in the West Bank. He warned, however, that if by then there was no agreement on the security arrangements, the troop withdrawals would again be postponed. Indeed, the final agreement, known as Oslo II, was not to be signed at the White House before October.

"His Majesty helped Israel and the Palestinians to extricate themselves from a very dangerous situation," a senior adviser to King Hassan told Edri at the end of the meeting.

In December 1995, after Rabin's assassination, Peres—now prime minister—went again to Rabat on his way back from Washington. Peres reported to the monarch that he had agreed with Clinton on the resumption of the negotiations with Syria, at Wye Plantation, on January 24, 1996. He was confident that he would be able to achieve a breakthrough with Syria "very soon." This hope, however, was soon to be dashed. One month later, on January 20, 1996, Foreign Minister Ehud Barak paid a short visit to Rabat and met with King Hassan. General (Res.) Barak had already visited Rabat in 1981, in his capacity as chief of military intelligence. Hassan knew, of course, that in Israel Barak was considered the "real" disciple of the late Rabin. He also knew that because of his many qualifications, Barak was likely to play an important role in Israeli politics. Therefore, Barak was accommodated in the official guest house in Souissi, which is normally reserved for heads of state. In his meeting with Hassan, Barak explored—among several other issues—the possibility of establishing full diplomatic relations between Israel and Morocco. The king, however, thought that the time was not yet ripe for such a move.[35]

Likud's victory in the general elections in May 1996 was received in Rabat in utter shock. Despite the geographic distance, but because of the large Moroccan Jewish community in Israel, King Hassan tried, in his own way, to help Peres win the elections. For example, he refused repeatedly to invite both Benjamin Netanyahu and David Levy to Rabat. He was concerned that such visits would be perceived in Israel as an endorsement of the Likud candidates.

After he was sworn in as the new prime minister of Israel, Netanyahu called several Arab leaders to assure them that he was committed to the Oslo Accords. King Hassan would not accept the call from Netanyahu. He decided to freeze all signs of public diplomacy with Israel. After the signing of the Hebron Accord with Arafat in January 1997, there were hopes for a thaw in Israeli relations with Morocco. Following a meeting with President Clinton in Washington, on February 13, 1997, Netanyahu wanted to stop over in Rabat on his way back to Israel. The king again said no. He told one of his aides: "I have no time for political tourism."

Nevertheless, and based on past experiences, one should not consider this public freeze in Israeli-Moroccan relations to be permanent. As a matter of fact, contacts between the two countries, on various issues, continue through other channels, as usual. Israeli officials who know intimately the history of Israeli-Moroccan relations are convinced that once the Arab-Israeli peace process is back on track, King Hassan's public relationship with the Israeli government will also be back on track.

RABIN'S IRAQI DILEMMA

Shortly after his return to power, in July 1992, Yitzhak Rabin was faced with a real dilemma: how to devise his Iraqi policy.

As defense minister in Yitzhak Shamir's cabinet, until the dissolution of the national unity government in the fall of 1989, Rabin was part of the decision to follow the American lead and to tilt toward Iraq against Iran. In a particularly low point during the Iran-Iraq War, he allowed secret meetings between Iraqi Foreign Minister Tariq Aziz and the director general of the Israeli Foreign Ministry, General (Res.) Abraham Tamir, in Geneva, in the years 1986–88. In August 1989, an effort was even made to arrange a secret meeting between him and Saddam Hussein, in Europe or elsewhere. The Gulf War in 1991, however, put an end to this tilt. In cooperation with its allies in the Persian Gulf, notably Kuwait and Saudi Arabia, the Bush administration decided that there would be no reconciliation with Iraq as long as Saddam Hussein remained in power. This tough anti-Iraq policy was couched in repeated public statements to the effect that reconciliation with Saddam Hussein was subject to his compliance with all UN resolutions. President Clinton had even sharpened this tough line. Acting upon the recommendation of his National Security Council, Clinton adopted a policy that called for the "double containment" of Iraq and Iran. In a later period, Clinton used the Kurdish "no flight" zone that the United States and its allies had established in northern and southern Iraq as a staging base for toppling Saddam Hussein. This covert effort, however, had not yielded any tangible results.

The "double containment" policy started from the assumption that both Iran and Iraq were pursuing policies fundamentally hostile to American national interests in the Persian Gulf and the Middle East. During the Cold War and following the ouster of the Hashemite monarchy in Baghdad, in July 1958, the United States had relied on Iran's military power and Saudi financial wealth to protect its interests in the Gulf. After the downfall of the shah of Iran in January 1979, American backing shifted to Iraq. After Desert Storm, however, President Clinton rejected the policy of building Iran and Iraq, one against the other, and preferred to contain both countries. Put in a broader strategic context, the double containment policy also helped promote the Arab-Israeli peace process and solidify American relations with the Arab world and Israel.

Not all of the U.S. allies in the Persian Gulf War agreed with this policy. Russia, France, Germany, and Egypt and other Arab countries argued that the UN mandate was to liberate Kuwait, not to topple Saddam Hussein. They preferred a carrot approach that would provide Saddam Hussein with the necessary incentives to modify and moderate his policies. They argued that by keeping the UN sanctions on Iraq and weakening Saddam's regime, the United States was practically providing opportunities for Iran to meddle and prey on this weakness. Eager to get a share in the reconstruction of Iraq once the UN sanctions were lifted, the Europeans, in particular, tried to circumvent the American policy by encouraging Saddam Hussein to join the Arab-Israeli peace process and to intensify his efforts for a dialogue with Israel. However, the sponsors of the Madrid Peace Conference in October 1991 did not invite Iraq to take part in that forum. The Bush administration was determined to rob Saddam Hussein of his ability to exploit the Palestinian problem for his own interests in the Arab world. The Madrid Framework established two tracks of negotiations between Israel and its Arab neighbors: a bilateral track, in which Israel negotiated in Washington with each of the Arab confrontation states and with the Palestinians; and the Multilateral Track, composed of five committees discussing various regional development plans. The Europeans, and especially France, encouraged Iraq to join this Multilateral Track. Isolated in the Arab world, his country torn by ethnic feuds with the Kurds in northern Iraq and with the Shiites in the south, his military capability considerably reduced and his nuclear infrastructure almost completely destroyed, Saddam Hussein had no cards at his hand. He had gone to war with the political and moral support of Jordan and the PLO. He had come out of the war with no friends at all. Thus, the European advice was the only option available to him, and he gratefully accepted it.

This "help Saddam" effort began shortly after the Madrid Peace Conference. During a visit to Jerusalem in January 1992, French President François Mitterrand explored with Prime Minister Shamir two initiatives for regional cooperation with Iraq: a Haifa-Baghdad railroad and an oil pipeline from southern Iraq to the Gaza Strip. If these two projects were approved, France was prepared to participate in the financing, which would necessitate an investment totaling $6 billion.[1]

By proposing those two projects, Mitterrand had two objectives in mind. First, he wanted to assure France a more active role in the reshaping of the New Middle East, after the United States had monopolized the bilateral Israeli-Arab peace negotiations. Second, two French oil companies, Total and Elf Aquitaine, were negotiating with Iraq two new oil concessions, and an Israeli agreement for a Baghdad-Haifa railroad, with French financial assistance, would provide the two companies with the political and economic support they needed.[2]

Since Iraq was not invited to the Madrid Peace Conference, it was easy for Shamir to reject Mitterrand's proposal. Similar ideas, however, from different players, were soon to follow.

It is this "Iraqi situation" that Rabin inherited from Shamir after his new Labor-led government was sworn in, on July 13, 1992. Rabin's top priority at this early stage was the peace process, not Iraq. After being defeated in the Persian Gulf War, Saddam Hussein had no military option, and he did not represent an immediate threat to Israel. Therefore, Rabin saw no reason to divert his attention from the peace process to the Iraqi problem. Moreover, after his meeting with President Bush in August 1992 and with President Clinton in March 1993, Israel's Iraqi policy was fully coordinated with that of the United States. In the following months and on several occasions, Rabin expressed public support of Clinton's dual containment policy. Rabin also opposed the lifting of sanctions on Iraq before Saddam Hussein complied with all UN resolutions. As for the peace process, Rabin agreed with Clinton that Saddam Hussein should be kept at arm's length and should not play any role in it. Clinton and Rabin believed that a strong Iraq would not only endanger U.S. oil interests in the Persian Gulf but also become a rallying point for a new confrontation with Israel. Hence, it was better to wait until a new Iraqi leadership took over from Saddam and then join the Arab-Israeli peace process in a responsible manner.

Accordingly, Rabin gave the following guidelines to the relevant government agencies:

- Israel was not to initiate any contact with Iraqi officials, at any level.

- Israel should reject any Iraqi initiative, through a third party. When the time came, all contacts had to be direct and official. This was meant to avoid a repetition of past experiences, when secret Israeli-Iraqi contacts were part of a deception scheme and a smoke screen to shield Saddam's aggressive intentions against Kuwait.

- Finally, in any future effort concerning Iraq, Israel should make it absolutely clear that it would not abandon the Kurds. For ten consecutive years, from 1965 to 1975, Israel had supplied military and humanitarian assistance to the Kurds in northern Iraq. This effort was conducted in cooperation with the Savak, the Iranian intelligence agency under the shah, and with the full knowledge of the CIA and other Western intelligence agencies. The legendary Kurdish leader Mullah Mustafa Barazani, who

died and was buried in the United States, visited Israel twice
after the Six-Day War of June 1967. Two of his sons, Idriss and
Massoud, also visited Israel and were trained by the Israeli army,
both in Israel and in Kurdistan. Israeli army officers were based
permanently in northern Iraq and advised the Kurds in their
fighting against the Iraqi army. On two occasions, on the eve of
the Six-Day War and the Yom Kippur War in 1973, Israeli army
officers, wearing the traditional Kurdish dress, were with
Barazani at his headquarters in northern Iraq when senior Iraqi
officers came to ask him to join in the war against Israel. He refused. On another occasion, former head of the Mossad Nahum
Admoni was with Mulla Mustafa Barazani when two Iraqi suicide
bombers attempted to kill the Kurdish leader. Admoni and
Barazani were not hurt. This Israeli assistance to the Kurds came
to an end in 1975, when the shah and Saddam Hussein reached
an agreement in Algiers on the navigation rights in the Shatt el-
Arab waterway.[3]

After the Persian Gulf War, the United States and its allies had helped establish an autonomous Kurdish region in northern Iraq. With the full encouragement of the United States, Israel resumed its contacts with the Kurds. Arab
press reports had indicated that Iraqi opposition leaders had helped Israeli
agents infiltrate into Kurdistan, with Turkish assistance.[4] At the instruction of
Prime Minister Shamir, Mossad operatives maintained regular contacts with
the two feuding Kurdish leaders—Massoud Barazani, the head of the Kurdistan Democratic Party (KDP); and Jalal Talabani, the head of the Patriotic
Union of Kurdistan (PUK). The Israeli effort to reconcile them had failed.

After he returned to power, in July 1992, Rabin continued contacts with
the two Kurdish factions. He also established contacts with Kurdish and Iraqi
opposition leaders in Europe and elsewhere and entrusted his minister of
health, General (Res.) Ephraim Sneh, the former head of the Israeli civil administration in the West Bank, with this task. Sneh met several times with representatives of the two Kurdish factions in London, Paris, and Washington.
Hence, in the face of repeated Iraqi efforts to establish a dialogue with Israel,
Rabin insisted that Israelis should always emphasize the need to safeguard the
legitimate rights of the Kurds.[5]

Despite these guidelines, however, Israel had witnessed intense diplomatic
activity in New York, Paris, Geneva, Rome, Amman, and Rabat aimed at encouraging an Israeli dialogue with Iraq. In February 1993, Saddam Hussein
told Yasser Arafat that he was very much offended because he had not been invited to the Madrid Peace Conference. Because of the "Kuwaiti crisis," he did
not expect the Arab countries to stand up for him. But because of the many sac-

rifices that Iraq had made for the sake of the Palestinians, he did expect Yasser Arafat to raise the issue of Iraqi participation with the American and Soviet sponsors. "In any event," Saddam told Arafat, "I want you to know that Iraq is not opposed to the peace process with Israel. At a certain point, I might even join it. Hence, you must continue your march toward peace with Israel. Despite the difficult situation that you are in, I know that you will do your best to get the maximum for your people."[6]

In April 1993, Morocco's King Hassan invited Barzan el-Takriti, Saddam's half brother and Iraq's ambassador to the UN in Geneva, to Rabat. He conveyed to him the message that because of the U.S. veto power, the UN Security Council wouldn't be able to lift the sanctions without Clinton's consent. He added that the only country that could influence the U.S. position was Israel. "If you want a reconciliation with Washington," the king told Barzan, "you should join the peace process. Despite Iraq's financial difficulties, you should also resume your financial assistance to the Palestinians." Upon leaving the royal palace, Barzan told the Moroccan and Arab press: "There is not even one Arab country that contributed to the Arab cause more than Iraq. If there are now Arab countries that challenge us to join in another war against Israel, we tell them that this time they will have to fight it alone. . . ."[7]

The Moroccan king followed up this conversation with Barzan by sending a special envoy to Baghdad to convey the same message to Saddam Hussein. The Iraqi dictator had to decide what came first—an unconditional reconciliation with the United States and Kuwait and joining the Arab-Israeli peace process, or lifting the embargo. He opted for lifting the sanctions first.

Nevertheless, when the Oslo Accords were signed in Washington, on September 13, 1993, Saddam Hussein's reaction was relatively mild. While the Iraqi Ba'ath Party issued a sixteen-page statement condemning the Israeli-Palestinian agreement, Iraqi officials told the PLO that "whatever is accepted by the Palestinians is also accepted by Iraq."[8]

Accordingly, when Farouq Qadoumi, the PLO "foreign minister" who opposed the Oslo Accords, came to Baghdad to seek Iraq's support, Saddam refused to meet with him. Saddam also refused to meet with George Habash and Nayef Hawatmeh, the leaders of the two radical wings of the Popular Front for the Liberation of Palestine, who were based in Damascus. Concerned that after his meeting with President Clinton in Geneva, in January 1994, President Assad would sign a peace treaty with Israel and curtail their terrorist activity, they came to verify if Saddam would agree to relocate their offices from Damascus to Baghdad. Iraq sent them back to Damascus.[9]

In October 1993, Iraqi Foreign Minister Tariq Aziz met secretly in Paris with a former Israeli official in an effort to open a direct dialogue between the two countries. The meeting lasted two days, and was also attended by Barzan el-Takriti, the Iraqi ambassador to the UN in Geneva. When published in an Israeli newspaper, it drew an immediate and angry U.S. reaction.[10] State Department officials feared that the Paris meeting, coming immediately after the Oslo Accords, which were negotiated secretly, without a direct U.S. involvement, was "another surprise," undertaken by Israel's Foreign Ministry without Rabin's knowledge. Foreign Minister Peres denied the report immediately. He told Israeli Radio: "Saddam Hussein is not a partner to the peace process. No Iraqi official approached us. It could be, however, that someone from Iraq met with someone from Israel, but this 'someone' was not empowered by us to negotiate with Iraq."[11]

In the summer and fall of 1994, Iraq became even more desperate to lift the embargo on its oil sales and to ease the UN sanctions. According to Israeli intelligence reports, the sanctions were taking their toll and Saddam's base had narrowed considerably. In the first six months of 1994, there were credible reports about five coup attempts, and unrest among the Iraqi elite was reported to be growing. Realizing that the United States had forgiven King Hussein and Yasser Arafat for their support of Saddam's invasion of Kuwait, Iraq decided to try to get a similar pardon. Saddam was now ready to follow Moroccan King Hassan's advice and to try entering Washington's gates through Jerusalem. Iraq tried to use the good offices of countries that had good relations with Israel: Turkey, Morocco, Jordan—and the PLO.

During a meeting between Arafat and Israeli Minister of Energy Moshe Shahal, the PLO chairman urged Israel to open a dialogue with Iraq. "I have a good and warm relationship with Saddam Hussein," Arafat told Shahal. "The moment you are ready for a dialogue with Iraq, let me know. I can easily arrange it."[12]

Born in Baghdad as Morris Fattal, Shahal was a classmate of Iraqi Prime Minister Adnan Pachachi and studied with several other senior Iraqi officials. He had gone to Israel in the early fifties. He had studied law in Israel, and after being admitted to the Israeli bar, he joined the Labor Party, was elected to the Knesset, and became a minister in Peres's, Shamir's, and Rabin's cabinets. Shahal reported his discussion with Yasser Arafat to Rabin, but the prime minister was not interested in a dialogue with Saddam Hussein at that stage. Nevertheless, and around that same period, the PLO did arrange a secret meeting in Istanbul between the former head of the Iraqi intelligence service who lived in exile, and a senior Israeli official. The meeting was inconclusive.[13] In a long article about the presumed "secret contacts" between Israel and Iraq, the editor in chief of the Egyptian paper El-Ahram challenged both Israel and Iraq to deny his story about the Istanbul meeting. They did not.

In July 1994, Iraqi Foreign Minister Tariq Aziz left for New York in an effort to persuade the UN Security Council to ease the sanctions on his country. On his way to New York, he stopped in Rabat and tried to enlist King Hassan's assistance. Morocco was well qualified for such a role. King Hassan had a good relationship with both the United States and Israel and with several Persian Gulf countries. Hassan met with Aziz twice during this trip. However, before committing himself to any action, King Hassan wanted to hear this "message" from Saddam himself. He sent one of his ministers to Baghdad, where he was told of Saddam's desire to negotiate with Israel. The report was leaked to one of the Israeli papers and was denied immediately.[14] Nevertheless, Arab ambassadors to the UN who met with Aziz in New York reported to Israeli Ambassador to the UN Gad Yaacoby about their meeting with the Iraqi foreign minister. "Aziz told us that Iraq does not consider itself a 'confrontation state' and would support any agreement between Israel and the Palestinians," an Arab ambassador told Yaacoby. Aziz added that he personally did not have any objection to recognizing Israel and normalizing relations with the Jewish state.[15]

While Yaacoby refused to identify the "Arab ambassador," other sources said that it was the Moroccan diplomat. He even suggested arranging a meeting between Aziz and the Israeli ambassador. Yaacoby called Rabin immediately and asked for guidance. Rabin again said no.

Weeks later, Rabin himself confirmed this Iraqi overture. In an interview with the Lebanese paper *El-Hayat*, the Israeli prime minister said: "A few weeks ago, Iraq tried to establish contacts with us, through a third party, in New York, more precisely at the UN. I know of no other place where a similar effort was made. I instructed all Israeli envoys that no one is authorized to maintain a direct or indirect contact with Iraq. This Arab country constitutes a very special case. We are part of the international community and we are committed to all UN resolutions concerning Iraq."[16] Rabin's unusual interview with the Lebanese paper was meant, in part, to divert attention from Morocco and the role it played in helping establish this contact. A few days earlier, the same Lebanese paper had reported secret contacts between Israel and Iraq in both Jordan and Morocco. The paper said that Tariq Aziz had met secretly in Rabat with Israeli Housing Minister Benjamin (Fuad) Ben-Eliezer. The Israeli minister denied the report immediately. A few weeks later, however, London's *Sunday Times* repeated the story and attributed it to MI6 sources—Britain's intelligence service.[17]

Like Shahal, Ben-Eliezer was of Iraqi descent. Born in Bassra, in southern Iraq, Ben-Eliezer went to Israel at the age of twelve and made his career in the army, where he reached the rank of major general. In 1976, he was sent by Rabin to Beirut to survey the needs of the Christian militias headed by Bashir Jemayel in their struggle against the PLO and its Syrian allies. He also served as commander of the Israeli forces in the West Bank. In his political orientation, he was very close to President Ezer Weizman and to Yitzhak Rabin. As such he was credited with being instrumental in Rabin's victory in 1992, which brought Labor back to power. Like Shahal, however, Ben-Eliezer too believed in a dialogue with Iraq. He was certain that once the sanctions were lifted, Iraq would join the peace process with Israel. As a man who reflected Rabin's thinking on Iraq, he explained: "Rabin too believed that peace with Iraq would serve Israel's interests. But he did not trust Saddam Hussein. Rabin thought that there can be no breakthrough with Iraq as long as Saddam is in power. He used to say that if the sanctions on Iraq are lifted, Saddam would use his oil revenues not to rebuild his country, but to acquire nuclear capability. With the large number of nuclear scientists in Iraq, Saddam could reach a nuclear capability even before Iran. Therefore, Rabin was totally committed to the U.S. strategy and he would not do anything behind President Clinton's back. It was not Rabin's style. He valued Israel's relationship with the United States and he would not do anything to undermine it. Besides, Saddam cannot stand on his feet. If he were a real patriot who cared for his people, he should have stepped down and let somebody else run the show. Should this happen—then everything is possible. . . ."[18]

After the signing of the "Washington Declaration" between Israel and Jordan, on July 25, 1994, the "Jordanian channel" to Iraq became particularly active. In early August, Israeli censorship censored a news item according to which President Ezer Weizman, in a telephone conversation with King Hussein, had said: "God willing, we will have soon peace with the man carrying your name," thus alluding to Saddam Hussein. A few days later, Iraqi Deputy Prime Minister Tariq Aziz held a series of meetings with Jordanian Prime Minister Abdul Salam Majali, amid rumors that Israeli and Iraqi security officials were meeting secretly in Wadi Arava, along the Israeli-Jordanian border. Without referring to these rumors, Jordanian Minister of Information Jawad Anani told an interviewer that "it is possible that Iraq would play an important role in the multilateral committees on development of regional water resources, environment, and economic cooperation." Iraq denied the report and criticized the Jordanian minister for speaking on its behalf.[19]

Despite these reports and their denials, Tariq Aziz made public his "moderate" views. In an article he published in an Arabic newspaper in East Jerusalem, the Iraqi minister reiterated his country's view that Iraq did not regard itself anymore as a "confrontation state." He added, however, that "there is a lot of exaggeration in the assumption that Israel is capable of convincing the United States to lift the sanctions on Iraq."[20]

Two months later, Tariq Aziz went one step further. In an interview with Eric Rouleau, an expert on Middle Eastern affairs and a former French ambassador to Tunis and Ankara, the Iraqi foreign minister made public an earlier secret decision by Saddam Hussein according to which there did not exist a "state of belligerency" between Israel and Iraq. "We have no joint border with Israel, nor do we have any direct conflict with Israel," Aziz told Rouleau.[21]

President Clinton's visit to Israel in October 1994, on the occasion of the signing of the peace treaty between Israel and Jordan, was presumed to put an end to all these "private initiatives" concerning Iraq. Replying to Clinton's address in the Knesset, Prime Minister Rabin reiterated Israel's position and his total commitment to the "dual containment" of both Iran and Iraq. The private initiatives, however, continued. In November 1994, former French defense minister Jean Pierre Chevenement wrote to Shimon Peres and to Tariq Aziz suggesting a high-level meeting between Peres and Saddam Hussein. Chevenement, who was married to a Jewish woman, was in France considered a friend of Israel. As defense minister, he had been involved in several arms transactions with Iraq, and he was considered a friend of Iraq as well. In January 1991, he had proved his friendship by resigning his cabinet position in protest against President Mitterrand's decision to join the U.S.-led coalition against Saddam Hussein. Hence, when Chevenement suggested a Saddam-Peres meeting, Tariq Aziz knew that the idea came from a man with no anti-Iraqi bias. Chevenement told Aziz that "such a meeting would ease Israeli fears and would help convince the Jewish lobby in Washington to try to urge President Clinton to ease the sanctions, if not to lift them altogether." Aziz replied that he would prefer that Chevenement himself discuss the subject with Saddam.[22]

Chevenement flew to Baghdad for a meeting with Saddam Hussein and then went to Israel via Jordan. In a meeting in Jerusalem, he reported to Peres about his discussion with Saddam and urged the Israeli foreign minister to agree to a secret dialogue with Iraq. Peres refused. He told Chevenement: "We have no enmity with the Iraqi people. The enemy of the Iraqi people is Saddam Hussein." Peres explained that the Iraqis were trying to use the "Israeli channel" as a venue to Washington. Saddam, however, was not a normal person. Once the embargo was lifted, he would revert to his old aggressive policies.[23]

In the fall of 1995, there were again persistent rumors about secret meetings between Israel and Iraq. The rumors were so persistent that the U.S. ambassador to Israel, Martin Indyk, raised the issue with Israeli officials. They denied it categorically. However, in order to avoid any misunderstandings with the United States, Peres issued a qualified denial. He told Israeli Radio: "There are no direct or indirect contacts between Israel and Iraq. We support the dual containment policy of Iran and Iraq. Any contacts which could have been made with Iraqis were made by self-appointed emissaries and not by Israeli government officials."[24]

The U.S. concerns and suspicions about Israeli back-channel contacts with Iraq were undoubtedly the result of a legitimate debate in Jerusalem and in Washington about the effectiveness of the dual containment policy. It is not a secret anymore that this policy did not enjoy the unanimous support of the U.S. political body. Within the administration, in Congress and in the business and academic communities, there were many who expressed doubts about the effectiveness of this policy. In Israel too, there were many experts and officials who challenged this approach and called for its revision. During a visit to Jerusalem in April 1995, members of the U.S. Foreign Relations Council suggested to both Rabin and Peres associating Iraq in the peace process, through the Multilateral Track for regional economic cooperation. They insisted, of course, on the need for Saddam Hussein to comply first with all UN resolutions. But once this was done and sanctions were lifted or eased, American oil companies would be prepared to invest in a new oil pipeline between Iraq and Israel. This was the same idea, but with minor variations, that had already been raised by French President Mitterrand in 1992.[25] Both Rabin and Peres rejected the idea and said that Israel would consider it "at the appropriate time."

This unshaken policy was based on the assumption, both in Israel and in the United States, that after so much pain and damage in Iraq, resulting from two unprovoked wars that Saddam Hussein had initiated, the Iraqi ruler would eventually be overthrown. They knew, of course, that the Iraqi opposition was divided and ineffective, but UN sanctions had driven the Iraqi people to the ground. If Saddam Hussein was still in power, it was not because of his successes, but because of his cruelty to his people and the divisions within the ad hoc Western coalition that had taken part in the Persian Gulf War. This tough anti-Saddam policy also took into consideration Syria's fears and concerns. Since President Clinton's meeting with President Assad in Geneva, in January 1994, Secretary Christopher and his peace team, headed by Ambassador Dennis Ross, had made a tremendous effort to achieve a breakthrough in the bilatral negotiations between Israel and Syria. After the Washington Declaration between Israel and Jordan was signed, on July 25, 1994, it was feared that President Assad would lose faith in the American peace effort and would suspect that the United States was trying to "isolate" him. Hence, in all contacts with Israeli officials, the United States discouraged any official contact with Iraq, at any level. In a discussion with an influential Lebanese newspaper, a senior American official was quoted as having said: "We believe that it is preferable at this time to concentrate on the Syrian-Israeli track. Lifting or easing the sanctions on Iraq could come only after a Syrian-Israeli agreement, not before."[26]

In examining the repeated Iraqi efforts to open a dialogue with Israel, one has to also take into consideration the Egyptian position and President Mubarak's ambition to play a leading regional role in the Middle East. In less than a decade, Egypt had moved from total support of Iraq in its war against Iran to a total rejection of Saddam Hussein because of his invasion of Kuwait. After Desert Storm, however, Egypt's policy became more nuanced. Publicly and officially, Egypt insisted on full Iraqi compliance with all U.N. resolutions. At the same time, Egypt opposed any new U.S. military action against Iraq and recruited an all-Arab support for this position. As to Israel, Egypt never concealed its opposition to any direct or indirect dialogue between Baghdad and Jerusalem. This change in attitudes reflected the changes in the regional balance of power in the Middle East. Immediately after the Gulf War, when the destruction of the Iraqi war machine had altered the balance of power in Israel's favor, President Mubarak came out publicly with his plan to denuclearize the Middle East and to ban all weapons of mass destruction. Mubarak's aides explained at the time that Egypt would never agree to a situation where Israel was the only nuclear power in the Middle East.

Mubarak's position did not come as a surprise to Israeli policymakers. As far back as Camp David in 1978, Egyptian policymakers had been divided on the issue of Israel's nuclear potential. Mubarak, then vice president, and his chief diplomatic adviser, Dr. Ossama el-Baz, suggested to Sadat not signing the Camp David Accords unless Israel agreed to sign the Nonproliferation Treaty (NPT). President Sadat rejected this advice. He was anxious to sign the agreement with Israel that guaranteed the return of Sinai to Egyptian sovereignty. He argued that once Israel withdrew from all the Arab-occupied territories, it would be reduced to its "natural size" and would not constitute any danger.[27] After the Oslo Accords between Israel and the Palestinians, Mubarak realized that Israel had not been reduced to its "natural size" but had become even stronger, militarily, economically, and politically. Egypt, the biggest and the most populous Arab country, had lost control of developments in the Middle East and was even being ignored by some Arab nations. King Hussein signed a peace treaty with Israel without even consulting Mubarak. Oman's Sultan Qabus invited Prime Minister Rabin to make an official visit, Qatar was prepared to sell natural gas to Israel, and now Iraq was ignoring Egypt's role in the peace process and was looking to other keys to open Israel's doors. Mubarak's main concern was that should a reconciliation between Israel and Iraq become possible, Egypt's role in American eyes would become considerably reduced, and this, in turn, could affect Egypt's strategic importance in the entire region.

It is against the background of these developments that we ought to see how drastically the U.S. and Israeli "Iraq policy" had changed, from a pro-Saddam tilt in the 1980s to a fierce struggle against his continued rule in the 1990s. The tilt toward Iraq was begun by the Reagan administration, as early as 1982. After the resumption of American-Iraqi diplomatic relations in November 1984, this tilt was later intensified by the Bush administration, and it remained unchanged until shortly before Saddam invaded Kuwait, in August 1990. Convinced by both the United States and Egypt of Saddam's "moderation," Israel too began to tilt toward Iraq in the spring of 1984. Unlike the United States, however, Israel did not completely shut its door to Iran. The Likud-led government of Yitzhak Shamir came to see Iraq as a "central element" in any future Arab-Israeli peace process. This was a clear departure from a consistent Israeli policy that saw Iraq as a "confrontation state" and a bitter enemy of Israel. In evaluating the military balance in the Middle East, Israel always took into consideration the added Iraqi military power on its eastern front.

There is no common border between Israel and Iraq, and a vast desert separates Jordan and Iraq. Nevertheless, since 1948, Iraq had participated in all Arab wars against Israel, and had sent troops either to Jordan or to Syria in an effort to defeat the Israeli army. Iraq was the only country among the confrontation states that had refused to sign an armistice agreement or a cease-fire agreement with the Jewish state. When President Sadat signed his peace treaty with Israel, in March 1979, Iraq had broken diplomatic relations with Cairo. Together with Syria, Libya, Algeria, South Yemen, and the PLO, Iraq formed the "Rejectionist Front" in an effort to derail the peace with Israel. Iraq also initiated the expulsion of Egypt from the Arab League and voted for the transfer of the league's headquarters from Cairo to Tunis.

This "rejectionist" policy began to change in the fall of 1981, after the breakout of the Iran-Iraq War and the assassination of President Sadat. The Islamic Khomeini revolution in Iran and the overthrow of the shah were seen by the United States and the Persian Gulf countries as a bigger threat to regional stability than Saddam Hussein's rule. Thus, acting under pressure from Egypt and Saudi Arabia, the Reagan administration allowed the transfer to Iraq of Egyptian surplus Soviet-made equipment, financed by Saudi Arabia and other Persian Gulf countries.

At this early stage of the war, Israel was not yet influenced by the developments in the Persian Gulf, and despite the Khomeini rhetoric, it continued discreetly to supply arms to Iran. Moreover, on June 7, 1981, eight Israeli F-16s took off from an American-built Israeli air force base in Sinai and flew eleven hundred miles eastward to destroy the French-built Iraqi nuclear reactor Tamuz, twelve miles east of Baghdad. This spectacular and imaginative achievement sent shock waves throughout the Arab world and drew angry condemnations by the international community, including the United States. Coming on the eve of new Israeli parliamentary elections, the air strike generated an ugly quarrel between the Labor and Likud parties and revived the personal and bitter feud between Shimon Peres and Yitzhak Rabin.

The destruction of the Iraqi reactor had its origins some six months earlier. Setting an example for coalition-opposition cooperation in matters of national security, Begin shared the secret of the planned destruction with Peres, in his capacity as chairman of the Labor Party. Begin said that the date for the air strike was not yet decided. "It all depends when the reactor will go 'critical.' If we want to save innocent lives, we will have to do that before then," Begin said. On May 9, 1981, Peres was informed by a "private source" that the air strike was imminent. Realizing that the date chosen was the date of the presidential elections in France, and since the Iraqi reactor had been built by France, Peres sent Begin a handwritten note, headed "Personal and top secret," urging the prime minister to postpone the operation until after the French elections. Begin agreed and postponed the operation. Begin, however, was shocked: How could Peres know the exact date of the operation, which was kept secret even from the cabinet ministers? Many years later, the "private source" identified himself—Professor Uzi Even, a senior researcher at the nuclear research center in Dimona and an active member of the Israeli left-wing party Meretz. In an interview with the Israeli daily *Ha'aretz*, Professor Even said: "While carrying out my reserve duties in the military intelligence, I learned about Begin's plan. I knew that it was a wrong decision. So I went to Peres and told him what I learned. Following my report, Peres sent to Begin the letter in which he urged him to postpone the operation."[28]

On May 10, Peres called François Mitterrand to congratulate him for his election as the new president of France. In the course of the conversation, Peres told Mitterrand about his initiative and Begin's positive response. Mitterrand was delighted. On June 5, 1981, a few days after he was sworn in, Mitterrand instructed his foreign minister, Claude Cheysson, to propose to his Israeli counterpart, Yitzhak Shamir, that France send a team of nuclear experts to Baghdad to exchange the enriched uranium in Tamuz with "Caramel"—a nuclear fuel that cannot be used for the production of an atomic bomb. Neither Begin nor Shamir responded to Cheysson's letter.[29] When Tamuz was destroyed two days later, Mitterrand was much offended. He told his aides that although there existed a latent state of belligerency between Israel and Iraq, France could not accept that a certain country, no matter how justified its motives, would settle its disputes through armed intervention and contrary to international law. Mitterrand believed that Begin should have had more trust in the French president, whose sympathy toward Israel was well known.[30]

Despite the fact that the parliamentary elections in Israel were to be held later in June, the infighting within the Labor Party was very bitter. Peres was outraged by Begin's action and called the destruction of Tamuz an "election gimmick." Rabin, however, took a diametrically opposed position. Interviewed by Israeli Radio, Rabin said: "Israel is unanimous in perceiving the threat posed by nuclear weapons in possession of an Arab country, especially a country headed by Saddam Hussein."[31] Thus, by not supporting Peres's view, Rabin only strengthened his assertion that Peres was an "untiring schemer" and that he was ready to sacrifice even the national interest for the sake of his personal ambitions. The election results, therefore, were not surprising: Peres lost again and Begin was given a second four-year term.

The first year of Begin's second term as prime minister was characterized by an ongoing tension with the Reagan administration. In December 1981, Begin applied Israeli law to the Golan Heights, effectively annexing it. In June 1982, he launched the war in Lebanon, with the aim of destroying the PLO infrastructure in southern Lebanon and expelling the Syrian and Palestinian forces from Beirut.

Responding to an American request, Saddam Hussein agreed to absorb in his country several thousand PLO members who had been expelled from Beirut. He made only two conditions: that the Palestinians arrive unarmed and as individuals, not as a group. Arafat had no choice but to agree. The Palestinians came to Baghdad via Syria in September 1982 and settled in Ramadi, in western Iraq.[32]

Meanwhile, at the request of King Hussein, President Mubarak, and Saudi King Fahd, President Reagan removed Iraq from the State Department's list of countries supporting terrorism. The door for commercial transactions with Baghdad was now wide open. The three Arab leaders also urged Reagan to resume normal diplomatic relations with Baghdad. They argued that Saddam Hussein had come to realize that Khomeini's threat to his regime, and to the entire region, was bigger than that of Israel. Reagan, however, wanted a more tangible proof of this theory before making a final decision.

By the end of 1983, the time was ripe for such a course. The political ruptures between Israel and the United States were now healed. Suffering from exhaustion and poor health, Begin tendered his resignation and Yitzhak Shamir succeeded him as prime minister. Shamir kept the foreign ministry in his hands and appointed Moshe Arens, the Israeli ambassador to Washington, as defense minister.

On November 29, 1983, both Shamir and Arens met with President Reagan at the White House. Following the meeting, Reagan announced the resumption of strategic cooperation with Israel, which had been suspended during the war in Lebanon. However, at the insistence of the Pentagon and the chairman of the Joint Chiefs of Staff, Israel's strategic role was limited to the eastern Mediterranean and was not included in CENTCOM (Central Command), which was responsible for the Persian Gulf. It was argued that if Israel was included in CENTCOM, the Arab countries would refuse to cooperate with the United States in the defense of the Persian Gulf.[33] At the same time, Reagan made important changes in key positions at the White House. He appointed Robert McFarlane as the new national security adviser, and Donald Rumsfeld, the former secretary of defense and former ambassador to NATO, became the new special envoy for the Middle East. By appointing such a high-profile envoy, Reagan was signaling to all parties in the Middle East that he meant to move ahead in all directions.

The first country to draw this conclusion was Turkey. A member of NATO, with one foot in Europe, Turkey was determined to play a more active role in Middle Eastern affairs. The Turkish government distrusted Syria and Iran and considered Saddam Hussein a lesser evil than Khomeini. Accordingly, the Turkish government encouraged Israel to open a dialogue with Iraq while it was still at war with Iran. In an effort to win Reagan's support, Saddam toned down his virulent anti-Israeli rhetoric. Through Egyptian and Turkish channels, Saddam communicated to Israel that he favored a political settlement of the Arab-

Israeli conflict and supported an Israeli-Palestinian deal. Thus, in the spring of 1984, the time was ripe for the reorientation of Israel's policy toward Iraq. Some Israeli policy planners saw some advantage in a dialogue with Iraq as a means of isolating Syria and Iran and creating a territorial buffer between Egypt and Syria.[34]

The Israeli tilt toward Iraq came to formal—although not public—expression during Rumsfeld's visit to the Middle East in March 1984. In a meeting with the Reagan envoy in Tel Aviv, Defense Minister Arens said: "Tell Saddam Hussein that we in Israel have considerable experience in fighting wars and we might be ready to assist him, if he were prepared to establish a direct contact with Israel."[35]

Rumsfeld's meeting with Shamir in Jerusalem was even more revealing. Early in 1984, the American Bechtel Corporation, which had business interests in the Arab world, was exploring the possibility of laying down a new oil pipeline from Iraq to the Jordanian port of Aqaba, with a capacity of one million barrels per day. Bechtel's plan coincided with an earlier Israeli proposal to reactivate the Kirkouk-Haifa pipeline, which had been shut down after the establishment of the State of Israel, in May 1948. In his memoirs, Secretary Shultz revealed that on January 5, 1984, Israeli ambassador to Washington Meir Rosenne brought him a message from Shamir suggesting the reactivation of the Kirkouk-Haifa pipeline. Shultz sent two emissaries to Baghdad to explore the idea with Saddam Hussein. They returned to Washington empty-handed.[36]

In its preliminary discussions in Baghdad, Bechtel did not meet any immediate rejection of its proposed Iraq-Aqaba pipeline. Saddam, however, wanted Israel's guarantee that it would not sabotage the pipeline, whose terminal would be in the immediate proximity of the Israeli border. In the event Israel did sabotage the pipeline, Saddam wanted a U.S. guarantee to cover the costs of the damage. Rumsfeld explored the idea with Shamir. He was positively surprised by the Israeli prime minister's reply. Shamir said that he was following the situation in the Persian Gulf very closely and that he had reached the conclusion that Iran was more dangerous to Israel than Iraq. When Rumsfeld mentioned the proposed pipeline, Shamir wondered why such a costly enterprise should be undertaken when there was another, less costly alternative. He suggested reactivating the Kirkouk-Haifa pipeline, which had been shut down in 1948. This pipeline was smaller than the one proposed by Bechtel, but it could transport oil and generate revenues almost instantly.

Rumsfeld took Shamir's proposal to Baghdad. He was unable to meet with Saddam Hussein, but he raised the issue with Iraqi Foreign Minister Tariq Aziz. When he heard Shamir's proposal, the stocky, spectacled Aziz turned pale. He asked Rumsfeld to take back his proposal as if it never existed. He said that he would not even dare to tell Saddam about the Israeli proposal, because if he did, Saddam would order his execution "on the spot."[37]

The idea of a new Iraqi oil pipeline was shelved for the time being, but never abandoned. The United States, however, continued to assist Saddam's regime. It provided satellite military intelligence, and the State Department lent its political support at the UN while the Department of Commerce urged the easing of trade restrictions. Finally, in November 1984, following a visit by Tariq Aziz to Washington, the United States and Iraq announced the resumption of diplomatic relations.

In the fall of 1984, following new parliamentary elections in Israel, a new national unity government was formed, with Peres and Shamir rotating the premiership. Yitzhak Rabin was appointed defense minister for the entire four-year term. There had never been in Israel such a strange cabinet, with so many contradictions. Prime Minister Peres accepted the formula of land for peace and favored a settlement with the Palestinians based on decent territorial compromise. Foreign Minister Shamir, in contrast, opposed any territorial compromise, and he preferred to retain the territories for the settlement of new Jewish immigrants. Regarding the Iran-Iraq War, Peres and Shamir shared the view that it would serve Israel's security interests if both countries continued to fight and bleed. But they also saw no reason why Israel should not continue to maintain an indirect dialogue with Saddam Hussein, without closing the doors on Iran.

In the spring of 1985, President Mubarak devised a regional policy based on an informal alliance of Egypt, Saudi Arabia, Jordan, and Iraq as a counterbalance to Iran and its Syrian ally. The United States, Turkey, and Israel supported this alliance, and on several occasions, President Mubarak intervened in Israel on Iraq's behalf and asked for the suspension of Israeli arms deliveries to Iran. Through the good offices of Egypt and Turkey, Israel also intensified its dialogue with Iraq. This "dialogue" had already been facilitated in 1984 with the appointment of Nizar Hamdoon—a Christian and a political activist in the Iraq Ba'ath Party—as ambassador to Washington. Born in Baghdad in 1945 to a wealthy family, Hamdoon studied in French Jesuit schools. In Washington he maintained good contacts with American officials, members of Congress, and the media. The new Iraqi ambassador did not limit his activity to Washington, but traveled across the United States and addressed many audiences, especially the business community and academia. He had the ear and trust of Saddam Hussein and in Washington media circles he was known to have a direct channel to Saddam, without going through the normal channel of the Iraqi Foreign Ministry. Hamdoon served in Washington until the summer of 1987, when he was recalled to Baghdad to become the deputy foreign minister. Saddam Hussein reassigned Nizar Hamdoon to the United States in February 1993, this time as his ambassador to the UN, a position that he holds to this day.

Hamdoon had several Jewish friends in the United States. Through them he was able to meet socially with some American Jewish leaders, on a private, noninstitutionalized basis. In one of those meetings, Hamdoon said that Iraq did not consider Israel a threat to its national security. He added that Iraq was now less interested in the Arab-Israeli conflict and was seeking a leadership role in the Persian Gulf region. He also said that Iraq no longer opposed the Egyptian-Israeli peace treaty, and that it favored a political solution to the Israeli-Palestinian conflict, based on Israeli withdrawal from the West Bank and the Gaza Strip and the establishment of an independent Palestinian state with East Jerusalem as its capital. "Our president, Saddam Hussein, is encouraging Yasser Arafat to espouse a similar policy," Hamdoon told his Jewish friends. Speaking about Iran, Hamdoon said that Khomeini's threat was not directed against Iraq only, but against Israel and all the pro-Western countries in the Persian Gulf. Hence, there should be a concerted effort by the United States and its allies to foil this Iranian subversion.[38]

What followed was even more dramatic: a meeting in Washington between the Iraqi ambassador and Israeli army general Avi Ya'ari, who was at the time the deputy chief of military intelligence. The two attended an academic seminar in Washington, and neither made any effort to ignore the other. The importance of the meeting was not in its substance—which was a repetition of what Hamdoon had said earlier to his Jewish friends—but in the very fact that it took place. The Iraqi ambassador knew exactly who Ya'ari was and what position he occupied in the Israeli general staff. Yet they met in Washington in what was considered to be the first face-to-face meeting between Israeli and Iraqi officials.

This, however, did not remain an isolated meeting. In the years to come, 1986 to 1989, direct contacts between Israeli and Iraqi officials intensified. With the encouragement of the United States, Egypt, and Turkey, General (Res.) Abraham Tamir, the director general of the Israeli Foreign Ministry, met twice, in Paris and Geneva, with Iraqi Foreign Minister Tariq Aziz; five times with Ambassador Nizar Hamdoon in New York and Geneva; and several times with Barzan el-Takriti, Saddam's half brother and the Iraqi ambassador to the UN in Geneva.[39]

Relations with Iraq being developed in the "right direction," Bechtel revived its plan for the Iraq-Aqaba oil pipeline. In the summer of 1985, U.S. Attorney General Edwin Meese, acting at the behest of his former law associate Robert Wallach, wrote to Prime Minister Peres recommending a careful examination of the pipeline idea. Meese's letter was handed to Peres by Bruce Rappoport, a former Israeli army officer and now an international businessman living in Geneva. Rappoport had been involved in a controversial oil transaction in Indonesia. He was an old acquaintance of Peres's, a fact that generated rumors that should the transaction with Iraq go through, Rappoport would contribute a sizable amount to Labor's elections fund. That was denied vehemently by Peres and all concerned. Once again, however, Bechtel's plan didn't fly. Saddam Hussein was not prepared to cooperate in a project that involved Israel, even if indirectly.

Despite the failure of this project, Peres, Shamir, and Rabin saw no reason to discontinue the dialogue with Iraq. They were much intrigued when, in the summer of 1986, they were told that Ambassador Hamdoon was prepared to meet in Washington with Moshe Shahal, the Israeli minister of energy. The proposed meeting was qualified as a "general discussion," with no specific agenda. Hamdoon, however, made one condition: that Israel undertake to stop its arms shipments to Iran. This was before the exposure of the Iran-Contra affair in November 1986. The very fact that Hamdoon made this condition showed to what extent Iraq was disturbed by the Iranian superiority on the ground, and it grossly exaggerated the importance of the small Israeli arms shipments to Khomeini. Shahal consulted with Rabin. The Israeli defense minister said that if Saddam Hussein would announce publicly that he favored a political settlement with Israel, he, Rabin, would be ready to state publicly that there would be no more arms shipments to Iran. Two days before the scheduled meeting, Hamdoon informed Shahal that the meeting had to be postponed because of "technical matters" that were never explained.[40]

A few months later, in the summer of 1987, during a visit to Jerusalem, an American Democratic congressman from New York whom Shahal refused to identify informed the Israeli minister that Hamdoon wanted to reschedule their meeting. The Iraqi ambassador suggested that the meeting be held in New York and not in Washington. Shahal agreed. Once again, however, the meeting was put off, because Hamdoon was appointed deputy foreign minister and had to return to Baghdad.

The "flirting" between Shahal and Iraq did not end there. In the fall of 1987, Shahal made a short visit to Cairo at the invitation of the Egyptian minister of energy. He paid a courtesy call on Mubarak, and the Egyptian president told him that a few days earlier, he had met in Cairo with Iraqi Foreign Minister Tariq Aziz, who had complained bitterly about the Israeli arms shipments to Iran. Aziz told Mubarak that he felt personally betrayed. On the one hand, he and Hamdoon were meeting with the Israelis, trying to find a peaceful settlement to the Arab-Israeli conflict. At the same time, the Israelis were supplying arms to Iran, thus helping Khomeini against Saddam. Mubarak claimed that he told Aziz: "What do you want from the Israelis? You all the time threaten them that once the war with Iran is over, the entire Iraqi army will move against Israel, to 'liberate' Palestine. Now you are complaining that the Israelis are helping Khomeini to defeat you." Shahal responded: "That's right. We are acting according to the principle that 'my enemy's enemy is my friend.' Were we not afraid of Saddam Hussein, we would never have sent one single bullet to Khomeini." Mubarak told Shahal that he was planning a visit to Baghdad in the next few days. He suggested that Shahal accompany him for a meeting with Saddam Hussein. Shahal was stunned. "I thought that Mubarak was joking. I told him that I was ready to go to Baghdad, but could he guarantee that Saddam would let me out?" Mubarak laughed and dropped the subject.[41]

The end of the Iran-Iraq War in August 1988 brought a growing stream of American, European, and Japanese businessmen to Baghdad, hoping to win contracts and to participate in the reconstruction of Iraq. In its effort to secure its businessmen a fair share of these contracts, the Bush administration offered loan guarantees and other assistance to the potential investors. One of the channels used at that time was Robert Abboud, an American banker of Lebanese descent with close ties to the Republican Party. On the eve of the Persian Gulf War, Abboud was among fourteen prominent Arab-Americans who were invited to the White House to express support for Bush's policy against Saddam.[42]

A native of Chicago, Abboud had served in the Marines and studied economics at Harvard. Upon graduating, he became director for investments in the Middle East at the First National Bank of Chicago. After the Yom Kippur War in 1973, when oil royalties almost quadrupled as a result of the Arab oil embargo, Abboud saw new opportunities for American businessmen in the Middle East. He was particularly involved in Iraq, and at his recommendation the First National Bank of Chicago granted substantial loans for business projects in Baghdad. In 1980, Abboud became the CEO of Armand Hammer's Occidental Petroleum. As such, he visited Israel several times, met with Israeli bankers and businessmen, and was introduced to several ministers in Menachem Begin's government. Four years later, in 1984, Abboud left Occidental Petroleum to become the chairman of the board of First City Bank Corp. in Houston. In this capacity and as president of the American-Iraqi Business Club, in June 1989 he led a delegation of fifty American businessmen to Baghdad. During that visit, he met with Saddam Hussein, and upon his return, the First City Bank Corp. granted the Iraqi El-Rafidein bank a loan of $50 million, guaranteed by the Bush administration, to encourage American business opportunities in Iraq.

It was during that June visit to Baghdad that the idea of a Saddam-Rabin meeting was first broached. In his discussion with Saddam, the American banker said that Iraq could not expect large investments for its reconstruction without an atmosphere of peace and stability in the region. He mentioned the fear in Israel that now that the Iran-Iraq War had ended, Saddam would turn his large army against Israel. Abboud suggested that Saddam follow the example of President Sadat, who had visited Jerusalem in November 1977 and instantly broken the "psychological barrier" between Israel and Egypt. A dramatic meeting between Saddam and an Israeli leader would have the same effect.[43]

Saddam Hussein did not dismiss the idea, he only wanted to know which of the Israeli leaders Abboud had in mind. Abboud said that he had Rabin in mind and knew an Israeli businessman, Azriel Enav, who could help persuade Rabin to agree. Saddam suggested that the meeting be held in Baghdad and that the PLO representative be invited to take part in the discussion. It was obvious that if there was PLO participation, Saddam could always argue—in case of a leak-age—that the meeting was meant to find solutions to the Israeli-Palestinian conflict.

In early August 1989, after meeting with Abboud in Texas, Azriel Enav flew to Israel to meet with Rabin in Tel Aviv. Enav was one of a small group of Israelis who grew up in the Haganah—the Israeli underground under the British Mandate, prior to the establishment of the State of Israel in 1948—then served in intelligence and were later able to combine business and intelligence in their civilian careers. Together with Yossi Harel, another intelligence operative whom Leon Uris portrayed as Ari Ben-Canaan in his best-selling book *Exodus,* Enav was a partner in Inkodeh, an Israeli factory for canned meat in Asmara, Eritrea. Inkodeh also served as an outpost for Israeli intelligence in East Africa. Moshe Dayan, Yitzhak Rabin, and other Israeli army generals visited Inkodeh on several occasions, prior to the Six-Day War, and studied plans for breaking the siege that Colonel Nasser had imposed on freedom of navigation to Eilat. When Dayan became foreign minister in Begin's first cabinet in 1977, Enav arranged for him a secret meeting in New Delhi with Murarji Desai, the Indian prime minister. Rabin was aware, of course, of Enav's role in Dayan's secret trip to India. He had known Enav for more than forty years, and they had even fought together in the battle for Jerusalem in 1948. He also saw him in action in Ethiopia. Hence, Rabin listened attentively to Enav's report on Saddam's discussion with Abboud and his suggestion of a meeting between him and Saddam in Baghdad. The report was similar to other intelligence reports about Saddam's presumed "moderation." When Foreign Minister Moshe Arens met with President Mubarak in Cairo on February 20, 1989, and expressed concern about Saddam's intentions, the Egyptian president told him: "You have nothing to worry about Iraq. Saddam had learned his lesson from his war against Iran. He is not going to war again. . . ."[44] Similar reports were coming from the United States and from Israelis who met with Iraqis on various levels.

Nevertheless, the ever cautious Rabin told Enav that before he gave his consent to a meeting with Saddam, he would like to meet with Abboud and get a personal impression of the man and his message. Since he was scheduled to visit the United States in September, at the invitation of Jewish organizations, he instructed his aide and speechwriter Eytan Haber to arrange with Enav a time and place for a meeting with Abboud. The meeting took place in Philadelphia, at the Windham Franklin Plaza Hotel. "In order to avoid media attention," Enav told me in Tel Aviv, "we had to go through the hotel's kitchen and to use the service elevator to Rabin's suite." Rabin asked many questions but remained uncommitted. However, he made two points absolutely clear: If there was a meeting with Saddam, it wouldn't be in Baghdad but in a neutral place, in Europe or even in Cairo; and under no circumstances would he, Rabin, agree to PLO participation in such a meeting.[45]

While Abboud was working his way through the ineffective and corrupt Iraqi bureaucracy, Rabin began to have second thoughts about the proposed meeting. He suspected Saddam's intentions. Immediately after the end of the Iran-Iraq War, Rabin had instructed the Israeli intelligence community to refocus its attention on Iraq, after several years of maximum emphasis on Syria. The Mossad was now reporting that Iraq was again recruiting scientists in Europe, mostly in Germany, in an effort to develop its nuclear capability. Iraq was also actively engaged with Egypt and Argentina in developing a ballistic missile, the Condor, which would be able to hit targets deep inside Israel. It was obvious that the destruction of the Iraqi nuclear reactor in 1981 had not ended Saddam's nuclear ambitions but only delayed them by ten years. Rabin was also told that in order to avoid a repetition of the destruction of Tamuz, Saddam Hussein had dispersed his new nuclear installations in several locations. No less worrisome to Rabin was a report by the chief of military intelligence that Iraq had become the largest producer of chemical agents in the Middle East. Mustard gas and nerve agents were produced in well-hidden facilities in Samarra, Falluja, and Salman Pak. Realizing that Saddam had used gas bombs against the Kurds, Rabin could not ignore the possibility—no matter how distant—that Saddam would be tempted to use the same mass-destruction weapon against Israel. Rabin feared that Iraq's "moderation" and the idea for a meeting with Saddam were only a smoke screen and part of a major deception effort aimed to shield Iraq's production of mass-destruction weapons.

As a matter of fact, while Rabin was meeting with Enav in Tel Aviv, three Iraqi nuclear scientists were participating in the Ninth International Symposium on Detonation, held in Portland, Oregon, August 28 to September 1, 1989. Israel knew that Iraq had had problems with detonation, so it was not surprising that Iraq had accepted the invitation to attend the Portland symposium. The three Iraqis were registered under the names M. Ahmed, S. Ibrahim, and M. Maher.[46] Anyone who is familiar with Arab names would easily detect that these were first names and not full family names. It was obvious that the Iraqi security services had made a concerted effort to shield the real identity of the three scientists. Furthermore, the Iraqis gave as their business address the Atomic Research Center, El-Qa'qa, P.O. Box 5134, Baghdad. The El-Qa'qa facility was registered with the International Agency for Atomic Energy in Vienna as a center promoting nuclear research for peaceful purposes. However, intelligence services in Israel and the West suspected that the center was part of Saddam Hussein's efforts to build an atomic bomb. Eventually, the El-Qa'qa facility was among the targets hit during Desert Storm.

Obviously alarmed by these reports, Rabin dragged his feet. Enav suggested that he travel with Abboud to Baghdad in order to get a personal impression of the Iraqi mood toward Israel. Rabin said no. His meeting with Saddam never took place.[47]

In the spring of 1990, following a major domestic crisis concerning the peace process, the national unity government in Israel was dissolved and Prime Minister Shamir was able to form a new government, without Labor's participation. Rabin's position as defense minister was now taken by Moshe Arens. Around that time, Saddam Hussein began implementing his "grand design" of invading Kuwait. Saddam shielded his troop movements in the Persian Gulf with belligerent statements against Israel. His "moderation" of yesteryear was now forgotten, and low-level meetings between Iraqi and Israeli scholars came to an end. In a speech on April 2, 1990, Saddam boasted that he was capable of producing binary chemical weapons and threatened that in the event of a new conflict, he would "burn half of Israel."[48]

Despite Saddam's threats, President Mubarak tried to calm Israel's fears. On April 5, 1990, Egyptian Ambassador to Israel Mohamed Bassiouni asked to meet urgently with Prime Minister Shamir. Bassiouni said that Mubarak had spoken with Saddam Hussein and had been authorized by the Iraqi president to inform Shamir that Iraq did not harbor any belligerent intentions against Israel. Mubarak wanted a similar reassurance from Shamir to Saddam. The Egyptian ambassador asked the Israeli prime minister to keep this exchange secret. Shamir agreed.[49]

In the following weeks, Israel grew more and more nervous about Iraq's intentions. Intelligence reports indicated that Iraq had constructed, on its western border with Jordan, fixed pads for launching Scud missiles into Israel. However, being engaged in a public conflict with the Bush administration over the peace process, Prime Minister Shamir was unable to convince the United States that Saddam's statements and actions were more than just rhetoric. Toward the end of June, Iraqi units engaged in joint maneuvers with the Jordanian army and Iraqi pilots flew reconnaissance missions over Jordan in the immediate proximity of the Israeli border. The entrance of Iraqi troops into Jordan was always considered a casus belli by Israel, and Shamir was determined to pursue the same policy even if it escalated into a full-scale war. Tension grew so high that two weeks before Saddam invaded Kuwait, Shamir sent Arens to Washington to discuss the situation with Defense Secretary Dick Cheney. Accompanied by the chiefs of the Mossad and military intelligence, Arens presented Cheney with all the information that Israel possessed. To Arens's surprise, the CIA already had this information and much more.

Iraq's invasion of Kuwait, on August 2, 1990, changed the entire situation in the Middle East. Overnight, Saddam's threats of the last few weeks had a totally different meaning. King Hussein endorsed the Iraqi move, and despite an advisement to the contrary from the local Palestinian leadership in the West Bank, Yasser Arafat too supported it. In consultations with the intelligence community and with the military command, Israel concluded that it would be involved in the crisis, if only because of Saddam's intention to split the Arab world and to draw a parallel between his action in Kuwait and the Israeli occupation of the West Bank and the Gaza Strip. After assuring President Bush of Israel's total support of his actions, Shamir devised a four-point policy concerning the Persian Gulf crisis:

- Israel was not a party to the crisis.
- Israel would not get involved in the crisis unless it was forced to do so. If Israel was dragged into the war, Israel would take care of its own defense, in consultation with the United States.
- Israel would stay out of the limelight and would not offer unsolicited advice. This was an essential point, since in the following weeks there were many commentators in the United States, Pat Buchanan among them, who accused Israel of pushing America into war so that the U.S.-led coalition would fight Israel's wars.
- There was no linkage between the Arab-Israeli conflict and the Iraqi occupation of Kuwait.[50]

Israel's Iraqi policy during the Persian Gulf crisis ran counter to Israel's security doctrine, which required an immediate response to an Arab aggression. Shamir was very much upset by the exclusion of Israel from the U.S.-led coalition, although he understood President Bush's reasoning. Getting Egypt and Syria to commit troops and join in a war against Iraq was a major American diplomatic success. It was not the first time that an Arab country had fought against another Arab country. But it was the first time that Arab countries had joined Western and foreign powers in a war against an Arab state.

In December 1990, it became clear that Iraq was preparing to launch Scud missiles into Israel. Saddam test-fired three medium-range missiles from eastern Iraq to western Iraq, near the Jordanian border. The Iraqis also built launching sites near Habbaniyah, an old air base that the British had built in the thirties along the now defunct Haifa-Kirkouk oil pipeline.

As the war drew closer, Israel felt diplomatically vulnerable. The Persian Gulf crisis had altered the diplomatic balance of power, both regionally and internationally. The Soviet Union, once the main supporter of Iraq, had now joined the American effort against Saddam Hussein. Israel, always considered a "strategic asset" of the United States, lost—temporarily, at least—its importance, its place taken by Egypt. King Hussein, a lifelong ally of the West, was forced to support Saddam Hussein; otherwise he would have lost his throne. Nevertheless, Jordan's importance as a bastion of moderation and as a buffer between tolerance and Islamic fundamentalism did not diminish. These new developments prompted Shamir in early December to take an urgent short trip to Washington. The sensitive issues relating to the Kuwaiti crisis were discussed

by Bush and Shamir only, with National Security Adviser Brent Scowcroft and
Ambassador Zalman Shoval taking notes. Bush and Shamir discussed three
main issues.

- The need for Israel to refrain from a preemptive strike against
  Iraq. Shamir agreed to the president's request.

- The need for Shamir to continue to show restraint if the war escalated. The Israeli prime minister could not promise to do so.
  He told Bush that Israel would "consult" with the United States
  before it took any military action. So that such a consultation
  could take place in the most rapid and secure manner, Bush instructed Scowcroft to ask Defense Secretary Cheney to install a
  secure hot line between the Pentagon and the Israeli Ministry of
  Defense. This was done even before Shamir returned to Israel.

- The strategic configuration of the Middle East and Israel's place
  in it. To the president's great surprise, Shamir spoke at length
  about Jordan and the need to take a "softer" stance toward King
  Hussein. Shamir told Bush that judging from the prevailing
  mood in Amman, King Hussein had no choice. Had he not expressed public support for Iraq, especially after Yasser Arafat had
  publicly embraced Saddam, the Palestinian majority in Jordan
  would have dethroned him. The president did not want to deal at
  length with the third issue at this stage. He wanted to concentrate on the Kuwaiti crisis. The strategic implications of the crisis
  would be discussed at a later stage.[51]

Despite Shamir's moderation and the relaxed atmosphere of the Bush-
Shamir discussion, Israel was still denied real-time satellite intelligence about
Iraqi troop deployment and had to rely on its own limited intelligence gathering capabilities. This was a very strange situation. Until Saddam's invasion of
Kuwait, none of the Arab armies on which the United States relied had considered Iraq an enemy. Hence their intelligence capabilities about Iraq were very
limited, much more limited than Israel's. This lack of Arab intelligence was to
weigh heavily on the military operations in the first days of the war. Egyptian
evaluations of Saddam's intentions were based more on expectations than on realities. A few days before the war started, a senior Israeli official in Cairo expressed concern about possible Iraqi missile attacks against Israel. A senior
Egyptian intelligence officer replied: "Don't worry about the missiles. Saddam
knows that when it comes to national security, Israeli leaders are reckless and
they would not hesitate to drop an atomic bomb on Baghdad. So don't worry."[52]
    In early January 1991 came a big surprise. Realizing that war was in-

evitable, King Hussein asked to meet urgently with Shamir. It was not the first time that King Hussein had met with Israeli leaders, but it was the first time that the meeting had been called with such urgency. It was obvious that despite his public support for Saddam Hussein, the Jordanian monarch had no illusions about the outcome of the war. He therefore wanted to avoid any misunderstanding with Israel, so as to spare his country another tragedy. Shamir flew to London, aboard a private plane, on Friday, January 4, before the Jewish Sabbath and met with Hussein at his private London residence, not far from London's Heathrow Airport, on Saturday night, January 5. Shamir was accompanied by Deputy Chief of Staff General Ehud Barak (currently the head of the Labor opposition party and a Labor Knesset member); Yossi Ben-Aharon, the director general of the prime minister's office; Elyakim Rubenstein, the cabinet's secretary; and Ephraim Halevy, the deputy chief of the Mossad, who enjoyed the king's utmost trust and confidence. Hussein was accompanied by General Zeid Bin Shaker, the chief of staff, who later became his prime minister; and Ali Shukri, the director of the monarch's office.

There was no time for small talk, and the king went straight to business. After analyzing the situation since Saddam's invasion of Kuwait, Hussein made it absolutely clear that he would not allow the entry of Iraqi troops into his country, nor would he allow the use of Jordanian airspace by the Iraqi air force to attack Israel. When Barak asked about the joint maneuvers by the Jordanian and Iraqi air forces, General Bin Shaker answered that the maneuvers were over. King Hussein explained that his support of Saddam Hussein was the result of his dependence on Iraqi economic and financial assistance, and not because he had aggressive intentions against Israel. Hence he wanted Shamir's assurance that if Israel did get involved in the war, Israeli warplanes would not violate Jordan's sovereignty and would not fly over its territory to hit Iraqi targets. Shamir made that commitment. He made it clear, however, that should Iraqi units enter Jordan, even without King Hussein's consent, Israel would retain its right to intervene as necessary to maintain its national security.

By making this commitment, Shamir clearly implied that he would stay out of the Persian Gulf War, as he had already promised President Bush in December. Indeed, despite the thirty-nine Scud missiles that landed in Israel, and despite the intense public pressure, Shamir did not retaliate. This responsible attitude won him the praise and admiration of the Bush administration. This restraint is even more remarkable in light of what was discovered after the war. According to evidence supplied by General Hussein Kamel, Saddam Hussein's son-in-law, who defected to Jordan in August 1991, on the eve of Desert Storm, Saddam equipped twenty-five Scud missiles with biological material, ready to be launched into Israel.[53] When asked why these Scuds were not launched, General Kamel replied that Iraq had been overwhelmed by the intensity of the allies' air strikes. This is considered to be only a part of the answer. Israeli intelligence officials now believe that Saddam did not engage in biological warfare only because he knew that Israel had a powerful response.

A few months after the war, on July 7, 1991, Shamir and King Hussein met again in London, to discuss the preparations for the Madrid Peace Conference. The Jordanian monarch opened the meeting by thanking Shamir for his restraint during the Persian Gulf War.

The road to peace with Jordan was now wide open.

PASSING THE TORCH:
THE RISE OF ABU MAZEN

In one of the stormiest sessions of the PLO's Central Committee meeting in Tunis on October 10, 1993, the walls were virtually shaking in the old and poorly maintained El-Quds elementary school. Abu Mazen, the Palestinian architect of the historic Oslo Accords between Israel and the PLO, was telling his colleagues that after the momentous handshake on the South Lawn of the White House on September 13 between Prime Minister Yitzhak Rabin and Chairman Yasser Arafat, it was now "time to take off the uniforms of the revolution and put on the business suits of the nascent Palestinian state." This remark, more than anything else in Abu Mazen's speech, strengthened the fear among PLO militants that in the process of building the new Palestinian institutions, they would be pushed aside and that key positions in the Palestine Authority would go to the Western-educated intellectuals and not remain in the hands of the PLO's "military wing," which had carried the burden of the Intifada, the Palestinian uprising, for the preceding seven years. This problem, which is still not resolved, will determine the fate of the PLO and whether the emerging new Palestinian elite will be able to assure the transition from armed struggle to statehood.

Attending the PLO meeting in Tunis was for me history in the making. The phrase may seem trite, but it was a unique experience for an Israeli journalist like me to visit Tunisia on such an occasion. This, after all, was the first time that Israeli journalists had been permitted entry into this North African country, a country with which Israel did not have formal diplomatic relations. By special arrangement, I did not go through the usual immigration and customs procedures. Instead, I was met at the airport by a smiling, friendly Tunisian Foreign Ministry official, who took my Israeli passport and handed me a temporary Tunisian permit. Within the hour I was in my hotel room in downtown Tunis, looking out at the landscape and breathing the air of this warm and hospitable North African capital.

The official told me that if I was to attend the PLO meeting, it was not sufficient to be accredited by the Tunisian press office. I required a separate press accreditation from the PLO as well. My new Tunisian friend kindly arranged for my temporary membership in the not yet born "State of Palestine."

Next evening, when I entered the heavily guarded hall of the El-Quds elementary school, it was unmistakably clear that the seeds of a Palestinian entity had taken a firm root. Palestinian flags were everywhere. The walls were covered with posters reading "Long live our intifada," "Struggle until victory," "Long live Abu Ammar." (Yasser Arafat's nom de guerre is Abu Ammar.) The fully packed hall held the Palestinian personalities who for years had captured world headlines by actions that ranged from terrorism to diplomacy. Arafat, with his trademark checkered, tricornered kaffiyeh, was seated on the dais, flanked by numerous armed bodyguards. He was listening attentively to Abu Mazen, the man who had orchestrated the secret negotiations with Israel in Oslo, and who under the encouraging mantle of President Bill Clinton, had signed with Shimon Peres the declaration of principles between Israel and the PLO.

Among the many participants, I spotted Ilan Halevy, a former Israeli who in 1974 formed together with four Palestinians the League of Communist Workers, which called for a two-state solution of the Israeli-Palestinian conflict. Halevy was a member of Ma'avak (Struggle), a small, radical anti-Zionist group that was an offshoot of Matzpen (Compass), an equally anti-Zionist and pro-Palestinian group. He and his French-Jewish companion Catherine were meeting clandestinely with various Palestinian activists in the West Bank, raising their political awareness and encouraging them to defy the Israeli government's authority. Because of this subversive activity, Halevy was considered a security risk at the time. To avoid arrest, he and Catherine hid at the Ramallah home of Hanan Ashrawi, the articulate and high-profile PLO spokesperson during the peace negotiations in Madrid and Washington. Catherine was eventually arrested and after interrogation was deported to France. Halevy followed her to Paris, where they were married. After the assassination of Issam Sartawi, a Palestinian intellectual who was murdered by radical Palestinians who were opposed to his contacts with Israelis and Jews, Halevy succeeded him as the PLO "observer" in the Socialist International. In the eyes of many Israelis, Halevy was still considered a traitor. But here in Tunis, he challenged the Israeli journalists and said, "It took you eighteen years to follow me."

Other participants at the PLO meeting included thirty-five political activists and military commanders of the intifada. Many of them had blood on their hands and were wanted by the Israeli army. Shortly after one of their leaders, Mohamed Ghneim (Abu Maher), stood at the podium and began his remarks, a Palestinian security officer approached me and said that I was not allowed to take notes. I readily complied, but a few minutes later the officer returned and said that he had been instructed to escort me out of the hall. Despite my protests, I was forced to learn this first lesson of "Palestinian democracy." I thought to myself, how fortunate I was that before being asked to leave the hall, I had been able to hear the speeches of Abu Mazen and a few other PLO officials.

There was no resemblance between the spectacled, elegantly dressed, well-mannered Mahmoud Abbas whom the entire world watched on the South Lawn of the White House on September 13, 1993, and the combative, gray-haired Abu Mazen who was now struggling to win the support of his colleagues for "his" accord with Israel. Undeterred by sharp criticism from some of the most prominent PLO leaders, Abu Mazen asserted that the accord with Israel "carried in its womb the fetus of the future Palestinian state." He said, "We Palestinians are educated and enterprising. As individuals, we helped build Jordan, Syria, Lebanon, and the oil-rich Persian Gulf principalities. Now, as a nation, we are facing the most important challenge of our long and painful history, the challenge of building our own country." The subsequent thunderous applause left no doubt that Abu Mazen had made his point.

While the PLO continued its deliberations, the multilateral committee on the Palestinian refugees—one of the five committees established by the Madrid Peace Conference—also met in Tunis. It was the first time that Tunisia had hosted such an international gathering with official Israeli participation. The Israeli delegation was headed by Yossi Beilin, the deputy foreign minister and one of the most dovish members of the Israeli Labor Party, who consistently called for an Israeli-Palestinian dialogue. His presence in Tunis was an opportunity for Arafat to thank him for the role he had played in initiating the secret talks that led to the Oslo Accords. For Beilin's meeting with Arafat, we were bused to the PLO chairman's modest two-story villa in Yaghurta, an elegant Tunis residential neighborhood. The road to the villa was blocked by Tunisian police, but the villa itself was packed with Arafat's bodyguards and security personnel.

When we entered the room for the routine photo op, Arafat was sitting on a large sofa in front of a rectangular wooden coffee table, his intense eyes searching for familiar faces, his balding head covered by the omnipresent kaffiyeh. He looked smaller and thinner than in his appearances on television. Many conflicting thoughts went through my head when I was face to face with Arafat. To most Israelis, Arafat is the eternal terrorist who has on his hands the blood of so many innocent victims. At the same time, I could not ignore the fact that to most Palestinians, he was bigger than life, a symbol of their national aspirations and the hope for their statehood. I had never met Arafat before, so I was very surprised when at the end of the photo op, he stood up and came straight toward me, shook my hand warmly with both his hands, and murmured a few sentences in Arabic. I still don't know what he said, nor do I know why I was singled out for this gesture.

Shortly after we left, Mahmoud Abbas—Abu Mazen—came to see Arafat and to discuss with him the language of the draft resolution that was to be submitted to the PLO's Central Committee. It is interesting to follow Mahmoud Abbas's career, as he represents the new Palestinian elite that will carry on its shoulders the burden of building the future Palestinian entity. Born in Safed, in the upper Galilee, in 1935, Mahmoud Abbas became a refugee at the age of thirteen. Safed, like several others during the British Mandate, was a mixed Jewish-Arab city. When the Palestinian leaders of that time rejected the November 1947 UN partition plan for Palestine, Arab residents of Safed took to the streets to prevent the birth of a Jewish state. They were defeated, and the Arab population of Safed took refuge in Syria.

Mahmoud Abbas completed his high school education in Damascus, and after graduating from Damascus University Law School, he moved in 1957 to the oil-rich sheikhdom of Qatar, where he was immediately offered a position as a high school teacher. During that period, Yasser Arafat was establishing his nationalistic Palestinian movement El-Fatah in Kuwait. Mahmoud Abbas joined the movement immediately and became its representative in Qatar, under the assumed name Abu Mazen.

In early 1963, after the dissolution of the Egyptian-Syrian union and the intense inter-Arab rivalry that followed, Arafat and his colleagues became disenchanted with all the Arab regimes. They lost hope in the Arab ability to reconquer Palestine, as was promised, and were now determined to engage in an armed struggle against Israel. They began to raise funds and purchase arms. Mahmoud Abbas was very successful in this endeavor, and he became the treasurer of El-Fatah.

From the beginning, however, there was a clear distinction between Abu Mazen and the other founding fathers of El-Fatah. Mahmoud Abbas, the lawyer and teacher, personified the scholar rather than the warrior. He chose to fill his leisure time studying Zionism, seeking to understand the reasons behind the Arab defeat. He was a fascinating mix of conservatism and pragmatism, always leaving his mind open to the winds of change in the Middle East and in the world at large. Mindful also of the powerful Soviet emergence, he tried to understand the Soviets' interest in the developing Third World and how they could help the Palestinian cause.

The summer of 1968 marked a turning point in the history of the PLO and in the personal career of Abu Mazen. Egypt's President Gamal Abdel Nasser, a diabetic, was seriously ill. He was hardly able to walk, and although the illness was kept secret, there was growing concern in Moscow that should Nasser die, the costly Soviet investment in Egypt would diminish, if not disappear. On the advice of Leonid Brezhnev's personal physician, Dr. Yevgeny Shazov, Nasser was flown secretly, on July 6, 1968, to the Soviet Union for medical treatment. On board the Soviet military plane was an additional "mystery" passenger— Yasser Arafat, soon to become chairman of the PLO. Arafat was introduced in Moscow as "Amin" and was described as "personal adviser" to Nasser. His real identity, however, was known to Brezhnev and the top Soviet leadership. In his discussions with the Soviet Politiburo, "Amin" was promised modest humanitarian assistance and training for the future Palestinian leadership.

Arafat's visit to Moscow was a bold move, and it is doubtful whether he grasped the full implication of his action at the time. By leaning toward the Soviet Union, Arafat made the PLO a part of the Cold War between the two superpowers. Abu Mazen, like the rest of the Palestinian leadership, supported Arafat's tilt toward Moscow, and he was later to be rewarded for his loyalty. In early 1980, Abu Mazen was a recipient of a Soviet scholarship, and he was accepted as a Ph.D. candidate at the prestigious Soviet Institute for Middle Eastern Studies. With his wife and three children, he lived in Moscow for over a year, and he is reported to have a good command of the Russian language.

He worked under the guidance of Vladimir Polyakov, an Orientalist and diplomat. His thesis, *Israel: A Country of Evil*, was published in 1983, in Arabic, under the title *The Other Side: The Secret Relationship Between Nazism and Zionism*. His incredible theory was that the Zionist movement cooperated with the Nazis during the Second World War and that the figure of six million Jews who perished in the Holocaust was "grossly exaggerated."

The most significant part of Abu Mazen's life in Moscow was not his academic achievements but rather his political activity. As a research fellow, he met with the top Soviet experts on the Middle East, including Igor Belayev, Boris Ponomarev, Yevgeni Primakov, and Vladimir Nussenko. His acquaintance with Primakov and Nussenko was to become particularly important. During the Persian Gulf War, Primakov, currently the Russian foreign minister, was Gorbachev's "troubleshooter," and headed the Russian intelligence service. Nussenko, a member of the foreign ministry, was at the time the director of the Soviet Foreign Ministry's Middle Eastern department and was the deputy chief of mission at the Russian embassy in Tel Aviv. Nussenko's appointment to his posting in Israel was announced shortly after Abu Mazen and Shimon Peres signed the Oslo Accords.

During Abu Mazen's stay in Moscow, he was introduced to members of the Israeli Communist Party—both Jews and Arabs—and it was also arranged for him to attend seminars in various Eastern European countries, Romania and Bulgaria in particular, which were also attended by Israeli Communists and left-wing scholars.

Life in Moscow convinced Abu Mazen that the Soviet Union would support the Palestinian cause, but not at the risk of armed conflict with the United States. Based on this conclusion, Abu Mazen redirected his political activity to Western Europe and to the conservative pro-Western regimes in the Arab world. Paris, not Moscow, became the center for future contacts between the PLO and liberal Israelis. Back in 1972, Michel Rocard, a leading French Socialist who later became prime minister, had met with Yasser Arafat in Beirut. Following the Yom Kippur War in October 1973, and especially after the PLO was granted the status of "observer" at the UN in 1974, Western European Socialist parties made a concerted effort to open a dialogue with the PLO. At the initiative of François Mitterrand, Austrian Chancellor Bruno Kreisky, and West

German Chancellor Willy Brandt, the PLO was invited to appoint an "observer" to the Socialist International. Israel, then led by the Labor Party, opposed this move, but to no avail. The PLO observer was Issam Sartawi, a brilliant Palestinian intellectual and an able cardiologist. Born in Acre and educated in Baghdad, Sartawi abandoned his practice in 1970 and turned PLO terrorist. In 1973, Sartawi masterminded an attack on a Lufthansa jet in Frankfurt, in which Israeli actress Hanna Marron lost a leg. He renounced terrorism in 1976 and became one of Abu Mazen's associates. From his office in Paris, Sartawi established contacts with moderate Israelis who were prepared to meet with the PLO and who recognized the Palestinians' right to self-determination. Owing to Kreisky's personal efforts, Abu Mazen achieved in 1976 his first success: The former secretary general of the Israeli Labor Party, Knesset member Aryeh (Lova) Eliav, met with Sartawi in Paris and in Vienna. Back in 1973, Eliav had aroused ardent dislike within the Labor Party for his extreme left-wing views. When the party secretariat met in Tel Aviv to approve a resolution that called for opening the territories on the West Bank to Jewish settlement, Eliav cast the single dissenting vote. His dovish allies, including then foreign minister Abba Eban, were fearful of Prime Minister Golda Meir, preferring to support a resolution that ran counter to their belief. By 1975, Eliav had resigned his position in the Labor Party. In 1976, under the auspices of former French prime minister Pierre Mendès-France, Eliav met secretly with Sartawi in Paris. Years later, Eliav confided: "I did not know that a man like Sartawi existed—an intellectual who renounced terrorism and became convinced that compromise was the only way to solve the Israeli-Palestinian conflict. When I approached Prime Minister Rabin, told him about my meeting with Sartawi, and suggested that there were elements within the PLO who were approachable, Rabin answered angrily: 'I will meet them on the battlefield.'"

For their efforts at establishing an Israeli-Palestinian dialogue, Eliav and Sartawi won the Kreisky Peace Price in 1980. When the picture appeared in the Israeli press, depicting Eliav and Sartawi smiling and shaking hands, many members of the Labor Party rejoiced that Eliav was no longer a liability for them.

Also in 1976, and over the objection of the Israeli government, Major General Mattityahu Peled met with Yasser Arafat in Paris. Peled, a hero of the Six-Day War, was among the first and strongest advocates of handing over territory to the PLO in return for a peaceful settlement with the Palestinians. Peled formed the Council for Israeli-Palestinian Peace and became its first chairman. It was in that capacity that he met with Arafat in Paris.

The May 1977 Labor Party defeat in the general elections was considered a setback to the PLO's efforts to maintain discreet contacts with liberal Israelis. The new right-to-center government, led by Likud leader Menachem Begin, forbade any contact with the PLO and opposed any territorial compromise in the West Bank and the Gaza Strip. Although these contacts continued, within a very short time Abu Mazen realized that his Israeli interlocutors had no mandate to speak with the PLO nor the power to change Israeli government policies.

President Sadat's visit to Jerusalem in November 1977 and the signing of the Israeli-Egyptian peace treaty in March 1979 were a terrible blow to the PLO. Over the objection of such conservatives as Khaled El-Hassan and Abu Mazen, who were supported by Morocco, Yasser Arafat joined the Arab "Rejectionist Front," together with Syria, Libya, South Yemen, and Iraq, in a futile effort to undermine the Israeli-Egyptian peace treaty. Arafat believed at the time that President Sadat had "expropriated" the Palestinian problem and that he had no right to negotiate with Israel an administrative autonomy on behalf of the Palestinians. The PLO decided to deepen its military involvement in Lebanon and to intensify its attacks against Israel, from bases in South Lebanon.

It is impossible to understand the "road to Oslo" without stressing the impact of the June 1982 war in Lebanon on PLO thinking and strategy. In early 1969, a few months after he was elected as the third chairman of the PLO, Yasser Arafat began to broaden his military presence in Lebanon. Yielding to heavy Egyptian and Arab League pressure, Lebanon signed in Cairo, on November 3, 1969, a nineteen-clause agreement that gave the PLO full control of the Palestinian refugee camps in Lebanon and freedom of action against Israel in South Lebanon. When the civil war in Lebanon broke out, in April 1975, the Lebanese army disintegrated and the PLO became the only cohesive military force in this ethnically divided country. The PLO soon lent its power to the Muslim communities against the Christian hegemony. Outnumbered and outgunned by the coalition of the PLO and the Muslim militias, the Christians turned to Israel for assistance. The Israeli government, headed at that time by Yitzhak Rabin, responded positively to the Christian plight. In return for Israeli arms, the Christians gave Israel valuable intelligence on PLO bases and activities in Lebanon. This newly born cooperation was at the beginning very limited and discreet. The Israeli leaders told the Christian leaders at that time: "We will help you to defend yourselves, but don't expect us to fight in your stead."

This cautious policy, however, was changed in the summer of 1977. The newly elected prime minister, Menachem Begin, after meeting in Jerusalem with leaders of the Lebanese Christians, admitted publicly that Israel was assisting the Christians militarily and promised to increase this aid in the immediate future. This was a major departure from the previous discreet policy and was to weigh heavily on future developments.

The change in Israeli policies was matched by a similar change in the PLO structure in Lebanon. From a conglomerate of lightly armed terrorist groups, the PLO began to develop an infrastructure for a regular army—the Palestine

Liberation Army (PLA), with fixed bases, heavier weapons, and a general command in Beirut. The Soviet Union, the Eastern European countries, China, Cuba, Libya, and Iraq all supplied the PLO with Soviet-made T-34 tanks, antitank rockets, and antiaircraft guns. Financed by Saudi Arabia and by other oil-rich Persian Gulf principalities, the PLO stored huge quantities of arms and ammunition in concrete underground bunkers in Beirut and in South Lebanon. As a result, PLO attacks against Israel became bolder and more sophisticated. Since the Israeli-Lebanese border was fenced and mined, the PLO developed new methods of infiltration, including attempts to use dinghies and gliders. Thus, the PLO presence in Lebanon became Israel's most important security problem and a key element in Israel's relations with the new Reagan administration.

The enhanced military stature of the PLO resulted in an improved political stature. This was particularly true in Western Europe. Taking advantage of the seeming paralysis in U.S. diplomacy, during the presidential election campaign in 1980 the European community injected itself into the Middle East peace process. At the conclusion of a summit meeting in Venice on June 13, 1980, Europe recognized the Palestinians' right to self-determination and statehood. Because of the improved political status of the PLO, many countries came to see a Palestinian state as a quite natural development and as a vehicle for peace in the Middle East.

In the summer of 1981, and shortly after Prime Minister Begin was re-elected to a second four-year term, the PLO expanded its zone of operations and initiated numerous attacks against Israeli and Jewish targets outside of the Middle East and mostly in Europe. In return, Begin was now determined to fight the PLO until it ceased to be a political or military factor in any peace process in the future. Moreover, the Begin government—in the words of Foreign Minister Yitzhak Shamir—was more and more convinced that "the defense of the West Bank begins in West Beirut." When Israel launched its war in Lebanon, on June 6, 1982, Prime Minister Begin and Defense Minister Ariel Sharon were convinced that without the expulsion of the PLO from Beirut, the war would not have achieved its political objectives. The United States, however, was very much opposed to the war. Nevertheless, on June 10, 1982, on the fifth day of fighting, the Israeli army was at the gates of Beirut and was threatening the Beirut-Damascus highway. Cutting the link between these two capitals would determine the fate of the Syrian brigade in Beirut and the PLO presence in the Lebanese capital. After a long and sharp telephone conversation with President Reagan, Prime Minister Begin yielded to U.S. pressure and ordered a unilateral cease-fire. The fighting, however, continued, and both Israel and the PLO accused each other of violating the cease-fire.

In an effort to avoid a precedent of Israel occupying an Arab capital, President Reagan, while insisting on a renewed cease-fire, empowered his special envoy to the Middle East, Ambassador Philip Habib, to work out a solution according to which the PLO forces would leave Beirut and be evacuated from Lebanon. As days went by and nothing much happened, Israel became increasingly suspicious of Habib's intentions. Israeli Ambassador to Washington Moshe Arens was feeding the government in Jerusalem with alarming reports that the United States was trying to transform the PLO into a political organization so it could be associated with a future peace process. In a cabinet meeting on July 18, Begin echoed these suspicions and said: "We can already hear some talk in Washington that the evacuation of the PLO from Beirut should be linked to the solution of the Palestinian problem, according to Security Council Resolution 242. If we continue to sit at the gates of Beirut without entering the city, we are inviting a national disaster. The PLO is already boasting victory because we did not enter West Beirut."

In light of intensified battles around Beirut, Ambassador Habib suggested to several Arab countries that they admit the PLO units into their countries. This proved to be more difficult than expected. For example, when he suggested to Saudi Arabia that they take two thousand PLO fighters, they looked at him as if they could not believe their ears. "They acted as if I had offered them a pork sandwich," Habib told David Kimche, the director general of the Israeli Foreign Ministry. Syria, Libya, and Algeria pretended not to have heard Ambassador Habib's plea, while Egypt first accepted and then retracted its original offer.

After exhausting negotiations, Tunisia eventually accepted the political body of the PLO; Yemen and Iraq accepted some military elements, while President Assad took only those Palestinians who were opposed to Arafat. In discussing this situation, Begin told his cabinet that the Syrian president was demanding not only an Israeli withdrawal from Lebanon and the Golan Heights, but also, as part of an overall settlement, that the West Bank be put under Syrian control.

This Syrian position was not new. It was consistent with Assad's thinking. Back in 1976, shortly before the Syrian army entered Lebanon—with the United States and Israel in agreement—Assad told Arafat: "I want you to remember that you do not represent the Palestinians more than we do. There is no such thing as Palestine. There is no Palestinian entity. There is only Syria and Palestine is part of Syria."

By the end of July 1982, Begin was alarmed that Arafat might accept Resolution 242, recognize Israel's right to exist, and renounce terrorism in return for U.S. recognition of the PLO. On August 1, 1982, Begin told his cabinet: "We have to finish off the PLO thugs as soon as possible. We have to deal them such a blow that there will be no more Palestinian partner for negotiations. We are now facing a real danger of an imposed American solution. The irony of this situation is that while we have defeated the PLO militarily, the U.S. is trying to reap the political fruits of our victory and is now ready to talk to Arafat."

On August 12, Arafat finally capitulated and informed Ambassador Habib, through Lebanese Prime Minister Shafiq el-Wazzan, that he was prepared to evacuate Beirut, under proper international cover. This was arranged, and the PLO evacuation was completed on August 31, 1982.

The war in Lebanon opened a new chapter in the Israeli-Palestinian conflict. The destruction of the PLO infrastructure in South Lebanon and the expulsion of the PLO headquarters from Beirut left Arafat with no operational base within reach of Israel. No Arab country bordering Israel would allow the use of its territory for PLO operations against Israel. In addition, President Assad, a longtime champion of the Palestinian cause, managed to split the PLO into two factions. The mainstream El-Fatah organization remained loyal to Yasser Arafat, who eventually came under Egyptian, Saudi, and Moroccan patronage. The other faction, consisting mainly of ten small radical groups based in Damascus, came under Syria's wings. This split made it very difficult to solve the Palestinian problem without Syria's participation, or so Assad believed.

American policymakers, however, were not yet prepared to include pro-Soviet Syria in any effort to solve the Israeli-Palestinian conflict. Instead, the focus of U.S. diplomacy shifted back to Jordan, leaving the PLO and Syria out in the cold. It was obvious that Reagan wanted to recapture the diplomatic initiative by proposing a plan that would go beyond the Camp David Accords and would exclude Soviet involvement in the Middle East peace process. This very intention, however, had a major flaw: It was not coordinated with the two major players, Syria and Israel. Kept officially in the dark, Begin was furious when Ambassador Sam Lewis handed him the Reagan Plan, shortly before it was made public.

The Reagan Plan tried to strike a balance between Israel's security needs and the political aspirations of the Palestinians, in conjunction with Jordan. It mentioned Lebanon only briefly, and it ruled out the annexation of the West Bank and the Gaza Strip to Israel.

Israeli rejection of the plan was quick and total. The PLO and Syria also rejected it, publicly and explicitly. Assad called the Reagan Plan "another Camp David," and he was determined to prove that the Arab-Israeli conflict would be more difficult to solve. Assad looked at the problem in the context of the Cold War. Moscow, under Yuri Andropov, gave Syria generous military assistance and helped restore Assad's self-confidence after his military debacle in Lebanon. Included with this largesse was a sophisticated air defense system based on SA-5 missiles manned by Soviet crews.

American eyes were now turned to Jordan. King Hussein visited Washington in December 1982 for talks with President Reagan and Secretary Shultz. In an effort to persuade the king to support the plan, the United States promised to supply Jordan with modern arms and generous economic assistance. Hussein, however, did not feel strong enough to go alone. He told Reagan that he needed the support of the PLO. Hussein then went to Moscow to seek Soviet support as well. But Yuri Andropov warned him not to endorse the Reagan Plan. Hussein got the message. On April 10, 1983, Jordan officially rejected the Reagan Plan.

It was at that dark moment in Palestinian history that Abu Mazen's star began to rise. Ignoring opposition from within his inner circle, Arafat appointed Abu Mazen as a member of the PLO executive committee, responsible for relations with nongovernmental organizations. As such he was also responsible for contacts with Israeli liberals and left-wing activists.

In a long, still officially classified document, Abu Mazen tried to explain what had happened in Beirut and tried to identify the mistakes made in Lebanon. He pointed out that with the right-wing Likud government in power in Israel, there was little the PLO could do to establish meaningful dialogue with Israeli officials. Jewish settlements in the territories began to proliferate. According to PLO estimates, 56 percent of the land in the West Bank and 22 percent of the land in the Gaza Strip were "state-owned." Accordingly, the Begin government could allocate more land for more settlements. Sporadic acts of terrorism were important, as part of the overall struggle against Israel. In reality, these acts of terror led nowhere. On the contrary, they only gave Israel a justification for harsher retaliation against the Palestinians. The war in Lebanon was the proof for this evaluation. In sum, Abu Mazen concluded, the PLO had no real military option against Israel, and he recommended a more intense political action. In his document, Abu Mazen suggested capitalizing on differences within the Israeli society and penetrating the Israeli political psyche. He recommended trying to reach out to activists of the Israeli Peace Now movement, whose mass demonstrations during the war in Lebanon had proved to be so effective. He also suggested exploiting the ethnic differences in Israel between Sephardi and Ashkenazi. Finally, Abu Mazen wanted to attempt to build a bridge with liberal American Jews, whose influence on Israel could be important.

The "Abu Mazen Doctrine," as the document was later to be labeled, was submitted to the sixteenth session of the Palestine National Council (PNC)—the Palestinian parliament-in-exile—in December 1983. It drew fire from all directions and was never formally adopted. Instead, the PNC decided to approve further PLO contacts with "moderate Israelis," on condition that these encounters be considered "private initiatives" that did not represent the official PLO position. Abu Mazen accepted this compromise, because it did give him some rope and a certain freedom to maneuver. But the price exacted was very high. On April 10, 1984, during a plenary session of the Socialist International in Albufeira, a picturesque Portuguese resort town on the Atlantic coast, Issam Sartawi was gunned down by the Abu Nidal Palestinian faction, which was opposed to any contact with Israel. At the suggestion of Willy Brandt, the head of the Israeli delegation, Shimon Peres, eulogized Sartawi as an "honorable opponent" who had shed his blood for the sake of peace. Lova Eliav, who was the first to meet with Sartawi, said: "He was the bravest of the brave. It pains me that the PLO hasn't done much to rehabilitate his memory."

A weaker and less determined person would have abandoned his efforts at this point. Not the stubborn and feisty Abu Mazen. At great personal risk, he was determined to implement his plan, confident of its success. With the encouragement of King Hassan of Morocco, he established very close contacts with prominent Moroccan Jews who maintained close relationships with their relatives in Israel or had close contacts with the Israeli left-wing parties. The most prominent among these Jews was André Azoulay, who later became King Hassan's economic adviser. The friendship between the two holds to this very day.

Abu Mazen's real success came only in the summer of 1992, when the Israeli Labor Party defeated the Likud in the general elections and a center-left government, headed by Yitzhak Rabin, was formed in Jerusalem. In his book *The Road to Oslo,* published in Arabic in Beirut, Abu Mazen revealed that the PLO encouraged Israeli Arabs to vote for the Labor Party, thus assuring its victory in the general elections. This strategy, more than any other factor, paved the road to Oslo.

CROSSING THE JORDAN

On February 12, 1995, King Hussein hosted at his Hashimiyah Palace in Amman a very special Israeli group: All of the men who had headed the Mossad since Israel's independence in May 1948 were invited with their spouses for a two-day official visit to Jordan. They were Isser Harel, under whose tenure Adolf Eichmann was captured in Argentina and brought to trial in Israel; General (Res.) Meir Amit, who was the first Israeli to meet with Morocco's King Hassan in 1964; General (Res.) Zvi Zamir; General (Res.) Yitzhak (Haka) Hofi; Nahum Admoni; and Shabetai Shavit, who had been involved in the last phases of the Israeli-Jordanian peace treaty.

The visit was organized by Ephraim Halevy, the deputy director of the Mossad and one of the two Israeli officials who, under Prime Minister Rabin's personal guidance, had orchestrated the Israeli-Jordanian peace treaty, signed on October 26, 1994. Of the six Mossad directors, only two—Isser Harel and Meir Amit—had never met the king previously. All six, however, had been involved in one way or another in the very complex aspects of the security cooperation between Israel and Jordan over the previous forty years.

No other head of state with whom Israel maintained an intelligence relationship had ever initiated such a gathering. It was King Hussein's way of saying thank you for the role Israel had played in saving his life and shielding his throne from the aggressive subversion of his more powerful Arab "brothers"— Egypt, Syria, and Iraq. According to one report, King Hussein had foiled seven attempts to overthrow him and escaped twelve assassination attempts.[1] Some of these attempts were foiled through tips from Israeli intelligence sources.

Shaking hands with General Amit, King Hussein did not have to be reminded of the chilling experience, in the spring of 1962, when two Syrian MIG-17s tried to intercept his plane on his flight from Jordan to Europe via the Syrian air corridor. The MIG-17s were detected by Amit's military intelligence, and two Israeli French-made Mystère jets took off immediately and intercepted them. Within minutes, they forced the Syrians to flee, and the Jordanian monarch returned safely to Amman.

And when he shook hands with General Zvi Zamir, whom the king had met on previous occasions, Hussein knew exactly how, during the Yom Kippur War in October 1973, the director of the Mossad had persuaded the Israeli chief of staff, the late General David (Dado) Elazar, to divert the Israeli artillery from a certain hill on the Golan Heights where King Hussein was addressing the armored brigade that he had sent to assist the Syrian army, in its fight against . . . Israel.

Indeed, of all the Arab confrontation states, Israel's relations with Jordan were the most enduring and the most trustful. The cooperation between the two countries was very modest at the beginning and was limited to strictly security matters. It included police cooperation along the border, in a joint effort to avoid infiltration and smuggling and to arrange the prompt return of innocent civilians who accidentally crossed the undemarcated border. Gradually it expanded to a struggle against subversion and terrorism. Then it moved to meetings at a political level, and eventually it led to an agreement on a fair sharing of the Yarmuk and Jordan water resources. After the Six-Day War, Moshe Dayan introduced the "open bridges" policy, which allowed easy movement of people and goods across the Jordan River. The bridges remained open even during the civil war in Jordan in September 1970, and during the Yom Kippur War in October 1973.

Over the years, all Israeli prime ministers exchanged with Hussein greetings and gifts on the occasions of birthdays and anniversaries, or on the eve of Muslim and Jewish holidays. The last gift, on the occasion of the Jordanian monarch's birthday, had been handed to King Hussein after Prime Minister Rabin's assassination by Rabin's bureau chief, Eitan Haber. In July 1976, King Hussein congratulated Rabin for the successful Entebbe operation, which led to the release of Israeli hostages whose Air France plane had been hijacked by a Palestinian terrorist group and flown to Uganda. On another occasion, Hussein asked Rabin to instruct Israeli patrol boats in the Gulf of Aqaba not to blow their horns in the afternoon hours, when Queen Noor and the monarch took their siesta.

Therefore, and because of the very special nature of this cooperation, it was not surprising that shortly after he returned to power in July 1992, Prime Minister Rabin revived his warm and trustful relationship with the king. Ever since his first meeting with King Hussein, in the suburbs of Tel Aviv in 1974, Rabin had been consistent in his support of an independent Jordan under the Hashemite rule. Hussein was also aware of the personal role that Rabin had played in September 1970, while an ambassador to Washington, in forging the strategic alliance between Israel and the United States that helped defeat Syria and the PLO in their joint effort to overthrow him.

In the summer of 1992, however, King Hussein was persona non grata in Washington. President Bush was unwilling to forgive him for his support of Iraq's invasion of Kuwait. Yet, Rabin could not ignore Jordan's geostrategic role as a buffer between Israel and Iraq. Jordan itself did not constitute a threat to Israel. In cooperation with Iraq, or with Syria, or with both, Jordan could change the balance of power between Israel and its Arab neighbors. The fact that since September 1970 King Hussein had not allowed the Iraqi army to enter his country assured the stability of the entire region. Furthermore, from his many conversations with King Hussein in the past, Rabin knew that the Jordanian monarch perceived Israel as a "strategic asset" for his country and as an "insurance policy" against Syria, Iraq, and Egypt. Nevertheless, during the fifteen years of Likud governments in Jerusalem, this Jordanian perception of Israel was accompanied by some fears. Various Likud leaders, especially Ariel Sharon, spoke openly of Jordan as being the "alternative homeland" for the Palestinians. King Hussein was forced to counterbalance this Likud perception by increasing his cooperation with Iraq.

Rabin sought now to reverse the trend, by reassuring Hussein that Jordan's existence as a sovereign state was a vital Israeli interest. Rabin also promised the king to intervene in Jordan's behalf in Washington.

This goal was easier for Rabin to achieve with the Clinton administration. Not sharing the intense anti-Hussein sentiment of President Bush, President Clinton showed that he was able to detach himself from his predecessor's policies and proved to be very open-minded about Jordan's strategic role in the region. Thus, acting upon the recommendation of Martin Indyk, his Middle Eastern affairs expert, Clinton met with the king at the Oval Office, for the first time, on June 18, 1993. The king was recovering from prostate cancer surgery at the Mayo Clinic in Rochester, Minnesota.

Clinton was impressed by King Hussein's warmth and sincerity. The king gave Clinton a firm commitment to pursue a road of peace with Israel. One week later, on June 24, the king followed up with a long personal letter to Clinton, describing his vision of peace. Clinton passed a copy of the letter to Israel. "My grandfather was committed to peace with Israel. He paid with his life for this commitment," Hussein wrote. "Had he not been assassinated, we could have avoided the bloodshed and we could have lived in peace for so many years."

On July 4, 1993, Clinton responded to Hussein's letter by pledging his full support for an Israeli-Jordanian peace. Soon after, Clinton asked Congress to resume military and economic assistance to Jordan.[2]

The Oslo Accords between Israel and the PLO were a kind of setback for Jordan. Although officially "disengaged" from the West Bank and the Gaza Strip, King Hussein never lost interest in the territories that Israel had captured from him in the 1967 war. He knew that more than half of his population were Palestinians. Because of this demographic reality, he had to navigate between conflicting trends. Israel did not always understand him, and on occasion Israel pushed him to take actions that he was not capable of taking. Rabin was well aware of this reality. Hence, soon after his handshake with Yasser Arafat on the White House South Lawn on September 13, 1993, and after his stopover in Morocco, Rabin's next destination was Jordan. Accompanied by his military secretary, General Danny Yatom (now the director of the Mossad); Ephraim Halevy, the deputy director of the Mossad; and his bureau chief, Eitan Haber, Rabin flew by helicopter to King Hussein's resort palace in Aqaba, on the Red Sea, on October 6, 1993. Rabin reassured the king that Israel would not sacrifice its long and friendly relationship with Jordan for the sake of Arafat. Rabin explained to the Jordanian monarch the complexities of the Oslo Accords, and he sought to counterbalance them with a declaration of principles with Jordan. Fully aware of the Egyptian military theory that the Arabs could never defeat Israel without the military cooperation of both Jordan and Iraq, Rabin wanted to eliminate the danger of Iraqi troop deployments in Jordan, thus reviving the now defunct "Eastern Front" against Israel. King Hussein was very forthcoming, but he made three conditions, from which he never deviated: Israel's guarantee of his "preferred status" in the Muslim shrines in East Jerusalem; Israel's withdrawal from a stretch of land of 381 square kilometers in the Arava, southeast of Beersheba, that the Israeli army had captured during the 1948 and 1967 wars; and a more generous partition of the water of the Yarmuk River, between Israel and Jordan.

A week later, King Hussein made public one of those three conditions. Without revealing his secret meeting with the Israeli prime minister, the king said the Hashemite Kingdom would "never give up its role as the Custodian of the Holy Places in Jerusalem."[3] King Hussein's attachment to the holy shrines in East Jerusalem was not surprising. It derived from the fact that he considered himself the forty-second generation direct descendant of the Prophet Muhammad, through the male line of the Prophet's grandson. In the more recent past, in 1951, King Hussein's grandfather King Abdullah had been assassinated in front of him, at the gate of El-Aqsa Mosque. Shortly after the Rabin-Hussein meeting in Aqaba, high-level negotiations between Israel and Jordan encountered their first major obstacle. On November 2, 1993, Rabin sent Foreign Minister Peres to Amman with a four-page document laying down the groundwork for further negotiations at lower levels. In coordination with Rabin, Peres was positive in his approach to the issues of water-sharing and border disputes, but he was less forthcoming on the issue of Jerusalem. Concerned that the definition of "preferred status" in the Muslim shrines in East Jerusalem would contradict the spirit, if not the letter, of the Oslo Accords, Peres suggested a language that recognized the "Jordanian status," not a preferred status in East Jerusalem. Hussein rejected this language outright. They both agreed, however, to continue the negotiations at a later date. Hussein had only one request: Since he was committed to Syria not to conclude a separate deal with Israel, he wanted to keep the meeting with Peres secret. Peres agreed. The next day, November 3, Peres was interviewed by Israeli television on various aspects of the peace process. While being made up in the studio, he told his interviewers "privately": "Remember the second of November." It wasn't long before this "private" remark was leaked to the press. The general conclusion was that a peace agreement with Jordan was very close.[4]

King Hussein was enraged. He felt betrayed. He was walking a tightrope, balancing between his desire to conclude peace "between the children of Abraham" and his commitment to Syria not to strike a separate deal with Israel. The king had already had a similar experience with Peres in the recent past. In a speech at Haifa University, on June 6, 1993, Peres had declared that "everything is ready for a peace treaty between Israel and Jordan. What is missing is . . . the pen."[5] When asked to comment on this remark, King Hussein said that he was sure that Peres's remarks "were taken out of context and were distorted by the press." As for Rabin, he dismissed his foreign minister's remarks by saying: "I am not interested in pens or pencils."[6]

Peres's remarks at Haifa University were made before the Israeli public became aware of his secret role in Oslo. Therefore, the Israeli press treated the remark at the time as "another Peres fantasy." This time, however, the leak about Peres's secret meeting with King Hussein on November 2 was more serious, coming at a time when President Clinton and Secretary Christopher were making a tremendous effort to assure President Assad that despite the Oslo Accords he would not be left out. It was feared that Peres's leak would derail the whole process with Jordan. Rabin immediately sent his Mossad troubleshooter Ephraim Halevy to Amman to calm the king's fears. Hussein, however, was adamant. He conditioned his agreement to continue the high-level negotiations with Israel on the exclusion of Peres. Rabin agreed.[7]

Indeed, from that date on, Israeli-Jordanian negotiations were conducted in two different venues. One was totally "compartmentalized" and directed exclusively by Rabin and Hussein. Involved in this track on the Israeli side were Ephraim Halevy, General Danny Yatom (Rabin's military secretary), and Rabin's bureau chief, Eitan Haber. Shortly afterward, Rabin added to his team Eli Rubenstein, the discreet cabinet secretary who also headed the Israeli delegation to the bilateral negotiations with Jordan in Washington.[8] On the Jordanian side were, in addition to King Hussein, Crown Prince Hassan, Prime Minister Abdul Salam Majali, and Hussein's military secretary, Colonel Ali Shukry, a descendant of a well-known Arab family from Haifa. His relative Suheil Shukry was married to Zippora Hacohen, a distant relative of Rabin's mother, Rosa. When he learned about this family connection, Rabin invited Colonel Shukry to visit Israel as his personal guest. Colonel Shukry was to accompany King Hussein to Rabin's funeral. At a later date, the king added to his secret negotiating team Fayez Tarawneh, the Jordanian ambassador to Washington and Eli Rubenstein's counterpart in the bilateral negotiations. After the signing of the Israeli-Jordanian peace treaty in the Arava, on October 26, 1994, King Hussein purposely decorated both Tarawneh and Rubenstein for their successful negotiation of the peace treaty.

The second venue of negotiations was public, and both Peres and Secretary Christopher were involved in it. This venue dealt mostly with joint Israeli-Jordanian economic projects. It was a direct result of an October 1, 1993, meeting at the White House, between Crown Prince Hassan and Foreign Minister Peres, under the auspices of President Clinton. During that meeting, it was agreed to form a tripartite committee to study joint economic projects in the fields of tourism, energy, and communications.

On January 24, 1994, Hussein was again in the United States for his semi-annual checkup at the Mayo Clinic. As is customary on such occasions, the king then came to Washington for a meeting with President Clinton and Congressional leaders. In a meeting with a group of Jewish leaders in Washington, on January 24, 1994, King Hussein spoke enthusiastically about regional development projects, such as building a highway to link Jordan to Egypt via Eilat, joint Israeli-Jordanian ventures in the Dead Sea and the Jordan Valley, etc. He did not say a word about the secret venue with Rabin and about the efforts to draft a joint declaration of principles (DOP) with Israel.[9]

Thus, while public attention was focused on the public activities and statements of the various actors, the real work was done behind the scenes and in total secrecy. After a meeting in London between Israeli and Jordanian air force officers, a secret air corridor was opened on December 15, 1993, between Israel and Jordan to allow negotiators from both sides to shuttle freely between Jerusalem and Amman in an effort to narrow the differences in the proposed DOP.

During all these months, King Hussein remained firm in his position that unless Israel accepted his three conditions—a recognition of Jordan's "preferred status" in Jerusalem, an Israeli withdrawal from an occupied Jordanian territory in the Arava, and a bigger share of the Yarmuk's waters—there could be no agreement on the DOP. Israel suggested following the example of the Oslo Accords and deferring negotiation on these three issues until after the signing of the DOP. King Hussein refused. As one senior Israeli official put it: "Hussein did not want to leave the chestnuts in the fire. . . . He wanted every issue resolved, before he agreed to sign the peace treaty with Israel." Indeed, in a closed meeting with members of the Senate Foreign Affairs Committee on February 14, Hussein said: "He who would agree to a DOP that would leave for a later date the decision on Jordan's status in Jerusalem, border disputes, and water resources would be paving the way for an unstable surrender treaty. . . ."[10]

During the next few months, Israel and Jordan exchanged several drafts of a proposed DOP, but no progress was made. In mid-May 1994, the Israeli negotiators, Ephraim Halevy and Eli Rubenstein, met in London with Crown Prince Hassan, in advance of a summit meeting between King Hussein and Prime Minister Rabin at the king's London home on May 19.[11] After summing up the points of agreement and disagreement between Israel and Jordan, Rabin told the Jordanian monarch that Israel was now prepared to grant him a "preferred status" in the Islamic holy shrines—El-Aqsa Mosque and the Dome of the Rock on Temple Mount. Rabin made no mention of the Christian holy places in the Old City of Jerusalem. That was a real breakthrough, and the negotiations on a DOP intensified.

The Hussein-Rabin secret meeting in London came one month after Israel and the PLO signed in Paris, on April 19, a comprehensive agreement that defined the parameters for an economic cooperation between Israel and the future Palestine Authority. To Jordan's great surprise, Rabin and Arafat signed in Cairo, on May 4, and in the presence of President Mubarak, Secretary Christopher, and Russian Foreign Minister Andrei Kozyrev, an agreement on Israeli redeployment in the Gaza Strip and withdrawal from the city of Jericho. Despite the mutual economic dependence between Jordan and the West Bank, Arafat did not consult with Jordan on this important issue. Instead, he continued to rely on Egypt's good offices. King Hussein was much concerned that his economy would be negatively affected by this Israeli-PLO agreement. Hence, once the "Jerusalem obstacle" was removed, Hussein told Rabin that he was now prepared to move faster in the effort to solve the remaining issues between the two countries.

In early June, both Rabin and Hussein conveyed to the United States the details of their meeting in London. In his determination to avoid any leaks, and according to his promise to the Jordanian monarch, Rabin kept Peres and his Foreign Ministry team totally in the dark. "In retrospect, it became clear to us that Peres knew about the secret Israeli-Jordanian negotiations only a little more than the Israeli press," commented a senior Foreign Ministry official.[12]

In June 1994, King Hussein again came to the United States. In a meeting at the White House on June 22, President Clinton told the king bluntly that if he really wanted to open a new chapter in his relationship with the United States, he would have to make a dramatic gesture on the peace front with Israel. Clinton suggested Hussein make his secret meetings with Rabin public. After the public handshake between Rabin and Arafat at the White House and in Cairo, Rabin's open visit to Morocco, and the readiness of other Arab countries to maintain a public dialogue with Israel, there was no reason why Hussein's numerous meetings with the Israeli leaders, "the most widely known secret," should remain secret. In such a case, Clinton added, Congress would certainly be more receptive to the idea of granting Jordan the economic assistance that it needed.

King Hussein responded positively to Clinton's advice and suggested the month of October as a convenient time for a public meeting with Rabin, in Washington. He expressed the hope that by then all the differences with Israel would be resolved and a DOP could be publicly signed at the White House.

On July 12, King Hussein surprised both Israel and the United States by proposing to advance the public meeting with Rabin in Washington from October to July 25. Despite the short notice, the White House on July 15 announced the plan for a meeting between King Hussein and Prime Minister Rabin, under President Clinton's auspices, on July 25. The pace of the secret Israeli-Jordanian negotiations for the drafting of the DOP intensified.

On July 19, the Israeli-Jordanian economic committee met near Eilat to discuss various development projects. The Israeli Foreign Ministry had a representative on that committee. At the end of the plenary meeting, however, the head of the Israeli delegation, Eli Rubenstein, conferred "privately" with his Jordanian counterpart, Ambassador Fayez Tarawneh. Upon his return to Jerusalem, the Foreign Ministry official reported to Peres on the Eilat discussions. He added that there was also a "private" discussion between Rubenstein and Tarawneh, from which he was excluded. Peres said nothing.[13]

The next day, July 20, Peres and Secretary Christopher met with Jordan's prime minister, Abdul Salam Majali, on the eastern side of the Dead Sea. The purpose of the meeting was to review the subjects that had been discussed the day before by their respective senior officials. Christopher, who was accompanied by Ambassadors Dennis Ross and Martin Indyk, later met separately with Crown Prince Hassan. The prince told Christopher that Israel and Jordan were "racing against time" in an effort to conclude the DOP before the Washington meeting on July 25. Upon his return to Jerusalem, Indyk went straight to the prime minister's office and asked for a copy of the DOP.[14] Since the final draft was not yet concluded, Indyk was shown the latest version and was promised that once the final draft was ready he would receive an advance copy. This final draft was handed by Rabin to Christopher in Washington on July 24, just one day before the White House ceremony. Meantime, and while Indyk was reading in Jerusalem the proposed draft of the Israeli-Jordanian DOP, a real drama occurred between Peres and Rabin. Upon his return to Jerusalem, Peres called Rabin and asked him if there was anything that he should know about the negotiations with Jordan. "It's good that you called," Rabin told Peres. "I was about to call you and invite you to accompany me to Washington, where King Hussein and I will sign a declaration of principles."[15]

Peres was stunned but said nothing. After all, he had done the same thing to Rabin with the secret Oslo channel. Peres had not informed Rabin about the Oslo channel until February 9, 1993, some five weeks after the channel was actually opened. That, however, was not the end of the drama. In his speech at the White House ceremony, Rabin did not mention Peres as one who had played a role in the negotiations with Jordan. The next morning, most of the Israeli papers criticized the prime minister for his behavior toward his foreign minister. Rabin was not deterred by this criticism. On the contrary. On July 27, Ambassador Itamar Rabinovich hosted a dinner for the prime minister, to which were invited the secretaries of state and defense, Congressional leaders, and other dignitaries. After all the VIP guests were gone, Rabin stayed at the ambassador's residence with a small group of senior Israeli and American correspondents. Rabin was very upbeat. He used that occasion to answer his critics in Israel regarding Peres. He said: "I didn't mention Peres in my speech at the White House because he was not involved in the secret negotiations with Jordan. The two officials who did the job, under my direction, were Ephraim Halevy and Eli Rubenstein." The Israeli journalists were taken by surprise. Until that moment it had generally been believed that Rabin and Peres had worked together on the Jordanian file. During his two-year tenure as prime minister, in the years 1985–86, Peres, more than any other Israeli politician, had been identified with the "Jordanian option." Therefore some of the Israeli journalists believed that, as had happened in Oslo, here too Peres had done the job and Rabin was only reaping the fruits. But now they were told by the prime minister, and for the first time, that Peres had been totally excluded from the secret Jordanian initiative.

Furthermore, before Rabin revealed the identity of Ephraim Halevy, the Israeli press was barred from identifying the deputy director of the Mossad. Now, however, the name and occupation of Halevy were fully exposed. Halevy, a brilliant British-born operative and a former station chief of the Mossad in Washington, was to pay dearly for his loyalty to Rabin and for his success. After signing the Israeli-Jordanian peace treaty, on October 26, 1994, Rabin wanted to appoint Halevy as the first Israeli ambassador to Amman. He was the ideal candidate. He was trusted by the king and his aides, he was witty, intelligent, and discreet, and—like Eli Rubenstein—he had gained enormous experience in Jordanian affairs. Peres, however, said no. Peres would not forgive Halevy for not even hinting to him about the secret channel with Jordan. After long delays, Rabin and Peres finally agreed to appoint a respected scholar, Professor Shimon Shamir, a former ambassador to Cairo, as the first Israeli ambassador to Jordan. As for Halevy, he was sent to Brussels as ambassador to the EEC. Nevertheless, until his assassination in Tel Aviv, Rabin continued to send Halevy on secret missions to Amman, not only without Ambassador Shamir's knowledge but also without the knowledge of Peres himself.

The Washington Declaration, as the Israeli-Jordanian declaration of principles was called, marked another historic station on the road of settling enmities that had plagued the Middle East in the past fifty years. President Clinton described the White House ceremony, on July 25, 1994, as "a new chapter in the march of hope over despair." It was obvious that the Clinton administration was trying to make the most of this new Middle East accord. Conducted at the same table that had been used for the signing of the Israeli-Egyptian peace treaty in March 1979 and the Israeli-PLO declaration of principles in September 1993, this White House ceremony was a welcome foreign policy success for President Clinton. To demonstrate his support for the new accord, Clinton presided over the ceremony and signed the document as witness. "History is made when brave leaders find the power to escape the past and create a new future," Clinton said.

In their DOP, King Hussein and Prime Minister Rabin declared, "with the world as our witness," that "after generations of hostility, blood and tears," Israel and Jordan had ended their long state of war. They publicly pledged to intensify negotiations toward a full-fledged peace between their two countries. "We have gone here a long way toward a full treaty of peace, and, although our work has not yet ended, it is my belief and hope that not long from today, we shall return to signing a permanent and final peace treaty," Rabin said.

For King Hussein, the Washington Declaration marked a dramatic break with Jordan's commitment to keep its formal relations with Israel within an Arab consensus. "Out of all the days of my life, I do not believe there is one such as this," the king said. "This ceremony would bring both nations 'security from fear' that has prevailed over all the years of our lives."

Despite these courageous words, however, Hussein did not hide his concern over Syria's reaction. Hence, just before the signing ceremony, President Clinton phoned President Assad and assured him that the United States would continue to mediate a peace accord between Jerusalem and Damascus. Clinton told Assad that for that purpose, he was sending Secretary Christopher back to the Middle East in mid-August to resume his shuttles between Jerusalem and Damascus.

Israel and Jordan had been blocked by almost half a century of "formal hostility" from developing cooperative economic projects that their similar geography demanded. To heal that breach, Hussein and Rabin outlined the following steps:

- Each country would prevent its territory from being used as a base for acts of terrorism against the other.

- Israel agreed to respect Jordan's interest in the Muslim holy shrines and to give "high priority" to Jordan's historic interest in these shrines when negotiations began between Israel and the Palestinians over the final status of Jerusalem.

- Jordan undertook to establish bilateral economic cooperation with Israel and to urge the Arab League to end its economic boycott of Israel.

In this context, and without waiting for a formal peace treaty, Israel and Jordan also agreed:

- To open direct telephone links between the two countries.
- To start negotiations on a proper allocation of the waters of the Yarmuk River.
- To link the two countries' power grids.
- To open two new border crossings—one between the twin southern cities of Aqaba (Jordan) and Eilat (Israel), and one in the north.
- To allow third-country tourists to travel easily between the two countries.
- To have their police cooperate to combat crime, particularly drug smuggling.
- To speed up negotiations on an international air corridor between Jordan and Israel.

In addition to his sincere desire for peace with Israel, King Hussein was looking for American economic assistance, especially a relief from Jordan's $700 million debt to the United States. Clinton promised to do his best to meet Jordan's requirements. In a rare joint appearance of Hussein and Rabin before both houses of Congress, the Jordanian monarch alluded to his financial needs, but without going into specifics. The warm welcome on Capitol Hill was a clear indication that Hussein would not be rebuffed.

After their return to their respective countries, Rabin and Hussein moved quickly to implement the Washington Declaration. For years there had been a secret telephone link between the leaders of Jordan and Israel. On August 7, 1994, they made this link public, in a telephone conversation between President Weizman and King Hussein. The next day, on August 8, Hussein and Rabin opened the first of the two new crossing points between their two countries, just north of Eilat. Immediately after the ceremony, King Hussein hosted a luncheon at his Aqaba palace in honor of Rabin, Peres, and Secretary Christopher, who had come for a new round of shuttle diplomacy between Israel and Syria.

More important, Israel and Jordan began working on a draft of a peace treaty. As expected, the border demarcation and the sharing of water resources were the main obstacles to overcome. In an effort to avoid a deadlock, Rabin flew to Aqaba on September 29, 1994, and spent several hours with King Hussein. A few days earlier, Ephraim Halevy and Eli Rubenstein presented to Crown Prince Hassan in Amman a first Israeli draft for a peace treaty. In his long discussion with Hussein, Rabin agreed to recognize Jordanian sovereignty over the disputed land in the Arava, southeast of Beersheba. However, since that stretch of land had been farmed by a nearby kibbutz for many years, Rabin suggested that Jordan lease this land to Israel for an undetermined period. Hussein listened attentively to Rabin's arguments, but did not respond. He wanted more time to think. Next day, on September 30, a Jordanian helicopter landed near the prime minister's office in Jerusalem. Colonel Ali Shukry, the king's military secretary, handed Rabin Hussein's answer to Israel's leasing proposal. It was a total rejection. After lengthy deliberations with the king and his brother, a possible compromise began to emerge. Accordingly, on October 12, Rabin flew again to Amman and proposed a new deal to Hussein: Israel would return to Jordan some 350 square kilometers, and not 381 as Jordan had demanded. Other land disputes would be settled by swapping territory. Part of the land Israel would return to Jordan would be leased to the Israeli kibbutz for a period of twenty-five years. The water needed for the irrigation of this leased land would come from Jordanian wells across the border. In return, Rabin promised to give Jordan an additional quantity of fifty million cubic meters of water from the Yarmuk River.[16] For this purpose, Israel agreed that Jordan could build a new dam on the Yarmuk, before it feeds into the Jordan. Jordan could built a second dam at a later date. Rabin also promised to take Jordan's needs into consideration when releasing water from the Sea of Galilee into the Jordan River. The water compromise was discreetly criticized by Peres. He told his aides: "Rabin didn't care about anything. He wanted the peace treaty and the ceremony. That's what mattered to him. . . ."[17]

King Hussein was pleased with the new Israeli proposal, but he still wanted more time to study it and to consult with his immediate associates. In an extraordinary move, Rabin assigned Eli Rubenstein and Ephraim Halevy to conduct nonstop negotiations in Amman until all the remaining obstacles were removed. It is obvious that both Rabin and Hussein were concerned that the issues would be talked to death. They both feared that the negotiations would slow down and the entire process dissipate.

Finally, on October 16, the negotiations came to a close. That night, Rabin returned to Amman for the third time. He negotiated with King Hussein until 3:00 A.M. on October 17 and took few hours of rest. The Israeli and Jordanian teams split into small working groups that labored through the night and completed the fifteen-page peace treaty. Shortly after breakfast, Hussein and Rabin went through the final draft and approved it. Immediately after the treaty was initialed by Prime Minister Rabin and Jordanian Prime Minister Abdul Salam Majali, Rabin and Hussein called President Clinton in Washington and informed him of their success. Clinton was delighted, and he accepted Hussein's invitation to attend the signing ceremony, not in Washington, but in the Arava, along the two nations' desert border, on October 26, 1994.

Glowing with pride, the Jordanian king and the Israeli prime minister addressed the dozens of correspondents who had gathered in Amman for this occasion. The joint press conference was broadcast live on Israeli TV, but not on Jordan's.

"I am full of hope that the future will be a future of peace," King Hussein said. He added that "this step will be a very important one for a comprehensive peace in this region. Hopefully, it is a new beginning and a fresh start. We will defend this peace, enjoy it, and cherish it. It's a peace with dignity."

Prime Minister Rabin called the occasion "a unique moment in history." He praised King Hussein's "courageous decision" to accelerate the negotiations and not to wait for other parties to catch up. King Hussein and Rabin explained that according to the treaty, Israel and Jordan would establish full diplomatic relations by the end of 1994, their borders would be opened for tourism and business, Jordan would end its economic boycott of Israel, and both countries were pledged to cooperate in the field of security, which had been handled by them secretly for the past forty-five years.

The treaty reflected what was widely known, that Israel's relations with Jordan had always been better and more trustful than those with any other Arab country. Hence, after so many secret meetings with Israeli leaders in London, Paris, and Tel Aviv and aboard a yacht in the Gulf of Aqaba, and after so many informal understandings in many fields, there was no need for complicated negotiations. The peace treaty only summed up these relations and gave them a formal, legal shape. In all these secret meetings, the discussions were always honest and frank. Moshe Dayan once told me that Israel and Jordan had reached such a degree of trust that each could conclude what his counterpart could or could not accept. Accordingly, both King Hussein and Prime Minister Rabin felt that this was the time "to cross the Rubicon."

Shortly after the joint press conference in Amman came the first reaction from Washington. "I am delighted," said President Clinton. "At a time when hatred, extremism, and threatening behavior still stalk the Middle East, this agreement reminds us that moderation and reason are prevailing, that nations can put conflicts behind them, and that courageous leaders can lead their nations to peace. . . ." The White House announced that President Clinton would attend the signing ceremony in the Arava on October 26 and would sign the peace treaty as a witness. A few months later, in a letter to King Hussein dated March 27, 1995, Clinton said that "attending the signing of that treaty . . . was one of the most moving acts of my Presidency. . . ."

As part of his first visit to the Middle East as president, Clinton embarked on a larger tour of the region. He visited Israel and Jordan and addressed the Knesset in Jerusalem and the Jordanian parliament in Amman. The president also visited Egypt, inspected U.S. troops in Saudi Arabia and Kuwait, and made a very controversial visit to Syria. That was a price that Clinton was prepared to pay, if only it allayed President Assad's fears that he would be left out of the Arab-Israeli peace process.

Unlike the Oslo Accords between Israel and the PLO, which sharpened divisions within Israel, the peace treaty with Jordan was welcomed enthusiastically by the entire Israeli nation. The treaty was approved by the Israeli Knesset by an unprecedented majority—105 to 13, with two abstentions.

This overwhelming Israeli support raised an immediate question: Why had this peace not been achieved before? King Hussein answered this question himself. In an interview with an Israeli newspaper, the monarch said: "I myself wanted to end the state of war long before. Unfortunately, it was impossible. Both Israel and Jordan had their own constraints. Each of us had a responsibility to shoulder. In the case of Jordan, my responsibility was related to the Palestinian people. Once this problem was solved, we engaged in intensive negotiations to conclude this peace treaty."[18]

The signing of the Israeli-Jordanian treaty was undoubtedly the most impressive achievement of both Ephraim Halevy and Eli Rubenstein. In a very warm letter to Rubenstein, Rabin wrote: "I simply cannot imagine the peace process with Jordan without you. You were the first violin in the peace orchestra for many years. You have invested in every word and every comma of this treaty your knowledge, expertise, and good sense." President Clinton too wrote to Eli Rubenstein, saying: "You have fulfilled the dream through your dedication and tireless efforts. I salute you for your personal contribution to peace. . . ."[19]

The signing of the Israeli-Jordanian peace treaty opened the way for its quick implementation. King Hussein demonstrated his intention to move in that direction in January 1995 by appointing General Zeid bin-Shaker as his new prime minister, succeeding Abdul Salam Majali. A former chief of staff of the Jordanian army and a relative of the king, General bin-Shaker had earned the reputation of a "strong man." He had assumed the premiership several times in the past, whenever the king faced serious or potential crises. The Israeli-Jordanian peace treaty was welcomed by the Bedouin elements in the kingdom, but met with some resistance among the Islamic fundamentalists and the Palestinians. Hence, bin-Shaker's appointment signaled a royal determination to carry out the king's policies and to ensure that the peace vessel sailed safely through the turbulent Islamic and Palestinian waters.

Indeed, on February 9, 1995, Israel and Jordan signed an agreement for security cooperation. This was the first of fifteen agreements that both countries had signed between February 1995 and January 1996. The other agreements dealt with problems of energy, sanitation, police, environment, commerce, agriculture, transportation (including aviation), science and technology, communications, and tourism. Among the fifteen bilateral agreements, the most meaningful, of course, was the one that dealt with security cooperation. It brought into the open the existence of the numerous "informal under-standings" that had been reached between the two countries in the last forty years. Once the agreement was signed, the Jordanian chief of staff and the commander of the air force went to Israel as the official guests of the Israeli army. At the end of the meeting, it was agreed to establish a direct link between the Israeli and Jordanian air forces and to arrange reciprocal visits at their air bases.[20]

A similar link was established between the naval commands in Aqaba and Eilat. Within a very short period, a personal friendship had developed between naval officers of the two countries. At the end of 1995, when Admiral Ami Ay-alon quit his command of the Israeli navy to become the head of the Israeli General Security Service (GSS), the commander of the Jordanian navy hosted a luncheon in his honor in Aqaba. Such an event could not have taken place one year earlier.[21] The Israeli-Jordanian security cooperation reached such a degree that in 1996, Israel expressed readiness to participate in the modernization of the Jordanian air force.

After Rabin's assassination and Labor's defeat in the general parliamentary elections, on May 29, 1996, King Hussein did not change his perception that good and trustful relations with both the United States and Israel remained the best guarantors of Jordan's independence. He also did not hide his intention that, in contrast to Egypt's "cold peace," his peace with the Jewish state would be warm. Hussein gave public expression to this desire. On January 10, 1996, when he and Leah Rabin inaugurated the Yitzhak Rabin Trauma Room at Ichilov Hospital in Tel Aviv, Hussein told Israeli correspondents: "We have no buffer zone or foreign troops to separate us. Our peace is a warm peace. . . ." On that occasion, the king also visited two Jordanian officers, one of them a pilot who had been wounded in Bosnia and needed special treatment that Jordanian hospitals were not equipped to provide.[22]

As expected, the warm relationship between Jerusalem and Amman drew sharp criticism from Damascus. In reply to a question about President Assad's statement that Jordan's relations with Israel were "too warm," King Hussein said: "Jordan's foreign policy is formulated in Amman, according to our own national interest." Jordan's foreign minister, Abdul Karim el-Kabariti, went one step further. He accused Syria of "hypocrisy." "While Syria is negotiating with Israel, it attacks Jordan for the very same reason," he said.[23]

In January 1996, King Hussein named Kabariti as prime minister, succeeding Zeid bin-Shaker. Kabariti kept the foreign ministry for himself, thus signaling a continuity in Jordan's regional policy and in its relations with Israel. In a country where powerful family connections are everything, Kabariti's appointment brought a new breed of Jordanian leadership to center stage. Born in 1949 into a prominent family in Aqaba, Kabariti had been studying geology at the American University in Beirut in 1970 when he was briefly kidnapped by

Palestinian groups angered at King Hussein's suppression of the PLO in Jordan. After his release, he returned to Amman, where King Hussein awarded him a medal for bravery. As foreign minister in Zeid bin-Shaker's government, Kabariti made tireless efforts to mend Jordan's relations with the Persian Gulf countries. This, in turn, meant distancing Jordan from Iraq. With the king's strong support, he put Jordan in open opposition to Saddam Hussein after the Iraqi dictator's sons-in-law defected to Amman, in August 1995. After becoming prime minister, and while Syria's negotiations with Israel foundered, he accused Damascus of helping Palestinian terrorists to infiltrate into the kingdom, on their way to Israel. Finally, at a Cairo summit in June 1996, he did not hesitate to engage in a public slanging match with Syrian Foreign Minister Faruq el-Shara'a over Jordan's warm relationship with Israel.

It is nearly impossible to explain this warm relationship between Israel and Jordan without detailing at length some of the "informal understandings" between the two countries, in the last four decades.

Following the assassination of King Abdullah in East Jerusalem on July 20, 1951, and the brief reign of his father, King Talal, Hussein was crowned king of Jordan, on August 11, 1952. His accession to the throne came less than a month after Egypt's Gamal Abdel Nasser toppled, in a military coup, the corrupt monarchy of King Farouk and declared Egypt a republic. Nasser's coup and his nationalist fervor had a tremendous impact on the Arab world. Very young and totally inexperienced, the new Jordanian monarch witnessed a succession of military coups in Damascus, which had also an impact on his British-commanded army. Facing growing nationalist pressures, Hussein was forced to dismiss all the British officers, including his chief of staff, Glubb Pasha, and to embark on the "Jordanization" of his armed forces. This move had weakened the army and undermined Jordan's stability. Nationalist army officers, including a newly appointed chief of staff, General Ali Abu Nawar, conspired against the king and, inspired by Nasserist sentiments, tried to overthrow the monarchy and declare Jordan a republic.

Israel followed these dramatic developments in Jordan with great concern. Senior Israeli army officers, including Chief of Staff Moshe Dayan, expressed doubts that the "Little King," as General Ezer Weizman called Hussein, would survive the intense Egyptian subversion. Prime Minister Ben-Gurion instructed the army to prepare contingency plans should Jordan disintegrate and cease to exist as a sovereign state. Israel's lightning victory in the Sinai campaign in October 1956 altered the regional military balance in favor of the pro-Western countries in the Middle East. Arab leaders who feared Nasser suddenly saw Israel as the only country capable of defeating him. The Egyptian-Syrian union in February 1958 increased the pressures on Jordan. King Hussein found himself sandwiched between Cairo and Damascus. In May 1958, a civil war broke out in Lebanon, fanned by intense incitement from

Egypt and Syria. The events in Lebanon led to unrest in Jordan as well. The kinship of the ruling Hashemite families in Jordan and Iraq led Iraqi King Faisal to send a mechanized brigade to the assistance of King Hussein. On July 14, 1958, the brigade commander, Colonel Abdul Karim Qassem, instead of marching to Amman, attacked the royal palace in Baghdad, killed the king and his ministers, and declared himself the ruler of the Iraqi Republic.

The Iraqi coup seriously upset the regional balance of power. Colonel Qassem took his country out of the pro-Western Baghdad Pact and asked for Egypt's assistance. He also turned to Moscow for military and political assistance. In the heat of the Cold War between the two superpowers, the Iraqi military coup was a net gain for Soviet diplomacy.

For a short while it looked as if, with Syria as a bridge, a vast Arab empire stretching from the Nile to the Euphrates was about to be established under Nasser's leadership. In a message to President Eisenhower, Prime Minister David Ben-Gurion urged the United States to put down the Iraqi revolution, if necessary by force. Eisenhower rejected this idea. Instead, and in an effort to avoid the collapse of American influence in the region, he sent the Marines into Beirut. This was the first American military intervention in the Middle East. Britain sent a battalion of paratroopers from Cyprus to Amman in order to shore up King Hussein's regime. Israel allowed the British soldiers to fly through its airspace.

In the face of growing Arab nationalism, Ben-Gurion changed his mind about Jordan's strategic importance. Until the establishment of the United Arab Republic (UAR) between Egypt and Syria, Ben-Gurion and many Israeli strategic thinkers had not considered Jordan a viable state. After the Iraqi coup, however, Ben-Gurion considered Jordan's existence to be an Israeli national interest.[24]

Ben-Gurion's new thinking laid the basis for the security cooperation between Israel and Jordan. Even before the Suez War in 1956, there was a modest infrastructure for low-level Israeli-Jordanian security cooperation. Israeli and Jordanian army and police officers met regularly at various points along the armistice lines and discussed ways to prevent infiltration of Palestinians into Israel. After the Suez War, and after the United States declared the Eisenhower Doctrine in 1957, this cooperation also became part of a regional framework aimed at blocking Soviet expansion in the Middle East. In July 1960, this cooperation found its dramatic expression in Israel's assistance in foiling two attempted military coups in Jordan. Thanks to hints passed on to King Hussein through the CIA and the shah of Iran, Hussein was able to uncover the conspiracy and arrest the conspirators.

In early August 1960, Nasser's long arm dealt Hussein a heavy blow. Syrian agents planted a powerful bomb in the desk drawer of Jordanian Prime Minister Hazza el-Majali. The prime minister and nine of his ministers were killed and many other officials injured. King Hussein wanted to take revenge on Syria. To do so, however, he needed his Israeli flank protected. A few days after Majali's assassination, the Jordanian liaison to the Israeli-Jordanian mixed armistice commission, Colonel Daud, informed his Israeli counterpart, Colonel Jerry Braverman, that King Hussein wanted a meeting with Israel "at the most senior level." The director of the Mossad, Isser Harel, suggested to Ben-Gurion a meeting with the Jordanian monarch at the shah's palace in Tehran. Before committing himself to such a meeting, Ben-Gurion wanted to know its purpose. He asked General Chaim Herzog, then chief of military intelligence, to meet with King Hussein's emissary. On August 14, 1960, Herzog met at Mandelbaum Gate in Jerusalem with Colonel Emile Jmeian, the king's military secretary. Jmeian was among the Jordanian officers who had fought against Israel in the 1948 war, and he subsequently published a book on the Jordanian army's role in that war. Herzog was stunned to learn from Jmeian King Hussein's intentions. The king wanted to invade Syria, but wanted an Israeli promise not to use this event in order to occupy the West Bank. He also wanted Israeli intelligence on Syria and on its troop deployments along the Syrian-Jordanian border.

"I hope that it is clear to you by now that Jordan's existence as a sovereign state, under the rule of His Majesty, is a matter of great concern to Israel," Herzog told Colonel Jmeian. The Jordanian envoy replied: "His Majesty appreciates Israel's position. We want you to know that Jordan is strong and the army is loyal to His Majesty. Syria cannot defeat us militarily. Our problem, however, is the Egyptian-Syrian subversion. We would appreciate it very much if Israel could help us combat this UAR subversion."

Herzog promised Jmeian to supply Jordan with the necessary intelligence. As for King Hussein's intention to invade Syria, Herzog said that he would report the subject to Ben-Gurion. Needless to say, Hussein's idea did not arouse much enthusiasm in Israel. According to Israeli intelligence estimates, the Jordanian army was no match for the combined Egyptian-Syrian army. With the subversive support of Iraq, Hussein was likely to lose his throne. At Ben-Gurion's request, both the United States and Great Britain persuaded the king to abandon his risky adventure.[25]

The Herzog-Jmeian meeting was the first high-level contact with Jordan, and it eventually led to the institutionalization of high-level military and political meetings between the two countries. This trend became evident one year later, after the dissolution of the UAR. On September 28, 1961, Syrian army officers staged the sixth military coup in that country's history. They dissolved the union with Egypt and restored Syria's independence. This development overturned the regional balance of power. Israel, Jordan, Turkey, and Iran gained a weakened neighbor on their borders. Egypt lost its foothold in the Fertile Crescent (Syria, Iraq, and Jordan), and Damascus became once again a theater of the battle for influence between Cairo and Baghdad. King Hussein lost his fear of Nasser, although he continued to face a hostile Syria. In the spring of 1962, Israeli air force planes intercepted two Syrian MIGs that tried to shoot down King Hussein's plane on its way from Amman to Europe via Syria. In August 1962, General Meir Amit, who succeeded General Herzog as chief of military intelligence in December 1961, met again with Colonel Emile Jmeian, at the no-man's-land near Latrun on the old Tel Aviv–Jerusalem highway. Amit and Jmeian discussed ways to combat Egyptian and Syrian subversion against Jordan. Amit suggested holding regular meetings between the chiefs of the Israeli and Jordanian military intelligence services. Jmeian, however, was not authorized to accept such a proposal. He suggested instead holding irregular meetings, as the need arose. This cautious Jordanian approach was explained at the time by the fact that in August 1962, Jordan and Saudi Arabia signed an agreement for military cooperation between them. Like King Hussein, the Saudi king too became a target of Nasser's subversion. Egypt accused Saudi Arabia of financing the military coup that put an end to the Egyptian-Syrian union.

The Jordanian approach was to change dramatically one month later. In September 1962, a Yemenite army officer, Colonel Abdullah Sallal, deposed his monarch, Imam El-Badr, and declared Yemen a republic. Hoping that Yemen would replace his lost "Syrian province," Nasser rushed to Sallal's assistance. He sent to Yemen a large army contingent to help defeat the royalist tribes that had received Saudi financial and military assistance. It was not long before Nasser realized that Yemen had become Egypt's Vietnam.

King Hussein was obviously pleased to see Nasser's subversive ability reduced because of his involvement in Yemen. Despite the defection to Cairo of the commander of the Jordanian air force, King Hussein felt relieved from the double pressure of Egypt and Syria. He was now prepared to deepen his contacts with Israel. In a meeting with the Israeli minister of police, Moshe Shahal, and his adviser Moshe Sasson, on February 19, 1996, King Hussein said that in his effort to conclude a peaceful settlement with Israel, he was guided by his grandfather's legacy. King Abdullah had wanted to sign a peace treaty with Israel soon after the 1948 war. Abdullah used to tell his Israeli interlocutors, among whom was Moshe Sasson's father, Elias, that "if there is no peace, there will be war, and another war and another war. Israel would always emerge as the victor."[26]

At the beginning of 1963, a series of events demanded Israel's and Jordan's immediate attention. On February 8, a group of Iraqi army officers led by Colonel Abdul Salam Aref and supported by the Iraqi Ba'ath Party staged a military coup in Baghdad. The Ministry of Defense, where President Abdul Karim Qassem resided, was bombed from the air. Qassem was killed in this thirtieth attempt on his life and his fifty-five-month tyranny came to an end. A month later, on March 8, a Ba'athist group in Damascus took over the Syrian government as well. The new Syrian regime sought an immediate cooperation with Iraq and began negotiations for a triple federal union with Egypt and Iraq.

The tripartite "unification agreement" was signed in Cairo on April 17 and roused great enthusiasm in the Arab world and many fears in Israel and Jordan. The renewed recognition of Nasser's leadership put the remaining pro-Western Arab regimes in danger. Riots broke out in Jordan, especially in East Jerusalem and Nablus. Police stations were stormed, Jordanian flags were burned, and thousands of demonstrators urged King Hussein to join the new tripartite union. The survival of the monarchy was again in doubt. The concept of Arab unity, so seriously damaged by the dissolution of the UAR, now gathered new momentum and gave ideological depth to the military strength on the banks of the Nile, the Tigris, and the Euphrates.

In personal letters to President Kennedy and to friendly leaders in Europe, Turkey, Iran, and Ethiopia, Ben-Gurion urged those leaders to help save Hussein's throne. He warned that Egypt's Nasser was liable to be tempted into adventures in less protected areas, such as the Persian Gulf principalities. Kennedy did not share Ben-Gurion's concern. European leaders too believed that Ben-Gurion overreacted. Indeed, a few weeks later, King Hussein was able to suppress the riots and the triple federal union was dissolved. By August 1963, Egypt, Syria, and Iraq were again at one another's throats.

Ben-Gurion's panicked letters were his last initiative as prime minister. As a result of an internal struggle within the ruling Mapai Party, he was forced to resign on June 16, 1963. Levi Eshkol, the finance minister, became the new premier. Eshkol appointed Abba Eban as deputy prime minister; Golda Meir remained in the Foreign Ministry, while Shimon Peres retained his position as deputy defense minister. On January 1, 1964, Eshkol appointed Yitzhak Rabin as the new chief of staff.

The summer of 1963 witnessed a dramatic development in Israeli-Jordanian relations. Relieved from Nasser's immediate threat and concerned about the nature of the Ba'athist regimes in Damascus and Baghdad, King Hussein sought to expand the informal security cooperation with Israel by adding a political dimension to it. Through his British-Jewish dentist, Dr. Emmanuel Herbert (Hertzberg), Hussein communicated to Israel his desire to meet with a trusted emissary of Prime Minister Eshkol. Hussein's mother, Queen Zein, was at that time in London. When Ephraim (Eppy) Evron, the Israeli deputy chief of mission (DCM), tried to contact her in order to set a time and place for the meeting with her son, Queen Zein—or the "Niece" as she was code-named in secret Israeli diplomatic dispatches—surprised Evron by saying that there was no sense in meeting with her. King Hussein (code-named "Prince Charles") was already in London, and he would be pleased to meet with the Israeli emissary in the British capital. Prime Minister Eshkol designated Ambassador Jacob Herzog— his political adviser and the brother of General Herzog—to meet with the king.

On September 24, 1963, Hussein and Herzog met at Dr. Herbert's London clinic, at 21 Devonshire Street. That was the first Israeli-Jordanian meeting at a political level. Herzog assured the king that Israel considered an independent Jordan an Israeli "strategic asset." As a gesture of goodwill, Herzog was authorized by Eshkol to promise Hussein continuing cooperation in the field of intelligence.

After a long review of the situation in the region, King Hussein expressed concern about President Kennedy's efforts to open a dialogue with Nasser. "Kennedy is trying to help America's enemies in the Arab world," the king told Herzog. One of the important subjects discussed in this first meeting in London was the problem of water resources. In the early fifties, President Eisenhower had sent a special envoy, Eric Johnston, to the Middle East to recommend the sharing of the waters of the Yarmuk and Jordan Rivers between Israel, Syria, and Jordan. Israel accepted Johnston's plan but the Arabs rejected it. Ignoring Arab objections, Israel laid a national water carrier from the upper Galilee to the Negev, intending to take its share of water according to Johnston's plan. King Hussein told Herzog that he too would take his share of water according to Johnston's plan, but in order not to antagonize Syria, he wouldn't announce his decision publicly. Hussein thanked Israel for its willingness to share intelligence estimates with him, but he also wanted Israeli assistance in securing urgent American financial aid.[27]

Prime Minister Eshkol was thrilled by Herzog's report. Golda Meir was in New York, attending the UN General Assembly. Eshkol asked Evron to travel to New York and report to Meir about the Hussein-Herzog discussion. He recommended that Israel support Jordan's request for American financial assistance. Indeed, while at the UN, Golda Meir met with Secretary of State Dean Rusk and explained to him the importance of helping Jordan financially. Rusk was willing to support King Hussein's request. In the meantime, however, President Kennedy was assassinated and the newly sworn-in President Johnson needed some time to reorganize his administration before he was able to turn to foreign policy matters.[28]

In early 1964, the water problem threatened to explode. Syria was pushing the Arab world into war with Israel and had submitted to the Arab League in Cairo a detailed plan for the diversion of the Jordan River sources, on the Golan Heights. Prime Minister Eshkol said that "water is like blood in our veins." He warned Syria that any attempt to divert the Jordan would be considered by Israel a casus belli.

Nasser considered the Syrian plan to be a trap. If he supported water sharing according to Johnston's plan, he would be accused by the Ba'athist regime in Damascus of "collaborating" with Israel. On the other hand, if he supported the Syrian plan, he would give Israel an excuse to launch a preemptive war against Egypt and Syria. In an effort to gain time and to seek Arab consensus, Nasser invited the Arab heads of state to meet in Cairo, January 13–17, 1964. Representatives of thirteen countries—nine of them heads of state, including the kings of Saudi Arabia, Jordan, and Morocco—attended the Arab summit. While the summit rejected Syria's call for an all-out war against Israel, it nevertheless adopted three important decisions:

- To divert only the Syrian tributaries of the Jordan River, which would deprive Israel of half the quantity of water that it was entitled to receive according to Johnston's plan.

- To form a unified Arab command, headed by General Ali Ali Amer of Egypt, in order to prepare the Arab armies for a future war with Israel.

- To establish the Palestine Liberation Organization (PLO), under the chairmanship of Acre-born attorney Ahmed Shukeiry, and to recruit volunteers to the Palestine Liberation Army (PLA). Egypt and Iraq had already formed their own Palestinian units, in the Gaza Strip and in Baghdad, and an effort was being made to persuade King Hussein to recruit Palestinians in Jordan as well.[29]

It was against this background that King Hussein met again in London, on May 2, 1964, with the Israeli emissary, Jacob Herzog. The king was obviously alarmed by the summit's decisions, especially those concerning the PLO and the PLA. Hussein gave Herzog the clear impression that he would never allow a Palestinian military force to operate in his kingdom. Israel supported this Jordanian approach. On May 15, 1964, the American embassy in Tel Aviv cabled the State Department in Washington that Israel was willingly fulfilling the duty of "Jordan's guardian" and one could assume that Israel would react forcefully against any change in the status quo in Jordan.[30]

Despite this muted opposition to the Cairo summit's decisions, on May 28, 1964, at the Intercontinental Hotel in East Jerusalem, King Hussein opened the first Palestine Convention that approved the establishment of the PLO. Three months later, on September 1, 1964, the first Palestine National Council (the Palestine parliament-in-exile) was elected in Jerusalem and adopted the Palestine Covenant, which denied Israel's right to exist. The very fact that Hussein participated in the creation of an organization that he opposed showed how narrow was his margin of maneuver. His hope to control the organization, and especially the demagogue Shukeiry, was soon to be dashed. A second Arab summit in Alexandria, in September 1964, confirmed the creation of the PLA and asked King Hussein to double the size of his army. The Jordanian monarch was in no mood to comply with this recommendation. Doubling the size of his army meant increasing considerably the number of Palestinian soldiers. He had no intention of taking this risk.

The decisions of the Alexandria summit were at the center of the third secret meeting between King Hussein and Jacob Herzog, in London, on December 19, 1964. In view of Hussein's concerns about the stability of his country, Herzog suggested a meeting between the monarch and Prime Minister Eshkol. Hussein refused. His situation was very precarious, and he could not afford to complicate it further by meeting the prime minister of Israel.

King Hussein associated the United States with his concerns. He told Washington that he urgently needed to strengthen his army. He was under tremendous pressure from Nasser to turn to Moscow in the event the United States refused to supply him with additional arms and military equipment. President Johnson was alarmed by this report. The Egyptian, Syrian, and Iraqi armies were already equipped with Soviet arms. Adding Jordan to Moscow's clients would constitute a net political gain to the Soviet Union and would create a new situation in the Middle East. Neither Jordan nor the United States wanted to see such a development.

In February 1965, President Johnson sent Ambassador Averill Harriman and Robert Commer to Jerusalem to inform Eshkol of his intention to sell Jordan one hundred M-48 tanks and twelve F-104 jets. In order to sweeten the pot, Johnson agreed to sell to Israel better tanks and a squadron of A-4 Skyhawk planes. In a meeting with Eshkol, Abba Eban, Shimon Peres, and Chief of Staff Yitzhak Rabin, Harriman explained Johnson's reasons for responding positively to King Hussein's request. A Jordanian army equipped with Soviet arms would create a situation where Soviet arms and experts would be deployed in the West Bank and in East Jerusalem. This could add substantial Soviet support to the Palestinians. Did Israel want this to happen?

Johnson's request placed Israel in an agonizing dilemma. The supply of military equipment to Arab countries was always a sensitive security problem for Israel. Deployment of American-made tanks in the West Bank would increase the threat to Israel's "narrow waist" between Tul-Karm and the city of Netanya. Israel had always used its influence in the United States and in Europe to prevent such a supply. Harriman, however, presented Israel with a totally new problem, which required new solutions. The "Averill mission" brought to the forefront the first conceptual conflict between Shimon Peres and Yitzhak Rabin. The Israeli deputy defense minister was a Europe-oriented politician, and he relied mostly on the French arms industry. He did not want to risk this arms channel by accepting American arms. In contrast, Rabin saw great opportunities for Israel in shifting gradually to the American arms market. Furthermore, as chief of staff, Rabin did not want Soviet arms and experts in the West Bank. He recommended accepting Johnson's decision to sell Jordan the small quantity of arms it needed. Without waiting for Israel's formal reply, Harriman continued his journey to Jordan to inform King Hussein of Johnson's decision. Since Peres was the only dissenting voice in Israel, Harriman took Israel's positive answer as granted.

He was wrong. On February 9, 1965, one day after Harriman's departure, I published in *Maariv* the details of Harriman's mission to Jerusalem. I did not expect the political storm that followed. On February 10, I became the subject of a criminal investigation by a government-appointed commission of inquiry headed by the attorney general and including a senior security service official and the deputy director general of the Foreign Ministry. This was the first case in Israel's history of a journalist's being interrogated under oath by a government-appointed commission with full judicial and criminal powers. In three different sessions, I was repeatedly asked about the source of my information and whether it was leaked to me by Peres or his aides in the Defense Ministry. The commission reached a dead end. Neither I nor my editors were prepared to divulge the source of my information.

As it turned out, the commission's inconclusive results did not really matter. Prime Minister Eshkol took this unique and unusual move not because he thought the publication would derail the arms transaction with Jordan, but only to convince President Johnson that he was determined to avoid further leaks. As to the source of my information, more than a year later, in June 1966, Prime Minister Eshkol told me: "You must be very naive to believe that I didn't know that you got your information from Peres's office." I was with Eshkol on his flight from Tehran to Tel Aviv after he had met secretly, on June 2, 1966, with Iranian Prime Minister Amir Abbas Hoveida. The prime minister said: "Both Harriman and I agreed that since all the participants in the meeting, except Peres, supported Johnson's proposal, then the only person who had an interest to leak the story was Peres." I remained silent and refrained from any comment.

The end of this episode was very positive for Israel. In a second meeting with Eshkol and his team, on February 25, 1965, Ambassador Harriman said that the "U.S. government recognizes that Israel's concerns over any reequipping or expansion of Jordan's forces, especially armor, depends partly on their location. Therefore, the U.S. government will seek a firm, private undertaking that Jordanian armor not be deployed to the West Bank of the Jordan River, provided that Israel—under no circumstances—divulge its knowledge of any such undertaking of the U.S.G. efforts to achieve it."[31]

The U.S. decision to respond positively to King Hussein's request was vindicated by some alarming developments in the following weeks and months. On January 1, 1965, a Palestinian group little known at that time, El-Fatah, launched its first terrorist act against Israel, across the Lebanese border. The leader of the group, Yasser Arafat, promised many more attacks in the future. With the active support of Syrian intelligence, which provided training and logistical assistance, Arafat kept his promise.

Arafat's terrorist activity caused some divisions within the Arab world. While Egypt and Jordan opposed Arafat's actions, Syria endorsed them enthusiastically. Syrian support, however, was conditioned by El-Fatah's willingness to coordinate its operations with Syrian intelligence. On one occasion, when Arafat planned to blow up the Saudi oil pipeline TAPLINE on the Golan Heights without coordination with Syria, Syrian intelligence did not hesitate to put him under house arrest. Arafat fled to Beirut, where he was again arrested. Finally, because of the intervention of the Syrian chief of military intelligence, General Ahmed Sweidani, Arafat was released from his Lebanese jail, but the lesson he had learned was very clear: Syria was determined to control the Palestinian decision. This Syrian position remains valid to this date.

These divisions and infightings were at the center of the third Arab summit conference in Casablanca, in September 1965. The summit ended in total failure. The head of the Unified Arab Command, General Ali Ali Amer of Egypt, submitted a very bleak report to the Arab heads of state. He said that none of the Arab armies was capable of launching a war against Israel within the next three years. In order to complete the preparations for war against Israel, General Amer urged King Hussein to allow the deployment of Iraqi and Saudi troops in his country. Hussein knew that this was a red flag for Israel. He also knew that he could not admit publicly that he was unwilling to comply with Amer's recommendation. Therefore, he conditioned his acceptance of Amer's proposal on a formal Arab commitment to provide him with the necessary air cover. Amer's report, however, clearly indicated that none of the Arab air forces was capable of confronting Israel in the near future.

Amer's report was fully confirmed by events on the Syrian front. After the Syrians began diverting the Jordan River, the Israeli air force, in August 1965, destroyed all the mechanical equipment on the diversion site. The Syrian air force was simply unable to challenge the Israeli air force. As for Nasser, he was bogged down in Yemen and could not realistically undertake another military adventure against Israel.

On his way back from Casablanca, King Hussein made a short stopover in Paris for a meeting with French President de Gaulle and for a political discussion with Israeli Foreign Minister Golda Meir. This was the first meeting with an Israeli cabinet minister, and the encounter with Meir was very emotional. In the past, Meir had met on several occasions with Jordan's King Abdullah. Now she was face to face with his grandson. King Hussein fell into Meir's arms and said: "I am so glad to meet you, Madame Foreign Minister. I wish this meeting had taken place long before."

The Meir-Hussein meeting took place in a private apartment in Paris and was very relaxed. Meir had already received a preliminary intelligence report about the deliberations in Morocco. Discussing the Casablanca summit, Meir repeated the publicly stated Israeli policy that opposed the entry of any foreign troops to Jordan. She also said that Israel opposed the deployment of any sizable Jordanian armor units in the West Bank. King Hussein had his own reasons for accepting Meir's position: He had used the Israeli warning as a pretext for his refusal to allow the deployment of Saudi or Iraqi troops in his country.[32]

The year 1966 witnessed increased tension along the Israeli-Syrian border and a sharp conflict between Jordan and the PLO. In the spring of 1966, a pro-Soviet faction took control of the ruling Syrian Ba'ath Party and pledged a "popular war" against Israel. Under the leadership of the party's secretary general, Colonel Salah Jedid, the new Syrian team pledged more active support of Arafat's El-Fatah group. The chief of Syrian military intelligence, General Ahmed Sweidani, helped Arafat's agents infiltrate into Israel via Jordan. King Hussein saw in such a move a Syrian attempt to destabilize his country. Hussein's relations with Arafat's rival, the pro-Egyptian Ahmed Shukeiry, were also strained. Therefore, on July 16, 1966, the king broke all contacts with the PLO. In January 1967, Hussein went one step further: He closed the PLO's office in East Jerusalem.

Much has been said and written about the circumstances that led to the Six-Day War. Hussein knew quite well that Israel had no aggressive intentions against him. The Johnson administration too had repeatedly assured the king that Israel harbored no ill intentions against his country. However, since Hussein ignored all the messages conveyed to him and decided to engage in the 1967 war, Israel had no choice but to respond to his attacks. The result was disastrous: Jordan's army was defeated and Hussein lost control over the West Bank and East Jerusalem.

The Six-Day War created a new situation in the Middle East. For the first time since 1948, Israel was now in full control of the land that after the First World War was given by the League of Nations to Great Britain as a mandate to establish a Jewish homeland in Palestine. For Israel, however, the question now was not only territorial, but also demographic: how to deal with the large Palestinian population in the occupied territories. The national unity government, under the premiership of Levi Eshkol, devoted four days—June 15 to June 19—to studying this new situation. While the majority of the ministers were in favor of returning the West Bank to King Hussein in return for full peace, two very influential ministers, Moshe Dayan and Yigal Allon, had different views. Allon, for example, suggested the immediate annexation of East Jerusalem and Hebron, the establishment of a Palestinian autonomy in the densely populated areas of the West Bank, and the creation of an Israeli "security zone" in the Jordan Valley, so that it could serve as a buffer between the Palestine autonomy and Jordan. Toward the end of June, Allon submitted a detailed plan along those lines, known as the "Allon Plan." Although the plan was never officially approved, all subsequent Israeli governments were guided by it. Yitzhak Rabin was its most ardent supporter. Dayan opposed the plan but he also rejected the idea of returning the West Bank to Jordan.[33] On June 19, 1967, the Israeli government decided to annex East Jerusalem only, and to leave the issue of the West Bank and the Gaza Strip for further study.

It was against this background that on July 2, 1967, barely three weeks after the war, King Hussein and Eshkol's emissary Jacob Herzog met secretly in London. Hussein got wind of the exploratory discussions that Israel was conducting at that time with West Bank leaders. He wanted to avoid a situation whereby he would lose the West Bank permanently. Hussein expressed regret for his decision to join the war. He accused Egypt's Nasser of misleading him to believe that he was winning the war against Israel. However, when Herzog asked him if he was prepared now to sign a peace treaty with Israel, in return of most of the West Bank, the king answered evasively: "Yes, but I need more time to decide. I must move cautiously, together with the rest of the Arab world. . . ."[34]

Nevertheless, toward the end of July 1967, two Israeli government-appointed committees recommended to Eshkol preventing the creation of an independent Palestinian entity and continuing the negotiations with King Hussein.

Israel, however, was not the sole player in the West Bank. Soon after the war, Yasser Arafat infiltrated into the West Bank, via Jordan, and established a clandestine base in Nablus. While he was recruiting guerrillas to his El-Fatah group, his companions in Damascus—including Faruq Kadoumi and Abu Mazen—sent him alarming reports about a new attitude of the Syrian government. "We have not one single tank to defend Damascus," admitted General Sweidani, the Syrian chief of staff, who as chief of military intelligence was a strong supporter of Yasser Arafat and his group. Sweidani added: "Any guerrilla operation by El-Fatah in the West Bank would be perceived by Israel as being directed by the Syrian Ba'athist government and would serve as an excuse for an Israeli retaliation against Damascus. So, wait a little with your operations." Other senior Syrian officials warned: "If Arafat goes ahead with his plans to resume guerrilla operations against Israel, we will crush you."

Kadoumi and Abu Mazen asked Arafat to return immediately to Damascus to deal with this new situation. At the same time, the rope of the Israeli security services was slipping around Yasser Arafat's neck in the territories. On September 1, 1967, Israeli security agents arrived at Arafat's secret hiding place in Nablus just one hour after he fled to Jordan, on his way back to Damascus.

Shortly after the UN Security Council adopted Resolution 242, on November 22, Israel and Jordan resumed their secret negotiations. The Johnson administration supported this approach, but also expected official negotiations, under the auspices of the UN special envoy, Swedish Ambassador Gunnar Jarring. President Johnson and Secretary of State Dean Rusk made it clear to King Hussein, however, that Resolution 242 did not necessarily mean an Israeli withdrawal to June 4 lines.[35] Based on this U.S. interpretation of Resolution 242, the Israeli emissary, Jacob Herzog, met in November 1967 twice with King

Hussein in London. The purpose of the meetings was to verify to what extent King Hussein was prepared to accept a territorial compromise in the West Bank. At the end of the second meeting, it became clear that Hussein was too weak to accept any compromise along the lines of the Allon Plan. Hussein insisted on total Israeli withdrawal to the June 4 lines, including East Jerusalem.

Meanwhile, Arafat resumed his terrorist activity against Israel, from bases in Jordan. In retaliation, Israel staged in March 1968 the first major ground attack against the main El-Fatah base in Karameh. Because of Jordanian army intervention, both Israel and Jordan suffered heavy casualties. According to Israeli intelligence reports, Yasser Arafat did not participate in the fighting. The moment he saw the Israeli mechanized column approaching, he fled from the Karameh camp on a motorcycle.

In the face of growing tension between Israel and Jordan, the United States proposed to both Israel and Jordan that they accept the UN envoy Gunnar Jarring's idea of meeting under his auspices in Cyprus. Israel accepted Jarring's proposal. On April 16, 1968, King Hussein rejected it. Instead, the Jordanian monarch met secretly in London—and for the first time—with Foreign Minister Abba Eban, in the presence of Jacob Herzog. The meeting, held on May 27 at the private residence of King Hussein's dentist, Dr. Emmanuel Herbert, at 1 Langford Place, was also attended by Hussein's minister of the court, Zeid Rifai. Originally, Hussein had wanted to meet with Prime Minister Levi Eshkol. The prime minister, however, decided to send both Moshe Dayan and Abba Eban to meet with the king. Dayan refused. He told Eshkol that he was still uncertain whether a settlement with Jordan was preferable to a settlement with the Palestinians.[36] In his meeting with King Hussein, on May 27, Eban detailed Israel's three conditions for a settlement with Jordan:

- No return to the lines of June 4, 1967.

- A united Jerusalem, under Israel's sovereignty.

- Border modifications according to Israel's security needs.

Hussein gave Eban an evasive answer, but Rifai told the Israeli foreign minister that any peace between Israel and Jordan had to be "honorable." A settlement that did not include the return of the holy shrines in Jerusalem to King Hussein's custody was not honorable, and was therefore unacceptable. Nevertheless, Hussein did not close the door to further secret contacts with Israel. He only insisted that a future meeting would have to deal with substance and not just with principles for agreement.[37]

For that purpose, Prime Minister Eshkol on May 29, 1968, convened a meeting with Abba Eban, Moshe Dayan, and Yigal Allon. Eban reported that

King Hussein wanted a clear answer as to the parameters of a possible settlement. He proposed that Eshkol himself should meet with the king. Dayan and Allon opposed the idea. They stressed that before a decision was taken, the entire political committee of the Labor Party should discuss the matter and decide on the issues. Dayan and Allon argued that at that stage, it was still unclear what the best option for Israel was—a settlement with Hussein or a settlement with the Palestinians. Eshkol said that in his meetings with Palestinian leaders in the West Bank, they had all suggested an agreement with Jordan and also made it clear that they would not participate in any autonomy talks without King Hussein's permission. Dayan replied that in such a case, Israel should retain responsibility on security, water resources, and land in the West Bank and transfer the authority in other fields to King Hussein. Because of these differences in opinion, no decisions were taken in that meeting.

On July 3, 1968, Eshkol convened twelve members of his party's political committee, including Dayan, Eban, Allon, and Eliahu Sasson, a veteran expert in Middle Eastern affairs with rich experience in secret meetings with Arab leaders, to discuss the parameters for peace with Jordan. Jacob Herzog reported that Zeid Rifai, a confidant of Hussein's, had conveyed to him the message that Jordan would oppose any territorial compromise, whether it was based on the Allon Plan or any other Israeli plan. As a result, Eshkol concluded: "In such a case, there is no need for me to meet with Hussein. Just to satisfy my ego, it is not that important." However, all the participants agreed not to close any doors and to hold another meeting with Hussein as soon as possible.

On September 20, 1968, Eshkol convened the full political committee of the Labor Party in advance of a meeting with Hussein scheduled for September 27. This forum was selected in order to avoid a premature debate within the cabinet, of which Menachem Begin was a member, as part of the national unity government that was formed on the eve of the Six-Day War. Eshkol suggested that Dayan and Eban meet with King Hussein. Dayan again rejected the idea. He told the gathering: "I am the last man who is suited for such a meeting. . . . Small talk is not one of my strengths. After two minutes, I would want to talk business and I would tell him what are my ideas for a solution, and it would all go up in smoke."

In view of Dayan's rejection, Eshkol decided that Allon and Eban, together with Herzog, would meet with the king. The meeting on September 27 was held in London at Dr. Herbert's clinic. Eban opened by stating that it was a historic moment and that it was the intention of Israel to verify whether Hussein indeed wanted a peaceful settlement with Israel. Eban had a veiled threat: If the negotiations failed, Israel would try to settle with the Palestinians independently of Jordan.

King Hussein replied that it was his dream to achieve peace. However, for peace to be achieved, it should be honorable. "If peace will be based on Israel's armed power," the king said, "then there is no chance for a settlement and the entire region will be in constant danger of continued war. You can win many battles, but you cannot afford to lose one single war. So Israel is vulnerable too, and needs peace no less than the Arabs need it."

Eban then presented Israel's conditions for a settlement with Jordan:

- Contractual peace.

- Considerable border modifications and no return to prewar lines.

- Demilitarization of the West Bank.

- A united Jerusalem under Israel's sovereignty, with a religious status for Jordan in the Muslim holy shrines on Temple Mount.

Israel would allow Jordan free access to the Haifa port and would cooperate with Jordan in the field of tourism. Israel would also consider a corridor to serve as a territorial link between East Jerusalem and the autonomous West Bank.

King Hussein replied that he understood Israeli security concerns, but Israel should ask itself what is security? Is it a few kilometers, or the sense of security of the population? "If there is trust and confidence between our two nations," the king argued, "then there is security for both. But if there is no trust, then a few kilometers won't give you the security you need."

Zeid Rifai played the role of the "bad guy." He told Eban and Allon that the fact that King Hussein did not address himself specifically to the problem of East Jerusalem should not be interpreted as an acceptance of the Israeli position. On the contrary, Rifai said, Jordan insisted on total Israeli withdrawal, including from East Jerusalem. "For the peace to hold, it should be honorable. Therefore, we reject the Allon Plan and we consider it to be totally unacceptable," Rifai concluded.

Two days later, on September 29, Rifai submitted to Herzog a written memorandum containing Jordan's answers to Israel's proposals:

- Jordan proposed that a settlement with Israel should be based on Resolution 242 and be achieved under UN Ambassador Jarring's auspices.

- Jordan accepted the principle stated in the preamble of Resolution 242, which spoke about the inadmissibility of the acquisition of territory by force. This principle should apply to the issue of East Jerusalem as well. However, if security concerns required border modifications, these should be made on a reciprocal basis.

- In East Jerusalem, Jordan was ready to accept Israeli sovereignty over the Jewish holy places only. The Muslim and Christian holy places should return to Jordan's sovereignty. Jordan also accepted that the city of Jerusalem should have a special status that would guarantee free access to all religions.

- As for security, without going into the question of who started the war, Jordan felt that its own security, and not Israel's, was at stake. Therefore, Jordan should be in a position that would enable it to defend the Palestinians on the West Bank. Jordan also rejected Israeli demands for permanent military presence and for the unrestricted right of Jews to settle in the West Bank.

Rifai's memorandum reiterated Jordan's position that the Allon Plan was "totally unacceptable," and he concluded by saying: "His Majesty's ability to contribute to a peaceful settlement depends to a very large extent on his ability to show the Arab world that peace is honorable and that it was not imposed. Therefore, before any date for a new meeting with Israeli leaders is fixed, the Israeli government has to say if it would accept these principles."[38]

Thus, from 1968 on, King Hussein consistently held the position outlined in Rifai's memorandum. The Jordanian position aroused many doubts in Israel about Hussein's ability to reach an agreement with the Jewish state. Moshe Dayan, in particular, expressed doubts whether King Hussein could reach an agreement with Israel by himself, without Arab consent. During a discussion in the Labor Party's political committee, Abba Eban admitted that during his September meeting with King Hussein in London, the king had admitted that he was too weak to conclude a separate peace with Israel. Hussein recalled that he had been in East Jerusalem when his grandfather King Abdullah was murdered in 1951 by Palestinians. He did not want history to repeat itself with him. He suggested that any peace process should begin in negotiations between Israel and Egypt.

That was the point that interested Dayan most. He was now strengthened in his belief that there was no chance for a "Jordanian option" and that therefore the Israeli effort should be directed toward Egypt. Nevertheless, the Israeli official position remained based on the Jordanian option and the meetings with King Hussein continued. Indeed, one month later, in October 1968, King Hussein and his chief of staff, General Amer Khammash, met secretly in London with the Israeli chief of staff, General Haim Barlev, to discuss Israeli security concerns in the Jordan Valley. The meeting was inconclusive. In reply to Barlev's concern that the king would allow an Iraqi contingent to be deployed in the West Bank, Hussein replied that he was prepared to give Israel assurances that the West Bank would be demilitarized, but the West Bank, in its entirety, should return to Jordan's sovereignty.[39]

The inauguration of President Nixon's administration in January 1969 brought an important change in the U.S. modus operandi. Secretary Rusk had promoted an Arab-Israeli dialogue under UN auspices, but Secretary William Rogers sought to reach an American-Soviet understanding on the parameters for a settlement between Israel and the Arab countries. When this failed, Rogers submitted his own blueprint for a settlement in the Middle East. The "Rogers Plan" was immediately rejected by Israel, and the Arabs too were not very enthusiastic about it. Golda Meir, who had succeeded Eshkol as prime minister in the fall of 1969, saw in the Rogers Plan an American attempt to impose a solution in the Middle East.

Two events in September 1970 brought profound changes in the region and had a direct effect on the Arab-Israeli conflict:

- On September 30, Nasser died from a heart attack. On October 6, he was succeeded by Anwar Sadat.
- Following a civil war in Jordan, King Hussein expelled all PLO forces from his kingdom. They moved, via Syria, to Lebanon.

Nasser's death affected the regional balance of power and the relations between the United States and the Soviet Union, and the civil war in Jordan had an immediate effect on the Israeli-Jordanian relationship. The dramatic events in Jordan began to unfold in early June 1970. Following an attempt to curtail the Palestinian military presence in Amman, a radical group—the Popular Front for the Liberation of Palestine (PFLP), which is still led by Dr. George Habash—ambushed King Hussein's car on his way to Amman's airport. Hussein was not hurt. Assisted by Syria, the PFLP called Amman "Hanoi" (making the connection with the Vietcong's fight against the United States) and claimed that the road to Jerusalem went through Amman.

The real challenge to Hussein's authority came in September 1970. PFLP terrorists hijacked four civilian airplanes and directed them to a deserted airstrip in eastern Jordan. After lengthy deliberations, the hijackers moved the passengers to Amman and destroyed the planes. His authority badly shaken, King Hussein decided to act forcefully against the Palestinian armed groups in his country. He concentrated the best Bedouin units in his army and launched an all-out attack on the Palestinians' military bases. Iraq threatened to move against Hussein if he did not halt his attack on the Palestinians. Through the U.S. embassy in Amman, Zeid Rifai asked the Nixon administration to ask what Israel's reaction to such an Iraqi move would be.[40]

In a desperate effort to deal with the situation, King Hussein appointed a military government, headed by Colonel Daud. The new prime minister flew to Cairo, supposedly to ask for Nasser's assistance against Syria and Iraq. Instead, he defected from Cairo to Libya. On September 15, Yasser Arafat declared the city of Irbid the "capital of liberated northern Jordan" and appointed himself "governor of Irbid." In advance of overthrowing the monarchy, on September 18, Arafat established in Irbid the "Free Jordanian Government." That same day, Syrian tanks entered Jordan in support of the Palestinian military revolt.

Egypt being unwilling or unable to help him, King Hussein had no alternative but to ask for Israel's assistance. At the beginning of the crisis, Golda Meir was in the United States. In a meeting with President Nixon and his national security adviser, Henry Kissinger, she was asked not to intervene in the Jordanian crisis. Nixon said he was considering a U.S. military intervention. Accordingly, Golda and Ambassador Yitzhak Rabin went to New York, where the Israeli prime minister was to meet with Jewish leaders and then return to Israel. The Jordanian crisis was handled in Jerusalem, at that time, by acting Prime Minister Yigal Allon, in cooperation with Defense Minister Moshe Dayan. On September 20, King Hussein informed Nixon that Syrian tanks had entered the city of Irbid. He wanted Israeli air intervention to halt the Syrian advance. Nixon and Kissinger expressed grave concern about this serious development. Syria was a "Soviet client state" acting militarily against an American ally. Should King Hussein be overthrown, the entire region would be destabilized and U.S. credibility would be severely damaged. Kissinger met with the Soviet ambassador in Washington, Anatoly Dobrynin, and warned him of the "serious consequences" if the Syrian tanks did not withdraw immediately from Jordanian territory.

In the face of Congressional opposition to a U.S. military intervention in Jordan and at King Hussein's repeated urgent requests, Nixon reversed his initial position and sanctioned Israeli air force intervention against the Syrian troops in Irbid. While Golda Meir rushed back home, Ambassador Rabin returned immediately to Washington and coordinated with Kissinger the Israeli effort to save King Hussein's throne. At the instruction of Allon, Rabin asked for and received an American guarantee that should Egypt or the Soviet Union or both attack Israel, the United States would rush to Israel's defense. This was the first ever U.S. strategic guarantee to Israel, and it was not made public at the time. Considering King Hussein's request for air intervention, Moshe Dayan thought that an air strike was not sufficient. He wanted to send an armored column to force Syrian withdrawal from Irbid and the return of the Syrian troops to their country. Pending the immediate return of Golda Meir from the United States, the Israeli cabinet delayed a decision on Dayan's proposal. Instead, it ordered Israeli air patrols over Jordan and deployed Israeli tanks along the Syrian and Jordanian borders. Kissinger's warning to the Soviet Union and the Israeli troop movements were sufficient. Syrian Defense Minister

Hafez Assad ordered the withdrawal of the Syrian tanks from Jordan. Assad also refused to allow any Syrian air activity against the Israeli air patrols over Jordan.[41]

While King Hussein's throne had once again been saved, it is interesting here to examine the positions taken by some of the Israeli ministers concerning the Jordanian crisis. King Hussein became aware of these deliberations, and they eventually affected his relationship with both Yitzhak Rabin and Shimon Peres. Golda Meir, the overwhelming majority of the Israeli cabinet, and Ambassador Rabin in Washington were determined to rush to King Hussein's assistance and help him defeat the combined attack of the Syrians and the Palestinians. In contrast, Shimon Peres opposed any Israeli intervention in support of King Hussein. He said: "We should refrain from any intervention in Jordan. The Hashemite Kingdom is closer today to a collapse than at any time in the past. Should this happen and a Palestinian state be established in Amman, I would not shed any tears."[42]

This was not the first time that Peres had spoken in favor of replacing King Hussein by a Palestinian regime. In May 1963, when Egypt, Syria, and Iraq were negotiating a new federation, Peres, then deputy defense minister, suggested to Ben-Gurion "crowning" an Israeli Arab Quisling as king of Jordan. In his diaries, Ben-Gurion wrote: "Shimon [Peres] suggested to me that should there be a change in Amman, we should not only take Mount Scopus [in Jerusalem], but also crown an Israeli Arab as the new king of Jordan. He, in turn, would negotiate with us a peace treaty."[43] Ben-Gurion rejected Peres's proposal.

Shortly afterward, Ben-Gurion resigned and Levi Eshkol, the new Israeli prime minister, aligned himself with the American position, which considered an independent Jordan, under the Hashemite rule, as vital to the regional stability of the Middle East. King Hussein, however, never forgot this Peres position. Although he continued to deal with Peres in his various functions, Hussein's attitude toward him was always that of respect combined with profound suspicion. Many years later, King Hussein was to pay back Peres for his positions during his time of need. In early 1996, when Peres became prime minister after Rabin's assassination and needed a photo op with the king in Amman as part of his election campaign, Hussein refused to meet with him. Instead, Hussein sent his personal helicopter to Jerusalem to bring Peres's Likud rival, Benjamin (Bibi) Netanyahu, to a public meeting in Amman.

Israel's assistance to Jordan in September 1970 led to the resumption of secret high-level meetings between King Hussein and various Israeli leaders. In November 1970, Hussein and Allon met in the Arava, along the Israeli-Jordanian border, just north of Eilat and Aqaba.[44] Hussein was accompanied by Zeid Rifai and was very relaxed. He thanked Allon for Israel's assistance. He told the Israeli deputy prime minister that although he did not feel threatened anymore, after the expulsion of the PLO forces to Lebanon and after Nasser's death, he nevertheless realized that henceforth he would have to take into account the Palestinians' political aspirations. He added that in the event of an Israeli-Jordanian agreement, he would grant the Palestinians an autonomy in the West Bank, but not an independent state. Hussein called Yasser Arafat a liar and he said that he would never again trust him.

This was the first time that King Hussein had departed from his usual demand for a total Israeli withdrawal from the West Bank and spoken about the need to satisfy the Palestinians' political needs. Allon did not respond to this suggestion before it was discussed by the Israeli government. Instead, he suggested to Hussein the opening of formal peace negotiations, under the auspices of UN Ambassador Gunnar Jarring. The Jordanian monarch refused. He did not think that the time was yet ripe for such an initiative.[45]

The Hussein-Allon meeting was very important because of the implied admission that the "Jordanization" of the West Bank, as practiced since its annexation to Jordan in 1950, was not practical anymore. The Palestinians needed to have a political identity of their own. This conclusion was the basis for King Hussein's plan for a Jordanian-Palestinian federation, which was officially launched on March 15, 1972. Addressing his nation, Hussein proposed the establishment of the "United Arab Kingdom," comprising two autonomous regions—one in the West Bank and the other in the East Bank of the Jordan River. The plan was immediately rejected by the PLO as an attempt to undermine the Palestinians' political aspirations.

Hussein's "federative" formula caught Israel by surprise, and Golda Meir rejected it outright. The plan was the main subject of discussion between the king and Meir on March 21, 1972. Golda thought that a plan that directly affected Israel's control over the West Bank should have been presented to Israel before its publication. Without committing herself to any future solution, Golda wanted Hussein to promise that:

- Jordan would not allow the deployment of Iraqi or Syrian troops in the kingdom.
- Jordan would not join an "Eastern Front" coalition against Israel.
- Both Israel and Jordan would prevent the establishment of an independent Palestinian state.

In his reply to Golda Meir, King Hussein explained that it was in the interest of both Israel and Jordan to prevent a situation where Syria and Iraq controlled the Palestinian decision. His plan for a federation with the Palestinians was aimed at ascertaining Jordan's supremacy in the new political entity.

Hussein handed Meir a position paper in which he undertook to demilitarize the West Bank once a final settlement was reached between Israel and Jordan. He wanted Israel to use its influence in the West Bank to persuade the Palestinians to support the federation idea. That proved to be not very practical.

In reply to Meir's question if he was prepared to sign a peace treaty with Israel, independently of the Arab countries, Hussein gave an evasive answer. He wanted first a clear Israeli undertaking to withdraw from all the territories occupied in the Six-Day War, including East Jerusalem.

Despite this basic disagreement, Meir told King Hussein that she would ask Moshe Dayan to meet with him in order to verify if there was a possibility of persuading the Palestinians in the West Bank to support the federation idea.

By the time King Hussein and Dayan met, on June 29, 1972, it was already obvious that the federation plan was dead. Yasser Arafat rejected it, Presidents Sadat and Assad broke diplomatic relations with Jordan, and the other Arab countries gave the plan a cold shoulder. Dayan's discussion with Hussein was focused, therefore, on other subjects. Years later, in a public lecture at Bar-Ilan University, Dayan revealed that he had proposed to Hussein a nonaggression pact. The Jordanian monarch rejected the idea. Dayan said that Israel was prepared to commit itself to Jordan's defense in return for a Jordanian commitment not to join an anti-Israeli Arab coalition.[46] Hussein, however, rejected the proposal.

Dayan's proposal came at a time of dramatic changes in Middle Eastern diplomacy. In a clear departure from Nasser's pro-Soviet policy, President Sadat, in July 1972, put an end to Soviet military presence in his country. Within a very short period, more than fifteen thousand Soviet military advisers and technicians were sent back to Moscow. It was a terrible blow to Soviet diplomacy and prestige. Moscow, however, had no choice. It had to comply with Sadat's decision.

The Nixon administration was obviously pleased with this development, but because of the U.S. presidential campaign it could not take full advantage of it. Arab leaders who met with both President Nixon and Henry Kissinger and asked for American pressure on Israel were told to wait until after the presidential elections.

It was against this background that Golda Meir and King Hussein met again in London on November 19, 1972. By then, Nixon had been elected to a second term. Egypt, Jordan, and Saudi Arabia did not hide their expectations that Nixon would now formulate a new Middle Eastern policy that would put an end to the Arab-Israeli conflict.

In anticipation of such an initiative, Hussein presented to Golda Meir a four-point peace plan:

- Jordan would conduct direct negotiations with Israel.
- In return for minor border modifications, Israel would transfer to Jordan's authority both the West Bank and the Gaza Strip. A territorial corridor would link the two regions.
- Jordan opposed Israel's annexation of the Jordan Valley.
- Instead, Jordan was prepared to allow the installation of several Israeli military outposts in the West Bank and would also allow the continued presence of the Jewish settlements, under Jordanian sovereignty.

The Israeli prime minister did not reject Hussein's plan in toto. She suggested dropping the issue of the corridor for the time being and concentrating on other elements of an agreement. She wanted a clear Jordanian commitment that after the Israeli withdrawal, the West Bank would be totally demilitarized. Israeli settlements would not be dismantled, and parts of the unpopulated areas in the West Bank, especially in the Jordan Valley, would remain under Israel's control.

It was this last point that aroused Hussein's strongest objection. He suspected that Meir was trying to propose a "Mini Allon Plan" that he had already rejected several times in the past.

Shortly after his second inauguration, on January 20, 1973, Nixon engaged actively in Middle Eastern diplomacy. King Hussein, Golda Meir, and the Saudi foreign minister visited the White House. President Sadat sent his national security adviser, General Hafez Ismail, for secret meetings with Kissinger, but no breakthrough was reported. In February 1973, King Hussein told Kissinger that Israel had rejected Jordan's four-point peace plan.[47]

Meir's visit to Washington in February 1973 coincided with the end of Rabin's ambassadorship and the appointment of Meir's trusted aide Simcha Dinitz as his successor. The visit was very successful, although it did not produce an immediate breakthrough. Preparing for Israel's parliamentary elections in October, the Israeli prime minister was not in a position to offer meaningful concessions to Israel's Arab neighbors. She preferred to wait until after the elections. President Sadat would not wait. The countdown to the Yom Kippur War began.

In the absence of any progress in the efforts to start a peace process, future secret meetings between Golda Meir and King Hussein dealt mostly with economic development projects. Among other plans, Israel and Jordan explored agricultural development projects in the Jordan Valley, joint extraction of potassium from the Dead Sea, Israeli assistance in recruiting foreign investments in Jordan, and low-cost housing projects in Amman. By that time, Hussein's relationship with Meir was warm and trustful. Unlike his grandfather King Abdullah, who had some difficulties in dealing with a woman, the British-educated Hussein had no such inhibitions. He liked Meir's directness and common sense and saw in her a figure of "mother." He was also impressed by her simplicity.

On May 9, 1973, Hussein met with Meir at a security installation north of Tel Aviv. This was the first time that the king had come to Israel. Other visits were soon to follow. Hussein came by helicopter to an airstrip north of Jerusalem and there boarded an Israeli helicopter that brought him to Tel Aviv. Because of the need to maintain secrecy, there were no waiters in attendance. Meir's most trusted aide, Lou Kedar, prepared the tea, and Meir served it. The contrast between Hussein's regal way of life and her simple one struck him. Hussein told her: "I have never been served by a prime minister." She replied instantly: "And I had never had the honor of serving a king."

Hussein complained to Meir that he was having difficulties in resettling the Palestinian refugees on the eastern side of the Jordan Valley. In the king's presence, Golda called Los Angeles and spoke with her friend and admirer Lew Boyar, a wealthy American Jewish builder and entrepreneur. "Lew," Golda Meir said, "I have with me a friend who might need your assistance. He needs a plan for a large low-cost building project." Boyar nearly fell off his chair when he heard who Meir's friend was. The next day, Boyar flew to Amman, and after meeting with King Hussein, he traveled to the Jordan Valley and inspected the development region. Boyar's plan was never executed because of lack of funds. Instead, Hussein undertook several smaller building projects that suited his needs and financial abilities.

Meir and Hussein met again in London on August 6, 1973. The most important meeting in 1973, however, was one held on September 25 at the security base north of Tel Aviv. The king went to Israel ten days after he had met in Cairo with both Sadat and Assad. As part of their preparations for the Yom Kippur War, Sadat and Assad made some goodwill gestures toward Hussein, hoping to enlist his support in due time. The presidents of Egypt and Syria did not share their secret with the king, although his intelligence told him about Syrian troop deployments on the Golan Heights that could indicate offensive intentions. Under the guise of military maneuvers, Egypt too was completing its concentration of forces along the Suez Canal. On September 9, Sadat met in Cairo with Yasser Arafat and his deputy, Salah Khalaf (Abu Iyad), and told them about his intention to go to war against Israel "very soon." A Lebanese newspaper quoted Arafat as predicting "a major Egyptian offensive, aimed at forcing the United States to apply a strong pressure on Israel."[48] Hussein did not tell Meir what he did not know, namely that Egypt and Syria were about to launch a coordinated war against Israel on two fronts. He sensed, however, growing tension in the region, and there were troop concentrations along Israel's borders. Hussein warned Meir that the stalemate was dangerous and could not continue. In the absence of negotiations, war would become inevitable. Despite the Israeli parliamentary elections in October, Hussein urged Meir to initiate a peace move as soon as possible.

In her meeting with Hussein, Golda Meir was accompanied by two senior army officers, one from the operations branch and the other from military intelligence. They interpreted Hussein's warning differently. The operations officer saw "nothing new" in the Syrian troop deployments on the Golan Heights. Israeli reconnaissance planes had detected these deployments in the last few days. In contrast, the intelligence officer suspected that a coordinated Egyptian-Syrian attack was possible.

Golda Meir was alarmed by Hussein's warning. Immediately after the king's departure, she phoned Moshe Dayan and told him about her discussion with Hussein. Dayan was not surprised. A day earlier, on September 24, the general staff had discussed the possibility of a limited Syrian military operation on the Golan Heights. One intelligence estimate said that President Assad could be tempted to launch short-range Frog missiles in the direction of Tiberias and medium-range Scud missiles in the direction of Tel Aviv. In light of Hussein's warning, Dayan ordered the chief of staff, General David (Dado) Elazar, to convene the general staff for another emergency meeting to discuss the situation on the Golan Heights. However, both General Elazar and the chief of military intelligence, General Eli Zeira, saw "nothing new" in Hussein's warning.[49]

The Yom Kippur War on October 6 created a new situation in the Middle East. Despite their initial military successes, Syria ended the war totally defeated, while Egypt could rightly claim a "half victory." When Henry Kissinger responded positively to Moscow's urgent intervention and arranged a cease-fire on October 21, the Israeli army was only thirty-two kilometers from Damascus and 101 kilometers from Cairo. Despite Israel's inability to dislodge the Egyptians from the solid bridgehead that they had established on the eastern side of the Suez Canal, Israeli troops crossed into Egyptian territory, encircled the Egyptian Third Army in the city of Suez in the south, and moved rapidly in the direction of Cairo in the north. It was due only to the strong American pressure that the Israeli army did not destroy the Egyptian Third Army and allowed food and water to be supplied to the besieged Egyptian soldiers.

Despite his bitter experience in the Six-Day War, when he lost East Jerusalem and the West Bank, King Hussein sent one armored brigade to the assistance of the Syrians on the Golan Heights. In one short battle, on October 16, the Jordanian brigade lost twenty-two tanks. Nevertheless, Hussein continued to send reinforcements of artillery and mechanized infantry battalions to the Syrian front.

For a short while, and in advance of the Geneva Peace Conference, held under the joint auspices of the United States and the Soviet Union, the United States tried to verify if there was a way of associating the Palestinians in the peace process. At the recommendation of Morocco's King Hassan, a former CIA official, General Vernon Walters, met in Rabat on November 3, 1973, with Khaled el-Hassan, one of the PLO founding fathers. This was the first high-level contact between the United States and the PLO. When asked what Arafat's conditions for joining the peace process would be, Khaled el-Hassan replied: dumping King Hussein and incorporating Jordan in a Palestinian state.

Needless to say, such a position prevented a U.S.–PLO dialogue for many years. Before and after a brief session of the Geneva Peace Conference, Kissinger negotiated the separation-of-forces agreements between Israel, Egypt, Syria, and Jordan. On January 19, 1974, King Hussein submitted to Kissinger his proposal for a separation-of-forces agreement with Israel. It called for Israeli withdrawal from the Jordan Valley. The Jordanian proposal was discussed in a secret meeting on January 26 between Meir and Dayan and King Hussein and Zeid Rifai. Meir and Dayan rejected Hussein's proposal. They suggested instead Israeli withdrawal from the city of Jericho only and free Jordanian access to the major Palestinian cities in the West Bank. Hussein rejected Israel's counterproposal. When Dayan asked what Jordan's "final border" in the West Bank would be, Rifai answered that they would be the pre-1967 lines. Rifai added that Jordan was prepared to accept a phased Israeli withdrawal, but the Jewish settlements in the West Bank would have to be dismantled and no Israeli military installations would be allowed to remain in the territories.[50]

This hardened Jordanian position was a clear departure from past positions. In his four-point plan submitted to Golda Meir in London on November 19, 1972, King Hussein had agreed to the continued presence of Israeli settlements in the West Bank, under Jordanian sovereignty. Hussein had also agreed to Israeli military outposts in the territories. After the Yom Kippur War, however, the general Arab perception was that Israel had weakened and hence the Arabs could harden their positions.

On March 7, 1974, Meir and Dayan made another unsuccessful attempt to persuade King Hussein and Zeid Rifai to accept a limited Israeli withdrawal from the city of Jericho. Hussein insisted on total Israeli withdrawal from the entire Jordan Valley, as a "down payment" for a phased withdrawal from all the territories, including East Jerusalem. Unlike the previous meeting, which was businesslike and relaxed, the March meeting was tense and uncompromising. Hussein told Golda and Dayan that by their attitude they were only strengthening Yasser Arafat.

In the summer of 1974, two major developments occurred in both Israel and the United States. After the conclusion of the separation-of-forces agreement between Israel and Syria, President Nixon made a triumphal visit to Jerusalem, Cairo, and Damascus. Shortly after his return from the Middle East, Nixon resigned because of his involvement in the Watergate scandal. He was succeeded by Gerald Ford, who kept Henry Kissinger as his secretary of state.

In Jerusalem, Golda Meir resigned, because of her blunders on the eve of the Yom Kippur War. She was succeeded by Yitzhak Rabin, who appointed Yigal Allon as foreign minister and Shimon Peres as defense minister. The new Israeli team put a growing emphasis on relations with Egypt, although the idea of a separation-of-forces agreement with Jordan was still on the agenda of both Israel and the United States. Henry Kissinger, in particular, was known at the time to be favoring an agreement with King Hussein, as a means of containing Yasser Arafat's growing political power. Yigal Allon supported Kissinger in this approach. In a speech in the Knesset, on August 6, 1974, Rabin gave some details of Jordan's proposal for a separation-of-forces agreement. Rabin said: "Several foreign sources have revealed that Jordan proposed an Israeli withdrawal from a stretch of land, ten kilometers wide, along the entire Jordan Valley. The U.S. government communicated to us the same proposal. We cannot accept it. Should Jordan submit other proposals, we will study them. So far, the Israeli government has not received any new Jordanian proposals."[51]

The Jordanian proposal of Israeli withdrawal from the entire Jordan Valley was a subject of a thorough discussion between King Hussein and the Israeli "Troika"—Rabin, Allon, and Peres—on October 19, 1974, at the Israeli security installation north of Tel Aviv. This was the last effort by Hussein to snatch an Israeli concession before an Arab summit in Rabat recognized the PLO as the "sole representative" of the Palestinian people. Despite an intense American diplomatic effort to prevent such a decision, the Rabat summit practically denied the right of King Hussein to speak on behalf of the Palestinians.

Nevertheless, Rabin continued to believe that at a certain stage, Hussein would agree to reengage himself in Palestinian affairs and would agree to a territorial compromise in the West Bank. This Rabin belief was based in part on the king's willingness to continue his secret meetings with the Israeli leadership. In a meeting with Rabin, Allon, and Peres on May 28, 1975, Hussein complained that had Israel agreed to withdraw from the entire Jordan Valley, the Arab summit in Rabat would not have recognized the PLO as the sole representative of the Palestinian people. In a second meeting with the "Troika," Hussein told the Israeli leaders that President Sadat had initiated the Rabat decision on the PLO only because he wanted to make sure that any future negotiations with the Palestinians would be conducted with Egyptian participation. Rabin assured the king that despite the Rabat summit decisions, Israel still refused to recognize the PLO.

The high-level Israeli-Jordanian meetings came to a temporary halt with the election of Jimmy Carter as the new president and after the election of Menachem Begin in May 1977 as prime minister of Israel. In a clear departure from Kissinger's step-by-step diplomacy without Soviet participation, Carter promised the Palestinians a "homeland" and sought the reconvening of the Geneva Peace Conference, under the joint auspices of the United States and the Soviet Union. Begin and Dayan, each for his own reasons, preferred a settlement with Egypt over a settlement with Jordan. This Begin approach led eventually to Sadat's historic visit to Jerusalem, to the Camp David Accords, and to the Israeli-Egyptian peace treaty.

However, before stressing this Israeli shift from Jordan to Cairo, one should focus briefly on how Carter's Middle Eastern policy was perceived by both Cairo and Jerusalem. During the 1976 U.S. presidential campaign, little was known about Carter's views of the Arab-Israeli conflict. In his only major address on the Middle East, delivered on June 6, 1976, the presidential candidate asserted that the precondition for peace was a change in the Arab attitude toward Israel. He said: "This change of attitude on the part of the Arab states must be reflected in tangible and concrete actions, including, first of all, recognition of Israel, which they have not yet done; secondly, diplomatic relations with Israel; third, a peace treaty with Israel; fourth, open frontiers with Israel's neighbors; lastly, an end to the embargo and official hostile propaganda against the State of Israel."

In the same address, Carter was also very explicit on the Palestinian problem. He said: "There ought to be territories ceded for the use of the Palestinians. I think they should be part of Jordan and administered by Jordan. I think that half of the people of Jordan are Palestinians themselves and that would be my preference."

However, once Carter became president, his Middle Eastern policy was in sharp contrast to what he had said in the past, and he was generally perceived by Israel as openly hostile. Israeli suspicions about Carter's policies grew even stronger after he had met in Washington with Prime Minister Yitzhak Rabin. Despite his promise to Rabin to keep the discussion secret, Carter made it partly public. In a speech on March 16 at Clinton, Massachusetts, Carter spoke for the first time of a "homeland" for the Palestinians. After meeting with President Sadat and King Hussein in Washington, Carter also met with President Hafez Assad in Geneva. After the meeting, Carter described Assad as "a strong supporter in the search for peace in the Middle East." If those meetings meant anything to Israel, they meant that President Carter was courting the most radical elements in the Arab world—Syria's Assad and the PLO's Arafat.

When Menachem Begin won the general parliamentary elections in Israel, in May 1977, he appointed Moshe Dayan as his foreign minister and General Ezer Weizman as his defense minister. Carter, however, was quick to remind the new Israeli government that the United States stood firm on its insistence that Israel surrender most of the West Bank and that it intended to bring pressure to bear on the new Begin cabinet to compromise on that issue. Begin, however, was determined not to surrender the West Bank to Arab sovereignty. As for Dayan, while the new Israeli foreign minister was amenable to a territorial compromise in the West Bank, he did not believe that King Hussein was able to "deliver." Accordingly, both Begin and Dayan dissociated themselves from the "Jordanian option" and shifted their attention to Egypt. Indeed, when Secretary of State Cyrus Vance came for the first time to Israel in the summer of 1977, in advance of Begin's own trip to Washington, the new Israeli premier asked for American assistance in arranging a meeting between him and President Sadat. Dayan also asked King Hassan to help arrange a meeting between Begin and Sadat.

However, before the Moroccan reply was received, Dayan wanted to find out if there was any change in King Hussein's position. In a meeting with the Jordanian monarch on August 22, 1977, at Dr. Herbert's clinic in London, Dayan asked Hussein if there was any chance for a territorial compromise in the West Bank. Hussein said no. Dayan wrote briefly about this encounter in his memoirs. Hussein, he wrote, was very blunt about the Palestinians. He told Dayan: "I have no intention of imposing myself on the Palestinians. If they will turn to me and ask for my assistance, I will help. Otherwise, I can live without them."

On the issue of a territorial compromise, Hussein told Dayan: "As an Arab ruler, I can't give Israel even one grain of sand." He insisted on total Israeli withdrawal to the pre-1967 lines, "including even the road leading to Mount Scopus."[52] In a personal discussion, following the Camp David Accords, Dayan said that he returned from London totally convinced that King Hussein was not yet ripe for a settlement with Israel. He quoted Hussein as having told him that he could not suggest that even one single village in the West Bank come under Israeli rule, and that no agreement could be reached with Israel unless East Jerusalem was returned to Arab sovereignty.

Dayan's meeting with King Hussein in London in August 1977 was the last high-level meeting between Israel and Jordan throughout Begin's tenure as prime minister. These meetings were resumed in 1985, when Shimon Peres became the prime minister of a national unity government, in which Yitzhak Shamir served as foreign minister and Yitzhak Rabin as defense minister.

The Israeli-Egyptian peace treaty was the single most impressive foreign policy success of the Carter administration. This success, however, could not be repeated with Jordan. In the secret negotiations between Israel and Egypt—not via the United States—there was a subtle agreement between the two countries to keep Jordan out of the process. Hence, when Hussein traveled to London and waited for a telephone call from President Sadat inviting him to come and join the Camp David negotiations, the king was terribly insulted when Sadat instead suggested that they would meet in Morocco on Sadat's way back to Cairo. Deeply hurt, Hussein criticized the Camp David Accords and joined the "Rejectionist Front," together with Syria, Iraq, Yemen, and the PLO. Years later, Sadat explained why he did not want Jordan at Camp David. He told Yitzhak Rabin: "It did not take me long to reach the conclusion that I should never allow King Hussein to join me at Camp David. If he did, there would have never been an accord. As you know, the man [Hussein] is perceived in the Arab world as a 'black sheep.' The man in the street does not have respect for him. Therefore, I thought that should Hussein join me at Camp David, he would have upped the bargaining and we would have never reached an agreement."[53]

The establishment of a national unity government in Israel in the summer of 1984 revived American-Israeli efforts to involve Jordan in peace negotiations with Israel. Despite the weakening of the PLO after its expulsion from Lebanon in 1982 and despite Jordan's rejection of Reagan's peace plan in 1983, the new Israeli prime minister, Shimon Peres, believed that there was a possibility of involving the Palestinians in the peace negotiations between Israel and Jordan. In advance of such an effort, King Hussein and Yasser Arafat signed, on February 11, 1985, an agreement for diplomatic cooperation. The accord was to serve as a mechanism for the implementation of Saudi King Fahd's peace plan, as approved by an Arab summit in Fez, Morocco, in 1982. Fahd's plan was the Arab response to Reagan's plan.

The Hussein-Arafat accord called for the convening of an international peace conference, with the participation of the five permanent members of the UN Security Council. The conference was to serve as an "umbrella" for direct negotiations between Israel and its Arab neighbors. The Hussein-Arafat accord was a marriage of convenience between an unfriendly couple. For King Hussein, the agreement with Arafat was a tool for circumventing the Rabat summit resolutions, which denied him the right to speak on behalf of the Palestinians. For Arafat, the agreement with King Hussein was a prelude to his being accepted as a "full partner" in a peace process with Israel.

On July 19, 1985, Peres and Hussein met secretly in London and agreed on a procedure for the opening of formal peace talks between Israel and a Jordanian-Palestinian delegation. The meeting was held at the private residence of Lord Mishkon, a Jewish Labor activist. Hussein gave Peres a memorandum of eleven points, all aimed at strengthening Jordan's position in the West Bank. Among other requests, Hussein asked for the appointment of pro-Jordanian mayors in four West Bank cities, various tax cuts, improvement of health services, and containment of pro-PLO activity in West Bank learning institutions. Hussein also asked for a total freeze of all Jewish settlements in the West Bank.[54] Indeed, on November 17, 1985, Israel appointed pro-Jordanian Zafer el-Masri as the new mayor of Nablus. He did not live long. On March 2, 1986, he was gunned down by the PLO, outside his municipal office.

The main stumbling block in a possible agreement between Peres and Hussein was PLO participation in the peace talks. Hussein insisted on formal PLO participation. Peres, however, as head of a national unity government with the right-wing Likud Party, was committed not to negotiate with the PLO. In an effort to remove this obstacle, Peres sent former ambassador Simcha Dinitz to Washington to meet secretly with Secretary Shultz. Ambassador Meir Rosenne was not informed about Dinitz's mission. In a meeting at Shultz's home on August 5, 1985, Dinitz reported to the secretary about the Peres-Hussein meeting on July 19. He said that Peres would agree to PLO participation in a joint delegation with Jordan that would first meet in Washington with Assistant Secretary for Middle Eastern Affairs Richard Murphy. After the meeting, the PLO would announce its acceptance of Resolution 242 and would renounce terrorism. Publicly, Israel would denounce Murphy's meeting with the PLO in Washington. Once the protest was made, Peres would accept the new fact that had been established in Washington. Both President Reagan and Shultz rejected Peres's "procedural" move. They insisted that the United States would not meet with the PLO unless Arafat accepted Resolution 242, renounced terrorism, and accepted Israel's right to exist.[55]

After the rejection of Peres's proposal, Assistant Secretary Murphy undertook to work out a document outlining the parameters for a conference under international auspices, as an umbrella for direct negotiations between Israel and a joint Jordanian-Palestinian delegation. As far as Jordan was concerned, its position on this issue was clear. In a speech before the UN General Assembly on September 27, 1985, King Hussein said: "We are prepared to negotiate, under appropriate auspices, with the government of Israel, promptly and directly, under the basic tenets of UN Security Council Resolutions 242 and 338. . . . It is Jordan's position that the appropriate auspice is an international conference, hosted by the UN Secretary General, to which are invited the five permanent members of the Security Council and the parties to the conflict."[56] In advance of Murphy's effort, Peres met again with King Hussein, in London, in October 1985. Peres told the king that in his speech before the General Assembly, he would include a sentence accepting the principle of an "international opening" to direct negotiations between Israel and its Arab neighbors. Indeed, after Peres's speech, King Hussein was pleased with this slight change in Israel's position.[57]

After these two public speeches by King Hussein and Peres, Murphy spent some eighty days shuttling between Jerusalem, Amman, London, and The Hague, trying to work out a language about an "international opening" that Peres could sell to his Likud partner Foreign Minister Yitzhak Shamir. The final draft was worked out on January 7, 1986, in a meeting in London between Murphy and King Hussein. Murphy's tireless efforts, however, failed. Both Arafat and Shamir rejected Murphy's plan.

Deeply frustrated by Arafat's attitude, King Hussein announced on February 19, 1986, that he revoked the agreement he had reached with Arafat a year earlier on a joint Jordanian-Palestinian political action.[58] Hussein said that the

Palestinians should now decide if they wanted Yasser Arafat to continue to lead them.[59]

After revoking his agreement with Arafat, Hussein embarked on a tough anti-PLO policy. In March 1986, he met secretly near Strasbourg, France, with Defense Minister Yitzhak Rabin. Hussein wanted Rabin to contain hostile anti-Jordanian activity in the West Bank. On June 19, Hussein closed thirty-five El-Fatah recruiting centers in Jordan and expelled Khalil el-Wazir (Abu Jihad), Arafat's deputy, from Amman. In line with the king's request, Rabin instructed the head of the civil administration in the West Bank to help establish the "Villages League" as an alternative pro-Hussein leadership in the territories. The leaders of the Villages League were armed, and in an effort to enhance their position they were able to get for their supporters various "favors" from the Israeli administration.

In July 1986, Peres and Rabin met with King Hussein in London. Hussein wanted them to help him get a U.S. loan of $1.5 billion to finance a five-year development plan in the West Bank. In an interview with *Maariv,* Rabin said: "The policy of the Israeli government is to strengthen Jordan's position in the West Bank and to undermine Arafat's prestige among the Palestinians."[60] All these efforts, however, did not alter the pro-PLO sentiments among the Palestinians.

In April 1987, Peres—now foreign minister under Shamir—made a last serious effort to work out a formula with King Hussein that would enable direct negotiations between their countries, under appropriate international auspices. Peres and Hussein met on April 11, 1987, at Lord Mishkon's home in London. Peres was accompanied by Yossi Beilin and the deputy director of the Mossad, Ephraim Halevy. King Hussein was accompanied by Zeid Rifai. Peres wrote in his memoirs that the mood was very relaxed. Lord Mishkon cooked the luncheon, and King Hussein suggested to Peres after the meal that they both wash the dishes.[61]

During the discussion, Peres proposed yet another formula for an international conference. Zeid Rifai took notes and wrote down every word. The draft did not mention the PLO, but said that Palestinians who accept Resolution 242 and renounced terrorism could participate in a joint Jordanian-Palestinian delegation. This ambiguous language served both sides. Israel did not accept *formal* PLO participation, but the participation of Palestinians who renounced violence. Peres could claim that the PLO, which didn't accept Resolution 242, would not participate in the negotiations, while Hussein could argue that since the PLO understood that in order to be invited to the international conference it had to accept Resolution 242, Arafat's attendance in the conference was guaranteed. This language was meant also to soften the U.S. position. On April 8, Rifai met in Washington with Secretary Shultz and was told that unless the PLO met the American conditions, it could not participate in the peace negotiations.

When the final text was approved, Hussein told Peres: "We won't sign the document. We will just add the place and the date—London, April 11, 1987."

The London Agreement was a genuine success. It supported the idea that the international conference would not have plenary powers. It could not impose or veto decisions made in the bilateral negotiations. Hussein and Peres agreed that there would be a ceremonial opening for the international conference, and immediately afterward the parties would split into bilateral working groups.[62] Despite this obvious success, the London Agreement was never implemented, and it created a credibility problem for Peres. The Israeli foreign minister had the approval of Prime Minister Shamir to meet with King Hussein. He did not have Shamir's approval for an international peace conference. In order to circumvent this obstacle, Peres and Hussein agreed to present the London Document as though it were an "American proposal." It was a convenient formula for both: Peres could claim that it was an American proposal and hence he had not acted behind Shamir's back; Hussein could argue that he had rejected all Israeli proposals but now accepted an American proposal. In order to convince the king that he was sincere in this effort, Peres hinted that should Shamir reject this "American proposal," he, Peres, would resign and would bring down the national unity government. Yossi Beilin, who participated in the drafting of the London Document, acknowledged that Hussein sincerely believed that Peres would resign.[63]

Upon his return from London, Peres immediately briefed the very able U.S. ambassador, Thomas Pickering. The ambassador had served in the past as ambassador to Jordan, and he knew King Hussein very well. Secretary Shultz was at that time in Helsinki, preparing for a summit between President Reagan and Mikhail Gorbachev. Instead of sending a cable to Shultz, Pickering suggested that Peres send Yossi Beilin to Helsinki, to meet there with Charlie Hill, Shultz's aide, and convey to him the importance of presenting the London Document as an "American initiative." Beilin's mission to Helsinki was not coordinated with Shamir.

Shultz refused to play this kind of game.[64] Shultz thought the London Document was good, and he was prepared to come to the Middle East, on May 1, to discuss it with both Shamir and King Hussein. He insisted, however, that Peres present his own document to the prime minister. On April 20, Peres informed Shultz that he had briefed Shamir and that the prime minister had some reservations. In his memoirs, Shamir wrote that Peres read him the document, but refused to leave him a copy, "out of fear of leaks."

On April 22, Ambassador Pickering delivered to Shamir a personal letter from Shultz. The secretary said in his letter that he planned to come to the region on May 1 and was ready to help close the gaps between Israel and Jordan. Shamir, however, informed Shultz on April 24 that he totally rejected the London Document. Just as Peres had not informed Shamir about Beilin's mission to

Helsinki, so did the prime minister send Moshe Arens to Washington without Peres's knowledge to try to persuade Shultz not to come to the region. In a meeting at Shultz's home on April 24, Arens told Shultz that his visit would be perceived as an interference in Israeli domestic politics. President Reagan agreed with this interpretation, and Shultz's trip to the Middle East was canceled. The London Agreement was dead.

This new development had deeply disappointed King Hussein. Extremely bitter, the Jordanian monarch expected Peres to resign and bring down the national unity government. Peres, however, did not meet this expectation. Facing strong opposition from Rabin and other Labor ministers, Peres abandoned his plan to quit the national unity government and call for new parliamentary elections. Peres was forced to continue as foreign minister, with clipped wings, in a Shamir-led government.

Despite this setback, King Hussein did not put an end to his secret high-level talks with Israel. On the contrary, he was now prepared to meet with Shamir also. Until the fiasco of the London Document, Hussein had met only with Labor leaders. Despite many efforts by Menachem Begin to meet with him, Hussein refused. He met only with Moshe Dayan, who was Begin's foreign minister and whom he met with several times in the past.

On July 18, 1987, Shamir became the first Likud leader to meet with the Jordanian monarch. The meeting was held in Hussein's new London residence. Shamir was accompanied by the director general of the prime minister's office, Yossi Ben-Aharon; the cabinet secretary, Eli Rubenstein; and Mossad operative Ephraim Halevy. The Israeli team left Jerusalem on Friday at midday and arrived at the king's residence in London just before sunset. The king attended the Friday-night dinner, which he had ordered from a London Jewish restaurant, and listened respectfully to the kiddush (the blessing on the wine), recited by Ben-Aharon and Rubenstein, both Orthodox and observant Jews. On Saturday night, at the end of the Sabbath, Hussein and Shamir engaged in a long discussion on the peace process and on the bilateral problems that concerned their countries. Although no breakthrough was reported, this precedent of Jordan talking to an Israeli Likud leader was to have sequels. Shamir presented the king with a gift—a Koran, the Islamic holy book, with a silver cover.[65]

On August 6, Shamir sent Justice Minister Dan Meridor to Washington to report to Shultz on his discussion with King Hussein. Meridor described the meeting as "positive." Hussein, however, reported to Shultz that he found Shamir "hopeless."[66] Although the contacts between Israel and Jordan continued through other channels, the fact remains that Hussein and Shamir did not meet again until January 1991, just a few days before the Persian Gulf War started. Developments in the region drew King Hussein's attention to other pressing issues. In November 1987, the king hosted in Amman an Arab summit meeting that welcomed Egypt back into the Arab family. Relations between

Egypt and most of the Arab world had been broken since President Sadat signed a peace treaty with Israel, on March 26, 1979. In December 1987, the Intifada, the Palestinian uprising, began in the Israeli-occupied territories. The Palestinian voice was heard loud and clear. King Hussein understood that his ability to speak on behalf of the Palestinians was reduced to nil.

In July 1988, Hussein drew the right conclusion from this new situation. He decided to disengage from the West Bank. Alarmed by the king's decision, Peres made a desperate effort to prevent this development. In a letter from Jerusalem dated July 26, the Israeli foreign minister urged the Jordanian monarch to remain committed to the London Agreement. The king's reply the next day left no doubt that the king's decision was irreversible. The language of the letters exchanged, as well as their form, is a case study in itself. Peres's letter and the king's reply were not written on official letterhead. Peres's letter was addressed to "Your Majesty," while Hussein's reply was addressed to "My friend." No names were mentioned in either letter. In the past, messages were telexed or, on occasion, hand-delivered by special emissaries who crossed the Jordan River. In recent years, however, modern technology had enabled faster and direct communication.

Because of the importance of the king's decision to disengage from the affairs of the West Bank, I present the text of both letters, in full.

Peres's letter to King Hussein:

Jerusalem, July 26, 1988

Your Majesty,

When we launched our effort to alter the tragic course of events in our region and to offer prospects of security and prosperity in peace to our peoples, we were under no illusions. We knew the undertaking was demanding. We knew the obstacles were many. Yet we were able to visualize the consequences of failure as well as of success. Reflecting on these four years, we can recall both gratifying as well as agonizing occasions. Moreover, in this process we have experienced moments when we misjudged each other's intention, or misunderstood a move, along with moments of instant understanding. I am prompted to send you this message out of concern that we may be in the midst of yet another move which may affect the future of peace.

We have heard that Your Majesty is contemplating policy changes regarding the West Bank. These published speculations have reinforced public perception in Israel that our policy, commonly dubbed the "Jordanian-Palestinian option," is no longer viable. Hence, the internal context and timetable made it imperative that we proclaim the availability of other options that are not necessarily in contradiction to this. Palestinians, for example, are not excluded from the Jordanian-Palestinian option. It is precisely for this reason that I am writing to reiterate my commitment to the London Document approach. Indeed, I am no less convinced today that it holds the most promising prospect for progress. May I add that the time of decisions at home should not be the time for hurried decisions and possibly irreversible steps abroad. Clearly, our ability to signal to each other, as well as to each other's audiences, our commitment to the desired course of action gave credibility to and hence solidified support for this option. The reverse may prove equally true.

When we are approached by Palestinians we indicate to them that the road to negotiations is open, provided the vehicle on which they travel is the one already agreed upon: UNSC Resolutions 242 and 338, the renunciation of violence and terror, and a joint Jordanian-Palestinian delegation.

Concurrently, we notice intriguing signs that the PLO is being forced to undergo a process of reevaluation of the need to renew its link to Jordan. Your Majesty has on many occasions introduced a voice, both sober and moving, in favor of peace. Your voice and policies in the days to come will be listened to with great care by everyone concerned.

With best wishes,

Sincerely yours,

Shimon Peres

King Hussein's answer:

TOP SECRET—PERSONAL

My Dear friend,

Thank you for your message and all the sentiments it contained. I wish to assure you that my total commitment to a negotiated peaceful settlement of the Arab-Israeli conflict remains unshakable. Any action which we might take is directed at breaking the impasse in the peace process which has prevailed for too long. We might disengage from the West Bank, but we will never disengage from the peace process. We might disengage from the administration of the people under occupation, but we can never disengage from the Palestinian people and the Palestinian problem. I still share with you the vision of peace and agree that the vehicle for peace is the international conference on the basis we arrived at in London. 42, 338, renunciation of violence and terror, and a Jordanian-Palestinian delegation to the conference will remain valid, even after our proposed actions. Indeed, we hope that our actions will cause the Palestinians to see the light and come to terms with the reality of what is required of them, if peace is to reign in our region.

   With best wishes for your continued good health, happiness, and every future success. May you continue your efforts to achieve our common objective of peace and good-neighborliness. You can always count on my friendship and support in this noble endeavor.

Hussein

27.7.88

Indeed, four days later, on July 31, 1988, King Hussein announced that he was breaking off administrative and legal links with the West Bank. The Israeli Jordanian option, in its old, traditional form, virtually vanished overnight.

   For a short period, King Hussein feared mounting domestic tensions, resulting from a combination of Palestinian, Islamic, and economic pressures. This fear pushed him into adopting tough public anti-Israeli positions. Appearing on Ted Koppel's *Nightline* program, Hussein said that the "flood of Jewish immigrants from the Soviet Union to Israel could push the Middle East into a new war." Ignoring the mounting pressure of the Bush administration on Shamir's government, King Hussein accused the United States of "doing nothing" to advance the peace process. He urged the United States to open a dialogue with the PLO and to agree to the convening of an international conference, as the proper venue for solving the Palestinian problem.[67]

   Hussein's pronouncements against the Soviet Jewish immigration were part of a wider Arab diplomatic effort in Moscow to halt the Jewish exodus to Israel. The campaign was orchestrated by the Arab League, and its prime mover was Egypt. The campaign, however, failed.

   Despite the sharp rhetoric, Prime Minister Shamir was not greatly disturbed by Hussein's pronouncements. The Israelis understood that the king was under mounting domestic pressures and hoped that Hussein would overcome the obstacles facing him. Indeed, neither the United States nor Israel expected total Jordanian disengagement from the West Bank. Even when the focus of American and Israeli diplomacy moved from Amman to Cairo, both Washington and Jerusalem sought to secure a role for Jordan in their effort to solve the Palestinian problem. This effort was partly successful in the Madrid

Peace Conference, in October 1991, when the Palestinians came to the Spanish capital as part of the Jordanian delegation.

By then, King Hussein had resumed his high-level contacts with Prime Minister Shamir. Iraq's invasion of Kuwait and Jordan's tacit support of this move created an explosive situation in the Middle East. Many Western countries, while disapproving of Jordan's position, were concerned that King Hussein would not survive the crisis. It is against this background that King Hussein invited Shamir to meet with him at the king's residence in London, on Saturday night, January 5, 1991. In addition to his usual team—Ben-Aharon, Rubenstein, and the Mossad operative Halevy—Shamir was accompanied by Deputy Chief of Staff Ehud Barak. Hussein had with him his chief of staff, General Zeid bin-Shaker. The king explained to the Israeli prime minister that he was forced to support Saddam Hussein because of Jordan's economic dependence on Iraq. Had he not supported Saddam Hussein, especially after Yasser Arafat embraced the Iraqi dictator publicly, the Palestinians in his kingdom might have tried to overthrow him. Now he was abandoned by the United States and ignored by Saudi Arabia and the oil-rich Persian Gulf principalities. King Hussein wanted Shamir to promise him that Jordan would not become a war zone between Israel and Iraq. In return for Hussein's promise not to allow Iraqi planes to fly over his country, he asked for a similar Shamir commitment not to fly over Jordan in case of a retaliation against Iraq. In reply to Barak's questions about the joint Iraqi-Jordanian air forces maneuvers close to the Israeli border, General bin-Shaker replied that the maneuvers had ended and would not be resumed.

While Shamir and King Hussein met again shortly after the Persian Gulf War, it was not until Labor's return to power, in the summer of 1992, and especially after the signing of the Israeli-Palestinian declaration of principles on the White House South Lawn in September 1993, that King Hussein reemerged as an active player in the Arab-Israeli peace process. This role was clearly displayed in the active involvement of Hussein in the Netanyahu-Arafat agreement on Israeli redeployment in the city of Hebron in January 1997. Even the Palestinians were forced to admit that Jordan's role was still viable.

A R A F A T   I N   G A Z A

Shortly after the historic handshake between Prime Minister Yitzhak Rabin and PLO Chairman Yasser Arafat, it became clear that both Israel and the Palestinians had exaggerated expectations that could not be instantly and realistically met.

When Israel signed the declaration of principles (DOP) with the PLO on September 13, 1993, Rabin and Peres sincerely hoped that Arafat would honor his commitment to end terror and violence, and that most, if not all, of the Arab countries would recognize Israel, establish diplomatic relations with the Jewish state, and end the economic boycott, thus helping Israel's integration into the region to which it geographically belongs. To achieve these goals, Israel reversed the positions it had taken in the bilateral negotiations in Washington. In return for the PLO's commitment not to declare an independent Palestinian state during the five-year interim period,[1] Israel agreed to transfer to the Palestinians in the Gaza Strip and Jericho—even before the election of a Palestine Authority—full responsibility in five domains: health, education, taxation, tourism, and social services. The remaining responsibilities were to be transferred after the elections. Thus, while the issue of sovereignty was not mentioned, the Oslo Accords did create a mechanism that made an independent Palestinian state a possibility. In practical terms, what this Israeli concession meant was that except for Jerusalem, the Israeli settlements, army installations, and other areas that Israel might retain for security reasons, the Palestinians would have jurisdiction over the remaining territories occupied by Israel in the 1967 war.

The momentum generated by the White House handshake strengthened this Israeli hope. Similar hopes were evident on the Palestinian side. Yasser Arafat, presiding over what seemed to be the impending financial collapse of PLO operations, saw in the White House ceremony a unique opportunity to reassert himself as the unchallenged leader of the Palestinian people. Isolated in the Arab world and deserted by many of his erstwhile closest associates, Arafat had on his agenda three major goals:

- To prove that the Palestinians, who had helped build the oil-rich Persian Gulf countries, were also capable of building their own independent entity.

- To make the Palestine Authority the nucleus of the future Palestinian government—a model for other Arab countries, especially in terms of economic growth, human rights, and a modern, effective, corruption-free civil administration.

- To make independent Palestine a bridge between the West and the Arab world.

These goals, however, were difficult to attain. Ever since its first encounter with the Zionist movement, in the early twenties, the Palestinian national movement had been characterized by its sharp divisions: the city versus the village; Nablus versus Hebron; pro-Jordan versus pro-Egypt; the Husseini clan versus the Nashashibis, etc. In the wake of the Oslo Accords, Arafat faced a similar situation. Not only the ten Damascus-based opposition groups but also two powerful Islamic fundamentalist groups—the Islamic Resistance Movement, known by its Arabic acronym, Hamas, and Islamic Jihad—had openly challenged his authority. Inside Arafat's own PLO Executive Committee, nine out of eighteen members either resigned or opposed Arafat's move.

In light of this situation, the late Yehoshafat Harkabi, one of the most illustrious Israeli Orientalists and a former head of military intelligence, called on Arafat to resign. Harkabi compared Arafat to Moses: "Just as Moses liberated the Israelites from slavery in Egypt but was unable to lead them into the promised land, so Arafat should vacate his place to a 'Palestinian Joshua' who will lead the Palestinians into Statehood," he said shortly before he died from cancer.

Nevertheless, as a result of the euphoric presentation of the Oslo Accords, the beginnings were quite promising. On October 1, 1993, President Clinton convened in Washington a meeting of forty-three countries that pledged a sum of $2 billion, over a period of five years, to help rebuild the infrastructure in the Gaza Strip and the West Bank. Of all the oil-rich Persian Gulf countries, only Kuwait remained adamant in its refusal to contribute, because of Arafat's support of the Iraqi invasion of Kuwait. "We would rather contribute to Israel than to Arafat," Kuwaiti officials told their American counterparts.[2]

On October 6, Rabin traveled to Cairo to discuss implementation of the Oslo Accords with President Mubarak. In advance of the negotiations with the PLO, Rabin sent to Tunis Generals Amnon Shahak and Ouzi Dayan to discuss various security problems with Arafat and his aides. The atmosphere in the Arab world in general was very positive. Unlike the angry Arab reaction after the signing of the Camp David Accords in 1978, when Egypt was isolated and expelled from the Arab League, the Arab reaction this time was surprisingly moderate. Morocco used the occasion to bring this secret relationship into the open. The Persian Gulf Sultanate of Oman, with which Israel had established a covert relationship in the early seventies and where an unofficial Israeli representative had resided since the early eighties, followed suit, and Sultan Qabus hosted a multilateral working group in Muscat, with Israeli presence, to study plans for regional development of water resources. Tunisia, like Morocco, announced its intention to open a low-level diplomatic interest section in Tel Aviv, and hosted a multilateral working group on refugees. Qatar and Bahrain did the same. Qatar even explored the possibility of selling natural gas to Israel and invited the Conference of Presidents of Major Jewish Organizations to visit Doha. Jordan opened up to Israeli correspondents and gave them access to senior Jordanian officials. All these moves were unthinkable before the signing of the Oslo Accords.

Based on promises made by Abu Ala, the senior Palestinian negotiator in Oslo, that Arafat would disarm the Islamic fundamentalist groups Hamas and Islamic Jihad and would end violence, Rabin and Peres expected terrorism to end immediately. Unfortunately, this did not happen and terrorism was not curbed. During an Israeli cabinet meeting on November 14, 1993, the chief of staff, General Ehud Barak, warned: "The Oslo Accords are very problematic. They create for the army a very complicated security reality."[3] His deputy— later chief of staff—General Amnon Shahak told the Knesset Foreign Affairs and Security Committee: "The Oslo Accords create for us a very serious security problem. If we cannot conduct preventive actions in the territories, the fight against terrorism would be more difficult than it is now. How could we provide security to Israeli settlements and settlers if the army would not be patrolling the roads of the Gaza Strip?"[4]

Indeed, the reality on the ground was diametrically opposed to the euphoric expectations. Violence not only did not stop, it was intensified. Arafat's record of using terror to further his political cause aroused immediate suspicions that the PLO chairman did not irrevocably abjure violence, unleashing it if not by command, then by a subtle acquiescence. The overall result was a gradual and substantial decrease of Israeli and Palestinian support for the DOP.

Complicating the situation was the ambivalent attitude of Rabin himself. The Israeli prime minister missed no opportunity to tell associates, friends, and American Jewish leaders that he didn't like the Oslo Accords, that he had been "dragged" into them by Peres and his "boys," but now that he had signed the DOP, he had no choice but to assume full responsibility for it.

In an effort to minimize the security risks, Rabin appointed General Shahak to negotiate the implementation of the Gaza-Jericho accord with the PLO's Nabil Shaath in Taba. Shahak's appointment signaled Rabin's intention to attend personally to the complicated security problems that had been neglected in Oslo. Rabin's move was ill received by "Peres's boys" in the Israeli Foreign Ministry. After negotiating the Oslo Accords, Peres's aides felt it was appropriate for them to continue handling the Palestinian file. Egypt and the PLO shared this view and preferred Peres over Rabin. In a well-orchestrated press campaign, Rabin was accused of "politicizing" the army. The Israeli prime minister, however, ignored the press campaign and gave Shahak and his team his full support. For him, the issue of security took precedence over any other consideration.

The declaration of principles dictated a very rigid timetable for negotiating its implementation. The negotiations started in Taba, on the shores of the Red Sea, on October 13 and were to be completed by December 13. The actual Israeli withdrawal from Jericho and the redeployment in the Gaza Strip were to take place on April 13, 1994. It was hoped that such a rigid timetable would force both sides to be flexible, if indeed they wanted to meet their deadlines. It was soon apparent that Shahak and Shaath were unable to solve the three key issues that the negotiators in Oslo were unable to resolve. These were the size of the "Jericho area," the security responsibility in all border crossings, and the PLO insistence on the Israeli military's total withdrawal from the Gaza Strip, its presence to be confined to the perimeters of the Israeli settlements.

The controversy over these three points concealed an even more serious problem. In signing the DOP, both Rabin and Arafat agreed that during the five-year interim period, the issue of sovereignty would not be discussed. Arafat, however, tried to "twist" the DOP and pretended to become the "sovereign" in the areas vacated by Israel. Hence he instructed Nabil Shaath, his negotiator in Taba, to present Israel with several demands, all of them relating to sovereignty and statehood. In Taba and in subsequent negotiations with Peres in Cairo, Arafat sought to gain full control of all the crossing points between the Gaza Strip and Sinai and between Jericho and Jordan; he wanted Israeli withdrawal not just from the city of Jericho but from the District of Jericho, which would bring him closer to the outskirts of Jerusalem. In later negotiations, Arafat also insisted that the Palestinians elect a legislature that would eventually become the constituent assembly of the future Palestinian state, with East Jerusalem as its capital. For this purpose, he also wanted some kind of "presence" in East Jerusalem, and wanted Palestinians residing in the city to be able not only to vote but also to stand for election; he also wanted a central bank that would establish a Palestinian currency, a Palestinian passport, and an independent postal and telephone service. All these issues, however, were in the DOP left to the final status negotiations, and most of them, not surprisingly, were rejected.

This conflicting approach to the negotiations was a result of conflicting interpretation of the DOP. Unlike Arafat, whose goal was a Palestinian state with East Jerusalem as its capital, the Israeli government did not exactly know where the Oslo process would lead. In a revealing interview years later, Yossi Beilin, one of the architects of the Oslo Accords, publicly admitted that one of the most important decisions since the establishment of the State of Israel in 1948 had been made without a proper decision-making process. He said that throughout the secret negotiations in Oslo, neither Rabin nor Peres held any serious discussion on the final status of the territories. Nor had the Israeli government held a discussion on this issue.[5]

As a result, Rabin defined in very general terms his "vision" for the final solution with the Palestinians. His position after Oslo was similar to the one he had taken during his election campaign in 1992. In briefings with senior correspondents, in meetings with various American Jewish leaders, and in his speech to the Knesset on October 5, 1995, Rabin defined his position as follows:

- There would be no return to the pre-1967 armistice lines.
- The Jordan Valley should become the "security border" of Israel with Jordan.
- Most Israeli settlements in the West Bank should be incorporated within the modified and recognized Israeli border.
- Jerusalem would remain united under Israeli sovereignty.
- A "Palestinian entity" would be more than an autonomy but less than a state.
- Final resolution of the Palestine refugee problem should be achieved by resettling the refugees in the various Arab countries and in other immigrant-absorbing countries in the world.[6]

Based on this thinking, Rabin's instructions to General Shahak in Taba were limited to the issue of redeployment in the Gaza Strip and Jericho area only. He also instructed Shahak to move cautiously, insisting on gradual progress and withdrawals. However, building mutual confidence between two neighbors sharing the same land proved to be more difficult than striking a deal between two enemies separated by clearly defined borders. Experience had shown that it was easier to conclude peace with Egypt and Jordan than to implement an ambiguous declaration of principles with the Palestinians.

Since Israeli and Palestinian negotiators were unable to agree on a number of critical issues, Rabin and Arafat met in Cairo on December 11 in an effort to narrow the gap between them. It was a disaster. "Arafat tried to give the DOP an interpretation which was already rejected in Oslo," said Rabin's political adviser Jacques Neriyah, who attended the meeting. In essence, it was a debate on "security versus symbols." For Rabin, it was an interim agreement, outlining a trial period for the Palestinians, during which they were to prove their ability to govern themselves and to curb terrorism and violence. For the PLO, the

Oslo Accords were a first step toward statehood. Hence, Arafat wanted to ensure the use of symbols throughout the interim period.

"There are no sacred dates," commented Rabin angrily after his return from Cairo. "There will be no redeployment in the Gaza Strip until I am satisfied that our security needs are met," he added. The Israeli prime minister was so disillusioned with Yasser Arafat that he didn't want to meet with him again before all the details of an agreement were worked out. He relegated the task of monitoring the Shahak-Shaath negotiations to Foreign Minister Peres.

In this atmosphere of mutual suspicion, Israeli Minister of Housing Benjamin (Fuad) Ben-Eliezer traveled to Tunis in December 1993 for a meeting with Arafat. General (Res.) Ben-Eliezer had been the military commander of the West Bank, and in that capacity he had ordered the arrest of Jibril Rajoub, one of Arafat's top aides, for his involvement in terrorist activities. After his release from jail, Rajoub became Arafat's choice for heading the Palestinian security service in the West Bank. It was Rajoub who initiated and arranged his captor's trip to Tunis.

"I want you to emphasize to Arafat that the whole Oslo process will collapse if he will not curb terrorism and if he will not meet Israel's security needs," Rabin told Ben-Eliezer. In his meeting with the Israeli minister, Arafat gave the first hint of his future tactic. He said: "I understand your security concerns. However, instead of a civil war in the Gaza Strip, I prefer to try to integrate the fundamentalist groups—Hamas and Islamic Jihad—into my future administration."[7] Arafat's tactic didn't work and terrorist acts against Israel continued with no interruption.

In this loaded atmosphere, Israeli and world public opinion were shocked by what was to become known as the "Goldstein massacre." On Friday morning, February 25, 1994, the American-born Orthodox physician Dr. Baruch Goldstein entered the "Ibrahimi mosque" at the Tomb of the Patriarchs in Hebron, wearing his Israeli army captain's uniform, and indiscriminately shot to death twenty-nine Muslim worshipers and wounded more than a hundred. It was the Jewish holiday of Purim, which coincided with the first day of the month-long fast of Ramadan. Goldstein was overpowered by the Muslim worshipers and was lynched.

The Palestinian and Arab reaction was instant. Violent riots erupted in Hebron and in other West Bank cities; Arafat suspended the talks with Israel; the UN Security Council unanimously "strongly condemned" the massacre (but not Israel) and called for a temporary international presence in Hebron. Despite the condemnation, talks with Israel were not resumed. It was obvious that Arafat was trying to score from this tragic event as many points as he could. As a condition for his return to the talks, Arafat demanded the evacuation of the Israeli settlers from the city of Hebron, the disarming of the Israeli settlers in the West Bank, the dismantling of the settlements in the Gaza Strip, and the deployment of a UN force in the territories—not just in Hebron—"in order to protect the Palestinians from Israeli terrorists." Rabin rejected these demands, although two members of his government, Shimon Peres and Yossi Sarid, did call for the evacuation of the Israeli settlers from the city of Hebron and the dismantling of the Israeli settlement of Netzarim in the Gaza Strip.

Peres's position on Hebron was influenced by the late Moshe Dayan. The legendary Israeli war hero was defense minister in Golda Meir's cabinet when a small group of ultra-Orthodox Jews, headed by Rabbi Moshe Levinger, celebrated their Passover Seder in the heart of Hebron. Caught by surprise, Dayan wanted to evict them by force, but he encountered a strong opposition from his government colleagues. In a recently released document, Dayan was quoted as having told Deputy Prime Minister Yigal Allon: "You know that Levinger's action is a provocation and illegal. If we adopted a policy of not yielding to Arab terrorists and we even risked the lives of innocent schoolchildren, how can we yield to Levinger's blackmail?" Dayan also spoke to Michael Hazani, the National Religious Party's minister of agriculture, and said: "I keep telling the Palestinians in Hebron that they have no choice but to comply with the army's orders. How could I explain to them now that Levinger and his extremist supporters do not have to obey the army's orders?" Interestingly enough, Dayan said that Yitzhak Rabin supported Allon's position on Hebron. Dayan concluded: "I knew that I had made a mistake. I should have resigned in protest against the government's position on Levinger's provocation in Hebron. I didn't. It was definitely a mistake."[8]

Dayan's mistake was to haunt Israel to this date. Finding himself on the defensive, Prime Minister Rabin made an extreme effort to revive the stalled negotiations with the Palestinians. During a visit to the Vatican, Rabin urged the pope to intervene with Arafat. He made similar efforts with Presidents Clinton, Yeltsin, and Mubarak. Norway's foreign minister, under whose auspices the secret Oslo negotiations were conducted, added his moderating voice to the Israeli effort. Eventually, and although the Oslo Accords precluded any UN involvement, Israel agreed—"in the interest of maintaining the momentum in the peace process"—to a temporary international presence in Hebron. According to an agreement reached in Cairo on March 31, 1994, General Amnon Shahak and PLO's Nabil Shaath agreed to deploy 160 observers in Hebron, for a period of three months. The makeup of the Temporary International Presence in Hebron (TIPH) was ninety Norwegians, thirty-five Danes, and thirty-five Italians. TIPH members were armed with pistols for their own self-defense, and had no military or police functions in Hebron. They enjoyed freedom of movement, and by their very presence they reassured the Palestinians in Hebron that the Goldstein massacre would not be repeated.

Shortly after the signing of the TIPH agreement, negotiations between Israel and the Palestinians were resumed. In order to make up for the lost time,

Israel agreed to accelerate the negotiations and to shorten the implementation schedules for the Israeli redeployment in the Gaza Strip and Jericho.

After the solution of the Hebron crisis, Rabin paid a short visit to Washington. In a joint press conference with Clinton on March 16, 1994, Rabin said that he was prepared to make "painful decisions" concerning the Golan Heights if President Assad would do the same.[9] Assad, however, was not forthcoming. Despite his meeting in Geneva with President Clinton in January 1994, Assad remained vague on the meaning of "normal relations" with Israel; he insisted on a total Israeli withdrawal to the pre-1967 lines and was uncompromising on the security arrangements that Israel requested.

After his return to Israel, Rabin consolidated his parliamentary majority by having Shas, the ultra Orthodox Sephardic party, rejoin his coalition government. In order to relieve himself from a dependence on the votes of five Arab Knesset members, Rabin was prepared to pay Shas a political price: He gave Shas a written commitment to the effect that no Israeli settlement would be dismantled during the five-year interim period, there would be no compromise on Jerusalem, and any agreement for withdrawals in the Golan Heights would be subject to a referendum. As expected, Rabin's commitment to hold a referendum on a possible withdrawal from the Golan Heights was sharply criticized by Syria. Misreading Israeli democracy, Syrians saw Rabin's letter to Shas as an indication that Rabin wouldn't withdraw from the Heights.

In the wake of the Hebron agreement, Hamas and Islamic Jihad introduced a new and deadly type of terrorism—the suicide-car bombings. Emerging during the intifada, these two fundamentalist groups opposed the Oslo Accords and were determined to derail the peace process. Because of its well-entrenched social infrastructure, Hamas enjoyed popular support in the Gaza Strip, estimated at 30 percent of the population, while its power base in the West Bank, especially in Hebron, did not exceed 20 percent. From September 13, 1993, to May 1, 1994, Hamas and Islamic Jihad were responsible for the assassination of thirty-two Israelis and the murder of nineteen Palestinians accused of "collaboration" with Israel. Inspired by the success of Hezbollah, the militant Islamic group in Lebanon trained and financed by Iran, Hamas's military wing, Iz el-Din el-Qassam, on April 6, 1994, blew up a car next to an Israeli bus in Afula, in the heart of Israel, killing nine Israelis and wounding forty-five. A week later, on April 13, a Hamas member strapped with explosives set them off on a bus in Hadera, killing six Israelis and wounding fifteen.

The fact that the two suicide bombings had been carried out inside Israel sent shock waves through Israeli society and increased Rabin's suspicion that contrary to his written commitment, Arafat was not doing enough to combat terrorism. What was of more concern was the growing Israeli difficulties in penetrating the military wings of both Hamas and Islamic Jihad. While Israel had a fair knowledge of the political and charitable activities of Hamas—both in the territories and abroad (including in the United States)—its knowledge of the military wing was more limited. According to Israeli intelligence sources, the number of suicide bombers did not exceed eighty candidates. Based on interrogations of Hamas prisoners, Israeli security sources managed to build a profile of a Hamas suicide bomber: eighteen to twenty-four years old, single, and of poor social and economic background. Recruited mostly in mosques, the suicide bomber was brainwashed to the degree that he believed that by becoming a *shahid* (martyr) he would go straight to Paradise, where he would be surrounded by pretty women. His family would be supported financially by Hamas. Israeli and PLO sources revealed that Iran had pledged a sum of $30 million to finance Hamas and Islamic Jihad activities against Israel. Leaders of both groups were reported to have visited Tehran on several occasions.

Investigation of several suicide bombings revealed that the operations were based on sound intelligence, logistical support, and well-indoctrinated training. Some of the Hamas members were trained to abduct Israeli soldiers and civilians. This training was based, in part, on Hezbollah's experience in taking Western hostages in Beirut in the mid-eighties.

Concerned that the intensified terrorism would lead to the collapse of the Oslo process, Arafat signed with Hamas in late April 1994 a six-point cease-fire agreement, according to which Hamas declared a one-month moratorium on terrorism and violence. Arafat needed this moratorium in order to enable him to conclude the Gaza-Jericho accord with Israel. Hamas, however, made it clear that the cease-fire was only temporary. In a leaflet distributed in the territories, Hamas defined its long-range goals as follows:

- Total Israeli withdrawal from the territories occupied in the 1967 war.

- Disarming the Israeli settlers and dismantling their settlements.

- Deployment of international forces to separate Israel and the territories.

Ignoring Hamas threats, and after months of tough bargaining, Prime Minister Rabin and Chairman Arafat signed in Cairo on May 4, 1994, the Cairo Agreement in the presence of President Mubarak, Secretary of State Warren Christopher, Russian Foreign Minister Andrei Kozyrev, and 2,500 guests. The ceremony, which was carried live by CNN and Israeli and Egyptian television, was marred by an embarrassing incident onstage. When presented with the maps attached to the ninety-eight-page agreement, Arafat refused to sign the maps delineating the Gaza Strip and the Jericho area, the Israeli settlements, and the zones of Israeli and Palestinian territorial and security jurisdiction in those areas. Jacques Neriyah, Rabin's diplomatic adviser, rushed to the stage to help the prime minister understand what was going on. When told that Arafat was refusing to sign the maps, an angry and red-faced Rabin wanted to leave the ceremony and return home immediately. He was certain that Arafat was pulling one of his last-minute tricks in order to extract more concessions. Shimon Peres had an angry exchange with Arafat, while Secretary Christopher and Ambassador Dennis Ross intervened with Mubarak in a desperate effort to avoid an irreparable damage to the peace process.

SIGN THE MAPS, YOU DOG, headlined the usually reliable London-based Saudi daily *El-Hayat,* paraphrasing the angry exchange between President Mubarak and Arafat.[10] While both Egyptian and Palestinian officials denied *El-Hayat's* headline, they did acknowledge that Mubarak and Arafat had a "very angry" exchange onstage.

The Cairo Agreement included the following:

- A twenty-four-member Palestine Authority would be established, which would assume responsibility for thirty-one executive and limited legislative functions, transferred to it by the Israeli Civil Administration. Judicial functions would be administered by an independent Palestinian body.

- The territorial jurisdiction would include land, subsoil, and territorial water.

- Israel would continue to retain authority over Israeli settlements, settlers, and Israeli army installations. Israel would also be responsible for external security—from sea and air—and would maintain "security presence" at all border crossings with Egypt and Jordan.

- As to "symbols," Israel agreed that the Palestine Authority would issue "passports/travel documents." The PA would also have a local TV and radio station and independent international telephone area codes for both Jericho and the Gaza Strip.

The exact size of the Jericho area remained unresolved. The maps that were the cause of the embarrassing incident during the signing ceremony in Cairo delineated the size of Jericho as sixty-two square kilometers. Rabin agreed, however, that this issue would be reviewed after three months and if the security situation allowed it the area could be expanded. Finally, it was agreed that the PA would not conduct foreign policy and would not establish embassies or consulates abroad, nor would it allow the establishment of foreign embassies in Jericho or the Gaza Strip. However, "routine dealings" with foreign states and international organizations, or with their representatives, would not be considered "foreign relations" and would continue as before.

The Palestine police force would comprise nine thousand men (seven thousand of them from abroad), and the policemen would be armed with light arms only. Finally, and as a gesture of goodwill, Israel agreed to release five thousand Palestinian prisoners and to allow the return of an unspecified number of deportees who had been expelled from the territories because of their involvement in terrorist activities.

In return for these gestures, Arafat renewed his pledge, in a letter to Rabin, to amend the PLO Covenant and to intensify his struggle against terrorism.

After his return from Cairo, Rabin said that the PLO's ability to govern and to curb terrorism would now be put to the test. "If they fail to impose their authority or if they prove unable or unwilling to end violence, they won't get anything beyond the Gaza Strip and Jericho," the Israeli prime minister said.[11]

The Cairo Agreement and the ugly incident with Arafat during the signing ceremony were not unanimously welcomed by the PLO leadership. Abu Mazen, Arafat's deputy and his heir apparent, who did not take part in the lengthy negotiations, commented: "The powerful Israelis imposed their interpretation of the Oslo Accords on the weak Palestinians."[12] Another Palestinian leader, Mahmoud Darwish, the most prominent Palestinian poet, who wrote the Palestinian Declaration of Independence in Algiers in November 1988 and who resigned his seat on the PLO Executive Committee in protest of the Oslo Accords, called the Cairo Agreement a "television peace."[13]

Once the Cairo Agreement was signed, Israel moved quickly to implement it. On May 18, one week ahead of schedule, Israel completed its redeployment in the Gaza Strip and handed over the responsibility for internal security to the Palestine police. On July 1, Yasser Arafat crossed into the Gaza Strip from Sinai and took charge of the newly created Palestine Authority. A new chapter in the bloody Israeli-Palestinian conflict had just begun.

This was the first time in Middle Eastern history that Palestinians governed Palestinians. Unlike many developing countries, the Palestinians had a good chance to build a modern and vibrant society. In most Arab countries, illiteracy is still very high, but the Palestinians in the territories were less than 5 percent illiterate. Many of them had studied abroad, mostly in Europe and the United States. Nevertheless, Arafat came to Gaza totally unprepared for this historic challenge. Many of the people he brought with him from Tunis were old and unfamiliar with the methods of a modern administration. He favored loyalty over talent, and it was obvious that he did not know where to begin. Instead of reconstructing the PLO in a manner that would invest more power in the hands of a young and Western-educated elite, Arafat preferred to concentrate all powers in his own hands. His refusal to relegate authority and his insistence on making all decisions created bottlenecks in the decision-making process and caused friction between him and his deputy, Abu Mazen. His transformation from a terrorist to a nation-builder proved to be extremely difficult. His modus operandi was also very peculiar. He created several security services, each competing with the others. At the initiative of President Clinton, the donor countries pledged an amount of $2 billion to help build the infrastructure in the Gaza Strip, over a period of five years. However, the lack of accountable institutions caused delays in channeling the funds. Moreover, money that was to be spent on long-term job-creating projects was eaten up by salaries for loyal functionaries. According to Israeli sources, some thirty thousand Palestinians entered the workforce every year, and Arafat was faced with the need to create jobs for them. In the absence of jobs, Arafat violated the Cairo Agreement by increasing the number of policemen from nine thousand to eighteen thousand, then to thirty thousand, and the figure now is close to forty thousand. Arafat explained to the bewildered Israelis that it was better to recruit more policemen and pay them salaries than to push the unemployed into the arms of Hamas and Islamic Jihad.

Troubling also was the way Arafat built his economic institutions. Arafat built two economic bodies, with no coordination between them. He surrounded himself with corrupt associates who were more interested in their "commission" than in the service they were supposed to provide. Israeli, American, Japanese, and European entrepreneurs were shocked to learn that Arafat granted—sometimes the very same day—the same contracts to competing companies. Furthermore, according to the Israeli-Palestinian agreement, Israel was to refund to the Palestine Authority various taxes collected from Palestinians working in Israel. In addition, Israel was to refund to the PA customs and gas revenues. To Rabin's great surprise, Arafat diverted the gas tax to a special account at a Tel Aviv branch of Bank Leumi, not to his government's budgetary operations. According to a report in the *Jerusalem Post* of September 10, 1996, and confirmed by the Israeli Finance Ministry, this "slush fund" of 200 million shekels ($65 million) was earmarked for Arafat's discretionary use, mostly to buy favors from political opponents, including Hamas and Islamic Jihad. This modus operandi aroused suspicions of corruption and created dissent among officials who felt they were being "ignored."

Furthermore, instead of spending more time in Gaza, Arafat preferred to travel abroad frequently. "Why is he traveling so much?" Rabin asked his associates. "Doesn't he understand that his first priority should be the building of his nation's institutions?"

Arafat ignored the criticism. Two weeks after he signed the Cairo Agreement, Arafat attended the inauguration of black-ruled South Africa. After meeting with Nelson Mandela and Israeli President Ezer Weizman, who represented Israel in that event, Arafat addressed a Black Muslim crowd in a Johannesburg mosque. Unaware that his speech was being secretly taped, Arafat called his audience to join in a jihad (holy war) "to liberate Jerusalem." He even hinted that once the Palestinians felt strong enough, they might revoke the Oslo Accords.

Arafat's speech in Johannesburg was leaked to the Israeli press and caused a furor. A furious Rabin was quick to warn: "Should the need arise, the Israeli army has contingency plans to reoccupy the Gaza Strip and Jericho."

Arafat's Johannesburg speech was not mere bragging—it was accompanied by a concrete action. In a letter to the chairman of PECDAR (Palestine Economic Council for Development and Reconstruction), the agency handling the funds channeled by the donor countries, PA Finance Minister Mohamed Nashashibi wrote in August 1994 that Arafat had allocated the sum of $15 million to establish a company whose task was to buy Jewish property in Jerusalem. Arafat's Arab Israeli adviser Dr. Ahmed Tibi was to become the CEO of the new corporation. Tibi denied the report, but Likud Knesset member Benny Begin said that he had a copy of Nashashibi's letter in his possession.[14]

Thus the "battle for Jerusalem" that was to be left to the final status negotiations was opened immediately after Arafat's return to Gaza. Fully confident that Israel would be unable to reverse the course set in Oslo, the PLO chairman allowed himself to ignore other commitments as well. Despite his two written commitments to Rabin to amend the PLO Covenant, no deadline was set for such an action. In private discussions, Arafat's aides were implying that because of the growing opposition to the Oslo process, Arafat would not convene the Palestine National Council (PNC)—the Palestinian parliament-in-exile—for amending the covenant unless he was assured of two-thirds majority, as the PNC's charter required. "So far, the chairman does not have this majority," the aides said.

At this early stage, however, Israel did not want to rock the boat. It was too soon to admit that Arafat was ignoring his commitments according to the Oslo Accords. Hence, on August 29, 1994, Israel and the Palestinians signed in Cairo an agreement for the early transfer of authority in the spheres of education, health, social services, taxation, and tourism. In an attempt to ensure a balanced budget for the Palestine Authority and to help fill the shortfall that would occur while the Palestinian tax system was being set up, Israeli Foreign Minister Shimon Peres urged the donor countries to open their purses to Arafat even though the appropriate institutions were not in place. Peres also encouraged investments in the Gaza Strip, so that the Palestinians would begin to enjoy "the fruits of peace."

From Rabin's point of view, however, the most important issue was security. Even before the completion of the negotiations in Cairo, Israeli intelligence services warned that the redeployment in the Gaza Strip and the withdrawal from Jericho could lead to more terrorism. They evaluated that the intensified terrorism had presented Israeli policymakers with three options: continuing the Oslo process, even at the price of making further concessions to the Palestinians; freezing the Oslo Accords; or forgoing the interim stage and moving straight to the final status talks.

Rabin had decided to continue the Oslo process. Once he made this decision, the Cairo Agreement was signed. According to that agreement, Arafat again pledged to "take all necessary measures" to curb terrorism and end all acts of violence. He again proved unable or unwilling to deliver. Israeli security officials became increasingly suspicious that the continued violence was tolerated by Arafat in order to force more Israeli concessions. Thus, instead of being a process of reconciliation, the Israeli-Palestinian negotiations sank into the quagmire of terror and retaliation. Like the French under the Bourbons, the Palestinians under Arafat had learned nothing from their long and bitter history. Hopelessly splintered into numerous feuding groups, the Palestinians approached statehood by attempting to derail the process of reconciliation, not only with Israel but also among themselves. Islamic terrorist groups like Hamas and Islamic Jihad reiterated their commitment to dissent, thereby confirming what Abba Eban once said: "The Palestinians never miss an opportunity to miss an opportunity." Attacks on Israeli soldiers and stabbings of innocent civilians generated a new cycle of violence that threatened to plunge the peace process into a new phase of hate and warfare.

Rabin insisted that Arafat honor his commitment to crack down on Hamas and Islamic Jihad and to apprehend and hand over to Israel terrorists who committed acts of violence in Israel. Arafat, however, felt that such a compliance would undermine his authority in the areas under his control. Therefore, roundups of Hamas and Islamic Jihad gunmen became farcical; they almost always ended in prompt release from jail. In the face of this attitude, Rabin delayed the release of five thousand prisoners to which he was committed under the Cairo Agreement. Rabin also delayed the first stage of the Israeli army deployment in the West Bank, which was due on July 13, 1994. The Israeli prime minister sensed that Israeli public opinion would not tolerate such moves while Arafat continued to ignore his commitment to end violence.

In October 1994, the wave of violence came to a frightening peak. An Islamic Jihad suicide bomber blew himself up on a bus in Tel Aviv, killing twenty-two Israelis and wounding forty-eight. Moreover, between June and November 1994, el-Fatah, Arafat's own group within the PLO, carried out twelve terrorist attacks, murdering eleven fellow Palestinians accused of "collaboration" with Israel. Two other factions of the PLO—the PFLP, headed by Dr. George Habash, and the DFLP, headed by Nayef Hawatmeh—carried out three more terrorist acts. Reporting to the Israeli cabinet on this serious security situation, the chief of staff, General Ehud Barak, admitted that the Oslo Accords had "improved the capabilities of the various terrorist groups to act against Israel."[15]

In an effort to avoid the total collapse of the peace process, and at the urging of Rabin, the CIA coordinated a high-level meeting in Frankfurt, Germany, between the Israeli head of the General Security Service, Yaacov Peri, and his Palestinian counterpart, Amin el-Hindi. Acting under the command of Abu Iyad, the head of the Black September terrorist group, Amin el-Hindi had been among the planners of the massacre of eleven Israeli athletes in Munich in 1972. El-Hindi was on Israel's hit list, which included all those who participated in the planning and the execution of the massacre. Ten terrorists were hunted down; el-Hindi was among the very few who survived. In his Frankfurt meeting with Peri, el-Hindi promised more cooperation in combating terrorism. Indeed, for a while there were signs of greater cooperation between the security services of Israel and the Palestinians. This cooperation, which was publicly appreciated by Rabin, was not sufficient to end the violence.

In early November 1994, the security situation again deteriorated and Arafat himself faced a chilling experience. Attending the funeral of Hani Abed, one of the military commanders of Islamic Jihad in the Gaza Strip, who had been killed by a car bomb presumed to have been planted by the Israeli secret service, Arafat was mobbed by angry demonstrators who shouted: "Arafat, Arafat! Remember what Islamic Jihad did to Anwar Sadat!"

This was not the first time that Arafat had faced death threats. He claimed to have survived forty attempts on his life. While this figure seems grossly exaggerated, there is no doubt that at various times, Israelis, Arabs, and Palestinians tried to hunt him down. But this was the first time since his return to the Gaza Strip in July 1994 that such a threat had been made. The threat became even more real when on November 3 Arafat entered the mosque where a memorial service for Hani Abed was being held. Accused of collaborating with Israel in hunting down this Islamic Jihad activist, Arafat was jeered and cursed, and eventually he had to flee the mosque barefoot and his trademark checkered black-and-white kafiyyeh was snatched off his bald head.[16] "It's a disgrace," said General Yousef Nasser, the overall head of the Palestinian security forces in the Gaza Strip and Jericho. "There can't be a situation where President Arafat can't go to a mosque and pray. He who would raise a hand against a brother Palestinian should know that we would cut it off." Hamas and Islamic Jihad activists were not deterred, however. Overnight, Gaza walls were painted with graffiti calling Arafat a "traitor" and an "Israeli agent." As a sign of contempt, Hamas prisoners in Gaza addressed their officers in jail in Hebrew, thereby indicating that they considered the officers "Israeli agents" too.

Arafat's political situation was further complicated by the signing of the Israeli-Jordanian peace treaty, on October 26, 1994. Arafat feared that he was suddenly pushed aside by Rabin. The Israeli prime minister was always perceived by both President Mubarak and Arafat as having "second thoughts" about the Oslo Accords. The PLO chairman was also aware of Rabin's suspicions that while he, Arafat, talked peace, in practice he did not do enough to curb terrorism. Rabin repeatedly admitted publicly that the Oslo Accords were "full of holes," and he vowed to rectify them, especially in the field of security.

In an effort to assure Arafat that the peace with Jordan was not at the Palestinians' expense, Rabin met with the PLO chairman on November 8 at the Erez checkpoint, north of Gaza. In advance of the meeting, Rabin convened a small group of ministers and senior army officers to discuss problems related to the delayed redeployment in the West Bank. Rabin felt that after Arafat's chilling experience in Gaza and in an effort to contain the constant erosion in Arafat's popularity, Israel should take some steps to enhance Arafat's personal position. Foreign Minister Peres and Minister of the Environment Yossi Sarid shared this view. Chief of Staff Barak, however, opposed it. Other ministers too expressed concern that an early redeployment without adequate "security valves" could be risky. After a private consultation with Peres, Rabin approved his foreign minister's idea of engaging in intense negotiations for an interim accord, aimed at resolving all issues related to Palestinian self-rule in the West Bank. Indeed, in his November 8 meeting at the Erez checkpoint, Rabin proposed to Arafat discussing in Cairo, beginning November 21 and in small working groups, all the issues simultaneously. According to one participant, this was really the first successful meeting between Rabin and Arafat since their historic handshake at the White House. "You could sense," the official said, "that the frosty relationship between them began to melt." Rabin candidly explained to Arafat that a redeployment in the West Bank could not take place before an agreement on the security arrangements. "The Israeli public would oppose such a redeployment if terrorism is not curbed and if the security of the settlements is not assured," the prime minister said.

According to the same participant, Arafat was very distressed. He told Rabin that he too was facing growing opposition to the Oslo process. He complained that the donor countries were withholding the funds that they had pledged, and he was unable to show his people the advantages of peace. The Israeli closure of the Gaza Strip, in retaliation to terrorist activity, had increased the hardships, since Palestinian workers were unable to work in Israel and provide food for their hungry families. This, in turn, had reduced the amount of taxes from Palestinian workers, which Israel was to turn over to the Palestine Authority. Hence, in the absence of funds and with unemployment growing, the Palestine Authority was unable to provide even minimum social services. In such a situation, there was a real danger that because of its vast social infrastructure Hamas would fill the gap.[17]

Nevertheless, and as a "routine" pattern, Arafat reiterated his promise to do more to curb terrorism. Three days later, on November 11, it was proved again that Arafat's promises were not sufficient. A Hamas suicide bomber rode his bicycle into an Israeli army post in the Gaza Strip and blew himself up, killing three army officers and wounding eleven soldiers.

This incident, coming right after his meeting with Rabin, placed Arafat in a very delicate situation. In order to salvage his credibility with both Israel and the United States, Arafat decided to act. He ordered a crackdown on the Islamic groups and the other Palestinian opposition organizations. Within days, ninety-five members of Nayef Hawatmeh's DFLP, based in Damascus, were arrested. Then, on November 18, came what was to become known as "Arafat's bloodbath." After Friday prayers, thousands of Hamas activists marched in a violent demonstration in Gaza, calling for Arafat's resignation. The Palestinian police, anticipating such a demonstration, used live ammunition to disperse the crowds. Within minutes, sixteen Palestinians were shot dead and more than two hundred wounded. The danger of a civil war was never so real.

Angry Hamas leaders passed a death sentence on General Youssef Nasser, whom they accused of masterminding the massacre. Other Palestinian groups suspended all contacts with Arafat and his Palestine Authority. Facing the danger of a civil war, Arafat retracted immediately. He declared a truce and called for a dialogue with Hamas. "We are not like the Serbs or the Croats. We and Hamas belong to the same people, although we differ over ideology," Dr. Nabil Shaath, the Palestinian negotiator, told correspondents. The fifty-five-year-old former Philadelphia economist added that Hamas leaders were capable of impairing Arafat's ability to stand up to them. "Arafat will look like Uncle Tom, wielding the machete for the plantation's white owner," he concluded. Indeed, in an interview with a Paris-based Arab weekly, Hani el-Hassan, a former close ally of Yasser Arafat who supported the Palestinian participation in the Madrid Peace Conference but who opposed the Oslo Accords, said: "Despite the strong Israeli and American pressure, El-Fatah's Central Committee refused to engage in the liquidation of Hamas. El-Fatah forced Arafat to retract, and that's what saved Hamas from annihilation."[18]

Thus, in the decisive moment when Arafat was called to prove his leadership, the PLO chairman chose a truce with Hamas over his commitment to Israel and the United States to curb terrorism. Such an attitude renewed doubts over Arafat's ability to deliver. This new situation was at the center of Rabin's meeting with President Clinton at the White House on November 21, 1994. In advance of the meeting, ambassadors Dennis Ross and Martin Indyk met with the Israeli prime minister at his hotel suite in New York. Their implied message was clear: As a signatory and a witness to the Oslo Accords, the United States would not like to see the peace process collapse. "We understand your frustration, but you have no other partner for reconciliation with the Palestinians," Ross and Indyk are reported to have told Rabin.

Indeed, despite their shared concern, both Rabin and Clinton decided to keep the Oslo process alive. However, in an effort to help cure Arafat's economic illnesses, the United States urged the donor countries to honor their pledges and provide the Palestine Authority with the necessary funds for its operations. In order to overcome possible Congressional opposition, the U.S. Department of State issued a report asserting that the "PLO complied with the provisions of the DOP." In a meeting in Brussels on November 30, the donor countries agreed to give Arafat $125 million—$102 million to cover current expenditures and salaries to policemen and $23 million to finance job-creating economic projects.[19]

During an interreligious dialogue in Madrid on November 30, Rabin and Arafat made another effort to solve the problems facing them. Unlike their previous encounter at the Erez checkpoint, the meeting in Madrid was tough and tense. During a cabinet meeting on December 4, Rabin revealed the contents of his discussion with Arafat. Rabin is reported to have told his ministers that he was "disappointed" with Arafat's performance. The PLO was not doing enough to curb terrorism, and therefore it would be "more difficult" to implement the next phases of the Cairo Agreement. Israel informed Arafat that it was prepared to transfer to him authority over health, education, social services, taxation, and tourism, but the army redeployment could not take place before an agreement on security arrangements.[20] The head of the General Security Service (GSS), Yaacov Peri, told the ministers that since Arafat's return to Gaza on July 1, 1994, the GSS had been encountering growing difficulties in penetrating the Palestine Authority. He revealed that there was an intensified Palestinian effort to smuggle arms and ammunition into the Gaza Strip, through tunnels from Sinai or by sea.

Nevertheless, the consensus among the Israeli ministers was that despite the difficulties, Israel had no alternative to Arafat's leadership.[21]

It was with this sense of "no choice" that Rabin, Peres, and Arafat met again in Oslo on December 10, on the occasion of the awarding of their shared Nobel Peace Prize. After the official ceremonies and festivities, Rabin, Peres, and Arafat had a long discussion that lasted until the early hours of December 11. After analyzing the problems that each of them faced, Rabin presented two options to Arafat: sticking to the Oslo Accords, but in a slower pace, until Israel's security needs were met; or a "symbolic" Israeli withdrawal from the major cities of the West Bank, in order to enable elections to the Palestine Authority without massive Israeli military presence. After the elections, Rabin and Arafat would meet again to discuss the continued implementation of the Oslo Accords.

Arafat rejected the two options and insisted on a strict adherence to the Oslo Accords timetable.[22]

Thus, a year after the historic handshake at the White House, it was obvious that Rabin had become aware of the Oslo Accords' shortcomings and was seeking ways to rectify them. Arafat's situation was no better. One of Arafat's closest allies, Abu Mazen, who signed the Oslo Accords with Shimon Peres, told a London-based newsmagazine that he was "very unhappy" with the way the negotiations with Israel were being conducted.[23] Professor Edward Said of Columbia University, one of the strongest opponents of the Oslo Accords, called on Arafat to resign.[24] According to Said, Arafat had gained nothing from the peace process. On the contrary, the city limits of Jerusalem were expanded, Palestinian prisoners were not released, elections were not held, a secure passage between the West Bank and the Gaza Strip was not granted, and sovereignty, even in areas under Palestinian control, remained in Israel's hands.

Amid this turbulent situation came another deadly terrorist act, increasing Israel's anxiety. On January 22, 1995, an Islamic Jihad suicide bomber blew himself up near a snack bar mobbed with soldiers at Beit Lid, to the east of Netanya, killing eighteen Israelis and wounding sixty. Shocked by this murderous act, President Ezer Weizman called for the immediate suspension of negotiations with the Palestinians, for thirty days, in order to reassess the situation. "We have to see if we did not err in choosing Arafat as our partner. You simply cannot trust a liar," the president said.[25]

Rabin and Peres were embarrassed by Weizman's intervention, but they decided to ignore it. In an angry meeting with Arafat at the Erez checkpoint, Rabin insisted that the Palestinian security services knew who the Hamas and Islamic Jihad terrorists were and who was assisting them. Realizing that the deteriorating security situation could derail the entire peace process, the Egyptian and Jordanian foreign ministers also urged Arafat to curb terrorism. The Russian coordinator of the Middle East peace process, Victor Posavaliuk, rushed to Gaza for an urgent meeting with Yasser Arafat. Dennis Ross phoned Arafat three times and tried to salvage the process. Needless to say, both Ross and Posavaliuk agreed with Rabin that President Weizman's call to suspend the talks should be ignored. They feared that a "temporary suspension" would become a permanent suspension and the whole process would collapse.

Weizman's call, however, was echoed by Abu Mazen. In an interview with an Arab daily, Abu Mazen said: "We have to suspend the negotiations temporarily, in order to draft a balance sheet and to decide how to proceed." Abu Mazen deplored the suicide bombing at Beit Lid and urged Arafat to disarm Hamas and Islamic Jihad, leaving arms in the hands of the Palestinian police only. At the same time, Abu Mazen acknowledged that the Oslo Accords were "vague" in many areas. He said that "it was a mistake" on the part of the Palestinians not to insist on a total freeze of Israeli settlement activity. He implied that it was also a mistake to accept the vague American language on the settlements. He revealed that because of the sharp divisions between Israelis and Palestinians, the United States had suggested a phrasing that said that neither side should take steps that could predetermine the outcome of the final status negotiations. "We should have insisted on a total ban on settlement activity," Abu Mazen said.[26]

In light of the deteriorating security situation, the United States initiated an urgent meeting in Washington, in February 1995, with the participation of the foreign ministers of Israel, Egypt, and Jordan. At Secretary Christopher's personal request, Arafat sent his negotiator with the Israelis, Dr. Nabil Shaath, to Washington. In an interview with a London-based Arab daily, Shaath admitted that "Oslo did not meet the expectations of both sides. Rabin really expected that Arafat would act against Hamas and Islamic Jihad. When this did not happen, Rabin was disappointed."[27] Shaath explained that unlike the bilateral negotiations in Washington, which sought a comprehensive peace with the Arab countries, the Oslo Accords called for a two-stage settlement of the Israeli-Palestinian conflict only. "Arafat preferred this approach, because it meant his return to Palestine rather than his continued exile," Shaath said. Finally, Shaath complained that by issuing their statements on their military operations in Gaza, both Hamas and Islamic Jihad were "complicating" Arafat's position, since he could not pretend that these actions were carried out from areas not under his control.[28]

The Washington meeting did not produce any tangible results. In reply to Palestinian complaints that Israel had not honored its commitment to redeploy its forces in the West Bank, Rabin suggested withdrawing first from the city of Jenin, and then continuing negotiations on further withdrawals. Arafat and Abu Mazen rejected Rabin's idea and claimed that "Jenin first" would split the redeployment process.[29] In a meeting with Shaath in Cairo, Peres suggested a sovereign Palestinian state in the Gaza Strip and continued negotiations on the future of the West Bank. Arafat rejected this idea too.[30] If these proposals proved anything, they proved that Rabin and Peres were becoming increasingly aware of the shortcomings of the Oslo Accords and were seeking ways to rectify them.

The continued stalemate in the Israeli-Palestinian negotiations was at the center of President Mubarak's visit to Washington in April 1995. Mubarak was "welcomed" at the White House with yet another deadly Palestinian terrorist act against Israel. On April 9, two Hamas suicide bombers blew themselves up near Kfar Darom, in the Gaza Strip, killing seven Israelis, one of them a former American. Briefing Egyptian editors on his discussion with Clinton, Mubarak warned that the Gaza Strip "could become another Afghanistan." He said that two months of Israeli closure of the Gaza Strip had increased economic hardships, since the Palestinians were denied work in Israel. The issue of the closure also came up during a joint press conference with President Clinton. In reply to an Egyptian correspondent, Clinton said: "The issue of the closure is really a tough question and I don't have an answer to it. If Israel opens the border and admits Palestinian workers, there is terrorism. And if Israel separates itself from the Gaza Strip, then there is unemployment and economic hardships. My advice to both parties is to continue their negotiations."[31]

Indeed, under strong American and Egyptian pressure, Israel and the PLO resumed their negotiations in Cairo. In an effort to avoid Arafat's downfall, Israel on April 25 urged the United States and the other donor countries to cover "immediately" the $136 million deficit in Arafat's $450 million budget for 1995. What was even more important, Peres locked himself into a June deadline for reaching an agreement on Israel's redeployment in the West Bank.

The June deadline, however, proved to be difficult to make. Refusing to evacuate the Jewish settlers from Hebron and insisting on effective security arrangements in the West Bank, Rabin proposed to delay the redeployment in Hebron to the final status negotiations. Arafat refused. On the other hand, and contrary to his pledge to leave the issue of Jerusalem to the final status negotiations, Arafat on April 10, 1995, decided to revive the dissolved East Jerusalem municipal council. This demonstrative act was meaningless. It challenged, however, Israel's claim to undivided sovereignty over a united Jerusalem.[32]

Amid this wrangling came yet another suicide bombing. On July 24, 1995, a Hamas suicide bomber blew up a crowded commuter bus during rush hour in Tel Aviv, killing six Israelis and wounding thirty-two. In mid-August 1995 came another suicide bombing in the heart of Jerusalem.

The lack of progress in the peace process and the continued terrorism in the big Israeli cities affected the popularity of both Rabin and Arafat. Better organized and certainly more vocal than the Palestinian opposition, the Likud Party and other right-wing opposition groups staged frequent demonstrations and called for Rabin's resignation. Extreme right-wing and religious groups called Rabin a traitor and accused him of betraying his promises to the electorate. Alerted by the security services to a possible attempt at his life, Rabin ignored the warnings. The former Canadian ambassador to Israel, Norman Spector, who is currently the publisher of the *Jerusalem Post,* recently wrote that as the term of his ambassadorship was ending, he made the final call on the Israeli prime minister, and in his trademark fashion, Rabin dismissed with a wave of hand the possibility that a Jew would ever kill another Jew.[33]

Rabin was aware, of course, of two facts:

- No country in the world, not even the United States, as had been proved at the World Trade Center in New York and the federal building in Oklahoma City, could totally eliminate terrorist acts. Rabin, however, expected Arafat to commit himself totally to combating terrorism. The security cooperation between Israel and the Palestinians was very important, but was quite insufficient.

- The overwhelming majority of the Palestinians were by now under Arafat's control. However, tens of thousands of Palestinians crossed daily from the Gaza Strip to work in Israel. The possibility of suicide bombers infiltrating into Israel with the innocent workers was therefore very real.

In the absence of any other alternative, Rabin and Peres became prisoners of their own slogans. After each terrorist act, they kept repeating that it was the job of the "enemies of peace." They also said: "We will fight terrorism as though there is no peace process, and we will continue the peace process as though there is no terrorism." This slogan, unfortunately, was wearing thin. Realizing that the peace process would not be suspended, Hamas and Islamic Jihad felt free to continue their carnage.

As part of the cooperation between the Israeli and Palestinian security services, Israel informed Arafat on August 15, 1995, that three Hamas activists were about to send another suicide bomber to Tel Aviv. Israel gave Arafat the name of the senior member of the team—Awad Slimi, who was suspected of having murdered Israeli colonel Mintz in the Gaza Strip. Arafat ignored the warning. Angered by this attitude, Rabin reimposed the closure of the Gaza Strip. Only then did Arafat move. On August 18, the Palestinian security services arrested the three Hamas terrorists, including Slimi, and brought them to trial. Shortly afterward, however, Slimi managed to "escape" from jail. He was recaptured only a year later, in September 1996, when Benjamin Netanyahu became the prime minister.

This inadequate security cooperation led the chief of the general staff, General Amnon Shahak, to tell the Knesset's Foreign Affairs and Security Committee that the extension of Palestinian autonomy into the next phase would fail if the Palestinian security agencies did not fully cooperate with Israel. It was obvious that Shahak's remarks could not have been made without Rabin's prior approval.[34]

In September 1995, two years after the historic handshake at the White House, it became clear that Yasser Arafat was not living up to his people's expectations. Instead of generating the kind of enthusiasm that might have attracted rich and educated Palestinians to build their new entity, Arafat created more divisions. Private investors—Western and Arab—had not renewed their initial interest and seemed to be afraid to take risks in this unstable situation. Furthermore, Arafat's record on human rights was worse than the record compiled at any time by Israel. Freedom of the press was suppressed, and on many occasions journalists were jailed and tortured and the distribution of their publications was banned. Calls for Arafat's resignation became more and more frequent. In Gaza, Dr. Haidar Abdul Shafi, whom Arafat had appointed to head the Palestinian delegation to the Madrid Peace Conference, called for the

ouster of Arafat. Hamas and Islamic Jihad leaders demonstrated their opposition to Arafat by intensifying their daily attacks against Israel. George Habash,
whose PFLP organization was headquartered in Damascus, called for the removal of Arafat from the chairmanship of the PLO.[35]

In this complex situation, the only Israeli leader who was pushing consistently toward an interim agreement with the Palestinians was Foreign Minister
Shimon Peres. His ambition to create a New Middle East blurred his sight, and
on many occasions he seemed to have lost touch with reality. Addressing the
Conference of Presidents of Major Jewish Organizations in New York in February 1995, Peres explained his new "vision" of computerizing education systems in the Arab world. Ignoring the deadly suicide bombings of Hamas and
Islamic Jihad, Peres threw in yet another proposal: a regional gathering of the
leaders of the three monotheistic religions in Israel and the Arab world.[36]
American Jewish leaders reacted to this "vision" with a smile.

Earlier, attending an interreligious dialogue in Madrid, together with Rabin
and Arafat, Peres said: "The Madrid Peace Conference was a diplomatic breakthrough; the Casablanca economic summit was a regional economic breakthrough; next year, in 1995, we shall witness an intellectual and cultural
breakthrough. We shall call for a conference with the participation of intellectuals from Israel and the Arab world."[37] Needless to say, no such conference
was ever convened, and Arab intellectuals remained the most vocal group in
opposition to peace or normalization of cultural relations with Israel.

More serious, however, was Peres's approach to security. Contrary to
Rabin's insistence that Arafat honor his commitment to apprehend and surrender to Israel terrorists who committed acts of violence in Israel, Peres suggested "not making it more difficult for Arafat," thus delaying further the
conclusion of the interim agreement. Peres believed that insistence on surrendering of terrorists would only "humiliate" Arafat.[38] This was not, however, the
feeling of many Israelis. A poll conducted by Haifa University showed that most
Israelis, while supporting the peace process, still considered Arafat "a terrorist
and a liar."[39]

Israel's problems with the Palestinians were intensified by a growing political tension with Egypt as well. Toward the end of 1994 and early in 1995, Israel
observed an important change in Egypt's Middle Eastern policy. The signing of
the Israeli-Jordanian peace treaty on October 26, 1994, without Egypt's involvement and the gradual normalization of relations between Israel and several North African and Persian Gulf countries aroused President Mubarak's
concern that Egypt was losing its leadership role in the Arab world. This sentiment was strengthened following President Clinton's four-day marathon taking
him from Cairo to Hafr el-Baten (Saudi Arabia's military headquarters during
the Persian Gulf War), Kuwait, Damascus, Jerusalem, and Amman. Clinton's
visit to Damascus was very controversial, but the president achieved his mis-

sion: President Assad promised him not to criticize the Israeli-Jordanian peace treaty publicly. Clinton's extremely warm address to the Knesset, in which he reiterated his promise to maintain Israel's qualitative edge in the region, was seen in Cairo as a proof that the United States was unlikely to pressure Israel to make substantial concessions in the negotiations with Syria and the Palestinians. Egypt gave the first hint of its change of policy during the Casablanca economic summit conference, on October 30, 1994. The conference was convened at the invitation of Morocco's King Hassan, with strong personal involvement of President Clinton and Foreign Minister Shimon Peres. Representatives from sixty-one countries—including Israel and thirteen Arab states—and 1,114 business leaders from all over the world gathered in Casablanca for a two-day conference to discuss regional economic cooperation. This was indeed a very impressive gathering. Ignoring several Moroccan hints to keep a low profile, Israel sent ten ministers—including Rabin and Peres—and hundreds of businessmen and journalists. It was obvious that in the face of the mounting terrorism, Peres was determined to prove that he was indeed leading Israel into a New Middle East of peace and prosperity.

To many Israelis, the Casablanca conference seemed the sweet fruit of the Oslo Accords. It proved to be, however, only a shield for the coming storm. "This is Peres's Golden Calf," joked Mustafa Amin, one of Egypt's leading editors, whose columns were reprinted across the Arab world. Amin reflected the views of Egypt's top policymakers, who were still influenced by the Nasserist nationalistic ideology. The leaders of this trend were National Security Adviser Dr. Ossama el-Baz, Foreign Minister Amr Mussa, former foreign ministers Ismail Fahmi and Ibrahim Kamel, former ambassador to Washington Abdul Raouf el-Ridi, and the current ambassador to the UN, Dr. Nabil el-Arabi. They all opposed Sadat's peace with Israel and they all called for a more assertive Egyptian foreign policy. For them, the Casablanca economic summit was proof of Israel's aspiration to dominate the economic systems of the Middle East. Egypt presented seven projects for regional economic cooperation, but none of them mentioned Israel as a potential partner. When asked about it, Peres dismissed Egypt's attitude as "sheer arrogance." In the euphoria of Casablanca, Peres did not want to read the writing on the wall and did not believe Egypt could prevent Israel's integration in the region's economy.

In this euphoric atmosphere, even Secretary of State Warren Christopher was carried away by exaggerated expectations. In a press conference in Washington on December 20, 1994, Christopher said that the U.S. Middle Eastern policy in 1995 would be to bring Israel and the Arab countries closer to a comprehensive peace. He expressed the hope that he would be able to persuade the Arab league to end the economic boycott of Israel and to encourage North African and Persian Gulf countries to establish diplomatic relations with Israel.[40]

The Republican victory in the Congressional elections in early November

1994 precipitated the change in Egypt's Middle Eastern policy. The Democrats' defeat led Egyptian policymakers to perceive Clinton as a "weakened president" whose authority had declined considerably both at home and abroad. Hence, shortly after the elections, President Mubarak traveled to Damascus for a meeting with President Assad. The Mubarak-Assad summit was followed in January 1995 by a tripartite summit in Alexandria, with the participation of Saudi King Fahd. The Alexandria summit sought to convince the United States that Egypt, Syria, and Saudi Arabia held the key for stability in the region. In the wake of the Alexandria summit, Egypt and Syria sought to balance U.S. dominance in the Middle East by an effort to improve Arab ties with Europe, Russia, Japan, and China.[41]

In a speech at Cairo University, which received little attention in Israel and the West, Dr. Ossama el-Baz gave public expression to this change in Egyptian policy. El-Baz said that during a recent visit to Washington, he had told his American counterparts that Egypt and the United States were divided on almost every issue in the Middle East. He bragged that Egypt was not a "client state" of the United States and that he had informed Secretary Christopher that Egypt opposed the continued isolation of Libya, that the U.S. policy of "double containment" of Iran and Iraq had failed, and that Egypt would never agree to Israel's remaining the only "nuclear power" in the Middle East. "There will never be an end to the Arab-Israeli conflict as long as Israel refuses to eliminate its nuclear arsenal," el-Baz said.

El-Baz's remarks about Israel's presumed "nuclear arsenal" did not come as a surprise to Israeli policymakers. As far back as Camp David, in September 1978, Egyptian policymakers were divided on Israel's nuclear potential. El-Baz argued at the time that Egypt should not sign the Camp David Accords before Israel joined the Nonproliferation Treaty (NPT). President Sadat, however, argued that once Israel signed a peace accord with all the Arab countries and withdrew from all the occupied territories, Israel would be reduced to its "natural size" and would not endanger the security of the Arab world. Mubarak, then vice president, disagreed with Sadat. When he became president, in October 1981, Mubarak made Israel's nuclear potential a pillar of his policy toward the Jewish state.[42]

Developments in the Middle East since the signing of the Oslo Accords proved that Israel was not reduced to its "natural size" but grew stronger—politically, militarily, and economically. The Alexandria summit was aimed, then, at containing this growth and blocking further normalization in Israel's relations with the Arab world. To divert attention from this change of policy, Egypt began to target Prime Minister Rabin. In private discussions with Israeli politicians and journalists, Egyptian diplomats accused Rabin of being "worse than Shamir." They played on the differences between Peres and Rabin, making no effort to conceal their preference for Peres.

By mid-1995, Egypt's efforts to contain the Israeli-Arab normalization had been partially successful. Despite repeated appeals by the United States, Persian Gulf countries refused to end their economic boycott of Israel without a formal decision by the Arab League. Since the implementation of Arab League decisions requires a unanimous vote, it was obvious that no decision could be made without Syria's consent. During a visit to Oman, Rabin urged Sultan Qabus to establish full diplomatic relations with Israel, but the sultan decided to wait for the "regional atmosphere" to improve.[43] Finally, in May 1995, and as part of a larger U.S. effort to encourage Arab states to normalize relations with Israel, Secretary Christopher urged Tunisia to open its promised liaison office in Tel Aviv. Tunisia, however, preferred to wait for further progress in the Israeli-Palestinian negotiations.[44]

In light of these developments, Prime Minister Rabin admitted, in a meeting with a group of American Jewish leaders, that Shimon Peres's "vision" of a New Middle East "had backfired, since it was stoking Arab fears of Israeli economic domination."[45] In this complex situation, Israel and the Palestinians decided to continue their intense negotiations for the conclusion of an interim agreement between them. Ignoring President Weizman's and Abu Mazen's calls for a temporary suspension of the negotiations, Rabin and Arafat said they would not yield to the "enemies of peace." They preferred to negotiate an interim agreement because they did not believe in shortcuts and in a jump to final status negotiations. The main object of the interim agreement was to broaden Palestinian self-government in the West Bank by means of an elected self-governing authority. In this process, the Israeli government embarked on a strategic course aimed at liberating itself of its control of another people and creating a new relationship with its Palestinian neighbors. Therefore, the interim agreement was not only a political ambition but also a solution to a moral predicament.

Unlike the secret negotiations in Oslo, where the teams were very small, the Israeli-Palestinian negotiations in Eilat and Taba involved more than one hundred people on each side. People from various walks of life—government officials, army and police officers, security agents—were engaged in intense negotiations for more than two months, working out critical issues that would determine the future of their two nations. It was not an easy experience. Because of Arafat's modus operandi and his reluctance to relegate authority to his subordinates, even the smallest detail had to be approved by him. This caused the Israeli and Palestinian teams many headaches and frequent crises. In one of the toughest meetings, in September 1995, Arafat stormed out of the room after General Ilan Biran, the Israeli officer commanding the Central Command, showed him a map separating two villages in the Jenin area. "This is Bantustan and I will never accept it," said Arafat in anger. After an immediate intervention by President Mubarak and Dennis Ross, Peres and Arafat were able to reach a compromise on that issue.[46]

During the long negotiations, monitored by Shimon Peres and Abu Mazen, Israel agreed that after the initial redeployment in the West Bank and the election of the eighty-two-member Palestine Council, Israel would undertake a "further redeployment." This was to be carried out in three stages. General Biran, whose command would be responsible for the redeployment, opposed this idea. He argued that before the Israeli government defined its final borders, it would be a mistake to give away territories and to be left with no cards for bargaining in the final status negotiations. Former chief of staff General Ehud Barak, who became Rabin's minister of the interior, supported Biran on this issue. Rabin, however, overruled Biran's opposition and authorized Peres to negotiate the details of the "further redeployment."

As expected, the security problems and the extent of each Israeli withdrawal were the most difficult issues to resolve. The Palestinians, for example, wanted to receive in each of the three stages of the "further redeployment" 30 percent of the land in the West Bank. When this was rejected, they asked for 20 percent. This was also rejected. Then they proposed that the extent of each of the three withdrawals be negotiated with them. Rabin again said no. Finally, Arafat agreed that the extent of the "further redeployment" would be decided by Israel alone.

Similar debates characterized the negotiations on almost every other issue. Eventually, after more than twenty meetings between Peres and Arafat and eight hundred hours of negotiations between the two teams, Rabin and Arafat made the necessary compromises and took the tough decisions. The result was a very detailed agreement, comprising more than three hundred pages and six annexes dealing with security arrangements, elections, transfer of authority, economic relations, legal affairs, and Israeli-Palestinian cooperation.

The agreement was approved by the Israeli cabinet and signed by Rabin and Arafat at a ceremony at the White House, attended by President Clinton, Egypt's President Mubarak, and King Hussein. Because of the continuing terrorism and the frequent crises, the ceremony did not generate the kind of enthusiasm and excitement that were generated by the first Rabin-Arafat handshake. Still, to have the presidents of the United States and Egypt, the king of Jordan, the prime minister of Israel, and the chairman of the PLO on the same stage at the White House was rather remarkable.

The interim agreement was based on gradual implementation and on better cooperation between Israel and the Palestinians. In presenting the agreement for ratification by the Knesset, Rabin explained that for the purpose of redeployment, the West Bank was divided into three zones:

Zone A covered 2.7 percent of the West Bank and included six Palestinian cities and Hebron with a special status. This zone would be fully controlled by the Palestinians.

Zone B covered 25 percent of the West Bank and included 450 small towns and villages, in which 65 percent of the Palestinians resided. This zone would be administered by the Palestine Authority, but the security would be controlled jointly with Israel.

Zone C comprised all the military installations, the Israeli settlements, and the unpopulated areas. Although this zone covered more than 70 percent of the land in the West Bank, the number of resident Palestinians did not exceed fifty thousand. This zone would remain in the hands of Israel for the "further redeployments" and pending the final status negotiations.

In order to assure the free and secure movement of the Israeli settlers and the Israeli army and police, new bypass roads were to be built to circumvent the Palestinian big cities. Rabin explained to the Knesset, on October 5, that during the interim agreement no Israeli settlements would be uprooted and building in the settlements for "natural growth" would not be hindered. Rabin added that the current arrangements for security and prayers at the Cave of the Patriarchs in Hebron and at Rachel's Tomb near Bethlehem would continue. The elections for the chairman of the Palestine Authority and for the eighty-two-member Palestine Council would be for all of the West Bank and the Gaza Strip, and would be held under international observance, to include observers from the United States, Canada, the European Community, and Japan. Israel agreed that Palestinian inhabitants of Jerusalem would participate in the elections and be able to stand for elections if they had additional residences outside Jerusalem. This was a major Israeli concession, which later served as a basis for the Likud's election slogan "Peres will divide Jerusalem." Finally, Rabin told the Knesset that Yasser Arafat had renewed his pledges to combat terrorism and end violence and also to amend the Palestinian Covenant so as to delete from it all passages that implied a destruction of the State of Israel.

The debate on the ratification of the interim agreement was very emotional and sometimes acrimonious. Outside the Knesset, the roads were blocked by angry Likud and religious demonstrators, who called Rabin a traitor and urged him to resign. In order to assure the ratification of the agreement, the Labor Party lured a Knesset member from the right-wing party Tsomet to vote with the government in return for his appointment as deputy minister. Indeed, after a long and stormy debate that lasted until the early hours of October 6, 1995, the Knesset ratified the interim agreement by only a tiny majority, 61–59.

Arafat's pledge to combat terrorism was immediately put to the test. On October 7, 1995, Peres, accompanied by the head of Israeli military intelligence, General Moshe (Bougi) Ye'elon, met with Arafat at the Erez checkpoint. Peres handed Arafat a list of twenty-five leaders of Iz el-Din el-Qassam—Hamas's military wing—and asked for their arrest. The list included Yehya Ayyash, "the Engineer," and his deputy, Mohamed Deif, who had masterminded all the recent suicide-car bombings. Although he had met with Deif one day after his return from Washington, on September 30, Arafat pretended to have never heard Deif's name. Peres ignored Arafat's lie and repeated his request. More than two years later, Deif was still at large; Yehya Ayyash was killed in January 1996 by a booby-trapped cellular phone, presumably by the Israeli secret service.

The month of October 1995 will be recorded in Israel's history as "Black October." It was characterized by daily violent demonstrations against Rabin and his team. The Likud and other opposition right-wing and religious parties denounced the interim agreement as a sellout to Arafat. The threats against Rabin's life became more and more alarming. Rabin dismissed them and continued to believe that a Jew would never kill a Jew. He was tragically wrong. One month later, on November 5, after addressing a huge "peace rally" in Tel Aviv, Rabin was assassinated by a single gunman.

Rabin's assassination and the subsequent defeat of Shimon Peres in the general Knesset elections, on May 29, 1996, had cast a heavy cloud over Israel's peace policies. The Arab countries in general, and the Palestinians in particular, would not "forgive" the democratically elected Likud's Benjamin (Bibi) Netanyahu for his victory over Labor. His insistence on reciprocity in the implementation of the Oslo Accords was perceived as an "excuse" for killing the Oslo process.

Nevertheless, after almost two years of Likud government, it is safe to assume that the Israeli-Palestinian peace process had crossed the point of no return. Despite their mutual distrust of each other, both Netanyahu and Arafat know that not only Israelis and Palestinians but also the U.S. and the international community would not let them miss this opportunity for peace between their two nations.

Appendix A

September 9, 1993

Mr. Prime Minister,

The signing of the Declaration of Principles marks a new era in the history of the Middle East. In firm conviction thereof, I would like to confirm the following PLO commitments:

The PLO recognizes the right of the State of Israel to exist in peace and security.

The PLO accepts United Nations Security Council Resolutions 242 and 338.

The PLO commits itself to the Middle East peace process and to a peaceful resolution of the conflict between the two sides and declares that all outstanding issues relating to permanent status will be resolved through negotiations.

The PLO considers that the signing of the Declaration of Principles constitutes a historic event, inaugurating a new epoch of peaceful coexistence, free from violence and all other acts which endanger peace and stability. Accordingly, the PLO renounces the use of terrorism and other acts of violence and will assume responsibility over all PLO elements and personnel in order to assure their compliance, prevent violations, and discipline violators.

In view of the promise of a new era and the signing of the Declaration of Principles and based on Palestinian acceptance of Security Council Resolutions 242 and 338, the PLO affirms that those articles of the Palestinian Covenant which deny Israel's right to exist and the provisions of the Covenant which are inconsistent with the commitments of this letter are now inoperative and no longer valid. Consequently, the PLO undertakes to submit to the Palestinian National Council for formal approval the necessary changes in regard to the Palestinian Covenant.

Sincerely,

Yasser Arafat
Chairman
The Palestine Liberation Organization

September 9, 1993

Mr. Chairman,

In response to your letter of September 9, 1993, I wish to confirm to you that, in light of the PLO commitments included in your letter, the Government of Israel has decided to recognize the PLO as the representative of the Palestinian people and commence negotiations with the PLO within the Middle East peace process.

Sincerely,

Yitzhak Rabin
Prime Minister of Israel

Yasser Arafat
Chairman
The Palestinian Liberation Organization

Appendix B

DECLARATION OF PRINCIPLES ON INTERIM
SELF-GOVERNMENT ARRANGEMENTS
September 13, 1993

The Government of the State of Israel and the PLO Team (in the Jordanian-Palestinian delegation to the Middle East Peace Conference) (the "Palestinian Delegation"), representing the Palestinian people, agree that it is time to put an end to decades of confrontation and conflict, recognize their mutual legitimate and political rights, and strive to live in peaceful coexistence and mutual dignity and security and achieve a just, lasting, and comprehensive peace settlement and historic reconciliation through the agreed political process. Accordingly, the two sides agree to the following principles:

Article I
Aim of the Negotiations

The aim of the Israeli-Palestinian negotiations within the current Middle East peace process is, among other things, to establish a Palestinian Interim Self-Government Authority, the elected Council (the "Council"), for the Palestinian people in the West Bank and the Gaza Strip, for a transitional period not exceeding five years, leading to a permanent settlement based on Security Council Resolutions 242 and 338.

It is understood that the interim arrangements are an integral part of the whole peace process and the negotiations on the permanent status will lead to the implementation of Security Council Resolutions 242 and 338.

Article II
Framework for the Interim Period

The agreed framework for the interim period is set forth in this Declaration of Principles.

Article III
Elections

1. In order that the Palestinian people in the West Bank and the Gaza Strip may govern themselves according to democratic principles, direct, free, and general political elections will be held for the Council under agreed supervision and international observation, while the Palestinian police will ensure public order.
2. An agreement will be concluded on the exact mode and conditions of the elections in accordance with the protocol attached as Annex I, with the goal of holding the elections not later than nine months after the entry into force of this Declaration of Principles.
3. These elections will constitute a significant interim preparatory step toward the realization of the legitimate rights of the Palestinian people and their just requirements.

Article IV
Jurisdiction

Jurisdiction of the Council will cover West Bank and Gaza Strip territory, except for issues that will be negotiated in the permanent status negotiations. The two sides view the West Bank and the Gaza Strip as a single territorial unit, whose integrity will be preserved during the interim period.

Article V
Transitional Period and Permanent Status Negotiations

1. The five-year transitional period will begin upon the withdrawal from the Gaza Strip and Jericho area.
2. Permanent status negotiations will commence as soon as possible, but no later than the beginning of the third year of the interim period, between the Government of Israel and the Palestinian people's representatives.
3. It is understood that these negotiations shall cover remaining issues, including: Jerusalem, refugees, settlements, security arrangements, borders, relations and cooperation with other neighbors, and other issues of common interest.
4. The two parties agree that the outcome of the permanent status negotiations should not be prejudiced or preempted by arrangements reached for the interim period.

Article VI
Preparatory Transfer of Powers and Responsibilities

1. Upon the entry into force of this Declaration of Principles and the withdrawal from the Gaza Strip and the Jericho area, a transfer of authority from the Israeli military government and its Civil Administration to the authorized Palestinians for this task, as detailed herein, will commence. This transfer of authority will be of a preparatory nature until the inauguration of the Council.
2. Immediately after the entry into force of this Declaration of Principles and the withdrawal from the Gaza Strip and Jericho area, with the view to promoting economic development in the West Bank and Gaza Strip, authority will be transferred to the Palestinians on the following spheres: education and culture, health, social welfare, direct taxation, and tourism. The Palestinian side will commence building the Palestinian police force, as agreed upon. Pending the inauguration of the Council, the two parties may negotiate the transfer of additional powers and responsibilities, as agreed upon.

Article VII
Interim Agreement

1. The Israel and Palestinian delegations will negotiate an agreement on the interim period (the "Interim Agreement").
2. The Interim Agreement shall specify, among other things, the structure of the Council, the number of its members, and the transfer of powers and responsibilities from the Israeli military government and its Civil Administration to the Council. The Interim Agreement shall also specify the Council's executive authority, legislative authority in accordance with Article IX below, and the independent Palestinian judicial organs.
3. The Interim Agreement shall include arrangements, to be implemented upon the inauguration of the Council, for the assumption by the Council of all powers and responsibilities transferred previously in accordance with Article VI above.
4. In order to enable the Council to promote economic growth, upon its inauguration, the Council will establish, among other things, a Palestinian Electricity Authority, a Gaza Seaport Authority, a Palestinian Development Bank, a Palestinian Export Promotion Board, a Palestinian Environmental Authority, a Palestinian Land Authority, and a Palestinian Water Administration Authority, and any other Authorities agreed upon, in accordance with the Interim Agreement that will specify their powers and responsibilities.

5. After the inauguration of the Council, the Civil Administration will be dissolved, and the Israeli military government will be withdrawn.

Article VIII
Public Order and Security

In order to guarantee public order and internal security for the Palestinians of the West Bank and the Gaza Strip, the Council will establish a strong police force, while Israel will continue to carry the responsibility for defending against threats, as well as the responsibility for overall security of Israelis for the purpose of safeguarding their public order.

Article IX
Law and Military Orders

1. The Council will be empowered to legislate, in accordance with the Interim Agreement, within all authorities transferred to it.
2. Both parties will review jointly laws and military orders presently in force in remaining spheres.

Article X
Joint Israeli-Palestinian Liaison Committee

In order to provide for a smooth implementation of the Declaration of Principles and any subsequent agreements pertaining to the interim period, upon the entry into force of this Declaration of Principles, a Joint Israeli-Palestinian Liaison Committee will be established in order to deal with issues requiring coordination, other issues of common interest, and disputes.

Article XI
Israeli-Palestinian Cooperation in Economic Fields

Recognizing the mutual benefit of cooperation in promoting the development of the West Bank, the Gaza Strip, and Israel, upon entry into force of this Declaration of Principles, an Israeli-Palestinian Economic Cooperation Committee will be established in order to develop and implement in a cooperative manner the programs identified in the protocols attached as Annex III and Annex IV.

Article XII
Liaison and Cooperation with Jordan and Egypt

The two parties will invite the Governments of Jordan and Egypt to participate in establishing further liaison and cooperation arrangements between the
Government of Israel and the Palestinian representatives, on one hand, and
the Governments of Jordan and Egypt, on the other hand, to promote cooperation between them. These arrangements will include the constitution of a
Continuing Committee that will decide by agreement on the modalities of admission of persons displaced from the West Bank and Gaza Strip in 1967, together with necessary measures to prevent disruption and disorder. Other
matters of common concern will be dealt with by this Committee.

Article XIII
Redeployment of Israeli Forces

1. After the entry into force of this Declaration of Principles, and not later than
   the eve of elections for the Council, a redeployment of Israeli military forces
   in the West Bank and the Gaza Strip will take place, in addition to withdrawal of Israeli forces carried out in accordance with Article XIV.
2. In redeploying its military forces, Israel will be guided by the principle that
   its military forces should be redeployed outside populated areas.
3. Further redeployments to specified locations will be gradually implemented
   commensurate with the assumption of responsibility for public order and internal security by the Palestinian police force pursuant to Article VIII above.

Article XIV
Israeli Withdrawal from the Gaza Strip and Jericho Area

Israel will withdraw from the Gaza Strip and Jericho area, as detailed in the
protocol attached as Annex II.

Article XV
Resolutions of Disputes

1. Disputes arising out of the application or interpretation of this Declaration
   of Principles, or any subsequent agreements pertaining to the interim period, shall be resolved by negotiations through the Joint Liaison Committee
   to be established pursuant to Article X above.

2. Disputes which cannot be settled by negotiations may be resolved by a mechanism of conciliation to be agreed upon by the parties.
3. The parties may agree to submit to arbitration disputes relating to the interim period which cannot be settled through conciliation. To this end, upon the agreement of both parties, the parties will establish an Arbitration Committee.

Article XVI
Israeli-Palestinian Cooperation Concerning Regional Programs

Both parties view the multilateral working groups as an appropriate instrument for promoting a "Marshall Plan," the regional programs, and other programs, including special programs for the West Bank and Gaza Strip, as indicated in the protocol attached as Annex IV.

Article XVII
Miscellaneous Provisions

1. This Declaration of Principles will enter into force one month after its signing.
2. All protocols annexed to this Declaration of Principles and Agreed Minutes pertaining thereto shall be regarded as an integral part hereof.

Done at Washington, D.C., this thirteenth day of September, 1993.

For the Government of Israel   For the P.L.O.

_____   _____

_____

Witnessed by:

For the United States of America   The Russian Federation

_____   _____

Appendix C

October 11, 1993

Dear Minister Holst,

I wish to confirm that the Palestinian institutions of East Jerusalem and the interests and well-being of the Palestinians of East Jerusalem are of great importance and will be preserved.

Therefore, all the Palestinian institutions of East Jerusalem, including the economic, social, educational, and cultural, and the holy Christian and Muslim places, are performing an essential task for the Palestinian population.

Needless to say, we will not hamper their activity; on the contrary, the fulfillment of this important mission is to be encouraged.

Sincerely,

Shimon Peres
Foreign Minister of Israel

Appendix D

May 4, 1994

Yitzhak Rabin
Prime Minister of Israel

Mr. Prime Minister,

With regard to the Agreement on the Gaza Strip and the Jericho Area, signed in Cairo on May 4, 1994 (hereinafter "the Agreement"), the PLO hereby confirms the following:

1. The PLO undertakes to ensure that the Palestinian Authority, including the Palestinian Police and other Palestinian Authority agencies, will function in accordance with the Agreement, and that the Palestinian Authority will activate the coordination and cooperation mechanism in a timely manner.
2. The PLO undertakes to cooperate with Israel, and to assist it, in its efforts to locate and to return to Israel Israeli soldiers who are missing in action and the bodies of killed soldiers which have not been recovered.
3. The PLO undertakes to submit to the next meeting of the Palestinian National Council for formal approval the necessary changes in regard to the Palestinian Covenant, as undertaken in the letter dated September 9, 1993, signed by the Chairman of the PLO and addressed to the Prime Minister of Israel.
4. When Chairman Arafat enters the Gaza Strip and the Jericho Area, he will use the title "Chairman (*Ra'ees* in Arabic) of the Palestinian Authority" or "Chairman of the PLO," and will not use the title "President of Palestine."
5. Neither side shall initiate or take any step that will change the status of the Gaza Strip and the Jericho Area pending the outcome of the permanent status negotiations.
6. Pursuant to Article IV, paragraph 3, of the Agreement, the PLO shall inform the Government of Israel of the names of the members of the Palestinian Authority in a letter that shall be provided within a week of signing the Agreement. The appointment of these members to the Palestinian Au-

thority shall take effect upon an exchange of letters between the PLO and the Government of Israel. Changes in the membership of the Palestinian Authority will take effect upon an exchange of letters between the PLO and the Government of Israel.

7. Immediately after the conclusion of the Agreement, early empowerment negotiations will commence pursuant to Article VI of the Declaration of Principles, and the two sides will explore possible expansion of the scope of these negotiations beyond the five spheres.

8. The two sides will intensify the negotiations on the interim arrangements consistent with the Declaration of Principles and guided by its target date.

9. The two sides reiterate their commitment to commence permanent status negotiations as soon as possible, but no later than the beginning of the third year of the interim period, as provided for in Article V of the Declaration of Principles.

10. As regards the relations between Israel and the PLO, and without derogating from the commitments contained in the letters dated September 9, 1993, signed by and exchanged between the Prime Minister of Israel and the Chairman of the PLO, the two sides will apply between them the provision contained in Article XII, paragraph 1, with the necessary changes.

11. The two Parties shall, within one month of signing the Agreement, invite the Governments of Jordan and Egypt to establish the Continuing Committee referred to in Article XII of the Declaration of Principles and in Article XVI of the Agreement.

12. The Government of Israel and the Palestinian Authority shall pass all necessary legislation to implement the Agreement.

13. The two Parties shall continue discussions on the following issues:
    a. the size of the Jericho area;
    b. the positioning of a Palestinian official at the bridge;
    c. additional arrangement in the Rafah passage; and
    d. all outstanding issues specified in the Agreement.

Sincerely,

Yasser Arafat
Chairman
The Palestinian Liberation Organization

May 4, 1994

Yasser Arafat
Chairman
The Palestinian Liberation Organization

Mr. Chairman

The Government of the State of Israel has the honor to acknowledge receipt of your letter of today's date which reads as follows:

With regard to the Agreement on the Gaza Strip and the Jericho Area, signed in Cairo on May 4, 1994 (hereinafter "the Agreement"), the PLO hereby confirms the following:

1. The PLO undertakes to ensure that the Palestinian Authority, including the Palestinian Police and other Palestinian Authority agencies, will function in accordance with the Agreement, and that the Palestinian Authority will activate the coordination and cooperation mechanism in a timely manner.
2. The PLO undertakes to cooperate with Israel, and to assist it, in its efforts to locate and to return to Israel Israeli soldiers who are missing in action and the bodies of killed soldiers which have not been recovered.
3. The PLO undertakes to submit to the next meeting of the Palestinian National Council for formal approval the necessary changes in regard to the Palestinian Covenant, as undertaken in the letter dated September 9, 1993, signed by the Chairman of the PLO and addressed to the Prime Minister of Israel.
4. When Chairman Arafat enters the Gaza Strip and the Jericho Area, he will use the title "Chairman (*Ra'ees* in Arabic) of the Palestinian Authority" or "Chairman of the PLO," and will not use the title "President of Palestine."
5. Neither side shall initiate or take any step that will change the status of the Gaza Strip and the Jericho Area pending the outcome of the permanent status negotiations.
6. Pursuant to Article IV, paragraph 3, of the Agreement, the PLO shall inform the Government of Israel of the names of the members of the Palestinian Authority in a letter that shall be provided within a week of signing the Agreement. The appointment of these members to the Palestinian Authority shall take effect upon an exchange of letters between the PLO and the Government of Israel. Changes in the membership of the Palestinian Authority will take effect upon an exchange of letters between the PLO and the Government of Israel.
7. Immediately after the conclusion of the Agreement, early empowerment negotiations will commence pursuant to Article VI of the Declaration of Principles, and the two sides will explore possible expansion of the scope of these negotiations beyond the five spheres.

8. The two sides will intensify the negotiations on the interim arrangements consistent with the Declaration of Principles and guided by its target date.

9. The two sides reiterate their commitment to commence permanent status negotiations as soon as possible, but no later than the beginning of the third year of the interim period, as provided for in Article V of the Declaration of Principles.

10. As regards the relations between Israel and the PLO, and without derogating from the commitments contained in the letters dated September 9, 1993, signed by and exchanged between the Prime Minister of Israel and the Chairman of the PLO, the two sides will apply between them the provision contained in Article XII, paragraph 1, with the necessary changes.

11. The two Parties shall, within one month of signing the Agreement, invite the Governments of Jordan and Egypt to establish the Continuing Committee referred to in Article XII of the Declaration of Principles and in Article XVI of the Agreement.

12. The Government of Israel and the Palestinian Authority shall pass all necessary legislation to implement the Agreement.

13. The two Parties shall continue discussions on the following issues:
    a. the size of the Jericho area;
    b. the positioning of a Palestinian official at the bridge;
    c. additional arrangement in the Rafah passage; and
    d. all outstanding issues specified in the Agreement.

The Government of the State of Israel acknowledges and confirms the undertakings and commitments contained in this letter.

> *Sincerely,*
>
> *Yitzhak Rabin*
> *Prime Minister of Israel*

Appendix E

Israel-Jordan
The United States
July 25, 1994

A. After generations of hostility, blood, and tears and in the wake of years of pain and wars, His Majesty King Hussein and Prime Minister Yitzhak Rabin are determined to bring an end to bloodshed and sorrow. It is in this spirit that His Majesty King Hussein of the Hashemite Kingdom of Jordan and Prime Minister and Minister of Defense Mr. Yitzhak Rabin of Israel met in Washington today at the invitation of President William J. Clinton of the United States of America. This invitation of President William J. Clinton constitutes an historic landmark in the United States' untiring efforts in promoting peace and stability in the Middle East. The personal involvement of the President has made it possible to realize agreement on the content of this historic declaration.

The signing of this declaration bears testimony to the President's vision and devotion to the cause of peace.

B. In their meeting, His Majesty King Hussein and Prime Minister Yitzhak Rabin have jointly reaffirmed the five underlying principles of their understanding on an Agreed Common Agenda designed to reach the goal of a just, lasting, and comprehensive peace between the Arab States and the Palestinians, with Israel.

1. Jordan and Israel aim at the achievement of a just, lasting, and comprehensive peace between Israel and its neighbors and at the conclusion of a Treaty of Peace between both countries.

2. The two countries will vigorously continue their negotiations to arrive at a state of peace, based on Security Council Resolutions 242 and 338 in all aspects, and founded on freedom, equality, and justice.

3. Israel respects the present special role of the Hashemite Kingdom of Jordan in Muslim holy shrines in Jerusalem. When negotiations on the permanent status take place, Israel will give high priority to the Jordanian historic role in these shrines. In addition, the two sides have agreed to act together to promote interfaith relations among the three monotheistic religions.

4. The two countries recognize their right and obligation to live in peace with each other as well as with all states within secure and recognized boundaries. The two states affirmed their respect for and acknowledgment of the sovereignty, territorial integrity, and political independence of every state in the area.

5. The two countries desire to develop good neighborly relations of cooperation between them to ensure lasting security and to avoid threats and use of force between them.

C. The long conflict between the two states is now coming to an end. In this spirit the state of belligerency between Jordan and Israel has been terminated.

D. Following this declaration and in keeping with the Agreed Common Agenda, both countries will refrain from actions or activities by either side that may adversely affect the security of the other or may prejudice the final outcome of negotiations. Neither side will threaten the other by use of force, weapons, or by any other means against each other and both sides will thwart threats to security resulting from all kinds of terrorism.

E. His Majesty King Hussein and Prime Minister Yitzhak Rabin took note of the progress made in the bilateral negotiations within the Jordan-Israel track last week on the steps decided to implement the subagendas on borders, territorial matters, security, water, energy, environment, and the Jordan Rift Valley.

In this framework, mindful of items of the Agreed Common Agenda (borders and territorial matter), they noted that the boundary subcommission has reached agreement in July 1994 in fulfillment of part of the role entrusted to it in the subagenda. They also noted that the subcommission for water, environment, and energy agreed mutually to recognize, as the role of their negotiations, the rightful allocations of the two sides in Jordan River and Yarmouk River waters and to fully respect and comply with the negotiated rightful allocations, in accordance with agreed acceptable principles with mutually acceptable quality. Similarly, His Majesty King Hussein and Prime Minister Yitzhak Rabin expressed their deep satisfaction and pride in the work of the trilateral commission in its meeting held in Jordan on Wednesday, July 20, 1994, hosted by the Jordanian Prime Minister, Dr. Abdessalam al-Majali, and attended by Secretary of State Warren Christopher and Foreign Minister Shimon Peres. They voiced their pleasure at the association and commitment of the United States in this endeavor.

F. His Majesty King Hussein and Prime Minister Yitzhak Rabin believe that steps must be taken both to overcome psychological barriers and to break with the legacy of war. By working with optimism toward the dividends of peace for all the people in the region, Jordan and Israel are determined to shoulder their responsibilities toward the human dimension of peacemaking. They recognize imbalances and disparities as a root cause of extremism which thrives on poverty and unemployment and the degradation of human dignity. In this spirit, His Majesty King Hussein and Prime Minister Yitzhak Rabin have today approved a series of steps to symbolize the new era which is now at hand:

1. Direct telephone links will be opened between Jordan and Israel.
2. The electricity grids of Jordan and Israel will be linked as part of a regional concept.
3. Two new border crossings will be opened between Jordan and Israel—one at the southern tip of Aqaba-Eilat and the other at a mutually agreed point in the north.
4 In principle, free access will be given to third-country tourists traveling between Jordan and Israel.
5. Negotiations will be accelerated on opening an international air corridor between both countries.
6. The police forces of Jordan and Israel will cooperate in combating crime, with emphasis on smuggling and particularly drug smuggling. The United States will be invited to participate in this joint endeavor.
7. Negotiations on economic matters will continue in order to prepare for future bilateral cooperation including the abolition of all economic boycotts.

All these steps are being implemented within the framework of regional infrastructure development plans and in conjunction with the Jordan-Israel bilaterals on boundaries, security, water, and related issues and without prejudice to the final outcome of the negotiations on the items included in the Agreed Common Agenda between Jordan and Israel.

G. His Majesty King Hussein and Prime Minister Yitzhak Rabin have agreed to meet periodically or whenever they feel it necessary to review the progress of the negotiations and express their firm intention to shepherd and direct the process in its entirety.

H. In conclusion, His Majesty King Hussein and Prime Minister Yitzhak Rabin wish to express once again their profound thanks and appreciation to President William J. Clinton and his Administration for their untiring efforts in furthering the cause of peace, justice, and prosperity for all the peoples of the region. They wish to thank the President personally for his warm welcome and hospitality. In recognition of their appreciation to the President, His Majesty King Hussein and Prime Minister Yitzhak Rabin have asked President William J. Clinton to sign this document as a witness and as a host to their meeting.

His Majesty King Hussein   *Prime Minister Yitzhak Rabin*

President William J. Clinton

Appendix F

Please call, *very urgent,* Mr. Leket, in Jerusalem: [telephone number follows]

Mr. Leket called to the Ministry for Foreign Affairs and asked us to forward the message.

Message from Arieh Fürth, representative of World Sionist Organization in Scandinavia [telephone numbers follow]:

Today on the 6 December I got a message from Chilik Leket through Amos Yovel who is assistant of Mr. Simcha Dinitz who asked me to forward to you:

1. Do not meet with Yassir Arafat.

2. If you do, Mr. Leket will demand from you to resign from all official Jewish positions.

You are kindly requested urgently to contact Mr. Leket in Jerusalem on one of the following numbers:

[telephone numbers]

NOTE FROM ABBA EBAN
TO MENACHEM ROSENSAFT,
DECEMBER 1988

I shall tell Leket that if you are removed, I shall resign from any connection with the International Labour Zionist movement.

A.

[handwritten note]

Appendix G

Dear Mr. Rosensaft

Greetings,

I received, a few days ago your letter of December 14, 1990 which includes your letter in *Newsweek* of February 11, 1990.

I would like to thank you for your frankness in expounding your ideas on the issue of peace in the Middle East. I do not know who told you that we are angry at you because of this frankness. Undoubtedly it is your right to expound your ideas as you like especially so that you do not hide your political positions and attitudes as a Zionist from the labour party and president of the Labour Zionist Alliance.

With due respect to your ideas, it is really regrettable to find that you are still prisoner of the stereotypes on the Palestinians and the Palestine Liberation Organization and of the propaganda and premeditated distortions of them. I had hoped that your participation at my meetings with the representatives of the American Jews in Stockholm on December 6, 1988 would have been an impetus at objectivity and reasonable dealing with one of the most complicated issues in the world.

Despite all this, I would like to affirm to you that the PLO, the sole legitimate representatives of the Palestinian people has made a historical compromise which is the corner stone of any just solution to this complicated issue.

The peace process in the area would not have witnessed this impetus and thrust had it not been for this solution proposed by the Palestinian people and their leadership. You know that the leaders of Israel refused until now all initiatives including Baker's five points for finding a peaceful settlement. Thus, peace cannot be made by one party. Israel has to make a similar historical compromise to achieve peace with the Palestinian people based on the recognition of our people's national rights including this right to freedom, independence and sovereignty.

I am confident that the chain of violence would definitely end if each of us makes the necessary steps to realize just and permanent peace.

With my thanks and appreciation.

Tunis June 25, 1990

Yasser Arafat
President of the State of Palestine
Chairman of the Executive Committee of the PLO

Mr. Menachem Z. Rosensaft

Appendix H

THE PRIME MINISTER

Jerusalem, le 17 août 1994

Votre Majesté,

Je suis particulièrement heureux de faire part, à Votre Majesté, par notre ami commun, M. Raphaël Edéry, de l'avancement significatif du processus global de paix, avec la signature de l'accord entre l'Etat d'Israël et le Royaume de Jordanie.

Plus encore que la signature de cet accord sous l'égide du Président Clinton, la sincérité et la chaleur apportées à cet événement historique, par Sa Majesté le Roi Hussein, m'ont convaincu qu'une étape essentielle vers la normalisation des relations entre Israël et ses voisins, et, surtout, la Jordanie et l'Autonomie Palestinienne, a été franchie.

Cette étape est devenue, je crois, décisive avec l'ouverture de la frontière entre Israël et la Jordanie, en présence des plus hautes Autorités des deux Etats.

J'ai l'honneur de vous adresser ci-joint une copie signée par les deux parties du texte en Anglais en attirant votre haute attention sur le paragraphe concernant les Lieux Saints d'Al-Quods.

Je peux assurer Votre Majesté, qua je continuerai, fort de cette évolution, à déployer tous mes efforts et ceux de mon Gouvernement, pour renforcer nos liens personnels avec Votre Majesté et pour concrétiser tous les projets de coopération que nous avons évoqués depuis notre rencontre dans votre Pays à l'occasion de nos différents échanges de messages.

Sa Majesté Hassan II
Roi du Maroc
Rabat

THE PRIME MINISTER

Je demeure également persuadé que Votre Majesté continuera à jouer un rôle essentiel dans la consolidation de la Paix et de la coexistence sincère entre Arabes et Israéliens comme entre Musulmans et Juifs, notamment dans le cadre des fonctions de Président de la Conférence Islamique et de la Conférence d'Al-Quods, que remplit avec éclat, Votre Majesté, depuis tant d'années.

Je tiens aussi à vous remercier de votre décision courageuse et historique qui m'a été transmise aujourd'hui par votre fidèle collaborateur et notre ami.

Permettez-moi d'assurer, une fois encore, Votre Majesté, de mon appréciation pour votre contribution et de mon estime et de la considération respectueuse pour Votre Personne et pour Votre Grand Peuple.

Yitzhak Rabin

Notes

INTRODUCTION: PERES'S DEFEAT

1. *L'Express,* Paris, Dec. 19, 1996.
2. Barry Rubin, in *Jerusalem Post,* Sept. 27, 1996.
3. *Jerusalem Post,* Sept. 27, 1996.
4. *El-Sharq el-Awsat* (in Arabic), London, April 11, 1997.
5. *El-Hawadith* (in Arabic), London, May 16, 1997.
6. *New York Times,* July 16, 1997.
7. *El-Hawadith,* May 16, 1997.
8. *El-Hayat* (in Arabic), London, May 19, 1997.
9. *Jerusalem Post,* Jan. 28, 1996.
10. *Maariv,* Tel Aviv, Nov. 16, 1996.
11. Ibid., Nov. 26, 1993; also discussion between Shetreet and author, Tel Aviv, June 25, 1997.
12. *Maariv,* Nov. 29, 1993.
13. Discussion between Shetreet and author, Tel Aviv, June 25, 1997.
14. Discussion between Rabinovich and author, Tel Aviv, Sept. 26, 1996.
15. IDF Radio, Galei Zahal, Jan. 5, 1996.
16. *Jerusalem Post,* July 10, 1977.
17. *Yediot Aharonot,* Tel Aviv, March 27, 1996.
18. *Jerusalem Post,* March 1, 1996.
19. *Yediot Aharonot,* March 6, 1996.
20. Kol Israel, Jerusalem, March 6, 1996.
21. *Maariv* and *Yediot Aharonot,* March 29, 1996.
22. Discussion between Peres and Israeli correspondents, Sharm el-Sheikh.
23. Interview with Peres, IDF Radio, March 29, 1996.
24. Israeli TV, Channel 2, July 10, 1997.
25. *Yediot Aharonot,* Oct. 4, 1996.
26. Kol Israel, April 22, 1996; *Maariv* and *Yediot Aharonot,* April 23, 1996.
27. *Maariv,* April 29, 1996.
28. *El-Nahar,* Jerusalem, May 16, 1996; *Yediot Aharonot,* May 23, 1996.
29. *New York Times,* May 24, 1996.
30. *El-Hayat,* May 2, 1997.
31. Yossi Beilin, *Touching Peace* (Tel Aviv: Miskal Publishing, 1997), pp. 212–15.
32. *Yediot Aharonot,* June 3, 1996.
33. Discussion between Ben-Eliezer and author, Jerusalem, Aug. 28, 1996.
34. *Maariv,* June 8, 1997.
35. Discussion between a Jewish leader and author, New York, March 6, 1997.
36. *Ha'Aretz,* Tel Aviv, Aug. 27, 1996.

37. *Jerusalem Post*, Sept. 12, 1996.

38. Ibid., Sept. 27, 1996.

39. Discussion between a participant and author, New York, Jan. 30, 1997.

40. Full texts published by Israeli government press office, Jan. 15, 1997.

41. *Maariv*, April 4, 1997.

42. Kol Israel, Jerusalem, April 30, 1997.

43. *New York Post*, Nov. 19, 1996.

44. *Yediot Aharonot*, Nov. 21, 1996.

45. *Le Monde Diplomatique*, Paris, May 1997.

46. *Yediot Aharonot*, April 18, 1997.

47. *Ha'Aretz*, May 20, 1997.

48. *New York Times*, May 21, 1997.

49. Discussion between Gold and author, Jerusalem, July 2, 1997.

50. *Jerusalem Post*, June 5, 1997.

CHAPTER 2: THE CONSPIRACY THAT NEVER WAS

1. Private discussion between one of those ministers and author, Tel Aviv, Nov. 17, 1995.

2. *Ha'Aretz*, Tel Aviv, Dec. 22, 1995.

3. Ibid., June 17, 1996.

4. Israeli TV, Channel 1, Dec. 8, 1995.

5. Summary of the Report of the State Commission of Inquiry into the Murder of the Late Prime Minister, Yitzhak Rabin. Ministry for Foreign Affairs, Jerusalem, March 28, 1996, p. 9.

6. *Ha'Aretz*, June 17, 1996.

7. *Maariv*, Tel Aviv, Oct. 11, 1995.

8. Summary of Commission of Inquiry Report, p. 3.

9. Ibid., p. 7.

10. Excerpts, *Maariv*, Nov. 5, 1995.

11. Israeli TV, Channel 2, Dec. 19, 1995.

12. Reuters News Agency. Quoted in *Maariv*, Nov. 24, 1995.

13. *Maariv*, March 18, 1996.

14. *Maariv*, Dec. 11, 1994.

15. I. Robert Friedman, *Zealots for Zion: Inside Israel's West Bank Settlement Movement* (New York: Random House, 1992).

16. Amnon Kapeliouk, *Hébron, un massacre annoncé* (Paris: Arlea-Seuil, 1994), p. 111.

CHAPTER 3: THE SWEDISH CONNECTION

1. William B. Quandt, *Peace Process* (Washington, D.C.: Brookings Institution, 1993), pp. 369–72, also 573–75; Mohamed, Rabi'e, "The U.S.–PLO Dialogue: The Swedish Connection," *Journal of Palestine Studies* 21 (1992), pp. 54–66.

2. *New York Times,* March 21, 1988.

3. Discussion between Freij and author, Jerusalem, Feb. 24, 1988.

4. Mahmoud Nofal, in *El-Hayat* (in Arabic), London, Feb. 28, 1996.

5. George P. Shultz, *Turmoil and Triumph* (New York: Scribner's, 1993), p. 1032.

6. *New York Times,* June 22, 1988.

7. Rabi'e.

8. Shultz, p. 1036.

9. Full texts (in Arabic) according to Cairo Radio, Nov. 16, 1988.

10. Shultz, p. 1038.

11. *Jewish Week,* New York, Feb. 10, 1989.

12. Shultz, p. 1040.

13. Author's interview with Rosensaft, New York, Nov. 23, 1993.

14. Ibid.

15. Rabi'e.

16. Shultz, pp. 1041–42.

17. Conference of Presidents of Major Jewish Organizations press release, New York, Dec. 7, 1988.

18. Shultz, p. 1043.

CHAPTER 4: THE MADRID PEACE CONFERENCE

1. *New York Times,* Oct. 2, 1990.

2. Discussion between Freij and author, Bethlehem, Feb. 6, 1990.

3. *Davar,* Tel Aviv, Sept. 15, 1990.

4. Mahmoud Nofal, in *El-Hayat* (in Arabic), London, March 2, 1996.

5. For full text of letter of assurances to the Palestinians, see William B. Quandt, *Peace Process* (Washington, D.C.: Brookings Institution, 1993), Appendix M.

6. Hanan Ashrawi, *This Side of Peace* (New York: Simon & Schuster, 1995), p. 100.

7. *New York Times,* Oct. 31, 1991.

8. See also Ashrawi, p. 149.

9. See also *New York Times,* Nov. 1, 1991; Yitzhak Shamir, *Summing Up* (London: Weidenfeld & Nicolson, 1994), pp. 238–40.

10. Text of speech, *New York Times,* Nov. 1, 1991; also Ashrawi, pp. 147–48.

11. *New York Times,* Nov. 2, 1991.

12. Nofal.

13. *Time,* Feb. 13, 1989.

14. Discussion between Likud minister and author, Jerusalem, Jan. 22, 1989.

15. Moshe Arens, *Broken Covenant* (New York: Simon & Schuster, 1995), p. 49.

16. *New York Times,* March 12, 1989.

17. Ibid., March 14, 1989.

18. *Maariv,* Tel Aviv, April 14, 1989.

19. *Le Figaro* and *Liberation,* Paris, May 3, 1989.

20. Kol Israel, Jerusalem, May 3, 1989.

21. *Newsday,* May 3, 1989.

22. Address by Secretary Baker, May 22, 1989. Distributed by USIA, Tel Aviv.

23. *Davar,* Tel Aviv, July 19, 1989.

24. Arens, p. 74.

25. *New York Daily News,* Oct. 11, 1989.

26. *Maariv,* Tel Aviv, Oct. 5, 1989.

27. Figures from Immigration Department, Jewish Agency, Jerusalem.

28. Arens, p. 117.

29. Israeli TV, Jerusalem, March 7, 1990.

30. *Jerusalem Post,* international edition, week ending March 24, 1990.

31. Radio Baghdad (in Arabic), April 1, 1990.

32. *Maariv,* April 5, 1990.

33. Kol Israel, Radio Baghdad, and Radio Cairo, May 30, 1990; also *New York Times* and *Washington Post,* June 1990.

34. *Times,* London, June 13, 1990.

35. *El-Masa,* Cairo, July 28, 1990.

36. Ashrawi, p. 69.

37. *Davar,* Oct. 18, 1990.

38. Discussion between Shoval and author, Tel Aviv, Oct. 7, 1996.

39. Shamir, pp. 221–22.

40. Reuters, Feb. 11, 1991; quoted in *Ha'Aretz,* Feb. 12, 1991. Also discussion with Shoval.

CHAPTER 5: STALEMATE IN WASHINGTON

1. Mahmoud Nofal, in *El-Hayat* (in Arabic), London, Feb. 28, 1996.

2. Discussion between Shoval and author, Tel Aviv, Oct. 7, 1996.

3. President Bush press conference. Text released by USIA, Tel Aviv. Also quotes from *Maariv,* Tel Aviv, and *Jerusalem Post,* Sept. 7, 1991.

4. *Yediot Aharonot,* Tel Aviv, Jan. 16, 1996.

5. *New York Times,* Sept. 13, 1991.

6. *Davar,* Tel Aviv, Sept. 14, 1991.

7. Moshe Arens, *Broken Covenant* (New York: Simon & Schuster, 1995), p. 249.

8. Discussion between Rosenne and author, New York, Sept. 20, 1991.

9. Shamir's briefing to Israeli correspondents, Washington, D.C., Nov. 22, 1991.

10. Nofal, March 2, 1996.

11. Discussion between Shash and author, Washington, D.C., Dec. 14, 1991.

12. Discussion between Shamir and author, Tel Aviv, June 17, 1996.

13. Nofal, March 4, 1996.

14. Discussion between participants and author, Washington, D.C., Jan. 14, 1992.

15. Nofal, March 4, 1996.

16. *Ha'Aretz,* Tel Aviv, and *New York Times,* Jan. 17, 1992.

17. Nofal, March 4, 1996.

18. Ibid.

19. Ibid., March 7, 1996.

CHAPTER 6: LABOR BACK IN POWER

1. *Davar*, Tel Aviv, June 25, 1992.
2. *El-Hayat* (in Arabic), London, June 25, 1992.
3. *Maariv*, Tel Aviv, June 26, 1992.
4. Rabin's speech to the Knesset. Text released by Government Press Office, Jerusalem, July 13, 1992.
5. Kissinger quoted in Robert Slater, *Rabin of Israel* (New York: Harper, 1996), p. 517.
6. Marlin Fitzwater's briefing, July 13, 1992. Quoted in Kol Israel, Jerusalem, July 14, 1992.
7. Leslie Gelb, "America in Israel," *New York Times*, June 15, 1992.
8. Quoted by Israeli Foreign Minister Ehud Barak in his address to the American Jewish Community Relations Council, St. Louis, Feb. 11, 1996.
9. *Yediot Aharonot*, Tel Aviv, June 19, 1992.
10. Kol Israel, Jerusalem, June 29, 1992.
11. *Ha'Aretz*, Tel Aviv, July 24, 1996.
12. *Yediot Aharonot*, Tel Aviv, July 24, 1996.
13. *El-Hawadith* (in Arabic), London, July 31, 1992.
14. Discussion between senior Israeli official and author, Jerusalem, July 22, 1992.
15. *New York Times*, July 4, 1992.
16. *Davar*, July 22, 1992.
17. Discussion between Shoval and author, Tel Aviv, Oct. 9, 1996.
18. Discussion between Hoenlein and author, Toronto, Oct. 27, 1996.
19. *Davar* and *Yediot Aharonot*, Aug. 12–13, 1992.
20. Discussion between Shamir and author, Tel Aviv, Nov. 11, 1995.
21. *Davar*, July 16, 1992.
22. *Maariv*, Aug. 26, 1992.
23. *El-Quds* (in Arabic), Jerusalem, Sept. 17, 1992.
24. *Davar*, Sept. 17, 1992.
25. *El-Hayat*, Sept. 17, 1992.
26. Shimon Peres, *Battling for Peace* (New York: Random House, 1995), p. 199.
27. Shimon Peres, *The New Middle East* (New York: Henry Holt, 1993).
28. *Wall Street Journal*, Sept. 21, 1992.
29. Peres, *Battling for Peace*, p. 199.
30. Discussion between Egyptian diplomat and author, Tel Aviv, Aug. 28, 1992.
31. Shaike Ben-Porat, "Talks with Yossi Beilin" (in Hebrew), *Hakibbutz Hameuchad*, Tel Aviv, 1966, p. 110.
32. Yair Hirschfeld, lecture, Tel Aviv University, June 13, 1996.
33. *El-Hayat*, Sept. 11, 1992.
34. *El-Ahram* (international edition, in Arabic), Cairo, Sept. 13, 1992.
35. *El-Hayat*, Sept. 14, 1992; *El-Hawadith*, London, Sept. 18, 1992.
36. Discussion between a member of the Israeli team and author, New York, Sept. 30, 1992.
37. *El-Hayat*, Sept. 16, 1992.
38. Government Press Office, Jerusalem, Sept. 18, 1992.

39. *Ha'Aretz* and *Yediot Aharonot*, Tel Aviv, Sept. 16, 1992.
40. *Los Angeles Times*, Sept. 15, 1992. Quoted in *Ha'Aretz*, Sept. 16, 1992.
41. *Maariv*, Sept. 22, 1992.
42. *El-Hayat*, Sept. 22, 1992.
43. Ibid., Sept. 24, 1992.
44. *El-Ahram*, Sept. 22, 1992.
45. Ibid., Sept. 15, 1992.
46. *Maariv*, Sept. 17, 1992.
47. *Al-Hamishmar*, Tel Aviv, Sept. 22, 1992.
48. Kol Israel, Sept. 30, 1992.
49. *El-Hawadith*, London, Oct. 16, 1992.

CHAPTER 7: RABIN'S BUMPY ROAD TO OSLO

1. *Yediot Aharonot*, Tel Aviv, Oct. 2, 1992.
2. Discussion between Hoenlein and author, New York, Oct. 22, 1996.
3. *El-Ahram*, Cairo, Oct. 17, 1992.
4. *Ha'Aretz*, Tel Aviv, Oct. 9, 1992.
5. *El-Sharq el-Awsat* (in Arabic), London, Oct. 20, 1992.
6. *El-Hayat* (in Arabic), London, Oct. 26, 1992.
7. Government Press Office, Jerusalem, Oct. 25, 1992.
8. Discussion between Aloni and author, Kfar Shemaryahu, Aug. 26, 1996.
9. George Gruen, *In Israel Under Rabin*, ed. Robert O. Freedman (Boulder, Colo.: Westview Press,), p. 54.
10. Discussion between Eini and author, Ramat Gan, Israel, Sept. 22, 1996.
11. *El-Sharq el-Awsat*, Feb. 26, 1995.
12. Shimon Peres, *Battling for Peace* (New York: Random House, 1995), p. 283.
13. *El-Watan el-Arabi* (in Arabic), Paris, Oct. 8, 1993.
14. Discussion between Ambassador Rabinovich and author, Tel Aviv, Sept. 26, 1996.
15. Transcript of press conference, Israeli embassy, Washington, March 15, 1993.
16. Discussion between Sarid and author, Tel Aviv, Sept. 27, 1996.
17. Discussion between Ben-Eliezer and author, Jerusalem, Aug. 28, 1996.
18. Nofal Mahmoud, in *El-Hayat*, March 7, 1995.
19. Peres, p. 285.
20. *Yediot Aharonot*, Dec. 9, 1994, and Jan. 27, 1995.
21. *Jerusalem Post*, May 4, 1995.
22. Nofal.
23. Ibid.
24. Ibid., March 8, 1995.
25. *Ha'Aretz*, Tel Aviv, July 6, 1993.
26. Nofal, March 8, 1995.
27. Peres, p. 293.
28. Nofal Mahmoud, *The Israeli-Palestinian Peace* (Beirut, 1995); *El-Hayat*, Feb. 8, 1995.
29. Abu Mazen, interview with *El-Sharq el-Awsat*, June 11, 1995.

30. *El-Hayat,* March 11, 1995.
31. *Yediot Aharonot,* July 15, 1993.
32. Peres, pp. 292–96.
33. Discussion between Aloni and author.
34. Nofal, March 8, 1995.
35. Telephone conversation between author and Amnon Barzilai, author of *Ramon,* Aug. 23, 1996.
36. Nofal, March 8, 1995.
37. Ibid.
38. Peres, p. 296.
39. Discussion between Sarid and author, Tel Aviv, Aug. 21, 1996.
40. *Maariv,* Tel Aviv, Aug. 9, 1996; Nofal, March 10, 1995.
41. Nofal, March 10, 1995.
42. Discussion between senior Israeli intelligence official and author, Tel Aviv, Sept. 4, 1996.
43. Nofal, March 10, 1995.
44. Private discussions between Palestinian officials and author, Tunis, Oct. 1993, and between Israeli officials and author, Tel Aviv, Sept. 1996; also Peres, pp. 298–99; Nofal, March 10, 1995.
45. Discussion between Hoenlein and author, New York, Oct. 22, 1996.
46. Peres, p. 301.
47. Nofal, March 10, 1995.
48. Discussion between Hoenlein and author.
49. Orly Azoulay-Katz, *The Man Who Could Never Win* (Tel Aviv: Hemed, 1996), p. 202.
50. Discussion between Ben-Eliezer and author.
51. Discussion between Ambassador Rabinovich and author.
52. Peres, p. 306.
53. S. Segev, "Point of No Return," *American Foreign Policy Interests,* Aug. 1995.
54. Quoted in Dore Gold, *The Middle East: Military Balance 1993–94,* ed. Shlomo Gazit (Tel Aviv: Tel Aviv University, 1995), p. 104.
55. Azoulay-Katz, p. 205.
56. Discussion between Eini and author.

CHAPTER 8: GEFILTE FISH AND COUSCOUS

1. *New York Times,* Dec. 13, 1993.
2. Eric Laurent, *La Mémoire d'un roi* (Paris: Plon, 1993), p. 233.
3. *Davar,* Tel Aviv, Sept. 9, 1993.
4. Israeli TV, Jerusalem, Sept. 14, 1993.
5. *Yediot Aharonot,* Tel Aviv, Sept. 15, 1993.
6. Laurent, p. 86.
7. *Yediot Aharonot,* Feb. 14, 1992.
8. Ibid., Feb. 5, 1992.
9. *Maariv,* Tel Aviv, Feb. 1, 1987.

10. *Ha'Aretz,* Tel Aviv, June 14, 1987.

11. Laurent, pp. 246–47.

12. Ibid., p. 249.

13. Ibid., p. 251.

14. Ibid., p. 267.

15. Samuel Segev, *Sadat: The Road to Peace* (Tel Aviv: Massada, 1979). Also *Yediot Aharonot,* Feb. 14, 1992.

16. Laurent, pp. 265–66.

17. Ibid.

18. Ibid., pp. 265–71.

19. Ibid.

20. Samuel Segev, in *Maariv,* Nov. 7, 1985.

21. Quoted in *Maariv,* Feb. 24, 1988.

22. Laurent, p. 271.

23. Discussion between American Jewish leader and author, New York, Oct. 1992.

24. *Al-Hawadith* (in Arabic), Paris, Oct. 1, 1993.

25. *Maariv,* Nov. 27, 1985.

26. Jacques Attali, *Verbatim,* vol. 1 (Paris: Fayard), pp. 889, 898–99, 905–6.

27. *International Herald Tribune,* Paris, July 24, 1986.

28. *Maariv,* July 23, 1986.

29. Segev, in *Maariv,* July 29, Aug. 1, 1986; Peres's speech in the Knesset, July 28, 1986.

30. Reuters News Agency, Aug. 6, 1986.

31. *Maariv,* Aug. 1, 1986.

32. Transcript of Clinton-Hassan joint press conference, distributed by press section of the White House, March 15, 1995.

33. *New York Times, El-Hayat,* and *El-Sharq el-Awsat,* March 16, 1995.

34. *El-Hayat,* May 29, 1995.

35. Ibid., Jan. 22, 1996.

CHAPTER 9: RABIN'S IRAQI DILEMMA

1. Personal briefing of author by a senior Israeli intelligence officer, March 1993.

2. Sa'ad Bazaz, "Ashes of War," *Al-Sharq al-Awsat* (in Arabic), London, June 7, 1995.

3. Briefing by Israeli intelligence officer.

4. Bazaz, June 14, 1995.

5. Briefing by Israeli intelligence officer.

6. Bazaz, June 14, 1995.

7. Bazaz, June 12, 1995.

8. *El-Majalla* (in Arabic), London, April 9, 1994.

9. Ibid.

10. *Yediot Aharonot,* Tel Aviv, Oct. 22, 1993.

11. Kol Israel, Jerusalem, Oct. 22, 1993.

12. Discussion between Shahal and author, Jerusalem, June 1994.

13. *El-Ahram,* Cairo, Sept. 30, 1994.

14. *Ha'Aretz,* Tel Aviv, Sept. 1, 1994.

15. Discussion between Yaacoby and author, New York, March 18, 1996.

16. *El-Hayat* (in Arabic), London, Aug. 23, 1994.

17. *Times,* London, Sept. 18, 1994.

18. Discussion between Ben-Eliezer and author, Jerusalem, Aug. 28, 1996.

19. *El-Hayat,* Aug. 12, 1994.

20. *El-Quds* (in Arabic), Jerusalem, Sept. 7, 1994.

21. *Le Monde Diplomatique,* Paris, Nov. 4, 1994.

22. Bazaz, June 14, 1995.

23. *Davar,* Tel Aviv, Nov. 6, 1994.

24. Kol Israel, Jerusalem, Nov. 6, 1995.

25. *Ha'Aretz,* Tel Aviv, April 6, 1995.

26. *El-Hayat,* Aug. 13, 1994.

27. S. Segev, in *Jerusalem Post,* Feb. 20, 1995.

28. *Ha-Aretz,* May 31, 1996.

29. Jacques Attali, *Verbatim* (Paris: Fayard), pp. 15, 32.

30. Ibid., p. 34.

31. Kol Israel, June 9, 1981.

32. Bazaz, June 14, 1995.

33. Howard and Gayle Teicher, *Twin Pillars to Desert Storm* (New York: Morrow, 1993), pp. 273–75.

34. Discussion between Tamir and author, Tel Aviv, July 26, 1995.

35. Moshe Arens, *Broken Covenant* (New York: Simon & Schuster, 1995), p. 48.

36. George Shultz, *Turmoil and Triumph* (New York: Scribner's, 1993).

37. Teicher.

38. Discussion between a friend of Hamdoon's and author, New York, Aug. 23, 1993.

39. Discussion with Tamir.

40. Discussion with Shahal.

41. Ibid.

42. *El-Wasat* (in Arabic), London, Oct. 2, 1995.

43. Ibid., also discussion between Enav and author, Tel Aviv, Sept. 29, 1996.

44. Arens.

45. Discussion with Enav.

46. *Ha'Aretz,* May 31, 1996.

47. Discussion with Enav.

48. Baghdad Radio, quoted by Kol Israel, April 2, 1990.

49. Moshe Zak, "Saddam's Choice—Deception," *Global Affairs,* April 1991, p. 2.

50. Discussion between Ambassador Shoval and author, Tel Aviv, Oct. 7, 1996.

51. Discussion with Shoval.

52. Briefing of author by senior Israeli official, Tel Aviv, Jan. 23, 1991.

53. *Ha'Aretz,* Oct. 18, 1996.

CHAPTER 11: CROSSING THE JORDAN

1. Diane Sawyer, on *Primetime Live,* ABC, New York, Feb. 14, 1991.

2. *Los Angeles Times,* July 26, 1994; also *Yediot Aharonot,* Tel Aviv, July 29, 1994.

3. Reuters News Agency, Nov. 4, 1993; quoted by all Israeli papers.

4. *Ha'Aretz,* Tel Aviv, Nov. 4, 1993.

5. *Maariv,* Tel Aviv, June 7, 1993.

6. *Al-Hamishmar,* Tel Aviv, June 7, 1993.

7. Discussion between a senior Israeli intelligence officer and author, Tel Aviv, Sept. 4, 1996.

8. Discussion between Haber and author, Ramat Gan, Sept. 4, 1996.

9. Discussion between an Israeli diplomat and author, Washington, D.C. The diplomat had been briefed on Hussein's meeting with the Jewish leaders, Jan. 25, 1994.

10. *Davar,* Tel Aviv, Feb. 15, 1994.

11. *Los Angeles Times,* July 26, 1994.

12. Discussion between senior Israeli official and author, Jerusalem, Oct. 4, 1996.

13. Ibid.

14. *Maariv,* July 29, 1994.

15. Discussion between senior Israeli official and author, Jerusalem, Oct. 4, 1996.

16. Eli Rubenstein, "The Peace Treaty with Jordan," *Hamishpat* (Israeli judicial quarterly, in Hebrew), Dec. 1995, pp. 10–16.

17. *Ha'Aretz,* May 1, 1995.

18. Interview with Hussein, *Yediot Aharonot,* Tel Aviv, Oct. 25, 1994.

19. *Yediot Aharonot,* Jan. 31, 1997.

20. Israeli air force journal (in Hebrew), June 1995, p. 21.

21. *Yediot Aharonot,* Dec. 29, 1995.

22. *Ha'Aretz,* Jan. 11, 1996.

23. *Jerusalem Post,* Nov. 19, 1995.

24. Samuel Segev, *The Iranian Triangle* (New York: Free Press, 1988), pp. 30–37.

25. Ibid. Also discussion between President Herzog and author, Herzliyah, Sept. 1981.

26. Moshe Sasson, in *Maariv,* Sept. 6, 1996.

27. Discussion between Ambassador Evron and author, Tel Aviv, 1984.

28. Ibid.

29. *El-Hayat,* London, Jan. 13, 1997.

30. Uriel Dan, *King Hussein and the Challenge of Arab Radicalism* (New York: Oxford University Press, 1986), p. 134.

31. Department of State, memorandum of conversation, Feb. 25, 1965. Declassified in January 1978.

32. Discussion between senior Israeli intelligence officer and author, Tel Aviv, May 10, 1969.

33. Meir Avidan, in *Davar,* June 2, 5, and 19, 1987.

34. Ibid.

35. Rusk's memorandum to Johnson, LBJ Library. Declassified Aug. 1, 1986.

36. Discussion between Moshe Dayan and author, Tel Aviv, Aug. 1976.

37. Samuel Segev, "Did President Carter Miss an Opportunity for Peace Between Israel and Jordan?" in Herb Rosenbaum and Alexei Ugrinsky, eds., *Carter's Presidency* (Westport, Conn.: Greenwood Press, 1994), pp. 131–39.

38. Ibid.

39. Discussion between Barlev and author, Washington, D.C., Feb. 1973.

40. Henry Kissinger, *The White House Years* (Boston: Little, Brown, 1979), pp. 598–99.

41. The sequence of the Jordanian crisis was recounted to author by Ambassador Rabin in February 1973 in interviews for a series of articles on Rabin's ambassadorship in *Maariv*, Feb.–March 1973.

42. Peres interview with *Maariv*, Sept. 18, 1970.

43. Ben-Gurion's diaries, Hebrew edition, entry of May 3, 1963.

44. *Time*, Nov. 16, 1970.

45. Discussion between Allon's aide Eliahu Hassin and author, Jerusalem, Nov. 18, 1970.

46. Dayan's lecture, Bar-Ilan University, April 20, 1975. Quoted in *Davar*, April 21, 1975.

47. Henry Kissinger, *Years of Upheaval* (Boston: Little, Brown, 1982), p. 220.

48. *El-Nahar* (in Arabic), Beirut, Sept. 21, 1973.

49. General (Res.) Aryeh Braun, *Dayan in the Yom Kippur War* (in Hebrew) (Tel Aviv: Idanim Publishing, 1992), pp. 38–40.

50. *Maariv*, supplement on Moshe Dayan, Sept. 9, 1992.

51. *Ha'Aretz*, Aug. 7, 1974.

52. Dayan's memoirs, Hebrew edition (Tel Aviv), pp. 36–38.

53. Yitzhak Rabin with Eitan Haber, *Discussions with World Leaders and Heads of States* (in Hebrew) (Idanim Publishing), pp. 97–100.

54. Matti Golan, *Peres: The Road to Peace* (New York: Warner, 1989), p. 310.

55. George Shultz, *Turmoil and Triumph* (New York: Scribner's, 1993), pp. 452–60.

56. King Hussein's speech to the UN, Sept. 27, 1985.

57. *New York Times*, Oct. 24, 1985.

58. Radio Amman, quoted in Kol Israel, Jerusalem, Feb. 19, 1986.

59. Hussein interview, *New York Times*, Feb. 23, 1986.

60. *Maariv*, Sept. 29, 1986.

61. Shimon Peres, *Battling for Peace* (New York: Random House, 1995), pp. 385–87.

62. The full text of the London Document was first published in *Maariv*. For the English text, see William Quandt, ed., *The Middle East: Ten Years After Camp David* (Washington, D.C.: Brookings Institution, 1988), pp. 475–76.

63. Shaike Ben-Porat, "Talks with Yossi Beilin" (in Hebrew), *Hakibbutz Hameuchad*, Tel Aviv, 1996.

64. Shultz.

65. Interview with Shamir, *Yediot Aharonot*, Feb. 4, 1994.

66. Shultz.

67. King Hussein interview, *Nightline*, ABC, New York. Quoted in *Ha'Aretz*, July 18, 1990.

CHAPTER 12: ARAFAT IN GAZA

1. Discussion between Oslo negotiator Yoel Singer and author, Washington, D.C., April 6, 1997.

2. Ibid.

3. *Maariv*, Tel Aviv, Nov. 30, 1993.

4. Ibid.

5. Interview with Beilin, *Ha'Aretz,* Tel Aviv, March 7, 1997.

6. Rabin's speech to the Knesset, Jerusalem, Oct. 5, 1995.

7. Discussion between Ben-Eliezer and author, Jerusalem, Aug. 28, 1996.

8. Dayan's discussion with Rami Tal, *Yediot Aharonot,* Tel Aviv, April 27, 1997.

9. *Davar,* Tel Aviv, March 17, 1994.

10. *El-Hayat* (in Arabic), London, May 5, 1994.

11. *Davar,* May 5, 1994.

12. *El-Sharq el-Awsat* (in Arabic), London, June 11, 1995.

13. Ibid., May 4, 1995.

14. *Jerusalem Post,* Oct. 20, 1995.

15. *Yediot Aharonot,* Oct. 21, 1994.

16. Kol Israel, Jerusalem, Nov. 3, 1994.

17. Discussion between a former senior Israeli official and author, Tel Aviv, Aug. 28, 1996.

18. *El-Waten el-Arabi* (in Arabic), Paris, Jan. 20, 1995.

19. *Ha'Aretz,* Dec. 1, 1994.

20. *Maariv,* Dec. 5, 1994.

21. Ibid.

22. Ibid., Dec. 12, 1994.

23. *El-Wasat* (in Arabic), London, Jan. 13, 1995.

24. Ibid.

25. Interview with Weizman, *Yediot Aharonot,* Jan. 27, 1995.

26. Interview with Abu Mazen, *El-Hayat,* Jan. 27, 1995.

27. *El-Hayat,* Feb. 13, 1995.

28. Ibid.

29. *El-Sharq el-Awsat,* March 31, 1995.

30. *Ha'Aretz,* April 5, 1995.

31. *El-Ahram,* Cairo: *Davar,* Tel-Aviv; *El-Sharq el-Awsat,* London, April 10, 1995.

32. Israeli TV, Channel 1, June 10, 1995.

33. *Jerusalem Post,* May 2, 1997.

34. Ibid., Aug. 25, 1995.

35. *El-Hayat,* Sept. 14, 1995.

36. *Jerusalem Post,* Feb. 14, 1995.

37. *Ha'Aretz,* Dec. 1, 1994.

38. Ibid., Sept. 15, 1995.

39. Alouf Ben, in *Ha'Aretz,* Sept. 22, 1995.

40. Kol Israel, Jerusalem, Dec. 21, 1994.

41. Samuel Segev, in *Jerusalem Post,* Jan. 20, 1995.

42. Ibid., Feb. 20, 1995.

43. *Jerusalem Post,* international edition, week ending June 3, 1995.

44. Ibid.. May 17, 1995.

45. Ibid., June 3, 1995.

46. *Ha'Aretz,* Sept. 8, 1996.

INDEX